American Annals of Education and Instruction
by Unknown

Address:
HardPress
8345 NW 66TH ST #2561
MIAMI FL 33166-2626
USA
Email: info@hardpress.net

AMERICAN
ANNALS OF EDUCATION
AND
INSTRUCTION,
FOR
THE YEAR 1834.

EDITED BY
WILLIAM C. WOODBRIDGE.

VOL. IV.

BOSTON:
PUBLISHED BY WILLIAM D. TICKNOR.
Press of Light & Horton.
1834.

... ASYLUM FOR THE BLIND. BY T. H. PERKINS, ESQ.

AMERICAN

ANNALS OF EDUCATION

AND INSTRUCTION.

JANUARY, 1834.

VISIBLE ILLUSTRATION OF BENEVOLENCE.

(With a view of the New England Asylum for the Blind.)

THERE is a depth, and strength, in the impressions produced upon the mind through the medium of the eye, which surpasses all that is discovered in the influence of the other senses. Why it is, we know not that any have pretended to explain. But the fact, we believe, none have doubted ; and on this principle have been founded the multiplied methods of visible illustration, adopted in the instruction of children.

But the truth of the principle is not less certain in adult age. The great public works which have traced the name of Napoleon in the memory of our race, in characters which centuries cannot obliterate, inspire more awe and admiration, than volumes of history, or scores of panegyrics. The traveller, who has seen the Bridge of Jena or the Column of the Place Vendome, or the Road of Mount Simplon, has perceptions, and *sensations*, if I may so speak, of the greatness and energy of the mind that conceived these works, which can never be known by those who only read of them.

The question has occurred to us — Why may we not employ this principle to aid the cause of benevolence? We never pass the noble edifice presented to the Institution for the Blind, once the abode of wealth and luxury and now devoted to the protection and redemption of the unfortunate, without an involuntary act of homage to the individual who conceived and executed this noble act of beneficence — without an earnest wish, that we could bring around it the wealthy of our country, and let them hear the soft but impressive voice which issues from it — GO THOU AND DO LIKEWISE!

It was only in the month of February, of the last year, this noble charity was destitute of funds, and its patrons were indebted, several hundred dollars, beyond the amount which they had contributed to send its teacher abroad, and commence the course of instruction. Within two months after, Mr Perkins offered his own family mansion as the future "Asylum for the Blind," provided a sufficient sum, not less than $50,000, should be raised before the expiration of the month of May, to provide for their wants. This single testimonial of interest for the blind roused others to effort; and a sum even larger than he required was raised, and devoted to this object, within the time prescribed. The institution, in place of a debt, now possesses a building valued at $30,000, and improvements and grounds that afford ample means for exercise and air, worth about $28,000 more, together with an available fund of not less than $35,000; and all this the result of a donation from a single individual, such as hundreds of others might make.

We present our readers with a view of the mansion which has thus been made the means of permanent blessings to the blind of New England. Does it not say to others,— GO AND DO LIKEWISE?

We have visited the institution; and we find its interior correspond to its imposing exterior. It is not a cast off, decaying mansion, which wealth was compelled to desert. Its large and airy rooms present the same substantial comfort, and means of health, to its present, as to its former inmates.

We were particularly struck with the provisions made for the physical comfort and education of the pupils of this institution. In addition to the regular provision of simple food, and proper clothing, they are kept in well ventilated rooms, during the hours of confinement. At other times, the play ground purchased for the express purpose, gives them more ample room to enjoy air and exercise, than were possessed by their wealthy predecessors. We rejoiced to find that here, as at Hofwyl, the house is closed at certain hours, in good weather, and the pupils compelled to remain abroad for recreation, as much as to attend to study during the hours of school.

We were not less rejoiced to find provisions equally liberal for personal cleanliness. The guardians of this institution believed that other parts of the body require washing, as well as the hands and feet. A bathing room is provided for the male pupils and another for the females; and every week each one enjoys a warm bath — a means of health and comfort possessed by the poorest among the ancients, but confined to a favored few, in these days of modern refinement. How few of our first schools furnish this best preventive of disease to their pupils, thus regularly! How many ever attend to the cleansing of the skin, during that half the year when increased clothing accumulates the secretions upon its surface.

But for whom have these ample and costly provisions been made? For the one thousand blind of New England. Are there none who will do as much for the hundreds of thousands of its indigent youth who long for the light of science, and can learn nothing but the elements of knowledge? Are there none who will exercise equal liberality in providing teachers for the million of ignorant freemen, just emerging from childhood in our favored country?

REVIEW OF MADDEN ON 'THE INFIRMITIES OF GENIUS.'

The Infirmities of Genius illustrated, by referring the Anomalies of the Literary character to the Habits and Constitutional Peculiarities of Men of Genius. By R. D. Madden, Esq, author of Travels in Turkey, &c. '*Qui ratione corporis non habent, sed cogunt mortalem immortali, terrestrem ætheræ equalem prestare indsutriam.*' — *Plutarch de Sanit Tuend.* In 2 volumes. Philadelphia: Cary, Lea & Blanchard, 1833. pp. 412.

A WORK embracing a range of topics so wide, and views and principles so interesting as the 'Infirmities of Genius,' deserves a more comprehensive title. Had it been called 'Effects of a Studious and Sedentary Life,' it would have excited the attention of some, who we fear will now neglect some of the most valuable hints for a student, which we have seen. That the evils it describes are by no means peculiar to that mysterious, overrated power, called 'Genius,' our observation, as well as our own sad experience, fully satisfies us. It is not the amount of *brain*, but of *mental action*, and of *bodily inaction*, which gives rise to these evils; and the ceaseless plodding of a heavy intellect, or the incessant tension of an anxious heart, or over-excited feelings, whether pleasant or painful; nay, even the ordinary cares of life, and the duties of religion, — if proper attention is not paid to air and exercise — will produce all the ills that 'flesh is heir to,' no less certainly than the mighty efforts of a Johnson, or the lofty flights of a Byron. By the testimony of this work itself, even these were not attended with evil, so long as the *body* received its due share of rest and attention; and the same neglect which produces 'the horrors' in a genius, may render any, but an idiot, a wretched dyspeptic.

The interest of this subject, and the work before us, is, therefore, by no means confined to the literary world. All who are ever 'liable to thought,' or who are capable of deep feeling, are concerned. In this day of intense activity, the politician, and the man of business, the zealous Christian, and the active doer of good, the advocates of improvement and reform, all need to understand the influence of the mind upon the body, and the dangers of excessive activity even in the noblest and most important sphere of human efforts. To none, perhaps, is this subject more important, than to *parents* and teachers, who feel the high responsibility, and the immense difficulty of their task; and to no others can we hope to gain access. We have long felt it desirable to say something, which should aid them in preserving and directing their own energy, and in avoiding that ruin of health, and that abridgment of life, which have too often been the result of faithful efforts in education. The work before us is an opportune aid; but we are painfully hurried on by the recollection, that the mere introduction of the subject, has consumed most of the stolen time, and the almost exhausted power of attention, which they have to devote to us.

Madden is a traveller, and a man of science. In the work before us he has described the infirmities of studious men, as presented in the examples of some of the most eminent authors, and traced the connection between the defects of the mind, and the diseases of the body.

The first question which suggests itself on this subject, is the effect of literary pursuits on the duration of life, and in order to throw some light on this subject, Mr Madden has formed tables of the longevity of twenty eminent men in each of the various walks of literature. A summary of the whole presents the following aggregate number of years for each class, and the average for each individual of the class.

	Aggregate Years.	Average Years.		Aggregate Years.	Average Years.
Natural Philosophers,	1504	75	Philologists,	1323	66
Moral Philosophers,	1417	70	Musical Composers,	1284	64
Sculptors and Painters,	1412	70	Novelists and Miscellaneous Authors,	1257	62½
Authors on Law and Jurisprudence,	1394	69	Dramatists,	1249	62
Medical Authors,	1368	68	Authors on Natural Religion, (Deists),	1245	62
Authors on Revealed Religion,	1350	67	Poets,	1144	57

When we recollect that these are among the most laborious and voluminous authors, and that their average age is 66, we think it cannot be inferred that literary labor is, on the whole, more unfavorable to longevity, than any other of the *sedentary* occupations, in our artificial state of society.

In regard to the effect of different pursuits, it is a striking fact, that the mere triflers in literature, have suffered more from its labors than its greatest benefactors. It appears that Philosophers have been most remarkable for longevity, and Poets the most short-lived among authors. Astronomers seem to have exceeded all other Natural Philosophers in the duration of life.

'In the Time's Telescope for 1833, there is a list of all the eminent Astronomers, from Thales to those of the last century; and out of eighty-five only twentyfive had died of the age of sixty, five had lived to between ninety and a hundred; eighteen between eighty and ninety; twentyfive between seventy and eighty; seventeen between sixty and seventy; ten between fifty and sixty; five between forty and fifty; and four between thirty and forty. In no other pursuit does the biography of men of genius exhibit a longevity at all to be compared to this. No other science, indeed, tends so powerfully to raise the mind above those trivial vexations, and petty miseries of life, which make the great amount of human evil.'

Authors on Revealed Religion, and Philologists occupy the middle point of the scale. Mr Madden remarks, that those pursuits in which the imagination is largely exerted, are least favorable to longevity. While this is unquestionably true, we are not inclined to ascribe it chiefly to this cause. So far as our own experience, or our knowledge of physiology can guide us, that occupation is *most exhausting*, which produces *most sensation*, either *nervous* or *intellectual*. In conducting the instruction of the deaf and dumb, we found the mimic exhibition of feeling, and the excitement it produced, incomparably more exhausting, than any amount of intellectual labor in examining or explaining mere science, provided there was nothing to call forth personal anxiety or apprehension, and we could ascribe to no other cause, the peculiarly prostrating influence of this occupation. An eminent musician, in feeble health, informed us, that too much use of a piano often exhausted him by the nervous excitement it produced; the harmonica or musical glasses, must be used with great care on this account.

On this ground, the wide difference in the duration of life between Natural Philosophers and Poets; between Moral Philosophers and Dramatists; Jurists and Novelists; Painters and Musicians, is easily explained. Could the fictions which rouse every feeling of the reader, and have produced every degree of nervous convulsion, from the mere sob to the hysteric, or the fainting fit, have been created without agitating every nerve of the author, and exciting him sometimes even to phrenzy? Could they have been imagined, and executed, without a corresponding inroad upon the constitution?

We cannot pass by the obvious bearing of this fact upon the reading of the young. Works of fiction are usually put into their hands as the means of amusement, or at least, they are suffered to be thus employed. But if these remarks be just, they require the full energies of the mind; for surely, the work, which, from its very nature, shortens the life of its author, by the excitement it produces, can scarcely relax the mind of the reader, who is capable of being deeply interested in it, and of reading every scene, and feeling every emotion. Indeed, we can well recollect that the stolen hours which we passed in this gratification, were far more exhausting than those which we spent in the hard study of the school; and we have never succeeded in making it a *relaxation* from severe thought, unless when the story was so familiar that it had lost its keenest interest, or when it could draw off the mind, for a time, from intense pain. The fact that deists, (as most of those here spoken of as 'Authors on Natural Religion' are,) should stand at an opposite and lower extreme of the scale, is a striking evidence that Christianity is 'profitable to the life that now is.'

Mr Madden presents in this connection the pernicious influence of premature cultivation, in the language of Tissot.

'The effects of study vary,' says this author, 'according to the age at which it is commenced. Long continued application *kills the youthful energies.* I have seen children full of spirit attacked by this literary mania beyond their years; and I have foreseen with grief, the lot which awaited them. They commenced by being *prodigies;* and they ended by becoming *stupid!* The season of youth is consecrated to the exercise of the body, which *strengthens* it, and not to study, which *debilitates* and *prevents its growth.* Nature can never successfully carry on two rapid developments at the same time. When the growth of intellect is too prompt, its faculties too early developed, and mental application is permitted proportioned to this development, the body receives no part of it, because the nerves cease to contribute to its energies; the victim becomes exhausted, and eventually dies of some insidious malady. The parents and guardians who encourage or require this forced application, treat their pupils as gardeners do their plants, who, in trying to produce the first rarities of the season, sacrifice some plants, to force others to put forth fruit and flowers, which are always of *short duration*, and are *inferior*, in every respect, to those which come to their maturity at a proper season.'

The examples of precocity which are presented, show the danger to the constitution, in a manner which we should think would destroy the mistaken anxiety, and check the cruel efforts of parents to secure it.

'Moore says, the five most remarkable instances of early authorship, are those of Pope, Congreve, Churchill, Chatterton, and Byron. "The first of these died in his fiftysixth year; the second in his fiftyeighth; the third in his thirtyfourth; 'the sleepless boy' committed suicide in his *eighteenth*; and Byron died in his thirtyseventh year."

'Mozart, at the age of three years, began to display astonishing abilities for music, and in the two following years, composed some trifling pieces, which his father carefully preserved; and like all prodigies, his career was a short one; he died at the age of thirtysix. Tasso, from infancy, exhibited such quickness of understanding, that at the age of five he was sent to a Jesuit Academy, and two years afterwards recited verses and orations of his own composition, he died at fiftyone. Dermody was employed by his father, who was a school-master, as an assistant in teaching the Latin and Greek languages, in his ninth year; he died at twentyseven. The American prodigy, Lucretia Davidson, was another melancholy instance of precocious genius, and early death. Keats wrote several pieces before he was fifteen, and only reached his twentyfifth year. The ardor of Dante's temperament, we are told, was manifested in his childhood. The lady he celebrated in his poems, under the name of Beatrice, he fell in love with at the age of ten, and his enthusiasm terminated with life at fiftysix. Schiller, at the age of fourteen, was the author of an epic poem. He died at fortysix. Cowley published a collection of his juvenile poems, called 'Poetical Blossoms,' at sixteen, and died at sixtynine.

'But it would be useless to enumerate instances in proof of the assertion, that the earlier the development of the mental faculties, the more speedy the decay of the bodily powers.'

The chapter on the influence of literary habits upon the character and health, deserve the perusal of all who censure or ridicule those who for their sake, and for their children, confine themselves to the study, or the school-room, because they have not the ruggedness of health, or the firmness of nerve which belongs to those who are breathing the free air, and using incessant and invigorating exercise. 'How slight,' remarks our author, 'are those alterations in health — almost imperceptible to the ordinary observer — which have produced or aggravated the gravest mental infirmities.' No one thinks of reproaching the sleepy child or the convalescent invalid for his peevishness, *as an act of his will*; and yet how few form any just estimate of the influence of disease and suffering, often far greater, upon those who are enabled only by the energy of the will to do the common business of life! How often do they reproach them for the diseased feelings which they have not been able to surmount, rather than accord that praise which they deserve, on account of those which they have overcome.

But this chapter contains a serious warning to all who commit literary suicide. The intemperate man is not excused for the consequences of his conduct, because he was intoxicated. On the same ground, says Mr Madden, (and we quote for ourselves as well as our readers,) —

'The literary man who indulges in habits prejudicial to his health, cannot be supposed ignorant of the effects that must arise from excessive application; and who can say he is guiltless of the infirmities he drags upon him?

'The studious man sets out with stealing an hour or two from his ordinary repose, — sometimes perhaps more; and finishes by devoting whole nights to his pursuits. But this night work leads to exhaustion, and the universal sense of sinking in every organ that accompanies it, suggests the use of stimulants, most probably of wine; alcohol, however, in some shape or other. And what is the result? Why, the existence that is passed in a constant circle of excitement and exhaustion, is shortened, or rendered miserable by such alternations, and the victim becomes accessary to his own sufferings.'

'In a word, if the literary man consume his strength and spirits in his study, forego all necessary exercise, keep his mind continually on the stretch, and even at his meals deprive the digestive organs of that nervous energy which is then essential to their healthy action; if the proteiform symptoms of dyspepsia at last make their appearance, and the innumerable anomalous sufferings which, under the name of nervous and stomachic ailments, derange the viscera, and rack the joints of the invalid; if by constant application, the blood is continually determined to the brain, and the calibre of the vessels enlarged to the extent of causing pressure or effusion in that vital organ; in any case, if the mischief there is allowed to proceed slowly and steadily, perhaps for years, (as in the case of Swift) giving rise to a long train of nervous miseries — to hypochondria in its gloomiest form, or mania in its wildest mood, or paralysis in the expressionless aspect of fatuity; (that frequent termination of the literary career;) who can deny that the sufferer has, in a great measure, drawn the evil on himself; but who will not admit that his infirmities of mind and body are entitled to indulgence and compassion?'

The 'advantages of literary pursuits,' we think, might be better exhibited. The 'abuses' of study are justly said to be 'its only disadvantages.' Moderation in all things (Ne quid nimis) would render this like every other occupation and enjoyment for which the Creator has qualified us, a source of increased happiness, instead of painful suffering, and humiliating injury to the character. There can be no doubt, that even the *bodily health* of those who plod on without a thought in the day labor of life, would be improved by exercise of the brain; and that the perfection of the animal frame can never be fully attained, while so important an organ is left in a torpid state. To use it to excess, however, is an offence, although less brutal, no less real or ruinous, than to gorge the stomach with gluttony, or to wear out the frame with licentiousness. We do not possess a faculty, or an organ which is not necessary to make us perfect beings, or whose *proper use* is not a means of *happiness* and *usefulness*, to *ourselves*, and to *others*. There is not one which it is not wrong and dangerous to neglect. It is a direct rebellion against the laws of Providence, to attempt to cultivate the intellect to the neglect or destruction of the affections and appetites, which unite us to our fellow-men, or to suffer any other idol to take the place of the proper objects of attachment. To our readers, we trust we need say nothing of the danger of sensual excess; but we fear many of them may need to be warned of the danger of intellectual excess; and perhaps we cannot do it more effectually than by referring to the book before us, as an evidence that the latter species of indulgence leads almost directly to the former.

The strong temptation to resort to stimulants, arising from intellectual exhaustion, has already been alluded to. More than one sad example in this volume shows, that the exhaustion and craving for some high excitement produced by excessive literary effort, produces a morbid state of the animal organs and propensities, which lead to gluttony and intemperance, and urge, even those whom principle ought to restrain, to wild and licentious indulgence. 'The prince of Moralists,' Johnson, was led into *all these excesses*; while he was deprived of the light and hope and peace, which his noble and expanded views of the value of moral truth placed within his reach.

Pope 'loved meat highly seasoned, and if he sat down to a variety of dishes, he would oppress his stomach by repletion, and though he seemed to be angry when a dram was offered him, he did not forbear to drink it.' Dr King his cotemporary and friend says, that he certainly hastened his death by improper indulgence of appetite. The intemperance of Burns is too well known. Cowley died of the consequences of a drunken fit. Dryden is said to have hastened his end by intemperance. 'Parnel,' says Pope, 'was a great follower of drams, and strangely open and scandalous in his debaucheries.' 'Churchill was found drunk on a dunghill,' and Prior was not more remarkable for his temperance. Byron 'the lofty minded Byron'—did not even limit himself to the 'gentlemanly liquors,' but sought 'inspiration for his muse' in the bottle of gin! Such are the results of intellect excessively cultivated, and unbaptized by the pervading influence of religion.

Nor can even religious influence always resist the overwhelming power of passion and appetite in a diseased constitution. The oppressed body often takes a dreadful revenge on the tyrannising mind, and urges its oppressor on to criminal acts, by the very excitement of feeling which was intended to destroy its legitimate influence, and paralyze the appetites which the Creator has bestowed for wise purposes. The records of the hermitage and the convent would often furnish evidence of this. The history of superstition and fanaticism in Europe presents many instances, in which base men have employed even religious influences, to excite the nerves to that point in which reason staggers, and *feeling predominates*, that they might prepare their victims for the most horrid cruelty, or the most brutal sensuality.*

But the votaries of literature should also remember, that by excessive effort they destroy the very power which they thus seek to render supreme. 'Surely,' says Ficinus as quoted by Mr Madden, 'scholars are the most foolish men in the world. Other men look to their *tools*. A painter will wash his pencils, a smith will look to his hammer, and a husbandman will mind his plough iron, a huntsman will have a care of his hound, a musician of his lute. Scholars

* See Christian Spectator for 1830, Vol. II, p. 104.

alone neglect that instrument (the brain) which they daily use—by which they range over the world, and which by study is so much consumed.'

In the language of our author, 'it seems little short of madness.' 'The balance of health can be maintained only when mental exertion is proportioned to bodily activity.' 'One is too learned, when it is at the expense of health.' To those who ignorantly, or fondly imagine that the mere flights of the immortal being, can have no influence on its humble and mortal companion, we commend the remarks of Tissot, which are quoted by Mr Madden.

'To comprehend the influence of mental labor on physical health, it is only necessary to remember, in the first place, that the brain is in action when one thinks; secondly, that the tendency of continual action is to produce fatigue, and that fatigue deranges the functions, because every debilitated organ performs its duties imperfectly and irregularly; thirdly, that all the nerves proceed from the brain, and precisely from that part of it which is the organ of thought, the common sensorium; fourthly, that the nerves are one of the most important points of the human machine, that they are necessary to every function, and that when once their action is deranged, the whole animal economy suffers from that derangement.'

We have rarely seen a work which combined sound theory with convincing practical illustration more happily for its great object than the 'Infirmities of Genius.' We earnestly commend it to the attention of all our readers who are called to think, whether they possess genius or not; and especially to those whose example is constantly operating upon the young. We feel confidence in assuring them that the faithful practice of its maxims will save them many an hour of bodily and mental suffering, and many an occasion of deep regret, or life-long repentance.

We cannot but hope to secure the indulgence of our readers for some of the defects in our own work, by quoting the following account of periodical authorship.

'The result, however, shows that the compulsory toil of a periodical composition has a greater influence on health, than voluntary labors to a far greater amount. This opinion is corroborated by an observation of Dr Johnson, no mean authority on any subject connected with literary history.—'He that condemns himself to compose on a stated day, will often bring to his taste an attention dissipated, a memory embarrassed, a mind distracted with anxieties, a body languishing with disease; he will labor on a barren topic till it is too late to change it: for in the ardor of invention his thoughts become diffused into a wild exuberance, which the pressing hour of publication cannot suffer judgment to examine or reduce. There is no labor more destructive to health than that of periodical literature, and in no species of mental application, or even of manual employment, is the wear and tear of body so early and so severely felt. The readers of those light articles which appear to cost so little labor in the various publications of the day, are little aware how many constitutions are broken down in the service of their literary taste.'

[For the Annals of Education.]

THE PLEASURES OF LABOR.

Mr Editor ; — As you have manifested some interest in institutions for combining manual labor with intellectual pursuits, and diminishing in some degree an evil so generally prevalent, viz. the ill health of literary men, I trust that the results of *experience* upon the subject, from however humble a source, may be acceptable to you. As I have spent the past season in one of the most distinguished institutions of this kind in the country for the express purpose of becoming acquainted with the system, I thought that among all the *theories* at present promulgated, it might not be inappropriate to give the result of some little *observation*.

The fact that bodily exercise, regular and systematic, tends to produce health, none I presume will question. Suffice it to say on this head, that I never saw one hundred and twenty more strong, vigorous and healthy young men together, in any place or circumstances.

They labor three hours each day. I do not consider this a sufficient amount of exercise to ensure health ; but they take, I believe, as much, or nearly so, as is taken in other ways, such as walking, sports, &c, by the students of colleges and academies where this system is not practised. As much I mean as 'good scholars' do ; not as some do who are no scholars, but spend their whole time in play.

The principal subject, however, on which I wish to remark at present, is with respect to the *disposition* with which labor is performed, because it is exciting some attention at present, and because some persons, in high stations too, entertain notions which I believe to be founded entirely upon error.

So far as my observation has extended, the hours of labor are looked upon with pleasure. So far from considering labor an unwelcome task, they delight in it; and so far from envying those who are too delicate or fastidious to engage in the same employments, they entertain for them a feeling of compassion, or the most profound contempt. I knew one young man, whose pecuniary affairs were such that he was obliged to leave the institution for some months in order to raise funds to pursue his studies, (for except mechanics, they only pay their board by their labor,) who was solicited by his friends to leave the manual labor school and enter one of our first colleges, they offering to furnish the necessary funds. He was a young man of great promise, but he declined, declaring that he would rather work his own way as he could, than conform to college customs. Did he consider labor as drudgery ? I believe that, in the school of which I speak, fortynine out of fifty, at least, would prefer decidedly to labor every day, could they be excused at their pleasure. Indeed, I do not know one among the 120, who would not. The fact is, the plan commends itself to every man who becomes practically acquainted with it.

It is a fundamental law of the human constitution, to desire that every thing we do may be of some use. 'What for?'— is the first interrogatory of a child when requested to do something, the utility of which he does not at once perceive. And it is only by much effort, or by bad example or precept, that the order of nature is reversed, and rational beings come to take delight in nonsense.

One of the leading periodicals in our country has recently given a very decided opinion in opposition to the *general* introduction of manual labor into our literary institutions.* The whole force of the writer's objections rest solely upon this principle — which is assumed altogether gratuitously, — that the labor is performed *as a task*, that the student goes to it for the same reason that the culprit goes to the gallows — because he cannot avoid it. It needs no other evidence than is afforded by this assertion, to satisfy me that the writer is entirely unacquainted with the subject of his review, except *theoretically*. He reasons only a priori, and thence, concludes that it is an irksome task to work. It may be to him, from his peculiar habits or feelings; and it will doubtless be to many who have lived lives of bodily inactivity; and to many others who despise labor. To those who have such habits or feelings, it is not indeed strange if manual labor is an 'irksome task' But to one who accustoms himself to viewing things in their true relations, it is not so. To *me*, the idea of a learned man's advocating the principle that mere child's play is better adapted to engage the attention of a reflecting mind (which every student should possess) than what is useful to himself or others, is superlatively ridiculous. However, I do not place my dependence upon any theory however obvious; but simply upon *facts*. If the statements I have made do not satisfy every one, that manual labor in connection with study is pleasant as well as useful, I hope they will examine for themselves, for they are certainly not aware of the state of facts, among those who are familiar with manual labor.

A COUNTRY TEACHER.

EDITOR'S REPLY.

We insert, with pleasure, the remarks of 'a Country Teacher,' and we regret that *some* of those to which he replies, found a place in the Christian Spectator. In consequence of the failure of our

* See Christian Spectator for September, 1833.

last number of this work, we met with them but recently, and must take another opportunity of expressing our views concerning them. In the mean time, we would observe to our correspondent, that the opinions of another may appear 'superlatively ridiculous' to him, without any decisive evidence against them; for this appearance always exists, where the constitution, or the habits of mind, or of body, produce great differences of character and feeling. The western hunter regards the *laborer* with contempt; and to the infidel, the belief in Christianity appears 'superlatively ridiculous.' We would add a few questions in reply to his — 'What for.'

Is the life more than meat, and the body than raiment? Is *strength* of more value than money, or furniture, or provisions? If so, that course which adds to the strength and the health of the body, and invigorates the current of life, need not shrink from the question,— 'What for?'— so long as it is *not in itself wrong*. We will submit a simple statement of facts to our correspondent, and to others who agree with him.

The Editor of this work was reduced to a state of debility in Paris, some years since, (the result of years of disease,) in which he was incapable of labor, and could walk but a short distance. He was directed by his physician to go in a carriage a mile and a half, to a Gymnasium, or place of gymnastic exercise, daily, and was there committed to the care of a judicious 'gymnastic trainer,' as he might be termed. This gentleman ascertained his strength by a few cautious trials, and then commenced a series of exercises, whose only object was to acquire strength, and to gain skill in using the limbs. He was made to walk on a mast laid horizontally, in order to teach him to balance himself, and to bring all his limbs into action; to climb a rope, at first a foot or two, and then more, as he could bear it; to suspend himself by the arms, and mark by the watch, how long he could remain; to hold out a weight at arm's length, increasing gradually the weight and the time; to throw a weight, and a variety of exercises too numerous to mention. Each of these was a new experiment on his strength and skill, and each followed by rest. At this period, he was unable to use any solid food, except four or five ounces of bread daily; and yet, at the end of a month, he gained the power of lifting forty pounds more than at its commencement. He could walk to the Gymnasium, exercise an hour and a half, and return on foot, without so much fatigue as a short walk had caused him previously; he could sustain an ordinary diet, and do a part of his ordinary business. He did not earn a farthing *in coin*. We leave it to our correspondent to calculate, how much he *really earned*, in saving his physician's bill, and in being enabled to gain twice as much as his support, for five years afterwards, instead of living a life of idleness and suffering.

We hope our correspondent will review his opinions, and will not forget, that in education as well as in medicine, it is but *quackery* to prescribe the same remedy for every diseased constitution, whether of body or mind. At the same time, we fully agree with him in the *utility*, and to those who are not in too morbid a state, the *pleasure*, of combining labor with study.

COWPER ON PHYSICAL MISEDUCATION.

In looking over the 'Private Correspondence' of Cowper, — a name which rejects an epithet, — we were struck with his remarks, elicited by an ill turn of his own, on the physical miseducation of the present day. They are so good a commentary upon some remarks in preceding articles, that we cannot withhold an extract.

Extract of a Letter from Cowper to one of his Friends.

'My silence has been caused by a malady to which I have all my life been subject, — an inflammation of the eyes. The last sudden change of weather, from excessive heat to a wintry degree of cold, occasioned it, and at the same time gave me a pinch of the rheumatic kind; from both which disorders I have but just recovered.

'I do not suppose that our climate has been much altered since the days of our forefathers, the Picts; but certainly the human constitution in this country has altered much. Inured as we are from our cradle to every vicissitude in a climate, more various than any other, and in possession of all that modern refinement has been able to contrive for our security, we are yet as subject to blights as the tenderest blossoms of spring; and are so well admonished of every change in the atmosphere by our bodily feelings, as hardly to have any need of a weather glass to mark them. For this we are, no doubt, indebted to the multitude of our accommodations; for it was not possible to retain the hardiness that originally belonged to our race, under the delicate management to which for many ages we have now been accustomed.

'I can hardly doubt that a bull-dog or a game-cock might be made just as susceptible of injuries from weather as myself, were he dieted, and in all respects accommodated, as I am. Or if the project did not succeed in the first instance (for we ourselves did not become what we are at once,) in process of time, however, and in a course of many generations, it would certainly take effect. Let such a dog be fed in his infancy with pap, Naples' biscuit, and boiled chicken; let him be wrapt in flannel at night, sleep on a good feather bed, and ride out in a coach for an airing; and if his posterity do not become slight-limbed, puny, and valetudinarian, it will be a wonder. Thus our parents, and their parents and the parents of both, were managed; and thus ourselves; — and the consequence is, that instead of being weather-proof, even without clothing, furs and flannels are not warm enough to defend us.

'It is observable, however, that though we have by these means lost much of our pristine vigor, our days are not the fewer. We live as long as those whom, on account of the sturdiness of their frame, the poets supposed to have been the progeny of oaks. Perhaps, too, they had little feeling, and for that reason also might be imagined to be so descended. For a very robust athletic habit seems inconsistent with much sensibility. But sensibility is the *sine qua non* of real happiness. If, therefore, our lives have not been shortened, and if our feelings have been rendered more exquisite as our habit of body has become more delicate, on the whole, perhaps, we have no cause to complain, but are rather gainers by our degeneracy.'

THE FIRST SCHOOL.

We remarked in our first volume of this work, that in our plans of education we ought to imitate, as far as possible, the measures which Divine Providence adopts in the education of our race. This is a subject upon which we have long dwelt, with great interest. It has been the clue which has guided us to many of our principles and views, and we have deferred a full examination of the subject, only because we considered it one of so great extent and importance. We venture, however, to commence, (in the hope of going on,) with an inquiry into the management of *The first school*, organized and conducted by the Great Educator of our race.

This school was established in the midst of the beauties and wonders of nature, in a fruitful spot, watered by four streams — a garden which contained every tree that is pleasant to the sight, and good for food. How different this situation from those provided by modern wisdom and benevolence, to form the mind, and senses, and tastes, of our children!

It is remarkable that the first school was a *manual labor school*. The first pupils were 'put into the garden—to dress it, and to keep it.' Let it be remembered too, that it was thus organized, when it was intended to be a scene of perfect enjoyment; and labor was appointed, of course, as a means of happiness.

The *first lesson* in this school was given upon objects and their names. Every beast of the field and every fowl of the air was brought to Adam; 'and he gave names to all cattle, and to every fowl of the air, and to every beast of the field.' How many of the pupils of our modern schools 'finish their education,' and even go to their graves, without having attained the knowledge imparted in this first lesson; and are compelled to employ but one, or at most a very few names, for 'the fowls of the air,' whose beautiful plumage or varied songs call forth their admiration. Such were the arrangements recorded by Moses, for physical and intellectual education. But in all the wonders of creation that surrounded the first man, there was nothing to call forth the feelings, except to their Author; nothing to develope the *human heart*; nothing to complete the *moral education*. He might have lived in Paradise forever, and still have been only an intellectual being, with the nobler half of his nature to a great extent unawakened, uncultivated, and perishing for want of exercise; and so far, made in vain. 'It is not good,' therefore, said his Creator, 'that the man should be alone.' 'I will make an help meet for him,' was the next decision; and Infinite Wisdom determined, that his companion to be '*meet*,' must be of a different mould of mind as well as of body. That this was not merely for the purpose of continuing the race, is evident from the fact, that the same wise Educator, in almost every school which has been organized *directly* by his own hand, has sent both sexes together.

It would have been easy for Almighty power, to have made one family of males and another of females, and thus to have formed those separate schools which modern wisdom has considered so necessary, and avoided those dangers which human prudence deems so great. But he has ordered otherwise; and the results are in accordance with our expectations, from the plans of Divine Wisdom. The evils apprehended have always existed in the greatest degree, where the sexes were most widely and carefully separated. The youth who avoid female society, are notoriously the most dissolute. The navy and the camp present a mass of corruption rarely found in mixed communities; and the monastery and the convent have produced and developed crimes, which are scarcely ever heard of in a family. The voice of experience, if it be listened to, will be found to have responded, to the first declaration of the Creator. '*It is not good for man to be alone.*'

In regard to the *direct methods* of moral education, the first school was constituted on the plan of absolute government. One of its prominent commands was given without any reason or explanation, and without any object which we can understand, except to test the obedience of the pupils. 'Of the tree of knowledge of good and evil, thou shalt not eat of it.' And this too was done in a school of adults, and not of mere children. At the same time, every thing necessary to enjoyment, was given 'freely.'

Punishment was among the means of government in this school, and this too, of the severest kind. 'In the day that thou eatest thereof, thou shalt surely die.' And we find no attempt to reconcile the pupils to this singular prohibition, and its severe penalty. It is simply, 'Thou *shalt not* eat of it.' 'In the day that thou eatest thereof, thou shalt *surely* die.'

We do not hear that it was thought advisable to offer any *rewards* for obedience, except the presence and instructions and favor of the Great Educator who would seem, from the occurrence after the fall, to have visited the first pupils regularly, 'in the cool of the day,' doubtless to impart lessons of temporal and eternal wisdom.

We hear of no interruption to the order, or the happiness, of the first school, until an enemy of the race persuaded one of the pupils, that the great command of the Educator was not reasonable, and that the penalty would not be executed; and artfully introduced *emulation* as a motive to action — its first appearance, so far as we know, in this world. 'In the day that ye eat thereof, then your eyes shall be opened, and *ye shall be as gods*, knowing good and evil.' The temptation was successful. The example and influence of one pupil overcame the other. This school of happiness, and improvement, and peace, was broken up; and its pupils were sent abroad into a world of storm and trouble, overgrown with thorns and briars, to begin the course of suffering involved in the penalty, 'Thou shalt surely die.'

[For the Annals of Education.]

ON THE MODE OF TEACHING THE ANCIENT LANGUAGES.

I. *An Essay on a System of Classical Instruction; &c.* London: Printed for John Taylor, 1829. 12mo.
II. *The New Latin Reader, Part I.* By S. C. Walker. Philadelphia.

There is one argument often set forth for the present method of learning Latin and Greek, by means of lexicon and grammar, and with no assistance on the part of a master, except what may be communicated on the examination of the pupil at recitation, — which commonly passes unanswered, and seems to be generally admitted as unanswerable: — it is this; that the present method took its rise in very ancient times, and has come down to us from those scholars, to whom Latin was the language of familiar intercourse.

But this is false. The present method of teaching Latin and Greek is the corruption of the system of teaching approved at that time; for that was diametrically opposed to the lexicon and grammar method. This corruption can be traced to no more respectable source than the indolence of schoolmasters; and it has been protested against at every stage of its progress, by the most distinguished scholars.

This is the first, and perhaps the most important thing, which the little work before us undertakes to prove; and most satisfactorily

* lexicons & grammars have not been in existence [illegible] years - The first grammar was written [illegible]

it is proved, by documents that bear directly on the subjects collected from the platforms of the first classical schools in England, and the writings of Roger Ascham, Milton, and Locke.

One of the first classical schools in England, was founded by Cardinal Wolsey, at Ipswich, in 1528; and when it was founded the mode of discipline and of teaching was given to the masters, in a letter yet extant, in the original Latin, under the Cardinal's own hand. This letter is headed, '*In what order boys admitted to the Academy should be taught, and what authors should be lessoned to them.*' The writer then proposes that the first class should be taught to pronounce the words, and to class them into the eight divisions, called parts of speech, being taught, without book, by the master. The second class were to be taught to form sentences, by being told the Latin forms for short English propositions, still without book. When this has been done a while, the children were to write down the sentences, 'in Roman characters;'

'And you will daily pay attention, (he continues) that each of the whole party have this note-book perfectly correct, and written as fairly as possible with his own hand.

'Should you think proper that, besides the rudiments, some authors should be given at this tender age; it may be either Lily's *Carmen Monitorium*, or *Cato's Precepts*; of course with a view of forming the accent.'

Thus far, no grammar, any more than dictionary, is mentioned. For the third class, however, to whom he recommends that Æsop or Terence should be taught, he adds;

'We should not disapprove your subjoining the little book composed by Lily, on the genders of nouns.'

For the fourth class to whom Virgil was to be taught, he says;

'Lily will furnish the past tenses, and supines of verbs. But although I confess such things are necessary, yet as far as possible, we could wish them so appointed, as not to occupy the most valuable part of the day.'

The fifth class is 'to be lessoned in some select epistles of Cicero.' No additional grammar is mentioned here. But, for the sixth class who are to read Sallust, Cæsar, or some history, he says;

'To these might not improperly be added Lily's Syntax; verbs defective and irregular; in short, any you may notice in the course of reading, as departing from the usual form of declination.' 'The party in the seventh form should regularly have in hand either Horace's Epistles, or Ovid's Metamorphoses or Fasti; occasionally composing verse or an epistle of their own. It will also be of very great importance, that they sometimes turn verse into prose, or reduce prose into metre. In order that what is learned by hearing may not be forgotten, the boy should reperuse it with you, or with others. Just before retiring to rest, he should study something choice, or worthy of remembrance, to repeat to the master the next morning. Lastly, for the eighth class, when by exercise of this kind the party has attained to some proficiency in conversation-style, they should be recalled to the higher precepts of grammar, as for instance, to the figures prescribed by Donatus to the elegance of Valla, and to any ancient authors whatever, in the Latin tongue. In lessoning from these, we would remind you to endeavor to inform yourselves at least on the points it may be proper should be illustrated on each present occasion. For example, when intending to expound at length a comedy of Terence, you may first discuss in few words the author's rank in life, his peculiar talent, and elegance of style. You may then remark how great the pleasure and utility involved in reading comedies; of which word you should explain the signification and derivation. Next, you may briefly, but perspicuously unravel the substance of the plot; and carefully point out the particular kind of verse. You may afterwards arrange the words in more simple order; and wherever there may appear any remarkable elegance; any antiquated, new-modelled, or Grecian phrase; any obscurity of expression, any point of etymology, whether derivation or composition; any order of construction rather harsh and confused; any point of orthography; any figure of speech, uncommon beauty of style, rhetorical ornament or proverbial expression; in short, anything proper or improper for imitation; it should be scrupulously noticed to the young.'

Such was the plan of teaching marked out for the oldest classical school in England. What a different thing it must have been for boys to learn Latin then, when, as there were no dictionaries widely diffused, on account of the imperfection of printing, the master construed the lessons to the boys, and they were not required to learn by heart even the regular verbs, till they had read Virgil, nor the irregular verbs, till after they had learned Cicero, while the peculiarities and niceties of grammar were left until they had advanced to the highest class! Boys will hardly call dictionaries and grammars facilities, when they have but increased their difficulties, by taking from masters all sense of responsibility in the preparation of their lessons! Nor did the ease and luxury of those days of study consist merely in reading the beautiful Latin authors with experienced scholars, instead of digging the skeleton of their meaning out of dictionaries and grammars. In those days, discipline was a very different thing. Listen to the Cardinal, in his directions about the studies of the fifth class:

'One point that we think proper to be noticed, as of first importance, is, that the tender age of youth be never urged with severe blows, or harsh threats, or indeed with any sort of tyranny. For by this injurious treatment all sprightliness of genius either is destroyed, or is at any rate considerably damped.'

And again, in the directions for the seventh class; —

'At intervals, attention should be relaxed, and recreation introduced; but recreation of an elegant nature, worthy of polite literature. Indeed, even with his studies, pleasure should be so intimately blended, that a boy may think it rather a *game at learning*, than a task. And caution must be used, lest by immoderate exertion the faculties of learners be overwhelmed, or be fatigued by reading, very far prolonged; for either way is alike a fault.'

Was this the direction of a mere theorist, who did not know the nature of a schoolboy? 'The Cardinal, says our author, was a schoolmaster, before he was a statesman.'

It is not proposed to recommend precisely this method of teaching Latin, to our modern schoolmasters, for several reasons. In the first place, few schoolmasters, in this age, when Latin has ceased to be a spoken language even among the learned, could be found capable of teaching the two lower classes. And in the second place, it is not necessary now that boys should learn to speak. But let it ever be remembered, that this natural and obvious method of teaching a language, was the first method proposed in the classical schools of England. Whatever arguments may be put forth, for the modern method, let it never be said that it was the method pursued by those distinguished scholars, whose Latin, though learned at school, was as a vernacular language. Let it be acknowledged, that as the first method of teaching it has declined, the ease and familiarity with which the language was formerly used, has declined also.

St Paul's school, at London, was founded by Dean Colet, a little before the Ipswich school. This school was also divided into eight classes, and the same course of instruction was adopted. Indeed, both Wolsey and Colet are known to have been intimate friends of Erasmus, who was the adviser of both in regard to these schools; and whose opinions, both in regard to the time and method of teaching Latin grammar, and with respect to the discipline of boys, is well known. On the latter subject he says, in his tract on the education of youth;—

'You may kill some children before you can make them one whit better by beating; and yet at the same time, with good words and good usage, you may do what you please with them. Of this temper I own myself to have been, when a boy. And my master, of whom I was a great favorite, because he was pleased to have conceived great hopes of me, having a mind to get a thorough knowledge of my disposition, did therefore make a trial how I could bear a sound whipping. Upon this a fault was cooked up, of which (God knows) I never so much as dreamed; and accordingly I suffered the discipline of the school. Immediately I lost all manner of relish to my studies; and this usage did so damp my spirits, that it almost broke my heart. From hence we may see, that these illiterate butchers (to give them no better term) ruin many a hopeful lad. And it is an observation, not ill grounded, that the most ignorant schoolmasters are generally the best at this exercise.'

The sentiments of Erasmus about Latin grammar, have already been given in Cardinal Wolsey's Letter. They are to be found again in his friend Colet's address to the St Paul's School, which he founded. Having recommended attention to nothing more in grammar than the mere distinction of the parts of speech, before entering on the study of the classic authors, the Dean asserts, that the study of such authors will better familiarize the pupil with the regular forms of language, than any dry rules given in the shape of abstract principles. His remarks are thus quoted by Taylor:

'In the beginning, men spake not Latin because such rules were made, but contrariwise, because men spake such Latin, upon that followed the rules and were made. That is to say, Latin speech was before the rules, and not the rules before the Latin speech. Wherefore, well beloved masters and teachers of grammar, after the parts of speech, sufficiently known in our schools, read and expound plainly unto your scholars good authors. And show to them every word, and in every sentence what they shall note and observe, warning them busily to follow and to do like, both in writing and in speaking; and be to them your own self also speaking with them the pure Latin very present, and *leave the rules*. For reading of good books, diligent information of learned masters, studious advertence and taking heed of learners, hearing eloquent men speak, and finally busy imitation with tongue and pen, more availeth shortly to get the true eloquent speech, than all the traditions, rules, and precepts of masters.'

Again, Erasmus himself, speaking of the importance of grammar, in his Ecclesiastes, says; —

'When I speak of grammar, I do not mean the inflections of nouns and verbs, and the agreement of one word with another according to its places; but the modes of speaking correctly and properly, which can only be acquired from multifarious reading of the ancients, who excelled in elegance of speech.'

He elsewhere refers expressly to the opinion of Colet, who

'Could not bear that the standard of a good style should be taken from the exact rules of grammar; which he would often affirm, did rather obstruct the purity of the language; not to be attained but by the reading of the best and purest authors.

After these quotations, it may be surprising to some readers to know, that Colet and Erasmus were authors of the Eton Latin grammar, with which Lily had less to do than either of them, although it bears his name. But this is not inconsistent. They did not intend to recommend a superficial study of language, when they withdrew abstract rules to the later stages of the course of study; or rather when they recommended, that the rules of language should be taught, by word of mouth, according to the present need of the scholar, instead of being learned, all at once, as abstract speculation. The science of grammar is not like the science of geometry, which it is useful to learn by itself, in the rigid forms of abstraction; and which may then be applied to natural philosophy, navigation, and other matters. For the science is not pure enough to hang together in the mind, without its natural exponents. If the student wants the discipline of pure science, (and every student does), let him take it in those studies which are especially appropriate to give it in the best manner. Let him learn geometry. But let grammar be learned in its applications, and then the various rules will take such hold of the memory as their comparative importance demands, and no more.

From the earnestness, however, with which all these great scholars exhort masters on this subject, it was obviously the tendency then, as now, for masters to give the abstract rules to the pupils, instead of lecturing upon grammar at recitation time. In the course of half a century, corruption grew on apace; 'and after a conversation on the subject, says our author, which took place at Sir William Cecil's, (then principal Secretary of State, afterwards Lord Burleigh) Sir Richard Sackville, treasurer of the exchequer, requested Ascham, who was one of the party, to commit to writing the opinions he had expressed. This was in 1566. 'At that period the defects of school discipline had become so great, as to attract the attention of many persons of chief consideration in the kingdom. The immediate cause of the conversation was the severity exercised towards the boys at Eton, some of whom had run away for fear of being beaten. The cruelty of schoolmasters was generally condemned by the company present, and it is particularly reprobated by Ascham in his treatise, which is called 'The Scholemaster.' But we shall omit all that he says upon discipline, except one passage worthy of especial consideration.

'This will I say, that even the wisest of your great beaters do as oft punish nature, as they do correct faults. Yea, many times the better nature is the sorer punished. For if one by quickness of wit take his lesson readily, another by hardness of wit taketh it not so speedily; the first is always commended, the other is commonly punished; when a wise schoolmaster should rather discretly consider the right disposition of both their natures, and not so much weigh what either of them is able to do now, as what either of them is likely to do hereafter. For this I know, not only by reading of books in my study, but also by experience of life abroad in the world, that those which be commonly the wisest, the best learned, the best men also, when they be old, were never commonly the quickest of wit when they were young.'

It is indeed curious to see how difficulties in school discipline have gone on, hand in hand with the abandonment of the natural method of teaching Latin; and while there was then, a severity of punishment scarcely known at this day, the general principles stated, are capable of application to many modern institutions.

MORAL EDUCATION.

We were rejoiced to find an Essay on Moral Education in the London Quarterly Journal of Education for July, and were deeply interested by its perusal. In this organ of the celebrated Society for the Diffusion of Useful Knowledge, we find it distinctly stated, and ably maintained, that —

'Instruction by itself, is an instrument of which either a good or bad use may be made. It is to moral education, so much neglected in these times, that we must direct the skill, the attention, and the capacity, of every one who devotes himself to instruction.'

The Editor concedes that the cultivation of the intellect will 'form *some* habits of order and industry.' But it is added — 'it is at least *insufficient*.' We use his own italics. He laments the 'total want or insufficiency' of schools for moral cultivation; 'the almost total absence of those exercises which are proper to form' the moral feelings, and habits, and the exclusive attention to the understanding. He remarks: 'The great thing which education neglects 'is the *formation of character and morals*.' He shows from the statistics of France, that ignorance does not produce a greater amount of crime, than misdirected knowledge — that something more than mere intellectual light must be given, to subdue the passions and govern the appetites, which civilization often renders more imperious in their demands. He quotes the remark of Seneca; 'Since learned men have abounded, good men are scarce.' He adds, that 'in the present day,'—'it appears that the formation of morals was never less attended to than since we have been so zealously occupied in the diffusion of knowledge.'

We would again express our gratification at this noble stand against the *knowledge-mania* of the day, and we thank the editor for his efforts '*to fix the basis of a good system of instruction, by putting moral education before all other kinds of education.*' Let knowledge be diffused! Let the intellect be cultivated to the greatest extent; but let not the *heart* be neglected, or we may still be but '*archangels fallen.*'

In regard to the *modes* of moral education, we should perhaps differ from the Editor. In our view, there are no sanctions but the commands of God and the prospects of a future world — no motives but the love of God and of the Saviour — which are sufficient to subdue the passions and control the appetites of *the mass of men.* We have seen — perhaps he is observing at this moment — men of intellectual strength — of 'power of will' which is seldom equalled — bending their necks to the yoke of appetite and passion — even to brutality. There is no security, in our view, but in that 'faith which is the evidence of things not seen' — which can look beyond temporary enjoyments and momentary results, and embrace the whole of our being, and estimate the whole consequences of our conduct, with a distinctness and confidence like that which strengthens the sailor to resist the storm, and emboldens him to direct his course to the place of destination, in the face of winds and currents.

Those of our readers who have perused the Sketches of Hofwyl, in the first and second volumes of the Annals, will recollect the simple yet excellent Vehrli, the devoted teacher of the poor children at that establishment. The following extract from one of his reports, will show his views as to the importance of religious instruction and the modes of giving it, derived from his experience with the most degraded children:

'In our morning intercourse, I endeavor to render habitual, a sense of acknowledgment to that God who has given us undisturbed repose, and who supplies us with the strength necessary to accomplish our daily tasks. In the evening I direct their reflections and their gratitude towards the same objects.

Religious views and sentiments are the best guides in life. Let me ask, what is man without religion! These are the first thoughts, and the first sentiments which should be engraved upon the infant heart, the first duties with which they should be impressed. During our labors in the field, circumstances and phenomena often present themselves, which afford opportunities of addressing to my children important questions, which I often improve as occasions for instructing them in the existence of a God, and his attributes, taking care to do it in such a way as to produce the greatest impression. I explain to them how we are favored with a knowledge of God and his views with regard to man, by his holy word, in which his designs towards us are revealed; and how he has manifested his kindness, in sending his Son upon the earth, in order to make us acquainted with his will, and to render us happy.

INDUSTRIAL SCHOOL AT MULHAUSEN.

In a late number of the Annals, we have urged the importance, — *the necessity* — of Citizens' or Middle Schools, to provide suitable education for those who are not destined to professional or literary pursuits, but who still need more than a primary education to fit them for their duties as men and as citizens. We have mentioned the fact that even in the monarchical governments of Europe, the measure is deemed necessary even to prepare men to be intelligent and useful subjects; and that the funds and the efforts of government, are constantly directed to the intellectual improvement of the laboring classes.

In one of the French Journals of Education we find the following account of a school of this kind at Mulhausen, one of the principal manufacturing towns of Alsace, which will give some idea of their organization abroad. The term 'industrial' we adopt from the rench.

In the Industrial School of Mulhausen, two courses of instruction are given, each of one year.

Before entering this school, the pupils, are expected to have acquired in the primary schools, a knowledge of French and German grammar; and must be able to write correctly in these two languages. They must be well versed in commercial arithmetic, and in linear drawing; they must also know how to measure surfaces and solids; and finally they must be well acquainted with the topography of their country and the geography of the globe.

The following is a list of the lessons given weekly:

FIRST SECTION.

Calligraphy,	2 lessons.		Demonstrated Arithmetic,	4 lessons.	
Ornamental drawing and the drawing of machinery,	6	"	Commercial Geography,	3	"
Correction of exercises in composition, in the two languages, prepared at home,	5	"	Practical notions of physics and of chemistry,	2	"
The history of France, as an exercise of the memory, and in translating,	3	"	Elements of the natural history of the three kingdoms,	3	"
			Composition for places,	2	"
			Together,	30 hours.	

SECOND SECTION.

Correction of exercises in composition,	6 lessons.		General geography and cosmography,	2 lessons.	
Book-keeping,	2	"	Practical notions of chemistry and of physics (Natural Philosophy),	5	"
Ornamental drawing, and the drawing of machinery,	6	"	Natural history with its applications to agriculture, to the art of preserving health, &c.	2	"
Explication of the rights and duties conferred and imposed by the charter and the laws of the organization,	1	"	Composition for places,	2	"
Practical and descriptive geometry, followed by surveying and mechanics,	4	"	Together,	30 hours.	

The persons employed in these establishments consist of a director, one professor of mathematics, three instructors, one assistant, two female instructors, two masters of drawing and writing, and five ecclesiastics of different denominations.

From this account of the lessons it will be perceived that in the industrial school, the pupils are expected to attain higher degrees of perfection in all the branches of knowledge previously studied, and to make new acquisitions.

Their exercises in *composition* are made more difficult, consisting of descriptions, narrations, and especially of essays, written in accordance with oral lectures delivered by the professor.

The linear *drawing*, taught at the primary school, may suffice for the simple joiner, or carpenter, the mason, the gardener, the stonecutter, the locksmith, &c. At the industrial school, the pupils attend to ornamental drawing and the drawing of machinery, a branch of the art which is indispensable to the mechanician, the architect, the sculptor, the surveyor, the engineer, &c.

The study of the *History of France* is particularly intended to lead the young people to a just appreciation of the institutions, and of the advantages of a free and constitutional government.

General and commercial *Geography* make known to them the surface of the globe, and indicate the countries where the most useful natural productions are obtained, and the places where these productions are wrought and transformed into manufactured articles, which are the objects of commercial exchanges. *Cosmography* explains to them the theory of the globe, and gives an account of the phenomena of the heavens, such as the phases of the moon, the eclipses, &c.

Demonstrated Arithmetic, besides giving the reasons of arithmetical operations and preparing the way for Geometry, assists in exercising the reasoning faculty and together with Geometry it constitutes, in one sense, a course of logic. Practical and descriptive *Geometry*, independently of its furnishing the key to surveying and mechanics, presents numerous applications to the arts and trades.

In a course of *Physics* and *Chemistry*, the pupils learn all that is most useful for them to know of the general and particular properties of ponderable and imponderable substances, of the laws of their motion, and meteorology, &c, as well as of the composition of ponderable bodies and of their action upon each other.

In studying the *Natural History* of the three kingdoms, the pupils find constant subjects for applications to the purposes of life. Thus, Mineralogy makes known to them the best materials for buildings, those which are most fit for the improvement of lands, in agriculture, or which may serve as combustibles, &c. From Botany they learn the structure and functions of plants, as well as the numerous uses which are made of them in the arts, and in rural and domestic economy. In a course of Zoology, they are taught the most important facts concerning animal organization, the classification of animals, and the uses to which man may apply them.

They are taught finally, to deduce from the laws of their organization, the means to be employed by man, in order to preserve the most precious of gifts, his health.

EFFECTS OF FAMILY EXAMPLE ON SCHOOLS.

Mr Editor; — There is hardly any subject upon which more is said than education; yet, with all our boasted improvements, I fear, there is not by any means so much done as is generally supposed. I have often asked myself why it is, that with all the superior advantages enjoyed by the youth of the present day over those of their progenitors, they are far from making those acquisitions, and having that energy of character and inquiring spirit, which should result from such advantages. Perhaps some may be sceptical upon this point, and, because much is said about the 'march of mind,' imagine that our infant schools and lyceums are filled with embryo Miltons, Franklins and Newtons. But nothing more is necessary, to convince them that their expectations are rather too sanguine, than to pass one day in almost any of our schools, with the teacher's means of making a correct estimate. Let them see the listlessness and want of interest manifested by one half of the pupils, whom nothing, but compulsion, can excite to learn anything valuable; and that so imperfectly, that the amount of error imbibed, almost renders the whole worse than total ignorance; and they will be convinced that there exists some radical defect. Take a boy from the wildest part of our country, whose means of improvement have been extremely limited, and give him an opportunity, and, with the slightest aid, he will soon outstrip many who have done nothing all their days but attend school. Whence this difference? for it is too great to be attributed wholly to novelty, the effects of which are but shortlived. There must be something, either in our school systems, or in our domestic arrangements, productive of indifference to improvement, and mental effeminacy.

I am thoroughly convinced that too much is done by instructors; or rather, that their exertions are misdirected, and too little by parents and the pupils themselves. Great exertions have been made to introduce more simple and expeditious modes of imparting knowledge, both in the books used and in the manner of instruction. Much, I am aware, has been effected in this way; but every innovation is not an improvement, and the present tendency is to make the teacher do all, and the student nothing. The *easiest* way of learning a thing is not always the *best*. The object of education is not the mere acquisition of a certain amount of facts; it should have a higher aim, viz. to discipline and strengthen the mind. It consists in no small degree, in laying a foundation upon which to build a durable superstructure; in supplying the pupil with an instrument, as ever may be wrong, — of completeness, wherever there may be defect.* A face of brass is an ill omen, as well in the republic as the individual. Vanity is as fatal to getting and keeping right, when it is the 'esprit de corps,' as when it is the spirit of the man. 'Seest thou a man wise in his own conceit? — there is more hope of a fool than of him.'

Yes, Sir, if you can make the people — the sovereign people — THE REPUBLIC — see and feel that they are *excelled* in the very matter of their self-glorying, *the education of the people,* by one of the old European dynasties — by an *absolute monarchy,* — you will do something effectual in the cause you serve — you will soon have something worthy to be recorded in the 'Annals' — you will have triumphed over *self-conceit,* the grand hindrance to all our good designs. I know not how much more power for good *the republic* may have than the *monarchy*; but this I am sure of, self-conceit must *palsy* that power. The proverb may be safely varied, admitting the monarchy to be the poorest of all institutions. *Seest thou a republic wise in its own conceit? — There is more hope of a fool than of* IT.

One reason why I value the 'Annals' is because it brings us wisdom from abroad. It is not all on our side the water.

T. T.

[For the Annals of Education.]

COMMON SCHOOLS AND COMMON EDUCATION.

NO. I.

I AM not sanguine enough to think that by some half-dozen numbers with the above title, I shall produce the much desired improvement of common schools, and therewith turn the *beau ideal* of popular improvements, into a glorious and enduring reality. I have no idea of such a magic power in what I can write in thirty or forty pages of the Annals of Education; I do not expect it from the *Annals* itself, although I honor it more than many thousands of the *friends of education*; for I am, and have long been, both a subscriber and reader.

But as I write, '*The power of the press, The power of the press,*' echoes from every wind, and I hear myself assured that I am laying my hand this morning on the lever of Archimedes, and so perfect, so powerful, that it needs but the gentlest touch in order to move

* I quote from recollection, not having your article on hand. You must pardon me if I make the spirit of your offending worse than the fact.

the nation and the world. An echo from all quarters — the repeated and repeated voice of the people — is it not true? I find myself half persuaded, even after the experience of more than a score of years of public life, I am tempted to be sanguine in spite of myself, and to say the Annals for 1834 will perfect the work, which has been carried on amidst discouragement, in preceding years.

But '*Where shall I stand*,' said Archimedes — '*If I had a place to stand on I could move the world!*' And I ask, in as great a difficulty as my mathematical predecessor, with some difference in my despair — how shall my lever *reach the weight?* *The power of the press!* What power can the press exert upon those who do not read? What can the 'ANNALS' do, honored as it is, by the testimonies of the wisest Patriots and Christians, or *my numbers* on *Common Schools and Common Education*, if they never reach the people? What can you do, or I, or the so styled friends of education, even if we write with the wisdom of sages and the fervor of youth, — if after we have written, the people will not read? *A thousand subscribers* or thereabouts — or *two thousand* for the New Year! — I must say the lever does not reach the weight. You see the predicament we are likely to be in; I mean that of the unfortunate stone-digger, who has reached only an outer flake at one corner of the rock, which as the lever is moved, is parted from the mass, and leaves still fixed and unmoved in its original position.

But there is another accident of the lever, which is quite as sure to defeat the skill of Archimedes, and the muscle of the most brawny operative — I mean, when the lever actually reaches the weight, but for want of sufficient 'hold' slips and leaves all things as they were, save it may be the falls and bruises of the laborer from the sudden failure. If you had a hundred thousand readers (I seem to hear you say, *I wish they would try me*) I mean a hundred thousand subscribers rather, for on the supposition, they would not be *readers;* — I fear as affairs now stand, your lever would slip for want of 'hold' — your *power of the press*, would leave the people unmoved even when it reached them. In good truth, Mr Editor, with the love of looking at pictures — the fondness for stories — the taste for the *everything* of the newspaper — the appetite for the summary, and even for the Annals, with its velvet pages and fine covering, — the habit of reading without thought, without plan or effort for personal improvement — and still more the habit of reading almost nothing at all — I would ask the most sanguine applauder of the power of the press, what you can do with a hundred thousand chances for improving common schools and common education, in such a condition of the people? Take *my* numbers, or take if you will 'the Annals' and 'the Journal', *all* the volumes — or, if you like something else better, take Locke, Milton and Abercrombie, and Edgeworth, and Babington and Hamilton, &c, and send them forth to your hundred thousand readers, all intent upon 'light reading,' while the numberless caterers to the 'public taste' furnish illustrations, until the principles to be illustrated are overlooked and forgotten — and men *glance* instead of *reading*, and read to avoid *thinking*; tell me — Will not the lever *slip* for want of 'hold?' I will not say that in order to good success, in attempts to improve common schools and common education, the people must be all *learned*; but I will insist, that great numbers of them must be engaged habitually in *learning*, studying, thinking, before they will be moved to much advantage by the power of the press. Without this, what does take place, will take place; the lever of the press, be it ever so long and so strong, will *slip* for want of 'hold.'

Good common schools, well taught and well learning, in districts regardless of personal improvement after leaving school! — It is impossible. Such districts will not employ good teachers; or, if they chance to employ them, will not like their ways, will not train the young for their school, nor in the paths of knowledge and improvement. *The common school system educating the country in all useful knowledge, in habits of study, and thought and wisdom, amidst a people indifferent to knowledge—incapable of study and thought!* It is impossible. If you had your hundred thousand readers, of such a sort, they would but glance and forget you; and all your accounts of modes of education, and principles of education, would have reached your hundred thousand, to be blessed and buried. A whole library on the subject of education — a selection of the wisdom of all times, would leave us where we are, unless study and meditation would give 'hold' to *the power of the press.*

I will venture, then, to say, that the true secret of improving common schools, will be found *in teaching the people how to do without them.* The best attempts will certainly fail in proportion to the expectation *that everything is to be done in them, and nothing after them.* You may work forever at common schools and common education — at *un*common schools and *un*common education — at the whole matter of *youthful* improvement, and you will never have success, much beyond the interest of the people in educating themselves. You will not get the mass of the young to learn *much*, unless you can show them their elders learning *more.* If you will have the stream clear and swift, it must run on. Every child knows how useless it would be to try to keep the stream rapid, and the waters transparent, as it fills the little pond which he has dammed up; and how soon he can see the bottom, and hear the rush of waters, after he breaks an outlet, and suffers the stream to run on. If you will '*clear away*,' and let education run on through families and neighborhoods, — it will run quick and clear through the schools, and push its way through all classes and improve all as it flows .

'Alas, then, for popular improvement ! We were hoping that however sluggish *the people* who have passed the school might be, they would take all needful measures for the education of the rising generation. Farewell to all hopes of improving common schools and common education, if *the people* are to be lifted, *before* the children, or *with them.*' A little consideration will correct this mistake. There *are already*, there have always been many of the people, whose own advantages have been from the common schools, and whose children expect no other ; who, after they have left school, keep learning more. These are the best friends of common education. If there had not been many such, the common schools would have been dead long ago. If their spirit and habit can be extended among their neighbors, they will be revived and perfected. I trust that spirit and habit will be extended, as I think it may at least, in part, by a more general circulation of the *Annals of Education* ; after all, there are many on whom to act effectually, if you can reach them. I wish you no higher prosperity, than to get upon your list one half of the considerate friends of common schools and common education, scattered through our land. Make your lever long and strong, and you will find a 'hold' after all, and the rock will be raised.

The following Dialogue is intended to show at once the ground of hope in the present state of the public mind, as well to use the best means of popular improvement. I will not say that I have found any one school district, which could furnish at once the circumstances and the interlocutions ; but if you will allow me the privilege of bringing characters together from more than one town or state, I may truly say that my *Dramatis Personæ* are real.

DIALOGUE, INTRODUCTORY TO A SCHOOL MEETING.

SCENE—*A School House — neighbors collecting for a School Meeting.*

Farmer P. Well, neighbor B. I believe this is about the fortieth time that I have been at school meetings on this spot, to make arrangements for the winter school.

Farmer B. Well, there have been great improvements in education in that length of time ; the children have a better chance now than when you were a boy.

Farmer P. Yes, yes, by all accounts as you say. So every body says, newspapers and all : and what every body says must be true. I hadn't much chance, by all accounts, — sure enough — I never went to school but three winters in my life, and only three or four weeks each.

Farmer B. Well then, *you* say, I suppose, like every body else, that the chance is a great deal better now than it used to be.

Farmer P. Yes, yes, to be sure — but what puzzles me, is, that on the whole I don't see that the young folks grow up *any wiser*, and but a precious little more *knowing*, than they did fifty years ago.

Farmer B. Why that makes me remember what I read the other day about Iceland, where they hav'nt any schools at all. Why, neighbor, without any *school system*, the children learn to read around the family fire, sure enough, like college boys, and read, and learn too, after they have learned to read. I fairly blushed with shame, while I read the account. Why, what a wise people we should be, if we made *such* improvement of the chance we have.

Farmer P. I tell you, neighbor, something is the matter. We build school houses, we raise money, we give all the children a chance to learn — and yet all they learn is, to read, write, and cypher, which all grows rusty, before they are thirty.

Farmer B. Well, I'll tell you what is the matter, in one thing at least. *We must have better teachers.* Them young upstarts, who know nothing themselves, are pretty fellows to teach wisdom to the neighborhood. I'm determined, if it cost double, to have a first rate teacher this winter. Let us try it, and see if we don't get the worth of our money.

Half a dozen voices. Aye to that — Let us try for once.

Farmer P. I agree to that — but don't say *for once.* You must give your first rate teacher half a dozen winters in order to make fair trial, and I don't think we shall be losers by it.

Farmer C. I am willing for that — only see, that if you give double, you get a man that is worth it; at any rate do the best you can for it. But I think we can make another improvement; it will cost a little, at first, but when it is once made it will remain for several years — I mean the *school apparatus* we have read of; it will not cost more than a dollar a family.

Farmer P. I am willing, if 'tis only for the novelty. The children will take an interest in it for a year or two at least, and I am for anything that will stir them up.

Farmer E. Yes, and they will have something to employ themselves about. I have thought a great many times, that a school was a sort of stupifying machine. Only think of it, neighbors, to sit on these seats six hours, with nothing to do only to fix their eyes upon these jaw-cracking words, (taking up a spelling book.) How long, neighbor P., would it take a right good school-master to make a lively little fellow into a sleepy dunce?

Farmer P. Not long. I guess neighbor we were about as well off forty years ago thrashing wheat, as to be dozing here over 'transubstantiation,' and such long words. Why, I remember how I read to my mother in those days in the Bible, and Pilgrim's Progress; yes, and as I grew older, we got hold of Rollin's Ancient History.

Mr F. Well. There will be another advantage from the apparatus. The scholars will know what they are about. I should be ashamed to tell how old I was, before I had a clear notion of the difference between a square and a cube; it was a great while after I could work the Cube Root.

Farmer B. There you hit my plan. You needed a better teacher to see whether you understood as you learned — to *make* you understand.

Farmer F. True, but his easiest way to do it would have been, to have set a square and a cube side by side.

Mr G. There is one more thing wanted — and that is to make the children come more regularly, and through the whole season. What can the best teacher do with the best books and apparatus, if the scholars are absent so much of the time, as to forget every lesson they are taught. And how can he teach them any thing worth remembering, if they come so irregularly that he cannot teach them in classes? If he is obliged to give sixty separate lessons of a morning, he might almost as well give none. Three minutes a piece, is about as good as no time. Let us alter in this matter; this will be a cheap and easy improvement.

Dr H. There's another subject, gentlemen, which I will name, if you will not be frightened. Your school-house is not fit for the use you put it to. When you get sixty children into this room, the air becomes, in a short time, unfit to breathe, so that if your other arrangements are ever so good, your school-house benumbs and sickens all the children's faculties.*

Mr I. The Doctor would not complain for want of fresh air, if he had been sitting where I have, with a stream of cold air coming in upon me.

Dr H. True, I forgot one evil while thinking of another; but I had good reason to remember it, and so have all my neighbors. My book tells sad tales of sore throats, and quinsies, and coughs, and fevers, very likely, by means of these very streams of air. If you build your school-house as it ought to be, I may be a loser, but you will not.

Lawyer K. Well, neighbor, saving the new school-house, which we can't touch this winter, I believe we shall be unanimous in all

* See November No. of Annals on this subject.

the points which we have named ; i. e. if neighbor Stingy does not come. For he would rather see the district as dark as the dark ages, than give a sixpence.

Farmer P. Well, if we are twenty to one we must not mind him. If he is stubborn, here is Lawyer K. will bear a hand at collecting, and we know it will be better for him and his children in the end.

Lawyer K. Well, if all these matters are 'cut and dried,' let us try one more, (looking at his watch), yes, and quick too, for it lacks only a quarter to seven, and then it will be, 'To order, gentlemen.'

All. Well, speak on.

Lawyer K. But first, I'll warn you all that if you adopt my proposal, you must look out, or I shall have more than one job at collecting.

Half a dozen. Well, let us see how we are going to get into the Lawyer's hands.

Farmer P. It will be the first time in my life, and I am so old that I shall not relish it now. However, let the Lawyer try and get a little business out of me, if he will.

Lawyer K. Well, if you don't try my plan you may try all the rest, and not accomplish much in improving your school ; and if you do take mine, with a forfeit, then ten to one a good many of you will have to pay, and I am not sure of escaping 'with a whole skin' myself.

All. Speak on.

Lawyer K. The secret of improving this school, and all the schools is short ; it can be told in less than the five minutes which now remain. If you wish the young to improve, *let the old keep learning*. Let the elder members of society be ever learning something new, useful and interesting, and we shall have no poor schools. When the children see that we are every day trying to learn more, that we are the better off for all we learn, they will catch our spirit. The young people who stand between, will get from both sides a stimulus to improvement, which they give back to the parents and the children. The children will not be made dull by the sleepy air about the chimney corner ; will not be frozen up by the cold of home ; but will feel the warm glow of an Iceland family, and be better off than they, because they will have *then*, good schools, as well as good homes. You see my plan. Gentlemen, you must settle the forfeit.

Farmer P. The lawyer is too cunning for us. But what if *we* should study '*like college boys*,' as neighbor B. said, then, Lawyer, you *will* lose your chance of collecting.

Lawyer K. Aye, but I might charge handsomely for advice

which was so useful. But this once, at least, I'll labor for the public good. If my clients will take my advice, they shall have it for nothing.

Mr L. Well, that is exactly what I have been trying to make out, as I have been sitting here without saying a word, seeing our good neighbor M. there, trying to make a fire. I hope neighbor M. will take no offence if I tell what has been in my mind.

Mr M. No, No; only I shall insist that you shall make the fire next time, for I have had trouble enough with it.

Farmer P. Well, I hope you'll contrive how to do it without all this bother, though I know not how, unless you have better materials and a better fire-place. As to your school, Lawyer K., you will never have a good school, in a smoky and cold house like this.

Lawyer K. Well, let us see how Mr L. is going to set the whole matter right.

Mr L. Well, then, with neighbor M.'s leave, we will consider what has been going on. First came a shovel full of coals, fanned by the wind, and looking bright enough to set the world on fire; and down they went upon the hearth, which you see has not taken fire yet, and never will; next came a dozen sticks of green wood laid half a mile from the coals; then to establish the line of communication between the fire and the fuel, came a peck of water soaked chips.

Mr M. Just such as school district No. 5, keeps dried in nature's wood-house — but what next?

Mr L. Why, what next, but the grand fire-making instrument that you have in your hands, *the bellows*, which I am sure you have been using a full half-hour, raising smoke enough to stifle us and put out our eyes.

Mr M. Ah, that's the fault of the chimney, the *draught is bad.*

Mr L. No wonder, then, that we have not a good school; for even with a good bellows and faithful blowing, we are likely to have no fire. If you want to have a good school you must have a good fire: so, then, to make the fire you must have — 1. Dry fuel, water will not burn. 2. The fire must touch the wood. 3. The fire and wood must be *above* the hearth, so that the air may pass through.

Mr M. And 4. I must come with the bellows!

Mr L. The bellows, man! no, not if I make the fire. Give me the bellows, and let me burn them up. All nature gives the bellows. Say then, 4. *a fire-place with a good draught*; let the chimney be the nose of the bellows.

Lawyer K. But what has all that to do with my proposition?

Mr L. Why a great deal. What are books and apparatus, but fuel, on which the love of knowledge may feed? And what the business of your best teacher but to lay them where the mind can take fair and fast hold of them, and where the flame may be fanned by all the motives of improvement?

Mr M. And then to take the bellows — rewards — places — — flogging, &c.

Mr L. Nay, man — to let it burn — if the chimney has a good draught, i. e. Lawyer K., to quote your words, *if the old keep learning something new, and useful, and interesting* — if the '*set*' of the neighborhood — of the family is towards useful knowledge — there'll be no need of a bellows. — I tell you what, neighbor, it is too much to expect good schools, in an empty-minded, idle-minded neighborhood. I don't mean to say that *ours* is so; for I'm sure we have talked long enough on this business to prove that we are not.

Lawyer K. Long enough, indeed. Twenty minutes past the time. *To order, gentlemen*, or we shall have no school at all.

ON TEACHING TO READ ACCORDING TO THE METHOD OF JACOTOT.

The higher branches of instruction are very properly confined to the school room: they are rendered more clear and interesting by the lessons of the professional teacher: he can assign its proper place to each, and consulting their natural order, prepare by one the way for the other. But there is another department of education in which the kindness and affection of a mother, will accomplish far more than the skill and experience of the teacher, when a word of tenderness will give a vigor and zeal, that cold encouragement and commendation can never inspire. It is in learning to read; the first, the simplest chapter, it is true, in the whole science of education, but for that very reason, the most interesting and the most important. The child may be harassed and disgusted on this threshold of his course, or he may be excited to a high degree of interest, and all his faculties brought into active exertion. It is the first bending of the twig; and although the pliant stem may, even long after this, be compressed into a regular and graceful form; yet, far quicker and stronger would be its growth, could we devote that time of correction to restraining its luxuriance, and preserving the tendency of its original direction.

In a former article I have stated the origin of the method of Jacotot. I will now endeavor to show by a brief illustration, that if his method do not fully accomplish this object, it does not, at least, fall far short of it.

It is by no means necessary that any particular work be generally adopted as the text of this exercise. The various circumstances, of which every teacher is the best judge for his own pupils, must direct in the choice. We will suppose that our little class has been told to commence with the Gospel of St John, and that each individual holds that work in his hand. Let them open at the first chapter, and be directed to fix their eyes upon the first verse. The instructor then pronounces the word *in*, and the class repeats it after him. 'This,' he then tells them, 'is the first word in the verse; it is represented by the two first marks that you see there. Now observe their shape, for you will soon meet them again, and of course you would like to recognise them. Can you describe them?

'*Yes Sir.* The first looks like a straight mark, the other has two marks instead of one, and there is a line across the top, that *unites them.*'

'That is very well described. Now let us take the next word, '*the.*' Look carefully at the letters. How many are there of them?'

'*Three.*'

'Are any of them like the two first?'

Here every eye will be running from letter to letter, in a diligent comparison.

'*No Sir, they are not at all alike.*'

'Well, now repeat these two words, and then we will pass to the next.'

'*In the beginning.*'

'This word,' continues the instructor, 'is very long, and you must take care to pronounce it distinctly. Now tell me whether you can find here any letter that you have seen before.'

Here the comparison recommences, and is attended this time with better success.

'*O yes, Sir; we find several.*'

'How many?'

'Two; the last letter of the first word is repeated twice, and then there is the last letter of the second word, too.'

'But point them out to me. Show me in which part of the word you find them.'

'The last letter of the second word comes directly after the first letter in this word.'

'That is very well done. But would not you like to have some name to distinguish that letter by, just as you distinguish your play-fellows, when you speak to them? It is very inconvenient to be obliged to say first letter and last letter, because it makes you say a great many words, in order to tell one thing.'

'*Yes, Sir.* Do give us a *name.*'

'I will give you one with a great deal of pleasure, but you must endeavor to recollect it. We call that the *letter e*. Now can any one of you tell why it is called so?'

This is apparently a difficult question for children. They will probably hesitate. Some may not perceive the answer until after several lessons; but they will at last decide that it is called *e*, because it is sounded so in the words in which they have seen it. The consonant sounds are more difficult to analyze, for it requires far greater effort to utter them. Perseverance, however, will ultimately succeed, and give the exact power of each letter, as far as they have been combined.

Should the scholar forget the name of any letter, his instructor should never hesitate to repeat it as long as he is satisfied that this forgetfulness does not proceed from neglect; for while the memory derives a large share of its strength from exercise, it is as useless to strain and fatigue it in a search after what is lost, as to hope that you can recall the impression to softened wax without imprinting it anew.

'Well, now,' continues the instructor, 'you say that this letter is called *e* because it represents that sound in the word. Now pronounce the whole word as slowly as you can. Separate the other letter from that which you call *e*, and then tell me what name you would give it.' Here the instructor will probably have to give an example of the drawled utterance that *b* requires, but he avoids attaching any name to the sound of the first letter. The class will soon perceive that the sound is imperfect by itself, and cannot be completed without calling in the aid of the next letter. They will here (as a natural consequence of the first observation) remark, that these two letters differ not in form alone, but that their power also is different. Leave them with this observation, and proceed to tell them the names of the two next letters that have been repeated.

They will remark, that *i* (to which I would give its elementary power) has, like *e*, an independent sound which is full and satisfactory by itself. Then by going back to *b* and uniting the *i*, first with the whole syllable as *ibe*, next dropping the *è*, and sounding the *ib* as a perfect syllable, and finally omitting the *b* also, they will separate without difficulty the two letters of *in*, and discover the exact power of *n*.

The instructor should now question them upon the letters.

'Are all letters alike?'

'No, Sir.'

'In what do they differ?'

'In shape.'

'Is that all?'

'In sound.'

'Well, how do they differ in sound?'

'Why, Sir, *e* and *i* are not alike.'

'But sound them; I wish to see where they differ.'

'*e* — *i*.'

'Very well. You are perfectly correct. But the other letters, *b* and *n* and *g*, are they alike?'

'No, Sir; they differ just as *e* and *i* differ. One makes *b*, the other *g*, and the other *n*; and then there is another thing in which they differ from *e* and *i*; they do not form a distinct sound when they stand alone.'

'How then can you give them a distinct sound?'

'By *uniting* them with *e* or *i*.'

Before we proceed farther, we should require the class to combine all the vowels and consonants in the lesson; *b* should be united with *i*; *th* with *ing*, and in short, the letters should be changed in every manner, and every description of combination formed that they will admit of. The class may then be told that the different kinds of letters that they have observed, have specific names by which we distinguish them, when we speak of all together, without mentioning each individual letter. That those which form a perfect sound, are called vowels; the others, consonants; and by explaining the derivation of these words, you will give them a stronger hold upon the memory.

The first lesson may end here. And I would now ask whether a faculty of those little minds has been left to slumber? Memory has caught the sounds and shapes of these new signs, and stored them up in her yet unformed reservoir. Comparison has lent her aid to mark the difference of form by which each is distinguished, and to discover the various powers and properties of each. And while analyzing their sounds, while composing new sounds by means of this analysis, has the progress of this class been confined simply to the knowledge that they have acquired in the art of reading; or have they from the first step in study, been shown that the results which they obtain are in proportion to their exertions, and that every species of intellectual acquirement must be earned by the full equivalent of intellectual effort?

Before we proceed to the second lesson we must require that each individual repeat the words and principal observations of the first. Some may have forgotten the words and names of the letters; they must in that case be repeated again. But the observations were the result of their own exertions. Now there is an important distinction between the recollection of arbitrary signs or unconnected facts, and that of an act of our own judgment. We cannot recover the former without returning to the first sources of our knowledge, but we carry with us a clue to the latter, and the same facts by which they were originally suggested, will always lead us back to them, even long after they have escaped the memory. While, therefore, we would assist a scholar to recall the name of an arbitrary sign, we would studiously avoid prompting his memory with regard to his own observations.

The first word of the next lesson is wholly new, — '*was*.' After it has been repeated it should be compared with the words of the first lesson, and the points in which they differ should be marked as minutely as those of their agreement. The vowels and consonants should be carefully noted down; each letter assigned to its proper class, and combined successively with the letters of the former lessons. The next word '*the*' will be hailed like an old acquaintance, nor will the re-appearance of *in* excite less pleasure. Whenever a scholar meets with words or letters that he has seen before, he feels that his knowledge is becoming more extensive and more perfect, and that he is approaching nearer to the period, when all the stock of forms and signs shall be closely and securely arranged in his memory.

With the remaining letters of this word, the —*ord*—you should proceed as with the other new letters: their powers should be ascertained by analysis, and they should then be combined with the other parts of the lesson. The very next word will show how much this course contributes to the real progress of the scholar. He has not seen this word before, he may suppose at first that it will be impossible for him to sound it; but every letter of which it is composed has entered into the composition of some of the words that he already knows; he has used them himself in the course of his various combinations, and by a few moments of trial and study, will readily discover their power and value in their present form. No new letters occur throughout the verse, and the new combinations can be easily read.

EXCESSIVE PUNISHMENT.

THE remarks of Colet and Ascham, in a preceding article, will scarcely be understood, or fairly applied, without remembering the peculiar severity of that day. '*Time was,*' when *pain* was considered the only sentiment which could be safely associated with knowledge in the mind of a child, as a means of inspiring the *love of learning*, and the rod was deemed as necessary a vehicle for conveying Latin rules to the mind, as syrup for administering a powder. 'Flogging' is as regularly administered to the young men, and it is an honor to the impartiality of 'the schoolmaster,' that we may add, young *noblemen*, in the great schools of England, as to her sailors. When we last heard of their *discipline*, an offender of whatever age was 'horsed,' or placed on the back of another pupil, and given over to the executioner employed for this purpose, to receive the appointed blows like a felon.

We do not remember ever to have seen a more complete exhibition of the system to which this belongs than in the following extract from the German 'Conversations Lexicon,' the basis of the 'Encyclopædia Americana.'

'Hauberle and Neuman relate, that John James Hauberle, the schoolmaster of a small Suabian town, during the 51 years and 7 months in which he performed the duties of his office, according to *a moderate calculation*, gave the youth entrusted to his charge, 911,517 blows with a stick—24,010 strokes with a rod—20,989 ferulings—136,715 blows with the hand—10,235 slaps upon the chops—7905 boxes on the ears—1,115,800 raps on the head, and 12,763 notabenes with the Bible, Catechism, Psalm Book, and Grammar. 777 times he made boys kneel upon peas; and 613 times upon a three cornered piece of wood. He obliged 5001 scholars to wear the picture of an ass upon the breast; and 1707 to hold out the rod; — not to mention the punishments which were inflicted *extempore*. Of the blows with a stick, 800,000 were for not learning Latin vocabularies, and of the strokes with a rod, 7,600 were for not learning passages of the Bible and hymns.

Without discussing the truth of an account taken from a work of so grave a character as the 'Conversations Lexicon,' or attempting to suppress the smile it will excite in our readers, we could almost weep when we think of the abuses we have ourselves more than once known. We only give place to this curious calculation, from recollecting the habits of some distinguished masters of the old school, whose ferule and 'taws' are now the food of worms. We shall never forget one, the shadow of whose authority made us quail, who applied the little instrument we have named, with its three fold lash, for *every error in Latin quantity* which occurred in a recitation! To reckon his blows, 'not to mention those inflicted extempore,' would, we fear, be almost hopeless.

One of our friends well remembers his receiving so severe blows in childhood, for forgetting his lesson, that his mother was compelled to apply remedies. And not many days have passed, since we heard of a poor boy who asked, why it was that when the master boxed his ears, his head turned, and he could scarcely hear what the master said, — a discipline to which a whole class were sometimes subjected! Are teachers, indeed, ignorant that such blows may produce deafness, and that they almost necessarily give rise to a temporary confusion of memory?

But we are not ready to concede, that because corporal punishment is not useful to *drive in learning*; or because it may be wrongly administered, that it is not sometimes important, (we believe very rarely) in subduing violent passion, or to form a counter motive to some inveterate propensity or habit.

As we have formerly remarked, the Great Educator of man employs bodily pain as a means of discipline; and multitudes, from the time of David to this day, have acknowledged its happy influence. We are persuaded, that in the days of childhood, the rod sometimes produced good effects on ourselves, and aided us to master feelings, in view of this object of terror, which might otherwise have assumed the tyranny of habits, before reason had learned to hold the reins of passion. We have had more than one pupil, whose confidence and affection we never gained, until we had assisted him, in this way, to govern himself. We believe that excessive punishment is ruinous to the character, while thorough discipline is indispensable.

mented with rheumatic toothache for years, from trying to 'harden himself,' by sitting with wet feet. The *January thaw*,' exposes a school very much to colds, and requires more caution than frosty weather.

Keep a thermometer in your room; for your variable state of body is no test of the proper temperature. Ventilate it well several times a day; but do not let your pupils be exposed to the cold, while in a state of perspiration.

THE WORLD.

Teach your pupils not merely to study at school, but to look abroad, and observe the face of nature. If they will watch the freezing of water, and the snow flakes, they will see the process of crystalization. Point out to them the changes in the air, produced by different kinds of weather. Let them look out for the Aurora Borealis.

VEGETABLES.

Let them mark how this is the season of sleep in the vegetable world; and show them how much better living plants resist the frost, than things without life. They may learn, however, even now, to distinguish the various kinds of evergreens and mosses; and may be taught to conceive of those countries where winter is perpetual. Do you find any insects or plants on the snow, in your region? If so, let them be watched and described.

ANIMALS.

Most of the birds have gone from the north, to warm climates. Let the departure of others be noted; and let the children observe how the robins, and snow birds, and partridges get their food.

The frogs and reptiles have buried themselves for the winter; and the bears and hedgehogs, where they exist, have generally gone to sleep for the season. The fox, the rabbit, the squirrel, and the deer, may be traced in the snow; and much instruction and amusement may be derived from watching their habits, in many parts of the country. Do not allow your pupils to pass over that change of color in the coats of several of the animals, by which the Creator enables them to conceal themselves in the season of snow.

THE HEAVENS.

The clear nights of winter show the stars in their greatest lustre. Teach your pupils the constellation of the Great Bear, if no other, and the situation of the north star. Point out the planets, when they are visible.

Venus, is the morning star until March, and is well worth the trouble of early rising in a clear morning. I have seen it cast a distinct shadow. *Jupiter* can be seen at any time in a clear evening. It is on the meridian (or south of us) at six o'clock; and of course sets after 10 o'clock. *Saturn* is visible at the same time as Jupiter, (if not obscured by its light,) a little lower down. The rings of Saturn and satellites of Jupiter, may be seen with a good telescope. *Mars* rises late in the morning, and sets before evening. *Mercury* may perhaps be seen at a very early hour in the morning.

In pointing out the wonders of Nature, forget not to lead the minds of your pupils to *Him who made them all.*

MISCELLANY.

Professional Education of Teachers.

It seems now to be felt by all parties on education that "*something must be done*" to prepare teachers for their responsible task. It is also conceded, that *practice* is indispensable to make a thorough teacher; and some believe that this is enough. One gentleman, himself concerned in an institution for the instruction of teachers, goes so far as to denounce the seminaries founded for this purpose as dangerous monopolies! We will not stop to examine the consistency of their course; for we are happy to find a large and increasing number of the friends of education, who deem it of the highest importance to communicate to the young teacher, a part of the experience of those who have gone before him; and who think that the science of Education and the art of teaching, are as important to an instructor, as the science of Physiology and the art of operating, to the surgeon. The last month furnishes many indications of progress on this subject.

Governor Wolfe, of Pennsylvania, in his late message to the legislature of that State, urges the necessity of such an arrangement for the education of its citizens as "should secure the education and instruction of a competent number of active, intelligent teachers; who will not only be prepared, but well qualified, to take upon themselves the government of the schools, and to communicate instruction to the pupils."

In New York the committee appointed at a public meeting of the Friends of Common Education, in July last, to promote the establishment of a Central Institution for the Education of Common School Teachers in that State, have recently issued an address setting forth the importance and necessity of such an institution, and warmly urging the friends of public instruction in all the Counties of the State, to hold meetings on this subject as soon as may be, and to unite in soliciting the attention of the Legislature to it, at their approaching session.

In the Oxford Academy, New York, which we should regard from its catalogue as flourishing, we find that a course of Lectures is to be commenced in School-keeping, for the benefit of those who wish to prepare for that profession, with a course of regular recitations on the subject. The same plan has been adopted in many other Academies.

Schools at the West.

The progress of efforts to promote education in "the West"—the great, the rising West—continues to be encouraging. The want of it is *felt*; and this is the first, and the most important step, towards procuring a supply. In our last number, we recorded the meetings of three conventions of teachers and friends of education, in Ohio and Kentucky; and during the present month, a meeting is to be held at Frankfort to organize a School Society for the State.

A similar association formed in Indiana, have been engaged in ascertaining the condition of education throughout the State, in order to rouse the people to action. The following are extracts from their report —

"*A large majority of the rising generation are destitute of any privileges of instruction.* In nine townships from which a full tabular report was returned, containing about 9,000 children between 5 and 15 years of age, only 919 attended school last year, and the larger part of those for three months only. But one in six are able to read; one in nine to write, one in sixteen have studied arithmetic; one in *one hundred* geography, &c. one in one hundred and fortyfive, grammar. In the three counties of Washington, Jackson and Lawrence, containing a population of 27,000, only 1,521 attend school in summer, and 3,433 in winter. Making an average in winter of one scholar to two families, and in summer, less.

"There are places in some of the oldest counties in the state where from 40 to 60 children have lived till now without any privileges of instruction, and others where it has been the fact for five or six years. Circulars from other parts of the state bring accounts equally gloomy. One reports a *township in which there has not been a school during the past year.* In one neighborhood where personal inquiry has been made in every family, out of 48 children under 21 years of age, six only could read, and two write a little. In another, among 60 children only eight could read."

Painful as these facts are, it is a matter of rejoicing that they are developed, for we cannot believe that Americans will rest, until some mode be found to enlighten this mass of uncultivated mind.

In Michigan, we perceive that this subject is receiving attention. It is stated by the Detroit Courier, in which we find some interesting essays on education, that the schools of that place are well taught, and that several literary associations exist for various objects.

Education and the Press.

It is no slight indication of interest in education, that it commands, to so great an extent, the services of that engine which moves the civilized world — the Press. Among the books with which it is continually burdened, a large part are designed for the young. No opportunity is lost of claiming for a book a place in the school; and no book will so readily find a publisher, as a good juvenile work. It is gratifying also to see, that the day of trifles is passing away; and that the name of "a Parley book" is becoming somewhat reproachful, from the fact, that so many of the attractive and highly embellished works under this title, are found to possess little permanent value.

The interest exhibited in this by the Periodical Press, is an omen not less gratifying. A great number of our newspapers not only copy and circulate articles on this subject, but often present valuable original essays.

Lancasterian Schools in Turkey.

It is stated on the authority of a letter from a gentleman in Constantinople that the Turks are becoming eager for instruction and are introducing the Lancasterian system of instruction among themselves. Two schools, embracing nearly seven hundred youths between twelve and twenty years of age, are already in successful operation. It is also added, that they are urging the English in that city to prepare books, maps, charts, cards, lessons, translations, &c. as fast as possible. They wish for the largest and best maps, which they can find, of every country. These, they copy, if not in their own language, and write their names in Turkish. They manifest much ignorance of the extent of the labor of preparing books, and suppose that a large geography can be be made in eight or ten days, with perfect ease!

Manual Labor Schools.

The combination of manual labor with study, as a means of economy and health, is gaining attention constantly. A number of institutions already existing, are beginning to adopt it, *as a part of their regular course of discipline* — the only mode in our view of making a fair experiment.

The Governor of Pennsylvania advises the adoption of this system in seminaries for teachers, proposed in his message, and the Seminary at Andover (Mass.) has made provision for the labor of its students. The interest in other states at the North, is manifested by the numerous applications for places at these schools, and the frequent inquiries of parents.

But we are most gratified to see the system embraced with so deep interest at the South. In the report of the Manual Labor School of the *Georgia* Presbyterian Education Society, it is stated that the experiment there made, furnishes satisfactory evidence that in that climate also, and with southern constitutions, labor promotes study as well as health.

The message of the Governor of Georgia presents it in the same view, and advises its introduction into the school system of that State.

NOTICES.

Alphabet of Botany for the Use of Beginners. By James Rennie, A. M. Revised and Corrected for the Use of American Schools, by Arabella Clark, Principal of Female Department Mechanics' School. New York: Peter Hill. 1833. 18mo. pp. 130.

An interesting introduction to Botany, adapted to the capacities of children, and calculated to excite a love for the study. Its arrangement is simple, and scientific terms are avoided as much as possible. Those which are used, are introduced with explanations which will render them intelligible, and illustrated by a number of well executed engravings. We rejoice to see it issuing from the "*Mechanics' School.*"

Lessons in Greek; a familiar Introduction to the Greek Language as a living tongue. By Theodore Dwight, Jun. Springfield: G. & C. Merriam. 1833. 12mo. pp. 104.

We have looked over this attempt to render the language of our sacred book more accessible, with great interest. It is a grammar, on the simple plan of nature, and proposes to let the pupil learn Greek as he learns English, by speaking and writing, analysing and spelling words, as they occur in phrases and combining them into new phrases, and thus presenting the theory, as he proceeds in the *practice* of grammar. It will find no favor with the "conservatives" in education; reformers will welcome it.

The Young Man's Guide. Boston: Lilly, Wait, Colman & Holden. 1833. 18mo. pp. 320.

So brief a title is a rare luxury to a reader, as well as to an editor, and printer. The book is marked, in general, with the same terseness and point; and we do not hesitate to recommend it as the best guide for young men to the common duties of life with which we are acquainted. It does not profess to refer to another world; and we think, does not bring forward the highest sanctions of duty, so much as it ought. But it presents those details of morals and manners, for want of which a christian character is frequently thrown into the shade, and sometimes rendered doubtful in the view of the world. The concluding chapters ought to be read by every teacher and parent. As our own copy was lent, we borrowed another, which we found had already been the means of destroying the box of an inveterate snuff-taker. If the author does no more, he will have the thanks of more than one of this generation, and perhaps some of the next. Like other works, this has its defects. The style needs attention; and the author sometimes mistakes his own peculiarities for universal principles.

Elements of Plane and Spherical Trigonometry, with its application to the principles of Navigation and Nautical Astronomy: with the Logarithmic and Trigonometrical Tables, by J. R. Young. Revised and Corrected by J. D. Williams. Philadelphia: Carey, Lea & Blanchard. 1833. 8vo. pp. 348.

We have just received this volume of the course of mathematics, by Young, and are able to give it only a cursory examination; but we find reason to believe it worthy of the author of the Geometry.

The Teacher's Gift for 1834. Boston: Brown & Peirce.

This little work consists of a series of brief maxims, one for each week, followed by a few remarks. A blank space is left below for references "To the Scriptures," "To History," "To Observation," for illustration or proof, which are to be filled up by the pupil for the weekly examination. We admire the plan. A book thus *compiled* by the pupil, would be worth fifty which he should merely read for amusement. It would teach him the most important of lessons — to think.

The Child's Annual. Boston: Allen & Ticknor. 1834. 18mo.

We were agreeably disappointed to find this a volume which we could cheerfully put into the hands of a child. The stories are written with good taste, in a spirit which discovers that the *welfare* of the children is not forgotten, in the attempt to please. Many of the other articles are instructive as well as interesting. The style of execution is handsome, without any expensive superfluity.

Scenes of American Wealth and Industry, in Produce, Manufactures, Trade, the Fisheries, &c. Boston: Allen & Ticknor. 16mo.

An interesting and instructive work, in a familiar style, and well adapted for the fireside companion of a child's winter evening, or a commentary on his geography.

Berquin's Children's Friend. 4 vols. 18mo. Munroe & Francis.

We have never seen a rival to this work of Berquin's, in its power of impressing principles by narrative and dialogue. It is confined, indeed, to morals and manners, but its author knew how to give a peculiar charm to truth. We rejoice that a new and well executed American edition has appeared. We have only to wish that it may soon be disposed of, and then we hope to see one more thoroughly Americanized in its character.

Youth's Sketch Book. Lilly, Wait & Co. 1834.

A book of uncommon beauty, and well fitted to cultivate the taste and the hearts of the young. To us, it has been highly interesting.

Exercises in Algebra and Arithmetic.

A series of "Exercises or examples in Algebra and Arithmetic," prepared by Mr Grund, have been published by Carter, Hendee & Co. together with Keys for the use of teachers. They are designed to accompany treatises on this subject, and to afford a variety of practical exercises.

MANUAL ALPHABET OF THE DEAF AND DUMB.

A a

B b

C c

D d

E e

F f

G g

H h

I i

J j

K k

L l

from instruction. To provide for these, we have six institutions: 1. The oldest and most northern, which has furnished teachers to most of the others, is the American Asylum at Hartford, Connecticut. 2. The New York Institution, of New York. 3. The Institution at Canajoharie, in the State of New York. 4. The Pennsylvania Institution, at Philadelphia. 5. The Ohio Institution, at Columbus. 6. The Kentucky Asylum, at Danville.

The American Asylum was nobly endowed by Congress. It is thus well provided with buildings and workshops; and is enabled to receive pupils below the cost of their board and instruction. It contains 130 pupils, a large part of whom are indigent, and are provided for by legislative grants, from every State except Rhode Island. Maine and New Hampshire sustain 15 to 20 deaf mutes, each, at this institution; Vermont, from 25 to 30; Massachusetts, 50; and Connecticut, 20 to 30.

The New York Institution has 124 pupils, and that at Canajoharie, 34. The State of New York supports 90 pupils at the institution in New York, and 24 at Canajoharie.

We regret to learn that the Institution at New York is suffering for want of funds. There are men of the spirit of Perkins, and there is a generous legislature, in that liberal State. Will they not furnish all the aid which these children of misfortune need?

The Pennsylvania Institution has 80 pupils. Of these the State of Pennsylvania provides for 50, and Maryland for 20. New Jersey supports 12 to 15 pupils, divided between the Pennsylvania and New York Institutions.

The Ohio Institution has 25 pupils, and that of Kentucky probably an equal number. A few of them are sustained by the public funds. We believe no States, except those we have named, have made any provision for the education of this unfortunate portion of the community; nor can we hope that they will gain attention, until the importance of general education is more deeply felt in the same States.

In the northern institutions, colored pupils are received as well as white; but of the 743 mutes of this class, a very small number are yet under instruction.

It is remarkable, that from some strange apathy or prejudice in the friends of the deaf-mute, or from the neglect of the more enlightened around them, the appropriations have almost always exceeded the amount demanded by applicants; and a portion of the fund appropriated by Massachusetts, has been devoted to the instruction of the blind, for want of subjects presented for instruction. It has been necessary in most of the States blessed with institutions, to make special efforts to search out, and bring to the proper officer, the children thus growing up, almost like the beasts that perish. In the midst of moral and intellectual light, they stand shrouded in utter darkness; and yet, there is often no kind hand stretched forth, even to point their parents to the means of illumination.

In a former volume, we have described the course of instruction adopted in these institutions. It is the American system, founded on the French system, as practised during the visit of Mr Gallaudet, (the first principal of the American Asylum) at Paris. The plan of Sicard, at that time presiding over the institution at Paris, was encumbered with forms and metaphysics from which it was happily freed at Hartford, and its spirit preserved in the more simple and enlarged method of nature. It is, in effect, to teach the deaf-mutes the tongue of her mother, as nearly as possible, in the same manner that she communicates it to her children who are blessed with hearing. It is to teach the signification of words by means of external objects, and the visible, natural signs or expressions, or of thought and feeling; to teach their combinations by incessant and varied practice; and *then, and not till then,* to combine examples into rules, and practice by means of principles. On this plan, the deaf mute makes progress in the use of language, which surprises all who notice it, and, like their companions in misfortune — the blind — acquire in months, a knowledge of the meaning and combination of words, which the absurd methods of many schools do not communicate in years, if at all.

We have said that this is done 'by means of external objects, and the visible, natural signs or expressions of thought and feeling.' In regard to the first, the process of pointing to the various objects around us, or their pictures, and in repeating the names, and requiring the pupil to repeat them, is too obvious to need description. 'The visible and natural expressions of thought and feeling,' are so much excluded by our sedate habits, and our fear of 'apish tricks' and 'theatrical manner,' that we almost deny their use, even to our orators. But who has ever witnessed unrestrained feelings — whether in the burst of eloquence, or the outbreakings of passion, or the overflowings of sentiment — that has not read more in the fixed attitude, and the impassioned gesture, and the illuminated or darkened countenance, and the glancing eye, than he *could* read in the mere words which were uttered? Who would not rather encounter volleys of reproach from the tongue, than that withering look of scorn, or that appalling frown of rebuke, which is inspired by some of our great minds?

We have formerly alluded to the diffusion of this *only universal language*, some of whose most abstract signs, such as 'truth,' and 'falsehood,' are individually the same, among the deaf mutes of France and Italy, and the Indians of the Missouri. In a visit to the great Reclusorio, or public poor house of Naples, we found ourselves perfectly at home with its deaf and dumb pupils, by means of signs acquired in the United States; while they were compelled to act as my interpreters, with the speaking beings around us. We have found this language equally familiar to the Spaniard, and the Italian, and the Frenchman, — to the Chinese, and the Sandwich Islander, and the North American Indian. And we may add, we have felt its influence more than that of any attempt we ever heard, to encumber, with articulate sounds, 'thoughts that breathe,' only when they glance with the lightning, from eye to eye. We may be considered enthusiasts — and so will he who talks of the power of music to those who never heard or practised it. Temperance societies have been formed in the Asylum at Hartford and New York, which have their meetings, and speeches by gesture, and seem to exert a happy influence on those who fall in the way of temptation.

There is another mode of communication, irksome indeed to the deaf and dumb, when compared with the striking rapidity of the language of gesture and expression, but still involving an algebraic precision, and a compressed form of abstract terms, which belongs only to words. It is by an alphabet of the fingers, known indeed to many, but which we have presented in this number, in the belief that it would be new and interesting to a large number of our readers, and useful to more. A slight experiment will show the vast superiority of this single-handed or Spanish alphabet, to the double-handed signs of letters, with which we were accustomed to transmit the mysteries of our childish days, that were too sacred or too dangerous for utterance. In this mode of communication, it is obvious that each word must be spelled. A slight movement of the hand indicates the close of the word; and only a practised hand, and a quick eye, are necessary to communicate the *substance* of an oral conversation, while it is going on. We have known this done in society; and a mute was enabled to write down immediately the principal remarks made. We present it, however, not merely as an object of curiosity. It is of essential service in the communications of a sick chamber, where the voice might disturb; or with a deaf friend. We have witnessed its convenience, in the intercourse of a lady with her domestics or children, on household affairs not interesting to a social circle. We believe these tangible signs would help to engage a child's attention to the less obvious forms of the written alphabet, and to assist his memory in spelling; and we have known it employed in spelling classes.

It is proper to add, that our Institutions generally provide instruction for their pupils in some branch of industry; and that they prove good workmen, and useful members of society.

THE RESULTS OF INDIVIDUAL EFFORT—

As exhibited in the Asylum for Poor Children, at Locle in Switzerland.

I RECOLLECT no narrative which interested my childish feelings more than an account of the Orphan House of Franke — now one of the noblest establishments in Germany — founded and sustained by the labors and prayers of a single, pennyless individual. I regarded it as one of the extraordinary occurrences of past times, which could neither be explained nor repeated. And yet it has been my lot to visit an institution scarcely less remarkable, founded and sustained, not by an eminent and well-known divine, but by a solitary female — not in the midst of a populous kingdom, but in a village, on the summit of Mount Jura.

Few objects interest a traveller, who regards his own species with interest, more than the contrast in the condition of the inhabitants on different sides of a boundary line. The industry, and neatness, and comfort of one canton or kingdom, is exchanged for negligence in agriculture, poverty in buildings, and wretchedness and beggary in the people, on passing the limits of another. None that ever passed from the canton of Vaud, to that of Friberg, can have failed to notice it. The transition from level, fertile France, to ,the mountainous, barren regions of Switzerland, is not less striking. In leaving France, I passed through a wretched village, in which houses are to be seen in every stage of decay, but none that bore the marks of recent origin, or even of repairs — and its tavern might have graced the 'Tail piece' of Hogarth, with the ruined world upon its tottering sign-post. The police officer who examined the traveller's passport, and dismissed him from the dominions of his 'Most Christian Majesty,' was the only individual who seemed to be much above the rank of mendicity, and scarcely an indication was to be seen of industry or comfort. A bridge separated the mighty empire from its insignificant neighbor — the canton of Neufchatel — and we began to ascend the Jura. A rugged road soon brought us to the summit, in view of a valley which is the original seat of the watch manufactory of Switzerland. The first dwellings I encountered, evidently belonged to a different order of beings. Simple as they were, the neatness of the buildings, and the care with which the grounds and gardens around them were kept, formed a striking and cheering contrast to the miserable huts I had left. The inhabitants were seldom visible ; but there was generally an appearance of comfort and cleanliness which made me think of *home*.

I soon entered the village of Locle, whose chief attraction was the Asylum of Mademoiselle Calame, for the education of poor children. My first inquiries were made of the landlord of the hotel at which I lodged. He knew little more of it, than that it was superintended and sustained by this lady — that the children appeared to be well-trained — that those who went into families conducted well, and were found valuable domestics. I had heard of it as distinguished for its religious character, and inquired of my landlord, (who was evidently not interested in this part of the establishment) — whether, in the conflicts of the Momiers, as the Pietists or Methodists, or Evangelicals of Switzerland are called, with the members of the establishment, any religious influence was exerted there which was not approved. He replied that the pupils were taught a great deal of religion, but 'he believed they never got so much as to do them any harm.' This was the only information I could obtain before visiting this institution.

At a little distance from the village I found the Asylum bearing the same marks of gradual progress as the farm of a settler in one of our new counties; and it was easy to trace the steps by which it had expanded, from an old Swiss cottage, so as to occupy several buildings, of respectable size.

On entering one of the buildings, I found it occupied by boys of from five to fifteen years of age. A part of them were in a school-room receiving instruction, and the remainder engaged in various mechanical employments adapted to their age and strength. In a neighboring building, the girls were divided in the same manner, a part in the school-room, and the remainder engaged in various occupations. In the whole establishment, I learned that there were 220 pupils, most of whom were girls, who had been rescued from poverty, and the still worse degradation of corrupt intercourse and education. Order and neatness pervaded most parts of the establishment. In one of the buildings which had been the first Asylum of these destitute children, there were some tokens of want, and its associate evils,—a memento of their former condition, which could not be removed until the new building, erecting for this purpose, could be completed.

This institution was designed to prepare its wards for the duties of the laboring class, either as domestics or mechanics, and depends entirely on charity for its support. On both accounts the children receive but an hour or two of instruction daily, and a succession of classes pass through the school room at different hours, so as to render a smaller number of instructors necessary. The greater part of the day is devoted chiefly to those labors which contribute to their own support, or to their preparation for future duties. Those who appear to possess extraordinary talent, receive more instruction, with a view to prepare them to act as governesses in families.

Lace and watch-work constitute the principal industry of the country, particularly the latter. This art gives employment to the greater number of inhabitants of this valley, 5000 at Locle, and 6000 at Chaux-de-fonds. Almost every house has its work-shop; and the daughters, as well as the sons, are employed in it. Each (after having learned the whole art,) employs himself with one particular part, such as escapements, pinions, spirals, rough work, finishing, polishing, &c. The finishing and polishing are chiefly done by women. There are 'establisseurs' who employ the workmen, each in his branch, and put the collected portions together, and then in turn sell to the great houses, for exportation.

This branch of industry is confined to a few villages. The neighboring villages of France do not attempt to imitate their industrious and thriving neighbors.

At the commencement of the establishment of Mademoiselle Calame, lace-making was the exclusive occupation of the children; but its price has fallen so much, that very little is now done. A part are occupied in this, some in sewing, and making the clothes for the family, mending, and knitting, some necessarily with the care of the house. These occupations are changed, so that each may be prepared to assist in every household occupation which is likely to devolve upon them, whether in their own families or those of others. The boys are employed in the tailor's and shoemaker's shops; a few of these still knit and make lace. Recently, some of both sexes were employed in some of the most simple branches of watch work. The proceeds are not indeed sufficient to sustain the establishment, but they aid materially in this; and they serve the more important purpose of forming the pupil to habits of industry, of preparing them to sustain themselves, instead of becoming a burthen to society hereafter. How could charity better promote the interests of the community?

Such is the aspect of the institution of Mademoiselle Calame to a stranger. After I became acquainted with her, I solicited an account of its origin and progress. The following translation of a statement drawn up by one of her friends and fellow laborers, at her request, will be more interesting to the reader, and give a more complete view of the character and views of this lady than any we could furnish.

The Institute at Locle.

'The establishment for poor children at Locle, which now contains 220 pupils, was commenced in 1815, with five children. It owes its origin to the compassionate heart of Mademoiselle Calame, which induced her often to visit the unfortunate; that she might succor them in their necessities. By this means, she learned that the misery of the poor was owing, to a great extent, to moral corruption, and made many vain efforts for their improvement. On seeing the insufficiency of all her care and toil to effect these objects, she reflected that if the young could be preserved from the bad example of their parents, another generation might find itself happier. As her own property was too small to allow her to undertake any plan for them alone, she made a proposition to her neighbors which was acceptable to them all, to give a single cruche a month. Almost every one smiled, and gave what they pleased. Mademoiselle C. then appointed a committee of twelve ladies to assist her in her labors. Notwithstanding all of these ladies, except two, were led in one way or other to resign this office, they continued to make semiannual collections, and to watch over their young charge.

'The famine of 1816-17, was a time of severe trial. Worldly prudence pleaded that the children should be sent to their homes, but their pressing necessities cried loudly for the increase of their numbers. Mad. C. listened to the dictates of compassion. She raised her thoughts above wordly considerations, and human policy; she implored the assistance of the Almighty, with confidence, that he who feeds the nurslings of the birds, would not forget the infants of men. Strong confidence in God filled her whole soul, and she said she had this same protector for her Asylum for the unhappy children, and would rely on him. Her constant desire has been to lead her adopted children to the knowledge of God their Saviour, and to train them to practice Christianity, by teaching them to live ever as in his holy presence. She believed that she found convicing proofs of his protection, in receiving providentially, from day to day, the necessary support for her numerous family, which increased every year. When her expenses increased, her receipts were always equally increased, though in a great measure unforeseen; and a balance of a few francs closed the accounts of the year.

'The Divine goodness was remarkable in preserving the family from all serious disease, and dangerous accidents. The angel of death has never entered their dwelling. But more especially she recognised the Divine favor, in the spirit of peace, and the love of God, which he was pleased to diffuse through the young hearts of those under her care.

'The children received instruction adapted to their disposition and talents. Many of them give delightful evidences of their improvement in the families where they are placed as instructors in different parts of Europe, and where they are both loved and esteemed. Constant applications are made to Mad. C. from the parents and friends of the family where they are situated, that she will send them similar characters; and the letters of the pupils themselves show, that the instruction they have received has been blessed to them, and may have already been able to alleviate the poverty of their families, and give substantial evidence of their gratitude, to the Asylum which nourished and educated them.'

The following extracts from notes made upon the spot, contain many details derived from Mad. Calame and others, which will serve to complete the history of the Institution.

In conversation with Mademoiselle Calame, I found her exhibiting the same spirit of energy, and perseverance, and entire confidence in Divine Providence, which is described in this narrative. Indeed, her confidence was carried on some points beyond what most Christians would consider proper; for she seemed to regard particular passages of Scripture as addressed to herself.

The children whom Mad. Calame first endeavored to rescue from the abodes of vice and misery were placed at her own expense, and as they increased in number, by the aid of friends, in families that were respectable, even in poverty. The dreadful neglect of body and mind which was thus made known, and the difficulty of superintending them while thus scattered, led to their being collected in a single cottage. The applications of want, and the sympathy of benevolence, soon filled a larger dwelling, and has ultimately required the erection of a large, new building, in which Mad. C. and one of her friends have placed the property from which they derive their support. When the children were first collected, their accommodations were so scanty, that it was necessary to put three in a bed; and I shall never forget the anecdote related to me by the superintendent of the orphan school at Bergin, near Basle, on this subject. Mad. C. visited that establishment, with an interest which seemed almost overwhelming. In entering the children's chambers, she burst into tears of mingled joy and grief, on seeing that each child was furnished with a bed for himself! Her children are still too narrowly lodged; and in many cases she is still compelled to assign two to one bed; a practice which I found generally disapproved of in the best schools of Europe.

She has found associates or assistants of her own spirit. She was not willing to engage any who were not disposed to enter as voluntary and cordial coöperators in these efforts to do good. She leaves it to them to determine their own compensation, which is usually, barely sufficient for their wants. She finds no difficulty in procuring all the aid she needs on these terms; and the principal Instructress receives but eight louis d'or a year — about thirtyfive American dollars. In short, the whole establishment has that aspect of entire devotedness to benevolent effort, which appears in the missionary stations of Greenland. As I have already observed, the supplies for her establishment are derived, like those of Franke, from voluntary contributions, with the exception of the monthly *cruche* collected in the village, and the pay of a few pupils sent here by parents or protectors who are able to make compensation. These are charged six louis per annum, — less than the estimated cost. All that is received goes into the general treasury. The people of the village wonder how the establishment can subsist. Some suppose it to be connected with a rich proprietor; others, with a foreign government; and at one time, it was placed under the inspection of police! Its resources have been in fact derived chiefly from the christian benevolence of foreigners, who discovered the institution, or heard of it from travellers. I first learned its existence from a benevolent lady of rank in Edinburgh; and subsequently found it was known to persons of similar character in London, Paris, Geneva, and Berne. Unexpected remittances have thus been received, frequently from strangers, of 20, 30, and 50 louis or pounds, and in many instances at the moment of the greatest want. In one instance, an almanac of Neufchatel, containing some account of the establishment, was carried to Petersburg. The leaf was torn out and sent to a lady at court, and a considerable gift was the result.

The pupils designed for a life of labor are taught reading, writing, arithmetic; and those who are most likely to need it, the German language. Geography and History are taught only to the more advanced. Instruction in vocal music was given twice a week; and the singing was agreeable. The Bible is read with them every morning; and the instructress spends an hour with the elder pupils in familiar conversation on religious subjects. The results are described as very happy, and their appearance, on these occasions, certainly gave evidence of deep interest in the subject. Mad. C. expressed an anxiety not to lead her pupils into what she termed 'a religious jargon,' which seemed to indicate, that she did not intend her pupils should be mere parrots in their religious lessons. She observed that she had sometimes received pupils who spoke with astonishing clearness and fluency on the subject of religion, but whose knowledge did not restrain them from falsehood and theft. The teachers of our schools cannot too often recollect that 'the letter killeth, but the spirit giveth life.'

Religious motives are principally used in discipline. The children are taught that they are prone to evil, and that they must not merely watch against it, but ask divine aid. They are continually reminded of the presence of God and their responsibility to him. Every effort is made to reform and improve them by gentle means. Solitary confinement has been found very useful, except to those who were stupid, for these would sleep. Sometimes a pupil is asked what her state of feeling is, after the punishment has been continued for a time; and the reply has occasionally been, that they were still illdisposed, intimating that they needed the continuance of their punishment. In other cases, it has been left to the offender to determine whether the punishment should cease, and he has decided that it ought to be continued.

Mad. C. remarked, however, that sometimes gentle methods would leave a violent temper unsubdued. One pupil, after being treated thus gently for a length of time, became so violent as to attempt to injure Mad. C. herself, whom most of the pupils love as a parent. Another, who was naturally very violent, could always be subdued by the voice of affection, and this was the means she employed. But on going into the world, where the same gentle and soothing forbearance could not be expected, where few had time or patience to exercise it, she became insupportable to all around her.

From such examples Mad. C. has been led to believe that corporal punishment is sometimes indispensable, to subdue violence, or to overcome habit. She considers it an act of kindness thus to aid the will of the child; and she finds, as we have done, that when properly and kindly administered, it rather secures than alienates the affections, and leads the offender to rely on his teacher as a kind guardian or protector against a violence or aberration of feeling which he has not yet learned to subdue. One striking example of this kind occurred at the school at Locle. A little boy had stolen, and was confined as a punishment. He escaped; but with filial feeling went immediately to the house of Mad. Calame. She asked what he had done, and he frankly told the story. She directed him to return to the Institution, and ask one of the teachers to whip him; and as he knew how much he deserved, he must determine the number of blows. He obeyed her orders, and prescribed the amount of his own punishment. The instructor was touched with his frankness, and inflicted the punishment very gently. 'Is it enough,' he asked at length. 'Not yet,' said the little fellow. 'Fool!' said a companion, — 'say it is enough.' 'Three more!' said the offender; and his punishment was completed.

In all her punishments Mad. C. reminds her pupils that they do not efface the crime; that only ONE can forgive sin; and that her discipline is not to avenge or blot out offences, but merely to serve as a memorial and preventive of future evil. She refers constantly to the fear and the love of God, as the motives to action; and finds them, as they have always been found, — whether in the school or the community, — the most efficient instruments of discipline, — the only means of permanent influence upon the character.

Such is the state of the institution at Locle. Whatever *theory* to be adopted account for its success, the *facts* are beyond controversy, that a single female, inspired by christian benevolence, by her own persevering efforts, in reliance on Divine Providence, established in ten years, an Asylum which provides the means of support and education for 220 children of misery and vice, and furnishes many families annually with faithful and skilful assistants, in the various duties of the household — an institution which would be a blessing to the rich, as well as the poor, of any country. Could our benevolent institutions be first endowed with a conductor of similar devotedness and energy, we should hear of fewer failures. Could those who possess this character be induced to devote themselves to such objects, they would do more for their prosperity than the most munificent patron could do; for without such a conductor, the most splendid endowments will often only be the instruments of evil.

[For the Annals of Education.]

ON THE MODE OF TEACHING THE ANCIENT LANGUAGES.

An Essay on a System of Classical Instruction; &c. London: Printed for John Taylor, 1829. 12mo.

The New Latin Reader, Part I. By S. C. Walker. Philadelphia.

Library of Education. Locke and Milton. Gray & Bowen: Boston.

In a former article I adduced from the 'Essay' the authority of Wolsey, Colet, and Erasmus, to show that the present mode of teaching the Greek and Latin languages is but a corruption of that which was practised in the early classical schools, and approved by some of the most distinguished scholars. I alluded to the opinions of Roger Ascham. Instructed by Sir John Cheke the tutor of King Edward the Sixth, adopting his methods, and testing their value in the education of his distinguished pupil Queen Elizabeth, his authority is of no small value. In his 'Scholemaster,' written in 1566, at the request of the Secretary of State, (afterwards Lord Burleigh), he says:

'After the child hath learned perfectly the eight parts of speech, let him then learn the right joining together of substantives with adjectives, the noun with the verb, the relative with the antecedent. * * * Let the master read unto him the Epistles of Cicero, gathered together and chosen out by Sturmius, for the capacity of children.' * * *

He directs that the teacher should then explain the subject of the epistle, construe it repeatedly to the child, and 'parse it over to him perfectly,' and instead of requiring him to spell it out from dictionary and grammar, simply call upon him to repeat it, as he has heard it. Let the child then translate it in writing, and after an hour has passed, retranslate his own English into Latin. It is not till after this *practice*, that *theory* is to be introduced.

'When the master shall compare Tully's book with the scholar's translation, let the master, at the first, lead and teach his scholar to join the rules of his grammar-book with the examples of his present lesson, until the scholar by himself be able to fetch out of his grammar every rule for every example; so as the grammar book be ever in the scholar's hands, and also used of him as a dictionary for every present use. This is a lively and perfect way of teaching the rules; *when the common way used in common schools, to read the grammar alone by itself is tedious for the master, hard for the scholar,* cold and uncomfortable for both.'

The next step of the course proposed by Ascham is, that the teacher should give him an English version of his own, to be retranslated into Latin.

* * * 'When he bringeth it translated unto you, bring forth the place of Tully; lay them together, compare the one with the other; commend his good choice and right placing of words; *shew his faults gently, but blame them not over sharply;* for of such missings gently admonished of, proceedeth glad and good heedtaking; of good heedtaking springeth chiefly knowledge, which after groweth to perfectness, if this order be diligently used by the scholar, and gently handled by the master. For here shall all the hard points of grammar, both easily and surely be learned up; which scholars, in common schools, by making of Latines, be groping at with care and fear, and yet in many years they scarce can reach unto them.'

He next proposes that the teacher should write a letter in English adapted to the child's capacity, and require him to translate it into Latin. After quoting the names of Cicero, Quintilian, and Pliny, in support of this method, he adds:

'I durst venture a good wager, if a scholar but translate after this sort one little book in Tully, he would come to a better knowledge in the Latin tongue, than the most part do that spend four or five years in trying all the rules of grammar in common scholes.'

Such were the views of a man of whom Sir Richard Sackville says; — 'Roger Ascham was the scholar of the best master and the scholemaster of the best scholar, that ever were in our time.'

This method of Ascham is in spirit the same as that of Wolsey, Colet, and Erasmus; but the peculiar modification of it, shows that Latin was already beginning to be used less in conversation, and more exclusively in the written intercourse of the learned. Hence, there is not so much attention to form habits of speaking Latin. But Latin, even in his time, was the only language allowed to be spoken in school. He objects, however, to its use, because it was spoken so impurely as to produce bad habits in the pupils.

About a hundred years after Ascham, lived Milton, who was also one of the finest classical scholars in England. In his letter to Hartlib on Education, he says:

'First, we do amiss, to spend seven or eight years merely in scraping together so much miserable Latin and Greek, as might be learned easily and delightfully *in one year*.'

He then goes on to speak of the method, and recommends that a book be 'lessoned thoroughly (*construed*) to them.'

'This,' he continues,' I take to be the most natural and the most profitable way of learning languages, and whereby we may best hope to give account to God of our youth spent herein.'

Speaking more particularly of grammar, he says:

'First they should begin with the chief and necessary rules of some good grammar, either that now used, or any better; and while this is doing, their speech is to be fashioned to a distinct and clear pronunciation, as near as may be to the Italian, especially on the vowels. Next, to make them expert in *the usefulest parts of grammar*; and withal, to season them, some easy and delightful book of education *should be read to them*.'

Soon after Milton comes Locke. He is very elaborate on the subject:

'As soon as a child can speak English, it is time for him to learn some other language. This nobody doubts of, when French is proposed; and the reason is, because people are accustomed to the right way of teaching that language, which is by talking it into children in constant conversation, and not by grammatical rules. The Latin tongue would easily be taught the same way if his tutor being constantly with him, would talk nothing else to him, and make him answer still in the same language.

'Latin I look upon as absolutely necessary for a gentleman. And indeed custom, which prevails over everything, has made it so much a part of education, that even those children are whipt into it, and made to spend many hours of their precious time uneasily in Latin, who after they are once gone from school, are never to have more to do with it as long as they live.

'But how necessary soever Latin be to some, and is thought to be to others to whom it is no manner of use or service, yet, the ordinary way of learning it in a grammar school is that, which having had thoughts about, I cannot be forward to encourage. The reasons against it are so evident and cogent, that they have prevailed with some intelligent persons, to quit the ordinary road, not without success, though the method made use of was not exactly what I imagine the easiest, and in short is this;—to trouble the child with no grammar at all, but to have Latin as English has been, without the perplexity of rules, talked into him; for if you will consider it, Latin is no more unknown to a child, when he comes into the world, than English, and yet he learns English without a master, rule, or grammar, and so might he Latin, too, as Tully did, if he had somebody always to talk to him in this language. And when we so often see a French woman teach an English girl to speak and read French perfectly in a year or two, without any rule of grammar, or anything else but prattling to her, I cannot but wonder, how gentlemen have overlooked this way for their sons, and thought them more dull or incapable than their daughters.

He then suggests what has probably occurred to most intelligent instructors that the 'true and genuine way' of learning Latin would be the same; but that if this cannot be accomplished, the '*next* best' is to give the pupil a *literal interlinear translation.* He proposes that they should read and copy this, and gradually be led to observe the inflections and rules of grammar by directing, and assisting their efforts, not by leaving them 'to be puzzled,' nor by rebukes, and punishments, which he considers too often 'the effect only of pride and peevishness in the teacher, who expects children should instantly be master of as much as he knows.' He requires no study of grammar rules —

'For languages being to be learned by rote, custom, and memory, are then *spoken in greatest perfection when all rules of grammar are utterly forgotten.* I grant the grammar of a language is sometimes very carefully to be studied, but it is not to be studied but by a grown man, when he applies himself to the understanding of any language critically, which is seldom the business of any but professed scholars.'

He advises next that the pupil should read some other easy Latin book with the aid of an ordinary translation.

'Nor let the objection that he will then know it only by rote, fright any one. This, when well considered, is not of any moment *against*, but plainly for this way of learning a language. For languages are only to be learned by rote; and a man who does not speak English and Latin perfectly by rote, so that having thought of the thing he would speak of, his tongue of course, without thought of rule, or grammar, falls into the proper expression and idiom of that language, does not speak it well, nor is master of it. And I would fain have any one name to me that tongue that any one can learn, or speak as he should do, by the rules of grammar. Languages were made not by rules or art, but by accident, and the common use of the people. And he that speaks them well, has no other rule but that; nor anything to trust to but his memory, and the habit of speaking after the fashion learned from those that are allowed to speak properly, which in other words, is only to speak by rote.'

To the natural inquiry — 'Is grammar, then, of no use?' Locke replies:

'I say not so: *grammar has its place also.* But this I think I may say, — there is more stir a great deal made with it than there needs, and those are tormented about it, to whom it does not at all belong; I mean children at the age wherein they are usually perplexed with it in grammar schools.

'If grammar ought to be taught at any time, it must be to one that can speak the language already; how else can he be taught the grammar of it?' When any one finds in himself a necessity or disposition to study any foreign language to the bottom, and to be nicely exact in the knowledge of it, it will be time enough to take a grammatical survey of it. If his use of it be only to understand some books writ in it, without a criti-

cal knowledge of the tongue itself, reading alone, as I have said, will attain this end, without charging the mind with the multiplied rules and intricacies of grammar.'

He then goes on to recommend the double translation of Roger Ascham, but it is not necessary to repeat it. Our object has been to give in detail a plan for beginning the study, which it is still in our power to adopt. Every master in our land can teach by interlinear translation; but how many could teach by conversation? All that is wanted is, a course of books, and many would be glad to see the course, published in London, 'for John Taylor,' reprinted in this country. It consists of six thin duodecimo volumes. In the meanwhile the 'New Latin Reader' will serve for beginners.

I have been thus copious in the extracts from the ancient friends of classical learning, because I believe, that a vague idea of the present method of classical instruction being 'the good old way,' is the main cause of its keeping the ground, against all the arguments adduced from common sense and reason, which have latterly been urgent against it. But so inveterate is the prejudice, or rather the habit, in favor of the present method, that I should not be surprised, if some should still refuse to believe the contrary, and again ask, 'How could the present method have become universal, in the public and private schools of England, when light has been advancing, if it were not that it is an improvement on those first methods?' The answer to this is not difficult. Even in the times of which I have spoken, the roots of the present system were in the schools, planted there by the indolence of schoolmasters; and there were obvious reasons why these roots should shoot forth, especially, in the public classical schools of England. Bulwer, in his late work on England and the English, (where he very strongly asserts that Latin and Greek *are never learned*, during the twelve years devoted to them in the preparatory and Eton schools), lays open other abuses in the endowed institutions of education, whose growth is much more difficult to be accounted for, than this corruption in the method of teaching. Masters and ushers, to whom salaries are secured for life, — whether they teach well or not, indeed, whether they have scholars or not, and who are never watched by any superintendent, — are very liable to neglect their duty. This has been the case, to a wonderful extent, in England. Their established school system is worse administered than their established church. And the public schools, have given the tone to the private schools, as they always will do.

But never did selfishness and indolence make a worse calculation, than in yielding to their own blind impulses on this subject. This irrational method of teaching the dead languages, has converted the school-room from a pleasant study into a gloomy place of the most irksome labor for the teacher, and of punishment for the scholar. 'The mysterious communion of wisdom with ignorance,' equally delightful to both parties, has been exchanged for a system of warfare, in which he that gains the most over the opposing will of the other, is accounted the best. It is true that no other branch of knowledge is attempted to be communicated exactly in the same unnatural manner; but the slowness with which Latin and Greek are learned on this plan, makes them usurp all the best hours of the first years of school-going; and thus they determine the character of the school-room, and cast a dark shadow over the whole course of education. The worst result is, that after all the sacrifice of knowledge on other subjects, of all really intellectual exertion, of so much happiness, and more especially of *moral education — the languages are not learned* at school, and rarely at college, unless other circumstances, not forming a necessary part of school influence, have roused the real classic enthusiasm.

'Are you a scholar, yourself, (says Bulwer to the fathers of the Eton young men who have passed twelve years in learning Latin and Greek), examine then the average of young men of eighteen, open a page of some author they have *not* read — have not, parrot-like, got by heart, open a page in the dialogues of Lucian, in the Thebaid of Statius. Ask the youth you have selected from the herd to construe it, as you would ask your daughter to construe a page of some French author she has never seen before, — a poem of Regnier, or an exposition in the *Esprit des Lois*. Does he not pause, does he not blush, does he not hesitate, does not his eye wander abroad in search of the accustomed 'Crib,' does he not falter out something about lexicons and grammars, and at last throw down the book, and tell you he has never learned *that*, but as for Virgil or Herodotus, *there* he is your man?'

This extract is not from an enemy to classic learning. Bulwer is a great friend to it, as his book shows; but he is roused to a protest against the present system of teaching Latin and Greek, because, by it, these studies are spread out over all the years of school-life, to the exclusion of various other branches of knowledge, which are equally important, to say the least, for the development of the mind, and the usefulness of life, as Latin and Greek.

I have said that never did selfishness and indolence make a worse calculation, than when they led masters to abandon boys to the lexicon and grammar methods of learning their lessons. And I repeat it. For suppose a master should take his class in Virgil, and construe to them their lesson; or if his scholars have something of a vocabulary in their minds, take the Latin words, two or three at a time, and giving them out in the order of the English, ask for their meaning, (when it is not ready, prompting it himself), and as he goes on, should point out the rhetorical and poetical beauties, and even, if he pleases, should parse it all over himself, and having finished a paragraph, should review it, giving the English in short phrases and requiring the scholar to give the Latin, and at last should require some one, or every one, to construe it himself; — what a pleasant exercise might thus be made of this painful task! What an opportunity he would have, for cultivating the minds of his boys! — While thus engaged with his first class, the other classes might be studying inflections, or reading with an assistant on the same plan, or studying something in their native tongue. To read the classic authors, with successive classes of intelligent boys, would be a never failing source of interest, to a master gifted with any power of discerning the shades of the human mind, and its modes of operation.

It is indeed marvellous that this method of teaching should not be pursued, when, as sometimes happens, a teacher has the care of a few scholars, or of a single one. Will it be said that the minds of young persons need to be tasked to labor more than this method of teaching would tax them? Very well. But why not discipline the intellect by some study, which does not admit of being communicated in this easy way? There are the sciences; — from the interesting deductions of chemistry to the pure abstractions of geometry. Let these studies strengthen the mind to habits of unaided labor, and solitary exertion. But let languages be taught in society, to which they belong.* Y.

OBJECTS TO BE ATTAINED IN TEACHING GEOGRAPHY.

Extract of a Lecture delivered before the American Institute of Instruction; by W. C. Woodbridge, on the Best Method of Teaching Geography.

THE *immediate*, and what are termed the *practical* benefits of the study of Geography, are generally supposed to consist in the superior skill it gives to the *sailor*, the *soldier*, the *missionary*, and the *traveller*, in their expeditions to various parts of the earth; or to the merchant, or the politician, or the man of benevolence, in his calculations of private or national affairs. It is indeed indispensable to all these. But by the very nature of our association, our attention is directed to this study as a *branch of instruction in our schools*, and he who should expect to qualify himself to circumnavigate the globe, or conduct the affairs of a shipping merchant, or the concerns of a nation, with no other knowledge than that which he obtains from the miniature outlines of the science which

* For the Editor's views, see Annals, Vol. I. p. 518.

are found in our school books, would meet with ridicule, as well as disappointment.

For purposes like these, a minute acquaintance with a particular country or portion of the world is often most essential. Every new subject may require a long period of special study; and the examination of authorities and maps far beyond the limits of a school-room. The method of study is here too obvious to be the subject of remark; for the object in view is, the *accumulation and recollection of every fact* which can be discovered on the given point. This, however, could not be attempted in a school, even if it were necessary to its pupils generally. We have then to consider what objects are *general*, and how the study can be arranged, so that *all* may derive the *utmost* benefit.

The first thought which presents itself to most parents, with reference to this study, is, that it is necessary to enable their children to *converse with others*, and to *take their station among* the well-informed community. Such a reason may be sufficient, with regard to the fashion of a garment or a mode of address; but in subjects of serious importance, we have high authority for saying, that this '*comparison of ourselves among ourselves*' is 'not wise.' There should be some *fixed standard*, to decide points so important as the studies of our childhood and youth; and the question must rather be — What *claim* has this science to be considered necessary to a well-informed man, and *why* is it useful as one of the studies of our youth?

It is said indeed to be one of the eyes of history; and without it neither the records of the past, nor the news of the day, can be understood. But the question still returns, what benefit is to be derived from these studies, which are, in fact, but branches of ancient and modern geography?

Perhaps we cannot answer the question better than by comparing those who are ignorant of this subject, with those to whom it is familiar.

The uninstructed knows not that there is a world beyond his sight. He has no idea that there can be other houses, or other modes of dress, or other articles of food, than those he sees. He knows not that there is another language on earth, or another country or town besides his own. His standard of excellence is, therefore, *just upon a level with the things that surround him.* There can be *nothing superior* in his estimation; and whatever is different, must be inferior, whether in manners, or dress, or arts, or sciences, or opinions, or faith. Whatever *appears* of a different character, however elevated it may in truth be above what he already knows, is received with contempt, or disgust, or prejudice. Such is the fact with the Chinese. To dress in white, for any other purpose but mourning, to salute a friend in the European style, or to eat with forks, in their view, indicates an inferior mind. Our arts and sciences are unworthy of their attention, our opinions and faith beneath their notice, and our pretensions, or those of our country to respect, are treated in the Celestial Empire, as those of a rustic would be in a fashionable assembly. All beyond its limits are '*barbarians.*' The whole effect of this 'comparison of ourselves among ourselves,' in a nation, or in a class room, is to excite and to gratify vanity; to establish a low and imperfect standard of right, and propriety, and beauty, and excellence of all kinds; and to check or destroy our respect for others, and our benevolence towards those who differ from us.

But let us now examine an individual at the other extremity of the scale, whose mind has been expanded by the only perfect mode of studying Geography, a survey of the various portions of the earth itself. A veteran traveller has long since ceased to consider the color of a dress, or the form of a salutation, as essential to good sense or respectability. He has found that there are varieties of climate, and soil, and food, as pleasant as his own. That the mind and habits and views of man, like the works of nature, are endlessly varied, and still without any imperfection. He learns to wonder without condemning, and to smile at some new appearance without contempt. He is prepared to receive, and to seek new articles of comfort or use, even from savages, and to acquire knowledge from the most ignorant. In short, one important support to his pride is taken away, one great obstacle to his benevolence is removed, and he is prepared to take his place as one of the family of man, instead of the mere citizen of a single state. He acquires an interest in the passing events of other countries, and is insensibly led on, if he have the spirit of benevolence within him, to desire, and even to seek, the happiness of his fellow men on the other side of the globe.

Such is, to some extent, the influence of the study of Geography at home, and such we should endeavor to make it upon the mind of a child.

But this study, like every other which is concerned with the works of the Creator, ought to be so pursued as to *elevate* as well as to expand the mind — to lift the heart to God through the medium of his works and his unceasing providence, — as well as to warm it towards our fellow men. It must ever be remembered, that the more knowledge we acquire of physical science, *of mere visible things*, without associating them with the invisible author, the more do we become attached to earth, and the less likely to rise towards heaven. To this cause it is, and not to the nature of their studies, that we ought to ascribe the frequent infidelity of naturalists; and the teacher of Geography should take care not to lead his pupil into this error.

[For the Annals of Education.]

THE INFANTILE FRAME.

Considered with reference to the present system of Infantile Instruction.

[We are indebted to Dr J. V. C. Smith for the following article, which we solicited in consequence of finding its leading principles in a sheet of a work on Physiology, which he is preparing for the use of schools. The subject is one of the deepest interest to teachers and parents.]

INFANCY and adolescence are particularly interesting and important periods in the history of our race, — requiring the unceasing vigilance, care and protection of those to whom young children are entrusted. Strange as it may at first appear, the dangers to which they are exposed, as it regards their physical welfare, are certainly greater in the more elevated walks of life, than in that humble mediocrity where rest is purchased by salutary labor, and mental excitement is invariably followed by a corresponding exercise of the body.

The rich man's child has no necessity for exertion. It sports on carpets and is carried to school in the arms of a servant. Its body is puny, nor will it ever have the ruddy cheek or the compact frame of the child that waits upon itself.

It is only in the highest and the lowest circles of society, that deformities are common. In the one, they are produced by not allowing the child to act in its own character ; and in the other, the same difficulties arise, by over-taxing the locomotive muscles, and the chills of poverty. The one is *over* nursed, and dies ; and the other dies for *want* of nursing. Wild animals are never deformed ; but those which have become domesticated, are constantly presenting anomalies. Exercise, of the kind too which children invariably select for themselves, is the best which could be devised. '*Natura ducit*,' was the text of the ancients — and she will always accomplish her designs, if not continually interrupted in her endeavors.

We fully believe there is a radical defect in all our systems of primary schooling. A false philosophy is in vogue, which obscures the early dawn of infantile intelligence, by forcing upon the mind, exercises and considerations which are not always agreeable even to their sovereign seniors, — when all that is most desirable could be obtained by an opposite course, far more pleasant to the child, more conducive to his present happiness, his physical perfection in manhood, and his respectability and comfort in old age.

In elucidation of these remarks, let us examine the organic structure of one of these cradle pupils, whose faculties, it is universally admitted, depend, in a great measure, upon the condition of the body.

At birth, the child, in reality, has not a single bone in its body, with the exception of those of the internal ear. The places are occupied by cartilage ; and so gradual is the process of the formation of bone, that at ten years of age, the extremities of the long bones are scarcely united to the main shaft. Bones are not flexible; but the cartilage, the model of what the future bone is to be, can be bent in any direction as it lies surrounded by the soft cushion of the muscles. Particle after particle of this semi-elastic substance is carried away by the absorbent vessels, and one of lime, the basis of the true skeleton, is deposited in its place. This *ossification*, as it is termed, or the gradual introduction of the bones into the beds which were primarily occupied by their patterns, is indeed a slow, unnoticed, but not the less wonderful operation. During this exchange of matter, distortions take place, and a multitude of maladies have an origin, which might have been averted by a knowledge of the first principles of anatomical science. The danger of distortion in the bones by improper or constrained positions, or long continued sitting, especially on seats without support, are too obvious to need illustration here.

The muscles were fashioned before our birth, but subsequently develope their energies in proportion to the cultivation bestowed upon them in all the after periods of life. Every internal organ belonging to the vital or digestive apparatus, like any new and beautifully constructed machinery, is in readiness to act, when the first breath is drawn.

But above all, the brain, that still poorly understood organ, by which man can alone manifest his superiority, for many years remains incomplete and imperfectly protected. Like the bones, however, it is daily undergoing modifications and developing new powers. It is not fitted, as sometimes supposed, to the exact capacity of the skull. No, the bones sustain an humble office, and accommodate themselves precisely to the condition of the brain; and never, in the records of physiological facts, have the sutures (the seams of the cranium) been known to be completely closed, till the encephalon, the thinking organ was finished, and nature said, in effect — seal up the treasure.

Next, let us examine some of the evils resulting from the hot-bed plan of infantile instruction, so popular in New-England. When children of two, three and four years old are crowded in badly ventilated apartments — pinioned, as it were, many hours in a day to a hard seat, — and drilled in the harness of class books which they neither love nor comprehend — the course is diametrically opposed to the clearest indications of nature.

Do not urge on the mind for the present. Take care of the body. Those splendid specimens of a well directed mind, which the mistaken teacher is so laboriously striving to produce, are best secured in the man, when a sure foundation is laid for it by a well organized body. When the edifice is in a condition for a tenant, seasonable notice will be given. Adopt the plan of the Infant Asylum of Geneva and some others in Europe, which aim chiefly at the physical health and enjoyment of the pupils, and give them only so much intellectual occupation as their feeble minds and immature bodies can endure, and then we may have the proper harmony maintained in the developement of children.

Children must play. They were designed to run, to eat, and to sleep alternately, and not to think profoundly. Were it not so, they would most certainly have been ushered into existence, manifesting the high pretensions of reasoning beings.

The restraints of the school-room are diametrically at variance with the physical laws of the animal economy. Without the free exercise of the muscles, the bones cannot be so speedily, nor so thoroughly finished, and distortions are always liable to follow. By limiting the action of the limbs, the internal organs suffer in a corresponding ratio. Lastly, the brain, in consequence of laying it under this pernicious course of early contribution, is overworked, and many formidable diseases, either mortal in the onset, or lingering upon the borders of the constitution, terminating in Dropsies, Imbecility, Insanity and Monomania, are assuredly among the evils which will yet exhibit themselves, and which will arise from our unnatural, unphilosophical system of public, infantile instruction.

[For the Annals of Education.]

EVENING STUDIES.

[The two following articles, on an important topic, were received from independent sources; and exhibit the views of individuals who have spent much thought, and have had much experience, on the subject of instruction. We shall be gratified to insert any remarks upon them.]

Mr Editor; — Thirty years ago, in many parts of New England, Arithmetic was not permitted in district schools during the day. The only means then enjoyed for gaining a knowledge of this branch was by studying evenings. For this purpose some teachers kept what was called a 'cyphering school' about twice a week. But of late the public sentiment has begun to tolerate arithmetic in the day school, as well as many other branches which were formerly excluded. There is now, therefore, less necessity than formerly for evening schools of any kind. And they were never very useful. It is true that an industrious individual, here and there, made considerable progress; but the greater part who attended, so far as regards intellectual improvement, might as well have been at home; and in regard to their morals, far better. Both sexes usually attended these schools; and they were viewed by both as scenes of recreation rather than improvement.

I have admitted, Mr Editor, that a few industrious individuals made some progress. This was undoubtedly the fact. But whether even their industrious habits would not, on the whole, have been as well promoted at home, is a matter of doubt. As to those who can have instruction on a given subject during the day, the case does not, as it appears to me, *admit* of a doubt. I am fully convinced that, so far as concerns those who make study their principal business during the day, the night was intended for relaxation and repose. To such, at least, evening studies cannot be on the whole improving, besides being injurious to their health, and especially to the eyes.

These remarks have been elicited by observing that evening lessons have become *fashionable*. Children of a very tender age, must not only have lessons during six or eight hours of the day, but during two or three hours of the evening and morning.

I am not averse to requiring children to study a suitable number of hours in a day. They *ought* to study, and to study *hard*. But I believe a greater amount of knowledge and mental discipline would be secured, if no child who has studied hard six or even *four* hours of the day were allowed to touch a book which requires much thought during the evening; for this is the period when body and mind require comparative rest. Let these hours be devoted to conversation. This conversation should involve the studies of the school-room, but not in a manner which will require much intellectual effort.

But these sentiments, if they were adopted by parents and teachers, would not be likely to have much weight. There is such a spirit of competition eternally at work, that it will find means to show itself somewhere. Could we establish the conviction that eating and drinking and dress are less worthy of regard, and knowledge more so, the same spirit which influenced our conduct in regard to the former, would still be connected with the latter. Parents, and teachers, and neighbors, would still strive to outvie each other in dressing the minds of their children, as they did before in adorning their bodies. And however heterodox the opinion may seem, the evil is, in many cases, not only as great, but greater; as much so as the abuse of the nobler nature is more to be deprecated than that of the mere animal.

Now in speaking of what, under certain circumstances, *would be*, I have exactly described, for some of our most fashionable circles, *what is*. The spirit of rivalry is abroad, and parents do not hesitate to devote themselves and their offspring to it, — a willing sacrifice. There are indeed parents who can encourage even greater excess in their children by their own example. Led on by the same rivalry in acquiring knowledge themselves, or by a false view of the importance of their own efforts, to the world, or by an anxiety for the business of life which christianity does not allow, they spend the hours of midnight in study or labor. Let them remember that they thus exhaust that vital energy which is

'My daughter's eyes must be protected,' she says, 'let what will be the consequence.'

This is exactly right; but it is not at all improbable that the other child is the one who is in greatest danger, only that the mischief is working within, — in the brain or in the digestive organs, — where it is concealed from view, and where it can go on without any striking external indications of its presence, until the injury is irremediable and recovery hopeless.

But we have almost filled the space we had allotted to our subject, and have hardly reached it yet. We will content ourselves, however, with these preliminary observations now, and conclude with recommending to our readers, and especially to parents, to propose the following questions to some physician in whom they have confidence. We have done it to a physician who called upon us while we were writing this article, and we give his replies.

'Suppose two children are employed a great number of hours each day, the one in mere copying, and the other in some perplexing work like arithmetic, so that the confinement and labor should be the same; will there be any difference in regard to danger to the health?'

'Yes; the latter will be decidedly in the greatest danger.'

'What part of the system is most likely to feel the effects of too severe or too long-continued mental occupation?'

'The digestive powers. Great anxiety, or any strong mental emotion, stops digestion almost entirely.'

'Which can bear the most intellectual effort without injury, children or adults?'

'The latter.'

'How many hours can children be safely employed in *study* daily?'

'The difference in individuals is very great; perhaps five or six upon the average. Besides this, they may read, or acquire information in light, easy ways, two or three hours more.'

If these views are correct, diligent study during school hours is sufficient for the immature powers of children, and their evenings ought to be spent in lighter pursuits, partaking, perhaps, of an intellectual character, but not severely tasking faculties already wearied with the labors of the day. A.

REVIEW OF PLANS FOR LIBRARIES.

***Plans for Libraries; By a Friend of Education.* 1833.**

THE indispensable necessity of the general diffusion of knowledge in our country, as the foundation of our prosperity — nay, of our permanent existence as the Republic of America, is universally admitted. Societies are forming in various parts of our country for the promotion of education, and a sense of its importance is taking a deeper hold on the community. In this state of the public mind it is very gratifying to notice the publication of a pamphlet like that whose title stands at the head of this article. Its design is to lead those who are particularly engaged in promoting the improvement of the American people, to take into consideration the formation of local, or parish libraries, as an essential branch of the system of general education. It is proposed to establish a well selected library in every parish or neighborhood throughout the United States; and it is worthy of notice that this subject has attracted attention almost simultaneously, both in Europe and in this country, and that in France and Scotland, efforts have been made to carry it into operation, with the prospect of success. The writer of the pamphlet before us appears to have studied his subject, and we would recommend it to all who feel an interest in the diffusion of knowledge.

The operation of knowledge on the community is two-fold: first, by its direct influence on the public character, in fitting it for a state of freedom; and again, by bringing to bear on the public mind, the instructions and warnings contained in the experience of the past. It is plainly the design of Providence, that both these means should operate in the advancement of human society. Man's nature is so constituted that it is impossible to preserve those very institutions which are indispensable to its full development and happiness, unless he also possesses certain internal personal qualities. A destitution, not only of a correct moral character, but also of an adequate knowledge of their natural rights, and of the principles of action and of government, has been the source of failure of all past attempts to secure a perpetuity of freedom.

But in our present imperfect state there is need also of the experience of the past as a guide for the future. It is so in respect to individuals; and doubtless it is equally necessary to the world as a whole. It is plainly the design of Providence, in the evils and miseries which are endured, that mankind may be taught by sad experience, if in no other way, the ruinous consequences of false principles and false conduct.

This lesson, the world sooner or later ***must*** learn. And ***we*** must either profit by the world's past experience, or learn the lesson too late in our own downfall, and become a final and effectual example, perhaps to some far distant age.

But if we, as a nation, are to read and understand the lessons of the world's experience, it must be by having access to the records of it. Nor is it sufficient that this should be done by a learned few. Where the people rule, and the laws and customs of the nation are only the acting out of the nation's character, it is necessary that this knowledge should be spread abroad, and perpetuated, and brought down as far as possible to every individual of our free, self-governing population.

This is the object which the writer of the pamphlet before us proposes to accomplish by the plan he suggests. He begins by some just reflections on the importance of the press, and proposes his plan as a means of giving the press its full power. We justly rejoice in the freedom of this mighty moral engine; but to be useful to its full extent, it must be ***applied in the most effectual way.*** And to be useful rather than destructive, it must be applied on the side of truth and right. At present, these desirable objects are attained but very partially, compared with what is easily practicable.

Now as an effectual means of giving the American press its full power, it is proposed to bring its influence to bear on the whole community of mind, by a system of town and parish libraries. In reference to this, he observes;

'The prominent inquiry is — How shall the press produce the greatest effect, and exert the most happy influence upon the public mind? In prosecuting this inquiry three things demand particular attention; viz. *The selection, and cheapness, and the circulation, of works published.*',

The first of these objects he would provide for by a judicious and well qualified committee, appointed for the purpose. The other two, he endeavors to show, will be best accomplished by the system he proposes. This system is as follows.

'The object is, that libraries may be commenced, as extensively as possible, on a system which will secure a regular increase of them. First, let a committee of judicious men, in whom the public will place confidence, be appointed to recommend books to be purchased or published, at stated periods of one or two years, for these libraries. Secondly, let these libraries be supported by subscriptions, by the purchase of shares, or by some other method, which may appear more practicable, each parish receiving an amount of books in proportion to its subscription. Thirdly, let an agent be appointed to visit parishes, and attend to the concerns of the libraries as may appear advisable.'

The committee mentioned in this statement, he considers of the highest importance.

'This committee,' he says, 'could ascertain the value of a work before they recommended it. The public would not be liable to be deceived by a captious title, a deceitful panegyric, nor by an address of an interested agent. The committee would recommend a better selection, than could generally be expected from individuals in the community.'

Our limits will not admit of a particular consideration of the plan; our object is rather to introduce the pamphlet itself, to the notice of those who are in circumstances to go forward on this subject.

Having stated and, explained his plan, the writer proceeds to compare it with the *itinerating* system, which has been carried into operation with some success in Scotland. He presents several considerations, tending to show that the system he proposes would be preferable. On the itinerating plan, a number of small libraries, about fifty volumes each, are connected together, on the principle that every two years the libraries in ten neighboring stations shall change places; each completing an entire revolution in 20 years, by which time the books are worn out. In comparison with this, he mentions several points of superiority in the local system. One advantage is, that the books being always accessible, *their value is enhanced.* He estimates it to be at least double that of itinerating libraries. From these, after a short stay, they are removed forever. 'It may be assumed,' he observes, 'that books remaining in a library twenty years, will, on an average, be of double the value of books which remain only two years. There is but one chance in this case to see the books, after which they are no longer within reach.' They are removed also, according to his estimate, when at least a fourth, or a third part are unread, on an average by each subscriber.

Again, by the system he proposes, there would be a much greater *speed of circulation.* The same book may be at once sent forth through the whole breadth of the land; whereas on the other, in each itinerating circle, it would be twenty years before it could be accessible to all. It would require ten or twenty years before access could be had to as great a variety of books, as on the other plan, would be always at hand, after the libraries were once well established.

Another prominent advantage is, that larger editions may be purchased or published, and consequently *books be furnished at a cheaper rate.* The number of independent stations being ten times as great, a much larger number of copies of the same book would be wanted. This is an important consideration. If by publishing a large edition, the books may be furnished 25 per cent cheaper, this would be a saving in every $1000, of $250, which of itself would purchase a valuable library. The itinerating system also requires the expense of transportation from station to station, which the other would avoid. The local plan, also, is susceptible of accommodation to the circumstances and wants of the people, to a far greater extent than the other. For these reasons, and several others which are considered at length in the pamphlet, the writer thinks that the system he proposes will be found preferable.

But it may be asked, how shall this plan be carried into operation? This subject deserves the particular consideration of *those societes which have been forming, or which may be formed, for the purpose of promoting popular education.* To them it seems naturally to belong, and it appears to us well calculated to promote their design. The value of libraries, as an aid in education, is obvious on the least reflection. The instruction acquired in a common school, embraces, of course, only the rudiments of knowledge, and rather excites a desire to know, than gratifies that desire. But if the youthful mind is left at this stage, it soon loses the appetite for improvement, and begins to think it knows as much as any need know. The conceit of its own attainment grows in proportion to its growing ignorance; all knowledge beyond the demands of the man's own narrow sphere, is despised; the children are instructed less than their parents, and ignorance advances from generation to generation.

But now suppose a well selected library at hand, regularly increased with new volumes, and affording a supply for every taste and age — the love of reading and desire of knowledge may take hold in the community — and time, which would be spent in folly and dissipation, is redeemed. The youthful mind, if properly excited by the studies of the school, is enabled to gratify the appetite for knowledge — and then it is in the path which often will lead up from the most menial employment to a more important sphere of action and usefulness. How many instances have there been, of the most eminent men, first excited to strive for intellectual excellence, by some sentiment or example, found in the reading of early life! Such impressions, ripening into strong desires, and firm resolves, exercised a controlling influence over their minds, and led them to high, noble and useful action. The intellect of the world has for the most part been slumbering for 6000 years. Iron oppression has chained it down — while a few have monopolized the privileges and enjoyments which are connected with intellectual development. The almighty, beneficent Creator, did not design it should be always so. Intellect is destined to be exerted on a larger and larger scale — and this country, we hope, is to be the favored spot. No one knows the hidden mines of talent which are concealed in the millions of minds which are now, and the hundreds of millions which are soon to be, in this land of Heaven's choicest blessings. *They will not lie dormant.* If they are not properly directed, their efforts will be a curse to themselves, and to the world. But if our native genius is properly cultivated, it may be expected to bring a long and bright day upon the destinies of man. Towards accomplishing this desirable result, we can see no more effectual ally, than well selected libraries, stationed within reach of all.

The author of our pamphlet also suggests that this subject is worthy the attention of our General and State Governments. None doubt their obligation to promote universal education; and our author quotes on the subject the opinions of many of our most distinguished statesmen. Hitherto almost nothing has been appropriated to the most important of all natural improvements, compared with the sums expended upon objects far less important. But this subject equally claims the consideration of towns and parishes, who feel an interest in their own and their country's welfare, and still more urgently, while it is neglected by our governments.

It may be remarked that this system, although it proposes to include the publishing of books, need not interfere with the interests of the booksellers; for it will be seen that it will only supply a want which itself has created, and by increasing the general habit of reading, the general demand for books will increase.

We cordially recommend this pamphlet, and the plan it proposes, to the attention of all who feel an interest in the progress of knowledge, and hope it will not lie a promising, but unnoticed scheme, for want of that attention which it so well deserves. As we have formerly suggested, we believe it will be the most efficient, if not the only means of giving life or permanency, to the valuable but declining system of local associations for mutual improvement.

[For the Annals of Education.]

FUNDAMENTAL PRINCIPLES OF FEMALE EDUCATION.

Mr Editor, — From the commencement of your 'Annals,' I have been convinced that your time could not be employed upon any subject more important to the present generation or their posterity. I rejoice that your efforts have met with the extensive and unqualified approbation of the wise and good. Were *due* attention paid to the 'Annals,' it is believed their number would be greater, and that your toil would not end in loss. You must

[For the Annals of Education.]

ADDRESS OF THE NEW-BORN.

NATURAL affection is enhanced and refined by the moral relations of a father. A little helpless stranger is introduced into his house and his heart. And a strange being it is! — such a one as himself was, a few years since. Till now, he knew experimentally, as little of a parent's heart as of his own infancy.

'Where, and who, and what art thou, little stranger?'

'The child of thy prayers, and hopes, and trembling fears! Quartered upon thee and thy companion — bearing her image — ever endeared to thine eye, thy imagination, and thy soul! Let the voice of Nature speak for thine infant child. Thine image, too, natural, moral, and immortal, is enstamped upon me. At thy request, the father of my spirit has committed my frail body to thy care. Years must it be watched, daily and nightly — resting on a mother's arm — clinging closely to a father's heart.'

'It is *new*, this care of providing for the child of my love. Thought of indeed, and talked of — but never realized until this day.'

'The frail casket of my feeble body, encloses a jewel of incalculable worth — an immortal mind — a spark of intelligence struck from the eternal rock, that shall live when 'suns shall rise and set no more.' Of this treasure, thou art the keeper! For this, thou must account to the father of spirits. My spirit bears the impress of his immortality — my body, of thy mortality. As such receive me, oh, my father! Provide for every want! To thee are they known by years of experience — but not to me. If suffered to live long enough to know myself, let me find my body nurtured to health, and my mind fitted to do its duty. Then shall I be taught how much of affection and duty I owe to thee.

'If thy spirit shall take its eternal flight before I am capable of estimating thy character, and thy love to thy son, leave me a written memorial of thy tenderness, and of thy deep concern for my immortal soul. Prepare thy surviving friends to love me, and furnish the portrait of my parents. So, though their voice be silenced, their example and writings may speak, and point the path to heaven, where I may meet them above the reach of Death!'

M.

DESCRIPTION OF THE VOCAL ORGANS.

[We are allowed to extract the following description of one of the most interesting parts of the human frame, from the Anatomical Class Book, by DR J. V. C. SMITH, — the pioneer, we believe, of popular text-books on this subject.]

BY voice, animals have the power of making themselves understood to their own species — and these sounds are either *articulate* or *inarticulate*.

Language is an acquired power, having its origin in the wants of more than one individual. Man, without society, would only utter a natural cry, which sound would express nothing but pain.

Supposing a human being to have been entirely forsaken by those of his species, in that stage of infancy, when he could have no recollection of anything pertaining to his race, his voice would, in essence, remain the cry of an infant, only strengthened in tone, at a particular age, by the development of the vocal organs, to their destined size.

But let two individuals be placed together, but without communication or knowledge of the existence of beings similar to themselves, the natural cry of each would undergo modifications: the one would make a sound, to express a particular sensation, which in time would be understood by the other: a repetition of the same note would be the sign of that sensation in future.

An additional sensation, having an intimate connexion with the first, would require a variation of tone, — and this would also become a symbol of two sensations. Here then would be the origin of language. Multiply the species, and each new member of the society would express some other sensation or want, by another modification of the original cry. Here we discover the certain commencement of a spoken language; these different sounds becoming classified, constitute a dictionary, in which each word is the mark or sign of particular sounds; — thus, if an individual can imitate the sound, or a series of sounds, he masters a language. Let it be remembered that man could never arrive to this perfection in sound or language, if his vocal organs were not differently constructed from brutes. Such is the mechanism of theirs, that so many sounds, and no more, can be made; but in man's organs, there is no limitation — no sound appreciable that he cannot imitate.

THE VOCAL BOX, OR LARYNX.

Directly under the integuments on the front side of the neck, is a cartilaginous tube, the *trachea* or wind-pipe, built up of a series of narrow strips, which are portions of a ring; therefore, it is always kept free and open. At its lower end it divides into two branches, going to the lungs on either side, but its upper portion is enlarged, just under the chin, and finally opens in common with the tube of the stomach and mouth. This enlarged part, quite prominent in man, is the *larynx* or vocal organ.

Several cartilages assist in its formation, viz, the *thyroid*, *cricoid*, the *arytænoid* and the *epiglottis*. The cricoid is the foundation; the thyroid is the wall around it; the arytænoid are appendages to the back of the cricoid, and the *epiglottis* is a valve, opening and closing the entrance into the wind-pipe, like the valve of a bellows.

Fig. 1. Fig. 2.

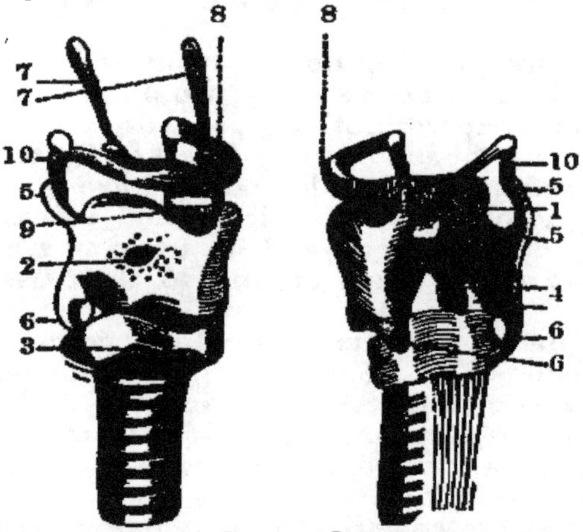

Explanation of Figs. 1. 2.

The five cartilages are.
1. The epiglottis.
2. The thyroid cartilage.
3. the cricoid auxiliary, and
4. The two arytænoid cartilages.
5. The two superior horns of the thyroid cartilage.
6. The two inferior horns.
7. The suspensory ligament of the os hyoides.
8. The os hyoides.
9. The azygos ligament, connecting the os hyoides to the thyroid cartilage.
10. The two lateral ligaments connecting the horns of the os hyoides to the superior horns of the thyroid cartilage.

One of these diagrams presents a front and the other a back view of the *larynx* or vocal box. The bone of the tongue is seen, like half of a hoop marked 8, in both plans. 2 is the front of the *thyroid cartilage*, felt under the skin — protruding in the form of an irregular tumor. The wind-pipe is the tube at the bottom of each larynx. The *vocal cords* — the membranes which vibrate to produce sound, as the current of air rushes by, are concealed, being placed inside. From the remarks in the text, together with the references, a very correct idea will be formed of the structure of this curious organ. By blowing through the wind-pipe of almost any animal, soon after it is slain, provided the larynx has not been injured, the vocal cords may be put in motion, and the sound which is produced will bear considerable analogy to the natural voice of the animal.

Within the larynx, and consequently below the valve, are four delicate membranes, two on each side, put upon the stretch — being in fact, like shelves, — their thin edges nearly meeting from the opposite sides, so that there is scarcely any space between them. These are the vocal cords.

When the air rushes out from the lungs through the wind-pipe, it must obviously pass through the larynx, — in doing which it strikes the tense edges of the cords, and produces a vibration. This vibratory motion given to the current of air, produces sound. In the cavities of the bones of the face, forehead and nose, its power is increased, and in the mouth it undergoes further modifications, and ultimately becomes articulate language. The teeth, tongue, lips, nose and fauces have each an influence in the production of articulate sounds. Hence grammarians have arranged the human voice under the appropriate divisions of *guttural, nasal, dental* and *labial* sounds, — expressive of the agency which each of these organs exert on the original tone.

Shrillness or roughness of voice depends on the diameter of the larynx, — its elasticity, lubricity, and the force with which the expired air is propelled through the *rima glottidis*, or slit like chink, between the vocal cords.

It is because the larynx is smaller in women, and more elastic, that their voice is of a different character. The breaking of the voice, *(vox rauca,)* noticeable in boys, at a particular age, depends partly on the enlargement of the apartments within the bones, which generally take place at that important crisis of their lives, when the whole constitution undergoes a sudden change.

But the mechanism of voice would have been incomplete, were there not a number of exceedingly delicate muscles, which graduate the diameter of the narrow slit through which the sound escapes into the mouth. Unconsciously, they effect the requisite contractions, forever varying, according to the rapidity, intensity, or strength of the voice, in singing, conversation or declamation.

Finally, the larynx is a musical wind instrument, of the *reeded* kind, on the principle of the hautboy. The nearness of the vocal cords to each other resembles the reed precisely. All the tones of reeded instruments are effected by finger holes, — but the tones of the human voice are varied by the extrinsic and intrinsic muscles, which shorten or elongate the vocal tube. Thus the same result is produced by this process, — increasing or diminishing the diameter of the larynx, that is accomplished in the clarionet, bassoon, flute and hautboy, by a graduated scale of finger holes.

Is not this another beautiful, mechanical evidence of the existence of a Being superior to ourselves ?

PRACTICAL LESSONS ON THE SITUATION OF COUNTRIES.

[The utter ignorance which we have formerly felt, and constantly seen, in regard to the relative situation of places, and the difficulty of conceiving of the position of countries in reference to our own, lead us to present sections of the earth from the Geographical Copy Book, and to write the dialogues accompanying them, as a specimen of the mode in which we think the subject ought to be explained by parents and teachers.]

Father. William ! here is another section of the Earth, in the Geographical Copy Book, and can you tell me what it is ?

William. Why, Sir, I see the two poles are marked upon it, and Washington. I suppose it must be a *section* through Washington and the poles.

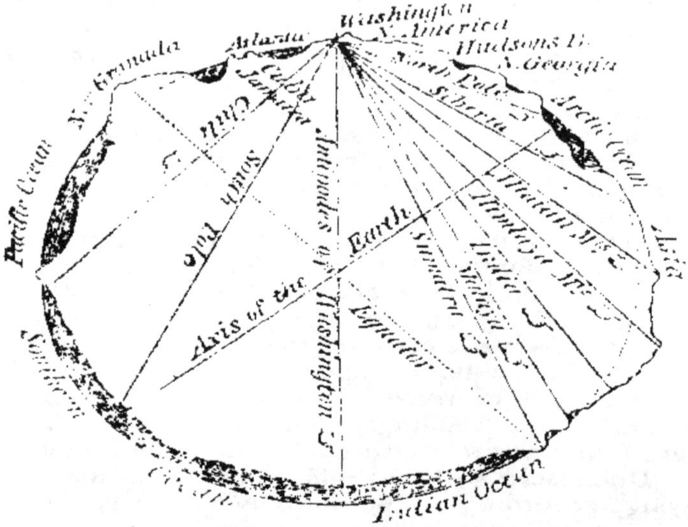

F. You are right. It represents the profile of the Earth, as it would appear if it were cut and divided, from north to south, through Washington. But do you understand yet what these indexes or hands mean?

W. In the other section that you gave me, they showed which way we must point to countries. I always thought we must point straight east to Africa; but I see now, as you say, I should only point to the Sun or the Stars; and I have learned to point eastward and downward, too, to show where Africa is.

F. When you stand with your face to the north, must you point to the north pole, straight forward?

W. No, father; but I never thought of that. It has always seemed to me that the north pole, was *above* me; but I see now, I must point *downward.*

F. You made a very natural mistake; for the north pole in the heavens, and the north star which shows us the north, are above us; but take care not to forget, that *up* and *down* are different in different places. If you will turn the section round, so that the people of the north pole (if there are any), are uppermost, you will see that they would be obliged to point *down* to us. But how would you point to Siberia?

W. Why — I must point down to that, too! I thought Siberia was east of us. It is about half way down towards my feet!

F. So it is east of us, my son; but the shortest way to it, if we could go that way, would be over the north pole — first north and then south — as you will see, if you will look at a polar map. But what mountains will you point to, if you point forward and lower down?

W. The Altaian and the Himlaya mountains, and I suppose Chinese Tartary, that lies between them. And then farther down is India, and Malaya, and Sumatra, and the equator. I never thought of pointing to them, with my face to the north!

F. It will be a long time before you will think of everything in Geography. But I am very anxious you should know, so well, which way places are from you, as not only to tell me *in words*, but to point to them. And what do you find our antipodes?

W. It is a spot in the Indian Ocean, father.

F. Yes; and perhaps one of our American vessels is just sailing over that spot; and the sailors are standing with their feet pointing upwards to the country they came from. Now tell me what you will find to point to if you look exactly south.

W. If I point a little down, I should point to Cuba and Jamaica; a little farther down, to New Grenada; and half way down, to Chili. And then, three quarters of the way down, is the south pole, directly opposite the north pole.

F. Right. And now look, and tell me how you would travel, if you should go directly round the earth, towards the south, and back by the north.

W. I must first pass over a part of the Atlantic Ocean and the West India Islands to the mountains of New Grenada, and then over a part of the Pacific Ocean to Chili. Then it would be all ocean, over the south pole to Sumatra and India. I must then go north, over India and Tartary and Siberia, to the Arctic Ocean, and across the ocean on the ice, to North Georgia and North America, and then *home again*. I never thought of travelling so before.

W. You will never travel so, I suppose; but I hope you will now think of countries, and of people, and of your friends when they go to sea, *just where they are*, and not as if they were in the sky — or you do not know where. Until you can do this, you will lose half the pleasure of studying Geography.

TEACHER'S ALMANAC FOR FEBRUARY.

THE SCHOOL-ROOM.

The days begin to lengthen; but as the greatest heat is after noon, and the highest tide after the moon has passed the meridian, the old maxim is often found true in a northern climate — 'As the day lengthens, the cold strengthens.'

Those who have not housed their wood, must now thaw off the ice and snow every morning; and those who have received it fresh from the forest, must have it carefully 'stewed,' (as the operation is called in the kitchen), before they can expect a fire. Either of these operations will occupy from one to two hours, and consume nearly half the fuel. In the mean time, cold and smoke will make it impossible for most of the children to *think* of anything else. Real *study* is out of the question; and if the teacher keeps his own temper, and that of his pupils, it is more than is generally done.

The portion of wood consumed to carry off the water, may be paid for by an additional tax. But we must estimate at least one hour, daily, lost to each pupil, forty hours already in the season, equal to seven school days. If it so continues for three months, twelve school days are lost to each scholar; or in a school of 60, seven hundred and twenty school days, or more than two years to the district! No tax will pay for time and knowledge, not to speak of the injury of temper and character so often resulting from cold feet, and cold fingers, and smoked eyes, and a mind absorbed by the sufferings of the body. Where does the blame belong? Who will correct the evil?

We have not estimated the loss of time from colds, and rheumatism, and chilblains; nor yet the physician's bills. Provide for all these, unless you keep your school-room warm; for if your boys must sit on benches, nature furnishes no means of warmth but by fire. Do you use a thermometer yet? Are the cracks stopped, and the windows all mended?

THE EARTH.

Still bound in icy chains at the north, there is little to observe upon the earth but the phenomena of cold and freezing. In your cellars, you may find occasion to show your children the sprouting vegetables, and that they do not grow green, without light. A few mild days may produce some buds in the trees; but like a child brought forward too early, or too fast, they will wither before they come to maturity. There is no change in animated nature, except that loss of life is visible abroad.

Our southern brethren will welcome spring and its buds, and blossoms, and birds, and perhaps some of its fruits, before the close of the month.

THE HEAVENS.

The heavens are still adorned with peculiar splendor; and during the last half of the month 'the moon will walk abroad in brightness.' Venus is still the morning star; and Jupiter will be visible early in the evening. Mars still sets so near the sun that it cannot probably be seen.

Among the constellations, you may yet see, early in the evening, the six beautiful stars in Taurus, or the Bull's head, in the form of a V; and the cluster of small stars not far from them, called the Pleiades, to which Job alludes. And not far from them is Orion — four large stars, in a rhomboid, for his shoulders and knees, and three in a row, for his belt.

At 9 o'clock, you will find near the meridian the six stars, three on each side of a rhomboid, with five others near them, of considerable brilliancy, which form Gemini, or the Twins. South of these and in a line with the belt of Orion, are the three stars in the head of the dog, and Sirius, or the Dog Star, the brightest in the heavens. In August, it rises with the sun, and is over our heads during the day. Hence the ancients called these days, dog days, supposing this star to produce the excessive heat.

A celestial globe, or 'Burritt's Geography of the Heavens,' will enable you to make the winter evenings' walk a delightful source of amusement, and instruction to your pupils. And if you will tell them but a little of the wonders of Astronomy, of the suns, and systems, and motion of the bright worlds above them, you may soon lead them to exclaim with an ancient observer; '*When I consider the heavens the work of thy fingers, — the moon and the stars which thou hast ordained — What is man that thou art mindful of him!*'

CORRESPONDENCE.

Letter from the Rev. Zerah Colburn, to the Editor.

[We addressed to Mr Colburn a copy of our review of his life, and a letter requesting some information as to the effect which time and other occupations had produced in reference to the powers of calculation, formerly so remarkable. We are gratified in being able to present to our readers his wishes for the future, as well as his account of his own state; and shall be happy to be the medium of any communication to him on the subject.]

Rockingham, Vt. January 11th, 1834.

Being at Springfield last week, I received from Mr Merriam your Periodical for October, 1833, (for which accept my thanks) and your request was communicated to me. I know not that I shall be able to answer your request more satisfactorily than I endeavored to do it in the Memoir. However, I will try.

My impression ever has been that if I had continued in the practice of my calculating faculty, I should have continued to progress, perhaps to an incredible extent. I do not think that the loss of my quickness in figures is to be at all attributed to repeated exercise, but to total neglect of that gift. I think, likewise, that had I continued in practice while at the same time, a course of arithmetical, or classical, or mathematical studies was enjoined upon me, there would have been nothing in these studies to destroy the mental gift, or the rapidity of its exercise. There was a time during my exhibition, that a Latin grammar was put into my hands, and all the attention which I devoted to it, had no effect upon my calculations. It was not long after I gave up public exhibition, before I had lost materially in point of readiness. Yet though nearly twenty years have elapsed, I do not know but I am now as well able to solve questions, as I was only six or eight months after I had thus retired.

I suppose, if I am not now as ready in giving answers as when I first commenced at the age of six years, a very little practice would serve to make me so. And I might even regain all my former quickness, were I in a situation that required such continued efforts of mind.

I shall be gratified if these few hints serve to satisfy you on the points embraced in your letter to Mr Merriam. I would now say that I thankfully receive the testimonies of public interest still felt in my case, from several public prints; and though last perused, not least, in the number of the 'Annals of Education,' which you were pleased to forward to me.

Under existing circumstances, I am thinking of seeking some pursuit that will least interfere with my ministerial usefulness, and enable me to support my family. I should prefer some employment that would most directly call into request my peculiar faculty, as I think I could in this way give better satisfaction than as a teacher of youth, from which my unfinished education seems to debar me. I think it possible that if the friends of science generally, knew my wish in this respect, some opening might be found. Might I request your concurrence in making known my wish?

Should anything else occur on the perusal of my book on which you wish for farther information, I shall be happy to afford it.

Very respectfully yours,

Zerah Colburn.

My present residence is at Lebanon, N. H.

MISCELLANY.

Convention of Teachers.

The Essex County Association of Teachers, held its fourth Annual Meeting at Topsfield on the 29th and 30th of November last. The number of Teachers and other friends of Education who attended, was considerable. Several interesting lectures and reports were given, and numerous discussions held on important topics. Among the subjects which occupied the attention of the Association, were the Carstairian system of Writing, Physiology, as a branch of study, the system of Jacotot, School Examinations, a County Depository for specimens in Botany and Mineralogy, and the enlarging and improving of the County Depository for School Books, Apparatus, Periodicals, and other works on Education.

It was stated, that since the Association was first organized, great improvements have taken place in the county, 'in the construction and ventilation of School Houses, and in the introduction of improved methods of teaching.'

A *Convention of Teachers* was also held at Wellfleet, in this State, on the 20th and 21st of December. The time was taken up with lectures and discussions. Lectures were delivered on Discipline, Mental discipline, Mode of Teaching Arithmetic, Reading, Grammar, the Lancasterian system, and the Qualifications of Teachers. At the close of each lecture, the subject of that lecture was introduced for discussion. In connection with the subject of Discipline, the question arose, 'whether corporal punishment is necessary in a school, on ANY occasion,' and was ably discussed at two several times. On taking the sense of the Convention on the question, it was decided in the affirmative. The question, 'whether writing ought to be taught in our common schools, with the other branches, was discussed at a similar length, and decided in a similar manner. The question, whether *short* reading lessons, with remarks and criticisms, were preferable to long ones, was also decided affirmatively.

In the progress of the Convention it was voted, 'to recommend to districts the globe and black board, to be used at the discretion of the teachers.' Resolutions were also passed, expressing a strong sense of the importance of having School Committees perform faithfully their official duties; and of having parents visit schools more than they have usually done. Another resolution recommended the general formation of County Associations, as a means of promoting the cause of education.

Agricultural Schools.

Several counties in the State of New York, are zealously circulating among the people petitions, to the Legislature, for the establishment of a *central* agricultural school for the State, and agricultural societies in each county.

Education in New Grenada.

Colleges and Schools. The government, under the presidency of Gen. Santander, are actively fostering education in various branches. Official information had been demanded from the different provinces, cantons, and parishes, concerning the condition of schools, &c, and partially obtained, even before the opening of the last session of Congress, at Bogota, so that the Report of the Secretary of Foreign Relations and the Interior, (Hon. Alejandro Velez,) gave us an interesting general sketch, particularly of the Colleges.

There are three University Departments: and the corresponding Universities are in the cities of Bogota, Popayan and Carthagena. The income of the latter, (having been increased partly by the funds of recently suppressed convents,) now amounts to nearly $20,000 annually. There are more schools in existence than perhaps our countrymen generally suppose; although in numbers and character they are very far from being what the government desire, or the imperative necessities of the people demand. Not a small part of them are Lancasterian.

We have received numbers of the printed schemes, or 'programas,' of the exercises at the annual exhibitions of the Colleges in the different provinces, in June and July last, in which are much more fully detailed, than at our commencements, the exercises of the pupils. Several of them form quarto pamphlets, of from ten to twenty pages, from some of which the general plans of many of the class books may be inferred. The number of pupils continues small.

Female College of Bogota.

The Female College, established last year at Bogota, held its first public exhibition on the 31st of June, (if we mistake not,) after it had been in operation eight months. The programa of this institution we perused with peculiar interest, as it is, we believe, the only one of the same name and destiny, under the patronage of any government in the world, and is likely to exercise a most extensive influence in South America.

It may, perhaps, hereafter affect Spain, whence a degraded plan of female education was received, and whose example has tended to discourage the intellectual elevation of woman. The President is a lady. There are three classes; the first with five pupils, the second with six, and the third with ten; total twentyone.

The first class debated the question—'What instruction ought a well educated woman to enjoy?' This subject was divided under several heads:—The general duties of women; their private duties; their disadvantages in society, and the means of removing them; how they may improve their condition in society, and perform their duties; false merit; external accomplishments; real merit; intellectual qualities; domestic arrangements, and cultivation of the intellectual faculties. The other exercises of the first class were in Castillian grammar, French, Christian Morals, Manners, Arithmetic, Drawing, and Music.

The intention of the government is, to add to the funds, the professorships, and the branches of study in this institution, as soon as circumstances shall allow; but to those who are acquainted with the state of society in South America, it will be perceived that it is already as important a step, comparatively speaking, as a well endowed female university would be in the United States. We hope to give more hereafter in relation to it.

Society for Elementary Education.

The latest accounts from New Granada afford us still further satisfaction. Vice-president Mosquera, during a visit to Popayan, his residence, devoted himself to the promotion of education with such zeal and success, that he had established a school society, called 'La Sociedad de Educacion Elemental Primaria de Popayan,' of the leading citizens; and under their care a Lancasterian school house was already nearly completed at the close of October, twentyfour yards long, to accommodate 200 boys; and preparations were making to provide another of the same description for girls, under the direction of a *Committee of Ladies*, acting under the

Society. The principle of gratuitous, popular coöperation for this important object, has therefore been at length commenced in South America. May its effects be equal to those it has produced and may produce in the United States.

Mr Mosquera has presented nearly $1,100 worth of books, slates, cards and other apparatus to the Society, and has opened a school for the preparation of teachers, containing one master, two general monitors, several class monitors, and twentytwo children. As soon as all these parts of his plan are in successful operation, he will bend his efforts to the formation of a high school, to fit youth for the University; and possessing great sway over the people, by his noble, and intelligent, and philanthropic character, as well as his talents and commanding eloquence, (having been called the first orator of Colombia,) we cannot but anticipate success. He has already done much for the schools in the country near Popayan; and has been invited to a rural banquet, as a mark of respect and affection.

The constitution of the Elementary Society of Popayan has been sent, to some of the gentlemen who have been honored with the appointment of Corresponding Secretaries and Fellows of that Association.

American Lyceum.

A number of distinguished friends of learning have been appointed by the Executive Committee of the American Lyceum to furnish Essays on a variety of interesting subjects; and invitations will be sent to these and many other gentlemen, in all parts of the country, to attend the Fourth Annual Meeting, early in May next, which it is believed will have much interest. The appointments made, it is to be understood, do not preclude volunteer communications.

Education of Teachers.

The necessity of educating men for the profession of teachers, as well as for every other, is gaining attention every month. In the State of New York, whose school system has been so useful, the Governor observes in his late speech: 'In this respect, there is, in my judgment, a manifest defect in our system. Little as yet has been done to provide teachers properly trained for this pursuit. Without well qualified and skilful instructors, the amplest funds will prove comparatively useless. It is scarcely less important to establish a wise plan of supervision, not so much for the purpose of securing a faithful application of the public moneys, as to introduce the most effectual modes of teaching, and the best system of instruction.'

He adds: 'I regret to see, that in this respect, we fall far behind even some of the monarchies of Europe. Several of the German states, particularly Prussia, are doing much more for the education of the people than we are.'

The Governor of Maine observes; 'Perhaps, however, the most profitable aid that can at this time be extended to the cause of primary education in our State, would be found in the establishment of a Seminary, for the better qualifications of instructors. It is not sufficient that towns are required to maintain schools, nor that schools are kept within the reach of all our youth; the desired result will seldom be attained, certainly not in its full extent, unless the several towns shall be enabled to procure faithful and competent teachers. I am convinced, that these cannot be obtained, in sufficient number to supply our rapidly multiplying districts, without additional facilities for their qualification, by the establishment of an Institution, in which they may be instructed in the interesting and important duties, which as teachers will devolve upon them.'

The Academician.

We have received the third number of the Academician and Southern Journal of Education, containing valuable essays on education, mingled with a considerable portion of miscellaneous articles. We earnestly hope, that this effort to engage the attention of the South to this important subject, may be encouraged.

Southern Manual Labor Schools.

A manual labor school in Georgia has been so conducted as to show that the pupils can pay for their board and tuition by their labor; and the town of Glynn has given 750 acres of land, chiefly cleared property, amounting to $3,800, to induce its teachers to remove it to their vicinity. The Presbytery of Alabama, as we learn from the Alabama State Intelligencer, have purchased land for locating a similar establishment on such a plan as to receive all classes of Christians. A bill has also passed the legislature of North Carolina to incorporate a school of this kind in that State.

Young Men's Associations.

We are gratified to see these associations extending throughout our country. That which is established at Boston has done much in circulating pamphlets on lotteries. That of Pittsburg issues a newspaper, entitled 'The Friend,' which is one of the most interesting we receive, and is sustained by the funds as well as the efforts of the Association. From a late report we perceive, that it contains nearly two hundred members. Another was recently formed at Albany, equally large. We believe that the New York institution is also prospering, although we are not favored with their paper. Our own work is regularly sent in exchange to some; and will be sent cheerfully, to all similar establishments.

Gratuitous Copies. We are compelled, however, after the present number, to diminish the list of gratuitous copies, and also of our exchanges; and we must beg those who have received them hitherto to recollect that we must use *every retrenchment,* in order to avoid further loss, unless our subscription is greatly enlarged beyond the present number.

Common Schools of New York.

An abstract of the Report of the Superintendent of Common Schools in New York, from which it appears that the State has distributed $100,000 for the support of the common schools during the last year, and that double the sum has been raised, in addition, from taxes and local funds. The influence of the system adopted in that State continues to be salutary. The whole increase of children from 5 to 16, in that State, has been 13,756 during the last year; but the increase of children at school has been 17,516. Ninety new districts have been formed; and 266 more have been reported than the last year. The whole number of districts, is 9690, of which 9107 have made returns. We are gratified to see that the superintendent urges the importance of embracing a wider range of knowledge in the course of instruction. He advises that the history and political organization of our country, and the elements of physical science should be taught in every school in our country. The whole number of children in these schools of New York, is now 522,618.

Great Value of Education.

The teacher's bill is often paid as reluctantly as the physician's; and those who seek for the causes which obstruct the progress of education, would do well to inquire whether one of the greatest does not arise from the maxim — 'The laborer is *not* worthy of his hire?' A lady within our knowledge, sent her children to a private school, and when the bill was sent in, called very politely, and said that she should be very glad to pay the bill, but she had no money' (i. e. after paying her milliner, &c). She wished, however, to continue her *patronage* to the school! Another lady of the same character observed, that education was of the first importance; and added; 'I am resolved to give my children a *good education*, if I am *never* able to pay for it.'

NOTICES.

Economical Black Copy-Book, to write with Water. By James Worcester. Boston: Published by the Author, No. 116 Washington-street.

We know of no system of writing superior to the Carstairan; and Mr Worcester presents its fundamental principles and elements correctly in this book. It is composed of a species of slate paper, on which letters may be distinctly traced with water, to acquire the habit of the several movements, or written with a white ink, which can easily be effaced. It thus combines the great economy of a slate, with the advantage gained by using a pen. We believe, it will be found very useful in schools which adopt this system, which is fully developed in Foster's work.

Topographical Map.

We have rarely seen a more beautiful specimen of topographical drawing than the 'Map of New-London and Windham Counties, Conn.,' from actual survey, by Wm. Lester, Jr. It gives a statistical as well as geographical view of these counties; and distinct Maps in the margin present us with the geological structure and plans of the principal towns. Why may not this be done for every county, at least, in the United States? The munificence of Massachusetts has already published a splendid work on its Geology, by Professor Hitchcock, which does honor to the State; and we learn that a geographical survey is also in preparation.

Parley's Magazine.

We have formerly mentioned the Juvenile Rambler, and its usefulness in schools. We did all in our power to secure it such a character as we approved; but its price and subscription list did not authorise a sufficient amount of illustrations. The Parley Magazine, with its splendid illustrations, only needed a change in its character, and the Rambler has been united with it, to accomplish the great object more effectually. The plan proposed for the future volumes will render it a valuable publication to every family; and the engagement of the late Editor of the Rambler to assist in it, will, we trust, secure its execution.

Scientific Tracts and Family Lyceum.

These two publications are united under the care of Dr J. V. C. Smith; and the appearance of the two first numbers leads us to hail it, as one of the most valuable agents in the diffusion of general and practical knowledge, in the families of our country.

AMERICAN

ANNALS OF EDUCATION

AND INSTRUCTION.

MARCH, 1834.

YOUTH WITHOUT CHILDHOOD.

CASPAR HAUSER. *An account of an individual kept in a dungeon, separated from all communication with the world, from early childhood to about the age of seventeen.* Drawn up from legal documents. By Anselm Von Feuerback, President of one of the Bavarian Courts of Appeal, &c. Translated from the German. Second edition. Boston: Allen & Ticknor. 1833. 18mo., pp. 168.

In passing through Germany, in the year 1829, we heard of an extraordinary being who had just 'come into the world,' as he subsequently expressed it, at the age of seventeen — a youth in form, and yet as ignorant of language, and of the use of his limbs, and even of the most common external objects, as the infant of a few months. He was observed on the evening of the 26th of May, 1828, near one of the gates of Nuremberg, in the posture of one intoxicated, who was equally unable to stand or to move. A letter which he held out, addressed to the Captain of a squadron of cavalry, gave no information except that he was born in 1812, and had never been suffered to leave the house, and that all inquiries concerning his origin and residence would be in vain. In reply to all the questions addressed to him by individuals and the police, a few unmeaning words and incessant moans were all that he could utter, and he pointed with marks of exhaustion, to his blistered feet. Meat, which was offered to restore him, he rejected with visible horror; but eagerly swallowed some bread and water; and on being conducted to the stable, stretched himself upon the straw and fell into a sleep so profound, that he could scarcely be awakened. His feet were as soft as the palms of his hands; his gait was that of a child, just beginning to step; and it was only with intense suffering that he could walk. His senses seemed to be locked up in torpor; and a wooden horse, brought to him by a soldier, in consequence of his frequent repetition of the German word for horse, 'ross! ross!' was the first and only object which seemed to excite interest. He seated himself by it, 'with a countenance smiling sweetly through his tears,' and passed hours and days, in moving, and feeding, and ornamenting it, as if it were the only being which called forth his social feelings.

It will be easily believed that such an appearance would excite intense curiosity. It was a case which set at defiance all the formal interrogations and arrangements of a German government; and it was difficult to decide whether he belonged to the asylum for idiocy, or the almshouse, or to the police office and the prison. After vain efforts to elicit something from him as to his residence or connections, to which he replied only in the same piteous moans and unintelligible phrases, he was committed to a tower over one of the gates, under the care of a humane jailor, and appears to have enjoyed all the comforts of which his case admitted. Common sense soon relaxed the severity of the law; and he was received into the family of the jailor, as a deserted, helpless child, and under the instruction of his children, *began to learn to talk!*

He was visited by crowds, who taxed their ingenuity in examining the poor youth, and wearied him almost to torture, by their inquisitorial efforts to discover something. But they could only ascertain that he was an infant of adult age; — in the expressive language of a London Reviewer, an example of 'youth without childhood.' He attempted, like an infant, to seize every glittering object which he saw, and cried if he was forbidden; and even when a lighted candle was placed before him, he tried to grasp the beautiful flame. In the midst of this seeming infancy, however, his guardians were astonished, on putting a pencil into his hand, to find that he could form letters distinctly. He filled a sheet with elementary characters and syllables, and closed by covering a page with the name — 'KASPAR HAUSER.'

This discovery of his name, usually so important in the records of a police office, furnished no clue to the mystery which enveloped this singular being. Destitute of the conception, as well as the names, of the most common objects, and averse to all the common customs and conveniences and necessaries of life, there seemed no alternative, in the language of his biographer, but to regard him as the inhabitant of some distant planet, or as one buried from his birth, and now just emerged into the world. Imagination was tortured to devise some mode of accounting for his character and appearance. Some dreamed of an experiment, made by modern theorists, to ascertain the state of a mind, left to advance to maturity in utter ignorance of the world, and thus realizing the fancy picture of a German story. Others supposed him the heir of some estate or diadem, of which he was unlawfully deprived. Others still conjectured, that this difficult and dangerous plan of burying alive, had been adopted to conceal the crimes attending his birth.

Such were the conjectures floating on the public mind in reference to this singular being, when we left Germany, unable to vary our route so far as to visit Nuremberg. It was not until subsequent education had enabled Caspar to clothe his own ideas in words, that any light was thrown upon his early history; and the following account, derived from the work whose title is at the head of this article, comprises all his recollections of childhood and youth:

'He neither knows who he is, nor where his home is. It was only at Nuremberg that he came into the world. Here he first learnt that, besides himself and 'the man with whom he had always been,' there existed other men and other creatures. As long as he can recollect he has always lived in a hole, (a small low apartment which he sometimes calls a cage,) where he had always sat upon the ground, with bare feet, and clothed only with a shirt and a pair of breeches. In this apartment he never heard a sound, whether produced by a man, by an animal, or by anything else. He never saw the heavens, nor did there ever appear a brightening (daylight) such as at Nuremberg. He never perceived any difference between day and night, and much less did he ever get a sight of the beautiful lights in the heavens. Whenever he awoke from sleep, he found a loaf of bread and a pitcher of water by him. Sometimes this water had a bad taste;* whenever this was the case, he could no longer keep his eyes open, but was compelled to fall asleep; and, when he afterwards awoke, he found that he had a clean shirt on, and that his nails had been cut. He never saw the face of the man who brought him his meat and drink. In his hole he had two wooden horses, and several ribbons. With these horses he had always amused himself as long as he was awake; and his only occupation was, to make them run by his side, and to fix or tie the ribbons about them in different positions. Thus, one day had passed as the other; but he had never felt the want of anything, had never been sick, and — once only excepted — had never felt the sensation of pain. Upon the whole, he had been much happier there than in the world, where he was obliged to suffer so much. How long he had continued to live in this situation he knew not; for he had had no knowledge of time. He knew not when, or how he came there. Nor had he any recollection of ever having been in a different situation, or in any other than in that place. The man with whom he had always been, never did him any harm. Yet one day, shortly before he was taken away, — when he had been running his horse too hard, and had made too much noise, the man came and struck him upon his arm with a stick, or a piece of wood; this caused the wound which he brought with him to Nuremberg.

'Pretty nearly about the same time, the man once came into his prison, placed a small table over his feet, and spread something white upon it,

* Probably water mixed with opium.

which he now knows to have been paper; he then came behind him, so as not to be seen by him, took hold of his hand, and moved it backwards and forwards on the paper, with a thing (a lead pencil) which he had stuck between his fingers. He (Hauser) was then ignorant of what it was; but he was mightily pleased, when he saw the black figures which began to appear upon the white paper. When he felt that his hand was free, and the man was gone from him, he was so much pleased with this new discovery, that he could never grow tired of drawing these figures repeatedly upon the paper. This occupation almost made him neglect his horses, although he did not know what those characters signified. The man repeated his visits in the same manner, several times.'

'Another time, the man came again, lifted him from the place where he lay, placed him on his feet, and endeavored to teach him to stand.'

At his final appearance the man took him over his shoulders, carried him, as he expressed it, up a hill, and brought him to Nuremberg. His recollections of his journey are very indistinct, and the fact that he sinks into a death-like sleep when he rides in a wagon, leaves it entirely uncertain in what way he was conveyed. After many ineffectual examinations, often leading to error, nothing remained but to provide the best means for alleviating his misfortunes, and supplying, in some degree, the loss of his years and childhood and youth, with the faint hope, that time might enable him to furnish a clue to his origin.*

The state of nervous excitement and disease, produced by the multitude of new objects and ideas that crowded upon him, emerging thus suddenly from darkness and solitude, led the police to exclude all visitors, and place Caspar in the family of Professor Daumer of the Nuremberg gymnasium, to receive such an education as he needed.

In the course of a year, he was so far advanced in the knowledge of language as to commence a memoir of himself. An attempt by some unknown person to take his life, excited, perhaps, by the apprehension of discovery, appears to have been the only interruption to the course of training by which we are told he came to be

* In recent newspapers, we find the following paragraph:

'*Caspar Hauser.* The mystery which hung about the origin and early life of this extraordinary young man, is said to be in a way of explanation. It seems, according to an account which we find in an English periodical, that Caspar Hauser was the fruit of an illicit amour; that a priest, the reputed father, took charge of the child from the moment of its birth, and finally inclosed it in a subterraneous hole or vault, in a convent where he was residing; that thus imprisoned and shut out from all human intercourse, the unhappy being passed his existence until within a day or two of his being found, as related in the history of his life which has been published, when the priest being compelled to quit the convent, and having no other place of concealment at hand, released and left the boy to his fate. The chain of circumstantial evidence, by which thus much of the story has been made out, is so well put together, as to leave little doubt that the true elucidation has been hit upon. The above outline has been communicated in conversation, by M. Kluber, the celebrated writer on Public Law, who first discovered and is still following the clue. When he has thoroughly sifted the matter, it is expected that he will favor the public with a memoir on the subject.'

'reckoned among civilized, and well-behaved men,' including, of course, many of the artificial wants and fashions which added neither to his happiness or worth. The narrative before us presents a variety of interesting details and anecdotes, concerning the childlike simplicity and amiable character of this youth, his singular views of life, and his peculiar propensities and habits, which well deserve perusal. Our limits only allow us to glance at a few of the most prominent points of the description, and the principles which they illustrate.

The darkness and seclusion in which Caspar had been kept, produced extreme sensibility to every external impression. After he recovered from that torpor caused by his entering the world, his senses were acute to a degree which was painful. Every object conveyed odors to him, which were, in a great measure, imperceptible to others, and some would produce shivering, and nausea, and fever. The touch of animals, or of metals, thrilled through his frame, and often produced unequivocal symptoms of pain and disease. His hearing and sight were also uncommonly acute, and several remarkable instances are given, in which he proved that he could discover objects and colors, as readily by night, as by day. He observed with attention and accuracy; and his recollection of persons and names, at an early period, was surprising. Colors were pleasing to him in proportion to their brilliancy; and he thought an apple tree would have been more beautiful if its leaves had been red, as well as its fruit!

The great principle was established in his case, as with infants, that forms and distances are not distinguished until the touch has corrected the errors of vision. He stated after he acquired the use of language, that in the beginning, the men and horses represented in sheets of pictures, appeared to him precisely like the men and horses that were carved in wood! He did not perceive the difference, until he had learned it by handling them. Another striking illustration of this principle is described. In this case he called a beautiful summer landscape which was seen from his room, — 'ugly! ugly!' — because, as he afterwards said, it appeared to him like a collection of spots of various colors on the window. Two or three years of instruction corrected these errors, and reduced his sensibility, on many points, to the common level; but he continued able to see distinctly at night.

His extraordinary memory declined with this acuteness of the senses, at the same time that his frame enlarged; and both were singularly coincident with a change in his diet. Caspar observed, in regard to his hearing, that 'its acuteness had been considerably diminished since he had begun to eat meat.' Professor Daumer, in his notes, observes, 'after he had learned regularly to eat meat his mental activity was diminished, his eyes lost their brilliancy and expression, and his vivid propensity to constant activity was diminished. The intense application of his mind gave way to absence, and indifference; and the quickness of his apprehension was also considerably diminished.' It is questioned by the author, whether it was the result of his food, or of the previous excitement. He now exhibits nothing of genius, or remarkable talent, no fancy or wit, but sound common sense, and persevering application.

His disposition was uncommonly mild and amiable, and his habits of obedience, produced as he said by early commands and punishment, were remarkable. He was equally remarkable for never yielding his preconceived notions to the authority, or even the testimony of others. He would not even believe the account given of snow, and of the growth of plants and animals, until he saw and felt it.

The same disposition to scepticism appeared in his reluctance to believe in the existence of his own, or any other spirit. Indeed, he did not seem for a long time to be aware of the difference between animate and inanimate objects, supposing all motion to be voluntary, and believing all matter capable of it.

His case furnishes some evidence on the long disputed question, whether man would naturally arrive at the idea of a Deity. Our intercourse with the deaf and dumb, and our inquiries of instructors at home and abroad, had long since shown us that the most talented and mature minds *do not* attain this idea, unassisted. In the case of Caspar Hauser, his biographer observes that 'he brought with him from his dungeon not the least presentiment of the existence of God, not a shadow of faith in any more elevated, invisible existence.' It was not until his faithful instructor led him to remark on the things which he *heard and saw within himself*, that he could believe in any objects but those of the external senses. Two of the most intelligent deaf mutes we have ever known, were for months, utterly incredulous of all that was said to them of an invisible being. But the example of Caspar Hauser, like that of the deaf mutes, also proves, that the idea of a Supreme cause commends itself to the reason and feelings of man, when his mind is cultivated. A touching incident which occurred in the course of his early education will illustrate this point, and must close our extracts from this interesting volume :

'His instructor showed him for the first time the starry heavens. His astonishment and transport surpassed all description. He could not be satiated with the sight, and was ever returning to gaze upon it. "That," he exclaimed, "is, indeed, the most beautiful sight that I have ever yet seen in the world. But who has placed all these numerous beautiful candles there? Who lights them? Who puts them out?" When he was told that, like the Sun, with which he was already acquainted, they always continue to give light, he asked again; "Who placed them there above, that they may always continue to give light?" At length standing motionless, with his head bowed down, and his eyes staring, he fell into a train of deep and serious meditation. When he again recovered his recollection, his transport had been succeeded by deep sadness. He sunk trembling upon a chair, and asked, with a burst of tears, "why that wicked man had kept him always locked up, and had never shown him any of these beautiful things."'

The whole story is a striking exhibition of the value of childhood, as a part of life — of the necessity of simultaneous progress in body and mind, in order to produce the man. It is an affecting illustration of that most criminal neglect, which leaves a human being to become 'in understanding and stature a man, but in knowledge a child,' — which allows him to acquire a power, most valuable or most dangerous, according to its application, without giving him the knowledge necessary to use it aright, or inspiring the disposition to employ it for good purposes. If the view of the starry heavens could rouse this gentle youth to such reproaches of the man to whom on other occasions he expressed affection, Oh! what will be the language of those benighted beings whom the neglect or oppression of civilized and Christian men, has shut up in intellectual darkness, when they see the glories of that world which lies beyond the firmament!

COMMON SCHOOLS IN NEW YORK.

Report of the Superintendent of Common Schools of the State of New York, made to the Legislature, January 8, 1834.

The report of the Superintendent of Common Schools in New York, is among the most interesting state papers. It informs us of the condition and progress of the most essential, but most valuable portion of the national capital — the minds of the people — and it derives a peculiar value from a circumstance which is by no means honorable to our country, that it is the only public document which furnishes this important information. The report for 1833, from the Hon. J. A. Dix, (the successor of Mr Flagg,) with which we were recently favored, affords gratifying evidence that its value is not likely to diminish. In addition to the sound principles of education which it contains, it presents accumulating proofs of the value of the New York system of schools, and of the happy effects of public aid, when given to encourage private effort, and not to render it unnecessary.

In that great State, a fund has been established, yielding only

$100,000 annually; little more than the product of the School Fund of Connecticut. In 1816, when the distribution of the School Fund was commenced, the whole number of School Districts in New York, was 2,755; the whole number of children 176,449, and of these only 140,106 were instructed. In 1834, we learn from the present report, that the whole number of Districts is 9,690, from 9,107 of which returns have been received, containing 522,618 persons from 5 to 16 years of age, and giving instruction to 512,475. Ninety new districts have been formed during the past year, and 266 have been added to the number that have made returns.

The amount paid to teachers for public schools, is stated by the Superintendent to be $677,429 44, by the aid of $100,000 from the State; and the whole amount expended for instruction in public and private institutions, is calculated at $1,000,000! It would thus appear, that the State of New York, by contributing 19½ cents for the instruction of each pupil, leads its citizens to contribute more than a dollar for each child, and inspires them with proportionate zeal for the extension and improvement of their schools. On the other hand, the State of Connecticut, by distributing a dollar for each pupil from its fund, has induced many districts to give up all efforts and contributions; and has encouraged the employment of inferior teachers and the neglect of duty in organizing and superintending the schools.

The average number of pupils to a school appears to be fiftysix — and the average period of schools has been eight months. Still the Superintendent remarks, 'that the whole number of children taught, are not to be considered as having received instruction during the whole average period of eight months, for which the schools have been kept; but that they have all, during the year, attended schools, and received more or less instruction'.

The productive capital of the school fund amounts to $1,754,-048 84. The unproductive portion, consisting of lands, is estimated at $173,664 20.

In reference to the increase of the capital, we would recommend the remarks of the Superintendent to all who are disposed to provide gratuitous aid.

'Experience in other States has proved, what has been abundantly confirmed by our own, that too large a sum of public money distributed among the Common Schools, has no salutary effect. Beyond a certain point, the voluntary contributions of the inhabitants decline in amount, with almost uniform regularity, as the contributions from a public fund increase. In almost every case, in which a town possesses a local fund, the amount paid for teacher's wages, above the public money, is about as much less, compared with other towns having no local fund, as the amount received from that source.'

He adds, we think with great wisdom :

'The sum now distributed from the Common School fund is as great as is necessary to accomplish every object of such a distribution. Should the General Fund at any future day be recruited, so as to admit of an augmentation of the capital or revenue of the Common School Fund, or both, the policy of increasing the sum annually distributed to the Common Schools beyond an amount which shall, when taken in connexion with the number of children annually taught in them, exceed the present rate of apportionment, would be in the highest degree questionable.'

The fact that sixteen out of seventeen districts, in eight hundred and twenty towns reported to the commissioners, and they to the fiftyfive clerks, and they in their turn to the Superintendent, affords abundant evidence of the admirable efficiency of the system and of the influence of the fund as there distributed.

In reference to the actual condition of Schools the Superintendent coincides with his predecessor, and with every observer, in the opinion, that they are far below the proper standard. He ascribes much of the defect to the want of competent teachers, and strongly advises that a department be organized in every Academy for the purpose of educating instructors for Common Schools. We rejoice to find this subject urged again upon the Legislature, and we hope it will not be without effect. We know not but the Academies may be the best place for providing this instruction. We do not perceive, however, that it will become necessary to secure places to the instructors thus taught, more than to the physicians educated at the Medical Schools, which are assisted by public bounty ; and it seems to us, that the public good demands provision no less liberal on the part of the State, for those who are to form the minds of its citizens, than for those who are to heal their bodies. We would also ask, whether it is consistent, while so much care is used to exclude improper persons from one profession, to leave the other open to every self-licensed adventurer ?

The Superintendent recommends some additional branches of instruction in Common Schools. He urges the 'great importance of giving to every child such a knowledge of history, especially that of our own country, and of our laws and forms of government, as is necessary to make him an intelligent and useful citizen.' He also speaks of the importance of calling in the aid of the periodical press in promoting the progress of improvement in education ; and we owe it to ourselves, and to some who have doubted the utility of special publications on education, to state, that he recommends this work as one which it is desirable to place in every Academy in that State.

We regret to find, amidst the many indications of prosperity of the Schools of this State, that 19,000 children remain unprovided with instruction in the city of New York ! Need we wonder at the progress of crime in that growing city ?

The Superintendent closes the report with a well merited commendation of Sunday Schools. He observes that 'although their utility is well understood, the whole amount of good which is accomplished by them, is not easily to be calculated,' not merely in reference to moral character, but to the intellectual habits of the pupils.

The documents appended to the report contain extensive statistical tables, which give a complete view of the number and resources of Schools, throughout the State.

SCHOOL SYSTEM OF FRANCE.

In our number for December last, we gave an account of the system of Common Schools in Prussia, derived from the report of Cousin. In a French Journal of Education, we have an account of the system organized for France, after a full examination of the best systems of the Continent.

The committee who introduced the law, first state the extremes to which the system of instruction has vibrated in that country — at one time leaving the whole subject to private effort, and at another throwing the burden of the Schools entirely upon the State — by one law placing them entirely under the control of the clergy, and by another, excluding the clergy from all concern in them — sometimes giving the care of them entirely to the local authorities, and at another subjecting them to the exclusive direction of the Government. They then observe, that none of these extreme, abstract principles ought to be adopted.

The three following heads, they believed, would embrace all fundamental questions concerning the subject: —

I. The subjects to be embraced in primary instruction.

II. The schools in which they are to be taught.

III. The authorities who are to preside over them.

I. The subjects to be embraced. Primary Instruction has been divided into two degrees. The first is considered as the lowest point to which it ought to sink — 'a degree of instruction which France owes to the inhabitants of its most humble hamlet, as well as in the largest city, wherever a human being is to be found.' It includes Reading, Writing, and Arithmetic, a knowledge of the legal system of Weights and Measures, and of the French Language, (so essential to the spirit of national unity,) together with Moral and Religious Instruction, which provides for a higher, but equally real order of wants, which God has implanted in all hearts,

—instruction necessary to maintain the dignity of human nature, and the good order of society. The religious instruction must be directed by such clergymen as the parents may desire; and the pupils of a school are confided to those of various denominations, where the schools are mixed.

This first degree of instruction is sufficiently extensive to make him who shall receive it, *a man;* while it is sufficiently circumscribed to be realized everywhere. But it is still far below the standard of that secondary instruction which is given in our private institutions and colleges; and yet in the present system of education, nothing is found to fill the intermediate space that is left between the two.

This want should be provided for, without compelling the citizen to incur an expense beyond the means of a large part of the community, or placing his children in an institution where they waste their time on acquisitions of no value to them,— unsuitable to their circumstances, and dangerous to their success.

The law, therefore, establishes a system of second, or Superior Primary Instruction, corresponding to that of the Middle Schools of Germany. In addition to the branches comprehended in elementary instruction, it embraces Linear Drawing, Surveying, and other applications of practical Geometry—a knowledge of Physics (Natural Philosophy and Chemistry) and Natural History, applicable to the uses of life—Singing—the elements of Geography and History, especially the History and Geography of France. To these may be added, such higher branches as the wants and resources of different places may render expedient.

II. The Schools in which they are to be taught.

France is divided into eightysix Departments, whose population is generally from 250,000 to 650,000. Each Department is divided into Arrondissements or Counties, each County into Cantons or Judicial Districts, and each Canton into *Communes.* A Commune is sometimes a part of a city, and sometimes consists of several villages, united under the direction of a Mayor and Council.

Every commune must maintain a school; and every one of 6,000 inhabitants, must have a Superior Primary School, corresponding to the Middle schools of Germany.

Every Department must maintain a School for Primary Teachers.

The qualifications required for a Teacher are, that he must be over 18 years of age, and must present a certificate of his freedom from all conviction of crime, and of his good moral character, from the Magistrate of his Commune, and a certificate of his qualifications for teaching, from the School Commissioners of the Department.

He shall receive a fixed salary, and a suitable dwelling, in order to attach him to his profession, and his local situation, and to enable him to teach the poor gratuitously; and a monthly compensation from each of his pupils whose parents are able to pay.

If there are no funds or revenues for schools, the authorities of the commune or district are to lay a tax for this purpose, and if this is not sufficient, the department must pay two per cent, in addition to other taxes. Should this sum be still inadequate, the Minister of Instruction is to pay from the fund for public instruction, so that every hamlet may in some way be furnished with the means of instruction.

A Savings Bank is to be established in each department, in which a part of the salary of the teacher shall be deposited, to be paid on his retirement, or, in case of his decease, to his family.

It will be perceived that this part of the law aims at two great objects. 1. To induce the teacher to remain permanently in his employment, and thus to render teaching a profession. 2. To compel every inhabitant of France to contribute to the support of Schools according to his ability, while he is still to receive aid, whenever his own means are insufficient to secure the education of his children. On the last point the Committee remark, in accordance with the principle we have so often advanced, that 'we profit most by things obtained at some sacrifice;' and that while the poor ought to pay *very little*, 'this trifling sacrifice will attach the child to the school, will excite the vigilance of the parents, and give them some importance in their own eyes.'

III. The authorities which preside over the Schools.

The schools of each Commune shall be under the direction of a local committee, consisting of the Mayor, the Curate (Catholic Minister) or Protestant Pastor, and three of the Councillors (Selectmen) chosen by the Council.

Every Arrondissement or County shall have a Committee composed of several public officers, and a minister of each denomination, who shall meet once a month.

The Communal or Town Committees shall inspect all the public and private schools of the Communes, watch over their health, and discipline; see that every child is taught; admit gratuitous pupils, and report candidates for teachers, and the conduct of teachers, to the County Committee.

The County Committee is bound to inspect all the schools in the County, and to report their state annually to the Minister of Instruction; propose reforms and improvements; and authorise and locate teachers; and after due examination, may remove them, subject to appeal to the Minister of Instruction.

In every Department there shall be one or more Boards of Commissioners, appointed by the Minister of public Instruction, whose duty it shall be to examine teachers, and give certificates of their qualifications, and to examine the intellectual progress of the pupils of the schools in their department, in frequent visits, and at irregular periods.

In this plan it will be seen, that the Committee have aimed at a combination of local and general authority. To place the schools exclusively under the local authorities, in their view, gives rise to 'a train of petty chicaneries' in regard to the management of the school, the choice of a teacher, and the influence exerted over him. While the teacher should be connected with those around him, by receiving his place either from their choice, or by their consent, respect should be secured for him, by making him amenable to a tribunal not subject to the influence of those local jealousies, which are so often destructive to the best interests of schools in our own country.

The French system of schools, in short, seems to us to supply the defects, which are obvious in the best systems of our own country. *It secures the existence of a school for every child in the nation*, by compelling every citizen to contribute his proportion, and yet providing a resource in case of his inability. It gives sufficient power to the local authorities to excite deep interest and a sense of responsibility ; while it guards against its abuse and secures a thorough system of inspection, by independent agents, whose pay enables them to devote their time to it. Above all, it provides for the education and permanent support of faithful, laborious teachers, without whom, the whole system is but an empty form of words.

METHODS OF THE FIRST SCHOOL.

After our views of 'The First School' were prepared, we had the pleasure of meeting with an article signed 'Clement,' in the London Sunday School Magazine, 'On the Education of Adam before the fall.' In the words of this writer, 'we discover a system of education, with *Nature for the School — God for the Teacher — Natural objects for the lesson — and Man for the scholar.*' It is obvious, as he remarks, that the first process of naming the animals, called the mental powers of our first parents into exercise. Attention — comparison — judgment, as to the varieties and peculiarities of animals — recollection of their forms, and colors, and characteristics, and memory of words, were all requisite. The first lesson, of the first man, was thus a key to his own faculties, and a guide to future efforts of mind. It was like the first attempt of a child to stand, when placed upon his feet, which gives to him the consciousness of a new power, and opens the way to a new course of action.

In this single lesson, we have indeed a key to the whole plan of intellectual education, which is vaunted by some as the modern plan, and derided by others as innovation. It is *to present objects of thought*, and then call the mind and the tongue into action, instead of attempting to impress merely our own thoughts, or transfuse our own ideas into the brain of our pupils. It is to present things, on which names may be inscribed, instead of a mass of names to be applied to things yet unknown, and to the pupil, inconceivable.

One circumstance to which we only alluded, is stated more distinctly in the Magazine; that 'Man was created, and sent forth to act as the ruler of creation.' We may add that he was *trained* to this high office, and that power was given him, in order to constitute responsibility, and to accustom him to its use. The idea of training a voluntary being, without giving him *power*, or to use an equivalent word in this case, *liberty* — of a state of probation in fetters — is as inconsistent with the plans of Providence, as with common sense. It would be as reasonable to train a child to walk, by carrying him in our arms. Who can *learn to govern himself*, if he is never left to make the attempt.

We shall never forget our impressions when the bolts of the novitiate school, in an Italian monastery, were drawn back, and we were pointed to the fundamental principle of the institution, inscribed upon its inner portal, —

'*Nolo et volo non habitant in hac domo.*'

'I will and I will not, do not dwell under this roof.' Nor shall we forget the still stronger impression produced by visiting a seminary of Jesuits, where every youth, even of manly age, was placed, at every moment, under the inspection of a master in his study, was compelled to follow him in his daily walks, and never allowed to leave his ranks; and even locked up at night in a little cell, where no vices could have access but those (the most horrible of all), to which his own passions would drive him, when released from the unceasing, inquisitorial torture of the teacher's eye. He might be trained thus, (if his spirit were not too lofty) to be the subservient instrument of a superior; but he could not be suitably prepared to be a man, and a freeman — to be the master of a family, or a member of a self-governing community.

We have regretted to see the same error pervading more than one family and school. The strong arm of power was used to stop every avenue by which the ebullitions of passion could escape, while nothing was done to subdue the fire within. As well might we attempt to destroy the force of steam, by closing all the valves by which it can issue; and as rationally might we wonder at the explosion, which follows the futile attempt to suppress an *accumulating power*, as at the out-breaking violence which often succeeds in the '*fetter system*' of education, applied to the strong, and every-day strengthening passions of the young. *He who is not taught to govern himself, will probably be ruined for want of a governor.* Watch his progress, and warn him of his danger; enlighten his ignorance, and assist his weakness; and if his strength is failing in the hour of trial, snatch him from the overwhelming torrent; but teach him to rule his own spirit, or he will be 'like a city that is broken down, and without walls.'

ELEMENTARY INSTRUCTION IN GEOGRAPHY.

Extract of a Lecture delivered before the American Institute of Instruction.

By W. C. Woodbridge.

The foundation of geographical knowledge must be laid in a knowledge of the relative situation of places, and this, the pupils of our schools must acquire chiefly through the medium of *maps*.

The pupil must therefore be first prepared to understand the true nature of a map, as a miniature representation of the mere outlines of objects on the earth. He must learn to conceive of a sheet of paper, as containing mountains, rivers, and kingdoms, to realize the imperfections of the representation, and to use it only as an aid to his imagination.

The map presents a shaded outline, which separates a large blank space, marked here and there with a dark spot, from another portion of the surface, crossed by crooked lines of various dimensions, marked with dots and little circles, and crowded with names. But this blank space, he must be taught, represents a wide, blue ocean, rolling in the majesty of its waves, and wafting navies on its bosom, or swallowing them up in its abysses. Those crooked lines are the emblems of noble rivers, flowing with irresistible strength, covered with ships, and teeming with animal life; and where they are crossed by another little line, he must imagine a cataract. Its banks, instead of being covered with *names*, are shaded with *lofty forests*, or spread into *beautiful, cultivated fields*, or enlivened by *villages*.

Where these circles are scattered up and down, there should be splendid cities and magnificent palaces, and crowds of ships, and a moving ocean of human beings. And those spots of various colors are the dominions of separate kings, and nations, inhabited by men

— so distant from us, that they never heard of our pupils — so numerous, that he might go among them, and come away, unnoticed.

In order to arrive at just conceptions of this kind, the study of Geography must commence with the elements. I do not mean with the *definitions* of land, and water, of mountains, and lakes, and rivers, and volcanoes, but with *the observation of the objects in nature around him,* which shall serve as the basis upon which these ideas may be founded. The name of mountain, and valley, and lake, and river, should be immediately connected with the observation of hill, and hollow, and pond, and brook; and the same process of enlargement should become familiar to his imagination, which is so beautifully exhibited in the 'Child's Book on the Soul,' in reference to time. He should be made to stand and watch the stream, and see it spread, and widen, and deepen, until it rolls on, a *mighty river*, whose farther bank is but just visible. He should be accustomed to gaze at the mountain, or the hill, until you can spread its base, and rear its top, and put on house after house, and village after village, and call him to climb step after step up the slow ascent, and then point him upward to the distant summit, until he is weary with the thought. He should stand and look at the cascade or the mill-fall, until, by the aid of description, the sound increases to a roar, and the bank deepens to a precipice, and the opening below becomes an awful chasm, filled with 'the noise of many waters.' Not till then should he hear the name of *Niagara*, which should embody all his loftiest emotions, and yet be presented as surpassing all that he *can* conceive.

But let us ask again — is it the *lines* and *spots* of the map, or the great *objects* they represent, which the pupil is to learn? If the latter, in what way is he to effect it? By gazing at these mystical marks, and committing to memory all the names attached to them? We have no patience with those who thus teach their pupils a science, which may be called *Chartology*, but has no more title to the name of Geography, than the giving names to an equal number of Chinese characters.

We have had the details of an instance in which a child of two years old, could point to every line and spot upon the map of Europe, only on hearing its name, before he could yet pronounce a word. But while we mourn over the mistaken kindness which could thus prepare an infant for the premature grave to which he descended, we do not envy the reputation of that teacher, who would be satisfied with making his pupils equally expert, in this parrot-like exercise. We fear there are many such instances — nay, we suspect there are many schools where the ideas derived from the map, are just such as would be obtained from studying those charts of human life which represent an event by a promontory, difficulty by a whirlpool, and death by a torrent or waterfall, terminating in the beautifully ornamented border, that surrounds this picture of time and history! We are only less liable to be imposed upon by that which pretends to represent invisible things.

The first step necessary to enable the pupil to acquire ideas from representation, is to teach him the relation of the one to the other. Even the effect of pictures is often lost upon the young mind for want of a practical knowledge, or perception of perspective; and he supposes objects smaller or higher, from their appearance on the picture, or darker from their shade, because he has never been taught to observe the effect of distance and light. How much more liable is he to error, in regard to the naked outlines, or mere indices of great objects, presented on a map. I know not any mode so effectual to make the pupil familiar with the nature of maps, as to teach him to construct them from nature, and this may be accomplished, at the same time that he is learning to observe the objects around him.

Let the course of observation to which we have referred, be extended to everything within his horizon, and let him learn the individual name attached to every object of importance. Let him learn to observe them from different points of view. Point out to him the varying position of the sun. Let him observe its direction in the morning, at noon, and at evening, — and then show him the north star, and he will thus find the marks for the four standard points to which he is to refer all descriptions of the situations of places. Let the terms, *east, south, west* and *north,* be attached to these points, only *when he has learned the need of them;* and not be employed before he has acquired distinct ideas of them. Let him observe the direction of the great objects of the landscape, first from one prominent point, then from another. Let him notice those which are in a range or '*row*' with each other from his station — those which are on opposite sides — those which would form a triangle — and those which would make a square, or a cross, and thus fix the positions of every important place in his mind, so that he could sketch a map of these points and lines from his imagination as well as from direct perception.

But he must in the mean time be taught the construction of maps of a much smaller space. Let him draw upon the slate, no matter how rudely, a square to represent the table upon which he is writing, or the room in which he is sitting. If practicable, let him look down upon it from the ceiling above, but in any event, let him mark the spot on which every object is placed, with its size and shape, as it *would appear* from above. As soon as he has repeated this so often that he perceives the want of accuracy in his rude representations, furnish him with a scale to measure the room or the table, and the distance of the respective objects from each other, and supply him with a smaller rule, adapted to the size of his slate, divided into an equal number of parts. Then direct him to transfer, after the measurement of every line or distance with the larger rule, an equal number of parts with the smaller upon his slate, until every object is represented in proportionate size, and relative situation, with a good degree of accuracy. This he will be told is a *plan* or *map*, and as his observations abroad are going on, he will probably be himself anxious, to employ the same method, to represent the various objects of the landscape before him. He should be led on, however, by graduated steps. Let him draw an entire plan of the house in which he lives, of the garden attached to it, and of the farm, or grounds around it. So far as it is practicable, let every effort be followed by *measurement*, as in the map of a room, in order that the habit of accurate observation so valuable in life, may be cultivated, at the same time that he acquires the correct idea of distances.

The pupil will now be prepared to delineate with more or less accuracy, the outlines of the country around him, and by observing carefully the ranges of objects, he may arrive at a tolerable degree of accuracy by mere inspection. He should be accustomed also to ascertain short distances, by paces, and longer ones by an accurate observation of the time which is spent in passing over them, either on foot or in a carriage, and to register all the circumstances which are necessary for his map. As his perception of accuracy increases, he may be taught to trace the deviations from a straight line in a stream or a road; and if circumstances admit, he should be allowed the use of a chain or tape measure and a compass, as soon as he is capable of employing them.

Such is the course it is desirable to pursue, in order to be fully prepared for the study of maps; and I know not how we can otherwise avoid the danger of false or imperfect conceptions, which will destroy half their value to the pupil. It is obvious, that it might be and ought to be commenced in the nursery, under the direction of the mother. It would serve as the amusement of many a listless moment, as soon as the child can use a slate and pencil. It might be carried on by any parent who can spend two or three hours in a week with his children, before they are ten years of age. If they are left to begin at school, no reason can be given why it should not be adopted by the instructor of a boarding-school. Indeed, there are few teachers of common schools, whose influence and usefulness with their pupils would not be increased, and whose labor would not be on the whole lightened, by the extra lessons and little excursions which it would render necessary.

After the pupil has become familiar with the construction of these simple maps, he should be taught to draw them on every variety of scale, until he ceases to think of the size of the map before him, and by immediate reference to the scale of measurement, should learn to perceive at once, through the medium of a map, the great objects which it represents, instead of the lines and points upon its surface, just as we perceive ideas through the medium of words. It will also facilitate his transition to other maps, if he be accustomed to draw a meridian through some prominent object, from an observation of the north-star or a shadow at noon-day; and to divide the map by other lines, drawn parallel and perpendicular to it, at regular distances. It will aid still farther in his transitions, if the central line from east to west be assumed as an *equator*, and distances be reckoned in both directions, from this and the first meridian.

It is scarcely necessary to add, that as no description can be equally useful with the view of objects themselves, it is desirable that the pupil should learn the geography of the neighboring country, as well as his own town, as much as possible, from *personal observation*, and be accustomed to describe and delineate its outlines. It should only be after his own sketches are executed, that he should be furnished with more complete, engraved maps, of the same region.

Let me not be told that this is *theory*, plausible upon paper, but impracticable in its execution. It is but the *history* of what *has been done* and *still is done*, in the schools of Pestalozzi and his followers in Europe; and is in substance what must be done, by every one who is designed to be a topographical or military engineer. It would require little more time thus to learn to delineate the great features of a country, if it were commenced at an early period, than it now does to imitate the letters of the alphabet. Every step is, in itself, perfectly practicable and easy. Only time and patience are necessary to combine them all, in an ordinary course of instruction. Where either of these fail, or where prejudice and avarice prevent the overtasked instructor from adopting this entire course, much may be done by devoting two or three hours in a week, for a short period, to this object. Some measures of this kind should always be taken, to prevent the blunders to which the uninitiated pupil is continually liable.

ON TEACHING A FOREIGN LANGUAGE ACCORDING TO THE METHOD OF JACOTOT.

By George W. Greene.

In a previous article, I have given a practical account of the course pursued by Jacotot in teaching to read, which may be applied to the mother tongue or to any other language. I now propose to give a similar description of the first steps in the study of a foreign language. It will be readily perceived that each of these courses depends upon the same principles, and that it is everywhere the aim of the method, to lead its pupils to regard themselves as their own teachers.

The first exercise in the study of language calls for a full exertion of good will in the scholars, and for patience on the part of the teacher. Nature has made a great distinction between men, in her distribution of the power of committing to memory. Those who, upon reading a page or chapter once or twice, can repeat it word for word, are remarkable instances of the tenacity of memory, rather than examples by which its general distribution can be estimated. There is much less distinction between boys. Some, indeed, can, without much effort, learn half a page, or even an entire page of a new language, at the first lesson. Others can scarcely repeat three lines, after long and assiduous study. The first, therefore have, in the beginning, an advantage* over the last in the study of language, and particularly according to the method of Jacotot. But the distinction is seldom kept up beyond the first quarter. If those whose memory is naturally dull, bring an unwavering resolution to their task, they will soon perceive that the obstacles gradually diminish, as their practice extends; the memory becomes more pliant, and forms itself step by step, to receive and retain the lightest impression.

While therefore we acknowledge the correctness of the student's plea, when he asserts that he cannot learn by heart, we still insist upon the effort, and bear with his blunders and hesitation and apparent dullness, until the exercise of his memory has made it prompt, and obedient to his will.

Taking it for granted, therefore, that every one who will make the exertion, can commit a lesson to memory, we place a text book in the hands of our scholars, and adapting our task to the power of the

*When I first formed a class in Latin, there were two scholars out of six who could scarcely learn six lines in a lesson. The next quarter one of these learnt his Greek epitome in a fortnight, and wondered that Greek should be so easy, and but a few weeks since brought me the first chapter of Genesis for his first lesson in Hebrew.

individual, we tell him to learn by heart a few words, or lines, or even a page.

On the opposite page, or interlined with the text, is a literal translation of every word of the original. Thus, while the student is learning the words, he learns also their exact or local signification. If, for example, the first lesson has been the preface to the lives of Cornelius Nepos, as soon as he has repeated the text, we call upon him to translate it; not from the volume itself, but by sentences and phrases, as we give them out. By this means he becomes accustomed to the sound of words as well as to their written form; and from the first, is learning (what all those who have studied language will acknowledge to be peculiarly difficult) to understand the observations which are addressed to him, or the conversation that is carried on in his presence.

'Non dubito fere plerosque, Attice, qui hoc genus scripturæ leve et non satis dignum summorum virorum personis judicent quum relatum legent, quis musicam docuerit Epaminondam; aut in ejus virtutibus commemorari, saltasse eum commode, scienterque tibiis cantasse.'

As soon as the sentence has been repeated, we ask for its translation into English.

At first, however, we have only the general meaning of the sentence, and there is no proof that the scholar knows which parts of the Latin and English correspond.

Non dubito fere plerosque, Attice, I doubt not, Atticus, that there are many, &c, &c.

We are thus brought near to the exact translation; but one step more must be taken, before we can ascertain the precise meaning of every word. The following questions will easily lead us to it. What is the meaning of *non?* What of *dubito?* What of *plerosque*, &c, &c.

If the scholar can answer such questions with promptitude and precision, there can be no doubt that he has learned his lesson perfectly. But we should have gained very little were we to leave the lesson here, and take it for granted that because he has recited it once, he will recollect it always. He must remember, as well as learn, and know the lesson of to-day, as well on the morrow, as at his first recitation. It is evident that this cannot be done without constant repetition. It is not enough to ask him to read it, or repeat it to himself — it must be repeated to another, and repeated aloud. Every new recitation, therefore, should be accompanied by a repetition of the old. The scholar should first repeat what he has learned today, and then go back to the lesson of yesterday, or last week, or last month.

As in large schools, or even in large classes, this is apparently difficult, I will give a short account of a method which I have seen practised with great success.

When we first form a class, there are generally several scholars who set out together from the beginning. Of course, their first lessons will not occupy more time than other duties allow for a large class. But by degrees, the scholars will separate. One whom nature has endowed with a ready memory, will soon be in advance of all his classmates. Another, perhaps, will follow him at a short distance behind, but a distance that every day increases. Behind these two we find a third, who, although unable to equal the first, still succeeds in keeping a little before the remainder of the class. The recitation bench will, in a certain degree, appear like a racing ground. The fleetest steed, with outstretched neck and panting breast, is far in advance of the rivals with whom he started; another follows him closely from behind. Here two contend with equal strength, and no effort can increase or diminish the distance between them; while the rear is filled up with the dullest of the ring, whom neither whip nor spur can drive out of a certain pace.

Now, in what manner can you keep so many scattering lessons together, and bring them within the compass of the same hour?

Each individual must, of course, repeat his new lesson, wholly and alone. And in this, the assistance of monitors will naturally suggest itself to every practical teacher. But the old lessons must be repeated attentively. When the new lessons have been recited, let the class remain at the recitation stand, in their usual order. You can call upon any member whom you please, to begin the repetition. If you would secure the attention of the class, you must show them that any individual may be called upon, without regard to the order in which they stand, and that, without any prompting from you, he must take up the sentence, or line, or word, just where the other has left off. It is in most cases best to allow to each but a few lines. The remainder of the class are apt to grow weary when called to listen for many minutes to the same scholar. There is a species of excitement in the rapid passing of words from one to another. Each little eye is attentively bent upon the teacher's face, and each ear eager to catch every word, when all know that it may be the last, but no one can tell who will next be called on to complete the sentence.

In this manner, let the first repeat the first sentence, or if it be too long, such a part of it as you think best. Let a motion of your hand be the signal for the next to break in. Let the sentence be long or short, according to the circumstances of the moment. If he take the wrong word, call upon the next, and pass it on in this manner, throughout the class, taking care not to prompt a pupil, unless it be absolutely necessary. As each scholar arrives at the end of his own lesson, let him return to his seat; and carry the repetition through, with those that remain. Above all, do not reject any external influence, that may increase the attention of the class, and the excitement of the exercises.

The limits of the epitome used for our introductory exercises varies in different schools; but it is generally thought that it ought not to contain less than 14 or 15 pages. While the pupil is still engaged in committing these to memory, various exercises may be introduced both to facilitate his task, and to give him better command of that which he already knows.

The first is a translation by words. Take at random any word in the epitome, and ask for its meaning, and construction.

'What does *domo* mean?'

'From home.'

'Where have you seen it?'

'Domo navibus proficiscens.

'Where do you find that sentence?'

'In the first section of Miltiades, where he receives the answer from the Lemnians.'

'Is that the only place you have seen it in?'

'No, Sir; I have seen it also in the second section.'

'Where is that?' &c, &c.

'Is that the only Latin word which you have seen for home?'

'No, Sir. Directly below the domo, in this last sentence, there is domum.'

'Well; how does that differ from domo?'

'I don't know, Sir.'

'Are they translated alike?'

'No, Sir. One is translated 'from home,' and the other simply 'home.'

'Which is from home?'

'Domo — in both sentences; in the first, domo proficiscens — departing from home; and in the second, domo profectus — departed from home.'

'Well, how do they differ, then?'

'Why, one is domum, and the other domo — that is all that I can see.'

'But the meaning. You have just said that they differ in that, too. Look attentively at the two words, and see if there be anything in them which represents this difference.'*

'How would you translate *from home*?'

'Domo.'

'How would you translate *home*?'

'Domum.'

'Why?'

'The book says so.'

'Where then is your *from*?'

'In *o*.'

[The conclusion is inevitable.]

* I have known a wilful boy pretend that he could not find any representation of this difference. It will not do, however, to admit this excuse. The difference is plainly marked, and every boy can see it.

'Which of these words would you use, if you wanted to say, at home?'

'Neither.'

'Why so?'

'Because I have seen that expression translated by domi, in the next section.'

'How many forms of home have you met with?'

'Three; domo — domum — domi.'

'Why does this word assume different forms?'

'To express different meanings.'

'Is the Latin language like ours in this respect?'

'No, Sir. Our language, instead of changing the forms of the words, unites with them smaller words, which express this distinction.'

'What is the meaning of proficiscens?'

'Departing.'

'Of profectus?'

'Departed.'

'Do you find in these two words, any such peculiarity as that which you just pointed out in domum?

'There is a far greater difference between them. Proficiscens is not so much like profectus, as domum like domo and domi.'

'But how large a part of each word is like the other?'

'The first four letters — *prof.*'

'Well, now examine the English words, departing, and departed.'

'I see, now, Sir; the *ing* in English is represented by the *ens*, and the English *ed*, by *tus*.'

'I am afraid that you have not seen facts enough to warrant such a conclusion. Two or three instances, you should remember, can never form a general *rule*. It is only by observing a great number of facts, and examining with great care a variety of examples that we can form rules of universal or even extensive application.'

'But I have more than one example, Sir. There is *hortatus* and *adjutus*, in the second section, both of them translated like profectus, with an *ed*; and there is *habens* in the first, and *interserens* in the fourth, and *dicens* in the third, which are translated with *ing*; and besides these, there is another word which only differs from these in its vowel, and is translated with the *ing*, also, — *dubitans*.

It is evident that the pupil cannot make such observations as these unless he be perfectly familiar with his epitome; and it is equally plain that these observations will be a great assistance in obtaining this familiarity. But another style of questions should be sometimes introduced. Question the class upon separate words. What is the meaning of *locum?*' 'Place.' 'Where have you seen it?' 'In the preface — *non primum*,' &c.

In this manner, the class should be carried through the epitome. The exercises I have described, should never be deferred until the whole be learned. Boys are not like men, who labor with some favorite object in view, and count each step that brings them nearer to it. They require every species of excitement, every variety of persuasion. All the influence within your control must be brought to bear upon them, if you would impart spirit and animation to their exercises. Neither will they, in general, be content to go on, without understanding the object and bearing of all that they do. The curiosity which distinguishes childhood is displayed in various ways. Every boy will seek to know why he is required to perform this exercise, or study that work. Nothing short of a reason will satisfy him; and that reason should be contained in the exercise itself. If he feels that every exertion is bringing him nearer to the goal — that every exercise has a direct bearing upon his progress — the exertion and exercise, however difficult, will still be pleasing, and the consciousness of successful effort will excite to further exertion.

THE SECOND SCHOOL.

The first school was The School of Innocence. The end in view, was the *immediate, unmingled happiness* of the pupils. The means were social and religious influence, combined with intellectual instruction, and bodily labor. The discipline was that of kindness, pouring forth incessant streams of bounty, to cheer and strengthen its objects, and lead them to love and to obey their benefactor.

But the pupils rebelled against this mild discipline; and they were removed from The School of Innocence, to *The School of Reformation.*

Their ultimate happiness was still the great object of their education. But transgression had rendered it impossible to attain this object, by conferring immediate enjoyment; for this would have cheered on the offenders, in the path of evil and misery. It could only be secured through the medium of suffering. The kind parent must perform the office of the no less kind physician. Instead of pleasant and invigorating food, he must administer disagreeable and painful remedies; and in place of affectionate embraces, he must resort to painful operations. Once, 'he led them in the green pastures, and by the still waters;' but now, he must send them forth in dreary exile.

Like other schools of reformation, it was attended with an unceasing course of privations; and the labor, which had been first prescribed as a means of health and enjoyment, was rendered so severe, as to involve, not merely constant toil, but frequent suffering. The body, which was formed to be the medium of external enjoyment, the instrument of executing the desires and plans of the soul, became, to some extent, its prison, and often checked its noblest flights, and disappointed its highest hopes.

The sentence of revelation is written upon the face of universal nature; — it is stamped upon the brow, and engraven in the history, of the children of Adam — 'Cursed is the ground for thy sake. In sorrow shalt thou eat of it all the days of thy life. Thorns, also, and thistles shall it bring forth unto thee. In the sweat of thy face shalt thou eat bread, till thou return unto the ground, for out of it wast thou taken.' Every cemetery, and every monument, and every record of the past, or the present, echoes the closing doom; '*Dust thou art! — and unto dust shalt thou return!*'

But even this sentence was not without its mitigations. With a merciful wisdom which marks all the discipline of the great Educator of our race, hope was mingled with the bitter cup of condemnation; and man was promised a final victory over the enemy, who had been the instrument of destroying his peace. Indeed, the toil which was the punishment of evil, was designed to be the means of delivering him from its slavery — of leading him back to Paradise!

Although the Creator closed the course of immediate, regular instructions which he had previously given, he appointed modes of approach to him; and he still maintained his intercourse with those whom he selected as monitors, in the system of mutual instruction, which was now adopted. It was not enough that man should suffer; he must also be *taught*; he must be called upon to reflect. He now received, what may be termed the first lessons of Bible instruction.

As soon as the spirit of emulation which produced the first crime, had found a *rival*, it burst forth into *envy;* and the first trangression of which we hear in the school of reform, was the murder of a brother, by the hand of a brother — because their Teacher 'had respect unto Abel and his offering; but unto Cain and his offering he had not respect'! It is remarkable, that this first murderer was condemned — not to death — but to a life of exile, and suffering, and comparative seclusion; and that he deemed this a 'punishment greater than he could bear.' Christian benevolence, and even modern policy, seem to be returning to this course. But the tremendous denunciation of the Giver of Life ought to ring in the ears of every man who lifts his hand against his fellow man, whether he be influenced by the lust of money, or of power, or like Cain, by the demands of mortified pride or disappointed rivalry, — even though they be self-baptised, with the name of 'wounded honor' —

'*And now art thou cursed from the earth, which hath opened her mouth to receive thy brother's blood from thy hand! When thou tillest the ground, it shall not henceforth yield unto thee her strength. A fugitive and a vagabond shalt thou be upon the earth!*'

Who of our readers cannot point to examples — perhaps living examples — of those who escaped the penalty of human laws, and yet stand, like the oak scathed by the lightning, bereft of beauty, and strength; or wander, shunned and gazed at by their fellow men, as if a visible mark were enstamped upon their foreheads! Who, indeed, that believes the Scriptures, can dare to honor and bless him, from whose bloody hand the tears of repentance have never washed away a single stain; and whom God hath cursed?

The progress of man appears to have been rapid, from the wandering life of a shepherd to the labors of agriculture and the arts. We soon find a record of an 'instructor of every artificer in brass and iron;' and a 'father of all such as handle the harp and organ.' But in this, as in every other school of reform, neither the progress of civilization, nor the cultivation of the arts, produced moral purity. Centuries of life were granted men for reflection and improvement; but this seems rather to have hastened, than arrested, the progress of evil. The Creator at length declared, that 'all flesh had corrupted his way, and that the earth was filled with violence;' and as the last resource which infinite wisdom could devise, resolved to expel these rebellious pupils, and reserve only a few, as the subjects of a second course of training. Still, we are told, he employed a faithful monitor, to warn the offenders of their transgressions, and their approaching doom. One hundred and twenty years were allowed for reflection and reformation; and not until this period expired, did he pour out the flood which destroyed them. How rarely does this patience and perseverance find any thing like a parallel, in the efforts of modern educators.

At length the appointed time had passed; the reform of the living was hopeless; and the last, desperate means of purifying the world was adopted. They were swept away from the face of the earth; and only a single family was preserved, to enter on another course of education.

[For the Annals of Education.]

FIRST STEPS IN EDUCATION.

The present is an age of simplification and improvement. The mysteries and pomp of learning must be thrown off; the minds of the people must be fed with those intellectual luxuries, that, a century ago, were the exclusive possession of the student in his c oset. Our *very infants* must be made philosophers, mathematicians, geographers and botanists. Everything must be '*brought down'* to their feeble comprehension. All this is well, if not carried to extremes. The fault of the past age has been, that children have been taught without understanding; and so far as the course adopted by the present age goes to remedy this evil, so far it is right.

But it should be recollected, that there is a time for everything under heaven, and a proper time too. Childhood is not the time for what is properly called, *study*. It is evident from the course of nature, that *confinement* of mind or body, for any length of time, is not proper for young children. The child must have varied, though not continued or severe exercise. He is constantly in motion, if not tied down; and unless he have this liberty of moving and acting, he is never happy. His mind is as volatile as his body. You cannot fix it long or intently, on any single object. This indicates what mode should be pursued in the education of children. It is a great mistake to suppose, that a child has not begun his education till he learns to read, and that he can acquire no useful knowledge, but from books, or in a schoolroom. Hence the reason, apparently, of the numerous works simplified for children, on subjects which do not belong, in this form, to their age.

It is said, 'the child has everything to learn.' Then let him learn it. Do not, before he has half learned one thing, begin to crowd into his mind half a dozen more. He begins to learn, as soon as his eyes are open to the light of day. And what does he learn? Why first, to use his own members, and secondly, by means of them, to make experiments on surrounding bodies. The child is more of a philosopher, than we are accustomed to think. As he grows, he examines everything he can find. He will put his hands into the water and into the fire, if you will allow him, to find out what they are; and in all this he learns, what he *must learn*, sooner or later.

As soon as he has learned to talk, he will begin to ask questions; and about what?—Not the abstract truths of Philosophy and Mathematics, but about such things as first attract his attention. The first teaching should be, in answering properly these questions, and directing the mind to suitable objects of inquiry. The first instructions will, of course be oral; and I should prefer, that for a long time they should continue to be so.

So late as five, or even seven years, according to the capacity of the child, seems early enough to commence what is called 'book-learning,' beginning with the alphabet. As much nearly, I believe, may be gained in time, by the child's superior capacity, and increased fixedness of mind, as would be lost by this delay. Neither would this time be wasted. It would, if the mother faithfully performed *her* duty, be devoted to lessons, as important to his interests as that of reading.

If it be asked why I would delay so long to teach reading, I answer, in the first place, at the age at which children usually begin these lessons, they have no conception of the use or advantage arising from this exercise. I have no doubt that many, by being driven to study that in which they could take no interest, have acquired in the outset, a disgust with study, which has lasted as long as their school days. A lesson, in my view, should not be given under the influence, either of rewards or punishments. The tendency of both is injurious. Better that the child be not taught at all, than that such measures be employed to insure his success.* If he be rewarded, he will begin to consider himself hired to learn, and will think himself wronged, if he is called upon to learn for nothing. In a word, he will consider study as a species of labor, by which he is to *earn* certain enjoyments or rewards. If he be punished when unable to learn his tasks, (and whether inability or neglect be the cause cannot in every case be decided,) or even when he has neglected them voluntarily, the invariable consequence will be, that study and punishment will be strongly associated in his mind, and dislike to study, and a fixed purpose of doing as little of it as possible, will probably ensue.

'But,' says the reader, 'if we delay to teach our children till they are willing to learn, they will grow up as ignorant as the cattle in the stall.' No. By no means,. You will find *some things that they will be willing to learn.* Did you never see a child listen with intense interest, to an amusing story? Here was manifested a willingness to be instructed. Present whatever you wish your child to learn, in an *interesting form*, place it as it were in his way, so that his mind will grasp at it, and seek to follow it out, and you need no rewards or punishments to make him willing.

There are many ways in which a child may be made interested in reading, as soon as it is necessary for him to learn. — And first, as to the manner of teaching, I would prefer a method something like the following, which should be practised by the mother, at home, if convenient.

In the first place let some book of stories be selected which shall be interesting and profitable for the child; let it be a book from which he has heard some pleasing narration read, and tell him you wish him to learn to read it, himself. Find some word with which he is familiar, the name of some well known object, and show it him, teaching him that that word is thus to be spoken. Find for him the same word in another place and make him recognize it, and

*In this point, if not in some others, our readers will see, that our corespondent's views do not accord with our own, nor, as we think, with the course of providential discipline. Still, the evil referred to is often serious. — Ed.

so with other words. Next teach him by name the letters of these words, and let him find the same letters in other words. Show him two words differing only in a single letter, and show him that one letter alters the sound of the word. Then give him a pencil, or a piece of chalk, and let him copy the letters, calling them by name, till he can draw their forms distinctly and legibly. He will, by this method, not only have sufficient variety to prevent the employment from being irksome, but he will at the same time, be learning to write. And here, let me remark, that I would never let a child touch a quill to paper, till he is able to *write* legibly every letter, with chalk or a pencil on a slate. More paper is spoiled, *absolutely wasted*, by children learning to write in common schools, than would pay twice for all the real good they get.

But I have one remark to make which it is essential to observe. The child must be under the government of the parent so completely, that he will be willing to do a thing *because his parent chooses it*, before the parent *can* form his mind as it is his duty to do. The principle of *cheerful obedience* must be early established, or it will be necessary, and too frequently it is so, to resort to harsh measures, or absolute compulsion, to induce obedience of any kind.

F.

[For the Annals of Education.]

COMMON SCOOLS AND COMMON EDUCATION.

NO II.

INTRODUCTION.

'THE true secret of improving common schools will be found in teaching the people how to do without them.' So I ventured to say in my former number. I remember that you qualified your assent to the assertion by saying, that this *teaching the people how to do without them*, must be accompanied by growing and unceasing pains, to improve the schools themselves. I agree, heartily, to the qualifications, so suitable, over your editorial table. I am not inclined to set forth, as the *only means* of improving common schools, an action *out of them;* for this is best promoted by an action *in* them. I will therefore, *now* say, The true way of teaching people how to *do without* them, is to show them how to do *with* them. No doubt a new spirit of self-improvement may be originated among the adult members of society, who have long passed the schools; and the press should exert its power for that purpose.

But in order to produce general self-improvement, there needs to be a constant influx from the schools themselves. Society will be effectually and thoroughly restored, mainly by means of those, who, previously to leaving school, have settled the principles, and commenced the practice, of a growing and endless self-improvement. If, as I said before, the stream must run *on*, it must also run *in*, or else the waters will subside below the outlet, and the stream be cut off. The influence must be mutual. The schools will not be much improved, without the aid of a self-improving public. The public will not grow self-improving, without the tribute of the schools. Thus would I *persuade*, if I may not *reason*, in a circle.

I beg your leave, therefore, to offer the MARCH ANNALS to the *Common Schools*, now closing their winter term. This is not the time to appeal to the School-meeting, but to the *schools* themselves, and especially to the highest class, who should at this moment be fixing the principles, and commencing the practice, of self-improvement. I write now, not for school-masters, but for *scholars*, and if I could have my will, this same *March Annals* should find its way into every school-house in the United States, and be read by the teacher to the scholars, and by the scholars to the teacher, and be indelibly impressed upon two or three hundred thousand minds, and give an impulse to self-improvement, which will be felt *in* school and *out*, from Maine to Georgia.

'Modest writer! So low in expectation in Number I. — so high in expectation in Number II.!' Nay, but I do not expect all this. I am not sanguine. I have lived too long to expect that Number II. will effect, what it does not blush to attempt — what it ventures to attempt with encouragement and hope. That writer who dares not hope, would better stop his pen. I *do* address the young, who in March, 1834, belong to the highest class in common schools, in the hope that I shall be listened to — why may I not say, be yielded to? While they read of powers and principles of self-improvement, perhaps, (must I doubtingly say *perhaps?*') *perhaps* they will make decisions, form plans, commence action — and hereafter, and forever, will seek after knowledge as for hidden treasure. Perhaps I shall assist minds, growing and immortal, and leave enkindled a flame, that will burn on earth, and burn forever.

I know, that for years, self-improvement has been here and there begun in common schools; which gives the evidence and the earnest of what may be done in them. But if it is done, it must be done by ascertaining the state of the pupils' minds, and then endeavoring to influence them.

In the dialogue which follows, I have endeavored to present distinctly, on the one hand, the views of many pupils, too often fostered by the example and influence of parents, and on the other, the feelings existing in others, which may be wrought upon, to lead them on when school days are over. Parents! Teachers! let me ask you to read this, and read it to your children now at school; and see, if in some mode the spirit of ***self-improvement*** cannot be waked up. It will surpass, in its effects, all that years of tuition can do. It will cause the seed already planted to spring, and to produce an hundred fold.

DIALOGUE II.

SCENE — *the Road — Thomas and Robert on their way to School.*

Thomas. Well, Robert, I have been thinking this morning that this is the last winter of our going to school.

Robert. And I suppose you have been thinking, that you are glad of it.

Thomas. No; I am sorry, I assure you; for I just begin to see that I know very, very little; and that I need a great deal that I do not yet know, and that I fear I never shall know.

Robert. I don't see any need of looking so sober about it. Poh! Thomas, *you* know enough. You have always been called one of the best scholars in the school. If you have not learning enough, what think you will become of the rest of us. I'm sure, you are a better scholar than I am; and I'll venture *my* learning. For my part, I am glad enough that I am so near through.

Thomas. I shall be *obliged* to leave off, whether I am ready or not; so I suppose that there is no use in groaning about it. And, after all, as I was thinking last night, I might as well get through; for, as I have managed, I have not gained much, these three or four years. Every winter I have been to school three months, and thought I gained a great deal; but summer followed, and I forgot almost all, before another winter came; and here I am, but a precious little wiser than I was four years ago. If I didn't 'turn over a new leaf,' as they say, I might go to school till I am twenty, and not be much better off than I am now.

Robert. I think I shall 'turn over a new leaf;' but it will be such, I believe, as every body else turns over, when they leave school. I have no notion of going to school all my life, or of turning scholar out of school.

Thomas. Ah! that's a good thought, whether you mean it or not. I shall remember that.

Robert. What?

Thomas. *To turn scholar out of school.* That would be a grand leaf to turn over! That would keep me from forgetting, and keep me learning, too. If I should turn scholar, out of school, I might gain something, after all. And besides, I could keep learning a great while — that is — if I live.

Robert. Well; I have no notion of being tied down to a book all my days. I do not mean to be either a doctor, or a lawyer, or a minister.

Thomas. Nor I. But I expect to be a *man;* and I should like to have as much knowledge, and as capable a mind, as a diligent man can have; and fit myself, as well as I can, for all I may ever have to do. I have learned already, in part at least, how to read, write, and cypher; and I should like to try, and see if I can't make use of what I know already, as the means of knowing more.

Robert. What! — after you leave school, and have no teacher?

Thomas. Yes. Why not, if as *you* say, I turn scholar after leaving school. What do you think of my brother William? He is now just six years old; I suppose if he lives ten years longer, he will know at least as much as I do now.

Robert. True enough. He will go to school for ten years to come; that's the reason why he will equal us, ten years hence. But then that will be because we shall not go to school.

Thomas. But then *we* shall be *almost* as ignorant as we are now. I don't like to think of that.

Robert. Nor I, either. But what can we do? We can't go to school with him; and we must work at home.

Thomas. Why, I remember, our teacher, last winter, took the Annals of Education, and he read to us one day an account of some poor boys at a school in Switzerland, who worked all day, to pay for their living. But they spent an hour in the morning, and an hour that they rested at noon, and an hour at night, in study, and learned more, and faster, a great deal, than they do at our school, in six hours a day. They learned all that we do; and besides that, they learned Geometry and Music, and could sing a great many beautiful hymns, to amuse themselves and their friends at home.

Robert. What do I care for geometry and singing!

Thomas. Well, if you don't care, it will show you what we can do. I am sure we can do as much as Swiss boys; and though we do work all day, if we study two or three hours *the whole year round*, it will be as good as going to school all winter.

Robert. I have heard of these Self-Supporting Schools. If I could go to one of them, and have a teacher —

Thomas. — Very likely you would not learn much! But you can have a self-supporting school of your own, and teach yourself, as Dr Franklin did.

Robert. *You* are welcome to, if you choose.

Thomas. Well, I mean to remember our two rules; the first was, *to turn scholar out of school*, and the second, *to be a scholar the whole year round*. I will write them down, so as to be more sure not to forget them. I am willing to mind them both, strictly, if I can but 'have an education.'

Robert. 'Have an education!' You have an education! Are you not going to be a farmer?

Thomas. Yes; and why should not a farmer have an education, if he can get it?

Robert. Why? Because it costs too much time, and too much money. There's my brother James, he is to 'have an education;' and I shall think myself well off, if I get as much to buy a farm with, as his education will cost him. You will be a pretty farmer, after you have spent the whole worth of your farm in getting an education.

Thomas. You talk wildly, Robert. Why, Master, all the 'education' I was thinking of, was what I may hope to gain, by keeping *strictly* to our two rules. Perhaps I may learn as fast as my little brother William will, in school, if I don't as fast as your brother James does, in college.

Robert. I have no notion of *getting an education*, and working too. I do not mean to torment myself all my life.

Thomas. Nor I. No, no — I want to find a plan that will please me rather than worry me, and that will make me *a better farmer*. Why, Robert, there is a great deal to study about farming. If I can study diligently, all my life long, perhaps I shall be happier, and richer too.

Robert. Fie! Thomas. Is that the way you honor *our fine system of schooling*, that they talk so much about, and print so much about? Here we have been trotting and running to school, these dozen winters, and we *are not yet fit to be farmers!* That 's the finish! Leave school at eighteen or twenty, and acknowledge yourself such a dunce that you must keep learning forty years longer!

Thomas. Yes, and more, too — twenty years more, if I should live to be as old as my grandfather. But I don't care for that. If I live *sixty* years longer, I am willing to study sixty years longer. I *choose* to do it. I am sure that I am the better off for learning to see, and hear, and walk, and talk, and think, and all the other little matters I have yet learned; and I am not willing to stop. I'll follow your advice and *try* 'to keep what I've got, and get what I can.'

Robert. Well, if I can't stop the boy's talk any other way, I must come to the Bible. You must die, Thomas, and there 's the end of it; and then, according to Scripture, 'Knowledge shall vanish away.' *Now*, what have you got to say, Thomas?

Thomas. Why, that the words you have repeated can't have any such meaning as you give them. Why, Thomas, the Bible is full of information, and will give us ten thousand times more knowledge than we have got. But stop, Robert; my mother made me learn *that* chapter by heart, and I can say another verse in it: — 'Now, I know in part; but *then* shall I know even as also I am known.' I don't pretend to understand the full meaning of this. But I'm sure of *one* thing — it *cannot* mean that all our knowledge will die, when the body dies, and that we shall never have any more. Death will not turn us into ideots, but our minister tells us we shall *know*, and *learn*, on a higher scale. So, Master Robert, instead of stopping me, you have only cleared the way before me, and set me lessons which I can *never* finish. I shall have to keep learning forever, that is, if I have 'charity.' Now the question comes back again — What have *you* got to say?

Robert. You are too *high* for me. But, Thomas, I shall have the most company, unless I turn and become of your mind. Where there is one like you there are a thousand like me.

Thomas. I don't wish to see a thousand like me, for we should all despair together. But if there were a thousand around me, minding our two rules, I should take courage. But I am determined to *try* — with few or with many.

Robert. Stop, Thomas, here is other business. Do you see the boys yonder, playing at *ball*? I'll promise to do my part at that.

Thomas. So will I; and after I get through, I shall be able to begin my work with good spirits.

Such are the feelings of some of the best pupils of our common schools. Should I have the privilege of addressing them, I would use such language as the following:

ON THE POWER AND PRINCIPLES OF SELF-IMPROVEMENT.

Addressed to the Highest Class in Common Schools, March, 1834.

Man was made for self-improvement! At his birth, he is feebler and less knowing than most other animals, and his early progress is much slower. The lambs can use their limbs as soon as they are yeaned; and their first days of life are spent in the most antic gambols. The chickens, as soon as they are hatched, begin to ramble alone, seeking after their food; and those birds which at first are so feeble that they must be fed in the nest, need but two or three weeks, before they can fly, with a swiftness exceeding tenfold the running of the most active man. God has given them *instinct*, by which we mean, that they have the use of their limbs and faculties, without learning how to use them. This gives them an advantage at first; but it is the very principle that prevents their ever knowing more than they knew at first. They were not made for self-improvement. At length the infant, which at first was much more ignorant and feeble than they, leaves them behind, and passes on, gaining both knowledge and power, without any limit.

At first, indeed, he knows nothing; not even how to use his eyes, or ears, or touch, or smell, or hands, or feet, or tongue. Nothing that has any capacity, can be thought of, less capable than an infant, to which God has given no more of animal instinct, than is just sufficient to keep it in a condition to use its higher and nobler power of self-improvement. It can breathe as well, and take its food as well the first day, as after it has lived fifty years. But it has, everything else to learn; and it has the power of learning everything. It is feebler and more ignorant at its birth, than birds and beasts, that it may be wiser and more powerful, afterwards and forever. For the first few days, you would not think, from any thing you see, that the little babe would ever equal the lambs and the fowls — so slowly does he learn. But as you watch, you see that he begins to know how to use his eyes and his ears, i. e. he begins to take notice of the sights and sounds around him. You see his unmeaning paddle, changed for reaching after, and taking hold of, the things that he wants, and for putting away from him the things that he dislikes. Soon, he shows that he understands what is passing around him, and his face is lighted with a smile, or darkened with a frown. He can even understand much of the thoughts and feelings of others, and as he lies in the lap of his mother, he looks deep into her very soul — already taught to read the language of her eyes and her face. Now, an experienced scholar, he begins to extend his plans of improvement. As he cannot reach all he wants, he attempts to move his body, and finds, that by adding the use of his legs to his hands he can do it. He first becomes a creeper; then, following the example of his elders, whose change of place is so much more rapid than his own, he tries his feet, and by the aid of chairs and stools, he learns to walk. Along with these improvements, so diligently and successfully made, are others, still more astonishing. He has seen the motion and heard the sound, of the organs of speech; — he has noticed the same sound, repeated again and again, until he has discovered its meaning. He tries to pronounce the same word, until he can speak the meaning of his soul. Now, he can think, and reason, and make known his infant thoughts, to those who are around him. What an instance of the power of self-improvement! He has done it all himself, by his own diligence and activity, commencing with the ignorance of a new-born infant. How inferior, two years ago, to a lamb or a bird! Now, how plainly it appears, that God made him to be wiser than the beasts of the field, and the fowls of the air!

Man was made for self-improvement! As he passes from infancy to childhood, he retains the activity of body and mind, by which he made his earliest improvements; but now, by means of his growing capacity of forethought and choice, he becomes capable of improvements on a higher scale, under the guidance of parents, teachers and masters, to whom for a season, his Maker has wisely subjected him. If forethought and choice submit to the guidance of experience, the improvements of childhood far exceed those of the earlier period of infancy. You need not go far to see the proof. Look upon the seats around you. Alas, there are some blockheads in the schools, and I cannot deny it, who seem to have *lost* the power of self-improvement, which they had for their two or three years of infancy, when they learned so fast, to see, and hear, and handle, and walk, and speak and think. But now, they live year after year — and year after year — are ten years old — are twelve years old — and are blockheads still; not because they *cannot*, but because they *will not* learn; because they choose not to submit to the guidance of their parents and teachers. It cannot be helped if they *will not* improve themselves, — blockheads they must be at twenty or fifty. But look again. There are other boys — and girls; — they are not *helped*, they are not taught, half so much as the blockheads I was speaking of; but they are educating themselves — submitting to the method which their parents and teachers point out. How easily, how freely they read. How well they understand every word, because they have tried to read and understand, over and over again, just as they learned the lessons and the arts of infancy. And as they learned their courage grew. From what they learned, they knew that they could learn more, and therefore tried other branches of knowledge. They began with the simplest numbers, and by following the rules and plans laid out for them, they are now capable of answering, with great ease and despatch, the most difficult questions in Arithmetic.

You see how the improvements are all in the line of labor and choice. I may give another instance, which shows, how it is only in that line, and in proportion to the vigor of that labor and choice. I refer to the trades, which in later childhood, the young begin to learn. A boy of fourteen foresees the necessities of life, and chooses an employment by which to earn his living; we may say, for example, of a Cabinet Maker. With the consent of his parents, he is apprenticed to a master of that trade. You may imagine how awkward he feels, as he passes for the first time through the warehouse, arranged with furniture of the finest workmanship and finish; how painfully he thinks that such a bungler as he is, can never learn so difficult an art. But he resolves to try. He follows the bidding of his foreman, and plies the tools again and again, until he begins to use them handily. He measures and fits, and measures and fits again, until he can construct, first, the boxes in which the finished articles are sent away. From month to month he looks and hears, and obeys, and tries, until at length he can build and finish, with as perfect a workmanship, as he saw, almost with despair on the first day of his apprenticeship. Before he was two years old, he felt the motives, and took the pains of infancy, and became a seeing, hearing, handling, walking, thinking child. Now, he has taken forethought of life, has chosen an apprenticeship, and by obedient diligence, has become an adept in the art by which he expects a comfortable and honorable maintenance in life.

Man was made for self-improvement! As he *passes* from childhood to manhood, he retains the active powers of infancy, and the forethought and choice of childhood, but he adds to these the power of *self-direction,* by which he again rises, by degrees, to a higher scale of improvement, if indeed, he *will now direct himself.* As childhood uses the attainments of infancy — so may manhood those of infancy and childhood, and increase every year in knowledge and in skill. Think of it! Do men lose their eyes, or ears, or hands, or feet, or their faculties of mind, or their powers of forethought and choice, as they pass from childhood to manhood? Can they not perceive, imagine, remember, reason? Can they not add knowledge to knowledge, and skill to skill? At manhood, we do but come into full possession of the means of improvement.

How great are those means! Even from the Common School, the young go forth with powers of improvement, to which no bounds can be fixed. They can read, write, cypher, and have some knowledge perhaps of Geography, History and Grammar. And are these *poor* instruments of knowledge and skill? With these, you may go forth to learn anything else, to learn *everything* else. Have you learned to read English? The English language, which you say you can read, contains all the knowledge and arts of mankind. It offers you a record of the experience and observation of all men — it offers you the wisdom of all ages. The schools are to be valued, not so much for what you learn *in* them, but for what you may learn AFTER them; not for the little knowledge which they furnish, but because they furnish *the means of all knowledge.* Shame to those scholars of the highest class, who are *doing up* their *last* studies, who are *finishing off* their education, by some *two months* more at school! Shame to those who grow up, and take this scanty education as enough! Shame to those who spend years in getting the key of knowledge, but who never intend to use it to unlock the store!

Man was made for self-improvement!—in all his powers and without any limit, in the present life and forever. The same kind, wise and powerful friend, who puts us in infancy, in a condition to fit us for the higher opportunities of childhood — and in childhood, offered us the guidance of parents, to lead us up to manhood; offers, also, to our first dawn of thought and in all our life, a guidance, suited to the necessities of our earthly path, and also to all the future periods of our being. He gives us his promise, that if we will acknowledge Him in all our ways, he will direct our steps, and bring us at last to that glorious world, where we shall know all that our hearts can desire, or our minds receive. Thus shall the mind and the heart be improved, and we shall grow wiser and better. This higher and endless path of self-improvement, he has not left us to find out for ourselves. God has not left us so ill provided at any stage of our existence; nor does he here. He has sent us his unerring word to teach us the way in which we should go. THE BIBLE is so simple that a child can gain instruction from it; and yet it is so full of knowledge, that the most studious can never finish it. With this guide you may go on to improve forever!

METHOD OF TEACHING THE ALPHABET.

WE have more than once expressed our opinion, that there is *no one 'best method'* on Education, as there is *no one 'best remedy'* in medicine.

In a letter from a teacher to the editor, in which we have to acknowledge his kind engagement to take five copies of the Annals for the next year, he gives the following account of a plan for teaching the alphabet. We insert it, because we doubt not that it may assist some, who are not prepared to adopt the plan most accordant with our habits and views.

'Before I conclude, I will take the liberty of describing to you the plan I pursue in teaching the alphabet —

'I had been aware for some time, that the methods pursued were very imperfect, so much so indeed, that it appeared to me very probable, that an aversion to learning through life was created, by the wretched mode in which the learner was made to ascend this first step. There seemed to me three great hindrances to the advancement of the pupil — the first, was teaching it by rote — the second, its not being associated with anything interesting to the learner — the third, the short space of time in which the mind was engaged with each letter. The first I could easily remedy; but the second and third involved more difficulty. I recollected however, that to keep important ideas in mind, I was accustomed to associate something with them with which I was quite familiar, and that this had assisted my memory in a very important degree; and I concluded, that if I could apply the same association of ideas in teaching the alphabet, it might prove very beneficial to the pupil.

In accordance with these thoughts, I immediately procured the picture alphabet — a card containing the alphabet, in and around each letter of which, there are drawn pictures of objects with which the child is most familiar, having under each their several names. I then gave the abecedarian a slate and pencil, and directed him to make the letter *a*, on his slate, so repeatedly that it became indelibly impressed upon his memory. In the same manner he learned *n* and *t*. I then pointed him to the word *ant*, and requested him to write it on his slate. I next told him, that he had written a word, that was the name of the little animal, of which that was the picture which was set before him — that those letters which he saw would spell all the words we use, such as cat, corn, &c,— and that as soon as he should learn these few letters, he could soon spell all these words. I then related some story respecting the ants, described their houses in Africa, their mode of flight, of clinging together in a flood, &c. Of course I did not inform him of all this at once; but at many different times, while he was engaged in writing the word. After writing an hour or two, and finding he would probably recollect the letters *a n t* by having them associated with *ant*, respecting which he had heard so many interesting things, I permitted him to learn the additional letters which were in the word *apple*, pursuing the same course, until he had learned the names of all the objects, and consequently, the whole alphabet. This he accomplished, in five or six weeks. I then put him on the

Infant School cards of natural history; when his progress in reading was proportionably rapid.

This is the plan I now pursue, and find it gives the pupil continual employment, and that of the most agreeable nature; while the association of ideas, fixes the letters indelibly in his mind.'

PRACTICAL LESSONS.

ANATOMY AND PHYSIOLOGY.

Extracted from 'The House I live in. By W. A. Alcott.'

[The author of the work which we have named, commenced a series of articles in the Juvenile Rambler, more than a year since, designed to illustrate the most simple principles of Anatomy to children. The body was described as 'The House' of the soul—the head being the cupola, and the limbs the pillars. The following lesson, which we requested from the author, furnishes, we think, a happy illustration of the proper mode of presenting such subjects to children. Each lesson has a portion which is figurative, and another, which is simply descriptive, in smaller type, indicated here by brackets.]

THE CUPOLA.

Structure of the Cupola. Of the covering. Reasons why the Cupola is so firmly covered. Doors and windows. Teeth. The brain,—where situated—its size, color, weight, and measure.

We come now to the cupola. The frame of this rests on the top of the great post. Seven out of the twentyfour pieces which go to make up that post, and which lie between the upper story and the cupola, form what is called the neck. Some of them are here shown in connection with the frame of the cupola.

This division of the frame is very strong. It consists of no less than 54 pieces; besides nine very small ones, which properly belong to the covering, for they are not to be found until the covering is put on.

[We shall see hereafter, that what may be called the 'covering' of the building, is pretty important; especially that of the head. The construction of this is such that the bones form the covering, as well as the frame; and they only have a thin layer of what we shall call 'shingles,' put on afterwards. In short, the bones all round the top of the head are framed together with so much exactness, that when you entirely strip everything off, you cannot stick the finest needle between them. *Besides* all this, they are very thick and strong.]

If you ask why the Builder took so much pains with the cupola, I can only say that, as some of my most valuable goods are kept here, and as they are things, too, which are easily injured, on the least touching or handling, it was necessary that the frame should be thus tight and strong. Indeed, it thus answers the purpose of frame and covering, both at the same time.

It happens also, that should robbers or murderers attack the house, they are almost sure to make their first attempts upon the cupola. Now he who built the house knew all this; and therefore contrived it so that it will bear pretty heavy blows before it can be broken in, especially those parts of it which are most exposed.

On coming to this place, as I was reading this chapter over to Charles, he started and said; Then it seems you did not build the house yourself. I thought people usually built their own houses. 'Sometimes they do, and sometimes they do not,' I replied. Nobody ever built such a *sort* of house for himself, *as I am describing*.

The truth is, my house was a thousand times more ingeniously contrived, and wisely constructed, than if I had built it for myself. I could not have adapted things to the purposes for which I now employ them, half so well as the wisdom and skill of the great Architect who planned the whole, has done it, without me. And I can never be thankful enough to him 'for all his benefits.'

I formerly spoke of the doors and windows, and observed that there were none in any other part of the building but the cupola. There are *two* windows. They are both in front, at the upper part. Some of the doors are in front, others at the sides. You only see *places* for them in the engraving; for the windows and doors themselves properly belong to the covering. At any rate, they are never seen except when the covering is on.*

Some of the timbers in the lower part of the cupola, at the fore part, are not very firmly connected with the rest of the frame. They may even be taken out without very great injury. Sometimes they drop out of themselves; at others, they become decayed, and are taken out. Generally, however, they do not decay, till the whole frame begins to decay, if they are taken good care of. You see the parts to which I refer. They stand in two rows, running crosswise, and parallel to each other. But we shall need another chapter, in order to describe these.

I ought just to say in this place, (though I do not expect you will fully comprehend my meaning,) that many people judge of the owner of a house, whether he is a wise man or a fool, by the front of the cupola, especially when the covering is on. If the part above the windows is wide, high and projecting, they are apt to think more favorably than if it is otherwise. They are rather apt, too, to think those the best people whose houses are the most beautiful. *You* may have been accustomed to think otherwise. You may think, perhaps, that many wise people live in mean, ugly-looking houses, and that a very dashing house shows folly rather than good sense.

[The brain, which is enclosed in the cranium or skull, is so important — and it is so difficult to understand the shape of the latter, without knowing something about the former, that I have concluded, (before proceeding with the story about the house,) to give a short account of it.

THE BRAIN.

The Brain — where situated — its size — measure.

When I was a boy and heard about the brain, I used to wonder in what part of the head it was situated. I had seen the brain of several domestic animals,

* I called the mouth, and ears and nostrils, doors — to keep up the figure; and, also, because these are in fact the principal avenues to the human soul, except the eyes, which may, with the greatest propriety, be regarded as windows. All sound, smell, taste, &c, come to us through these passages, and the machinery or organs near and within them. Why then may they not properly be called doors?

the ox, the calf, the swine, and the lamb; and as in these it appeared to occupy only a small part of the head, I concluded that the *human* brain did also. Some person, as ignorant as myself, told me that the brains lay in the forehead; and this opinion I grew up with.

The color and general appearance of the human brain are not unlike those of domestic animals, but it is a great deal larger. Man has a larger brain, in proportion to his body, than almost any other known animal.

To give you a more accurate idea of its exact size, however, just take a piece of twine and tie it round your head from the bottom of the eye-brows or edge of the forehead to the nape of the neck, letting it come down close behind the root of the ear. Now all above this string, except the skull itself and the skin, flesh, hair, &c, is brain: and the whole covering, bone, flesh, skin, &c, can hardly be more than half an inch thick, in the thickest part, and in some places scarce a quarter of an inch; so that there is a very considerable quantity of the brain, as you see. There is even a *little* brain below the line of the string; but not much, unless you call that *brain* which runs down into the hollow cavity of the spine, like a large whitish cord, and which I have already told you is the *spinal marrow.*

At the beginning of the last chapter, I presented you with a picture of the bones of the whole head. Now if the bones of the face and neck were taken quite away, and nothing left but just the hollow brain-case, the appearance would be very different. Here is the front view of a skull, from which the bones below have been thus removed.

You see in front the top of the cavity, or socket, for each of the two eyes, and on one side the place where the ear should be in the living person. This braincase is composed of eight bones, most of which are closely united by a rough edge, like that of a saw, the notches of which shut into each other as exactly as saw teeth would.

The seams, as a tailor would call them, are by anatomists called *sutures.*

One of the most important bones of the skull or brain-pan, is that which stretches across the whole forehead, and is called the *os frontis*, or frontal bone. Another across the back side of the head, and shaped thus Λ, is the *os occipitis*. The sharp top reaches to the crown of the head. Another piece, shaped a little like a clam-shell, lies around each ear. It is the *os temporis*. There are, of course, two of these. On the top of the head, surrounded by those already described, are the two *parietal* bones, (*ossa parietalia.*) Surrounded by them all, in the bottom of the skull, is a large bone, the *os sphenoides*; and a smaller one, the *os ethmoides.*

Now, as I have already told you, this whole space is filled up with brain. In an adult, the brain weighs from two and a half to three and a quarter pounds; or it measures a quart or more. In a few instances, it has been found somewhat larger.]

TEACHING THE GREEK LETTERS.

From 'Lessons in Greek. By Theodore Dwight, Jr.'

[The recent declaration of a Professor of Languages, that few carry from college any knowledge of Greek which is worth the time spent in acquiring it, is confirmed by the observation of most persons acquainted with our public institutions. Any plan is welcome, which promises to remove this reproach. The attempt is made by Mr Dwight, to give the Greek, to some extent, the interest of a living language, on principles derived from various modern plans. We insert the first lesson, which will serve, at least, as an example of the thorough, productive mode of teaching. Let its success be tested by an experiment with an intelligent child; or a similar course be tried with English. The Modern Greek pronunciation is adopted.]

Let these words be written on the black board, or on a slate or paper, before the class assemble, and placed where all may see them distinctly from their seats.

'Εγὼ	*γράφω*	*ἐπιστολήν.*
I	*write*	*a letter.*

The following questions may be put to the whole class; but it is generally better to put questions to one scholar at a time, sometimes in order as they sit or stand, and sometimes selecting them without regard to order, to keep them attentive.

How many Greek words are here? How many letters are in the first? Write the first letter. This capital, or large épsilon, is like what English letter? Epsilon sounds like *e* in *met*, or *a* in *mate*. Now write the second letter. Gamma,* you see, is made long: the pen being carried down below the line, and brought up again. That is the Greek *g*. Now write ómega. Gámma, omega spell *go*. What is the whole word? Speak it. Erase it. Write the first letter. What is it? How does it sound? Write the second. What is it? How does it sound? The third. What is it? How does it sound? Put the little mark before or over epsilon, which is the soft breathing, and shows that the ancient Greeks used to sound it as if *h* came before it. Mark the long accent over omega. That shows that you are to speak it more strongly than the rest of the word: ĕgó, not égo: ĕ must be sounded like *e* in *met*, or *a* in *mate*; and ē like *e* in *me*.

Now erase it, and write the word again.* What is the first letter? Second? Third? What must you put over the first? Why? What over the third? Why? Erase and write it again.

How many letters are in the second word? What is the first? What is it like? What does it sound like? Write the second. Ro, as you see, goes below the line, but does not come up to it again. Write álpha. That is the Greek *a*, and sounds like *a* in *father*. Spell this first syllable after me: gámma, ro, alpha — *gra*, [pronounced *grah*.] Erase it. Write it again. What is the first letter? Second? Third? Write the fourth, *phe*. What is the last? What does phe, ómega spell? Put the sharp accent over alpha. That shows that it is sounded more strongly than any other part of the word, as *a* is in *father*. It is spoken grápho, not graphó.

Erase the two words. Write the first. The second. Erase them again; &c.

* Speak gamma as if spelt gammah; and omega, as if spelt ómĕgah.

[A similar course is adopted with the third word.]

Make every scholar speak the sentence many times, with the proper accents, until all are familiar with them. Make all write them over and over again, and spell them, naming all the letters, till they know them by heart.

What letters are used more than once in these three words? What are used only once? Let each write down in a line all the different letters, with the names and sounds against them: thus,

E ε	epsilon	like *e* in met.
γ	gamma	g
ω	ómega	o

and so go on with the other letters.

O-μέγα, or omega, means great or long o. *O-μικρὸν*, or omikron, means small o. *E-ψίλον*, or epsilon, means sharp or small e. Write *μέγα*, *μικρόν*, and *ψίλον*. What letters are here which were not given before? Write them under the others, with their names and sounds against them. μ is called me, and sounds like m. κ is called kappa, and sounds like k. ψ is called pse, and sounds like ps. How many letters have you now in all? There are in Greek only 24 letters. In English there are 26.

THE TEACHER'S ALMANAC FOR MARCH.

THE SCHOOL-ROOM.

Many of the public schools have now broken up, perhaps with some grand display of wooden swords and paper shields, or grotesque finery, to gratify the vanity of younger children, and amuse older ones. It is hoped, however, this system is passing away; and that the progress of a school will no longer be tested by the capacity of the pupils to strut upon a stage.

'Cold, blustering March' will find its way into the school-room, and its moisture and chills will expose the health of the pupils, in the inactivity of school-days, even more than 'frosty January.' '*The head cool, the feet dry*, and *the body warm*,' will still be a good maxim, for teachers and pupils.

This is a favorable opportunity to 'post up' the accounts of the winter. What has been lost by the pupils, for want of room, or fuel, or fire? What have they gained in health or comfort, by the care of the teacher? What have they gained in the improvement of the mind, and the heart, by his aid or example? Who is better, as well as wiser? What has the teacher gained? for he must be a poor teacher, who, in the early periods of his employment, does not improve more rapidly than his pupils.

THE EARTH.

The fetters which have bound the earth and the waters at the north, will soon be loosened, and vegetation will awake from its sleep. Let your pupils watch these wonderful processes. Let them ascertain for themselves, the depth to which the frost has penetrated the ground, and the gradual process of the season in dissolving it. If any great stream is near, do not fail to let them witness its 'breaking up,' sometimes one of the grandest scenes in nature. Call upon them, also, to watch for the first evidences of life in vegetation, and the first appearance of animals and insects, which have been absent or torpid.

THE HEAVENS.

Call upon them to remark the connection of the changes on the earth, with the greater length of the days, and the elevation of the sun at noon. If there is no other mode obvious or convenient, let them mark the shortening shadow of some fixed object at noon. Do not fail to make them note the day of the Equinox, and the time of sunrise and sunset.

Among the constellations, Cancer, which is one of the signs of the Ecliptic, will be on the meridian at 9 o'clock, on the 3d of March, and of course, a little later on every succeeding day. This constellation gives name to the Tropic of Cancer and it is when the Sun is in this part of the Ecliptic, that it turns to the south. A globe, or Burritt's maps, must be referred to, to gain a correct idea of this and other constellations now rising. None of the brilliant planets will be visible in March.

MISCELLANY.

Teachers' Society of Georgia.

The Teachers' Society of Georgia, held its last Annual Meeting at Savannah, on the 16th, 17th, and 18th days of December last. The first day was occupied by an Introductory address by Mr Wm. H. Williams, the arrangements for the business of the succeeding days, and an address from Mr Holbrook, of Boston, on the importance of County Lyceums. A Committee was appointed to draft resolutions on that subject.

On the second day of the session, a report was made on the adaptation of the higher branches of mathematics to female education. Reports were then received on the condition of schools in various parts of the State. Though the condition of the common schools, and the apathy of parents and trustees are represented as deplorable, yet it is believed that the spirit of improvement is abroad, and the people of the State, generally, are awaking to the importance of education. Many new schools of a higher order, especially female seminaries, have lately been established, and the county classical schools are improving in their character. 'Efficient teachers are also more in demand, and more liberally patronised than formerly.'

A committee was appointed to prepare a circular, giving a brief exposition of the plan and advantages of County Lyceums, with the form of a Constitution. It was resolved to invite Teachers and other members of the society, throughout the State, to assist in establishing them. Cabinets of Natural History for Schools and Lyceums, were also recommended. The remainder of the day was devoted to a discussion, on the most successful modes of teaching the various branches of science, and in making arrangements in regard to future meetings. The 'Academician and Southern Journal of Education' was recommended to the attention and patronage of teachers and friends of education.

On the last day of the session, a report was made by Mr W. Baird, on

'Examinations and Exhibitions,' which was highly acceptable to the Society; and it was subsequently resolved that the subject of 'Examinations' should be discussed at the next annual meeting of the Society. A long discussion took place on 'Systematic Benevolence,' and on the best methods of securing female influence and efforts in the cause of education. The 'Annals of Education and Instruction,' was recommended to Teachers throughout the State. The committee appointed to draft the Circular, on County Lyceums, presented a brief, but interesting and valuable report. An exhibition was made, by Mr Holbrook, of his apparatus, with an explanation of its uses.

Before adjourning, Committees were appointed to report on the following subjects.

1, The propriety of making the Bible a text-book, in schools and academies; 2, Chemistry; 3, Lyceums; 4, Manual Labor Schools; 5, Free Schools; 6, The most suitable school manuals, both English and Introductory Classics; 7, The Construction of School Rooms, — and Apparatus; 8, School Governments; 9, Trustees of Academies; 10, Gymnastics; 11, The Monitorial System; 12, Importance of Rhetoric, and the best modes of Teaching it; 13, Lectures in Schools — how far useful; 14, Best Method of Teaching the Greek and Latin Classics in Grammar Schools; 15, Instruction in the Modern Languages; 16, Education of Teachers, and Importance of Institutions for that special purpose; 17, Importance of Cabinets of Natural History, connected with Schools and Academies; 18, Propriety of forming Juvenile Libraries in Schools and Academies; 19, Propriety of forming County Maps, embracing Geography, Geology, Agriculture, Statistics, &c.

The next semi-annual meeting of this Society is to be held at Mount Zion; and the next annual meeting at Milledgeville. We are gratified to see so many important subjects of inquiry presented; and hope that this Society, with the Journal recently established, may do much for education.

Schools among the Indians.

Returns have been made to the National Government, during the past year, from 20 schools among the Indian tribes; which, with those returned in former years, make up the number of 53 Indian schools. Of these, 31 are under the care of the American Board of Foreign Missions, 10 under the care of the Baptist General Convention, 6 under the Roman Catholics, 5 the Methodists, and 1 the Episcopalians. The whole number of pupils is estimated by the Gambier, (Ohio) Observer, at 1835.

Among this number, we may mention, more particularly, the following. 1. A school at Upper Sandusky, Ohio, sustained by the Methodists, with 50 to 60 pupils, some of the oldest of whom write, and study grammar and arithmetic. They have a neat school house. 2. An establishment, embracing 110 scholars at Green Bay, under the care of the Episcopalians. The pupils are instructed in the branches taught in our best common schools. It is intended soon to set apart a portion of each week, for the purpose of giving the boys a knowledge of farming and the mechanic arts; and the girls, of housewifery. 3. A school near St Thomas, on Grand River, beyond the Mississippi, among the Creeks. The pupils are said to be constant in their attendance and interested in their studies.

In addition to these, the agent for the Choctaws, who have removed to the west of the Mississippi, has devised a plan, with the approbation of the chiefs, for building, during the present year, 12 new school houses. The expenses, together, with those of the necessary teachers and books, are to be paid from an appropriation of $6000, made by the treaty of 1816. 'The buildings are to be plain, substantial log structures, and the teachers, married men, steady, sober, industrious and religious, who will take their families with them, and who will devote themselves to their calling. Both sexes are to be taught the usual English branches. The boys are also to be instructed in the arts of husbandry, and the girls in spinning, weaving, and housewifery. Three schools among them, of a higher order, are also contemplated.

Class Book of Physiology.

We are gratified to learn, that the time for presenting manuscripts for the premium offered by the American Lyceum, for a text book on Human Physiology, is extended to October next. The object in view is highly important, and ample time should be allowed to produce a complete work.

Lectures before the American Institute.

Those who are best qualified to deliver Lectures on Education, are among the most busy men of our community. In many cases, it is not easy for them to prepare their manuscripts promptly for the press; and the Institute is, of course, bound to wait their convenience, in this gratuitous, and often expensive service. It is on this account, that the publication of the lectures has been hitherto so much delayed. We learn that the lectures of 1833 are just published, by Carter, Hendee & Co.; and we believe they will form one of the most interesting volumes which has appeared.

School Fund for Massachusetts.

The Committee on Education, of the Legislature of Massachusetts, have recently presented a report, in reference to the formation of a School Fund. They observe, that according to the last returns from 99 towns, the amount paid in the average, for instruction, is one dollar ninetyeight cents, for each pupil — a greater amount, we suspect, than is paid in most other states. The result, we believe to be, that the schools are much better, though still below the proper standard of a free state, and far below what is generally supposed. They propose, not to relieve the people from a tax, which is not burthensome; but to establish a fund, to render this more efficient, and to afford aid, proportioned to the contributions and efforts which are made by those immediately concerned. We are gratified to see that it is proposed in the first place to appoint Commissoners to examine the state, and wants of the schools, before deciding on the mode of employing the fund.

New Institutions.

From recent papers and documents, we heard of the establishment of a Manual Labor School, at Fayetteville, North Carolina, and of 'The Episcopal School' on an excellent plan at Raleigh, of which Mr Cogswell, recently of Northampton, is expected to be Principal. A new Theological Institution has also been established at Windsor, Connecticut, under the Presidency of the Rev. Dr. Tyler. The Lane Seminary, at Cincinnati, as it appears from its last report, is in a highly flourishing state. We hope to say more of these Institutions, hereafter.

Boston Primary Schools.

We noticed on the cover of our last number, what should have been inserted in the text, that there are usually from eight to twelve pupils absent in each of the Primary Schools, and therefore, that the room usually allowed to each pupil, is somewhat greater than would appear from the numbers on the books of the school.

We are gratified to learn, that the Committee are going on, and receiving aid, in their plan to procure better rooms; and we regret that any should misinterpret our efforts to promote better views in the community on this subject. To a correspondent who complains of our 'tone,' in reference to the 'Report,' we would merely observe, that more than one concerned, regards it as far less severe than the case demanded.

☞ Since these pages were in type, we have received intelligence of the *assassination of Caspar Hauser!* — at the city of Anspach, in Bavaria.

NOTICES.

The Common School Arithmetic; prepared for the use of Academies and Common Schools in the United States, and also for the use of the Young Gentlemen who may be preparing to enter the Military Academy at West Point. By Charles Davies, Professor of Mathematics at the Military Academy at West Point, and author of Elements of Descriptive Geometry, Surveying, and a Treatise on Shadows and Perspective. Hartford, Conn. H. F. Sumner. 1833. 18mo, pp. 270.

We have heard some parents of late, expressing a desire that their children might learn Arithmetic in the *good old way*, of rules and examples. The present work is constructed on that plan. The rules are concise and definite, and the operations are distinctly explained; the character of the author is a guarantee for the accuracy of the work. In regard to this mode of teaching the elements of arithmetic, our opinion has been fully expressed; but we suppose that it is often necessary for those who are to enter the counting house.

The Class Book of Anatomy, designed for schools, explanatory of the First Principles of Human Mechanism, as the basis of Physical Education. By Jerome V. C. Smith, M. D.

——'for I am fearfully and wonderfully made.'

Boston: Allen and Ticknor. 1834. 12mo, pp 280.

We are gratified to see this attempt to introduce a new subject to ordinary students. It is wonderful that civilized man has been so long willing to remain ignorant of the residence of his mind, and the instruments by which it operates. The book before us abounds in information in which every adult reader will feel a deep interest, and from which all may derive valuable lessons, of a practical kind. We are gratified to see frequent references to the Great First Cause of life and motion. It is to be regretted that so much of a technical character should have been introduced into a class book, and that the author should not have employed the terms of common life more generally in his descriptions; but we cordially wish success to this enterprise, in a path almost untrodden. In our last number we gave an extract from the work.

A Universal History, in twentyfour books, translated from the German of John Von Müller. In four volumes, 12mo. Boston, Cottons and Barnard. 1834.

The character of Müller as a writer, and the value of his history, are beyond our feeble praise; and an American edition of the translation is a valuable gift to the library of standard works. While he is far above Hume and Gibbon, in reference to religion, it is to be regretted that a history so complete and elaborate, should call in question the records of the sacred books, concerning miraculous events, and the origin of its prophecies, and thus require so much caution in its use with the young.

Good's Book of Nature, abridged from the original work; adapted to the reading of Children and Youth; with Questions for the use of Schools, and Illustrations from original designs. Boston: Allen and Ticknor. 1834. square 16mo, pp. 224.

A valuable abridgment of an excellent work; but adapted to *youth*, and not to children.

AMERICAN

ANNALS OF EDUCATION

AND INSTRUCTION.

APRIL, 1834.

ON THE POWER OF EXPRESSION.

In gazing at the speaking marble of the ancients, or in reading the effusions of savage eloquence, who has not wondered, that modern civilization and refinement have done no more to perfect that power of expression, which is the chief distinction of man above the brutes — which gives to the painter and the musician, the poet and the orator, all their influence over the human heart. To those who are familiar with the language of the deaf mute, and see the finest thoughts, and the deepest and most delicate emotions, pourtrayed without the aid of words, and with a strength and beauty which words cannot describe, it is still more a matter of surprise, that this talent, which evidently belongs to our nature, should be so buried, and this power of expression so generally lost.

The same train of thought has passed through our minds, in observing the contrast of infancy and manhood. We see the child pouring forth its thoughts and feelings in every look and movement, making every limb expressive, and giving a voice to every feature; and we find the same child, when arrived at manhood, with muscles which scarcely move, except when '*something is to be done,*' with features far less animated than those of ancient statues, and eyes scarcely less vacant. We hear him, as soon as he gains a command of words, uttering them with tones which give life to language, and teach us the meaning and modifications which he intends, with a precision which no formal definition, or rule of rhetoric, could rival. In youth and manhood, all this is changed for the monotonous drawl, or the formal measurement of tones and stops, which pervade our schools and our assemblies, and even ascend our pulpits, whose themes *ought* to awaken every feeling, and call forth every power of expression. This faculty certainly exists in childhood; and it constitutes that secret charm, which scarcely any heart can resist. And yet, with all our efforts to cultivate, and refine, and elevate the human character, it is lost. To what this loss is to be ascribed, and how it is to be avoided, are questions which we have often asked, and we have been gratified to receive the following article, from a teacher well qualified to answer them.

The recent improvements in the methods of cultivating the power of expression in the young, are subjects of just congratulation among all who are interested in the advancement of education. But the beneficial changes thus effected, are not adequate to the eradication of the evils arising from the neglect of early and seasonable culture. The utmost care in pruning and training the plant, is of little avail, unless we enrich the soil. Expression has its life-spring in a deeper stratum than that of formal education. Open the *sources* of expression, and the *stream* will flow. At present, we are busied in digging the channels after the most improved form; but we leave the fountain sealed. The artificial cultivation of eloquence can never create the power of expression. It may mould and modify the *forms* of language; but it cannot give that which *causes* language. It may be a very feasible and a very salutary process in communities which, like those of antiquity, have carried fertility of mental resource, finish of thought, depth of feeling, and vividness of imagination to their highest point of cultivated excellence. But the formal study of eloquence, amidst comparative sterility in the sources of mental power, in the absence of the exciting causes of eloquence — empassioned feeling and teeming imagination — must ever lead to mannerism, rather than genuine excellence, and to a merely imitative, if not an affected style of expression.

If we would see man resume his ancient capability of expression, we must cease to expect such a result from the narrow scope to which human culture is now confined. We must cease to demand of the limited faculty of the understanding, the combined offices of intellection, feeling, and imagination. We must learn to respect and cherish the affections, — to deepen and vivify them. We must afford a generous encouragement to the ideal tendencies. We must cease to repress the intense aspirations of humanity after the great and beautiful.

Man has unquestionably enlarged the sphere of the understanding, since the time when ancient eloquence expired. But it is by no means certain that he would not have made a much more glorious progress through the domain of knowledge, had he duly preserved the unity of his constitution, and retained the impulse imparted by the deep-felt emotion and glowing imagination of antiquity. Let Bacon be referred to as a modern example of the rigor of philosophy maintained amidst the play of a luxuriant fancy. See how, in his page, the august and beautiful features of Truth are preserved, as well as its characteristic exactitude of outline—how the spirit of life is breathed into the whole form, and diffused around, as a sensible presence.

The absence of eloquence from the circle of the arts, is not a comparative evil only. *We* disparage the ancient regard paid to expression, and fondly imagine that, if we *are* suffering from our neglect of it, we suffer only in the regions of feeling and fancy, which, we arrogantly presume, we can afford to dispense with. But the life of the mind does not lie in the intellect. The springs of action and of power lie deeper in our nature; they work in the seats of the animal and the affective constitutions. To influence man as an agent, it is not enough to exhibit, to state, or to demonstrate. Truth must be imbedded in feeling, and enkindled by imagination, that it may be transfused into our whole nature, and identified with our being. The mental action of modern times, being, in general, restricted to the observation and the exposition of facts or principles in the department of science, exerts little influence on human character. It does little to lift up and impel the soul, or to renovate and strengthen it for those stupendous efforts which have stamped antiquity as the era of the sublime, or to adorn it with that finished and perfect grace, which modern art despairs of approaching. The genius of modern life employs the acquisitions of intellect for the improvement of condition, rather than the elevation of character. The spirit of ancient culture was, perhaps, too purely ideal, and its aim too ambitious: its end, too generally, was glory. Yet, we must not forget that, to the ancients, glory was the comprehensive designation of universally acknowledged excellence. *We*, on the other hand, are too prone to measure mental exertion by the degree in which it contributes to comfort. What an interval separates these two ends of human endeavor!

The spirit of Christianity, it is true, would redeem us from this degrading tendency of our times, were it, as it ought to be, the ascendant influence in human affairs. But, what with the pressure of entailed evils of condition and of education, the Christian spirit does not predominate in society. Commerce, improvement, enterprise, are the absorbing interests of life. Convenience is the paramount consideration. Let the enormous sums lavished on modern facilities for the despatch of business, and the scanty pittance that has usually been doled out for the advancement of mind, or the melioration of character, bear testimony to the truth of the assertion. What, on the contrary, might be the state of man, were the physical improvements at which he has now arrived, but the 'lower works' of his creative energies — the external means of facilitating the attainment of higher forms of character, by contracting the time, and abridging the labor hitherto devoted to the provision for real or imaginary wants!

The prevalent neglect of the liberal arts, in present systems and modes of education, leaves us destitute of one great counteracting force, by which the degenerating tendencies of mind might be resisted. Man inevitably sinks, when he neglects the culture of those arts which embody the workings of his whole nature, and impart life and unity to his aspirations after whatever is higher and better than the present. No degree of civilization, no pitch of artificial refinement, can compensate for the absence of those primary impulses of our constitution, which interpret its inner laws, and to which the fine arts, in general, so intelligently and faithfully respond. But none of these arts is so indispensable to human progress, as that of expression, whether oral or written, poetic or prosaic, in form. The essence, indeed, of all the fine arts, is expression — the embodying of thought and feeling, by that wondrous, and as yet, ill-defined power, which traverses and connects the external and the internal sources of conception, and to which is assigned the office of evoking the image of every impression enstamped, whether from within or from without, upon the human soul.

Cultivating this art which, unlike the processes of mere intellect, embraces the unity of his constitution, and concentrates all its powers, man must necessarily ascend in the scale of character. The understanding, the memory, and all other recipient faculties may be exercised in high perfection, while the vital powers of the soul remain inactive and morbid. Not so with the forms of mental action, which create expression: these elicit feeling, incite imagination, and vivify the intellect. Expression, as an art, is, at its very lowest power, a step upward from the material, or rather, through the material to the spiritual. It tends to the beautiful and the sublime, in the moral, not less than the intellectual and the physical; and, in all its higher efforts, it is so manifestly impelled by a breath of inspiration, and reveals so clearly an internal power, that it necessarily sheds a spiritual light. This noble office it fulfills, when cultivated in modes analogous to its own nature, or rather, to that of man himself; and when such effects do not result from its cultivation, the blame is to be laid on defective modes of discipline, and not on the inadequacy of the art itself to produce these effects.

But what relation is there between such an art, and the process of reciting from a formal and pedantic treatise on rhetoric; of being exercised on common places, or drilled on vocal inflections and prescribed lines of gesture and attitude? The young mind might, it is true, rise above the deadening influence of these soulless operations; or, if felicitous in imagination, might even succeed in wringing from them a grace of art, were the internal sources of expression supplied. But towards this effect, education contributes nothing. The student has his head well stored with knowledge, his memory replete with ideas of the understanding; but his heart has not been stirred, nor his imagination impressed; and he is commanded to give utterance to thought, without ever having been placed under the experience of those quickening pains and pleasures of feeling, which compel expression, and without having been indulged in the contemplation of those forms of nature and of art, which would elicit his unconscious yet eloquent admiration, and invest him with the full power of glowing expression, ere he was aware.

The adequate cultivation of language, as of every other expressive art, demands that the whole nature of the human being be early and effectually trained to it. The discipline of intellect will, no doubt, contribute to the desired end; but it is utterly incompetent for the full effect to be produced. It is, indeed, of less importance in this than in any other branch of mental culture. To attain expressive power, the affections must be exposed to strong and deep yet salutary impressions; the heart must be impelled, the will quickened, the imagination enkindled, the emotions powerfully excited, the fancy enriched by all forms of exterior beauty. Fertility, life, and creative power, having been thus imparted, the pliant season of childhood and youth must be moulded by genial methods, to those ideal and impassioned forms of habit, which render true, rich, strong, and vivid expression the spontaneous function of the man. Education, if so directed, will cease to convey a dead letter, instead of infusing a quickening spirit.

It is in vain that we expect expressive power of individuals or of communities that have not been subjected to the discipline of empassioned emotion, and surrounded by grandeur in the features of nature, or perfection in the products of art. Nor is this discipline at all incompatible with the moral unity of man. There is a salutary agitation of our nature implied in all the severer forms of human experience. There are provisions, alike in our constitution and our condition, for a profound and beautiful troubling of the waters; and the angel has express commission to descend, on his renovating office, at appointed intervals.

Did the force of feeling, or the vividness of imagination, or the intensely exciting influence of circumstances, to which the young Greek or Roman was early habituated, impair the vigor of his constitution, either physical or mental? What then might we not expect of the young Christian aspirant after immortality, for whose spiritual nature so magnificent provision has been expressly made, in a revelation addressed to the primal and commanding principles of conscience, faith and love? What are all the cherishing influences of nature or of art, in comparison with that emanating from the divine source of his spiritual life? What form of mental character ought to be so rich, so noble, so pure, so fraught with all the finest elements of expression, as his? What can more deeply penetrate humanity, than the motives of his daily life? What can more exalt it? What can transcend the glory of that future, which his imagination depicts, and his faith realizes? What an inexhaustible treasury of mental resource is implied in his spiritual vision! Yet how unjust is education to this favored being — how it paralyzes and impoverishes him! Not one of these sources of inspiration is he early and habitually led up to, that he may imbibe its invigorating and purifying stream, to prepare him for efforts worthy of his nature and its opportunities. As if to quell his ingenuous aspirations, the guides of his youth coldly assure him that the era of primitive mental power is elapsed; and as for expression, he may account himself fortunate if, haply, as the reward of his utmost exertions in striving after the great models of the past, he succeed in catching something of a dim resemblance to their manner. It may be that effort is even discouraged, and ultimately abandoned, on the plea that the purer style of thought to which the genius of modern life inclines, needs not the laborious cultivation of expression, enjoined in ancient discipline; as if that the universal diffusion of intelligence renders the influence of emotion and imagination unnecessary for the production of mental effect — as if eloquence were not a purely moral effect; — as if questions of right and wrong, of truth and duty, of patriotism and self-devotion, of justice and humanity, of the good and the beautiful, any light could be shed by a more general knowledge of chemistry, mechanics, or astronomy.

Enough has been said to call forth an inquiry into some of the defects of education as it regards this subject. We can only mention one of the most obvious, at present.

Those powers and faculties of man, which constitute him a social and communicative being, suffer, in common with all other parts of his nature, from *the sedentary habits of modern life.* The modes and character of expression are most intimately connected with the condition of the physical frame. The latter may be, and too generally is, kept, through the habitual neglect of invigorating measures, at too low an ebb for natural, energetic, or vivid expression. A feeble condition of the organic frame, and a consequent imperfection in its functions, have, in their degree, the same effect with actual sickness, in quelling activity and communication. They produce a suspension of sympathetic intercourse, by deadening the interest felt in external relations, and throwing the attention inward upon the morbid sensations arising from impaired vitality. The tendency of the modern student to habits of seclusion and reserve, to the deadness of sympathy, and consequent inefficiency in communication, is owing, in no slight degree, to the absence of enlivening, physical action, one of the main springs of energetic and impressive character. The formation of morbid habits commences even in infancy, and their confirmation is aided by that continual deterioration of health, which necessarily accompanies the perpetually extending requisitions of study, in the course of education. The individual who began his scholastic career with the comparative advantage of three or four hours' recreation a day, closes the critical period of adolesence with the allowance of exercise afforded by his walk, twice a day, to and from the lecture room. What infatuation can exceed that of expecting from this lifeless mechanical being, the attributes of living, eloquent expression, or even of forcible conception or effective diction? Expression, like all other forms of communication, implies that the mind has passed from the negative and the passive, to the positive and the active states. Language, whether oral or written, is a mode of action; and whatever impairs or relaxes activity, quenches expression.

The claims of health on the attention of the studious have, of late years, been enforced with the impressiveness which their vast importance merits, by the sanction of professional authority. Improvements have been effected, also, in some particulars of great moment to the health of childhood and youth, during the progress of education. But nothing adequate to the demands of the human constitution, has yet been attempted; and, certainly, nothing adequate to the cherishing and quickening of those powers which are peculiarly dependent on the condition of the vital functions. A pining and drooping organization affords no possibility of expressive force and life. Nor can the modes of communication ever rise above a barely tolerable mediocrity, or a mere artificial excellence, without the thrilling impulse of pure and vivid health. The stream of feeling must be full to overflowing, in order to impart to thought an effective force, or a wide diffusion.

THE EFFECTS OF DISCIPLINE; A VISIBLE ILLUSTRATION.

'It is *impossible* that persons of so different disposition should harmonize' — says an observer of the quarrels of neighborhoods. 'How can I keep children from quarrelling, when their tempers are so different'— says the parent of a large and ill-governed family, or the teacher of an ill assorted school. We know of no more satisfactory answer to the complaints and difficulties of these unfortunate educators, than the visible illustration of the effects of discipline, which is exhibited in the engraving and the following description. They will see what *kind, judicious, and patient discipline can accomplish,* with the most unpromising subjects.*

'There is a little menagerie in London, where singular associations may be witnessed upon a more extensive scale, and more systematically conducted, than in any other collection of animals with which we are acquainted. Upon the Surry side of Waterloo Bridge, or sometimes, though not so often, on the same side of Southwark Bridge, may be daily seen a cage about five feet square, containing the quadrupeds and birds which are contained in the annexed cut. The keeper of this collection, John Austin, states that he has employed seventeen years in this business of training creatures of opposite natures, to live together in content and affection. And those years have not been unprofitably employed! It is not too much to believe, that many a person who has given his half-penny to look upon this show, may have had his mind awakened to the extraordinary effects of habit and of gentle discipline; when he has thus seen the cat, the rat, the mouse, the hawk, the rabbit, the guinea pig, the owl, the pigeon, the starling, and the sparrow, each enjoying as far as can be enjoyed in confinement, its respective modes of life, in the company of others, — the weak without fear, and the strong without the desire to injure. It is impossible to imagine any prettier exhibition of kindness than is here shown; the rabbit and the pigeon playfully contending for a lock of hay to make up their nests; the sparrow sometimes perched on the head of the cat, and sometimes on that of the owl — each its natural enemy; and the mice playing about with perfect indifference to the presence either of cat, or hawk, or owl. The modes by which this man has effected this, are, first, keeping all the creatures well fed; and secondly, by accustoming one species to the society of the other, at a very early period of their lives. The ferocious instincts of those who prey on the weaker are never called into action; their nature is subdued to a systematic gentleness; the circumstances by which they are surrounded are favorable to the cultivation of their kindlier dispositions; all their desires and pleasures are bounded by their little cage; and though the old cat sometimes takes a stately walk on the parapet of the bridge, he duly returns to his companions with whom he has so long been happy, without at all thinking that he was born to devour any of them. This is an example, and a powerful one, of what may be accomplished by a proper education, which rightly estimates the force of habit, and confirms, by judicious management, that habit which is most desirable to be made a rule of conduct. The principle is the same, whether it be applied to children or to brutes.'

* The account and engraving are from the 'People's Magazine,' a publication which has gained great popularity, and promises to be very useful.

[For the Annals of Education.]

REPLY ON MANUAL LABOR SCHOOLS.

Mr Editor, — I beg your indulgence, while I offer some explanation of the views of the writer of the article upon 'The Pleasures of Labor,' published in the Annals for January last, and some reasons for the peculiarity of those views.

I never thought that labor was better for students than other kinds of exercise, simply because it would make them possessed of a few more pieces of '*coin*,' at the close of their term of study, than they would otherwise own. Doubtless, it is one advantage of the system, that it enables those who are not in affluent circumstances, to obtain an education, which they otherwise could not. But I am far from considering this the principal reason, in favor of Manual Labor Schools.

I do not prefer labor to any substitute for it, which will secure to students a greater amount of physical, intellectual and moral strength. On the contrary, that system, which will do this, shall have my decided preference and cordial support. You ask, 'Is not the life more than meat, and the body than raiment?' I answer, certainly; and that, which tends to make the one longer, happier, or more useful, and the other stronger and better fitted for the vicissitudes through which it must pass, is worthy of all acceptation. Thus much for what I did *not* mean.

I *did* mean, and still believe, that manual labor, in connection with literary pursuits, is the best course that has been devised, to promote the sound exercise of the bodily and mental powers. I did not then, and do not now, intend to interfere with the Medical profession, or to condemn any of their prescriptions. Hence I do not say that the course prescribed by the Paris physician, was not the very best which could have been pursued. I leave invalids to cure themselves or get cured, as they best can. I had, and still have, reference to *Schools* for those who have been less unfortunate — who have never known the miseries of dyspepsia — who, at least, are not considered invalids. *They* cannot be induced to comply with the Paris prescription, for the sake of *preserving* their health, for they know neither the danger or evils of losing that treasure. I believe 'an ounce of preventive is worth a pound of cure,' and, therefore, I think it important that *some* course be adopted, which will secure the health of those, who are not already within the vortex of those diseases, which, it is well known, mar the happiness, and seriously diminish the usefulness of a large part of our literary men.

I have been at some pains to 'review my opinions' upon this subject, and I am yet compelled to believe, that the happiness and interest of every person will be best promoted by a regular system of manual labor. Even though an adult invalid be sufficiently convinced of the imperious necessity of exercise for the body, to induce him to perform daily, a course of gymnastic evolutions; yet, I think I need not ask whether he would not be happier, and relish his exercise better, did he know that himself or some one else was to be directly benefited by what was done, aside from the effect upon his physical powers. Some would be pleased only with that which brought the 'coin' into their own pockets; but I am happy in believing there are few such. But would not the person going to his gymnastic exercise feel more satisfaction in what he was doing, if, for instance, it was the means of establishing a good school, or of improving one already established, or of sending to some one destitute of them, liberty, science, religion, or anything to increase his comfort or happiness? The answer need not be given.

But, to leave this ground, which I had not in my imagination the most distant idea of touching, in my last communication, can gymnastic exercises be made to answer the purpose of labor, in schools generally? It is evident that to leave them without either, is but to suffer students to pursue the broad, beaten track, through the regions of dyspepsia and disease, in its thousand forms and with its attendant miseries, to a premature grave. For students, left to themselves, without any regular and systematic course of exercise, in which all are *required* to join, will never take that amount of exercise, which their physical natures demand. The experience of all ages teaches this, and especially is it proclaimed by our own. Can then, any substitute be found, for labor, which shall be efficacious? Let *facts* answer, for I am fond of reasoning, which is based upon them.

Patronage, in a free country, must surely be considered as the test of popularity, in schools at least. How is it with the schools established with gymnastic exercises? I believe I might begin with the justly celebrated Round Hill and Mount Pleasant institutions in Northampton and Amherst, and almost 'go the rounds' to every school in the land, established upon that plan, and find them — empty — absolutely empty — or rather, the *houses*, for *they* are not. How is it with the gymnastics of Yale? After sending an able agent abroad to collect information and select the best models, and expending large sums to carry their plans into execution, in the best manner, they very soon found they must give up the project. The scheme was unpopular — the students would not conform to it — and now, if I am correctly informed, 'at a great distance in the country,' the instruments are returning to the dust, as they were with great rapidity. Amherst College, I visited last autumn, and gymnastics there were in a wofully dilapidated state. In short, I know not of a school established upon this principle, but has failed; I know not a college which has adopted it, but has relinquished it — failed for want of patronage — relinquished it because they could not sustain it. I do not say there *are* no such schools — but they are unknown to me. I do not say no other causes contributed to their downfall — but I believe this was the principal. Why else have all such schools failed, and no others?

Next look at Manual Labor Schools. Why do we see every one of them constantly full, and rejecting every year, more applicants than they admit, for want of room to receive them? Is not this very strong evidence that students are fond of the system? Besides, I know from personal observation that those, who have never been accustomed to labor, are not less fond of it, after a little practice, than those to whom it is familiar. I have seen young lads too, direct from the city, who had never attempted anything like work, placed at some suitable employment, who would seem to take as much delight, and manifest as much care and attention, as a farmer or planter, whose fortune depended upon his care and success. The consequence is, the exercise is beneficial. But attempt to make a set of school lads or of young men, go through the various movements of the gymnastic exercises; and, as soon as the novelty is over, farewell to all interest in the performance; and then, farewell to most of the benefit they might derive from the exercise properly performed. I wish to keep in view, what I consider a fundamental principle, that, other things being equal, that system of exercise is best, in which most interest is felt by students.

And what do *facts* — what does experience say — is that system? With one accord, so far as I know, they declare that, every system, except that of manual labor, which has yet been adopted for general use, has utterly failed to effect its object. They say, that wherever and whenever that system has been established on a permanent basis, its success has equalled the expectations of its most sanguine friends. It has been found to secure the health of students, and not to retard their intellectual advancement, while, at the same time, it promotes their happiness; and, as a *fourth* advantage, I will add, it confers a pecuniary benefit.

It was with these reasons pressing upon me, that I said in the former article, already alluded to, 'to me the idea of a learned man's advocating the principle that mere child's play is better adapted to engage the attention of a reflecting mind, than what is useful to himself *or others*, is superlatively ridiculous.' After having carefully 'reviewed my opinions,' I am compelled to think as before; because it is contrary to the principles of the human mind, that it should be so, and experience shows that it is not so. Those who have suffered much from disease may be induced to take such exercise, *as medicine;* but healthy youth and children never can. At least, with all the efforts that have been used, they never have, to my knowledge, taken it cheerfully, and, for a long time.

After a little more of *my* experience, I shall no longer intrude upon your readers. With the miseries of dyspepsia, I have been for several years of my life, daily conversant,—I have drunk the dregs of the loathsome cup. Now, probably, few more robust and healthy persons than myself, can be found. A change of diet and a regular course of bodily exercise have produced this result, to effect which I tried many physicians, mineral springs, and even the ocean, in vain. It is exercise, and nothing else, which keeps my physical powers in tune. Of this, I have *convincing proof,* whenever I neglect it. I have labored and received remuneration. I have labored with as much pleasure and assiduity, where I did not expect or receive a 'farthing in coin'—I have taken, and, from necessity do daily take exercise, in ways different from either of these; but it has not that charm which attends that taken in the other cases. For instance; I walk five or six miles before breakfast; but, if I accomplish nothing except to obtain the exercise, it confers but a small share of the benefit or pleasure, which I should derive, could I walk three miles, and induce a man to subscribe for the Annals of Education, and then walk back. Or, if I could, in any other way, advance the cause of truth, or increase the happiness of a fellow being, or better his condition, the result would be the same. If there lives a man, who would take pleasure *rather* in that which is useless in other respects except to his bodily health, I would advise him, by all means, to seek exercise of that kind.

If there be one who cannot find labor to perform, I advise him by all means, to *exercise in some way* his physical powers. Still, it is true that, since students generally cannot be prevailed upon to take sufficient exercise, in any other way, the idea of a wise man's opposing the general introduction of manual labor into literary institutions appears 'superlatively ridiculous' to me; *not* without any decisive evidence against his opinions,' but because they are opposed to important and unchanging truth.

A COUNTRY TEACHER.

We leave it for our readers to compare the remarks of our correspondent with our own. We would only add, that many of our *Manual Labor Schools* have failed; that some of the most valuable of our High Schools still exist, perhaps as many as of the

Manual Labor Schools — and that we consider their success or failure, in both cases, as often arising from causes entirely foreign to the subject of labor. Our correspondent will admit, that public opinion or prejudice, is not argument, and that the prejudice of Americans is no more evidence of the inutility of gymnastics, than former prejudices were, of the folly of building steamboats; and *we* shall not cease to maintain, that manual labor is *generally* the best mode of exercise.—EDITOR.

MANUAL LABOR DEPARTMENT OF THE LANE SEMINARY.

THE fourth Annual Report of the Lane Seminary at Cincinnati, Ohio, has recently appeared, and contains much that is interesting in reference to manual labor.

This institution is another of those 'Visible Illustrations of Benevolence,' which are so rapidly and so happily multiplying in our country. It owes its origin to the benevolence of a single merchant, and its broad foundation to individual contributions; and the fact that these were chiefly presented by '*the East*' to 'the West,' affords gratifying evidence that narrow, local feeling is not yet predominant over the spirit of beneficence. The Seminary has three professors in the theological department, and three in the department of preparatory study, which is designed for those whose age or circumstances prevent their pursuing a collegiate course. One building for one hundred students, and two houses for professors, are already built, and a chapel is soon to be erected. In consequence of the provision of funds, the expenses of each student do not exceed $60 or $80 annually.

But the principal peculiarity in this institution is in its provisions for manual labor, and the ground on which it is placed. It is with peculiar pleasure that we find '*physical education*' spoken of, in connection with 'talents and acquisitions,' and the 'spirit of holiness,' as '*of fundamental importance* to ministerial energy and success.' When will the acknowledged truth, that 'the mind is influenced by the state of the body,' be adopted *practically*, in our schemes of education! On the subject of manual labor in connection with study, the Committee remark in general:

'Whatever may be the theoretical objections of good men, practically unacquainted with this system, to its practicability and importance, it is to the directors no longer a matter of experiment, but of sober fact, resulting from three or four year's experience, that the connection of three hours daily labor, in some useful and interesting employment with study, protects the health and constitution of our young men; greatly augments their physical energy; furnishes to a considerable extent, or entirely, the means of self-education; increases their power of intellectual acquisition; facilitates their actual progress in study; removes their temptations to idleness; confirms their habits of industry; gives them a practical acquaintance with the useful employments of life; fits them for the toils and responsibilities of a newly settled country, and inspires them with the independence of character, and the originality of investigation, which belong peculiarly to self-made and self-educated men.

They make one remark, which we presume will explain more than one of those failures which have led some to doubt the practicability of the system:

'No small injury is threatened to manual labor institutions, and no small embarrassment has been felt by this Seminary in common with others, in consequence of the erroneous impression too commonly prevalent, that no funds will be needed in a manual labor institution, even when the student has no trade, no knowledge of any kind of business, no power of accomplishment, and little disposition to perform the labor offered him, as a means of paying his expenses.

'The committee need not inform such young men, and the community generally, that no institution can long sustain itself and prosper under such circumstances.'

While they consider the pecuniary benefit of the plan as of minor importance, compared with the health and vigor it produces, the report furnishes encouraging evidences that much may be done in this respect under favorable circumstances. In consequence of the contiguity of the Seminary to Cincinnati, printing has been introduced as one branch of labor, and the novelty and success of this department renders the details interesting.

'During the early part of the last year, an arrangement was entered into by the committee, with Messrs Corey & Fairbank, booksellers of Cincinnati, to furnish the students with several printing presses, and with stereotype plates for printing Webster's spelling-book. This establishment has been in operation nearly a year, and now embraces six presses, furnishing work for twenty students.

About 150,000 copies of the above named work have been printed, and about 1000 copies per day are now issued from the presses.

The students have recently commenced the printing of an edition of Dr Eberle's treatise on the diseases of children, a valuable medical work, which requires fine paper and the best workmanship; and it is believed that in all respects the execution of the work is highly satisfactory to the employers.

The report from which we are quoting, is a very handsome specimen of the skill of the students. In regard to pecuniary results, the Committee state:

'The average amount earned by six printers in ten months by working about three hours per day, ...	$120,00
'Average amount earned at the same rate in a year, . .	144,00
'Amount now earned by twenty students per week, .	50,82

'Average amount (by each student), ...	2,54
'Average amount earned by twenty students at the same rate as above per year, ...	132,08

'In view of these results, and the small annual expense of this institution, it is hardly necessary to remark, that the students in this department have the high satisfaction of providing the means of their own education without aid from friends, or from the benefactions of the church.

'This arrangement is the more important for our young men, from the fact that a knowledge of the business is easily acquired; several of the students having gained such an acquaintance with the employment in three or four weeks, as to be able to earn fortysix cents per day, or two dollars and seventysix cents per week, by working three hours per day.

'This operation is highly satisfactory to the Committee, not only as furnishing a useful and advantageous employment to the students, but as it is unattended with any expense to the institution in furnishing presses, or in the printing and disposition of the books. From nearly a year's full experiment the Committee are fully persuaded, that this branch of our manual labor has peculiar advantages in respect to its simplicity, its appropriate exercise, its general utility, and pecuniary results.

'In accordance with the special request of the printers' association of this institution, it is intended, as soon as practicable, to adopt measures for the extension of this establishment; and from the facilities here enjoyed for conducting the printing business, it is hoped that a large portion of our students, at no very distant period, may enjoy the advantage of this employment.'

In the cabinet shops connected with the Institution, materials have been furnished, and work paid for, by an establishment in Cincinnati. The whole is placed under the superintendence of some of the most skilful workmen among the students, who are responsible to the employers for all that is done, and have secured a pecuniary profit of $701,35 in five months. The profit to individuals is thus stated by the Committee:

'Several of the best workmen have earned from twelve and a half to fifteen cents per hour, and have received for their services during the time above specified, from forty to sixty dollars each; while those who have recently commenced learning the business, have earned from ten to twenty dollars each.

'While the fact is here rendered obvious, that a first rate mechanic is entirely independent in this Institution, and can support himself by his three hours' labor without infringing at all upon his study hours; the Committee wish it to be understood that such results are secured only by young men of energetic, industrious, and economical habits; and that those of different character, and who have little or no knowledge of tools, ought not to rely, to any considerable extent, at least for the first year, upon their labor as the means of paying the expenses of the institution.'

A farm of 110 acres, is also annexed to the institution, from which, additional advantages are anticipated.

Such are the results of one of the most recent experiments on the manual labor system, and they seem to us to confirm the position we have maintained, that while this, like every other system of education, needs *a foundation* on which to rest, and the faithful, persevering efforts of skilful agents — it may be made a means of *economy* in education, and of imparting that vigor of constitution which renders that education doubly valuable, and secures to the individual, enjoyments and hopes which are beyond all price.

HINTS TO YOUNG TEACHERS.

Mr Woodbridge, — To you, sir, I have taken the liberty to address this letter, for several reasons. A strong and eloquent appeal, by a late writer in the Christian Examiner, — said to be the Rev. Dr Channing, — in favor of education, and your work in particular, as most useful in its cause, attracted my attention to it, and led me to think it possible, that some occasional papers, illustrative of the effects of certain commonly pursued methods, whether evil or good, — of the great diversity in the characters of children — and the variety of effects which the same treatment would consequently produce, under the same and different circumstances — together with results which a critical attention to minute experiences has taught me, &c, &c, — might be useful and not inappropriate to the pages of your periodical. They may also serve to illustrate the erroneous ideas entertained of school-keeping as a profession, which are referred to in the article I have mentioned.

Experience.

HINTS TO YOUNG TEACHERS. NO. I.

A good Teacher must unite, in a greater or less degree, all the qualities requisite in a good parent. Let us examine if this assertion be not strictly true. If it were proper to speak of any one *essential* more necessary than others to the perfection of school-keeping, I should mention *moral discipline;* and where is the degree of patience, gentleness, moderation, firmness, self-command, judgment, feeling, intelligence, not demanded for this? Without all these qualities in the instructor, his pupils will not be led to love and reverence him — if they cannot love and reverence, they will not obey him; if they do not obey, they will not receive his instructions. Doubtless, there have been teachers who have commanded affection *or* fear, (I question if *both*) without having the art of imparting knowledge; and some who have possessed this power, without the others. But I would give little for what a child would acquire under such circumstances. Even a *greater* degree of *decision of character* and knowledge of human nature, is required in the teacher of a miscellaneous school, than in a parent, because the variety of dispositions and capacities, which he has to manage and direct, each requiring different treatment, is greater. The teacher, while he is necessarily uninfluenced by the ill judging, and often injurious partiality of a parent, has not, on the other hand, the warm affection which a natural claim inspires; to cheer him through his arduous undertaking. At the same time, forbearance and tenderness are equally required of him, and no one can deny, that as much, at least, of genuine and scientific knowledge should be the property of the teacher as of the parent.

These remarks might be very disheartening to young teachers conscious of imperfections, and with an humble estimate of their own capacity, were it for a moment to be imagined that all this is to be accomplished and acquired at once. On the contrary, it will be only after long practice, much effort, and the strongest desire that all, or any of these results can be obtained; but with these, there is little doubt, that success will follow. There are, indeed, many teachers, who undertake the employment, from mixed, and perhaps, *wholly selfish* motives, and who go on for years without learning to feel one great aim — one noble purpose — who pursue their occupation as a task, finish it as soon as they can; and when out of their hands, put it out of their thoughts. Yet, let us observe, that these persons know nothing of the elevated delights of their employment; they have all the drudgery indeed, but they have none of the pleasures, the rewards of the exercise. As Fenelon so beautifully says of religion — 'They perceive what it deprives them of — but they do not see what it bestows; they exaggerate its sacrifices without looking at its consolations.'

Others beginning to teach from the very same motive, indeed, without realizing that there can be any other, very soon begin to discern the world of thoughts and action, beyond the limits of their first feeble view — begin, perhaps painfully, to realize all they should, but do not, accomplish; and will be discouraged or stimulated, according to their peculiar character, by this conviction. If discouraged they often do injustice to themselves, their pupils and their God. If stimulated, still, it is only after long, anxious experience, and perhaps extreme mental suffering, where the character is sensitive, that any degree of the desired preparation is obtained. It is to persons in these circumstances that I would venture to present my own history, as a young teacher, with many of the feelings which have been described.

At an early age, and with only such knowledge as the best public schools of the time afforded, (for my parents were too much straitened to afford me any farther education,) I was led by the strong stimulus of duty to my parents and myself, to open a private school. I had no distinct idea, at the time, of benefiting others. Having no experience, I had little knowledge of what was in fact required by my Creator, for so responsible an office, farther than this — I had been blessed with the purest moral and religious, and, I may add, intellectual instruction, from the best of parents; and my motto had always been, that whatever we think we can do, and resolutely determine to accomplish, may, in fact, be done, and done well; and in this belief, and with the highest standard as to what a good Teacher *ought to be*, but with scarcely any idea of the difficulties and trials of the preliminary steps, I set about my arduous task.

The most painful discipline I ever endured, was in *learning to teach*, or rather, in learning *to govern myself*. Government of my pupils, and all other externals of school-keeping, I found perfectly easy; but it was not till the last six months of the several successive years, during which I was engaged in the occupation, that I was able to reach the standard I had marked for myself, without a degree of mental endurance, which the strongest motives could have alone enabled me to bear. During these last happy months, however, I had the exalted privilege of believing, that while ministering to the improvement of others, I had conquered myself, and that the moral and intellectual fruits I was enabled to mature in the minds committed to my charge, were yielded with as much ease and delight to them, as to my own heart. Perhaps I should be permitted to observe, that my success in every outward view had been very great; far beyond my most sanguine expectations; and had my own approbation but equalled that I received from others, my present recollections of the period, would be entirely satisfactory. But it was not so — my conscience sensitive — and my standard proportionably high — bitter have sometimes been my feelings, on realizing how far below it, I have frequently fallen.

In these remarks on myself and my situation, I would not be understood to suppose, that all those I am addressing are in parallel circumstances; some of them may have precisely contrary difficulties; some of them may have found self-government easy, and that of their pupils, difficult; while others, again, may have found both a minor trouble, while the power of *making their pupils learn*, may be the prime object of their solicitude; and, in short, a catalogue of different trials connected with school-keeping, might be brought forward by each. It is my earnest wish to make use, both of my success and of my failures, for their good; to give practical remarks or examples of those parts of the employment, in which I was so happy as to succeed; and to offer them the benefit of my experience in those, in which I had the grief to fail.

[For the Annals of Education.]

EXTREMES IN EDUCATION.

The maxim is not more trite than just, that 'human nature is prone to extremes.' If verified nowhere else, it is true in the world of education. There is constantly a tendency among instructors, when departing from what has been found to be an error, to diverge as widely from truth in the opposite direction.

One instructor finds he has been in the wrong, not to keep his pupils constantly employed. In his solicitude to furnish them with something to do, he is apt to overlook utility, or at least he does not attend sufficiently to their capacities and their health; and *jades* them with *employment* as he had before disgusted them with *confinement* and *monotony*.

Another, who has long been in the habit of trying to make his scholars 'study hard *continually*' under all circumstances, finds, at length, that it is one thing to hold a book before the face, and quite another to study it; and concludes to give up the forcing scheme. But in so doing he usually departs to the other extreme — that of leaving them to choose whether they will study or not, and of suffering them to float down the stream of indolence. He forgets that in leaving human nature to its own course, he leaves it sadly in danger of going wrong; that nothing is gained in the intellectual or moral world without active effort — without *opposing the current;* — and though he may not believe with the celebrated Dr Good, that no human being would lift a finger if he could help it, he will probably be compelled to the conclusion, that it must never be wholly optional with children, whether they will study or not.

He who has long been in the habit of inflicting corporal punishment, but who has seen instances where it did not produce the expected results, and perhaps the contrary, adopts a new theory. He believes that *all* punishment which produces bodily pain is wrong. This may go well for a time with some teachers, and in some schools; but in large establishments, the inmates of which have been collected together suddenly, especially if the teacher has neither been taught nor disciplined himself, it will never succeed. For though force should rarely be used, even with the rod, (which is, perhaps, the least objectionable form,) yet there must be power in reserve, and the scholars must know it.

One teacher has become convinced that he has been too reserved with his pupils. But in becoming more familiar than before, he loses their respect. Why so? Because he goes too far, and in putting off *distance*, becomes a mere playfellow. Just so in regard to school books and school lessons; and a hundred other things that might be mentioned, did my limits permit.

Some of the more prominent errors to which I have alluded, deserve a further consideration. And first, the present disposition among parents and teachers to dispense with *hard study*. There can be no doubt that children have formerly been tasked too much; or at least, in an improper manner. They have been confined too long at once to a subject which was beyond their capacity, to benches and air which were uncomfortable and unwholesome, to discipline which was unmeaning, and to books which needed much explanation and illustration. None of these circumstances are necessarily connected with study; and yet quite too many of them have pretty uniformly been *associated* with it.

At the present time, more attention is, in some instances, paid to the physical condition of children than formerly, and they are not so rigidly confined. The discipline is less tyrannical, and where it is not wholly *lost*, more parental. Books and apparatus of almost every kind are provided, and with means so abundant, he is regarded as stupid, who will not try *some* method of awakening in the minds of his scholars an interest in their studies.

But now too, all the rage is for excitement — frequent or constant excitement. In furnishing books which shall be intelligible, we are falling fast into the habit of furnishing those which *require no thought*.

All the scholar has to do, is to glance along superficially, over their lines and pages. Their meaning, when there is any, is on the surface. There is no purer water or finer gold discovered, by digging deep. The scholar acquires, and perhaps retains for life, the habit of looking over the surface *only*.

The same effect is *often* produced by *apparatus* and all other sorts of labor-saving machinery. The pupil uses all these, which are intended only as *aids* in his progress, and which in this view are of great value, as *substitutes for hard study*.

I might have adverted to the *arrangement of class books*. To *aid the teacher*, by leading him to a thorough and practical course of examination on the lessons which he assigns his pupils, many of our most valuable class books are provided with *questions*. Though seldom if ever intended, the result of this arrangement is, that the *pupil* seizes eagerly on the questions, and does not attempt to think for himself. Perhaps the teacher, to save time and labor, not only allows the practice, but even encourages him in it. Here then, mechanism, and consequent superficiality come in. The pupil is apt to *associate* the question with the answer, without fully understanding either; and only secure a little of the outside of the mass of knowledge, while the pile of richer ore remains untouched.

Let me advert to one thing more, in the catalogue of labor-saving machinery. The multitudes of teachers, or rather of monitors, in some of our large schools, is exceedingly unfavorable. Not that a great number of teachers, is in itself undesirable. With thorough discipline and proper arrangement, at least as many teachers in a school, as there are different branches taught, might be useful. But even in that case, each should be master of his art. It is true, that great good is often done by means of monitors *from the classes*; but who can doubt for one moment, that much greater good would be the result, were the acquirements of the monitors more extensive and thorough?

Their instructions readily become superficial, and are also *substituted, often, for hard study*. Recitations are, indeed, more frequent, but their results are not apt to be permanent on the mind of the pupil. It is otherwise, I admit, with the monitor; for if he does *his* duty, whatever becomes of the pupils, *he* must *study* —and study *hard*, too — and as 'teaching we learn,' monitors themselves usually make very considerable progress.

If the foregoing remarks are not true, how happens it that the pupils in many of our schools — and, of the more popular ones, too; — always appear to disadvantage in practical life, when compared with some of those whose facilities for improvement fall far short of theirs; — I mean when we compare *means*, as well as results?

Nothing seems to me more obvious, than that both sexes in New England, were far better qualified to fill stations of *usefulness* — real, solid usefulness in society, as society was fifty years ago—than they now are. In other words, instruction was far better adapted to the *times* than it now is. I am well aware of the truth of the remark, that while *young* men are ever looking *forward* to the 'golden age,' *old men* are as constantly dwelling on the wisdom and excellence of past things and times; and though I do not yet belong to the *latter class*, I have not made my statements without some allowance for the partialities of the aged.

Fifty years ago, there was, of necessity, no way of accomplishing anything, *but* by hard study; and this gave energy to the mind. No picture-book manufacturer had then arisen to *enervate*, while he enlightens by his labors; and by a multitude of dishes highly seasoned, and by the choicest condiments, to tickle and please the palate, for a short time, to spoil the appetite in the end, and thus defeat his better intentions. No apparatus builder had then blessed us with his labors, till we had learned to turn the fruits of those labors into curses. *What was done*, was better — far better — done then, than now.

But the worst evil of labor-saving machinery, in all of its forms, is, that while it indirectly renders study unfashionable, mental *discipline* at the same time, is sickening and dying. Each pupil should come from school, well disciplined — rendered a good soldier for life. He should *not* come forth in the wretched habit of having *every thing done for him*, by books, and apparatus, and instruction; but in the more rational habit of *doing every thing for himself*; and of compelling all around him — men, things and circumstances — to become, in a certain sense, his books, apparatus, and teachers. X.

[For the Annals of Education.]

COMMON SCHOOLS AND COMMON EDUCATION.

NO. III.

OBSERVATION, EXPERIENCE, READING.

In the Annals for March I addressed the highest class in common schools. Before this number is issued, many of these will be dispersed, and the rising youth will be mingled with their elders, in the various employments of life; amidst which, young and old together are wont to be without plan and effect for their own improvement. I will come now to neither portion of society, separately, as in my two former numbers, but as more suited to my double title, to the mixed community, to the youthful and adult population — to suggest the *method*, from the *sources* of improvement.

It were folly to write on this subject merely for the young, as if they, *only*, were susceptible of improvement, or as if they could be advanced amidst gross, public, (especially parental) indifference and neglect. We have tried this long enough. It is time to address society as it is; to urge *all ages* to what belongs to all, and what can only be secured by the combination of all. It is time to think, and write, and speak of 'education' *out of school*, and *after school*, with all the earnestness we have been wont to urge it *in* school, if we would secure the improvement of society at large, or even of the schools themselves. I mean, then, what I say for all, *in* school or *out*, well-inclined or disinclined; in short, *for every body*. I am ashamed of my countrymen, and countrywomen as well as of the schools of men and women, as well as of boys and girls, that do not improve themselves. How idly they live! How little they learn! What mental drones! How little they advance, in wisdom and skill, and virtue, from sixteen to seventy! We have set half Europe mad, by our boasting of the improvement of 'the people.' We have declared ourselves wise enough to instruct in the halls of legislation, to direct the councils of government, and to bless ages yet unborn. And yet how idly we live! how little we learn from sixteen to seventy! Fie upon us, to keep up this noisy boasting, when nine in ten of us take as little pains to improve ourselves, as if wisdom *grew* upon Republicans, upon Americans, like fruit upon the trees; or as if *we* were wise by instinct, like the beasts and birds! Fie upon us, to boast of our wisdom, when we leave off the toil of getting it, as soon we are left to ourselves; when we drop the miner's tools as soon as our parents or masters have shown us the way to the veins of gold! Fie upon us, to boast in our manhood, when we have left the diligence, and pains, and progress, of even our infancy and childhood! Fie, fie upon us, to be boasting aloud before all the world, that *we* can steer across the sea of self-government, and give convoy to all the nations of the earth, when we will not even study the navigation of our own little bark along the narrow streams of common life. I write, then (good for little as my words may be), for all who need '*schooling;*' and they are many, even from childhood to grey hairs. I should be glad to be read in every school, at every fireside, in every parlor in this land. I shall not, I trust, write so ill as to be useless, if I am read. Let me then try, again, my 'circle of persuasion.' If I succeed with the scholar, I shall send *him home*, an example to the family, to influence father and mother, and brother and sister, by his diligence and success. If I succeed with the family, I shall send a new set of pupils to the school, and in both ways justify my double title —'*Common Schools and Common Education.*'

I proceed, then, in my present number, to address THE PEOPLE — *youthful and adult*, — on the *method*, necessary to reach the *sources* of improvement. It is by *observation*, *experience and reading*, that we draw from the sources of improvement.

What *observation* is, and how it is concerned in improvement, may be explained from the history of infancy. The infant begins 'to take notice.' How significant, now, is that eye, which a little while ago seemed but to shut and open, but to sleep and wake! What meaning it expresses — what delight — what dislike! How it proves itself the organ of communication with the inward soul! The ear, indeed, does not, like the eye, indicate, by any expression of its own, what influences pass through its winding passages, but the whole countenance and every motion of the limbs tell us that the child does 'take notice' of sound, in all its varieties of tone and articulation, and is roused to feeling, and thought, and action by its wonderful power: and it is especially by means of the ear, he becomes a student and an adept in his own mother tongue. The same is true of all his other senses. 'He takes notice' of impressions which are made upon them by surrounding objects, by men and things; and thus becomes gradually and rapidly acquainted with the little world in which he moves. The infant is an *observer*. He learns from *observation*.

And what is *experience?* That, too, may be explained by the history of infancy. The infant increases in knowledge and skill by *trying experiments* upon what he observes, — by adding experience to observation. Every one of those little philosophers 'tries experiments,' and thus learns the uses and abuses of all that he observes. Eyes, ears, hands, feet, the floor, the chairs, the blocks, the toys, and his own feelings and thoughts, everything around him, and within him, he brings to the test of experiment, with surprising activity and diligence; and after trying again and again, he comes at length to know, what is the use and abuse of all he meets with in his little world. As observation extends to the character and conduct of others, he keeps testing everything by his experiments, and learns by experience how to conduct himself in the little society into which he was born. Happy are those children who find, in the world of living beings around them, the principles of rational, moral and religious life, true and pure, — like the laws of nature, which were the first objects of their observation and experience. Happy are those, whose parents are not guilty, by their folly and false principles, of making their children either knaves or fools; who, when their children try experiments on *them*, give no sanction to falsehood and deception, no premium to ignorance and weakness!

The powers of observation and experience, thus exerted in infancy, are undoubtedly greater and more various in childhood and manhood; while higher motives prompt to their exertion, and better aids are given at every step in the progress of life. Self-improvement must, of course, depend upon the use or abuse of these growing powers — of our increasing opportunity. Our own listlessness and indolence, the misguidance of others, and the misgovernment of ourselves, may check, and almost stop, the hopeful beginnings of infancy. Whoever will not 'take notice and try experiments,' will gain little or nothing, as he reaches constantly a wide and still wider field of observation and experience. He may pass the 'smoke of his chimney,' may leave his neighborhood, or his country, may mingle in all scenes, and be called to acts, opinions, and decisions, and remain as ignorant and unskilful as before. '*There* is a man,' said Dr Johnson, pointing to an old friend, 'who had lived fifty years without experience!' This man had the opportunities of advancing life, but he had lost *the methods of infancy*, and became neither more wise, nor more skilful. Thus, in ten thousand cases, improvement ceases, or at least falls short of the growing powers and necessities, as soon as men have reached the point which secures a moderate supply to their animal wants; — as soon as by their rational nature, they have secured the bare purpose of the instinct of the brutes! No wonder at the corresponding fact — which claims the attention of all who are anxious for the improvement of the rising generation — that parents and teachers, the 'educators' of the young, should prove mistaken and misguiding guides, in a path from which they so early turned aside!

On the other hand, improvement *must* be secured to all the periods of life, if the methods which Providence has secured to infancy, be pursued — in proportion as we are well guided and well governed by ourselves and others. Whoever will 'take notice,' and 'try experiments,' as diligently, as constantly, and with as free scope as an infant, cannot fail of improvements, more and more rapid and extensive, at every period of life, from childhood to youth, and from youth until the powers shall decay in extreme old age. No situation in life, open to the air and light, amidst the works of God and the ways of men, can be so retired, as not to afford boundless scope to observation and experience — as not to furnish objects and subjects for the longest life. All that is wanting is, that the child, with new advantages and new motives, should keep up the observation and experience by which it made the improvements of infancy, and that the man, again, with new advantages and new motives, should keep up the observation and experience of infancy and childhood. Look and try, amidst all the scenes of nature and society. The fields, groves, beasts, birds, insects, stones, plants, the family, the neighborhood, yourself — are not these subjects enough for your observation and experience? Are not these inexhaustible sources of improvement? Keep eye, and ear, and every sense, and every faculty attentive and alert, and the improvements of childhood and manhood will proceed, as did the improvements of infancy.

A familiar illustration of 'observation,' is given in the pleasant dialogue of 'Eyes and no Eyes,' in the 'Evenings at Home.' Two boys are represented giving an account of their walk over the same ground. They both had eyes. One boy returned from a *dull* walk — had seen nothing interesting — had learned nothing useful, because, though he had eyes, he had '*no eyes*;' i. e. he did not use his eyes to see with; or, did not take notice of what he saw, so as to make it the subject of thought. The other boy had eyes and *used them*; saw and took notice of a great many agreeable objects, and was led by seeing them, to a great number of useful reflections. How many people, young and old, are like the former boy — they have eyes, and no eyes — ears, and no ears — senses, and no senses — faculties, and no faculties — reason, judgment, memory, and no reason, judgment, and memory. Amidst ten thousand wonders, they see nothing, hear nothing, learn nothing.

The Rev. Mr White, of Selbourne, England, was himself a striking instance of observation, as we learn from his book, entitled 'The Natural History of Selbourne*;' and his example shows, what an ample range every one has, without going far from home. If your observation should be limited to your own neighborhood or parish, you would never have finished all that would be new, interesting, and instructive; you would be still finding novelties, beauties, wonders, as long as you should live. Try, and see!

All the improvements that you have made, or seen made, in common sense and practical wisdom, or in any of the arts of life, are so many illustrations of the effects of observation, united with experience. The mechanic, the farmer, the merchant, the scholar, the physician, the statesman, the divine, having all attained skill in their respective arts, owe it in a high degree to the united effect of observation and experience. They have taken notice and tried experiments. So is it with all who have become wise in conducting affairs public and private. All the improvements which have been made in the powers by which machinery is moved, and in the use of machinery, all the inventions and discoveries which have added to the blessings of life, are the results of Observation and Experience. Thus Franklin's observations and experiments, in the ways of men, gave him his practical wisdom, and common sense; those on lightning, have given us the lightning rod. The observation and experiments of Watt, and Fulton, and others, have given us the steam engine and steam boat, a steam loom and printing press, and travelling car. Thus, also, Whitney invented the gin, which picks the seed from the cotton; and Arkwright, the jenny that spins it; and thus inventions have been multiplied, until one man can conduct the work of hundreds. In like manner, too, have the greatest wonders of science been performed. Observation and experiments have enabled astronomers to measure the distances and size, determine the motions, and calculate the times of the planets, and prepared telescopes which show to us innumerable stars, unseen by the naked eye.

But these illustrations of observation and experience cannot be gained nor could they all exist, without *reading*, which gives the observation and experience of others. You must *read*, in order to

* Republished by G. & C. Merriam. Springfield.

guide, correct, extend, and perfect, your own observation and experience. You cannot of yourselves go to all the sources of knowledge. You would need more than ten thousand lives, to learn the internal structure, or the outer surface, or the infinitely varied productions and inhabitants, of the world you live in. And, certainly, a thousand lives would not enable you to find out what has been, and thus to lay the foundation for wisdom, as to what is or will be. You must go then to BOOKS — to the records of the observation and experience of other men — and by the aid of their remarks improve your own methods of observing, and correct the results, and ascertain general principles by comparison. Observation and experience, without reading, are often like a watch without a regulator — ever too fast or too slow.

PRIVATE SCHOOLS OF PROVIDENCE.

THE 'First School' was taught by the Creator himself. The Second School was confided to the care of monitors, and was divided into *private classes or schools*; increasing in number, with the multiplication of our race; and thus, each man is made, to some extent, responsible for the welfare and character of others, as well as for his own. The constitution and organization of these private schools, emanating, as they do, from Infinite Wisdom, deserve to be examined in detail.

I. Two monitors were appointed to each school, and uniformly, *one of each sex*. In the expressive language of a German writer — 'Man and Woman are the corner stones, of human life, the personification of power and love — man is the reflection of the DIVINE ALL POWER — woman, of the DIVINE ALL LOVE.' In the deity, both are united. The union of both is necessary, in order to conduct education aright; and we constantly find a deficiency, where it is confided to either sex, exclusively.*

II. The office of these monitors is permanent. They are usually appointed and removed only by the Creator; and are invested with absolute power, no control or interference being allowed, except in cases of gross neglect or ill treatment. With these exceptions, their rights have been held inviolate, by human laws, except in a

* It is surely false philosophy, which deems this necessary, only in mixed establishments; for each pupil *naturally* possesses the character of his own sex; and if the design be to modify or perfect the character, it must be accomplished by the reflection of other qualities, from the other sex.

few small communities, now passed away; and are questioned, only by a few visionary theorists, in modern times.

III. By the ordinance of the Creator, this absolute power is placed under the direction of undying, self-forgetting, parental love — and unfortunate is he, who has an instructor that is destitute of this qualification for his office.

IV. The pupils of these schools are almost always sent singly — never more than two or three at once — and at distant intervals. The monitors are thus gradually prepared for their important task, and are enabled to train the first, as guides to those that follow.

V. Each of these schools is intended, at the same time, to be a seminary of monitors; and those who superintend them, are expected to prepare them for this office.

VI. In order to give education its full influence, the pupils are sent, before their dispositions and propensities are strengthened by habit, to be continued in the same school, and subjected to the same influences, until their education is completed.

VII. The number of pupils in each school is limited — seldom exceeding ten, and scarcely ever reaching twenty.

VIII. These schools are generally composed of pupils of both sexes; and it is remarkable that a plan, generally considered dangerous, proves so safe in practice. Although the pupils are accustomed to the most constant and familiar intercourse, from infancy to childhood, and even to old age, these schools are distinguished for a degree of purity far beyond those of a single sex, although subjected to a discipline incomparably less severe. Let him that doubts, compare the *families* of any country, with its *boarding schools*, or *colleges*, or *monasteries*, or *camps!*

IX. Objects and their names are the first subjects of instruction; and observation, experiment, and imitation are the principal methods employed.*

X. These schools are organized for *education*, in its widest sense; and the most careful training must be combined with instruction.

To those who have visited one of these private schools, conducted as it should be, by the union of enlightened power and chastened love — who have seen the spirit of heaven, which breathes through its atmosphere — we need say nothing to prompt a wish that such could be the only schools of childhood, and a sigh, that any other should be necessary.

* See p. 172 – 3.

[For the Annals of Education.]

NAUTICAL SCHOOLS.

Dear Sir, — Amid all the interesting matter touching the cause of education, with which your pages abound, I do not remember to have seen any article on the particular subject of *nautical education.*

It is undoubtedly true, that the importance of education in its fullest acceptation, and, more especially, elementary education, is not duly appreciated by any community on earth — I mean if we are to judge of the views of mankind by their every day practice. It is, however, no less true, that public attention, in many parts of our country, has been more directly turned to this subject of late, and that great efforts have been made, and are still making, to wake up the benevolent, the enlightened, the patriotic, and the Christian, to the immense and paramount importance of an increased education of the people, who are to decide the destinies of this immense and growing republic. But in looking at a subject in its general bearings and relations, we often lose sight of its particular divisions and the relative importance of its various parts. It has thus happened, probably, that the education of seamen, as a class, has attracted but little attention and interest.

The time was, when all the claims of seamen were dreadfully neglected — when they were used only like the vessels they manned, and the sails they unfurled to the breeze or reefed in the gale, to bear the cargoes of their employers to foreign lands, and return with the produce of other countries, to enrich their owners. Under such a state of things, what could be expected of seamen, exiled from society, for the greater part of the time, exposed to hardships and perils, unknown to landsmen, with no guide but their passions? Is it surprising, that when released from the temporary restraints of their captains, and from the duties of the ship, they should riot in vice and misery?

Such was the history of seamen, to a lamentable extent, at home and abroad. *At home* — they felt like strangers and outcasts, and were welcomed to no society, but that which would enervate their bodies, and pollute and destroy their souls — filch their money, and debase and paralyze all the finer feelings of their nature. *Abroad* — they were induced to seek the vicious indulgences to which they had been trained at home.

But the scene is now changed. American Seamen, at least, are beginning to be regarded as men — as immortal — as having rights and immunities, sacred and valuable. Those who have hitherto fattened on their misery, have begun to tremble.

Their claims are heard — thought of — respected ;— their wants, in a measure, provided for ; — their morals considered and guarded. Hence we see *Bethels* arising all through the land in our cities, where they may meet to worship God — *Boarding Houses*, where they can resort in safety, and be free from temptation — *Savings Banks*, where they may lay aside their earnings, to provide against age, sickness and want, instead of ministering to their appetites and vicious propensities ; — and hence we hope to see *Seminaries*, intended and adapted for their instruction in common branches of education, and in nautical science.

I am aware, that one or two such schools have been established, and that more are contemplated ; but it is highly desirable to call the attention of the public generally to this subject, and to impress them with the importance and the expediency of establishing many such institutions.

It would be unnecessary to detain your readers by any remarks as to the importance of education in the common branches, to any individuals in the community. But I will say, that seamen need such instruction, especially, and that they are in peculiar danger of being overlooked.

They need it especially. If they are untaught when they go to sea, as too many of them are, pride and shame will tend to keep them ignorant. If they cannot read or write, how many hours at sea will be wasted, that might else be profitably employed ! Their minds will be stored with vice and profanity, for lack of better instruction. But the evil does not stop here. If they are ignorant of the rudiments of knowledge, they cannot learn navigation as a science ; and are shut out from all hope of rising above the rank of a common sailor.

They are in peculiar danger of being overlooked. Most seamen go to sea when they are young, and of course, if not early instructed, they are left entirely to themselves for life. Others, of their age, may be also neglected in youth ; but change of place, or circumstances, may favor them with instruction in the family, the store, the familiar lecture, or some association for mutual improvement.

Some such system as the following, might be adopted to advantage.

1. Let merchants and captains give preference to young seamen who can read and write.

2. Let a Nautical school be established in every seaport town in the country ; where not only Navigation shall be taught at a moderate price to all who desire to be instructed, but connected with which shall be a master devoted to teaching elementary branches of common education.

3. Let merchants, and others interested in seamen, recommend

to their crews to resort to these schools, and perhaps pay a bounty, to such seamen as bring certificates of proficiency from the instructor.

Should you deem the subject suitable to your work, I shall be happy to furnish you with some remarks from one who has had experience in conducting a nautical school.

A Friend of Seamen.

ON PREMATURE COLLEGIATE EDUCATION.

Presented to the Literary Convention of New York.

[The following is the introductory portion of an essay presented to the New York Literary Convention in 1831, by the editor of this work. We still consider the subject as of high importance, and regret that some measures of this kind are not taken to secure the existence of institutions in regular gradation. Nothing can be more certain, than that so long as degrees are granted on conditions which can be fulfilled by those who are just emerging from boyhood, the spirit of economy and the pressure into '*life*' in this country, will never allow high schools of an elevated character to flourish.]

At the first meeting of the Convention, in October last, I ventured to make the following remarks:

'In all comparisons of European institutions with our own, it is important to remember, that in Europe, the line is distinctly drawn between the students of different ages, and in different periods of advancement. In our institutions, those of all ages are mingled. There, there are schools adapted to every age. The Latin schools and the Gymnasia take the place of our Colleges; and young men do not often appear in the University, until the age of eighteen. During the earlier periods they are placed under constant inspection, and parental restraint. In the University, they are expected to govern themselves in a great measure. The difficulty of government in our Colleges, arises from attempting to educate men and boys in the same establishment. The same regulations, the same inspections, the same system of discipline, cannot be applied to both. It will be too relaxed for the one class, or too restricted for the other; and distinction would be invidious. There seems to be no mode of obviating the evil but to establish some line of separation. Let our Colleges gradually raise their requisitions: until they shall receive only *young men*, and let them be treated accordingly. Let them provide Gymnasia and higher schools, where *younger* pupils shall be under constant parental care and inspection at all hours, and not thrown into the midst of the temptations and facilities for evil, which our Colleges present, while neither reason nor experience are sufficiently matured to protect them.'*

This division of institutions appears to me not less important in reference to the literary than the moral progress of their members; and in perusing recently a work of Dr Chalmers, I have been happy to find the same principles in regard to the organization of colleges, maintained by this eminent man as essential to their prosperity. The opinion of such an individual, founded on the experience of colleges modelled like our own, will probably be interesting to the Convention, and I beg leave to offer the following extracts for their consideration:

'The radical error of our system lies in the too early admittance of our youth to universities. Generally speaking, whether we look to their age or to their acquisitions, they are too soon translated from the pedagogy of a school to the more liberal discipline of a college. The change wanted (and on it every other desirable improvement could be easily suspended,) is, that a far higher than their present average scholarship should be exacted from them ere they are admissible as students. As it is, we pass a great deal too early from the treatment of them as boys, to the treatment of them as men. In the majority of cases, they take their departure from the grammar school, without even the first elements of Greek, and without being able to translate extemporaneously the easiest of our Latin authors. It would be well, we repeat, if, ere they could be received into a college *for any professional* object, they had a far higher practical acquaintance with both languages; and if, by their tried and ascertained expertness in the work of translation, they should evince both that they have a large command of vocables, and that they are thoroughly grounded in syntax and grammar. But, for this purpose, it seems absolutely indispensable that the period of their boyhood, with its appropriate drudgeries, should be considerably extended. They should be kept at least two or three years longer at drill; whereas, at present they are handed over to the professor before the schoolmaster has finished his work upon them; and, by the existing method of our university tuition, the one is in the worst possible circumstances for executing what the other has left undone. All the vigor and vigilance that can possibly be put forth from the academic chair, never will replace the incessant taskwork, the close and daily examinations of the school-room. What should be done is, that, ere the university course shall commence, the scholastic course, instead of being cut short, as it now is, should be allowed to attain its proper and adequate completion. It is assuredly in the rudimental part of education that we are defective; and it is in this that we are so much excelled by our southern neighbors. We are weak throughout, because weak radically. A failure at the root is seen to be indicated by a general sickliness, a lack of strength and stamina, even in spite of that gay and gorgeous effervescence which disguises the frailty that is underneath. The characteristic freedom, exuberance, and activity of our college system, we hope will remain unchecked and untrammelled; but certain it is, that these would yield a produce far more enduring, were they grafted on the deep and well laid foundation of English scholarship.'

* Journal of the Convention, 1830.

Dr Chalmers's remarks on the practical reasons of this course, are not less applicable to our own country than to Scotland. Here also, as we were formerly obliged to let down the system of education for the purpose of drawing more students to college, so now, as the number is so greatly increased, we may raise the system. Formerly, the want of professional men made it necessary to admit them with imperfect qualifications. Now, the overflow of the secular professions gives the full opportunity of demanding such qualifications as they ought to possess; and thus of elevating the professions in character and skill, instead of merely adding to their numbers, already too great.

Such a plan would also have a happy effect in leaving room for the support of scientific schools of an elevated character, to which those might resort who are not designed for professional life. Many are led by the empty name of a degree, whose value is daily becoming less, to spend their time in a manner totally unsuited to their peculiar talents and their future destination; or become the mere residents of a college building, and examples of idleness and corruption to those around them; when pursuits congenial to their taste might have roused them to industry, and prepared them for usefulness.

I am aware that much has been done by our colleges on this subject, and with happy effect; but much remains to be done, before we can see the plan realized which is proposed by Dr Chalmers.

AN EVENING AT THE FLUSHING INSTITUTE.

[We have met with nothing which so strongly reminded us of the aspect and spirit of Hofwyl, as the following sketch of an evening at the Institute at Flushing, Long Island, extracted from a number of its interesting journal.]

'It is a little after seven, and the bustle of returning from tea has subsided. The boys (for so we call the long coat of eighteen as well as the roundabout of twelve) are at their desks; except the junior class, who have rooms of their own, and the junior section, who have a study of their own. The instructers are at a meeting of the *Eumathean Society*, and it has fallen to our turn this evening to 'keep the study.' Seated at one of the ordinary desks, for there is no pedagogic throne in the room, with pen, ink and paper, we shall be the faithful chroniclers of the important events of the evening. All is as quiet as the restlessness of sixty young mercurials will allow. The business of the day is over, and the evening they are left to employ as they please, provided that during the first hour they are silent, and that no one disturbs his neighbor. And how are they all employed? Students, aspirants after literary fame, they are communing with the master minds of antiquity! Not satisfied with the acquisitions of the day, they are digging still deeper in the mines of classical lore! Their grammars, their lexicons, and their text books, are their delight! — Your smile of incredulity, gentle reader, rebukes me, and sends me back to the unvarnished truth.

There is one who has already fallen to sleep. Tired with skating in the afternoon, he has taken his dictionary for a pillow, and in his dreams is repeating his pleasures on the pond. — There is a fidget — a perpetual motion — now he stands up — now he sits down, moving about as much as possible within the precincts of his liberty. Presently he will be nodding, too, for the quicksilver of his nature is rather in his body than in his mind, and when one is obliged to be still, the other soon sinks to rest. A book, at this hour, except it be a fairy tale, operates upon him like an opium pill. — There is another devouring the Arabian Nights, whose taste will be considerably elevated when he thinks the *Iliad* superior to *Sinbad the Sailor* or the *Forty Thieves*. * * *

Mr ——, I say to one leaning on his elbow, 'Would it not be well for you to devote a part of your evenings to your lessons, that you may stand a little higher in the ranks? Your friends are mortified in seeing your signature so low down.' I give the advice, as physicians do medicine to an incurable patient, more for conscience than for hope's sake. Nature seems not to have designed the young gentleman for a scholar; and yet it will offend his parents to tell them that anything more than a plain English education will be wasted on him. Besides, what shall they do with him for a few years to come? Turning over the leaves of Latin and Greek books is at least an innocent employment: and after all, his instructors may be mistaken: good minds are sometimes very slow in unfolding: the acorn gives no promise of the oak. Now yonder little volatile is a boy of talent, and would make a fine fellow, if his mind would only hold still long enough to receive an impression. M—— is preparing a hoop for the 'graces;' C—— is adjusting one of the buckles of his skates; B—— is entertained with his picture in a looking-glass, &c, &c.

But we must not do injustice to our adopted family. These are the minority, and if they are not turning their time to the best account, it must be remembered in their behalf, that business hours are over. Their recitations during the day make no part of the present scene. — The majority are so quiet that they do not attract our attention, and hence we have little to say concerning them. But we have our eyes on students in earnest. Some with works of useful information or entertaining knowledge, others with their classics or mathematics, and some with still better books, are making a profitable use of their time. — The bell-ringer leaves his seat — a general movement of impatience.

Three tolls of the bell say that the hour is gone. Not much mourning at its decease. Every one shoots from his place. The sleepers awake. The 'graces,' battledoor, &c, are all in motion. The five minutes of liberty, bustle and noise, soon fly past, and the ringing of the 'big bell,' echoed by the jingling of the 'little bell,' restore the study to order. — 'The letters — the letters.' How many bright eyes of expectation, and eager voices in every quarter 'anything for me? anything for me?' as the sprightly post boy distributes his packet. 'It's too bad,' says one, 'I hav'nt heard from home these three weeks; I'll not write again until I *do* hear.' While some glad hearts are as enraptured with a letter from home, as if they had received a valuable present. Now and then we observe one who will lay aside a letter from 'home, sweet home,' and not read it until he has finished his play — a worse sign, by far, than an ill recitation. The mail has brought a favor for ourselves. After a few lines of introduction we read 'How is ——— coming on? We should be glad to hear from you about him, as often as it suits your convenience to write. Your silence has left us in suspense.' Would that we had the faculty of Dr Dwight for dictating to three amanuenses at once! for then we might communicate with parents about their sons to the extent of their wishes. Our numerous engagements allow us to do but little in this way. We make it a rule however always to answer letters of inquiry; and we are glad also to receive such letters, as they serve to direct our attention more particularly to individual boys.

We hope our friends will understand this; and there is another thing on this subject, that we would request of them, which is, that they will not measure our attention to their children by our attention to *them*. We are alive to the responsibilities we have assumed. Our pupils are our family. Between them and us there are no intervening objects either of interest or affection. That we are not forgetful of his boy, every parent or guardian should feel assured, although he may not receive a line of intelligence from us during the session. To take care of our pupils is our duty; to write frequent letters about them, may or may not be our duty. We repeat again, that we are happy in receiving communications from parents, inasmuch as they serve to bring particular boys to our mind, and we invariably sooner or later reply to their inquiries. It is a deficiency in making voluntary reports, that we would explain. — But we have wandered from the study. What are the boys about?

'The last hour' they spend *ad libitum* with an extension of the liberty of the first hour, but not to their leaving the room. A couple here are playing at checkers, and there at chess; a few keep to their books if the rattling tongues and restless motion of their companions will permit them; for the majority prefer talking and moving about. And of what are they talking? What are the themes of such incessant discourse? What the unfailing excitement of such constant clatter? One would suppose, that, secluded from the world, and forming a community so entirely among themselves, they would find conversation (to use one of their own favorite words) rather 'stale.' But no, it is as fresh and as brilliant at mid-session, as when they have just returned from the novelties of the vacation. — Beside the music of tongues we have the piping of rare musicians; a dozen flutes are going in all the varieties of melody, from the gamut to the sonata. In one corner two are playing *duos*, entertained with their own harmony, regardless of the Babel of tongues and the chaos of notes around; a happiness we cordially wish every family that our journal visits. — The bell rings out another hour; the little bell calls to order, and all is perfectly still for fifteen minutes before repairing to the chapel — an interval of quiet appropriated to the reading of the Holy Scriptures. Thoughts here possess the mind too deep, and in this medley, too solemn for utterance. The service in the chapel is short. The boys hasten back to the studies and prepare to retire. They linger round the stoves, talking about its 'freezing hard to-night,' and wondering if 'the bay will be frozen over this winter.' With 'good night, good night,' we give them hints to be gone. Some three or four light the lamps at the desks, and by permission go to reading or studying again until the bell rings ten. The rest are away to their dormitories — a little racket on the stairs — here and there a straggler — and the house is still. The solitary lamp diffuses its dim light through the dormitories — the instructor on duty paces the floor. Some of the alcoves we trust are closets of prayer, since there are bended knees beside the beds without. They slumber quietly; not one on the bed of sickness — *Gratias, Domine.* — The watchman strikes ten — the curfew of our little world.

Thus it is, night after night — night after night. — Truly we ought to learn something of 'patient continuance,' if not 'in well doing.'

Tuesday, 10 *o'clock P. M., January* 21.

PRACTICAL LESSONS.

VERBAL ANALYSIS OF SENTENCES.

The articles which we have published in former numbers in reference to the old methods of teaching the languages, as presented by Colet, Ascham, and Milton, and Locke, may perhaps have increased the number of those who wish for some new manuals to aid in their application. A Greek work with an interlineary translation, was published sometime since by Mr W. R. Johnson, of Philadelphia. Some of Taylor's translations of the modern languages have been reprinted, and those of the ancient languages would be, if the demand should justify it. Mr Dwight, in the 'Lessons in Greek,' has sought to render the languaguе of the New Testament accessible to all, on the same general principles. We gave a part of his first lesson on the letters, in our last number, and now add other specimens of his plan.

After teaching the entire alphabet, he goes on in the several lessons to *illustrate* practically, and *then define*, the parts of speech, requiring the pupil continually to spell, read, write, and repeat from memory, every word which he learns, in the spirit of the method of Jacotot, described by Mr Green. After giving the inflections of the article and the declensions of nouns, he proceeds, in the sixth lesson, to give the following example of the verbal analysis of a sentence.

Ἡ	νὺξ	ην	ηδη	περὶ	την	τετάρτην
	Night	*was*	*now*	*about*	*the*	*fourth*
ὥραν,	η	σεληνη	ἐλάμψε	την	πεδιάδα,	
hour	*the*	*moon*	*lighted*	*the*	*plain*	
καὶ	τὸ	πληθος	τοῦ	βαρβαρικοῦ	στρατεύματος·	
and	*the*	*fullness*	*of the*	*barbarian*	*army :*	

What kind of word is η? What do you think it to be? What does it mean? What do you change it into, to say — *of the* — *to the?* And in speaking of many things, how? What nouns are changed like this? Is η used with a noun that means a man, a horse, or any other male creature? What is? Tell its changes. What nouns are changed so? Or is it used with a noun meaning a stone, water, or other lifeless things? What is? Tell its changes. What nouns are changed like this?

How is νὺξ changed; or to what declension does it belong, the first, second, or third? Does it end in η, α, ας, or ης? Does it end in ος or ου? Does it end like any of the words of the third declension? How do they end? How does νὺξ end? What is the end of nouns of the second declension, in the second or genitive case? Has the genitive case just as many syllables as the nominative? Which has more? How many more? How can you make a new syllable ending in ος for νὺξ? If you put os to nux (neex) it would make a hard word: νυξος. The Greek language is soft; and when a word would sound harshly if regularly chenged, they generally put in some smoother letters: so here, they do not say νὺξ, *night*, νυξὸς, *of night;* but νὺξ, νυχτὸς. We do so in English sometimes, to make a pleasant sound, or, as the Greeks say, εὔφωνη, (euphony).

η νὺξ, *the night;*
της νυχτὸς, *of the night.*

Write the third or dative case; the fourth; the fifth. The first, plural; the second; &c.

Is ηδη a verb? What then? What is περὶ? What is την? What does it belong to? What does it show? [That there is a noun in the feminine gender, singular number, and accusative case.] *Τετάρτην* — what does this belong to? What kind of word is it? Ὥραν — what is that? What case? What declension? Why? Give all the cases.

What does η show? [That there is a feminine noun, in the nominative plural, to which it belongs. By seeing the article η you would know that there is to be some *one* thing spoken, and no more; and that the name of that thing is feminine, and — in what declension? Why the first or third?] Give the cases of σεληνη. What is — *the moons* — in Greek? What is — *of the moons?* What is — *to the moons?* What is — *O! moon?*

Πεδιάδα is πεδία in the first case, and πεδιάδος in the second. What declension does it belong to? How do you know? Give all the cases. What is τοῦ? What might we know from seeing τοῦ? What kind of word must come after it? In what case? Why? — Declension? Why? Why might it not be in the first declension? What sort of a word is βαρβαρικοῦ? What does it belong to? What would you know of any other word to come, by seeing this? Might this word and τοῦ belong to the same nouns, or not? The first case of the next word is στρατεύμα: what declension does it belong to? Why? Why not the first? Why not the second?

Now write down alone the first noun, νὺξ. Tell me all you know about it. [Any of the former questions may be repeated]. What is the next? What do you know of this? The third? &c, &c.

An intelligent teacher will easily apply the principles of the method to our own, and any other language.

EXPLANATORY METHOD OF READING.

We have just given an example of *verbal analysis* of a sentence. The Sessional School of Edinburgh, which we described in a former volume, has done no little service to education in its admirable illustrations of the explanatory mode *of teaching reading* or *intellectual analysis.* In the language of Mr Wood, 'Its object is threefold. — 1st. To render more easy and pleasing the acquisition of the mechanical art of reading; 2d. To turn to advantage the particular instruction, contained in every individual passage which is read; and above all, 3d. To give the pupil, by means of a minute analysis of each passage, a general command of his own language.'

In the introduction to Emerson's 'First-Class Reader,' we marked for future use, an example of this analysis, furnished by the author, as a guide to teachers, and now present it to our readers. It contains a model for examinations at the first and second reading of an article.

APPEAL IN BEHALF OF THE BLIND.

The author of the book of Ecclesiastes has told us, 'that the light is sweet; that it is a pleasant thing for the eyes to behold the sun.' The sense of sight is, indeed, the highest bodily privilege, the purest physical pleasure, which man has derived from his Creator:—to see that wandering fire, after he has finished his journey through the nations, coming back to us in the eastern heavens; the mountains painted with light; the floating splendor of the sea; the earth waking from deep slumber; the day flowing down the sides of the hills, till it reaches the secret valleys; the little insect recalled to life; the bird trying her wings; man going forth to his labor; each created being moving, thinking, acting, contriving, according to the scheme and compass of its nature; by force, by cunning, by reason, by necessity.——— Is it possible to joy in this animated scene, and feel no pity for the sons of darkness? for the eyes that will never taste the sweet light? for the poor, clouded in everlasting gloom?

'If you ask me why they are miserable and dejected;' I turn you to the plentiful valleys; to the fields, bringing forth their increase; to the freshness and flowers of the earth; to the endless variety of its colors: to the grace, the symmetry, the shape of all it cherishes, and all it bears. These you have forgotten, because you have always enjoyed them; but these are the means by which God Almighty makes man what he is; cheerful, lively, erect; full of enterprise, mutable, glancing from heaven to earth; prone to labor and to act.

This is the reason why the blind are miserable and dejected——— because their soul is mutilated, and dismembered of its best sense; because they are a laughter, and a ruin, and the boys of the streets mock at their stumbling feet.

Therefore I implore you, by the son of David, have mercy on the blind. If there is not pity for all sorrows, turn the full and perfect man to meet the inclemency of fate. Let not those who have never tasted the pleasures of existence, be assailed by any of its sorrows. The eyes that are never gladdened with light, should never stream with tears.

First examination on the foregoing extract.

What is the title of the piece? Who is the author? What sacred writer does he quote? What is the quotation? What is the 'highest bodily privilege?' What is meant by the word 'bodily?' What is *here* meant by the word 'physical?' What pleasures are higher and purer than bodily or physical ones? What other senses have we, besides that of sight? Whose gift are they? What is the 'wandering fire,' mentioned in the text? Why is it spoken of as 'coming back to us in the eastern heavens?' What are the effects of its rising, so beautifully described in the text? What wakes the insects and the birds, and sends man forth to his labor? What are the effects of its return, on other created beings? Do these effects of light, prove the truth of the sacred writer's assertion quoted above? What feeling should our enjoyment of the morning light, excite towards the blind? What beautiful objects of sight are spoken of? Why do we forget their beauty and value? What is the effect of the beauties of nature on man? Why are the blind sad and dejected? Why are the blind peculiarly entitled to our compassion?

Second examination on the foregoing subject.

What is the meaning of the word 'author?' What is the equivalent word applied to a female? What is the meaning of 'highest?' Of 'purest?' What is the effect of adding the syllable *est*, to a word expressing a quality? Give some examples. What is expressed by the word 'physical?' To what class of words do most of those which end in *al* belong? When the termination *al* is added to a noun, into what is it changed? Define 'Creator.' From what verb is it derived? What is the meaning of the word 'wandering?' From what is it derived? What is the effect of adding the termination *ing* to a verb? Give examples. What does the termination *ing* generally express? *Ans.*—Continued action. What is the meaning of 'finished?' From what is it derived? What are some of the other derivatives of the same word? What does the termination *ed* generally express? Give examples. What is meant by the word 'nations?' What adjective is formed from nation? How? Define 'eastern.' From what is it derived? What other adjectives are derived from the same word?

What is the meaning of the word 'heavens' in this connection? What other meaning has it? What adjective is derived from the word *mountain*? What is meant by 'the mountains painted with light?' Is this a literal or a figurative expression? What other instances occur, immediately afterwards, of the same figure? What is the 'floating splendor of the sea?' What is meant by 'the earth waking from her deep slumber?' Point out the words, in this part of the piece, used metaphorically. Why is the day represented as 'flowing down the sides of the hills?' What is 'painted' derived from? Name other derivatives of the same word. From what is the word 'waking' derived? What other words have the same derivation? Give some of the derivations of the word 'deep!' Of 'slumber,' of 'day.'

How do 'hills' differ from mountains? What is the diminutive for 'hill?' What are 'valleys?' Why is the term 'secret' applied to them? What is the meaning of 'recalled?' What does the first part of the word 'recalled' signify? Can you give any other examples of that syllable having the same signification (as *remit, revert*, &c.) What does the latter part of 'recalled' signify? Give examples; (as *miscalled, uncalled.*) What is the meaning of 'life?' What are some of the derivatives and kindred words. (As *lively, lifeless, livelihood*, &c.) Define 'bird.' How does a 'bird' differ from an 'insect?' Define 'trying.' Give the derivatives of *try*. Define 'wings.' Give the derivatives of it. What do you consider to be comprehended in the term 'created being?' Is it limited in the text to living beings? Is the term, properly speaking, more comprehensive? What is the origin of the term *being*? Does it apply to unorganized or lifeless matter, as well as to living creatures? Define, and give some of the derivatives of the following words; *move, think, act, contrive, possible.* What kind of animals obtain their food by 'force?' What animals by 'cunning?' What by 'reason?' Is it common to find the word 'joy' used as a verb in prose writing? What is the meaning of 'animated?' Its origin? Its kindred words? What is the original meaning of 'scene?' Is it applied in the text literally or metaphorically? What is meant by the term, 'sons of darkness?' What figure of rhetoric is this an example of? What figure of rhetoric is used in the expression, 'eyes that will never taste the sweet light?' &c.

The above specimens are deemed sufficient to show the nature and character of the proposed system.

THE TEACHERS' ALMANAC FOR APRIL.

THE SCHOOLROOM.

The month of showers and sunshine and flowers is come. All nature begins to smile, even at the north. Our southern friends have enjoyed spring for some time, and begin to think of summer. The past winter has been one of unusual mildness; but we have scarcely reason to expect that it will yet give way entirely to its smiling successor, without a parting salutation of frowns and storms, perhaps frost itself. The active spirits of the young are more restless than ever, from the very influence of the season. The blood swells in the veins and courses more rapidly through them. The impulse to movement indicates its *necessity*, in order to balance the increased excitability; and the attractions without, render the impatience of confinement still greater. The true wisdom of the instructor is to mark these animal changes, which he may discern in the horse, snorting and prancing as he leaves his stable, and the lambs, skipping in the fields, and *yield* in some degree to that which the pupil himself cannot entirely control. Allow him longer intermissions; encourage active games; do not demand so rigorous application as in winter; you are not yourself capable of it. Warn him that he will have stupid afternoons, if he eat a winter's dinner in the spring; and do not let its influence spoil your temper.

THE EARTH.

But now begins the golden season for instruction abroad; and in reply to a correspondent who asks our opinion about the introduction of natural history into schools, we would say, — Do not suffer one change at this interesting season to pass unnoticed. Avail yourself of every opportunity to teach the name and character of each object around as it is presented.

Let your pupils observe the birds as they return to the north from their migrations — the wild geese, the ducks, the singing birds — and call upon them to mark the first appearance of each. The animals that have slept for the winter are roused, and the reptiles and insects are beginning to appear. The shad, salmon, herring, sturgeon, are ascending the rivers to deposit spawn. The shad was seen at Savannah early in the last month, and in the middle of it, in New Jersey. The mackerel, and smelt, and eel, are departing from the coast, under the influence of the same law. Let the periods at which the new comers are first seen, be noted in a book, to be preserved from year to year. It will be a valuable record, and serve as a means of comparing seasons.

Let them observe and note with similar care the budding and flowering of plants and trees. The following tables from a work of uncommon accuracy, and of great value to a teacher, 'The American Almanac,' will show the manner of constructing these tables, and some interesting facts concerning the difference of climate in different sections of our country. Observe and record in the same manner the operations of agriculture, and the results.

FLOWERING OF FRUIT TREES.

The average period of flowering near Boston, is as follows: Peach, (14 years) May 2. Cherry, (19 years) May 4. Apple, (17 years) May 16.

		Peach.	Cherry.	Apple.
In Marietta, Ohio,	1828	March 11—18,		April 1,
	1829	April 17—22,	May 1,	May 4.

Times of the Flowering of the Peach, Cherry, and Apple trees in 1817, at different places.—[Dr J. Bigelow, Mem. Amer. Acad., Vol. IV.]

	Lat.	Peach.	Cherry.	Apple.
Montreal, Canada,	45,35	May 12,	May 24,	May 25,
Brunswick, Me.	45,53		" 16,	" 29,
Albany, N. Y.	43,39	" 12,		" 15,
Boston, Mass.	42,23	" 9.	" 9,	" 18,
New-York, N. Y.	40,42	April 21—26,	April, 25—30,	" 4,
Philadelphia, Pa.	39,56	" 15,	" 20,	April, 20,
Baltimore, Md.	39,21	" 9,	" 8,	" 14,
Lexington, Ken.	38,6	" 6,—15		" 10,
Richmond, Va.	37,40	March 26—April 6,	" 4,	" 10—18,
Charleston, S. C.	34,44	" 6—12,	March, 24,	" 4,
Fort Claiborne Ala.	31,50	" 4		

THE HEAVENS.

The large and splendid constellation of Leo will appear on the meridian in the middle of the month; and deserves to be studied on a globe, or Burritt's maps to his 'Geography of the heavens;' a work which ought to be in every school library. Regulus, one of the brightest stars in this constellation, deserves particular notice, because it is so frequently referred to by mariners. The Hydra and its rhomboidal head should also be noted. Venus is now the evening star. Mark the progress of the Sun to the north, at noon, and observe how the shadow of the school house, or a tree, at that hour, grows shorter as the season advances. Mark the influence of this in reviving the vegetables and the animals, in bringing life out of death, and ask your pupils, *who* it is that sends them 'seed time and harvest, summer and winter.'

MISCELLANY.

Instruction in England.

A recent article in the Edinburgh Review presents a melancholy picture of the state of instruction in England. The writer endeavors to show the fallacy of the statements which suppose that nearly all the children are taught. It appears that of 700 prisoners tried in four counties, 'upwards of 260 could not read, and only 150 could write, or even read with ease; and nearly the whole number were totally ignorant in regard to the nature and obligations of religion.' In the riotous districts, a large proportion of the population is still altogether uninstructed. In one county only 24,222 out of 41,017 individuals could read. In London, 150,000 children are left uninstructed. In a village of 1,467 persons, only 562 could read — other villages of 1000 or 2000 inhabitants, have *no school.* The British and Foreign School Society, feel themselves compelled to say, that '*England is yet uneducated.*' Great exertions have indeed been made by benevolent institutions; but they have not yet kept pace with the increase of population, and now it is next to impossible to overtake it. From a statement in the Scottish Guardian, it appears, that in Glasgow only one-fifteenth of the population are at school, and of course that two-thirds of the children are without instruction! — so that even Scotland has not increased its schools in proportion to its population. Are not these facts a warning to us to lose no time in completing a system, which shall reach every child in our country, and extend as our numbers increase? In Manchester, only 3,000 out of 250,000 children receive *daily* instruction.

The Reviewer strongly urges the adoption of the principles of the Prussian system, and especially the foundation of schools for teachers. In proof of the necessity of something more than Sunday School instruction, he quotes the remarkable declaration of the committee of the General Assembly of the Scottish church — that, in their Highland schools, while they have taught 'Reading, Writing, Arithmetic, Geography, Mathematics and *Latin*, "they have impressed a religious character on every school;" and that if they were to specify such as in that respect have been found *most distinguished*, they could not hesitate to name those schools *in which the greatest variety of secular instruction is imparted*.'

Instruction in Louisiana.

We learn from the Superintendent of Schools in this State, that there are no less than 12,000 children, between the ages of 5 and 15, who are utterly shut out from the benefits of instruction, by the supineness of the parish authorities, in carrying into execution the liberal legislative enactments upon this subject. The whole number at public schools the past year was only 1500; and yet the sum drawn from the treasury, during the same period, in support of public schools *only*, (to say nothing of near $25,000 to the two colleges of Louisiana and Jefferson) was over $30,000.

N. O. Bee.

Schools of France.

The French government have directed that the *New Testament* be placed in the hands of every child in the public schools.

School System in Pennsylvania.

We are gratified to learn by a letter just received from the Hon. Samuel Breck, the author of the bill for the public schools in Pennsylvania, that it has passed both branches of the legislature, with only '*one nay*, in the house of Representatives, and *three* in the Senate, making a very extraordinary degree of unanimity.' The bill as passed, directs 'an appropriation out of the public treasury of $75,000 per annum, until 1840, when it will be increased to $100,000,' which is used as a stimulus to raise funds by voluntary taxation among the people, and 'will enable them to instruct 512,000 children.'

We are indebted to Mr Breck for the entire report; but must defer our notice of it to a future number.

School Fund in Ohio.

A correspondent of the New York Observer states, that the quantity of land given by the General Government, to the State of Ohio, for school purposes, has been in all, 678,576 acres, valued at $1,200,000. About half of these lands are sold, and the amount received in part payment is already $400,000. This constitutes a school fund; and is annually increasing. 'The legislature have not, however, relied on this fund.' Within five years they have commenced a school system, 'which requires a tax of three-fourths of a mill on the dollar of taxable property, to be applied under certain regulations, in each township, to support schools.' The wisdom of this measure is seen in the results. 'School districts are formed, school houses erected, committees annually appointed in each township, to visit the schools, examine teachers, &c. Last year, (1832) about $60,000 were raised by taxation for the schools.'

Addresses on Education.

When the plan for establishing a Journal of Education, was first proposed in this city, a gentleman of great intelligence and cultivation remarked to the proprietors — 'Why, gentlemen, you may publish *a few pamphlets* on education; but as to a *periodical* on the subject, you can never find *materials!*' *Eight volumes of this work* have now been published, and materials are still abundant — substantial, important materials. Our library is crowded with materials; but, unfortunately, too substantial and important for the present state of the subject in our country; and we are compelled to seek from other sources, articles adapted to the public demand. Even the materials of the day, however, are superabundant; and we can only give a passing notice to several valuable addresses, recently received. Those of President Woods, before the Alabamian Institute — of Joseph Hall, Esq. before the North Carolina Institute of Education — of D. D. Barnard, Esq. before the Young Men's Association, Albany — and of the Rev. Dr Dana, in the Ipswich Female Seminary all abound with interesting and important views of various topics, in reference to education. We have marked passages from all of them; but must omit them, to make room for articles unpublished, which our plan requires.

The address of Dr Dana is devoted particularly to the subject of reading. The opinion of Dugald Stewart is quoted and maintained, that 'Nothing has such a tendency to weaken, not only the powers of invention, but the intellectual powers in general, as *a habit of extensive reading without reflection;*' *mere reading*, it is added, loads, oppresses, enfeebles, and with many is a mere substitute for thinking. Valuable directions are then given for the selection of authors; and we could wish they might be addressed to every seminary in our land.

Bristol College.

The Episcopal School at Bristol, Pennsylvania, under the direction of the Rev. Chauncey Colton, has received a charter as a college. It contains between 80 and 90 students. The course of studies is stated to be as extensive as in most of our colleges. Manual labor, '*as a specific requisition*' — fills up a part of the intervals of study, and is found to be highly useful as well as economical.

Donaldson Manual Labor Academy.

A Manual Labor School has been recently founded in Fayetteville, N. Carolina, under the name of the Donaldson Academy. It has two departments, the preparatory and classical; and it is proposed to add a teachers' department. Manual labor is to be voluntary. The pupils are required to attend religious services, selecting such as they prefer.

Episcopal School of North Carolina.

An Episcopal School will be opened on the first of April, near Raleigh, in North Carolina. It is to be superintended by Mr Cogswell, recently of the Round Hill School at Northampton, assisted by a chaplain and teacher. The prospectus treats *instruction* as only *a part of education*, and presents physical education and the discipline of the mind, the formation of the character and of religious principles, as essential objects in such an institution. The pupils are to constitute one family, and the whole will be under the entire control of the principal and rector. No honors or distinctions will be conferred; the spirit of emulation being considered only a temporary excitement, and are inconsistent with Christian principles. Systematic instruction is to be given in the Bible and in Religion, as regularly as in the Classics and Mathematics. Parental supervision and training is intended to supply the place of premiums and severity.

Assassination of Caspar Hauser.

The assassination of Caspar Hauser could only be noticed in our last number The following are the particulars of this melancholy catastrophe, which took place at Anspach, from the Algemeine Zeitung.

'Hauser was invited, at 9 o'clock in the morning, by a stranger, who said he had something important to communicate to him, to meet him in the Palace Garden in the afternoon, and inconsiderately complied with the invitation, without communicating it to any body. At half past three, Hauser, breathless and confounded, rushed into the room of his tutor, and dragged him, with unconnected expressions, towards the garden, but fell down exhausted on the way. The tutor then first perceived that Caspar was wounded, conveyed him home, and sent a police officer to the garden, who found a small purse of violet silk containing a scrap of paper, on which was written in a disguised hand, "Hauser can tell you well enough why I appear here, and who I am; to save Hauser the trouble, I will tell you myself whence I come; I come from the Bavarian frontier, on the river ——. I will will also give you the name of M. L. O." We since learn that Caspar died of his wounds on the 17th. The wound was inflicted with a two-edged instrument, three-fourths of an inch broad, and was only three-fourths of an inch below the heart.

'The following, says the Berlin State Gazette, is a letter from Anspach, dated the 18th. Caspar Hauser was not able to speak much during the last hours of his life, and only in broken sentences, yet he gave utterance to the gratitude he felt towards his benefactor, Lord Stanhope, and his worthy tutor, Mr Meyer. A deputation from the Court of Justice was present until the moment of his decease, and took notes of all he said. Four days have elapsed, yet no traces of the assassin have been obtained.'

CORRESPONDENCE.

Extract of a letter from a Teacher in the Southern States.

Dear Sir, — In addition to a wish to speak to you a word of encouragement, in the great work in which you are engaged, I avail myself of an opportunity to meet your request, that practical teachers would convey to you, the results of their experience in training the mind and morals of youth. A teacher for many years, I have myself felt the want of that interchange of opinions, and communication of modes of instruction, which you design to employ.

Nowhere is such information more wanting, than in the South and West. A lamentable ignorance of the science of education prevails, in all the schools with which I am acquainted. When this shall be better understood, the respectability it will confer on the profession of teaching, will do much to enlist and secure for education, those talents which seek more conspicuous fields for exhibition. A teacher from inclination, I have sought to employ every means within my reach, for elevating this profession to greater usefulness, and higher respectability. I have discouraged its pursuit for temporary purposes; and have declined ever offering a situation to any individual, who has not determined to devote to it all his energies and find his principal reward in its exercise. Believing, myself, that the office of the faithful educator far transcends every human pursuit, in responsibility, dignity and importance, I have accustomed myself to consider it as the great field in which all my energies are to be expended, and all my pecuniary means bestowed. In furtherance of its great objects; I have erected a large and beautiful building, furnished with apparatus, engravings, a library, and all the aids that experience has taught me to facilitate the development of the powers of the immortal beings, subject to my control.

The influence of this recent establishment is as yet scarcely perceptible; it will require much time to rouse the intelligence of the country from a shameful lethargy to its highest interests; to divert the forecast of prudence from the absorbing pursuits of business, in which all the nobler feelings are repressed, to those more pressing wants of the rising generation, which are now sacrificed to Mammon.

It is really terrifying to the philanthropist to look over the southern and western States, and see the moral and intellectual degradation which everywhere prevails — to enter the wretched hovel where the tyrant of childhood holds his imperial sway, and reflect that here is the guide of a future people to intelligence and happiness! To learn the general sense of the community — thus *practically* displayed — of the little importance of the example and precepts of the teachers of youth. The system of common school instruction is here worse than useless; so little benefit is esteemed by all to arise from it, and consequently such the indifference with which it is received, that a majority of parents, even though no fee is required, neglect to avail themselves of it. Still these free schools prevent the rise of others, that would be comparatively useful. I say, *comparatively useful* — for, indeed, many of our private schools are schools of vice, and tend to degrade the cause of education by their almost utter insufficiency.

To establish my authority, a thing before unheard of in a teacher in this country, I am at first obliged to contend with the parent and the child alike. No parental coöperation was given — no precept at the fireside aided in repressing that spirit of uncontrol which so strongly marked every condition of this people. In my instructions, I now appeal to no slavish motive — I excite no emulation — I promise no rewards, and present no punishments. You may conclude from the state of things around me that my exertions are inefficient. Not so. I have appealed to the results of experience — I have shown the necessity of uniform rule in the family and school-room — I have succeeded to some extent in rooting up vicious habits, and planting the seeds of virtue — and I have pointed to the change in the intellectual and moral character of youth around me. I have thus touched the chord of interest as well as reason of the parent. The youth, I endeavor to *allure* to intellectual effort, and I lend an encouraging hand. If a rugged ascent is to be surmounted, I seek to crown it with a wreath of flowers; and I retain none who cannot find in knowledge the reward of their exertions.

The 'Annals' is a perpetual remembrancer to me of my duty — an encourager in the laborious task of public instruction — a guide and monitor to unwearied exertion, in the best and noblest cause to which man can consecrate his energies. That it will be sustained I have little fear; and with the spirit which is evinced in sending forth the message of philanthropy to an intelligent people, that intelligence must be recreant to itself if it suffer it to sink.

We are much indebted to our correspondent at St Petersburg for the account of the state of instruction in Russia, which will appear in our next.

We have also to acknowledge the receipt of documents from M. Fellenberg, which indicate the progress of Hofwyl. They reached us after this number was ready for press.

NOTICES.

The Introductory Discourse and the Lectures delivered before the American Institute of Instruction, in Boston, August, 1833, including a list of Officers and Members. Published under the direction of the Board of Censors. Boston: Carter, Hendee, & Co. 1834. 8vo. pp. 318.

We announced the publication of this volume in our last number; and our expectation, that it would be one of the most interesting which has appeared, are not disappointed. There is little of the 'fine writing' objected to by the London Reviewer. There is a great deal of sound, practical instruction, founded upon the experience of careful observers. We were interested particularly, with the views of Mr Perry in this respect, as applicable to common education, and those of Professors Packard and Hale, and Mr Greene, in reference to higher schools. We have spoken of other lectures before; and we know not where to stop if we attempt to describe them more fully. The whole volume is replete with interest to those who mean to make teaching a profession instead of a trade; and we think might satisfy those who would take the trouble to examine it, of the value of associations for the improvement of education.

The Constitutional Class Book, being a brief exposition of the Constitution of the United States, designed for the use of the Higher Classes of Common Schools. By Joseph Story, L.L. D. Boston, Hilliard, Gray & Co. 12mo. pp. 166.

The appearance of a second Class Book on this subject, is gratifying evidence of an increasing demand for instruction of the highest importance to Americans. We wish that every citizen of the next generation, may be able to decide on the character of a work, of which we do not feel ourselves capable of giving an opinion.

Angell's Union Series of Common School Classics.

1. Child's First Book. 2. Child's Second Book. 3. Child's Third Book. 18mo.

Lessons for Reading and Spelling, Arithmetical Tables and Exercises, Mental Arithmetic, Orthography, &c. 12mo. pp. 252.

Lessons for Reading and Spelling, with Exercises in Mental Arithmetic, Abbreviations, Definitions, &c. 12mo. pp. 296.

The Select Reader, designed for the Higher Classes in Academies and Schools. 12mo. pp. 504.

This is a series of six books, prepared by a practical teacher, under the quaint title of Union No. 1 — Union No. 2, &c. In the early stages, Spelling Lessons are given, which are immediately followed by Reading Lessons, containing the same words; and a set of simple questions are added to each lesson of the first five books. The plan we think good; the selections, so far as we have been able to examine them, are interesting and well graduated; but we could not venture to give any opinion of the whole series — so extensive — and composed of so various materials — without an examination which our duties, render impracticable. We observe that several instructors who have introduced them, have found them very useful. We can discern no sufficient reason for connecting one part of the plan, we mean the *Arithmetic*, with the lessons of a reading book; unless it be intended to excite attention to the subject in those parts of the country where mental arithmetic is still unknown.

AMERICAN

ANNALS OF EDUCATION

AND INSTRUCTION.

MAY, 1834.

[For the Annals of Education.]

PUBLIC INSTRUCTION IN RUSSIA.

We have been favored by our correspondent at St Petersburg, with the following account of the Schools and Literary Institutions of Russia, translated from authentic documents. So little is known of the condition of this vast empire, and of the elements from which its future progress is to be estimated, that we present it to our readers in its original form.

PROGRESS OF INSTRUCTION IN RUSSIA.

The Academies for educating the clergy, founded in ancient times, remained as the only nurseries of science in Russia, a long time after the important reforms which the Emperor, Peter the Great, introduced into various other branches of his government. With the exception of the gymnasia of the academy of Arts and Sciences, founded in St Petersburg in 1747 — two attached to the Moscow University in 1755—those of Slobodo—Ukraine and Kasan — some superior schools in the East Sea provinces, and some schools in a few government towns, this mighty empire possessed no other permanent establishments for the diffusion of knowledge, until nearly the close of the eighteenth century. In the year 1783, the Empress Catharine, anxious to remedy this evil, established a new system under her own especial superintendence, with a view to reform all the schools, already founded, to establish others, and to endeavor to render education general. To carry this plan into effect, Jankevitch de Marievo, director of the Schools in Austria, was invited to Russia. A trial of the new system was made in Petersburg, and, proving satisfactory, the founding of schools in other parts proceeded so rapidly, that in 1790, no less than one hundred and seventy were flourishing in various parts of the Empire. By the regulations published in 1786, they were divided into two classes, upper and lower. The inspection over them was confided to the governors of provinces, and they were supported by the funds of the government courts. All private schools, at the same time, were furnished with rules and regulations.

A new era was introduced during the reign of the emperor Alexander — every branch of public instruction experienced his watchful care and fostering hand. New life was given to the Imperial Academy of Arts and Sciences, and to other learned institutions, by the extension of their privileges, and liberal grants of money; by the acquisition of valuable libraries and scientific collections, which were thrown open to the public; and by the liberal assistance granted, in order to perfect various learned and literary undertakings. The system of education received a new and improved form. A minister of public instruction was appointed, and all put under his direction. The department to which was confided the care of the various schools, published their plan in 1803. By the new regulations, there were to be four classes — Universities, Government Schools or Gymnasia, District Schools, and Parish Schools. To each University was attached a circle of several Governments or Provinces, under the superintendence of an approved Inspector or Rector. For the support of all hese establishments, excepting the circles of Dorpat and Wilna, (which have separate funds) 1,800,000 rubles, or $360,000, were annually granted by the government. Universities were founded at Karkov, at Kasan, at Dorpat, and afterwards in St Petersburg. Those already existing at Moscow and Wilna, received new laws and regulations. Besides these public establishments for educating youth for the walks of civil life, especially for the government service, during Alexander's reign of twentyfive years, a great number of new schools were founded, having a more definite object in view, and those already established were improved and remodelled. From 1804 to 1808, when the new system was introduced, one hundred and forty new schools were opened, and this increase was continued, in proportion to the actual wants of the country, and the means of support which were granted. For extending their utility, and for greater order, and in conformity to the principles on which they were founded, in 1826 it was deemed needful to commit to a special committee, the task of preparing a new code of regulations for seminaries, from the highest to the lowest grade, and this was published in 1828. At the same time, the establishments for education, founded in Siberia, were altogether confided to the inspection of the governors of the various districts; as it was impossible, for the University of Kasan, to superintend that extensive tract of country. In the following years the academies in the governments of Moghilet and Vivebsk were disunited from the circle of Petersburg, and placed under the care of a separate inspector, and designated the circle of White Russia. The establishments in Odessa and Bessarabia were also placed under separate inspections. A code of regulations was promulgated, adapted to the situation of the schools established beyond the Caucasus. A new Institute called the 'Pedagogical,' for the training of teachers, was opened in St Petersburg.

Reports for 1830 *and* 1831.—The annexed tables, show by a comparison of these two years, the state of all the seminaries of learning, in this empire, under the direction of the minister of public instruction.

Changes in the Circles of Instruction.—At the commencement of 1831, a new distribution of the various schools was settled, by which the Moscow Circle was transferred to that of St Petersburg the schools of Novogorod Government, and to Karkov, those of Voronez. The St Petersburg Circle transferred to the Moscow Circle, the schools of Smolensk and Kaluga Governments—those of Minsk were transfered from Wilna to White Russia; and Volhynia and Podolia to the Circle of Karkov.

Reasons for the decrease of Schools in 1831.—Owing to the Cholera in 1831, in many parts of the empire the schools were closed. The Moscow University shut up in 1830, resumed its public lectures 13th January, 1831. In the Universities of St Petersburg and Dorpat, the vacation commenced earlier than usual. In Wilna Government, the Cholera and Polish war, put a stop to everything, and this was the case also in the surrounding governments. On recommencing the year, only six Gymnasia, and sixteen district schools were opened. In the University of Wilna, it was not deemed prudent for the students to assemble in any number, until things were more settled; only the medical lectures were given, and those only to such students, as were educating at the expense of the government.

On the recommencement of instruction in the various schools of Volhynia and Podolia, further reforms were introduced. In consequence of the disturbances, during the revolt of the southern provinces, the Gymnasia of Vennitsk, and the Lyceum of Volhynia, were closed, as well as several private Roman Catholic schools of the clergy, and of the monks of St Basil, in the governments of Volhynia, Podolia and Kiev.

Table I.

Literary Institutions under the direction of the Minister of Public Instruction.

Circles.	Universities.	Schools of first class.		Gymnasia.		District Schools.		Parish and Village Schools.		Private Schools.		Total.	
		1830	1831	1830	1831	1830	1831	1830	1831	1830	1831	1830	1831
St Petersburg,	1			8	7	50	45	74	63	111	80	217	196
Moscow,	1	2	1	11	12	[illegible]	89	153	171	[illegible]	36	306	310
Dorpat,	1			4	4	25	21	68	11	138	154	236	191
Wilna,	1	1		12	7	59	22	261	45	60	17	394	92
Kasan,	1			8	8	51	53	39	40	4	8	103	110
Karkoff,	1	1	1	12	13	93	97	87	91	26	31	220	234
White Russia,				4	7	10	21	22	33	9	15	47	78
Odessa,		1	1			6	[illegible]	1	3	5	6	13	18
Beyond the Caucasus,				1	1	3	7					4	8
Siberia,				2	2	20	20	13	13	1	1	36	36
	6	5	3	62	61	[illegible]	[illegible]	[illegible]	[illegible]	402	345	1610	1277

Table II.

Number of Teachers and Students at the Universities and Head Pedagogical Institute.

Universities.	Teachers.		Students.	
	1830	1831	1830	1831
St Petersburg,	37	42	202	236
Moscow,	79	78	754	814
Dorpat,	72	73	619	529
Wilna,	116	95	1321	120
Karkoff,	100	95	308	313
Kasan,	56	54	113	146
Head Pedagogical Institute,	21	25	95	94
	481	462	3412	2295

Table III.

Number of Schools, Teachers, and Scholars in the Various Circles.

Circles.	Schools.		Teachers.		Scholars.	
	1830	1831	1830	1831	1830	1831
St Petersberg,	246	195	303	309	9489	8714
Moscow,	305	309	1012	932	15575	14969
Dorpat,	235	193	725	762	7310	7625
Wilna,	393	91	880	306	19079	6654
Kasan,	107	109	435	456	6667	6881
Karkoff,	219	233	676	827	15068	14648
White Russia,	45	78	85	301	3407	4712
Odessa,	13	18	62	142	754	1214
Beyond the Caucasus,	4	8		35		709
Siberia,	37	37	105	100	2075	2241
	1604	1271	4283	4170	79420	68367

Table IV.

Degrees taken at the Universities.

	Petersburg.		Moscow.		Dorpat.		Wilna.		Kasan.		Karkoff.		Total.	
	1830	1831	1830	1831	1830	1831	1830	1831	1830	1831	1830	1831	1830	1831
Drs. of Divinity								7						7
Masters of Arts							23	11					23	11
Candidates	16	10	31	5	17	19	71	19	4	1	9	10	148	64
Actual Students	11	21	73	19	23	25	56	12	17	2	31	35	221	114
Drs. Medicine			3	4	10	3	9	5		1			22	13
Inspectors of Hospitals				3	1	2							1	5
MedChirurgeons			1				1						2	5
Accoucheurs			2	2	3							3	5	5
Midwives					7	7	7	11		1		2	14	28
Surgeons			8	26	9	6	75	66	8	7		30	100	135
Apothecaries					1							1	1	1
do, Assistants			3	8	8	8	7	8		2		8	18	34
do do, low'r class			6	10	28	21	6	3	5	2		10	45	46
	27	31	132	77	112	91	255	145	34	16	40	99	600	457

In 1831, the reform of the department of instruction was continued according to the regulations of 1828, and all schools not conducted agreeably thereto, were closed. This will account for the decrease in the number, as stated in the tables.

Private Schools attached to the Gymnasia. — By the regulations of 1828 in laying down the schools attached to the Universities, it was arranged to remodel by degrees, those belonging to the government Gymnasia for the children of the nobility, and officers of the service. As these schools had depended on the resources of those for whose benefit they were founded, until the present time, they had been entirely under the control of the nobility; but in Simbirsk, a school of this kind, on the new system, was opened for ten poor scholars as a trial, under the name of 'Charitable Institute of the nobility,' to be continued until the full number of scholars appointed by the regulations, was complete.

Measures for improving Private Education. — One great desideratum of the government reform, was to have more attention given to the private education of children, and especially to superintend the masters of schools — private tutors, and governesses. In the regulations of 1828, rules were laid down for admitting foreigners and private persons, to the situation of teachers; and for the maintenance of due order, in all private schools under their care. In the Ukase, of 1831, regulations were most amply detailed, placing all under a kind of visitation or superintendence of the police, who were required to watch over the conduct of all foreigners engaged in educating youth, whether in schools or in private families.

ON THE CULTIVATION OF EXPRESSION,

AS A BRANCH OF MENTAL DISCIPLINE.

To the Editor of the Annals of Education.

In the communication inserted in the last number of your work, I mentioned some of the causes which conspire to depress the character of modern eloquence, and to obstruct the development of the power of expression.

Another of the evils of modern education, which tend to impair the power of expression, arises from the *inertness and degeneracy of feeling* which are necessarily consequent upon our modes of discipline. Much of the evil now alluded to, has its origin in the neglect of health, to which we have already adverted. But, among its usual causes, we cannot overlook the cramping of the young powers, and the stinting of youthful experience, which so strikingly characterise the influence both of the nursery and the school. The child, generally speaking, is left to labor and lag in his progress, from a paucity of objects for observation, from the tedium of monotony, and from the prevailing want of living and varied interest in the circumstances by which he is surrounded. His nature, not less than his experience, becomes limited and impoverished. His impulses are few and feeble; and his character consequently becomes stagnant. How different the result from that for which man's complicated constitution and inexhaustible capacities seem designed! How different, often, is the result, in those favored instances in which the spring time of human life happens to be spent under the genial influences of a country residence, amidst the full enjoyment of freedom and variety, and strong natural excitement — as contrasted with the majority of cases in which the period of childhood is passed under the restrictions and privations, or artificial incitements, inseparable from the forms of city life!

If it is true that we can express well only what we have felt, and if expression is necessarily an important end of cultivation, for all the purposes of social man, education should be so contrived as to deepen, enlarge, and vary the avenues of early experience, in order to quicken, invigorate, and expand the vitality of mind. Change, vicissitude, novelty, penetrating and arousing sensation, are an indispensable part of the discipline of a human spirit. By these is it impelled to all its higher forms of action, and especially in the exercise of its expressive powers. Nothing is more easy than to quell the susceptible spirit of childhood by inducing morbidness of the animal nature, to lull it in mental inaction, or to stupify it by senseless routine, whether of passive or of active experience, — of neglect, or of monotonous tuition. Nor is the excitation of one class of faculties, at the expense of the rest, at all different in its ultimate consequences. Look at the wearied and hackneyed victims of premature lessons and ever renewed tasks, in whom the freshness of the soul is worn out in childhood. Here, it is not cultivation that we see, but systematic destruction. The early education which prepared the mind for those matchless examples of expression, to which we still revert with increasing admiration, was vivid, penetrating, various, invigorating, and inspiring in its influence. It was liberal in exposure and hardship, in sunshine and recreation, in contact with nature under all its aspects, and in the exhibition of perfect specimens of ineffably beautiful art. It cherished romantic and enthusiastic impulse, as well as exacted severe self-discipline and rigorous restraint. The tone of feeling was raised to its highest capability. No wonder that an instrument thus created, thus finished, thus cherished, should give forth sounds that have not yet ceased to vibrate on the ear of man.

The claims of the human affections, particularly in their earliest experience, demand an extent and variety of provision, which have not hitherto been exemplified in modern experiments in education. On this part of our nature is morality grounded. Yet nothing, and, generally worse than nothing is done, to develope the capabilities of this soil. Except the primal care of the mother, what good influence is shed upon this productive field? What is effectually or wisely done to deepen, enrich, and vivify it? Is the tilling hand put forth to expose it to the warming sun, or the salutary frost, to irrigate it when parched, or to renovate it when exhausted? Higher considerations, indeed, than these connected with our present subject, urge the reformation of education in this respect; and nothing short of an entire remodelling of the plan of education, will suffice, either for the particular end in view in these suggestions, or for the more general ones, of meeting the demands of human nature in the moral relations, and of providing for the expanding mind that spiritual nurture of pure and exalted affections, which is drawn from the highest of all sources.

In the preceding paragraphs, only general principles are advanced, which may be carried out into more minute and practical application, in subsequent numbers.

Another impediment to progress in this department of education, is to be traced to the utter neglect of early culture, in relation to the imaginative faculty; and in no community is this neglect so prevalent as in those in which the English language is the vehicle of communication.

Imagination is the power which gives form to ideas, and renders them susceptible of distinct and impressive character. Destitute of this power, thought would escape us in vapid abstraction, and feeling would be so dim and vague, as hardly to become a subject of consciousness. Imagination confers on us the power of assimilating our inward being to the surrounding universe, by associating the fleeting shadows of conception with the more palpable objects of the perceptive faculties. We thus realize the analogies of our nature and our conditions, invest these with the unity of conscious life, and amplify and inspire our being, by quickening and strengthening it at once from within and from without. This accumulative and concentrating energy becomes the vital force of expression, in all its forms; not only conferring on language the charm of imagery, but giving body and figure to abstraction, and rendering thought communicable.

The inert and lifeless character of imagination, in the youth of England and America, as contrasted with those of other nations, is mainly owing to three circumstances: the absence of elevated and inspiring association in the modes of early culture; the predominance of mechanical convenience and routine, in the aspect of surrounding condition; and the too exclusive exercise of the memory and the rational faculties, in all the stages of education.

The discipline of the nursery is generally very defective, as regards a prospective influence on association. Still less attention is paid to this important point of early cultivation, by the teachers of elementary schools. Childhood is spent, for the most part, in intellectual inertness and ennui, caused by the perpetual presence of the same uninteresting forms and sounds, and the same mechanical and insignificant occurrences. Life is thus rendered stale, at its very outset; and the wearied imagination soon learns to subside into a lethargic acquiescence with the character of circumstances. Tameness of conception, and flatness of expression, are the necessary results of such experience in childhood. How different this effect from that designed by the generous provisions of nature, which surround the child with every variety of form, and color, and sound, with magnitude and minuteness, with majesty and grace, with motion, and action, and life, in endless diversity. The teeming and ever changing world around him, was evidently intended to cherish a rich and prolific growth of associations, to multiply the resources of mind, and to endow the human being with a measure of creative power.

To put man in possession of this portion of his great birthright, we must cease from restriction and routine, in the management of infancy and childhood, and study how to amplify, rather than how to abridge, man's early privileges and natural relations. The tendencies and requisitions of the human constitution, the demands of the great law of ceaseless renovation — to which life, both animal and mental, is subjected — must be faithfully observed. The nursery and the elementary schools must be assimilated, in degree, to the scene of power, and grandeur, and ever varying beauty, without. The charm of freshness and vicissitude must be infused into the consciousness of life. The ingenuity of the mother and the teacher must be tasked, to furnish both food and stimulus for the imaginative power, that its vigor and buoyancy, and creative facility, may ultimately contribute their powerful aid to the completion of character, and to fertility of thought and language. The human being must find, as he advances in ability, that the sphere of influence, and the scope for action and observation, are expanding around him. He must not be left to feel the depressing burden of power not exerted, the ennui arising from conscious capability unemployed. He must feel that his mind is a faithful copy of the stirring world of reality — alive, and active, and productive, sustaining and renewing itself, forever, from the importations of creative energy.

To this end, the mental discipline of human beings must undergo a vital change. The over-worked intellect, and the gorged memory, must be relieved: a healthful revolution must take place, in favor of powers long and deeply injured by neglect, yet indispensable to sound character and true happiness. The whole drift of our early discipline, at present, is, to overload the lower order of faculties, and impoverish those which are the fountains of man's higher life. We lay no foundation for sentiment; and we consequently have none for eloquence, which is the utterance of sentiment. The noblest power of intellect, conception, the creative power of mind and character, is overlooked. Expression, as the original offspring of the soul, can hardly exist in such a condition of the mental being; and not until the conceptive faculty is restored to vitality, by efficacious modes of early culture, can the power of just and forcible expression be attained; for it is to this faculty, germinating in the blended soils of sensibility and imagination, that a true analysis will ever trace the reproductive power of vivid and inspiring communication.

But it is not merely in the disproportioned exercise of the different classes of the intellectual faculties, that existing education is defective, in regard to the cultivation of expression, as a branch of early mental discipline. We are chargeable with a great neglect of the moral powers, the mainspring of all effective communication on those topics which usually form the finest field for eloquence, whether in speaking or in writing. Sentiment, which is the embodying of our moral impressions and principles, and hence the very soul of language, is not at the present day, an object of attention in the culture of the young. To this circumstance is chiefly owing the sterile and insipid character of our modes of expression. Under the guidance of ancient discipline, on the contrary, the passion for glory, the love of distinction, the impulse of patriotism, the pride of character, the admiration of excellence in all its forms, physical, moral, and ideal, were unceasingly employed as stimulants of the youthful soul. The forms of such incitement, it must be conceded, were sometimes qestionable. But the spirit which they kindled, and the impulse which they imparted, gave the loftiness and the glow of inspiration to all the mental productions of antiquity, and leave us to infer what might be effected by a more pure and elevated course of training, such as should be prompted and sanctioned by the genius of Christianity.

The Christian spirit as originally exemplified, was noble, ardent, self-denying, generous, and irrepressible. The enfeebling influences of modern life have, it is true, abated its heroism. But its main trait, an unlimited and unwearied benevolence, still exists, though under less magnanimous and impressive forms. From this source should early education be enriched with copious nurture for the youthful spirit, invigorating and dilating the heart to a force and expansion of feeling, far transcending the limits of the ancient ideal. Yet the moral tendency of modern education is to discourage an excursive and enterprising spirit; we are prone to regard Christianity as an influence exhibited in passive and negative virtues. We look too exclusively at 'the patient continuance in well doing,' and too seldom advert to the considerations of 'honor and immortality.' The young are seldom made to feel that Christianity is a vocation to 'glory and virtue,' soliciting and sustaining the noblest action of the soul, and designed for the ample development of all its powers. Education, therefore, is defective in its moral incitements; and the heart is, in general, left too inactive, for the higher efforts of expression, all of which must breathe an atmosphere fraught with the elements of moral life.

To aid man in attaining the full use of his expressive powers, much of his early culture must be directed to the affections and the will, and be made to consist, not in the mere inculcation, but the practice of active and arduous virtue. We consume the youthful period of life in a wasting exercise of exclusive and unintermitted intellection. Never, thus, can we see attained, the standard of those noble effusions of mind which distinguish the era of antiquity, or of which, in later times, such an example was furnished in the revered character of Milton, whose high wrought personal virtues gave the tone of inspiration to whatever he wrote — to his ephemeral pamphlets on politics, not less than to his Paradise Lost.

INFLUENCE OF THE 'PICTURE SYSTEM' OF EDUCATION.

Mr Woodbridge, — In this day of pictures, when many are anxiously inquiring — Where will these things end? — every friend of children ought to reflect on the use and abuse of the picture system, and the ultimate tendency of introducing them into school books.

In regard to the utility of such pictures, there are two opinions. One class of men, and their number is not small, believe that all pictures are useless. They do not regard them as positively *mischievous*, except in so far as they engross the attention and time of the young, and encroach upon the contents of the purse. Could some parents have the full quota of labor, which their mistaken views of education or their avarice demands of their child, and could the pictures be afforded gratis, they would have nothing to say.

Another class believe in the utility of pictures, but differ greatly in their views of the extent to which the system should be carried.

Some suppose that they should be confined to the mere illustration of science; others think they may be studied, as so many lessons of themselves. There are some, also, who would use engravings of a good character to cultivate the taste, the imagination, and the habits of attention and observation.

I am well acquainted with a father, who selects from books and periodicals the best engravings he can find, pastes them into a book, and presents them to his infants, as soon as they will pay them the least attention. He has found that when they come to go abroad among objects of which they have before seen representations, they observe them with much more interest than they would otherwise have done. Besides this, they return to the *study* of their pictures on a future occasion, with new interest and increased delight. Sometimes the mere infant will study its picture book silently, for an hour together.

Again, there is another and a very numerous and increasing class of the community, whose great object, in the use of engravings, seems to be to amuse. All books, papers, periodicals, school-rooms, and even parlors are to be strewed in profusion with pictures, not so much to illustrate science, or cultivate taste, imagination, or the mental faculties, as *to please*; or as some of them say, 'to make children happy.' They are willing they should study, but the objects to which they would have their attention directed, are only such as can be observed and studied as mere play. They are wholly opposed to pressing upon the juvenile attention, that which is not first made alluring by pictures, or conversation, or both.

In conformity with the views of this portion of the community, a considerable number of writers have turned their attention to the art of juvenile book-making. All children's books, even those of the gravest character, and for the gravest purposes, must be highly embellished, often with the richest engravings. Ordinary cuts will not answer. And books without any cuts, meet with a reception still less favorable.

Foremost in the list of those who have forwarded the picture system is the popular author under the fictitious name of Peter Parley. This author, while he has written some books in a most excellent style, and led many minds into the same track, has published others which, were it not for their engravings, would neither instruct, or amuse; and some which would obviously mislead.

Those who measure everything by what they call its *utility*, declaim loudly against all this. 'Let the course be pursued a few years longer,' say they, 'and our youth are ruined.' 'Even now,' they continue to observe, 'children will not read as they once did. If a book is not 'full of pretty pictures,' it is untouched.

Even a school book which does not abound with them, has no charms.'

But the evil, it is added, has gone further. They will not study anything, *however beautified*, as they once did. The book which is set off with the finest engravings, is not now studied with half the intensity of interest with which books *were, thirty years ago*, which had no pictures. When just received, the pictures are run over hastily, and perhaps, some of the shortest stories or articles *partially* perused. It is then thrown aside; or if its lessons are resumed, it is only as drudgery, or with the same disrelish with which the epicure returns to plain food, after having lived a considerable time on delicacies.

It is insisted that even adults are, in some measure, affected with the same form of mental disease. The cry for short chapters, in the gravest works and on the gravest subjects, short articles in the newspaper and the magazine, short prayers and short sermons, is supposed to be increased, if it is not produced, by the picture system. Nothing will go down now, we are told, till it is highly seasoned, to please the caprice of a capricious palate and stomach.

While, however, we admit the justness of many of these views, and regret the existence in the public mind of any disposition to confound study and play, — business and relaxation, — we cannot admit that all the mischief alluded to arises from this source — the *picture* mania. We believe that the injudicious portions of Parley's books, and of others of a similar stamp, have had their influence. But we believe that much of the evil lies deeper than all this, even in the domestic and social habits. Artificial wants have multiplied disproportionally to the means which most families enjoy of gratifying them. This involves parents in a perpetual whirl of occupation, which leaves neither time, nor strength, nor disposition for thought. Sometimes several occupations are followed. Almost nothing is *read* but the newspaper; and nothing but business, and fashions, and amusements, conversed upon. Under such circumstances, in a moral and intellectual atmosphere so unfavorable, how can the love of knowledge or the habit of thought be implanted? Or if implanted by the labor of the teacher, how can it thrive?

When we look at the actual condition of most families in this busy, money-making, money-seeking, community, — even christian families — we cease to wonder at the unwillingness to study, of which so many of our most thorough teachers of common, sabbath, and high schools complain. There is room, it seems to me, to account for it all, were there no serious charges to bring against the picture system. And I am even inclined to think, that the picture system, is only the natural but noxious growth of a soil already prepared by parental mistake and neglect. Still its tendency, in some instances, whether it shall be found to sustain the relation of cause or of effect, is most unhappy: and it becomes the intellectual no less than the moral guardians of the rising generation to arrest the evil, if possible — before it bears off like a mighty flood, every vestige of that national character for which we were once preëminent. X.

[For the Annals of Education.]

COMMON SCHOOLS AND COMMON EDUCATION.

NO. IV.

READING AND STUDY.

In my last number I addressed myself to all classes of the community on the importance of continuing and perfecting our education by continuing the habits of *observation* which we began in infancy, and thus of gaining *experience*. I closed by urging the necessity of *reading*, in order to avail ourselves of the experience of others, as well as to guide and correct our own observations. By resorting to BOOKS we may gain more than a thousand lives would enable us to acquire by personal observation; and may learn much that it is impossible to acquire except from the records of the past. However great the value we place on experience, it cannot then be complete without books. It is *idle* to despise book learning. Be not so vain as to think that you know enough to neglect what others have learned before you. If your own Observation and Experience are worth something, the Observation and Experience of others are worth much more; and your own is mainly valuable because it prepares you to learn by that of others. If a man *will*, he may improve by his own; but if he *will*, he may improve a thousand fold more by a due use of the Experience and Observation of others. He may see with ten thousand eyes, work with ten thousand hands, and have ten thousand lives, who by *reading*, does in one single life, take in as far as he can, the wisdom and skill of other men of his own and all past times. This is true certainly to us, who have, in our own English language, a key to the whole store of ancient and modern wisdom.

Yet, to the knowledge and skill, which may be derived from books, your own observation and experience must prepare the way. It is only by your own, that you can understand and apply the observation and experience of others. Without it you may read, either to forget, or only to retain a mass of lumber in disorder and confusion. If you rightly use your own opportunities of observation and experience, you will be prepared to survey every subject to which you may wish to apply the observation and experience of others: and in every case, will but enlarge by books, the knowledge which, without them, you have begun to obtain. Thus the knowledge accessible without books, prepares us for that which books afford, and that afforded by books does but direct, guide, extend, and perfect, that which is gained without them. What is Arithmetic, but calculation perfected from our first thoughts of number and quantity: from our first observation and experiment that two and two make four, or two from three leave one? What is Geography but extending the knowledge of place, which you gained in the first observations and experiments of infancy and childhood; — or Chemistry, but a nicer, fuller view of the secret principles of nature, of which you have taken some notice in the growth and decay of plants and animals, in heat and cold, in water and steam, in soap-making, bread-making, boiling, baking, brewing; — in the most common operations of nature and art? Or what is Natural History, but a fuller view of what you have observed of the forms, structure, habits, relations of the plants and animals around you; — or Natural Philosophy, but the science which you put in practice in every motion of your body — which you apply, or see applied, in all the labors and arts of life? The hoe, the plough, the spade, the well-sweep, or wheel, or pump, are all concerned in Natural Philosophy, as truly as the complicated machinery, moved by water or steam. What again is History, of all nations and of all times, but a larger view of what you have taken notice of, in yourselves or others? Certainly 'book knowledge' is the best aid to knowledge without books; and knowledge without books the best aid to 'book knowledge.' Man cannot be wise according to the capacity of his rational nature, without the wisdom of other men. Neither can the wisdom of other men make that man wise, who brings not what he reads, to the test of his own observation and experience.

But reading brings you to *more* than the experience and observation of other men and other times. One *book* there is, rich in the history of men — of individuals and nations, — which with that history, reveals all that most concerns man to know; as the word of Him who knoweth all things. The Bible reveals the great principles of our duty and welfare, now and forever, more clearly than we could find them out by any length of existence — or by the history of men and nations for any duration of their being. It gives the experience and observation of men, as far as it can, and then supplies the defect of that communication, from the stores of infinite wisdom and knowledge. Let us be thankful that we can learn something from our own observation and experience ;— that we can learn something from the observation and experience of others ; but more thankful still for the word of our Father in Heaven, which meeting what we have felt and seen, is, in matters of our highest need, above and beyond all the observation and experience of men. The Bible is to us, what the instruction of parents is to their children ; or of teachers to their pupils, or of books of science to beginners. It meets us with lessons suited to our observation and experience, and requires our faith in the ascending steps which it opens before us. We listened to our parents when they opened before us the path of life. We followed our teacher, and our book, when we were required to believe in the numerous principles of science, until our faith was turned to knowledge in our progress. Let us in like manner proceed from our observation and experience of good and evil, to learn what the Infinitely Wise teaches us in regard to this life, and the life to come, until at length our religious faith may be turned to knowledge. In order, however, to the improvement of our minds and hearts, our *reading* must be *study*, or rather observation. All men grow up and live amidst opportunities of observation and experience, but with what different results! How little, for the most part, do they learn. So multitudes read — with as little profit, as if they read not. They read thousands of pages in a year, tens of thousands in their life time, yet grow very little or no wiser. They had eyes and no eyes, alike in all their intercourse with men and things, and in all their perusal of books. They neither think nor act to better purpose, for themselves or others, for all they have seen, felt or read. What a pity to live so long, to see, hear, feel, try, and read so much in vain !— as if a child after two years activity and diligence, were to remain still like an infant of a month old !— or as if a youth after being schooled a dozen years, would be found with no more knowledge and skill than a child of two years old ! What a pity — after the observation and experience and reading of fifty years — to have the wrinkles of age, and the knowledge and skill of a mere young man ! In order to make reading the means of improvement, and by it to perfect observation and experience, you must *study* Let me give an instance which will make my meaning plain.

Suppose a boy of fourteen, to take the Arithmetic for the first time. It is a small book, of two hundred pages. He can easily *read it through* in a day or two ; but would this reading do him any good ? Why has he gained nothing by reading his Arithmetic through in two days — every word and figure — from beginning to end ? Plainly, because he has not *studied* it. He must indeed *read* his Arithmetic, but it is a sort of reading which he cannot finish in two days. He cannot read it to purpose without taking months for the task; and even then he must *study* it; that is, he must read it with such *attention* and in such *order* that he may understand what he reads, with such *repetition* as will fix in his mind what he reads, and with such *reflection* as shall enable him to use his knowledge. The same course is required, in all books, if we would read to purpose—if by reading we would become wiser and better. All books will not require equal time, or attention, or repetition, or reflection; but each must have its share; or hundreds of books may be read in vain.

Nothing can be learned, no art can be acquired, without *attention*. Nothing has been. In infancy you gave attention to the voice, that you might hear exactly the words you would understand, and learn to speak; and to the lips and tongue and mouth, that you might see exactly the motion of the organs of speech. You gave attention when you learned to write, or read, or cypher. At this moment, I am taking a lesson on the importance of attention. I am sitting in a room where a Music teacher is giving lessons on the Piano-Forte, without giving *attention*. But just now, I heard the pupil say, 'I had to stop and think,' i. e. 'I had to give attention. Now the Piano rings again. But hark! the teacher's voice. 'You are wrong, you did not attend, you must not be in a hurry, you must give *attention*.'

But to attention you must add *repetition*; you must do over and over again; you must practice until 'practice makes perfect.' You must repeat observation, experience and reading, until the truth be distinctly perceived, and the habit fixed.

But attention and repetition must be in such *order* as is fitted to the condition of the faculties. The child must not attempt what is suited only to manhood, nor the ignorant what is suited only to the more learned. The first lesson in Arithmetic should not be the rule of three, or the square root; and if it be, attention and repetition will be in vain. The first attempt of an apprentice should not be to make the article which belongs only to a master of the trade. The reading book of a novice should not be that which cannot be understood without years of previous study. 'I bought,' said one of the wisest and most learned men, 'when I was in college, Young's Night Thoughts and tried to read them, and gave them up in despair because I could not comprehend them. I laid them by several years, and read them at length with ease and great delight, because my mind had become prepared.' Read then,—study then,—*in order*. Let the next be indeed the next.

'The purest way for a learner,' says Locke, 'is not to advance by jumps and large strides,—let that which he sets himself to learn next, be indeed the next; i. e. as nearly conjoined with what he already knows as possible; let it be distinct, but not remote from it. Let it be *new*, and what he did not know before, that the understanding may advance; but let it be as little at once as may be, that its advances may be clear and sure. All the ground that it gets in this way, it will hold. This distinct and gradual growth in knowledge is firm and sure; it carries its own light with it, in every step of its progression, in an easy and orderly train.'

But to attention—repetition—order—*reflection* must be added, in order to profit by observation, experienee and reading. It is impossible to tell how much reflection there is in infancy, or how much it aids infant observation and experience, because every one forgets that early portion of his own life. Yet it is plain that infants must improve themselves as *rational* creatures, i. e. by the exercise of their thoughts. This explains the twofold improvement which we perceive, viz. in each particular matter which they learn, and in those rational powers which at every moment must direct their observation and experience. The infant on its mother's lap, or on the floor, looking, hearing, feeling, tasting, smelling, trying its hands and feet, is not a mere animal; neither does it belong to the idle-minded class of human beings, which is made up always of its elders. Its *mind* is as busy as its body; while it inwardly reflects upon the use and abuse of all it meets with.

In infancy (let us be thankful for the wise arrangement of heaven), reflection is spontaneous. If it is not a contradiction to say so, God has given to infancy the instinct of willing and active thoughts, which ceases not until reason has grown strong enough for free thought, choice, decision. Thenceforth, it must invigorate and perpetuate itself. Reflection must thenceforth exist of choice decision, and self-government. The field of observation and experience must, in a word, be voluntarily studied. All books of knowledge must be studied. The book of revelation must be studied, with attention, repetition, just order, and with the reflection of reasonable beings, that we may learn the use and the abuse of all that comes before us.

What shall we say now, of 'common schools and common education?' Are not 'men and things' before the 'PEOPLE,' and may not each one improve without limit, by observation, and experience, and reading? What else can hinder any one, but his having eyes and no eyes, ears and no ears, senses and no senses, faculties and no faculties, books of every science and no reading, and no studying, the book of books and no heart to search it, to meditate upon it and apply to their proper use the blessed principles it contains? Alas, what is liberty to the idle-minded!—what the privilege of being an American and a Republican, to those who will not improve by observation, experience and reading? What the blessing of being rational and immortal, to those who will not seek the wisdom of reasonable and immortal beings?

[For the Annals of Education.]

SCHOOL LIBRARIES.

MUCH has been said, within a few years, of the importance of School Libraries. Like every other proposed innovation upon ancient usage, they have had, and still have, both advocates and opponents.

Their opponents insist that children read by far too much already; that he would be doing them more good who should lessen the amount of their reading than he who should increase it. That the reading of so many books will increase the feverish state of the mind, already too visible, and draw off the attention from severer studies.

The friends of school libraries say, that instead of interfering with other studies, facts show that other things being equal, the general progress will be the greater for it; and that a good library proves, in some measure, a substitute — a cheap one too, — for vicious amusements.

Now is it not obvious that both of these views may be correct? Admit that children read too much, is this an argument against furnishing them with a new set of books, better assorted and selected, and might not this course, under judicious management by parents and teachers, secure the great point which the opponents of libraries suppose is defeated, that of leading them to read better books, and fewer in number; and at the same time, reading them more thoroughly? Admit, too, the feverish state of the public mind; is there any way of correcting it but by appropriate food or remedies, applied to the mind itself?

To starve the mental stomach *entirely*, — will it not be to induce excess at the first opportunity? Surely there is a medium between starvation and gluttony. And will not school libraries, well selected, with a reference to their intellectual and moral tendency, be most likely to correct that morbid or feverish tendency in the public taste, which it must be admitted is too obvious?

The points of difficulty will be, in making the *selection* and the *loans*. How to contrive a plan which shall be satisfactory to pupils whose rights are equal, and at the same time secure to each individual, at each drawing, the book best adapted, at that period, to promote his mental and moral progress, is no easy task. But if this can be overcome — (and under the guidance of judicious teachers it probably may) the effects of School Libraries must it is believed be most happy.

Teachers' Libraries have been long ago recommended. In this day of fancied improvement in Education it is strange that a subject like this should require to be urged; and yet nothing can be more obvious than its necessity. In making this remark in this place it was our object to suggest the importance of adding to each school library for the pupils, a few books for teachers. Unfortunately, there are not a very large number specially intended for them. If every school cannot afford even this small number, let the Library in the centre of the town, or the Lyceum library, contain them, and let teachers have access to their use. We believe, too, that most teachers would derive great aid in fulfilling their arduous and responsible task, by reading the books designed for their pupils. It often happens that a parent or a teacher will derive quite as much benefit from a well written book for children, as from one designed for his own use. He will also be prepared, in this way, to converse with those pupils who read them, and ascertain how thorough has been the perusal.

These remarks on School Libraries were elicited by reading, in the Lynn Weekly Messenger, an account of the Library in a ward of that town. This library contained, at that time, nearly two hundred volumes. It was collected chiefly by the contributions of individuals — often of those who derived no benefit from that particular school.

In addition to these contributions, each scholar who is a member of the school, pays at least one cent a month; and some more. A few books were also presented to the Library; and during the past year, the committee contributed five dollars.

Besides the library, the school has, for two or three years, been furnished with apparatus of various kinds, a black board, maps and charts, periodicals, &c. Among the maps and charts, mentioned, are fourteen maps of different counties on pasteboard; and among the periodicals, twenty copies of the Juvenile Rambler were taken. It should also be observed, that considerable attention has been paid by the school to Geology; and the pupils have collected many specimens, both in Lynn and elsewhere.

It is stated, that a third part more knowledge is acquired, in the same space of time, since the use of a library, apparatus, periodicals, &c. 'Most of the scholars feel a deep interest in perusing the library books, and are able to give a pretty correct account of their contents.'

We are sorry the writer does not state the manner of distributing the books, as we conceive that much of their usefulness will depend on this circumstance; and facts of this kind, as affording the results of experience, are highly useful. But without this, the account of an experiment of this kind not only illustrates the subject we had selected for our remarks, but deserves, of itself, a place in the 'Annals of Education.'

CHALMERS' REMARKS ON THE LOCAL SYSTEM.

A work was published in numbers, several years since, by Dr Chalmers, entitled, 'The Christian and Civil Economy of large Towns', which well deserve the attention of all who are endeavoring to do good, in any form, to a large population. He urges, that whether we attempt to supply the bodily necessities of men, or their intellectual and moral wants, it is important to adopt a *local system*. He proposes, that in all beneficent efforts, a town or city should be divided into districts, each of which should be assigned exclusively to an individual, or committee, to be explored and supplied as the object may require. The general and obvious advantages are; that in this way all the suffering or want will be discovered,—that none will be neglected for want of some responsible agent—that the agents themselves will feel deeper interest in a field which they cultivate constantly and permanently,—that they will become better qualified by their knowledge of the people to operate in the best manner,—and that they will have a great advantage, in gaining the confidence and affections of those with whom they are conversant.

The plan was applied in Glasgow, to the subject of instruction both in Sunday and day schools for the poor; and in looking over our papers, we find the following summary of remarks on this subject, made by Dr Chalmers, at Edinburgh, in conversation with the Editor, several years since. We present them to our readers as they were noted at the time.

'The Local System is chiefly valuable as it searches every corner, and brings every child under its influence. It is *cultivating a small portion of ground thoroughly*, instead of scattering the seed over a large tract. It is giving an example of *what culture can do*, to stimulate all around to action. It has the advantage of proximity. It enlists the gregarious feeling in its support. It flatters the pride of the parent, or conciliates his good will. It is generally effectual in bringing out nine-tenths of the whole teachable population of the whole two hundred inhabitants.' 'There are Sabbath schools of thirty children, generally one to every district.'

'One teacher is employed for each school, usually an humble man. He is found fully sufficient. If a sufficient number of teachers cannot be obtained, begin with a smaller district, and extend.'

'It is not made the great object to cultivate the memory. On this ground, Dr C. prefers Watts's Catechism. He would never carry the memory beyond the understanding. Owen's school gave him new views, as to the capacity of the young mind. He does not see any ground for continuing in religion the *rote system*, which is abandoned on other subjects. He does not require over one verse to be committed to memory a Sunday. As to storing the mind with passages, he believes learning a verse, or reading a chapter daily will be as effectual in furnishing topics. He does not see the advantage of continuous narrative.*

'There are four day schools, (in Glasgow) on this plan, two of which are devoted to reading. Two others are commercial schools, and teach writing and accounts. Each master is compelled to spend four hours daily for his school in these branches. During the remainder of the day, he has the building to use for instruction in other branches, and the people are thus led on to the higher grades of instruction.'

[For the Annals of Education.]

HINTS TO YOUNG TEACHERS.

NO. II.

Before I proceed to speak of my individual experience, — on one subject, I would earnestly address youthful teachers.

There is a common, and at a first and cursory view, a very natural opinion, prevalent among men, that the respectability, dignity, and even importance of an Instructor, depend on the studies, and the ages of his pupils, consequently, that those who fit boys for college, or instruct young persons in the superior branches of education, are highest on the scale of teachers ; and that the younger the children, and the less they learn, the less important and dignified is the station they enjoy.† Now I would beg leave to reverse this

* The thought suggested by his remarks was, that a *principle* deeply rooted in the understanding or the conscience, is more likely to be efficacious than a *sentence* imprinted on the memory. The radiations from a single point of truth or a single passage of Scripture will produce more valuable light, than the crossing, interfering rays from many. — Ed.

† A short time after I opened a school, composed of quite young children, I received a letter from a very intelligent friend who was preceptor of a large seminary in the West, in which I found the following remark : 'I am sorry to hear

order; — and I trust the reasons I can offer, with examples I may hereafter adduce, will suffice to show, that the opinion, is not only a false one, but pregnant with danger and mischief, not only to the teacher but to the taught.

As a comparison, though a most imperfect and inadequate one, let us suppose the artizans employed in laying the foundation of a building were told, or persuaded themselves, that their office was a very humble or unimportant one — that as they only worked on the lowest parts of the great design, and on parts which when the edifice was completed, would no longer be visible, they were not obliged to take particular pains with their work, except to accomplish it as *quickly* as they can — in *what manner*, is of little importance. But is not the whole superstructure to be raised upon this very foundation? Are not the form and size of the building determined by it; and does not its strength, and duration, and value, depend greatly, if not entirely upon it? This, however, as has been before observed, is a very imperfect comparison, for the mason may perhaps go through his task, and perform it well, without knowing the whole design of which his work makes a part; he may do it mechanically, and with his attention confined to it alone. But the teacher of *young children* should see the whole course before them; *he* should have a clear and a correct knowledge of all the *details* of the edifice which he is assisting to raise. He is, in com-

you are devoting your time and talents to an A B C school; you might do something better.' By this time I was just beginning to find out what an A B C school was, or rather what it might and ought to be; and being of a contrary opinion, I answered my correspondent accordingly.

[That our readers may know something more of our correspondent, we subjoin the following extract from a letter.

'I have long since given up the labors, and the trials, and the privileges, and the rewards peculiar to school keeping, circumstances having rendered it as imperative a duty to resign as to assume it. The occupations in which I am at present engaged, still leave me some time to devote to pursuits unconnected with them; and I am desirous that it should be productive of something possibly useful to others.'

We would add, that, for ourselves, we think that the view of one who has withdrawn from the excitements and bustle of the school room, and looks back, and looks on as a mere spectator, is to say the least, not less likely to be right than that of those whose *personal feelings* are still concerned. We earnestly commend to the attention of our readers, the first sentiment of this article. We consider the error it attacks as serious. We believe that it must be eradicated before our schools can be placed on the proper basis. We believe that careful observers will bear us out in the opinion that there are ten men qualified, as society now is, to address a public assembly, for one who is capable of speaking with effect to a collection of children. And thus it must ever be, so long as it is considered a trivial, easy, childish employment—so long as the foundation is deemed less important than the superstructure. Better deprive the youth of competent instruction, than the child, if either is necessary; for the youth is capable of instructing himself, if the proper means be placed in his hands. — Ed.]

parison with other teachers, like a traveller who should undertake to point out the way for a great distance to some stranger inquiring of him, when compared with another who should attempt to describe the route to the place, from one much nearer to it. The first certainly requires a far more thorough acquaintance with the road, more clear and distinct ideas of the journey as a whole, he should have a more familiar idea of the objects in his mind's eye, and more distinctness of delineation in his descriptions of them, than one who is preparing the stranger to go from a shorter distance,—if, for no other reason, because if he should *set out* on a wrong track, he would have the more steps to retrace. Though it may be justly said, that the pupil goes but a small part of his journey by the direction of his early teacher, yet during that short time, impulses may and ought to be given him, which will continue to operate through life. The stimulus to many an after important step, to many an excellent resolution, or virtuous triumph, whose source is hidden even from his own perception, may arise from the moral and intellectual incentives received at what is called, in contempt, an A B C school: and what responsibility does the conviction bring, that if good seeds are not planted, some injurious ones, whose effects are equally unnoticed and unknown by the hand which perhaps thoughtlessly scatters, them ; may, nay *must*, be implanted? No period of our progress, however short, from infancy to our graves, passes unmarked by some strong influences. They may nourish and improve the mind, as the dews, the rains and the snows fertilize the earth ; or they may blight and destroy its best capacities, like the worm, or the noxious vapors which prevent vegetation, or produce poisonous plants ; while the causes are equally hidden from all but the great Creator.

Certainly, then, the instruction as well as the care of early childhood is all essential, and should be intrusted only to those who are aware of its importance, and humbly, yet with confidence, acknowledge its responsibility. And yet how can this be, if the world attaches little or no consequence to it ; if the teacher is led to think that his first school is merely a sort of experiment in which he may try his hand, and that if he finds himself successful, he may hope for something *better* and *higher?* How can it be, if parents consider it of so little importance as to think and to say, as I have a thousand times heard them ;—'Why, really, I cannot give an extravagant price for the schooling of so young a child ;' or, 'It is not of so much consequence, you know, what school he attends now, he is so young. I shall soon send him to a higher one.' And these observations were from parents, otherwise sensible, intelligent, and deeply interested for the welfare of their children. If, I say, the great mass, even among the most cultivated and morally wise persons, entertain such opinions as these, how can different ones be expected, from those who undertake this comparatively difficult office? Their motives must necessarily be personal ones, and though possibly of a pure nature, yet quite unconnected with the degree of good or evil they may unconsciously effect. Other and better views, if they come at all, must come afterwards.

Here I would beg to observe, that I do not refer to 'Infant Schools,' commonly so called, for their importance is of a different order, and stands on a different ground from those of which I speak, and are besides, but of recent origin. I have not sufficiently investigated the subject to speak of their relative or even actual value, though it strikes me strongly that the parent, if *capable and favorably situated*, is the fittest guardian for his child's tender mind, until old enough to begin what is termed school-education; but if not, (and on this point I speak with confidence,) at least let an Infant School be confined to the infant age, to three or at most four years; for I know, by sad experience, the ill effects on the minds of children who have continued at these schools long after that period, of which I shall hereafter have occasion to speak.

Among those things which I learned only by experience, on which I would venture to advise young teachers, is the importance of receiving pupils of as nearly the same age as possible. This, and the following remarks, refer, of course, to private schools only. I do not mean exactly an equal number of years, but I mean only that the elder, and younger, and middling classes, should not be together at the same school. So convinced did I become, of this, that as I began to instruct *little* children, I could never afterwards be induced to take those of more advanced age and attainments. Had I done so, I should certainly have given up the younger ones; and the facts which proved this to my mind, I shall, perhaps, hereafter, be enabled to specify. Another plan which I would advise is, that as soon as practicable, the number of pupils collected should be *small* and *limited*. I know custom has made it appear very strange and somewhat preposterous, perhaps, thus to limit the number in a school for *young* children, but it is because the employment is considered of such trifling importance. 'Oh! you can as well teach thirty, as twentyfive or twenty,' is the common remark; how very *erroneous*, every conscientious and zealous teacher can affirm. That this plan is wondered or sneered at, is no argument whatever against it, if it be really right and proper. Exclusive of its advantages in a worldly point of view, (for there is no common saying more true than that, where things are to be had with difficulty, they are most eagerly sought, certainly by those who reflect least on the subject, and these unhappily, make up the larger class of those who send their children to school,) there are others I would particularly desire to point out. One is, that a teacher is able, in that case, to preserve much greater regularity and order than where the changes among the pupils are incessant, and where new faces are consequently ever interrupting the attention of the little students; and this order and regularity are more necessary to the well being of a school and its teacher, than either are generally aware. Another weighty reason in favor of this practice, is, that the instructor is not obliged to class his scholars so much. He can pay more particular attention to each mind, and discover its individual capacity, *corporeal as well as mental*, for sometimes the one depends in a great measure upon the other. He will then be enabled to adapt his teaching to the peculiar need of each little intellect, and not be in danger of demanding too much of some, and not enough of others.

It may be said, and justly, I fear, that the compensation considered sufficient for the tuition of young children, is inadequate to the support of a Teacher, unless he receives a very large number. To this, in some respects, conclusive argument, I would only reply, that a reform in that point, in prevailing opinions, is very necessary; and that unless there are some to be found, properly informed on the subject, and disposed to promulgate higher and more correct views — these views can, of course, never be promulgated — but fortunately for the teacher, however unhappily for mankind, there are other motives swaying men, besides those of moral advancement. If a school be limited to a small number, it will soon have the credit of being what is called a *select school*, and as fashion is a powerful incentive to those who have no higher ideas on the subject, — and there are doubtless some who from a better motive, may really prefer to send their children to this select school — it will soon be found that a *higher price* is no barrier, and rather a help to success in this respect; and thus both objects will be attained. Of course I mean to imply, that the school really has that moral worth which will enable it to maintain the stand it assumes, for, otherwise, sooner or later it will fall in the opinion, at least, of the wise and good. But the difficulty is, that the greater number of schools have not sufficient worth to support them; and if they stand, adventitious causes must account for the circumstance. Yet this fact is a consequence, again, of the very effects of which we have been speaking; and the evils constantly act and react on each other; — and it is the intention of the preceding remarks, to induce parents and teachers to view the different parts of this important subject in their true point of light.

I would venture to suggest one more hint, while on the subject of selecting and arranging the kind of school of which I speak;

it is, that the teacher should *not take any assistants.* The propriety of this advice may at first appear doubtful, but I will give the reasons which appear to me conclusive, and then leave this point, with the others on which I have been writing, to the decision of my readers. In the first place, if my previous assertions are correct, it would follow that no assistant could be needed; since a small, limited number, could be readily managed by one person. It must also be allowed, that uniformity of management, of discipline, of culture, is exceedingly important to the young; and even supposing the methods pursued, and the manner of pursuing them, to be equally good, allowing that the teachers perfectly agree, (which, if both were *independent*, conscientious, and zealous, would be very unlikely) — the very change, from one to the other, dissipates and puzzles the mind of the pupil. He is oftentimes occupied in trying to find out the road by which the one teacher came to a conclusion, as he may see it is a different one from that by which he has just been led; while the Instructor, unconscious of this, is endeavoring to carry him on to another point, or showing him the uses to be derived from that he has attained. This observation is equally applicable to the regulations and discipline, and I feel confident, after much reflection on the subject, that the conclusion to which I have arrived is a just one, — viz. that one teacher, *in such a school,* is better than two, or a dozen.

I trust I shall not be misunderstood in the purport of the preceding remarks and animadversions. My desire is to show that some of the prevailing opinions on many points of school discipline, instruction, and order, are erroneous; and how and why they are so. The young teacher is burthened by many difficulties, which it requires all his self-command to meet, and his every virtuous effort and resolution to strive against; but it is better that he should be aware of them, and know which should be attributed to his own defective management, and which to circumstances beyond his entire control, perhaps, but which may be modified and their consequences rendered less injurious, if he be aware of and prepared for them. Nor do I, with regard to the *plan* and *outward formation* of the school, propose anything impracticable, or even difficult; since I, myself, was enabled to effect it, with entire success; in what manner, and by what means, I will take the liberty to show in a future article, if I can presume on the interest and kind wishes of my readers.

[For the Annals of Education.]

ON THE CONNECTION OF LITERARY INSTITUTIONS.

It is a common saying, that every class of society depends, for some portion of its happiness, upon the other classes of the civil system; and that every individual, however insulated in feeling and devoted to self, derives a share of his enjoyments and advantages from his intercourse with others. This observation loses none of its force, when applied to the different institutions for education, through which we pass, in the successive stages of our progress toward manhood. The faults of the Primary School are preserved in the Academy; the faults of the Academy extend to the University. Although the professor who concentrates all his powers upon one subject, may feel superior to the instructor, whose efforts are scattered over the humbler field of elementary science, it is upon him that he must in a great measure depend for the pleasure and success of his own labors. If the first elements of knowledge be imparted in a manner that excites the child's curiosity, and calls into exercise all the powers of his mind, the principal of the Academy will have only to cherish the flame, that his predecessors have kindled. And when, after an active pursuit of his academical course, the scholar reaches the halls of the University, the professor will derive from the animation and interest of his pupil, a new animation, and a new interest, in revealing to his delighted eye the inner beauties of the temple, whose portal he had but reached. These also must he leave, and mingle with the active world that lies beyond. And here the habits which, roughly formed in the Primary School, were cherished in the Academy, and received their last culture and bent at the University, will extend their influence to thousands, through the medium of commercial speculation, in the keen debates of the bar, or the grave precepts of the pulpit. Some, who have been guided by them to professional eminence, must, in the course of time, become related to a new generation, in the solemn bond of parent and child. The principles that have influenced their own lives, will then be impressed upon the minds of their children; these, in turn, will transmit to their posterity the same rich legacy; and thus the cord, that was first touched in the neglected hall of the Primary School, may vibrate onward to remote posterity.

The order and arrangement, therefore, of every institution for education, becomes a subject of the greatest importance to every class of instructors, as well as to every class of society; and he who draws closest the bonds of their natural union, will contribute most to the true interests of education. But obstacles and difficulties have accumulated to a degree, that must defeat the efforts, not only of any single individual, but of any single institution. A long course of error has given them the sanction of experience, and the veneration of age. The path of the Primary School has long been marked out by iron-handed custom; neither can the academical course pass beyond certain limits. The inconvenience in the former case, is comparatively slight; but leads, in the latter, to the most fatal results.

In this country, where a profession is often chosen before the first elements of knowledge have been secured, the scholar generally comes to the Academy, in order to prepare for the counting room, or 'for College.' If he be designed for the counting-room, he confines his attention to a few elementary studies, with a rapidly gained knowledge of which, he hopes to mingle equally and honorably with his fellow merchants. Neither is he guided in his choice of these, by any other considerations than those of immediate profit. Arithmetic, he can apply to his accounts; Geography, to his connections with other countries; and a knowledge of one or two modern languages may give new facilities to this communication. But the cultivation of mind that secures real superiority in every profession, the discipline of reason that guides to correct decisions upon the old routes of commerce, and opens the way to the discovery of new, and, above all, the taste, that softens the roughness of commercial intercourse and tempers the love of gain by refining the feelings and purifying the heart — all these are sacrificed to his aversion to the labor of study, or his eager desire of immediate distinction.

If a collegiate education be his object, he is directed to a certain number of classic authors, through which he must pass before he can obtain admission. At this point, we find schools divided into two distinct classes. In one, the student lingers out a long and dreary course, wasting his best efforts by improper methods, and careless instruction. In the other, rapidity of progress is the great test of genius, and he who can prepare for college in a year, receives the highest rank. With his eyes fixed upon College, he commences the task. The grammar is mastered in a few lessons, and the astonished pupil hurries with bewildering pain, through every variety of declension, and conjugation, and grammatical form. He springs forward to the second course, without stopping for breath; and dashes through this with equal swiftness. His cry is still — Onward! — his eye is still fixed upon the goal, and his gaze grows more intense as he draws nearer to its bound. But no sooner is it gained, than, like the alpine traveller, he finds a new object beyond. This soon fixes his attention, he loses sight of the intervening space, and dizzy and confused with the rapidity of his course, he hurries by the first goal, with the same velocity that had marked his approach.

This picture may seem too highly colored; but we fear there are but few instructors, who cannot bear witness to its truth. If the knowledge of Latin be presented to the student as the object of his labor, is he taught to write it, that he may feel the beauty of its idioms — to read, that he may store his mind with the noble thoughts of its classics, or improve his taste by an attentive study of its models? Or does he suppose that his task is accomplished, when the first definition of his lexicon is given for each word; and a paragraph which he cannot understand in the original, is rendered into an English, equally unintelligible? The acquisition of a science is overlooked, and the accomplishment of a fixed task is made the object of study. Few students inquire how much they know of the language or science that they are studying, so long as the customary course of prescribed reading has been passed over. It matters not that they cannot point out to others, or feel themselves, a single beauty of Virgil; they can scan each line with mathematical exactness. No matter that they cannot perceive the rich flow and harmonious arrangement of Cicero's sentences; they can parse them, word for word, and their ambition is satisfied: and although the mighty instruments of Newton and La Place lie rusting in their hands, they can answer every question, solve each theorem, and they ask for nothing more.

The University is not less bound by the same circumstances. The scholars who present themselves for admission can seldom do more than read and parse the preparatory works. Many can scarcely do this, and know as little about the real sense of their text-books as if they had never read them. It is impossible that such students should enter upon an elevated course. The time that should have been given, to a thorough preparation in writing and reading the languages, has been wasted in a fatal attempt to hurry over certain authors; and as a natural consequence of this course, the years which should be devoted to a study of the classics, for classic beauties, and of science for a scientific discipline of mind, must be bound down to the dictionary, and the grammar, and the very elements of liberal study. And even if (as sometime happens) the University rejects such applicants, and sends them home to prepare anew, will their preparation be more perfect under the direction of the same guide, that has once formed them to habits of haste and superficiality? They know but little of the force of intellectual habits who believe that it will — but little, of the fondness with which we cling to the path we have once pursued, or how the mind will go on believing, hoping, that it is in the right track, but unable to examine or estimate its progress, until the time for correction is past.

But if in this course, the instructor has only sacrificed his own judgment to the urgent instances of parent and child, he can scarcely hope to receive his pupil once more under his care. If his application fail at one institution he will surely be received at another; and thus under most circumstances, the student attains his chief object — 'admission to College.'

This false and fatal preparation, however, does not depend more upon an improper use of the course required, than upon some errors inherent in the course itself. It is generally supposed, that a College is an institution in which we can give a more perfect and graceful form to the materials that have been collected at school. No one looks for a perfect and extensive course of science, or expects that the student should have acquired that discipline of mind, and extent of information, which can only be gained by years of active and diligent labor. But a general knowledge of the details of science, a thorough acquaintance with its leading principles, a foundation of rigid mental discipline, a taste for all that is beautiful in literature, and a familiarity with the feelings and nature of man, as they are revealed in the history of his actions, a bold, enlarged, inquiring mind, — these certainly should be the fruits of a liberal education.

From what seed must they spring?— A grammar rigidly exacted but seldom understood, because half its precepts can never be applied?— a text-book chosen without regard to the knowledge and mind of the pupil, connected with facts of which he has never heard, referring to a hundred customs of which he is wholly ignorant, and which, if it be understood at all, must be understood by intuition, because the train of its thought is too far in advance of its reader? Can a child understand the orations of Cicero, who would not understand the speeches of Webster? Can he translate the noble figures and labored expressions of Virgil, when the simpler diction of Dryden would be unintelligible? And yet the subject of Webster's discourse, is also the subject of conversation at the table, and in the evening circle; and every idea is made familiar, by allusions to objects and subjects that are familiar. The language of Dryden is the language of his daily exercises; and many of its richest expressions are echoed in the glad tones of his youthful sports, or the free effusions of domestic intercourse. But the mind must be familiar with facts themselves, before it can understand the language that represents them; and no one can wonder that a child should stop, confused, before the thousand combinations of language and thought, that he meets in the classics, while his mind is still occupied in collecting the simpler ideas of daily life. Yet this is the situation of hundreds of our youth; and Virgil and Cicero are given to boys, who, at best, know but the outlines of Roman history, and who must turn to the dictionary, or a translation, at every step. O! ye inconsistencies of man, how large a space do ye still occupy in the history of his mind! Such is the beginning from which we expect noble results. We scatter our seed to the winds and still look for the blush of harvest; we waste in disconnected efforts the vigor and energy of life, and wonder that they no longer remain, when we have at last discovered their true application.

We return therefore to our first position, that the connection between school and college is so close, that every circumstance which affects the one, must necessarily extend to the other. As well might we expect the head to be clear, and prepared for thought, while every vein is burning with the heat of fever, as that one institution should implant pure and vigorous principles, while another is wasting the powers of the mind, and corrupting the sources of its energy. A reform, therefore, must be general, if we would make it effectual. It must extend from the primary school to the University — it must spread throughout the whole of that important period of life, in which the education of one human being is directed by the views of another.

ON THE STUDY OF ANATOMY.

We have recently received the following note from a gentleman at the South.

[To the Editor of the Annals of Education.]

Some circumstances lately led my mind into a train of thought, some of which were new to me, and I venture with unfeigned deference, to submit them to you personally, and to your readers if you see fit. The subject of education occupies much of my musings; and the particular point, the value of the knowledge of a subject hitherto almost entirely neglected in the instruction of our children, I mean the knowledge of ourselves. This may be divided into many distinct branches, one of which is our material formation, which may still again be divided and subdivided, I know not to what extent. I was thinking of the utility of drawings, one example of which we have in 'The House I live in,' in the Juvenile Rambler. It occurred to my mind that a real skeleton, or parts of a skeleton, if they could be obtained, would be better than the best drawings, and indeed the very best kind of apparatus for a school;— for instance a hand and arm, a foot and leg, or a skull. I thought the advantages of such furniture would be great and various. It would afford instruction directly in anatomy, and what is still more important, would accustom our children to contemplate such subjects rationally, seriously, and minutely, and entirely take away that dread of such things, which we have received from our nurses.

After I had gone so far, I went on with a number of bold inquiries, quite new to my own mind. Such as, would it not be very beneficial, morally, religiously, intellectually, and practically, for the bodies of deceased persons, by consent of their friends, and their own previous approbation, to be publicly dissected, accompanied with appropriate lectures—and that all mystery, secrecy and reserve should be removed from every department of knowledge, that all might be accustomed to the true, philosophic examination of every truth, every reality, every material exertion, and mode of operation; and every relation which the mind of the learner was capable of embracing understandingly. The inquiry is, whether all things should not be called by correct and appropriate names, the accurate import of which should be generally known. And whether this would not have a direct and strong tendency to prevent crime, and increase holiness and goodness, and instead of light, trifling, and injurious, to make men truly enlightened, serious, and benevolent; and finally to advance the race of man with the greatest possible celerity, in its destined career of moral and physical improvement.

I have for the moment, I can hardly tell why, answered all the inquiries to my own mind, decidedly in the affirmative; whether I am right or wrong, or whether I go too far, must be determined by greater light and experience. But whether right or wrong, I have a favor to ask as an individual, and an answer will, I think, be of public utility. Can such articles as I first named, skeletons and parts of skeletons, be obtained, and what would be the cost of them? My present design is to have my school room and my dwelling furnished with every article I can afford, which is calculated to communicate instruction concerning this wonderful and most interesting creature, man. C. O.

We consider the general object of our correspondent's communication highly important. There is no intrinsic difficulty in accomplishing the first plan proposed, and we doubt not that the vender of apparatus, who shall embrace this among the objects of attention, will meet with ample encouragement and remuneration. We do not know at present any regular mode of procuring parts of a skeleton; but we hope this communication will call the attention of medical gentlemen to the subject, and induce them to aid in the important step in education. We trust too that the premium proposed by the American Lyceum, for a class-book on human physiology, to be awarded in October next, will lead to new interest on the subject, and furnish new openings for efforts of this kind; for it was the intention of the movers of this plan, that the outlines of Anatomy as well as of Physiology should be embraced in the plan, as the necessary basis of physiological knowledge. It is not to be hoped that our schools would pursue these branches separately.

In order to illustrate still farther the interest and simplicity of Anatomy as a study for youth, we have added another unpublished lesson from 'The House I live in.'

In regard to the publicity of dissections, our correspondent is stepping upon *dangerous ground*. Let him remember that our Creator has implanted within us feelings on subjects of this kind, which are intended to be the safeguards of moral purity. Let him recollect, that the nations which have broken down these barriers against evil, have become *sinks of pollution;* and that *chastity* has not long remained, after *natural modesty* has been banished, either in individuals or communities. On the other hand, we admit that there is among us much of *artificial modesty,* which often unfits us for some of the most important duties of benevolent and active life, which perverts the conscience by leading us to associate the appointments of the Creator with the guilt of crime, which confounds knowledge with crime, which leads to the concealment of facts of vital importance to the health, and purity, and life of the young. In some instances within our knowledge, this ignorance has led to the very vice it was intended to prevent, and in one, to mania and suicide! We tremble too when we read, that nothing which '*maketh a lie*' shall enter into heaven, and then recollect the amount of this crime produced by this '*artificial modesty*' — the number of conscientious parents we have known, who would be guilty of falsehood without hesitation, under its impulse. Surely there is *something wrong* in this subject; for truth and duty must be consistent with themselves.

ON THE STUDY OF THE GREEK LANGUAGE.

To name this subject to an American scholar is to call up a blush for his country. Whether we consider the intrinsic beauty, and philosophical structure of the Greek language, or the noble models of reasoning, and eloquence and style which it furnishes, or its importance in the interpretation of that book by which we believe that 'LIFE *and* IMMORTALITY *are brought to light*' — every argument which can be adduced for the study of a language not immediately necessary to the business of life, would seem to apply to the Greek, preëminently. And yet, the few scholars among us look in vain for companions in their labors or their pleasures; and the multitude of *graduated tyros*, are compelled to confess and lament their ignorance, or to palliate the shame by a sneer at antiquity.

An admirable series of articles in the Quarterly Register of the American Education Society, and the lecture of Professor Felton before the American Institute, present with great force and beauty the arguments in favor of the cultivation of Greek literature. But with the question — 'What good will it do?' — so constantly sounding in our ears, and with the constant argument of our country that a study which does not promote directly, either *wealth* as one part of the community demand — or *moral improvement*, as another portion require, — is of no value, we feel little hope that they would convince any who are not yet persuaded of the importance of having a greater number of thorough Greek scholars among us. We will venture, however, to address to one of these parties, a portion of an eloquent appeal by Professor Stuart on the union of classical and sacred studies.*

After urging upon his readers the necessity, in a christian nation, of comprehending the scriptures in the original, he insists that this knowledge should be spread among the laity, and not confined to the clergy — for he adds — 'This has once been tried, and the shadow of death spread over the nations;' and he thus meets those who admit this, and yet neglect classical studies.

But what has all this to do with *classic* study? Much; very much indeed. The Bible is a revelation by *language*. To know what it teaches, *language* must be studied and understood. The most important part of the Scriptures, is in the *Greek* language. Greek then must be understood in order to read it. But how is this to be accomplished? To read the New Testament only, can never give one such a knowledge of Greek, as to enable him to understand and interpret it with any good degree of reasonable confidence. The laws of Greek grammar and of Greek philology in general, must be made to bear upon the New Testament. When God speaks to men, it is in language such as men employ. It is subject, therefore, to the like rules and methods of interpretation. If this be not so, then a new revelation must be made in order to guide the interpreter. If it be so, then the more extensive one's knowledge of Greek is, the better he can interpret the New Testament. There are hundreds of words and phrases in it, which can be fully understood and satisfactorily illustrated only from the Greek classics. With all the *Hebraisms* it contains, it contains also a great deal of classic Greek, i. e. Greek which in its idiom fully accords with that of the Greek classic writers. Unless mira-

* Quarterly Register of the American Education Society. Vol. III. p. 164.

cles are to be wrought anew, then, how can any say that the Greek classics need not be studied in order to interpret the New Testament? It is in vain to say this. There never was a good interpreter, there never can be, without such a knowledge. The nature of the case carries along with it a full demonstration of this. All right interpretation must be founded in the idiom, the *usus loquendi* of language. How can a man acquire this by studying only the New Testament, or even the Greek Testament and the Septuagint? It cannot be done. Those who know nothing by experience may maintain that it can be; but those who speak from experience, must certainly know better.

But parents and students will say — 'What more can be done? Are not the most precious years of life completely absorbed by these studies? Is not the time, and often the vigor of our youth wasted away in reaching even that point of ignorance in the classics, which is the subject of such bitter taunts?' To this we must reluctantly answer in the affirmative; and mourn over that 'weariness, of the spirit as well as of the flesh, which so generally results in the mere consciousness of mortifying ignorance. But the question naturally arises — 'Is all this *necessary*? Is there no defect in the modes of instruction, which produces the waste of intellect?' Some of our scholars will tell us — 'Undoubtedly — There is not enough of hard study, not half enough of the *grammar* and *lexicon* and *drill*.' But where or how is it practicable in our country to have more of these, without lamentable ruin of constitution, or that utter neglect of other studies which will make our young men mere magazines of philosophy?

But from other quarters we hear a more cheering reply.— 'Our *methods of instruction* are wrong. We have departed from the simplicity of nature, and we only pay the just penalty, in being left to grope our way in darkness; or, if we reach the goal, to find the course long and painful.' We are pointed to some of the first classical scholars of olden times in England,* to show that we have deviated even from 'the good old way' of our country, on this subject. These eminent men forbid that tyros should commence with the abstract theory and forms of language, as we now do, a task which is rarely accomplished without painful and injurious compulsion. They urge that the inductive plan should be adopted, that nature and the natural progress of the mind should be consulted, that it should be pursued in such a manner as to lead the pupil on by the interest of the study itself. This last point, all experience shows cannot be attained with most minds, without attending to the first — without furnishing the pupils first with so much of the material of the language as shall render it a pleasing medium for the acquisition of ideas, before he is repulsed with ab-

* Annals of Education, Vol. IV. pp. 19 — 65.

stract rules and skeletons of forms, which he is not prepared to understand or apply. We would ask an objector, whether he who is familiar with our own language is not best able to understand its grammar — if, indeed, any other can be; and we would again ask, why the same familiarity with a foreign language should not be equally useful. With the application of these principles in the school of Fellenberg, and in the system of Jacotot, our readers were made acquainted in our first volume. The evil has been felt by many of our own public teachers, and the value of the remedy admitted.

Some efforts have been made to apply to these principles in elementary books. But until recently for the force of established habit, or the cry of 'Innovation ! Quackery ! 'superficial scholars!' from the 'censores literarum,' little progress had been made. Public schools would not allow improvements, and private teachers would be discountenanced by many of our colleges, if they should venture upon it.

Within a short period, the views to which we have referred, have been gaining ground. They are fully developed by Professor Ticknor in reference to the modern languages, in his lecture before the American Institute of Instruction,* and have been applied by him in the instruction of classes in the University of Cambridge. He observes '*They coincide with the suggestions made by Lord Bacon — and with the system pursued by Milton and Locke, and by the vast majority of skilful teachers in those parts of Europe where Education, at the present time, is the best conducted and advanced the farthest.*'

In a recent lecture before the American Institute, Professor Packard of Bowdoin College expresses the same views.† He argues that the *facts of language* should be acquired like those of science, by selecting and arranging, and then reducing them to order ; and then deducing and illustrating the general law, which is then rendered at once intelligible and interesting. The irksome task of committing a grammar to memory as the first step in learning a language, he considers not only useless, but *injurious to the habits and mind of the pupil ;* and he adds — '*I am not aware that a mode of proceeding so contrary to nature is now pursued by any enlightened instructor.*' Not many years since, it was made a question whether in republishing 'Locke on Education,' that portion which relates to this mode of instruction should not be omitted, in order to avoid exciting prejudice against the work ! We rejoice at this happy change.

In reference to the Greek we have hitherto known only two el-

* Annals of Education Vol. ii. p. 49.

† Lectures before the American Institute for 1833, p. 155.

ementary works on this plan. An introductory work, with an interlinear translation, was published by Mr Johnson of Philadelphia, which, in skilful hands, might be rendered very useful. A simple collection of simple phrases, designed to illustrate in the usual grammatical order, the forms and rules and syntax of the language, was published by Professor Goodrich of Yale College; and we have known it used with success, in gaining a sufficient knowledge of that language to read the New Testament with ease, with very little instruction.

Both of the works we have named, were designed rather as instruments, than directories, in a course of instruction; and neither of them were *fully* adapted to self-instruction. In the 'Lessons in Greek, by T. Dwight,' from which we have already made some extracts, the attempt is made to draw out in detail that inductive plan which is often so much misunderstood, and misrepresented; and in such a form as not only to enable every intelligent instructor to employ and extend it, but to permit all who desire it, to ascertain the amount of the difficulties which are considered as obstructing every avenue to this noble, and to us, sacred language. We have already given it our welcome, as the first of this kind. Although it will naturally be expected to have the defects of a first essay, we believe it will be found worthy the examination of those who teach the elements of the language, as well of those who wish to pursue the study. That we have full ground for the remark, aside from all theoretical views, we think our readers will be satisfied by perusing the following letter, recently received from a lady in New York.

New York, April 5, 1834.

To the Editor of the Annals of Education.

'Dear Sir—I have recently been so highly gratified by a new source of pleasure and improvement, which has been opened to me, that I cannot forbear asking the favor of making known to others, through your interesting journal, what I cannot but deem a valuable acquisition to the young student, as well as to all who have any desire to penetrate the mysteries of Ancient Languages, but are kept from the undertaking by the dry and uninteresting, as well as *tedious* process, by which they must acquire them. Just one month since, I *accidentally* met with the lessons in Greek, recently published by Theodore Dwight, Jr. of this city. I had not at the time the most distant idea of studying the language, but was induced from mere curiosity to look at the first page. I became so much interested, that without being aware of the time that had elapsed, I found I had finished the first lesson, and was disappointed that some interruption caused me to leave my book.

The next day I resumed it with equal interest, and by devoting one hour a day for the last month, to these books, I am now beginning to read the New Testament with ease and pleasure. Every step of my progress has been so interesting, that I have gone to the study entirely as a relaxation, and have learned to read the New Testament, without having taken a single hour from any other employment; that is, I have had *no fixed time* for study, but have taken up my book at leisure moments; and since I have commenced translating, I usually read a few verses before retiring to rest for the night, which is often the only time I devote to it. I have been continually astonished at my own progress, for from having formerly attended a little, to Latin and French, in the common mode of plodding through uninteresting grammars, I had no idea that any language could be acquired so rapidly, or the study of it made so delightful.

I have tried to analyse the sources of my pleasure in studying. So far as I understand them they are these. There is nothing to be learned, that is not fully understood; and at every step, the learner is made to feel that something is *accomplished.* The great charm about this work seems to be, that it introduces you at once into the very heart of the language; and the mind, instead of being *driven* into it, earnestly seeks for itself the knowledge of all the peculiarities in its formation.

It is so simple that the very young student can fully comprehend it; and if it were introduced into schools, I doubt not that the Greek language would be learned in one sixth part of the time that is usually consumed upon it.

Some young ladies, who live near me, observing how interested I had become in the study, purchased the book, and without informing any of their friends, they managed by studying half an hour every evening, after they had retired for the night, to obtain sufficient knowledge to commence the New Testament, which they are now reading with me. We have had no instructor; but when I applied a few evenings since to a friend, who called accidentally (and who is a professor of languages) for some information about a passage I was reading, he expressed great astonishment on being told the short time I had devoted to the study, and said he never met with such an instance before.

I sincerely wish, for the benefit of those who are so often obliged to weary their patience over the pages of uninteresting grammars, as well as for ladies and children, this simple work might be extensively made known; and with this view, I have taken the liberty of addressing you.

It is a great mistake into which some have fallen to suppose that the work is for *Modern* Greek. It teaches Ancient Greek. Mr Dwight adopts the modern mode of pronunciation merely, but the work may be studied with equal advantage by those who prefer to retain the other system, as the only difference is in the sound of a few of the letters.'

Our readers will not forget, that this novice in Greek, as well as the author of the work in question, would smile at the idea that '*a* *knowledge of the Greek language'* was attained in this short period, and by the use of this *elementary work.* To adopt the metaphor of Prof. Packard, Mr Dwight merely attempts to open the gates to the temple of antiquity; to remove some of the obstacles which have rendered it so difficult of access; and to introduce the student into its vestibule, and place him in a situation from which he may proceed to examine its treasures. Much less would this be deemed sufficient to prepare one to become an interpreter of the New Testament, as will easily be inferred from the remarks of Prof. Stuart which we have quoted. In the lecture before the Institute, to which we have referred, it is well observed;—'It is not enough to make the student a mere *translator;* knowledge of language is of little value except as it admits the possessor to a new field of thought, and a new view of men.' The customs and institutions of ancient times are so interwoven with their languages, that the one cannot be thoroughly understood by him who is not familiar with the other; and we would urge the tyro in language to beware of assuming the character of a commentator, especially in our sacred books*; although he will often find a beauty and force in the original, which no translation has rivalled.

But we find here, satisfactory evidence that the first difficulties of the language were overcome, and the student made 'a translator' during a period which would scarcely be believed, were not the authority unquestionable. And how has this been accomplished? Simply by leading on the mind in a natural course, by substituting the inductive for the synthetic mode of instruction.

In the first lessons of which we have given a specimen, the pupil is made familiar with the Greek letters; but we trust none of our readers were so far misled by the simple title which *we* gave, as not to perceive, that while the student is there primarily occupied with spelling and reading, he is also learning a portion of the language itself, and impressing indelibly on his mind some of its elements. In subsequent lessons, as we have already remarked, the author goes on to present each part of speech distinctly in examples, to illustrate its

* An instance of misinterpretation, which occurred within our own knowledge many years since, impressed this deeply on our own mind. A person accustomed to give public religious instruction, and to whom we often listened with interest, came to us to receive lessons in Latin, in the hope of gaining a little more knowledge of the Scriptures through the medium of the *Latin Translation.* We had often found him raising his voice (as we supposed from the impulse of feeling) to a pitch which was exhausting and dangerous to his feeble frame; and we ventured to remonstrate with him on its inutility, and evil effects. He listened patiently; but replied with great calmness—'Ah, Sir, you do not understand that passage, 'Cry aloud! Spare not! Lift up thy voice *like a trumpet!*' To such an argument, thus urged, there was no reply intelligible to one ignorant of eastern metaphor; and I could only regret that he could fortify himself against argument, by an appeal to a supposed knowledge of Latin.

nature and use, and then to embody what is thus discovered, in a definition or rule. The inflections of nouns and verbs are taught at first in the same inductive mode, and the pupil is first furnished with examples of each, is called to observe and classify the terminations, and finally is presented with complete formulas, or paradigms, and the trunk and branches of the Greek tree.

All this is done in connection with the study of *Greek phrases*, each of which are to be *spelled*, *read*, *translated*, *written*, *analysed*, *and repeated*. The meaning, origin and form of each *new* word is given, while the pupil is required to rely on his previous knowledge of those which have been taught; and he will gain from this unpretending work, a knowledge of the accents, breathings, and different classes of letters, and many other little circumstances, which would be welcome to some of the perplexed graduates of our colleges. The mystery of dialects is explained, in a manner which will enable a child to comprehend it. The author maintains that the modern Greek is but a dialect; and adduces many authorities in favor of the opinion, among others, that of a Greek Professor, Mr Negris — to whom both are as familiar as our maternal language. In the absence of any standard of pronunciation which has authority, he proposes and employs that of the modern Greek, as having the best claim on the score of expediency, as well as of its probable antiquity.

The work is closed by a series of lessons from various authors, which are gradually made more difficult and accompanied by less illustration, and a vocabulary of the words introduced, until the student is finally thrown upon his own resources and efforts. It embodies more of the inductive system as we were accustomed to practice it in the instructions of the deaf mute, as we have seen it in the schools of Pestalozzi, and Fellenberg, and Jacotot, and as it has been recommended by some of the most able teachers of language in our own country, than any work we know. Indeed, it is the only one we have seen, which will give any distinct view of this mode of instruction to an inexperienced person; and while it has the imperfections of a pioneer work, and inaccuracies, many of which would doubtless have been remedied if the author had been in the neighborood of the press, we are sure that instructors and pupils who are not fettered by the trammels of precedent and habit, will find it well worthy of attention.

The author employs music as an aid in the acquisition of the accent and pronunciation, in a manner which we hope to notice hereafter.

LESSON IN ANATOMY.

THE HUMAN HAND.

From 'The House I live in.'

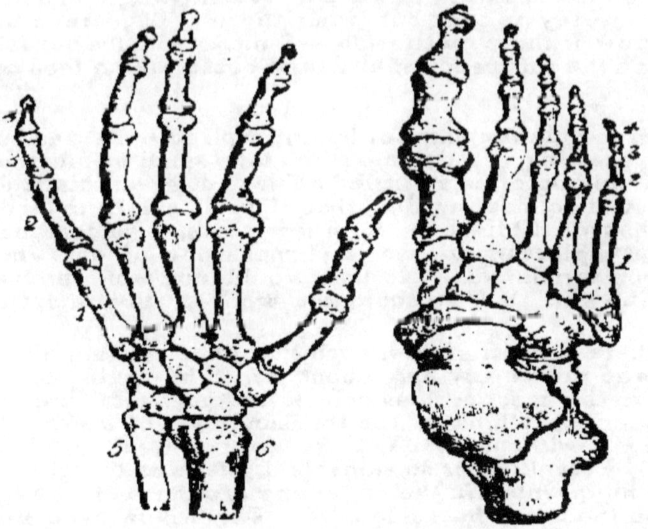

I have shown you both these parts of the frame before, but not so plainly. They were much smaller, and you saw them in connection with other parts. They are engraved, here, on a much larger scale, and much plainer. At present, I shall not say much, except about the one on the left hand. That on the right, I may tell you about at some other time. This chapter will be long enough without it, for there is much to say about the other. A gentleman in Europe has just written a whole book, a great deal larger than this, about nothing else.

The left hand figure, you will see, represents the parts which in the engraving at the head of the last chapter, we find at the end of those long, hanging, ladder-like frames; and forms a part of them. I told you about the rapid motion of those parts; but though they can be made to move swiftly, they could not accomplish much without these pieces at the end.

You might easily guess that this part of the frame was made to be active. For when you go into a factory or any other building, and see a contrivance not larger than a man's hand, which consists of twentyseven pieces of metal, besides a great many ropes, pulleys, hinges, &c, you at once *think*, if you do not *speak* it; 'All this *means* something.' So the piece of *frame* now before you *means something*. There are fifteen or more hinges in it; and the number of ropes, pulleys, &c, is almost innumerable. Those last I cannot tell you about till we come to the next chapter.

Small as this member of the 'frame' is, it is a part of the utmost consequence. Even if 'the house I live in' was a palace, or if it had cost as much as St Peter's church at Rome, or the pyramids of Egypt, it would be of little use without it. And if all the 'houses' in the world were without it, neither those houses, nor anything else, would long be worth much. The farmer could not sow his grain, or plant his corn, or weed or hoe it while growing, or collect it when ripe. Nor could the miller grind it, or the baker make it into bread, if it were grown. Neither could we raise anything else to eat, in its stead. We might get along a few years with what is already raised, but what then? The fruits and roots and nuts which grow without cultivation — I mean without our labor — would not last us, and the thousands of birds and beasts which feed on them, very long.

* * * * * * *

The human tongue is spoken of by an inspired writer, as being a 'little member,' yet boasting great things. So this small member of the frame, which we are talking of, is a 'little' affair; but great things depend upon it. It is a sort of connecting link, that, if used, serves to bind the human soul to 'the house' it 'lives in' for a few years, — seldom more than 100. Without it, or neglecting to use it, (I speak now of our whole race) our lives must soon terminate. 'He that would not work, neither should he eat,' is a Divine law; but he could not work much without this little instrument.

[Perhaps there is not a greater curiosity under the sun than the *human hand*. Yet who thinks anything about it? The truth is, many of the best, as well as the most curious objects in the world, are neglected in the same manner. Think of the thousand uses of *water*. What living thing could exist without it? Yet we do not think much of all this; and are we ever thankful for so valuable a gift as water is?

The bones represented in the engraving are those of the *left* hand, and you look upon the *top* or backside of it. The whole hand and wrist contain twentyseven bones; nineteen in the former, and eight in the latter. The bones in the hand have a general resemblance, though some are much *longer* than others. The four longest, opposite the figure 1, support the *palm* of the hand, and are joined at one end *to* the wrist bones, and at the other to the first joint of the fingers. They are called the *metacarpus*.

The bones of the wrist are called the *carpus*. They are situated between the *ulna* (5) and the *radius* (6) on the one side, and the metacarpal bones and the first bone of the thumb on the other. They are wedged together like the stones of a pavement, only not so firmly.

The first four bones of the *fingers*, opposite figure 2, are the longest. Those opposite 3, are shorter; the last, or those marked 4, shorter still. The thumb has one bone less than the fingers. All the joints of the hand — and there are fourteen, besides the wrist — are the *hinge* joints, and the ends of the bone are made a little like door hinges. They only bend in one direction, of course. Where the fingers join to the metacarpal bones, there is much more freedom of motion, than at the hinge-like finger joints. But the joint at the wrist admits of motion, very freely, in every direction.

When the bones of the hand are not quite so naked as they appear in the engraving, but are dressed up in muscles, tendons, membranes, nerves, arteries, and veins, and covered with skin, nails, &c, in a manner which I cannot fully describe in this volume, the whole presents a most beautiful appearance. Beautiful and useful as it is, however, and placed before our eyes from the time we see the light, till we sleep in death, there are few things in the whole visible world of which, not only children, but adults, are so ignorant!

To prepare the young reader for a full description of this member in Part II, I here transcribe a few lines from Bell's Bridgwater Treatise on the Hand, lately published.

'The difference in the length of the fingers serves a thousand purposes, adapting the hand and fingers, as in holding a rod, a switch, a sword, a hammer, a pen or pencil, engraving tool, &c, in all which a secure hold and freedom of motion are admirably combined. Nothing is more remarkable than the manner in which the delicate and moving apparatus of the palm and fingers is guarded. The power with which the hand grasps, as when a sailor lays hold to raise his body to the rigging, would be too great for the texture of mere tendons, nerves, and vessels; they would be crushed, were not every part that bears the pressure, defended with a cushion of fat, as elastic as that which we have described in the foot of the horse and the camel. To add to this, there is a muscle which runs across the palm of the hand, and supports the cushion on the inner edge. It is the muscle which, raising the inner edge of the palm, forms the drinking cup of Diogenes.'

It is the *top* of the *right foot*, which is shown in the engraving by the side of the hand. The bones of the foot have a strong resemblance to those of the hand. The figures, 1, 2, 3 and 4, which stand along by the side of the little toe, refer to the different rows of bones opposite to them, as in the case of the hand.

The foot, itself, has just the same number of bones that the hand has; but at the instep or ankle, there is one less. The seven bones of the ankle, have much less motion than the eight wrist bones have.]

THE TEACHER'S ALMANAC FOR MAY.

THE SCHOOLROOM.

What though the teacher, in the summer season, receive but a scanty remuneration, and is assigned to a narrow school-room? This, for the time, is the trial to which her Creator calls her. Let her make the most she can of her circumstances. What though but one scholar in three or four has any books or other instruments of instruction? What though she is deluged with pupils — three or four times as many as she can take care of — and is obliged to suspend many of them 'between the heavens and the earth,' on benches six inches wide? What though she cannot prevail with the parents to send them to school in the 'cool of the day,' before the sun gets more than half-way to his burning meridian. *She has engaged* — let her do what she can. Somebody else might do *worse* than herself for the heterogeneous mass upon which she is called to act. She may be consoled by the reflection that

> 'Who does the best his circumstance allows,
> Does well; acts nobly; — angels could no more.'

If she has not money — even by drawing heavily upon her scanty wages, to purchase books, and seats with backs for her pupils, let them go out into the pure air of heaven, occasionally; (at least when the weather is fine) and study some of the ten thousand lessons in the great book of nature. Or let them occasionally *stand;* and perhaps make letters, or write words or sentences on slates. These last cost very little, and will richly repay the teacher who labors even for fifty cents and her board a week.

Let every teacher remember that the air of the school room is rendered impure by *respiration,* at the rate of a gallon a minute; and this too whether the temperature of the room is high or low. — That cool air falling upon the human body, when in a profuse perspiration, especially in currents through a window, door, or crevice in the wall or floor, exposes to colds, rheumatisms, fevers and consumption; and that though the robust and vigorous should not feel its effects immediately, the *feeble* must; and the strong *may* in the end. — That the lungs are inevitably injured by breathing dust often; whether it be from sweeping the school room without first sprinkling it with water, playing in the sand, or exposure to a road which is constantly travelled.

THE EARTH.

The air, the earth, the waters, are teeming with life; and we can no longer point to any particular objects in so wide a field. Let your pupils learn now, if they never have before, to read the great book of nature, in all its pages. If possible, let each one be supplied with a note book, to make memoranda of the facts they observe; and let them daily, or weekly, give an account of them in writing, if they are able — if not, orally — a mass of facts will soon be accumulated in this manner which will surprise and delight them; the habit of observation will be formed; and more progress will be made in composition and 'the art of speaking and writing the English language correctly,' than in months spent in 'the grammar book.'

A new branch of natural history may now be pursued with pleasure. Encourage your pupils to bring you specimens of the minerals they find, let them describe their qualities carefully; and if you do not know their names, send the description to others.

Can you not find the opportunity to lead your pupils into a garden, or to engage each in cultivating a little spot at home, that they may acquire some practical konwledge on the subject? Can you not at least keep a few flower boxes in your school-room, or sow some seeds on wet cotton?

THE HEAVENS.

This will be a favorable season for studying the constellations about the north pole — the Great Bear, Little Bear — Cassiopeias Chair, and the Hair of Berenice. The last is a collection of nebulous (indistinct) little stars, which will be in the meridian at nine o'clock in the middle of May. In a straight line between this and the last star, in the tail of the great bear, or the first in the handle of the dipper, is a very bright star called Cor-Caroli, or Charles's heart. The constellation of the Virgin, one of the signs of the Zodiac, will be in the meridian in the evenings of the latter part of the month. Spica, one of its most beautiful stars, is much used by navigators, and may be distinguished by its solitary and peculiar brilliancy at the south.

MISCELLANY.

PENNSYLVANIA COMMON SCHOOLS.

We rejoice that the great state of Pennsylvania has at length adopted a system for the management and direction of her common schools, and that its features are, in the main, so excellent. From the report acknowledged in our last number, from the Hon. Samuel Breck, to whom the state is indebted for preparing and carrying through the measure, and the amended act since become a law by the signature of the Governor, we learn that the fund established in that state in 1831, for the aid of common schools, now amounts to $546,563, and will soon be $2,000,000. The new bill appropriates $75,000 of its revenue for the year 1835, and the same annually thereafter, until the fund yields $100,000, to be applied to those districts which comply with the conditions of the new act. This act makes each county in the state a school *division*, and every ward, township, and borough in each, a school district, which district shall contain a sufficient number of schools for the education of all within its limits who shall be offered. This new division of the state does not, however, interfere with the special regulations made by former acts for the city and county of Philadelphia.

The new statute requires that every district shall have six school directors, two of whom shall be elected annually. Their duty is to determine the number of schools which shall be necessary; to procure proper buildings, 'to appoint capable teachers, at liberal salaries,' and provide generally for the operation of the schools. They are to receive no compensation for their services, but an exemption from serving in the militia, or in township and borough offices. Two or more of the directors must visit the schools, at least once a month, and make an annual report to the *inspectors.*

The inspectors are two persons in each district, appointed annually by the courts of quarter sessions. Their business is to visit every school at least once in three months; to inquire into the moral character, learning and ability of the teachers, examine candidates for teaching, and grant certificates, for one year only, to those who shall be found qualified. They may require teachers to be examined publicly. They must also investigate the condition of the schools, as to the progress of the pupils, and their discipline; the character of the teachers; the branches taught, &c, and report annually, to the superintendent; which report must be published. Their only compensation is the same as that of the directors.

The Secretary of State is to be the Superintendent of the schools, whose duties, as defined by the statute, are nearly the same with those of the Superintendent of Common Schools in the state of New York. He must also settle all controversies that may arise in regard to the duties of inspectors and directors, and in regard to school money.

In order to prevent the school fund from excusing individual exertion, and to make it operate as a stimulus, an annual joint-meeting of one delegate from each board of district directors in a county, together with the county commissioner, shall be held, who shall determine whether a tax is necessary to meet the school expenses. If they determine a tax to be necessary, it shall be levied; but no tax shall be less in amount than *double the sum furnished them from the revenue of the school fund.* But if they determine that no tax is necessary, the districts whose delegates voted in the negative shall not be entitled to any aid from the school fund for that year; but the money to which they would otherwise have been entitled, shall be divided among those districts whose delegates voted in the affirmative. If no tax is voted, the old law shall be considered in force, without any regard to the school fund. If a tax is agreed upon, a public meeting of the citizens of each district shall be called, who may increase the tax, if they think it necessary. This last is one of the most valuable portions of the bill.

A majority of four in six of the directors may connect manual labor with study, in their several districts, and purchase the necessary materials, and employ persons to instruct the pupils in the mechanic arts and in agricultural pursuits, whenever they think it expedient.

The Bill as it came from the hands of the Committee made provision for the education of teachers,* but the amendments of the Senate excluded it. A less important section which required the teachers in the several *divisions* to adopt, yearly, *a uniform course of study* to be pursued by *every school in the division*, shared the same fate.

Oberlin Collegiate Institute.

We have given some notice of the origin and objects of this institution in a former number. From a recent circular we learn the following particulars.

The system embraces instruction in every department, from the Infant school to a Collegiate and Theological course. Physical and moral education are to receive particular attention. The institution was opened in December last, and has sixty students; about forty in the academic, and twenty in the primary department. All of them, whether male or female, rich or poor, are required to labor four hours daily. Male students are to be employed in agriculture, gardening, and some of the mechanic arts; females in housekeeping, useful needle-work, the manufacture of wool, the culture of silk, certain appropriate parts of gardening, &c. The Institution has five hundred acres of good land, of which, though a complete forest a year ago, about thirty acres are cleared, and sown with wheat. They have also a steam mill, and a saw mill, in operation. During the present year it is contemplated to add fifty acres to the cleared land, to erect a flouring mill, shingle machine, turning lathe, a work shop with an extensive boarding house, (which together with the present buildings will accommodate about one hundred and sixty students) furniture, farming, mechanic, and scientific apparatus; and begin a library.

During the winter months, the young men are at liberty to engage as agents, school teachers, or in any other occupation they may select. The expenses of students in the seminary for board at the table spread only with vegetable food, are eighty cents a week; and ninetytwo cents a

* One *petition* was presented against the provision for the education of teachers. The following letter of a schoolmaster from the same county, which we copy *literatim* from the Philadelphia Gazette, may suggest the reason.

'I take the pen in Hand to Notice you That I wand that money Where your Son went to School to me last Winter to me Henry Krebs In ———— and I shall write you the bill of his Schooling Where he went is 42½ Cents and a half and the amount of the Rens 11 Cents and so the whole amount is 53½ cents and So I have no more to write at present Henry Krebs his hand and pen august the 15th 1833 &c

Henry Krebs'

week for the same with animal food twice a day. Tuition is from fifteen to thirtyfive cents a week. The avails of the students' labors have thus far varied from one to eight cents an hour. The average has been five cents. A majority of the male students have, by their four hours' daily labor, paid their board, fuel, lights, washing and mending, and some even more; and this without any interference with their progress in their studies.

The time to be spent at this Institution, in preparation for the various professions and employments of life is not yet defined, nor a single course of study marked out as the only one through which an individual can attain a desired station. Diplomas are not to be given according to the time spent in study, but to the student's real acquirements.

Circuit Schools in Illinois.

There is room for much encouragement to the friends of common education in Illinois. The Illinois Patriot, the Gazette, and the Pioneer and Western Baptist, are ably advocating the cause; and a late number of the latter paper gives notice that a number of well qualified circuit teachers can find employ in that state by making application as there directed. We are glad to find that among the qualifications recommended, are *aptness to teach, conciliatory manners, and good moral character.* With these pre-requisites, the course proposed is as follows: The teachers being provided with suitable books and lessons on cards, are to take two, three, or more schools in different neighborhoods, visit each once, twice, three or more times in a week, hear the scholars recite their lessons, lecture, and explain the subjects, and thus enable those of any age who are disposed to learn, *to learn to teach themselves*, by the aid given them by their teachers. It is stated, moreover, that there are already a number of settlements, where the people are desirous of having the circuit system put in immediate operation.

Circuit Schools, and Lyceum Anniversary in Georgia.

Circuit schools are also attracting much attention in Georgia. In the 'Pioneer' of Illinois, for March 26th, is a letter from a Georgian to his friend in Illinois, in which he speaks with the highest confidence of this mode of teaching, as applied to the Southern States. A pamphlet is also mentioned as having been recently written on this subject, and circulated among the citizens of Georgia.

We are glad to find both the southern and western states turning their attention to a plan of instruction that promises so much, especially to new or thinly settled states. The Pioneer justly remarks that we have only to apply to other branches the same principle which has long been applied to schools for teaching singing. It is well known that these have been taught on what is substantially the 'circuit system' (at least in many parts of our country) for a century or more.

We are also glad to learn that the friends of education in Georgia, and particularly in Athens, the literary metropolis of the state, propose to hold a Lyceum or Common School anniversary at the next commencement at that place, to be attended by delegates, visitors, teachers, &c. They purpose to invite collections in Natural History for deposit, exhibition, or exchange, to be explained and illustrated by experiments and descriptions, by the professors of the college, by teachers, or by those who present them. A course of Lectures on School teaching, is also under consideration, and will probably be given at a future season, if not during the present.

Public Schools of New York.

We learn from the official report of the Public School Society, published in the New York Weekly Messenger, that the society has now, in operation, fiftyone schools, embracing 6631 boys, and 4831 girls, of whom about seventy per cent were in daily attendance on the first of February. This is an average number of 163 to each school, in actual attendance. The society employ fortyseven teachers, twentyseven assistant adult teachers, and seventyfour monitors; whose salaries for a year amount to $34,975. The monitors generally have a salary. Thirtyone of the schools are kept in only thirteen buildings; the others are generally kept in rooms hired for the purpose. The course of instruction in these schools embraces, besides the elements taught in the primaries, arithmetic, geography, grammar, composition, declamation, book-keeping, history, astronomy, algebra, geometry, and trigonometry. The schools are mainly supported by taxation; and are represented as being, 'with little exception,' in fine order.

New-York Institution for the Deaf and Dumb.

We have just received an interesting report from the New York Institution for the Deaf and Dumb. The whole number of pupils in December last, was 134. It has been necessary to provide additional teachers, accommodations and mechanical shops, for the increased number. A course of lectures has been given three evenings in a week, in the language of the deaf mutes, to explain the principal phenomena of nature, illustrated by means of apparatus, and to give the pupils general ideas in other topics. A library of 100 volumes has been collected for the use of the pupils. Instruction has also been given to a class in linear drawing, an art which ought to be taught to all the deaf mutes.

The resources of the Institution, although considerable, are not adequate to the execution of various plans of improvement proposed, or to the completion of those already commenced, and the building is still encumbered with debt. We cannot think, however, that a state so liberal, and individuals so benevolent and able, as many in New York, will allow so important an institution to suffer.

Donaldson Academy, and Manual Labor School.

The establishment of this school, at Fayetteville, North Carolina, was mentioned in a late number. We have just received a pamphlet embracing a 'Report on the state of that Institution,' in March last, and a 'Catalogue.' We are happy to learn that the prospects of the school are very encouraging. It was opened on the first Monday in January last, and on the twentieth of March it had, in both departments, eightyeight students.

One thing in the pamphlet, in particular, strikes us very favorably. The Trustees and others concerned do not set out with the idea of making the avails of labor too prominent an object. Their great purpose is to secure the *health of the students*; and while, *as a secondary object*, they wish to make the best possible use of all labor in defraying expenses, they do not intend, in ordinary cases, to require or permit a greater amount of it than is compatible with the highest degree of physical, intellectual, and moral progress.

MATHEMATICAL AND GRAMMAR SCHOOLS OF CHRIST CHURCH HOSPITAL, LONDON.

AMERICAN ANNALS OF EDUCATION AND INSTRUCTION.

JUNE, 1834.

THE BLUE COAT SCHOOL OF LONDON.

There is a splendor in the endowments for the education of the poor in England, which strikes an American very powerfully. It indicates a value for the object, an interest in the children of the poor, to form and to devote such noble establishments and extensive funds to their use, which surprises and gratifies us, in a land of aristocracy, whether we trace it to the benevolence of some individual, or the providence of the government. Nor is this beneficence confined to the Universities and higher institutions, which in our country we think excite too exclusively, the interest of those who have the means and the disposition to do good. Many of these funds also provide for the early and elementary education of the destitute and neglected, in the best manner which the knowledge or taste of the age could point out; and though generally less necessary in our country, yet similar beneficence, devoted to the same object, in a manner suited to *elevate* instead of sustaining our schools, might do incalculable good.

Among the charitable endowments for education in London, none is more likely to be known to a stranger than Christ Church Hospital, or the 'Blue Coat School,' as it is familiarly called — for he meets its pupils daily in a dress that shows their connection with some by-gone age. It is said to be the nearest approach to the monkish costume which is now worn in England. An outside coat or close robe, with long skirts of dark blue cloth, is the ancient tunic. It is fastened with a girdle round the waist. With this, is singularly contrasted the under tunic of yellow, and the yellow worsted stockings; and the peculiarity of the dress is rendered still more conspicuous, by the small, round, flat cap of black worsted, which forms the only covering for the head of the 'Blue Coat Boy,' whatever may be the weather; for the dress is rigidly required as a condition of their education. It is not a little amusing, to see one of these shadows of another generation moving through the modern crowd of a London street.

The school was established by Edward VI. at the instance of the eminent Ridley, in the surrendered monastery of the Grey Friars, and endowed with its revenues. These, with subsequent donations, now amount to about $200,000 a year. The whole number of pupils maintained is about a thousand, one hundred and fifty being received annually. A part of them are kept in their earlier years, at a country establishment connected with this. The greater number leave the institution at fifteen years of age, after acquiring the usual elementary branches of instruction. Those who are designed for classical or mathematical students remain longer, to prepare for the University, or the Navy; but are still 'Blue Coat Boys.' Several are constantly maintained by the institution at the Universities, until they complete their education.

The buildings are chiefly modern. The engraving represents one front of the building for the Mathematical and Grammar Schools recently erected, and will give some idea of the extent and splendor of the establishment. A new and noble hall for a chapel and dining-room, has also been built of granite, to receive eight hundred pupils, one hundred and fiftyseven feet in length, by fiftytwo in breadth; and the whole space beneath it is formed into open arcades, with unusual providence and kindness, to afford a play ground for the boys in bad weather.

The internal regulations of the school are in many points not less singular than the costume of the pupils, and its *plan* would not serve as a model for us. But we should rejoice to see the *spirit*, which founded this noble institution, pervading the possessors of wealth and the officers of government in our own country, — the spirit which deems a princely revenue well bestowed, for the *common education* of *the children of the poor*.

A VISIT TO HOFWYL.

We have believed that no service we could render to the cause of education in our country, would be so great as to present the epitome of the modern improvements which we found at Hofwyl. It was with this view that we published the letters on this subject in the first and second volumes of the 'Annals,' and time has not changed our opinion. We have been astonished, however, to find intelligent men, who would give it no attention — would scarcely read it — because it was 'foreign!' — and to be told that some of the American advocates of education were jealous, because their plans were not more talked of! — and that the Annals would be rendered unpopular! We should *be ashamed* to believe this. We rejoice to learn that by those who *read* them, these articles are regarded as among the most valuable in the work — to hear from a common school teacher, that they were of more practical value to her than any others — and to find parents who discover the rich mine of instruction, which is found in the system of Fellenberg. We ask others to read them. We cheerfully leave to time the decision on this point; and present as a confirmation of our views of Hofwyl, the following account of a recent visit, in a letter published by the able editors of the London Penny Magazine.

We have received the following interesting communication from a correspondent upon whose accounts we can place a full reliance. The establishments for education, which have been founded and matured in Switzerland, by the public spirit and laborious perseverance of M. Fellenberg, have now existed about thirtytwo years. Their high merits have been long familiar to the English public. At the present time, we understand that certain political dissensions, which have produced much ill-will and unhappiness in the canton of Berne, have had the common effect of all violent contests of opinion, — they have made men indifferent or opposed to those institutions for the amelioration of the human character, whose great object is to elevate our species above intolerance and narrowness of party-feeling. We trust that the open or concealed hostility which, it is said, now threatens the excellent establishments of M. Fellenberg, will speedily be put to shame by the good sense of the people of Switzerland; who will perceive in such institutions the surest preservation against the outbreaks of a mistaken zeal for freedom, on the one hand, and the tyranny of exclusive pretensions, on the other.

'In the month of August, 1832, I travelled into Switzerland for the purpose of making myself acquainted with the schools and institutions at Hofwyl. Situated about three leagues from the picturesque capital of Berne, amidst a beautiful scenery, composed of a cultivated vale, the Jura ridge of mountains, a pine forest, a small lake, and the glaciers of the Bernese Alps, stand the extensive buildings of the establishment, surrounded by about two acres of farm land. Upon my first arrival, before I could obtain an opportunity of presenting my letters to the benevolent founder, I wandered about in various directions. All was business and activity. Here was a troop of lads cutting the ripened corn, while another troop was engaged in conducting it to the barns. Here was the forge in activity; and there some little gardeners performing various operations in small plots of ground that were portioned out. Here was a group of little girls gleaning; there others carrying water, most of them singing, while thus employed. But my attention was peculiarly arrested by about one hundred men, who in a large, open building, erected in a recess of the garden, appeared to be engaged like boys in a school-room; over the entrance was inscribed this motto, "The Hope of their Country."

'I was at last fortunate enough to be admitted into the study of M. de Fellenberg, — a man somewhat advanced in years, with a countenance beaming with intelligence and kindness. De Fellenberg was, by birth, one of the ancient aristocracy of the country, and in possession of the hereditary property of his family. He determined upon devoting his fortune, and the labor of a life, in the endeavor to effect the regeneration of his native land, by the means of education. "I will infuse good habits and principles into the children." For thirtytwo years has he pursued his steady course, increasing in influence, and extending his establishment as his scheme grew upon him, until it has become what he described to me. "This," said he, pointing to a large building, "is the institute for the boys of the higher classes. Here are their dining-rooms; — arranged on each side of yonder galleries, are their dormitories. Here you see their gardens, their museum, their work-shops, their school-rooms; here their gymnasium where they exercise themselves in wet weather, here their stream of running water where they bathe every day; study is their employment, bodily labor their recreation, — but bodily exertion I insist upon. There is no health, no vigor of mind, no virtue without it. Those persons grown to manhood, who are mixing with the boys, are placed by me to observe every action, and catch every expression. My grand object is to comprehend thoroughly the character of my pupils, in order that I may work more efficaciously upon them. These persons are by no means considered as spies by the boys, — they are their companions. At Hofwyl, all that is not in itself wrong is permitted. I never like to forbid a thing when I am unable to assign a reason for doing so; it creates a confusion in young minds with regard to principle, a thing most dangerous to their future happiness. We have no boundary-mark, yet my boys stay at home: we interfere not with their pleasures, yet they cling to their duty.

"Within this enclosure is my eldest daughter's poor school for girls. She has about a hundred under her direction, who are fed and clothed by the establishment. To these she devotes her entire time. They learn all that in after-life will be of service to them: — to clean the house, — to cultivate the garden, — to sew, — to make all those little necessaries which are of so much importance in the cottage; to read, and sing, — to be cheerful, and to be happy. Unless our women be brought up in modesty, and with industrious and religious habits, it is in vain that we educate the men. It is they who keep the character of men in its proper elevation.

"Here is my school for the middling classes, — here all instruction has reference to practical purposes. Man was born to have dominion over the earth, and to subdue it, but it is by the intellect alone that he can do so. His unassisted strength, what is it? To conquer Nature he must understand her. Look in here, and you will see the laboratory of the chemist, and the lever and the pulley of the mechanic.

"In these two buildings are my poor school for boys, who are boarded and clothed by the establishment. And well they earn their maintenance, for the little fellows work ten hours a day in the summer; and the expense that I incur in their behalf is nearly repaid by their exertions. They study for two hours each day, and this I consider sufficient. The case here is the reverse of the Institute, for bodily exertion is the labor and study the recreation. The habits I bring them up with are those which I desire should continue with them through life; they consequently have reference to their probable position in society. The habit of continued study would ill-become a person destined to gain his livelihood by his hands. Although there are now one hundred boys assembled here, mine were but small beginnings. I had but one pupil at first. It was long before I could find a master in whom I could confide. Do you observe those little patches of garden-ground? Each poor lad has one to himself; and the produce belongs exclusively to him. They usually dispose of it to the establishment, which either pays them the money at the time, or lodges it for them in a little bank I have founded. Many of them have very considerable sums there. It is here that they obtain a habit of passing the greater portion of their time in continued labor; — they become acquainted with the value of labor, by the produce of their little gardens. The instruction that I give them, although somewhat more elevated than what is generally obtained by persons of their rank in life, is directed to the rendering perfect the senses and reflection, — to make them better practical men; drawing, the sciences of arithmetic and geometry, a useful selection from the other sciences, all taught in the most unostentatious manner; the history of their native country, and an acquaintance with the different natural objects around them, together with music, form the extent of their literary instruction.

"Religion is inculcated in every way. Public prayer, both at church and at school, is regularly performed in common with the schools of other countries. Besides this, these poor lads are taught to see the Creator in his works. When their admiration is roused by a natural object, they are accustomed to direct their thoughts to its Maker.

"But here," said my venerable companion, "is the engine upon which I rely for effecting the moral regeneration of my country, (and my attention was directed to the men whom I had before seen in the morning); these are the masters of village schools, come here to imbibe my principles, and to perfect themselves in their duty. These men have *six thousand* pupils under them; and if, by the blessing of God, I can continue the direction of them, success is certain."

'To insure success M. Fellenberg spares no pains, — no expense. There are no less than thirtytwo professors solely devoted to his establishment, who inhabit a house to themselves upon the premises.

'In all, there are about three hundred and fifty individuals in this little colony. Despite of his enemies, the spirit of De Fellenberg is spreading throughout Switzerland; and after having seen the parent institution I visited several of his establishments in some of the remotest cantons.

'A week closed my short sojourn at Hofwyl. I quitted it with a heavy heart; and the recollection of the moral beauty of what is there witnessed, will remain riveted on my memory forever.'

EDUCATION AND THE PRESS.

We are thirteen millions, and we have not less than one million of children *wholly uninstructed*, and not less than one million more, whose means of instruction are shamefully scanty. *Education*, in its comprehensive sense — as a preparation for life — for the life of an American Citizen as he should be — we need not say how rarely it is to be found! Millions of parents, and teachers, and school inspectors, scattered over our vast republic, are ignorant or unmindful of those duties to the children, on whose faithful performance the future purity, and prosperity, and the very *existence* of our country depend. How can such a mass of ignorance be enlightened — such a mass of prejudice as it brings in its train, be overcome? How can the apathy and avarice which stop every ear be removed? Can a single periodical accomplish this? Can we with a thousand, or even two thousand subscribers, effect it? We have never dreamed so wildly. We have but struggled, till our strength and means were exhausted, to preserve *the last beacon light* on this subject. It is for this only that we have proposed to others to aid in its preservation. We and our work are powerless in effecting this great object in view, unless we can enlist the aid of others — unless each of our readers will endeavor to circulate and to apply the principles which we endeavor to furnish for this purpose, and scatter abroad the light which one work can only scatter in feeble separated rays to a few points of our country — merely to make the obscurity visible which reigns over this subject. We would gladly ascribe this result to the defects of our own work; but the brief existence of several kindred publications shows that there is some other and more extensive cause than our defects. Indeed, the mortifying fact that enterprising publishers could not venture to publish more than *two hundred and fifty copies*, of a volume so replete with instruction for teachers, both theoretical and practical, as the lectures of the American Institute for 1833, is a sad evidence of the prevailing apathy on the subject.

To remove this apathy — to circulate valuable information on this subject, and excite the interest of our newspaper-reading community, none can do more than the conductors of the newspaper press. We cordially rejoice to see the increased interest taken in this subject by our newspapers, within a few years. A subject which, by common consent, seemed to be excluded from their columns, is now frequently discussed in an able and interesting manner; and if we should render this work a compilation, the essays, addresses and reports which we constantly receive on this subject, would furnish a sufficient stock of materials, of real value, to fill every number of the Annals. We appeal to our fellow laborers of the press, to continue and extend their efforts as they value our morals or our institutions. And we shall devote a large portion of our numbers to extracts which will show the increase of interest thus exhibited; and cheerfully offer our pages for their use.

'DOES MERE INTELLECTUAL EDUCATION BANISH CRIME?'

No one doubts at the present day, that ignorance is a fruitful source of crime, and that the diffusion of knowledge is one indispensable step to moral improvement. In a recent number of the London Eclectic Review, we find the following testimony to this effect referred to by our newspapers.

The condition of the agricultural districts is stated, in the report of the British and Foreign School Society for 1831, to be most distressing.

'Debasing ignorance prevails to an extent which could not be credited, were it not verified by the closest investigation. The facts which have been elicited respecting the moral and intellectual state of those counties which have been disgraced by riots and acts of incendiarism, are truly affecting, and yet they are but a fair representation of the actual state of our peasantry. We call ourselves an enlightened nation, an educated people; and yet, out of nearly seven hundred prisoners put on trial in four counties, upwards of two hundred and sixty were as ignorant as the savages of the desert; they could not read a single letter. Of the whole seven hundred, only one hundred and fifty could write, or even read with ease; and, in the words of one of the chaplains to the jails, nearly the whole number were totally ignorant with regard to the nature and obligations of true religion.'

Farther proof of the inadequacy of existing means for the instruction of the people is furnished in the reports of the same society for 1832-3. We shall quote only one or two.

'In September last (1831,) out of fifty prisoners put on trial at Bedford, only four could read. In the month of January (1833,) there were in the same prison between fifty and sixty awaiting their trials, of whom not more than ten could read, and even some of these could not make out the sense of a sentence, though they knew their letters. At Wisbeach, in the isle of Ely, it appears from a memorandum on the calendar, of a kind which ought to be affixed to every similar document, that, of nineteen prisoners put on trial, only six were able to read and write; and it is added, the capital offences were committed entirely by persons in a state of the most debasing ignorance.'

The statement which the Committee of the General Assembly have lately made, that, in their Highland schools, those in which the greatest variety of secular instruction is imparted, are most distinguished by a religious character, is one which we should have been quite prepared to expect. Man is distinguished from the brute, not less by improvable reason than by the capacity for devotion; and these two are not opposed the one to the other. The more truly enlightened any man becomes, the more his reasoning faculties expand and are purified by an enlarged acquaintance with external nature — the more inexcusable is he, if he remain unimpressed by the consideration of 'things which are unseen and eternal.' Irreligion is wilful stupidity: 'The *fool* hath said in his heart there is no God.'

The connection of ignorance with crime is more certain in a reading community like ours, where, *hitherto,* the mass of influence thrown upon the mind through the press has been in favor of morality. But the question naturally arises, Does mere knowledge banish crime? Unhappily it is a truth which cannot be forgotten, that the basest heart has often been connected with the most cultivated mind; and we need but a Byron to show us, how consistent even the most exalted genius may be with the most debasing moral qualities. Such an individual will not indeed rob, or murder, or oppress, to gain pelf which he does not need; but his own soul may become a sink of pollution, reeking with deadly miasma, and infecting all within its influence. The following article from the Scottish Guardian, although not correct in all its statements or reasonings, deserves deep reflection, and we have been gratified to see it circulating extensively through our newspapers.

Two Magistrates of Paris recently made a tour through the United States, and in the course of two years collected important information regarding the statistics of crime and education. In the state of New York, 500,000 children, out of two millions, are at public schools; that is, a *fourth* part of the population, and £240,000 are annually expended for this purpose. Yet in this state crime increases, and that, too, though the means of subsistence and employment are so much more easily obtained than in any other countries. In Connecticut, education is still more extended, and nearly a *third* part of the population is at school. Yet crimes multiply to a frightful extent. The Journal of Education, stating these facts, draws this cautious conclusion, — 'if knowledge cannot be accused of *causing* this increase of crime, at least it has not *prevented* it.'

On turning to France, and examining tables of the comparative proportion of instruction in its different departments, during a period of three years, the western and central provinces have been found the most uneducated, — 15, 14, 13, 12, and 8 per cent. only being able to read and write; but, according to an essay on the moral statistics of France, presented to the academy of sciences, the *minimum* of crime is to be found in these uneducated departments, and the *maximum* in Corsica and in the south eastern provinces, and in Alsace, where nearly half the population can read. The different employments of the population may account for this difference in part; yet still we may again draw the cautious conclusion, that if education has not *caused*, at least it has not been seen to *prevent* crime.

The only ascertained moral effect of intellectual education was stated in last March by the Lord Chancellor, in the House of Lords. In Russia, where education can scarcely be said to exist, out of 5,800 crimes committed within a certain period, 3,500 were accompanied by violence; while in Pennsylvania, where education is generally diffused, out of 7,400 crimes, only 640 were accompanied by violence, being in the proportion of 1-12th of the whole number, instead of 3-5ths, as in the former case. Thus the only ascertained effect of intellectual education on crime is to substitute *fraud* for *force* — the *cunning* of civilized, for the *violence* of savage life. Nor would even this small change be permanent. A highly intellectual community, without moral principles and the habits of self denial which religion imposes, would only prove a sleeping volcano, ready to awaken every moment, and overthrow those very institutions under which it had been fostered. To increase the intellectual power, and enlarge the knowledge, of a man void of principle, is only to create in him new desires, to make him restless and dissatisfied, hating those that are above him, and desirous of reducing all to his own level; and you have but to realize universally such a state of society, to fill the cup of the world's guilt and misery to the *brim*. What do we say then? Not certainly that education is to be withheld from any member of society, — for that question is now decided, whether we will or not, — but that from the infant school, upwards to the university, it must be a thorough *Christian* education, in which our youth shall be trained in the ways of virtuous self-control, and piety and righteousness wrought into the understanding and into the whole habit of man. A perfunctory religious education will no longer serve — not mere Bible reading — but Bible education. The understanding must be enlightened, and the heart must be gained over to the side of truth and righteousness. In short, *the grand aim of education* must become, not merely the formation of intellectual habits, or the acquisition of secular knowledge (as is too exclusively the case in present times,) but the formation of the christian character. Men have hitherto been prone to take for granted, that it was only necessary to teach the art of reading, and before this new power all vice and error would flee away. These are dreams of men ignorant of themselves, and ignorant of our poor nature. Men must be trained to piety and virtue as they are trained to any other habits, whether intellectual or physical; and the moral man must advance contemporaneously with the intellectual man, else we see no increase from our increased education, but an increased capacity for evil doing.

The following application of this truth to our own country and its peculiar dangers, from the Northampton Courier, is another gratifying evidence of the increased interest taken in the subject.

We believe that there is much truth and justice in the remark, that other influences beside that of force, must be exercised, to keep the Union of these states permanently together. Statutes may be enacted, constitutions framed, and interests multiplied, but if there is not a primary feeling of moral obligation and fraternal duty, to cement and enforce them, the duration of this government, like all others, is extremely questionable and uncertain. Pecuniary interest, and common defence, and general prosperity, are but transient ties, which can be thrown off to suit the excited spirit of the times, or changed to meet any pressing emergency. They are but selfish bonds, which yield at the rude touch of popular disaffection, and are easily rent by the misguided voice of public sentiment, and vindictiveness, and clamor. But if legal enactments and obligations, and physical wants, and common defence, do not constitute security against dissolution, what influences can be exerted to sustain and strengthen a civil compact of such stupendous weight and importance as our own? If these things fail, what iron will enter the souls of men, to enforce their moral obligations, and to impress upon them the maxim of 'union,' with certain safety and security?

We think a *moral* obligation, and religious feeling, and fraternal affection, which is founded in the heart, and has its emanations from the soul, if rightly cultivated, will insure this purpose, and guarantee its permanent duration. Some deep abiding sentiment, some strong affection of the mind, some radiating influence from the heart, which rises above selfishness, and pecuniary wants, and sordid interest, which all feel and acknowledge, is what should be cherished and cultivated, to bind with adamantine chains the different parts and sections of this our own favored country together.

Yes; it is by cultivating the sense of 'moral obligation and religious feeling' and the 'fraternal affection' which is their necessary concomitant and result, that our own union is to be maintained, (for we are unwilling to add the qualification which is chilling so many hearts) and not by constitutions of parchment, or even by the arm of power. If our laws are not supported by our feelings, and principles, the force which we use to maintain them, may indeed make us *fellow prisoners*, or *fellow subjects*, but never can unite us as *brethren* or *fellow citizens*. France has long sought to establish moral principle on some other basis than that of Christianity; but she has renounced this visionary plan, and now requires the *New Testament* to be employed as the text book of morals and religion in every school in the empire. Let us profit by her example, and retain the precious legacy of our purer, happier ancestors.

[For the Annals of Education.]

ART OF MISEDUCATION.

HOW TO TRAIN A CHILD TO CONSIDER MONEY-GETTING AS 'THE CHIEF END OF MAN.'

RULE. — *Make trade, and bargains, and prices, the principal subject of conversation before him. Tell him to buy everything as cheap as possible. Admire his good bargains, and tell of your own.*

'DID I not get a good bargain?' said a boy about twelve years of age, to another boy, a few mornings since, just as they were going into the school-room. 'I bought a bow,' he added, 'for a shilling, and sold it again for twentythree cents!' — In connection with this anecdote, an able teacher, and a very close observer of men and things, remarked to me, as follows:

'The times have strangely altered, within the last twenty years. Boys *now*, are not at all what boys were *then*. Then, there was such a thing to be found here and there, as a boy who loved study, and studied *hard*. Then, if there were fewer class books, and those sustained an inferior character, they were, at least, better studied. Then, if a smaller number of branches were taught in our schools, they were taught much more thoroughly. But now you can seldom find a hard student, in our schools. If a boy has lessons, such lessons as boys of similar age and capacity used to get, and get cheerfully too — 'Oh, they are too *hard!*' He dislikes his teacher. His parents learn the fact, and acquaint the teacher with it; and wonder why he can't make his school as agreeable to his pupils as Mr Such-an-one does his. Or, what often happens, they withdraw them from the school, without much ceremony, and send them somewhere else. However, after they have been transferred from school to school, a year or two, till their minds are rendered twice as volatile and dissipated as they were before, it often happens that they come back again, and apply for re-admission.'

'But though boys *will not study*, they *will make bargains*. Every boy, from one yard to two in height, is an adept in buying, selling, and swapping penknives, pencils, combs, skates, sleds, bows, &c, &c; and ten to one but their trading occupies half their thoughts and some of their hands, even during the school hours.'

'Now what is to be done? If this fondness for trading were confined to a few individuals in a class, or a school, the case would be less discouraging. But it is nearly universal. The children of pious parents are often as full of their buying, selling, and swapping, as those of the vicious.'

'The representation you make, is indeed a painful one,' I replied. 'But is it not obvious whose the fault is, and where we ought to look first, for a reformation? Is it not in parents? Are not their hearts, from morning to evening, set on buying, and selling, and getting gain? Observe the general current of conversation, in our best families; and can you continue to wonder what the matter is with the children? The work of reform must begin here — with the parents — or it never can begin at all, at least till you can change the laws of nature, and make the stream ascend, by its own power, higher than the fountains which feed it.'

The following extracts on this subject, which are taken from Abbott's Magazine, are too much in point to be omitted.

> 'Richard, why don't you obey at once' says the father, 'when your mother speaks to you? My love, you know I leave the children entirely to you.' 'I know you do, my dear; but I can't help thinking *you* ought to govern the boys.' 'You are at home, my love, all the time, and really you ought not to expect much from me, occupied as I am continually, — business pressing from Monday morning till Saturday night. I want to be *quiet* when I am in the house; I must have a fire in my room in future.'
>
> * * * * * * * * *
>
> 'Father,' says Thomas, a grown up son, 'I am distressed about little Mary — she is so disorderly at table, and pays no attention to what mother says; I am afraid she will turn out like B. C. Mr F. makes his little girl obey.'
>
> 'Oh! Mr F. is a teacher; it is his business to make *experiments* in education. You used to behave just so; and I don't see but you have turned out pretty well.'
>
> 'But I am afraid we children don't set the best example we can. Spurzheim says, "we must be what we would have little children." Little Mary imitates all we do.'
>
> 'Well — I can't attend to it now; I must be off to the store. I have got 5,000 dollars to pay before two o'clock.' And thus — days pass away, and weeks, and months, and years — the father having always such a press of business on hand, that he has no time to study the philosophy of education. The 5,000 dollar note at the bank must be met — and as to the children, why 'Mrs B. must attend to them.'

And this is a faithful picture of many a father, who will say and think that he loves his children more than everything else on earth! — who professes to feel it his duty to train them up in the right way! And this '*paternal affection*' will sacrifice the minds and souls of his children, in order to fill their pockets, — to provide an inheritance which, for want of proper education, they are only prepared to abuse as the instrument of evil, to themselves and others! Surely the writer before us is not too decided in saying — 'It is a *fatal error* which has crept into the bosoms of our men of business, that they must give their *whole souls and bodies* to it; that doing an *extensive* business, is the great object of life.' Nor is the judgment of God too severe, which so often gives to such a father his heart's desire, and allows him to provide a fortune for his child, and leaves him to waste it to his own ruin — and often to break the heart of his parents; when he does not succeed in teaching him that 'money-getting is the chief end of man.'

[For the Annals of Education.]

ON THE UTILITY OF NAUTICAL SCHOOLS.

In our last number we inserted an article from a gentleman who has been conversant with seamen, on the subject of Nautical Schools, and we rejoice to have any plan presented which is designed to benefit a class of men of the highest importance to our country, and yet among the most neglected. We have been favored by our correspondent with the following letter, from a nautical teacher who has passed twenty years upon the ocean, in all the various situations on shipboard, from that of common sailor to that of master, and during this period constantly assisted in the education of some of his ship-mates. It will present more fully the practicability and importance of these Institutions, and we would respectfully ask our readers in seaport towns, to read it, with the question before them — 'Is it not our duty and our interest to establish such a school for the seamen of our own port?'

'Dear Sir, — The first question you propose is, 'Whether seamen generally avail themselves of the advantages which a Nautical Institution offers.' As far as my experience goes, I believe that by far the greater number of our own seamen, in this section of our country, not only attend our Nautical Institution, but appear to manifest a deep interest in its prosperity. There is no other institution of the kind in this state; you will not be surprised, therefore, to hear that young men from all parts of the state, even the most remote, enter it for their nautical education: indeed, I have had several from our largest seaports. I have found, generally, that lads from the country, who for the first time are about embarking upon the ocean, appear to consider it highly important that they should have some nautical knowledge previous to undertaking this, their first voyage. But many of our young lads in this city make one voyage first, and afterwards attend to their nautical studies. Most of them pursue their studies, from voyage to voyage, embracing all the important branches in Navigation and Nautical Astronomy. They all, without exception, acquire a taste for this kind of study; this may be accounted for, that the plan of instruction is altogether practical. To such as feel an interest in the education of seamen it would afford them much pleasure to see fifteen or twenty, each waiting their turn to measure the distance between the sun and moon, stars and moon, or planets and moon, in order to determine the latitude and longitude of their position. These observations are made from the top of our building. It would also afford such much gratification, to return with them to the *room*, and observe the interest which they all take in ascertaining the result of their observations; they would find the most perfect order among them. Indeed, I have never had occasion in the whole course of my instruction, to reprove one of them for idleness, or for the least misdemeanor. When the hours for study have expired, instead of that anxiety which we find in other schools among young lads to hasten from their studies, I am frequently obliged to persuade them to leave. These remarks are made in order to give you some idea of the interest which seamen take, in acquiring that information so necessary to a good navigator. A further proof of its being a pleasure rather than a task to them, to be well versed in that which we may consider of the utmost importance is, that I have many whom I consider to have belonged to the institution for four years, and have no doubt they will continue for some time to come.

There is no situation in life which I should prefer to that of a nautical instructor, provided, I could realize a trifle more than a mere livelihood; for, I assure you, it affords me much pleasure to instruct that class, among whom so great a portion of my life has been spent. As a final answer to the question proposed, it is my opinion that the seamen of our own country generally would take advantage of a good nautical institution; and I cannot but express my surprise that there are so few good institutions of this kind in the country.

Very little dependence could be placed on foreign seamen, towards the support of an institution of this kind. There are quite a large number who sail from this port. Of such I have had but very few; they are men generally without education, usually indulging in all the evil propensities to which human nature is liable, without the least restraint on their passions.

Your next question is, 'What proportion of masters and mates do you find well qualified for their stations?' Probably you may be surprised at my answer; for I have generally found their education very limited.

First, of the masters. I have had in the institution about forty in all, four or five of whom were men of decent education, the remainder extremely limited. I should be unwilling to say more on this subject, although much more might be said. I have had quite a large number of mates; their qualifications were about equal to the masters. This will not appear strange when we take into consideration that those of whom I am now speaking, entered the sea-service very young, with little or no education. Indeed, many of them have told me, that all the education they then had, they had acquired, themselves, on the ocean. The fact is, they were naturally enterprising, ambitious men, and worked their way onward to be mates and masters, much to their credit. From the acquaintance which I have had with our navigators, at home and in foreign countries, I believe I am warranted in saying, that not more than one in twenty are well qualified for the important duties of Master and Factor. This does not apply to the masters of our India-men, neither to those who navigate the Pacific ocean; for they, generally, have had the advantage of an early education. Indeed, I have met with some in India whom I consider men of the first rate talents.

Your next inquiry is, 'What benefit is such an institution to young seamen and boys?' In my estimation the advantages which they would derive from such an institution could not be estimated. In the first place it adds much to their character, gives them a standing in society, improves their morals, and prepares them for the faithful discharge of that duty to which Providence, in his wise dispensation, has called them. Now, as vice generally follows ignorance, we must certainly acknowledge, that the education of any class of our fellow beings, is of the utmost importance; particularly of such as are exposed to temptations, without a friend to admonish them.

How often have I heard seamen, when reproved for intoxication and other vices, answer, 'I care not what becomes of me; it is immaterial whether I live or die. I have no education; and consequently can never be promoted; *I have "lived hard, fared hard"* — and the sooner my end comes, the better.' Without an education you will perceive, Sir, they have no stimulus — nothing to induce them to excel in any one thing; hence, they are easily persuaded and led astray by the designing, to commit any act of violence. They are naturally confiding, and consequently, through ignorance, become the dupes of landlords, grog-sellers and the brothel; and by them are eventually ruined.

The good effect of education on our seamen would not be confined to them alone, for it is a public benefit, as our ships would then be navigated by men looking forward for promotion; and we may naturally conclude that their conduct would be such as to entitle them to the respect and consideration of their employers, which would be an additional stimulus for them to continue in well-doing. Let us inquire here — among what class of seamen are found the projectors, aiders and abettors, of such schemes which have frequently ended in mutiny and murder on board some of our ships? From the experience which I have had, I have no hesitation in saying, among that class usually denominated '*old salts*,' that is, men without education, and of course without the least hope of promotion. I have witnessed many serious disturbances, on board my own, as well as other ships, and generally found the plans laid and executed by this class. On the contrary, I never knew a young man of decent education aid in any such nefarious transactions. I firmly believe, there is more to be apprehended from a crew of ignorant men, than from one hundred crews of decent education. The reason must be obvious. So well convinced have I been of the fact, that I have invariably avoided shipping such men.

This leads us again to inquire — are many of our young seamen destitute of such an education which would give them preferment? If so, is not their education of vast importance both to themselves and to the community. Do we not generally find that people of education deem it important that the Sabbath should be respected; and do they not, at least for example's sake, attend on divine worship? Hence, if education gives the seaman a rank in society, would he not be likely to conform to the established customs of society, instead of profaning the Sabbath? In a word, I believe that education would have the most salutary effect.

Having answered the questions proposed, and given you my opinion without reserve, I would beg leave to suggest the following for your consideration. If you intend to establish a first rate Nautical Institution, the situation should be such as to admit the Sun, Moon, &c, being seen, at least when not more than eight degrees above the horizon. If the eastern horizon could be seen from the top of the building it would be far better. The top should be flat, at least a portion of it, so as to admit one to go on it, with safety. The farther the school room is from the street the better, even the fourth or fifth story. How would it answer for you to engage an able instructor, allowing him a certain sum for educating a limited number of scholars annually, giving him the privilege to instruct such as could afford to pay for their education? This plan undoubtedly would lessen the expenses to your society. If the support of the institution is to depend in part upon such as will pay for their education, no doubt it would be of the utmost importance to have a first rate instructor. He should be a seaman in every sense of the word, thoroughly acquainted with every branch of navigation and nautical astronomy; should also be well acquainted with the nature and construction of nautical instruments, and with their use.

Give the seaman to understand that he may be elevated to a respectable rank in society, and no one would be more desirous to improve. On the contrary, let him but think that he is despised, and the community indifferent to his fate, and it will harden him in sin and profligacy.

The cause is a good one, and my prayer is to our common Parent, that he may abundantly bless all your endeavors; indeed, I feel assured that he will. I shall esteem it a privilege to contribute my mite towards this great and good object; for I believe our seamen have been too long neglected. If my remarks be true, can this subject be urged too strongly on the minds of the public respectfully?'

BERNE SOCIETY OF TEACHERS;

SWITZERLAND.

Among other evidences of the continued and active influence of Hofwyl in the cause of education, we have recently received a file of a Gazette for Teachers, issued by its indefatigable guardians. It is intended as the organ of communication for the friends of school improvements in the Canton of Berne. Several of its numbers are devoted to the proceedings of the *Cantonal Society of Teachers*, whose efforts seem to promise much for the cause in Switzerland.

This society was formed by the teachers assembled for instruction at Hofwyl, in the summer of 1832, and consisted of one hundred and fiftyfour members, with few exceptions, teachers of ordinary schools. Fellenberg was chosen President, and Vehrli, the excellent teacher of the farm pupils of Hofwyl, Vice President. Its constitution presents, as the great objects of the society, union and coöperation in promoting the education of the people, and elevating the character of the schools. The means proposed were, free communications between its members, consultations concerning the best modes of advancing the cause of schools and improving the condition of teachers, and direct efforts to excite the attention of the people to the defects of present plans and methods of organizing and instructing the common schools of the country. The last object seems to us highly important, and too much neglected among us. May we not derive an important hint in regard to our own duties? No great object has yet been effected, until *a class of men*, more or less numerous, have devoted themselves to it; and so busy is every one in our country, that none are disposed to assume a task which does not necessarily devolve upon them — or even to attend to a subject, which is not directly connected with their business. The modesty and the isolation of teachers, the fear of being charged with interested motives, and too often, we are sorry to say, indifference to the object itself, have led those who were engaged in education to neglect all direct effort to excite the interest of others. But if we hope for the promotion of improvement in education, from whence must we expect it, unless from those directly concerned, and most able to speak and write on the subject? Why does it not belong to teachers to speak, and write, and act upon society, in reference to education, as much as upon clergymen to exert their influence on the subject of theology? How much would it elevate the character of the profession, how much would it do to excite interest in the subject, if the *army* of teachers in New England would come forth from their school houses, and *unite* in enlightened efforts to spread just principles, in reference to the importance and the methods of education, among those around them!

Among the important topics in the school itself which are proposed by the society of Berne, to be presented in the meetings of its auxiliary societies, the first named is a careful inquiry into the condition of the pupils of their schools, and the proper means for their moral improvement. For this purpose they urge, that every effort be made to give the pupils *constant employment*, and to guard them against the temptations of idleness — to preserve a mild but firm course of discipline — and to promote *fraternal affection* among them. They urge, that every branch of instruction, from the highest to the lowest, be discussed at these meetings; and that there should be a steady effort among the teachers to *advance in knowledge and skill*. Would that the last object could be impressed upon the minds of the multitude of teachers in our country, who wrap themselves up in the consciousness of having attained the *ne plus ultra* of skill and knowledge, or lie down in listless apathy, after their daily task is performed, with no anxiety but to 'get through' the business of tomorrow, as early as possible.

The second meeting of the Berne Society of Teachers was also held at Hofwyl. It was opened by an interesting address from the President, full of truth and energy, of which we can only give a few opening sentences.

'Guardians of the spiritual life, the personal wealth, of the children of our people! we have assembled to ratify our bond. We have pledged ourselves, that in our schools, shall grow up a noble, well-taught generation of the people — true to the principles of the gospel, devoted to God, and faithful to men — a people whose characters shall not be unworthy of the scenes of grandeur and beauty which the Creator has assigned as their native land.'

'In this great object we shall succeed only so far as we follow the Saviour's example, and imbibe the fulness of his love to man, and trust in God, in forming the hearts of those who are committed to us, in extending the influence of the school to every household, and in warming the hearts of parents as well as children. God will reward such labors, even if they are not rewarded on earth. The God who feeds the ravens and clothes the lilies, will never forsake the faithful guardians of *his* children.'

Among the evils suggested at this meeting of the society, as requiring a remedy, were some familiar to our own schools — the want of faithful visitation, for which responsible and *paid* officers were considered the only remedy — neglect and difficulties in obtaining suitable teachers — imperfect school books and means of instruction — the want of a periodical for teachers — the unhappy difficulties arising from the dependence of the teacher on the caprice or convenience of individuals for his scanty pay, and claims of parental dictation often founded upon it. One serious evil, not found among us, is the duty imposed upon teachers of attending funerals, and performing, to some extent, the weekly as well as Sunday duties of clerk of the parish.

After the meeting was closed, the band of music of the farm pupils of Hofwyl, called the assembly to a repast prepared for three hundred and sixty persons by the liberal founder of Hofwyl. It was opened by him with prayer, acknowledging the favor of God to their association, and intreating his blessing upon their future efforts. A scene of social enjoyment and familiar intercourse then followed, suited to cheer the hearts of these fellow-laborers in an arduous and too often thankless office. Occasional songs, of that elevated and heart-stirring character which we have formerly described, were sung by the farm pupils, and united in by the chorus of teachers, and toasts were drank in the common wine of Switzerland — a liquor of less strength than the cider of our country. While we trust that the progress of the principles of temperance will speedily satisfy the friends of morals, that social drinking, and the useless, if not censurable practice of toasts, are but the handmaids of intemperance to many who might otherwise have been sober, we translate one sentiment given by a teacher, as a specimen of those offered on this occasion.

'There is *one means* of making the happiness, and the delight, which we feel to day, UNIVERSAL. There is *one unfailing means* to convert ruined families into families of joy, — to dry up the sources of poverty and misery — and to stem the torrent of overwhelming vice; to secure our liberties and those of our children against all the power of treachery — in short, to secure the purity and the happiness of the people. And this unfailing means is CHRISTIAN RATIONAL EDUCATION OF THE PEOPLE, and especially of the poor. *To all then, who understand this mighty cry, and put their hands to the holy work* — LONG LIFE! HEALTH *to all the friends and promoters of rational education of the people, and the poor — far and near!* LONG LIFE TO THEM!!!'*

*This imperfect translation of the German '*Lebe Hoch!*' is the best that occurs to us.

Such animating sentiments were followed and impressed by some of the noble 'Männerchoren' — or hymns for male voices, which the Swiss music furnishes, to cherish social, and benevolent, and patriotic, and devotional feeling, in place of the bacchanalian, and amatory songs, which so often disgrace our social meetings.

During the summer of 1833, a course of instruction was given to teachers, under the immediate direction of Fellenberg. It was closed by an examination, at which a considerable number of persons were present, and the Cantonal Society of Teachers held its third meeting immediately after. It was attended by two hundred teachers and friends of education — or *school men*, as they are all styled in simple German — many of whom were new members.

The time was occupied chiefly in business measures, relative to the organization of the society and its branches. A petition was offered, signed by many teachers, soliciting the government to remove the obstacle thrown in the way of attending the summer course of instruction for teachers at Hofwyl, of whose value they speak in the highest terms. This was adopted unanimously by the society, and ordered to be urged upon the attention of the public authorities.

Several communications were presented on the defects of the course of 1832, under the direction of a principal appointed by the government. One of these, signed by fiftynine teachers, testifies that, while the previous course had been grossly defective, the course pursued under the direction of Fellenberg had met their wants entirely ; and that it was entirely unjust to ascribe to Hofwyl and its founder, difficulties which originated in the incompetency of the director appointed by the government. Indeed, we find much evidence that this was another illustration of the danger of committing to political men, the management of literary institutions ; and we have abundant reason to know, that the determined hostility of the Bernese Aristocracy to the plan for the education of the people, which Fellenberg has pursued for thirty years with so much ardor, is sufficient to account for the new course of petty persecution to which he has been exposed. We trust, nay we are persuaded, that his zeal and faith, and that of his son, who now so ably coöperates with him, will not yield to clamor, or be subdued by opposition.

It was announced to the Assembly that another course of instruction would be given to teachers at Hofwyl, to commence in May of the present year, and continue until August, and the next meeting of the Society was appointed to be held at that time. We trust that a large body of teachers are now witnessing scenes, and enjoying privileges, which cannot fail to exert a most salutary influence on them and on their schools. Would that we could witness such a movement in any considerable portion of our own country. Could we see some individual who had the faith to invite, and the influence necessary to collect such a body of teachers, to listen to instruction and consult for the good of their schools for three months, in any state in the Union, we should expect more benefit to the cause of education than from any amount of school funds: for, important as they are, under proper regulation, they can never supply the place of an intelligent and well-trained body of teachers.

'WHAT'S THE USE OF EDUCATION?'

COMMON SCHOOLS AND COMMON EDUCATION.

NO IV.

Mr Editor, — I have been more than half inclined to yield to your objection to my Dialogues: more especially as I quite despair of sending them down to the two hundred thousand common readers whom I have been so modest as to ask for. I have therefore been revising my rough draught; but alas! have found myself obliged to leave this third dialogue very much as when you cast your eye over it months ago; for the plain reason that my characters will, in spite of all my pains to the contrary, discourse in their own homespun way. I am compelled, against my will, sometimes even to allow them to introduce trivial circumstances, which are immaterial to the point in debate; for they insist very pertinaciously upon this privilege of common conversation, though I tell them that they indulge themselves in this and some other faults, until they prove that their minds are not half educated; that they are a plain, homespun, farming set, and have no claim at all to be termed gentry or literati, and are quite unworthy of the station to which I am elevating them, by bringing them out in the 'Annals.' I console myself, however, with the thought that I shall gain one thing at least by their obstinacy; that my dialogues will thus appear what they really are, 'collectanea from the walls and homes of the common people,' instead of being 'made up' by my own literary industry. Thus, perhaps they will be more readily taken as illustrations both of *a will and a way* for the improvement of common schools and common education. Allow me to make one request before I finish my preamble, viz. — Let your editorial scissors spare my *vulgarisms* — perhaps I may better say my *idioms of common life.* I hesitate on the word 'vulgarisms,' because the friends, whom I have had passing before me as my 'Dramatis personæ,' ought not in truth to be called 'vulgar people,' for they have in their homely way a refinement, which I have often failed to meet, amidst much higher pretensions.

WHAT IS THE USE OF EDUCATION?

DIALOGUE III. SCENE — *the Road.*

Robert. Here's a book Thomas, just suited to your mighty plans: *Biography of self-taught men.* As it suits me, I thought I would bring it to you: but very fortunately I saw you coming down the hill, and waited here to give it you, so you can take it home and make the most of it. It is the very thing for you: for I've peeped into it a little. You can learn here how to be a great man to your heart's content. I suppose you mean to be a Franklin or a Sherman, and then how you will laugh at all the College learned men, as you leave them far and far behind: while poor I will be still at the plough-tail, as I have been all day long, until half an hour ago.

Thomas. Poh! Robert, have I made a fool of myself, or is it only you who are making a fool of me? I have read Franklin's life long ago, and have read it more than once too; and I feel a stronger resolution to improve myself every time I read it: but I am sure, I never dreamed of getting into Franklin's track at all. Unless I learn ten times faster than I've ever done yet, I shall have enough to do to learn what every common farmer ought to know.

Robert. But now Thomas, you will own that you have a little expectation, that you will be as great a man as Franklin, some thirty or forty years hence.

Thomas. Not I, Robert, any more than I have of being as rich a man as Stephen Girard, who you know died a while ago, the richest man in the country. I expect to be industrious, but I dont expect to be worth fifteen millions of dollars. I mean to study, but don't expect to know as much, or to be as famous, as Franklin.

Robert. Then what's the use of all your toil and trouble; your studying all winter and all summer, in school and out of school, and all your life long? What's the use, if it will not make a great man of you, say a member of Congress, or a Judge, or a Governor?

Thomas. And what's the use of your ploughing and digging and hoeing and planting and harvesting, all summer long, and every year, as long as you live?

Robert. Why, to feed and clothe me, and shelter and warm me, to be sure. We should soon be in trouble if we would not work for what we would need, till we were sure of getting a thousand times as much as we need.

Thomas. That's right, Robert. How nicely you set the matter right, whether you will or not. We should be badly off too, if we would not learn what we need to know, because we could not get what we do not need to have. Why, Robert, I don't *need* to be a governor, or a judge, or a member of Congress; but I do need to know more than I do, and to have a stronger and more active mind. What say, Robert, are you sorry that you have as much learning as you have — that you can read, write and cypher, because you cannot be as great a man as Franklin? Would you be willing to part with all your learning, and be as ignorant as Casper Hauser?

Robert. To be sure I would not. I should make a poor shift at getting a living, if I were like him: I would not be like him for all the millions in the world.

Thomas. Well, Robert, if what you have got is worth so much, why not get more? why not keep on learning, if a little knowledge is worth so much? For my part I mean to try, and see if the things I don't know, will not prove as useful as the little I do know. I cannot think it possible that I shall ever learn all that will be useful to me, though I expect to be a true working farmer all my life long. Why should not I try to be a wiser and happier man? Why should I not try to know more and more, all that can be useful to me, or my friends. I don't see why study will not bring its reward as well as work. If I grow wiser that will be good pay. So, Robert, you see I have not changed by passing from February to May — nor by turning from the school to the farm.

Robert. Yes; but do you gain anything? Are you any more learned?

Thomas. No: not as we commonly mean by 'learned;' for I am not learned at all, but it seems to me as if my mind had grown a little greener.

Robert. Greener? How?

Thomas. I was thinking of the grass. I have been watching it and watching it this spring, but I have not seen it grow. Yet I see it has grown, it looks greener. I can't see that I gain, but I can see that I have gained. I was going to say, my mind seems as fresh and cheerful as the spring. I know I have gained but very little, but to that little I can apply the proverb; 'Knowledge is pleasant to the soul.'

Robert. You make me think of the violets. I have watched them to see them come forth; but I could see no rapid advance; but this morning, as I went singing along, I saw them blossoming beside the path. So Thomas (you see I always give you a lift when it comes handy) if you will drink the dew and the showers, and the sunshine, wisdom will blossom on your modest path. I say that, because you are content to be a plain farmer.

Thomas. Why, here we are! How short the road has been! Well, Robert, you see you have got home with me. So come in, and if father begins upon me as he did last night, we shall have our subject continued in-doors.

Robert. Well, if you are likely to have a Dialogue, I will go in for half an hour; only mind — I go as a hearer, not as a speaker.

Thomas. As you please — only come in.

WHEN WILL EDUCATION BE FINISHED?

SCENE — *the House — various members of the family.*

Father. Good evening, Robert. What's the good news?

Robert. Why nothing very good, except I have brought Thomas a book, which is to make him as great a man as Dr Franklin.

Thomas. Why Robert, I thought you gave that up, before we got half way home. I am sure I told you plainly enough, that I hadn't any such foolish notions.

Robert. Yes, yes. Thomas says he means to be a real student, summer and winter, winter and summer, and yet be a plain, plough-jogging farmer all his life long. That's a likely story! Study fifty years, and be still at the plough tail! isn't that a likely story?

Lucy. Why in a quarter of that time, Thomas, you'll learn out. When you have learned all you can turn to account, Thomas, your zeal will cool.

Thomas. Yes, Lucy, when I have learned all that I can turn to account; but when think you that will be?

Lucy. Oh, now you have got your new shoes on, I suppose in a half dozen years, by the time you are three and twenty at farthest; then our Thomas will know all that is to be known that is of any use, unless he should become a great man like Dr Franklin, as Robert says. Then, how his zeal will cool!

Father. Thomas, never mind if they do try to make fun of you. I am forty years older than you are, and though I haven't studied so much as I now see I ought to have done, yet I have taken some pains to learn, and I am sure I have not 'learned out.' All I can say about it is, that I see ten times as much to learn, as I used to see forty years ago: and I think that if you should learn ten times as fast as I have done, and should live on this farm forty years hence, you will find more to learn after that. Here are Lucy and Robert, perhaps they 'will learn out.'

Thomas. Oh Lucy is only trying to make fun of me. She does not think me vain enough to think I am going to do any great things; and I know she is not thoughtless enough to say seriously, that either I or she can learn all that we need, in half a dozen years, or half a dozen times that.

Lucy. No, Thomas, I am not so thoughtless; and as you do me that justice, I will agree that you are not so vain hearted. As to me, I am sure there's no danger of my 'learning out;' of my getting through all that lies in my narrow circle, second mistress of the kitchen, and the garden, and the children, as I am. I shall need half a dozen years at least before I shall complete my education for the kitchen, and the house, and the garden.

Father. Yes, and six times that, before you would know all that would be pleasant and useful to know.

Lucy. And then if I were to get Mr White's spirit, (you know Thomas the book that Mr W. sent me a few days ago) it would take me a dozen, dozen years to study all the plants and animals, within sight of the smoke of our own chimney. And then the newspapers; may a young girl like me, Thomas, read the newspapers?

Thomas. Father says they are not all fit to read, and I believe so myself. Yet we can't help looking for the good, amidst more or less evil. So my judgment is that you may read the newspapers.

Lucy. But then I am sadly puzzled often. I find variety enough, but in order to make it pleasant and useful to me, I see I must understand Geography, and History, and half a dozen sorts of Philosophy. Thomas I shall not get through in a dozen, dozen years, if I should live so long.

Father. And then the Bible — the book of books — easy for children to understand — but how much better we can understand it, the more we know of geography, and history, and your half dozen philosophies. And *there* is a study for you, which you will not need to leave off, Lucy, at the end of a dozen, dozen years.

Mrs Elizabeth. Well, Thomas, what do you think of me, with my half dozen children? When think I shall learn out?

Thomas. Why, as you are a woman, and cannot therefore expect to rise to high places like Franklin, and as you are obliged to keep at home with your half dozen children, according to some people's notions, you haven't anythingto learn. But let me ask you one question. Pray, sister, have you learned yet all you need to know — I mean all you need as the mother of my little nephews and nieces?

Mrs E. All? No, brother. I am in trouble every day on account of my ignorance, for the duties of my own narrow sphere. I have no wish for high places — I do not know yet enough for my low one — though it is a high place too. All I wish is, to learn as much as I can every day, that I may know how better to take care of the children that are in my little home school.

Lucy. That is, how to teach them A B C, a-b ab. That requires very profound learning!

Mrs E. Why yes, Lucy, I believe I am competent to that already, and can without great difficulty teach them that lesson, as soon as is needful for them. But I have found by trial, that there is much more to be learned, in order that I may bring up my children aright. So I have determined to learn as much of their bodies and minds, and of all that they need to learn, as possible.

Lucy. Oh you have only to let them grow up. Who studies and tries to improve herself, that she may train her children better? Where are your studious, thinking, philosophic mothers? Fie, sister, take it easy.

Mrs E. So then you will study half a dozen years to make out your kitchen, and garden education, and advise me to let the plants of my little garden take care of themselves.

Lucy. Ah, there you've caught me. So we must come round, and be all on Thomas's side, at last.

Robert. Well, Thomas, I see you carry the day. So I'll leave my book for the plough-boy, and let him study and be a plough-jogger all his life, if he will. So good night, and I hope after all, you'll get to be as great a man as Dr Franklin. (Exit)

Lucy. Well, Thomas, Elizabeth is on your side, and father is on your side, and I half believe Robert is on your side, and as I have so much to learn, I shall be obliged to be on your side.

Father. Well, then, let us take more pains, and keep learning until we have 'learned out.' Come let us close the day by reading the 104th Psalm, which will show us subjects of knowledge, more than we can ever finish.

[For the Annals of Education.]

HINTS TO YOUNG TEACHERS.

NO. III.

I HAVE observed that I had a high standard of what a good teacher ought to be, even when I first began to instruct, — but little or no idea, by what means to become such an one myself. When I first realized, in practice as well as theory, the extreme difficulty of the task I had undertaken, (for I had resolved to be in truth a *good teacher,)* my fears overcame my hopes, and despair would have sometimes tempted me to resign the employment, had I not motives to impel me, superior to all merely personal considerations. —*Patronage* I abhorred; and resolutely determined not to become the protegé of any overbearing or even kind hearted and prudent director. I had seen the evil of this system, in more than one instance, — in which friends of my own had opened schools, through the assistance and under the recommendation of some 'high in authority,' and thus, holding on another's sleeve, were compelled, not only to stand or fall with him, but to submit themselves, their judgment, their arrangements, even their principles, to his decision. I therefore did not apply for the children of my friends — but simply mentioned to all I met, that I should like to take a few pupils. I began with the first that was offered, and I soon had more; and these first pupils continued with me as long as I was willing and able to retain them; and this fact will, perhaps, sufficiently show that the parents, at least, were not dissatisfied with my exertions. Yet here I would take occasion to observe, that the standard of the parent's *expectations* should be no boundary of the teacher's endeavors; — to say that parents in general, do not require half what we have laid down as necessary to the perfection of an instructor, would be only to *add* to, *not diminish* his responsibility, — since it is in the sight of Heaven we are to act, — it is to God we are accountable for the performance of all our duties; it is before the judgment of His holy tribunal, that we are to stand; and the favorable testimony of every parent, of whose child we had the care, would be insufficient to acquit us, if our consciences, or our Divine Judge condemned. Let not the young teacher, then, begin, by setting before him the hopes or even the desires of a parent, as the measure of his duty. Of course I shall not be understood to mean that such desires should be disregarded; on the contrary, respect should be paid to them, as far as they are compatible with his own convictions of duty. But as the penalty of differing from the parents, or exciting their displeasure, can at worst, fall but on himself, by causing the loss of his pupils, it should be esteemed as dust in the balance, when compared with the necessity of following every dictate of conscience. I beg leave to affirm, however, that where the instructor of a school really acts from these high motives, he need have no fear of the consequences. The very uprightness and dignity of his resolves will inspire him with active power to fulfil them, — the very purity of his motives, and the disinterestedness of his feelings, will actuate and sanctify his every exertion; and if he lose one pupil through wayward caprice or ignorant dissatisfaction, he will gain numbers by steady perseverance, in the path he thinks the best calculated to ensure success. I could cite several instances, in which I was urged by those most respected, to alter my views and arrangements in minor matters respecting their children. I was sorry to disoblige or displease them; a few scruples as to the result of persisting, troubled me for a while; then I looked to a *higher 'director,'* examined carefully what would be best for my school, and for my own performance of duty in it — and then decided accordingly, unbiassed by the wishes even of those I sincerely desired to please, and often in contradiction to them.* Yet never did I have cause to repent it, even in reference to my own interest. The request was generally yielded to my convictions, and I never lost a pupil in consequence.

The preceding remarks have reference only to trifling and unimportant matters. In those which concern the nearer interests of the pupils, I do not even consider it a duty to know, much less to regard individual opinions, if the teacher is, and certainly he ought to be, capable of making up his own opinion. To those who may still differ from me on this point, I would make a few further observations.

In the first place, setting aside the fact, that scarcely any two persons would agree, with regard to the peculiar kind of discipline, — degree of instruction, &c, &c, they would wish their children to receive, it is fair to take it for granted that an intelligent parent will satisfy himself of the nice judgment and conscientious delicacy of the mind to which he intrusts his child, before he subjects him to its jurisdiction. But secondly, no parent is bound to place, or even to keep his child at a school, in the instructor of which he has not the most entire confidence; and every teacher should hold himself at all times, not only ready but willing to part with his pupils, however much he may desire to retain them for their sake and his own; since on that ground alone, he holds his right to exercise his individual judgment and views of study.

I have said more on this topic than may seem requisite, in the prosecution of my plan; but I cannot help thinking, it is one of the points on which young teachers oftenest mistake. It is a prevalent idea that school keeping is in many respects like a *trade*, or *mechanical employment*, in which it is the *first* duty of the artizan to satisfy his employers, and to finish the work, as far as he has the charge of it, in the *precise* manner in which it is ordered; and that any variation from such orders would be reprehensible.

This opinion might be correct, if we acknowledge, at the same time, *that we have but one grand employer, and who that employer is.* In forming the character of a child, and fitting it for Heaven, the CREATOR engages numerous instruments, both human and

* It should not be forgotten, here, that our correspondent addresses those who intend to be private, independent teachers. It is of course understood, that the teacher who enters a school under the direction of fixed rules, or of trustees, is bound to adhere to those rules, and obey the directions of those who employ him, so far as their power extends, or to resign his station. Unhappily, this power is often exercised in a way which destroys his usefulness, and drives him to private efforts. — EDITOR.

divine, that is, HE works through the parents, friends, and instructors of the child, — and through circumstances which HE arranges in respect to its best temporal and eternal interests. The teacher of a school of children, therefore, is indeed accountable to his EMPLOYER — but it is to GOD alone — and to HIM let the whole force of the expression be applied. Then the more clearly it is proved that he is answerable for his work, for the *materials* of which it is composed, and the perfection with which it is completed, the more firmly will my previous positions be established. This is a necessary inference.

My experience has in all respects coincided with the views I have here expressed. While my school maintained its situation for years, several in the same neighborhood, whose teachers were quite as well, and probably in many respects better, calculated than myself for the office, all things considered, failed and were broken up, solely, as I was led to think, from the mistaken idea, that it was proper and necessary to give satisfaction to each and all their patrons, — and at length, like the old man and his ass in the fable, by trying to please every body, satisfied no body. This must be the case, unless there are higher grounds to go upon than man's approbation or applause. Having established my school, the next point was to decide on the number I was competent to instruct faithfully. When this was settled I made a great mistake — being so foolish as to mention the number and limit it, before I had received pupils sufficient to make it up; and I discovered the folly of this by finding it was generally supposed that my school was full, and many children sent elsewhere, who would have been offered, and whom I should have been glad to receive.

At length, however, the mistake was explained, and I obtained the requisite number; after which the applications increased, so that I found it highly proper, as well as desirable, to make another arrangement, which was to have the same terms for all, whether boys or girls, from three to seven, eight, or ten years of age, (I took none older or younger) and I gradually established this, and at the same time increased the terms of tuition; — and I seriously believe, that I owed much of my success to those very arrangements. The value of everything in this world depends, in a great measure, on the difficulty there is in procuring it; and when it was found that my small number was not to be increased, those persons whose children made a part of it, were anxious they should remain; while others were equally desirou for theirs to join it. Thus I soon had a list of applicants, as is common in large and, as some will have it, more important schools, and only when I had a vacancy, admitted a new scholar. Many went out of town for months at a time, and even attended other schools while absent, who yet were considered still as my pupils, unwilling to lose their places, and were paid for accordingly. This gave great advantage to me, and likewise to those who were left; since the smaller my school was, the more I could do for those still under my care. I was anxious that any advantage I might gain from a lessening of care, should be amply shared by them in other ways — while the fact, that the children who were absent were my pupils, gave us each a claim on the affection and interest of the other, which supported the relative and endearing ties of teacher and pupil.

With regard to the advice I have given, not to admit any assistants in a school for small children, I have but a few words to say as to my own opinion, and the grounds on which I support it. I was frequently solicited to 'go into partnership,' as it is called — or to unite myself with persons who had a smaller number of pupils, receiving the instructor as an assistant. In every instance, the applicants were older than I was, and more experienced — consequently I could not think for a moment of placing them under my dictation; and having no desire to subject myself to theirs, I uniformly and promptly declined. There must in all cases be one established head in every school — or there will necessarily be anarchy and confusion.

But on every other consideration I was satisfied that my decision was a correct one. On the score of emolument, surely it can make little difference whether one teacher instructs a small, or two teachers a large number of pupils; certainly it ought not, since the recompense would be divided proportionably. And I have seen the bad effects of such a division of labor, of influence and of affection — in a school of this sort. I have felt them in the schools I myself attended when a child; and I also know what the effects must be by a close observation of those produced in the minds of my pupils by every change of treatment, and even by the changing state of my own mind, as it was operated upon, either physically or morally. It will be acknowledged, that even when the opinions and principles of parents with regard to education, differ materially, the effects are discoverable, often painfully so, in their children. Yet here there is every claim of nature and affection, every adventitious circumstance to aid the moral operation of each parent on the other, and on the child — claims and circumstances which are, of course, denied the teachers of a miscellaneous school. I do not say that an assistant teacher never did, or never could increase the worth and the happiness of a school; but I do say, that if it does, the school is not so well conducted as it may be; and that two teachers can hardly effect so much, as one truly good teacher can and ought to effect among a number of small children.

I have been endeavoring, if possible, to describe what may be accomplished by placing before us the most correct standard; and by applying to the object all the effort and perseverance, all the fortitude and strength of mind, all the judgment and energy of character, we can obtain. But I would not by any means decry the beneficial results of what has been done, even by those who have had no such standard, and make use of but little of the penetration and force of character they may, perhaps, possess — possibly, indeed, from not considering the occupation of sufficient importance to demand it.

These plans respecting the arrangements and external formation of a school, must of course, be accommodated, in every instance, to the peculiar circumstances in which each individual teacher is placed; and after all, they are of minor consequence compared to the exercise of those internal virtues and energies, which insure and stamp the character of a school and its instructor.

INANIMATE ELOCUTION.

We have received another interesting article on the neglect of the power of expression among us, but must defer it to our next number.

The following remarks from the Geneva Gazette, on the public exhibition of the college in that place, furnish a striking illustration of the defect to which our correspondent alludes. We wish this were a solitary example; but we believe almost the same remarks may be made concerning a large proportion of similar exhibitions in our country.

'The compositions ranked above the ordinary character of such productions: and when examined in a purely intellectual point of view, it must be acknowledged that they were distinguished as developing minds well disciplined, careful in research, discriminating in judgment, refined in taste, deeply imbued with classic lore, and possessing highly cultivated imaginations. We are sorry, however, that we cannot award equal commendation to the delivery of those compositions. Although the subjects were admirably designed for the most splendid demonstrations of oratorical power, yet there was a coldness in their recitation that ran counter to the elevated and inspiriting emotions which such pieces were so well calculated to awaken. There was little gesticulation, and too great monotony of voice. We could discover no revelation of intense passion and spontaneous feeling in the speaker; no indignation at the cruelty of the tyrant; no admiration in the victory of the patriot. The brow was calm and unclouded; the lips scarce told there was utterance *there;* the eye, the soul of eloquence, exhibited no concentrated expression, no mental illumination. There was *some* gesture, but it was neither free, nor bold, nor energetic. There were no outpourings of passion; none of the majesty of intellectual achievement; none of the transcendency of impassioned eloquence bursting forth with native and original fire; no signs indicating that the speaker felt his subject. There was too much of the formality of the ball-room — too much of the chilling indifference of the stoic. More attention to this subject would be of infinite advantage to the great majority of speakers.'

We would merely add the question — Of what avail are arguments or persuasions which proceed from one who seems neither to feel, nor to believe what he is saying? — *Si vis me flere*, &c.

[For the Annals of Education.]

SCHOOL REFORM IN DORCHESTER, MASS.

Reform, in the civil world, appears to be the favorite watchword. Why should it not be so, in the world of Education? True, it is not every innovation which is entitled to the name of reform; but no reform can be effected without innovation. Ought prejudice to be a stronger barrier, here, than in matters of government and religion?

Dorchester, in Massachusetts, is one of the oldest towns in New England. Here the first church was organized; here, as from a centre, the Puritan spirit was diffused; here, emphatically, is 'the land of steady habits.' To this day the people dread, as much as any other known community, the progress of innovation, and the spirit of reform, lest the result should be, — what it often has been — that things which ought to be permanent, should, in the general agitation, become unsettled, or be swept away. Yet here, even *here*, in Dorchester, a great revolution has, within a few months, been accomplished; and without any violent commotion except that of public sentiment.

The common or public schools of Dorchester, like those of the Puritans generally, received early attention; and compared with other things, were for a century and a half prosperous. If they did not keep pace with arts, mechanics, agriculture, and manufactures, they did not, for a hundred and fifty years, fall far behind. But of late years, like the schools of New England generally, —

they have been suffered to fall quite in the rear, in the march of general improvement. In 1830, Dorchester had over four thousand inhabitants; and according to the usual proportion in this country, the number of children between the ages of four and sixteen years must have been at least one thousand. For this population, there existed six public schools, containing not far from six hundred and fifty pupils. There were, however, several private schools, continued a part of the year, and a select school for the more advanced pupils. Besides, many of the more wealthy families sent their children to Roxbury, Boston, and other places, for the whole or a part of their instruction. Of the three hundred and fifty children not found in the public schools, therefore, a considerable number can be accounted for, without supposing, in their case, a total neglect of instruction. It is however true that not a few, between the ages of four and sixteen years, were in effect excluded from the public schools, (and consequently many of them from any school at all,) by a rule which required that no one should be admitted 'till he knew his letters,' and could 'read words of two syllables.'

There was one thing more, which operated to exclude children of this class. The average number of pupils belonging to each school, was of course about one hundred and ten. These were of all ages, and were consigned to school-rooms by no means large or commodious. No school had more than one teacher. Often, there were in daily attendance from seventy to eighty pupils. These all required attention, not only in regard to discipline, but the lessons of instruction; and a large proportion of them were studying from three to six or seven branches every day. As the monitorial plan of instruction had never been adopted, lessons and pupils were sometimes wholly neglected. The 'little ones,' especially, were apt to be overlooked; and this became so obvious and general an evil, that some of the parents omitted to send them.

During the last winter and spring, the Dorchester Temperance Society, which had resolved itself into a Lyceum, and held weekly meetings for lectures and discussions, not only on subjects connected with the cause of temperance, but on other important topics, took into special consideration the improvement of their public schools. It was soon discovered there was a very general dissatisfaction with the existing state of things in this respect; but what could, what ought to be done? Evening after evening the subject was discussed; sometimes with considerable warmth. As might have been anticipated, there was opposition; but the friends of reform, if not more numerous, were stronger than their opponents. District meetings were held in some of the districts in the town, and committees were appointed to consider the matter Finally the question on reform came up in general town meeting, and after much debate and one adjournment, the new measures were carried by an overwhelming vote.

By this new arrangement, five primary schools are to be established in the town; one in each of five out of the six districts; and these are to be supplied with buildings, and books, and apparatus, and teachers. This will greatly lessen the number of pupils in the annual grammar schools, and leave no teacher more than forty or fifty (instead of seventy or eighty) daily pupils.

The schools in Dorchester have hitherto been supported by a general tax; but the highest sum ever raised for this purpose was two thousand seven hundred dollars. The new system requires the town to raise four thousand; of which sum a reasonable proportion is to be appropriated to the support of the primary schools. Their teachers, who are to be females, will receive $3,25 a week for their services. All these are to be continued throughout the year, and some of the former schools which had been discontinued a part of the year, are, we understand, to be made permanent.

When the people of Dorchester shall have added to these a Classical or High School, they will be on a footing, in this respect, with Boston, Worcester, Springfield, and Lowell; and their schools may be confidently expected to rise to a rank which they ought long ago to have sustained. There will be no necessity of sending their children to other towns and states for education.

It was curious to watch the progress of men's minds during the *revolution*. Some persons — we mention it to their honor — who had no family, and whose tax will be much increased by the new measures, were among their warmest advocates. Others, however, were 'disinterested' only, where they saw that the public sentiment would support the proposed *innovations*.

But the work of reform is accomplished, and Dorchester is emancipated. We hope the spirit of improvement which has effected changes so desirable, will be extended throughout the commonwealth, and throughout New England.

FOURTH ANNUAL MEETING OF THE AMERICAN LYCEUM.

We regret our inability to attend the recent meeting of the American Lyceum. We find the following account of it in the New York Daily Advertiser.

'The American Lyceum, after a session of two days and a half, in this city, adjourned on Monday last. There were fifty or sixty delegates from different parts of the country, and the subjects deliberated upon were of general interest. Measures were taken for the extension of the Society's operations and connections, by the formation of Departments and Classes of Science, Literature, and the Arts, and the invitation of scientific persons to coöperate. Future annual meetings will probably thus present attractions to a large portion of the intelligent men of the country, and lead to extensive benefit in the various branches of knowledge.

'The foundation of a cabinet of natural history, the plans for establishing an uniform system of meteorological observations in the Union, the procuring of town and country maps through local lyceums, as well as other measures taken or meditated by the society, have rendered necessary the extension of their operations.

'The Society have also provided for a more general publication of their objects and designs, especially in this city, which it is to be hoped may serve as a successful appeal for that support which they deserve; and for the drafting of a plan for the proper constitution and management of local lyceums, so as to render them interesting and useful. They will also promote the establishment of a central school for teachers, and have appointed a committee to report on the applicability of the monitorial system, in any form or degree, to the common schools of the country.

'The information communicated to the Lyceum by several members was listened to with great interest; particularly that on the state of Education and Lyceums in Massachusetts, by Hon Mr Calhoun; on the Monitorial System, by Samuel W. Seton, Esq, of New York; on the New Jersey Lyceum, by Rev. W. R. Weeks; on the state of Education and the thirteen new Lyceums of Georgia, by Judge Clayton.'

Among other valuable communications, several were received from abroad. We have only room at present to insert the official account of the proceedings.

FOURTH ANNUAL MEETING.

New York, Friday Morning, May 2nd, 1834. The fourth Annual meeting of the American Lyceum was organized in the District Court Room of the United States, at half past ten. President Duer in the Chair, and William B. Kinney, Secretary.

Messrs Pinckney, Dwight, and Rogers having been appointed a Committee to examine the credentials of members, reported the following.

Massachusetts Lyceum. — Hon. William B. Calhoun, Prof. A. H. Everett, C. Dewey, Frederick Emerson, Josiah Holbrook, William C. Woodbridge.

New Jersey State Lyceum. — Rev. William R. Weeks, D. D., Rev. Isaac V. Brown, Prof. Stephen Dodd, Dr S. H. Pennington, Mr E. E. Wines, Prof. John McLean, Prof. J. Henry, Dr Isaac H. Hampton.

Wesleyan University, Middletown, Connecticut. — Rev. Heman Bangs, Dr D. M. Reese.

Yale College. — Mr Davenport.

Albany Young Men's Society. — Leaman N. Woodruff, Peter Carmichael.

Brooklyn Lyceum, New York. — Rev. D. L. Carroll, Judge P. M. Radcliff, Mr Eames, Prof. Haskell.

Naval Lyceum, Brooklyn, New York. — Captain Sloat, Lieut. Pinckney, Thomas S. Smith.

New York Lyceum of Natural History. — Joseph Delafield, M. D., Dr Torrey, Dr J. Van Rensselaer, Dr L. D. Gale.

Newark Mechanics' Association and Lyceum. — Dr S. Congar, Nathan Hedges, I. W. Sanders, Dr L. A. Smith.

Essex county Lyceum, N. J. — Dr William Pierson, Rev. Rainsford Wells, J. B. Whiteley, Ab. G. Rogers, D. A. Hayes.

Hamilton Lyceum, Brooklyn, N. Y. — Alden I. Spooner, C. R. Marvin, Alexander Hadden.

Nottingham Lyceum, N. J. — Dr A. B. Howell.

Orange Lyceum, N. J. — Albert Pierson, Ira G. Munn, Jesse Williams, Rev. George Pierson, Nelson Lindsley.

Washington City Lyceum, D. C. — Rev R. R. Gurley.

University of Georgia. — Judge A. S. Clayton.

The following gentlemen were also received as members of the Lyceum on invitation.

The Marquis Aycenena, —— Aycenena, from Mexico; Tomas Gener, President of the Constitutional Cortes of Spain, Consul for Columbia; Dr Tobin of London; Prof. James Renwick, from the New York Lit. and Phil. Society; Timothy R. Green, Esq. President of National Convention of Young Men's Societies; Robert G. Rankin, Esq., of New York; A. B. Johnson, Esq., of Utica; Samuel W. Seton, Agent of the Public School Society; Mr Stamatiades, from Athens in Greece.

Messrs. Dwight, Clayton, and Gale, having been appointed a Committee of Arrangements, reported the following order of business, which was adopted, viz.

1. The sessions shall open at nine A. M., with prayer, and at two P. M., except when otherwise ordered.

2. The business shall be arranged as follows. Reading of the minutes, Reports from Committees, Reports from Lyceums, Schools, &c, to be in order half an hour after the opening. Essays in order, one hour after the opening. Discussions of Regular Questions in order one and a half hours after the opening. Resolutions, two and a half hours after the opening. Resolutions may be offered at any time on leave.

Questions for discussion at the fourth Annual meeting of the Lyceum.

1st. Is the establishment of a Central School for Teachers desirable in the United States, and on what plan should it be founded?

2d. Is the Monitorial System in any form or degree appropriate to our Common Schools?

3d. Ought corporal punishment to be inflicted in our Common Schools?

4th. How far and by what means may Natural History be introduced into common education?

5th. Should the Ancient Languages constitute a part of education in Common Schools?

Reports on Lyceums and Schools were presented by several gentlemen, in the order of States, on invitation by the President.

The Monitorial System (the 2d regular question) was taken up, but on motion postponed, when the Lyceum adjourned till afternoon.

Friday Afternoon, 4 *o'clock*. The Lyceum met, and Judge Clayton was called to the Chair.

Mr Dwight, first Corresponding Secretary, read a letter from Mr C. D. Arfwedson, consenting to furnish an essay on the state of Public Schools in Switzerland, on his return to his country, and apologizing for his absence from the 4th annual meeting.

On motion, the offer of Mr Arfwedson was accepted by the Lyceum.

A letter was read from Mr William C. Woodbridge, regretting the necessity of his absence, and his inability through ill health to furnish the report assigned to the Committee on Foreign Correspondence, appointed at the 3d annual meeting. Mr W. also suggested an alteration of the plan authorized by the resolutions of last year, relating to a Text-book in Physiology. On motion resolved, that the Executive Committee be requested to make the alteration proposed.

An essay on raising the standard of Female Education, by Mrs Sigourney, was read, whereupon

Resolved, that the thanks of the Lyceum be presented to Mrs Sigourney, and that the essay be referred to the Executive Committee for publication.

Extracts of correspondence with Mr Joaquim Mosquera, Vice President of New Grenada, were also read, conveying interesting information of the progress he has made in Popayan and Pasto in promoting education.

Dr Weeks presented, in detail, an account of the formation of the New Jersey State Lyceum, on the 3d of April last.

The first regular question was then taken up, and discussed by Messrs. Dwight, Clayton, Weeks, Carroll, Howell, Reese, Green, and Dewey.

The Lyceum then adjourned till tomorrow.

Saturday Morning, May, 3*d*. The Lyceum met at half past nine A. M.

Mr Calhoun made a detailed statement on Lyceums, Schools and Academies in Massachusetts.

Mr Hayes made a report of the Essex County Lyceum, New Jersey.

An invitation was read, from Mr Whitlaw, for the members to attend his introductory lecture on Medical Botany, on Monday evening next, at Clinton Hall.

The Corresponding Secretary read an essay on education in the Mexican Republic, from Mr Lorenzo De Zavala, Minister Plenipotentiary from that country to France.

On motion, resolved, that the thanks of the Lyceum be presented to Mr Zavala, and that his essay be referred to the Executive Committee for publication.

The discussion of the first regular question was resumed by Messrs Dwight and Hedges.

On motion of Dr Rogers, resolved, that a Committee, with power to add to their number, be appointed, whose duty it shall be, during the recess of the American Lyceum, to correspond with persons in different parts of the country, whose attention has been particularly directed to the business of instruction; to collect information, and otherwise to promote the establishment of a Central Seminary for the education of common school teachers. The following gentlemen were constituted such Committee. Messrs Dwight, Rogers, Weeks, and Carroll.

On motion of Mr Carroll, it was resolved, that a committee be appointed to prepare and report some plan for raising funds, for defraying necessary expenses. The following gentlemen were appointed — Messrs Carroll, Green, and Weeks.

On motion of Dr Pennington, it was resolved, that a Committee be appointed to collect information, and report on the best plan for conducting and rendering interesting and attractive the proceedings of Local Lyceums. The following gentlemen were appointed such Committee — Messrs. Pennington, Carroll, and Hedges.

Mr Seton, General Agent of the Trustees of the New York Common Schools, being invited, communicated his views of the second regular subject of discussion, after a few remarks by Messrs Hedges and Howell.

On motion of Mr Kinney, it was resolved, that a Committee be appointed to produce an essay on the second Regular Question.

The Lyceum then adjourned.

Monday, May 5th. The Lyceum met at Columbia College at eleven A. M. On motion of Judge Clayton, it was

Resolved, That the Executive Committee be requested to take measures to organize classes or departments, for the promotion of Moral, Political, and Physical Science, the result of whose labors during the year shall be made known at the session of the next annual meeting.

Resolved, That each class or department be empowered to call to its aid such scientific gentlemen as they may think proper, though they be not members of the Lyceum; and that the same be invited to take part in the business of the next annual meeting.

Resolved, That the Executive Committee be requested to organize a Department of Literature and the Arts, subject to the same regulation as those for the Department of Science.

The following report from the Committee on raising funds was adopted.

'The Committee appointed to propose some plan for raising the requisite funds to defray the annual expenses of the Lyceum, beg leave to report and recommend, that a committee be appointed to prepare and publish an address to the public, explaining the nature and designs of the American Lyceum, showing its facilities of receiving and communicating the most valuable information, on topics of general education, its influence in the formation of local Lyceums throughout the country, the reform and improvement it is destined to effect on the system of common schools, and the relation which it holds to the good interests of learning and knowledge. That said committee make arrangements for holding a public meeting as soon as practicable, when addresses shall be delivered, bringing the nature, operations, and objects of the Lyceum prominently before the meeting — and that the committee then make a personal application as extensively as possible, to individuals either to become annual subscribers or life members, or to contribute liberally to the funds of the society.

'It is confidently believed that an efficient committee for the purpose contemplated, might, after a spirited appeal to the public, be able to procure a sufficient fund, not only to meet the current expenses, but to enable the Lyceum, through the medium of the press, to make its influence on the cause of popular education, knowledge, and improvement felt to the extremities of the nation. D. L. Carroll.'

On motion it was resolved, that Mr Carroll, Dr Gale, and Prof. Renwick be a committee to carry into effect the plan recommended in the report.

OFFICERS.

The following list of officers, reported by the Committee on Nominations, were chosen.

President — William A. Duer, President of Columbia College.

Vice Presidents — 1st, Alexander Proudfit, D. D., Salem, New York ; 2d, Roberts Vaux, Philadelphia ; 3d, Hon. Edward Everett, Boston ; 4th, Thomas S. Grimke, Esq. Charleston, S. C. ; 5th, Philip Lindsley, D. D.

Recording Secretary — William B. Kinney, Newark, N. J.

Treasurer — William Forrest, New York.

Corresponding Secretaries — 1st, Theodore Dwight, Jun'r, New York ; 2d, J. L. Comstock, M. D., Hartford, Conn. ; 3d, Josiah Holbrook, Boston ; 4th, Judge Clayton, Athens, Georgia ; 5th, Prof. J. M. Sturtevant, Illinois ; 6th, William C. Woodbridge, Boston ; 7th, Rev. B. O. Peers, Kentucky ; 8th, Hon. William B. Calhoun, Springfield, Mass. ; 9th, Thomas P. Jones, Washington, D. C. ; 10th, Abraham Woods D. D., Alabama ; 11th, Prof. John Griscom, Providence, R. I. ; 12th, President Cushing, Hampden Sidney College, Virginia.

Additional members of the Executive Committee. Prof. Olmsted, Yale College ; S. H. Pennington, M. D., Newark, N. J. ; Prof. J. S. Rogers, N. Y. ; J. Kearney Rogers, M. D., New York ; A. P. Halsey, Esq., New York ; James Donaldson, Esq, New York ; Prof. James Renwick, New York ; Prof. Vethake, New York ; John D. Russ, M. D., New York ; Dr Torry ; Dr L. D. Gale ; Dr J. Van Rensselaer ; Rev. D. L. Carroll, Brooklyn ; Robert G. Rankin, Esq, New York.

On motion of Judge Clayton, it was

Resolved, That the thanks of the Lyceum be presented to the President, for his valuable book on Constitutional Jurisprudence, published at the request of the society, and that a copy of it be placed in the library.

A letter and an essay on the means for promoting civilization and education among the Western Indians, by Henry R. Schoolcraft, was read, whereupon,

Resolved, That the thanks of the Lyceum be presented to Mr Schoolcraft, and that the essay be referred to the Ex. Committee for publication.

On motion of Mr Dewey, it was

Resolved, That the thanks of the Lyceum be presented to Mr Woodbridge, for his attention and liberality in regard to the publication of the proceedings of the last annual meeting, and that he be requested to continue to publish the proceedings in the Annals of Education.

The following essays written for the American Lyceum, were laid before the Society and referred to the Executive Committee for publication, and votes of thanks were passed to their respective authors.

An essay on Education in Mexico, by Juan Rodriguez, a member of the Mexican Congress, of the Indian race.

An essay on Education and Literature, in Poland, by a young Exile, seventeen years of age.

An account of the higher branches of education in the Island of Cuba, by Justo Velor, Rector of the principal College of Havana.

The Report of the Corresponding Secretary was referred to the Executive Committee.

The Report on Young Men's Societies, presented by Timothy R. Green, Esq. was referred to the same Committee.

On motion of Judge Clayton, it was

Resolved, That the Lyceums which are now, or may hereafter be established, be requested to unite with this society as branches thereof, and that they be represented in its annual meetings; and in the event of a failure so to be represented, they favor this society with a Report of the state and condition of their respective institutions, to the end that the great objects of this society and its associate societies be promoted, and their benefit more generally diffused.

Prof. Haskell, of Brooklyn, exhibited and explained his family and school apparatus to the society, and the further examination of it was referred to the Executive Committee.

The Lyceum then adjourned.

THE TEACHER'S ALMANAC FOR JUNE.

THE SCHOOL-ROOM.

More care than ever will be necessary to keep the school-room in such a state, that the languid, heated bodies of your pupils need not entirely overpower their mental faculties. Do not, however, in any case, expect as much from them as at some other season; for they are not *physically capable* of it; and punishment for bodily languor would be tyranny, not discipline. Give them as much of free air exercise as possible. Fifteen minutes' relaxation will often do more to secure order and good lessons than many angry words, or even strokes of the rod.

But some of our readers have left 'the school room.' We hope they have not forgotten 'the school,' the centre of affection to *faithful teachers*; and may all our teachers be such! Remember to lay up in summer leisure, the provision for winter. Your mind, at least, is at leisure. Look around you, and observe men and things. See what the life is, for which your pupils are preparing; and consider how you can best fit them for it. Observe the face of nature, and the course of events; and collect facts and illustrations to instruct and amuse your pupils during the winter. Store your own mind with the practical knowledge which you ought to impart to them.

THE WORLD.

The world is now teeming with life, in every form. The insect tribes are fully developed, and you can find ample amusement for the leisure hours of your pupils in teaching them to observe and classify them, according to their habitations, their food, their appearance, their useful or injurious effects, and the birds that feed on them. Every hour, every place almost, will afford some opportunity for remark; and the troublesome housefly, the disgusting spider, and the humble ant, if carefully observed, will afford lessons on animal instinct and divine wisdom, as precious at least as the maxims of the spelling-book, and probably more durable. Can you not procure a microscope, or at least a magnifying glass, to show your pupils the wonderful structure of insects?

The earth is gemmed with flowers and plants also. Encourage your pupils to observe and gather them. Tell them all you know of their names and qualities, and assist them to learn more. If you do not understand Botany, let them compare the forms of the leaves, the number of the petals or flower leaves, their color, texture, and other cirumstances; and help them to observe the progress of bud, flower, fruit and seed. But we can only point you to the book of nature, and leave you to read it by the aid of the proper guides. The garden will be an interesting portion of it; and the exercise of cultivation will cheer and invigorate the little observers.

THE HEAVENS.

Make your pupils observe at noon the progress of the Sun to the south, and of the shadows to the north, the increasing length of the days, and *the solstice*, on the 21st. On the same day, *a total eclipse of the Moon* will be visible throughout the United States, beginning at Washington about half past one in the morning, and terminating from four to five o'clock. It is three quarters of an hour earlier by the time of the Western States, and a little later in New England. In South Africa and the neighboring Oceans the sun will be partially eclipsed on the 7th of June; but it will not be hidden from us. Ask your pupils how this can happen. Among the constellations, the beautiful Corona Borealis or Northern Crown will be at the meridian on the 22d, at nine o'clock; and at the same time the Little Bear, so important from containing the star nearest the pole, but not at the pole. See 'Geography of the Heavens.' The Serpent may also be traced, and *Libra* is now to be on the meridian in the evening. Mars, Jupiter, and Saturn will also be on the meridian now in the course of the evening. Venus is very near the sun at its setting.

MISCELLANY.

Premium Work on Physiology.

The American Lyceum have recently decided, that the class book on Human Physiology for which they have offered a premium, should also embrace the elements of Anatomy. It is to be comprised in 250 pages. Manuscripts should be forwarded to one of the corresponding secretaries, by the first of October next. *Simplicity of style* will, we presume, be a primary requisite.

Examples of Self Education.

It is not a little encouraging to those who long for the advancement of society, to see the results of that education which is gained by some in the school of nature and providence, with little of the aid of man — and in this view we publish the following examples.

Ohio. Mr Ewing, U. S. Senator from Ohio, is perhaps the most conspicuous man in this State at the present time, unless Judge McLean be an exception. Although he has been in Congress but a single session, he has acquired a high reputation as a statesman. I should think him to be about forty. He is a self-made man — a striking exemplification of what a man can attain to by merely *personal effort*. He is a native of this State, and was born poor. In his youth, his principal employment was wood-chopping. Being very athletic, he excelled in the labors of the axe. At length, when he had become what would be called, 'a great, overgrown, awkward, brawney young man,' by a fortunate jostle, a desire for an education waked in his bosom, — he directed his steps to this institution, where he completed his education preparatory to the study of the law. In term time he chopped wood at the College door — and in vacation, it was his custom to swing his axe upon his shoulder, and go forth in search of a job; which he would accomplish, and return with fresh vigor at the commencement of the next term. In this way he sustained himself while in College, and came out with a constitution as vigorous as when he entered. And now he is a senator of the United States.

Scotland. [*Extract of a letter from the Rev. George C. Potts.*]

Philadelphia, December 20, 1833.

Rev. and Dear Sir, — You requested me to state a reminiscence of early life, concerning two young men at the University of Glasgow. They were natives of the Highlands of Scotland. The first had been a *sailor* in the whale fishery in the northern seas: the other was a *shoemaker*, who had served a regular apprenticeship to his trade.

In Scotland there prevails an ardent desire in the minds of most young men to acquire a classical education. The parish schoolmaster is generally a man of erudition, for he is appointed by the law of the land. Through this means and by the instruction of the parish minister *they* acquired a knowledge of Latin and Greek — engaging at intervals in their different occupations to procure for themselves a subsistence. Being youth of ardent piety, they resolved to devote themselves to the Gospel ministry; and knowing the necessity of a collegiate course, as preparatory to that office, they determined with their slender means, to earn, by hard industry, *sufficient* to pay the professors' fees. These young men entered the University of Glasgow, depending for their weekly support on the work of the shoemaker, who made three pair of shoes every week, for which he received one shilling and ten pence. This was their only resource. The *sailor* studied the recitations in Greek, and the departments of philosophy and mathematics, and read them regularly over to the *shoemaker* while he was at work: and when the work was done, they read over carefully the lessons of the succeeding day. Thus they were well prepared, and maintained a reputable standing in their class.

Indiana Teacher's Seminary.

This Institution is situated near Madison, Indiana, and was opened on the first Wednesday of March last.

Its design is to prepare young men to teach Common Schools. Much of the instruction is to be communicated in Lectures, of which there are to be two courses. The *first* is intended to exhibit the most easy, rapid, and successful mode of teaching the common English branches, beginning with the Alphabet, and the best means of exciting interest, and governing a school.

The second is to enable every teacher to explain to his pupils the nature of those things, and animals, which are mentioned in their studies, and the *reasons* for pursuing a particular course rather than any other. Lectures to be illustrated by apparatus. In connection with these lectures there will be regular recitations on the ordinary branches. Particular instruction is to be given in speaking, writing, and sacred music. A session will consist of forty weeks. During the remaining twelve weeks — (Dec. Jan. and Feb.) the students can *teach*, as a means of defraying, in part, their expenses. None are admitted under fifteen years of age.

A seminary library will be provided, and all class books and other books be loaned.

But the institution is also to be a manual labor school. 'The use of a fertile farm, well stocked and supplied with tools and machinery, will be given to the students, by means of which every individual of sober and industrious habits,' of the required age, 'can pay for his board by his own labor, without retarding his progress in study.

Seminary for Teachers at Andover.

We have insisted upon no point more earnestly, or with more confidence, than the *necessity of a professional education for teachers*, as indispensable to the permanent improvement of our schools. We are rejoiced to learn from an appeal to the friends of Common education, received as our number is closing, that the Trustees of Phillips' Academy have resolved to place the Seminary at Andover on a broader and more permanent basis, for the accomplishment of this object. They have been urged to this measure by the success of the plan thus far, and the numerous calls for teachers from the destitute portions of our country. In addition to the large building and apparatus already used for this purpose, a farm for manual labor, lodging-houses and a hall for boarding, have been provided as the means of diminishing the expenses of the students. It is confidently believed that many young men, well qualified for the office, are ready to devote themselves to the business of teaching as a profession, provided they can receive a little aid in addition to the means of support now offered. The Committee believe that a donation of *sixtysix dollars*, to be furnished only as a loan, and thus perpetuated, would be sufficient to secure the *continued residence of one candidate* for this important office, at the seminary; and they ask the aid of the friends of education in this form. We trust they will not ask in vain; for of what avail will all other means of benevolence prove, if our *schools* are not supplied with faithful and competent teachers?

Huron Institute.

A manual labor school under this name has been established at Milan, Huron Co. Ohio, which contains eightyseven students; twentyfour in the classical department, and in the English department, thirtyfour males and twentynine females. The board in the Institute is given at cost, varying from seventyfive to eightyseven cents per week; and the tuition is only twelve or sixteen dollars a year.

Education Convention in Missouri.

We are gratified to see that a convention on the subject of education has been called in *Missouri*, which was to meet on the 15th ult. We earnestly hope 'the great West' will awaken to its own wants, and make efforts proportioned to its power. Who will go from the 'land of schools' to aid them?—for the too common result of such efforts is, that the interest and hope excited, sinks into despair, from the *impossibility* of procuring competent teachers.

Boston Farm School and Asylum.

We are gratified to learn that the Boston Asylum for Indigent Boys, has been united with the Farm School. A farm, removed from temptation, has been secured on Thompson's Island, at a short distance from the city; and buildings are soon to be erected to receive the pupils.

Periodicals on Education.

It is encouraging to find new efforts made, in various directions, to establish periodicals on education, for they indicate an increased interest in the subject on the part of the community, for want of which the few that exist have languished. 'The Mothers' Magazine,' from assuming a distinctive religious character, has gained an extensive circulation, and we are told, has been republished in England. 'The Fathers' Magazine' has been established the present year, at New York. The 'Southern Journal of Education,' in Georgia, has reached its eleventh number. A spirited paper called 'The Inciter,' has been published by a teacher, in Lancaster, Pennsylvania, which contains much that is useful on education. 'The Journal of the Flushing Institute' has an excellent character. In addition to these we have just received the first number of 'The Schoolmaster, and Academic Journal,' published at Oxford, Ohio; and should be much interested to see this, or some other periodical on education, gain an extensive circulation at the west.

Eclectic Academy of Music in Cincinnati.

A Society has been formed under this title, at Cincinnati, with two objects in view; first to promote the introduction of *vocal music as a branch of school education*, throughout this country; second, to promote improvement in church music. The Trustees express their conviction, founded on the entire success of the plan abroad, and the happy results of the experiments in Boston and Philadelphia, that it is *practicable* to make it a branch of *common school education.* They hope to convince the public of its importance, and eventually to secure the proper instruction of teachers in this art. A course of instruction is to be given by a professor acquainted with the system already introduced by the Boston Academy. We cordially hail every kindred institution; and hope that music thus early implanted, may become one of the rational recreations of the rising West.

House of Refuge in Philadelphia.

From the last report of the Philadelphia house of refuge for juvenile offenders, it appears that during the year past ninety persons, rescued from juvenile crime, have been sent from it into families or places of respectable occupation, and that most of those who have left the institution during the five years of its existence, have given satisfaction to their employers. The managers also state, that the number of individuals who needed the aid of this refuge has been less than usual during the past year; and the number reformed, greater. They ascribe not a little of this to the removal and reform of those who were corrupting their companions. Such institutions are a blessing to our country. But how much better will it be, when their necessity is in a great measure anticipated, by a course of education, moral as well as intellectual, which shall extend to *every child in the community* — from the earliest age!

PUBLIC SCHOOLS OF PHILADELPHIA.

Sixteenth Annual Report. These schools have now on the rolls 6767 pupils, of which number 3713 are boys, and 3054 are girls. In parts of the city where the population is too scattered to admit of the establishment of public schools, the children are placed in the private schools nearest to the residence of their parents. The number thus provided for is 1098, making the total number of children educating at the public expense 7865. A new and excellent brick school-house has been erected in the city, and although it had been opened only three weeks at the time the report was made, nearly 400 children were already in attendance.

The expenses of the year were $74,170; but this amount includes $40,620 expended in purchasing ground and building school-houses. The report thus concludes:

'In presenting this brief outline of proceedings in the sixteenth year of their labors in a branch of public service of incalculable importance, the controllers again beg permission most earnestly to solicit the attention, influence, and active coöperation of their fellow-citizens in the promotion of this great work. It is one to which every individual may effectually contribute by advice, exhortation, authority, and explanation afforded to the proper subjects for these establishments. It is to *sound, practical,* Christian education that we must look for improved morals, judicious industry, for the maintenance of truth, order, and justice, for the intelligent assertion and manly support of those principles upon which alone our free and happy institutions can be preserved from destruction. This is a work which every friend of man — every lover of his country and of freedom, ought to lend his most zealous and unwearied efforts to promote; it is one in which combined effort is demanded, and in which the united strength of the philanthropist, the patriot, the christian; of the good and the wise, will be sustained by Divine aid, and ultimately crowned with universal and triumphant success.'

CHARITY SCHOOL SOCIETY OF PHILADELPHIA.

This is a society supported by vested funds and contributions, which has a large school house in Walnut, between Sixth and Seventh streets. There are now 260 boys in the male department, and 250 girls in the female. The girls are instructed in sewing as the common rudiments of education. The total expense of instruction, including teacher's salaries, books, stationary, press, &c, was $2002, and the average number of pupils being 510, it is seen that the annual cost of each scholar is but three dollars and ninetythree cents. — *S. S. Journal.*

We sometimes hear an expression of surprise that certain books are not noticed in this work. Some, indeed, which are sent are left unnoticed, because we consider them unworthy of notice; and some, because they are foreign to our object: but these are *comparatively few.* In *many* cases we do not receive valuable books, although we ascertain, subsequently, that the authors have endeavored to send them; in others, a long and laborious examination would be necessary to justify any expression of opinion; and we must frankly say, that the receipts of this work do not justify the purchase of books for criticism, or the devotion of so much time to the preparation of half a page, although we have sometimes done both. We will merely add, that books sent to our agents in cities, will generally reach us safely; and we shall *hereafter* insert the title at least of all new works on education which we receive, not in our view of an injurious tendency.

We intended to devote a *larger* (not *large*, as incorrectly printed) portion of our number to extracts, which will show the state of public opinion. We are obliged to defer much that we designed to use in our present number.

NOTICES OF BOOKS.

A Compendium of Natural Philosophy, adapted to the use of the General Reader, and of Schools and Academies. By Denison Olmsted, A. M., Prof. of Mathematics and Natural Philosophy in Yale College. New Haven: H. Howe. Boston: Carter, Hendee and Co. 1833.

The publications of Professor Olmsted, for the use of Colleges, have established his reputation as a man of science, and will give teachers of our higher schools a confidence in this work, which they cannot accord to the republications of foreign works, by professed bookmakers. It will be highly valuable to the mechanic and the self-educator also, and to those who desire to revive the knowledge they have once acquired, and to keep pace with the progress of science. It is written in a simple, perspicuous and interesting manner, and presents very happily the practical applications of philosophical principles. For novices, we should much prefer the inductive plan; but as a 'compendium' of the science, we think it excellent.

Mental Culture, or the means of developing the Human Faculties. By J. L. Levison. Boston: Allen and Ticknor. 1834.

This is a republication of a work on Education, based on phrenological principles. The first part is occupied with an account of the mental philosophy of phrenology, which deserves the attention of every teacher, whatever may be the final result of the investigation as to the conformation of the brain, or the external exhibition of its organs. The second part presents the practical results of these opinions in the management of the young, and contains many valuable maxims on education. Indeed, the coincidence of these results with those deduced from the experience of the ablest educators, and the simplicity and obvious good sense which will commend them to most unprejudiced minds, is, in our view, one of the strongest presumptions in favor of the truth of the system by which they are sustained.

This work is free from the sceptical and anti-Christian views which deform some others of the kind; and sustains religious instruction and daily religious worship, as essential to a sound education.

Outlines of Human Physiology, designed for the use of the higher classes in Common Schools. By George Hayward, M. D. Boston: Marsh, Capen and Lyon. 1834.

We cordially welcome another work on the human frame, designed for the use of schools, more extensive in its range than the Class Book of Anatomy. A work prepared by a physician of reputation, evidently with great care, on a subject of so much importance, and abounding in interesting facts, we need scarcely say, deserves attention and experiment in our high schools. We wish its arrangement and style were less technical, and more adapted to common minds.*

A Lecture to Young Men. By Sylvester Graham. Providence: Printed by Weeden & Cory, 1834.

We are rejoiced to see a work published in our country, on a topic in Physiology which the 'artificial modesty' to which we have formerly alluded has

* We would take this occasion to suggest to professional and scientific men, who prepare works for common schools, that immense advantage might be derived from the counsels of a practical teacher, or from experiments with a few pupils, as to the manner of giving instruction; and should this be deemed disrespectful, we would remind them that Dean Swift considered it not unworthy of him to read his sermons to his kitchen-maid, in order to attain simplicity. The world would be spared a deluge of useless words, and sentences, and books, if modern writers, sacred and secular, would follow his example. We would remark, however, that the work before us is by no means to be charged with *redundancy*; and that we only regret the want of *greater simplicity* in the language and methods of illustration.

covered up, until a solitary but fatal vice is spreading desolation through our *schools* and *families*, unnoticed or unknown. The experience of teachers, the case-books of physicians, and the painful exposures which accident or the dreadful diseases which follow in its train, have occasionally produced, have, at length, forced it upon public attention, and we hope it will not again be forgotten. The work before us is the result of extensive observation and study; its usefulness has been tested by its influence as a lecture, and its views of this evil are in accordance with the experience of the few teachers whom we have known, possessed of the moral courage to encounter it. We would offer it to some who have earnestly desired a work on the subject, as one adapted to their purposes. We would recommend its perusal to *every parent* and *teacher*. We would warn them, that those who were most confident of the safety of their charge, have often been most deceived; and that the youthful bashfulness which seems to shrink from the bare mention of the subject, is *sometimes* the blush of shame for concealed crime. We feel bound to add, what abundant and decisive evidence has shown, that ignorance on the subject is no protection from the vice, nay, that it is often the original cause or encouragement of it; that it gives tenfold power to the evil example and influence, which are so rarely escaped; and that a cure can be effected only by the most careful instruction and long continued discipline, both physical and moral, directed by such experience as is presented in this work. We regret that the work of Tissot on this subject could not be divested by an able physiologist of some of its obsolete views, arranged on a plan more simple, and especially pruned of much which is dangerous to the infected.

The Family at Home, or Familiar Illustrations of the various Domestic Duties, with an Introductory Notice. By G. D. Abbott. Boston: Carter Hendee and Co. 1834.

'The Mother at Home' and 'The Child at Home,' by the Rev. Mr Abbott, of Worcester, have been followed by the 'Family at Home,' by his brother. Like the Family itself it is a *miscellany;* a series of articles not connected by any such plan or system as well trained minds delight in; but perhaps on that very account more likely to arrest the attention and improve the habits of the miscellaneous minds which form so large a majority of every community. It presents distinctly the religious views of the editor, or rather of the 'evangelical' in England, by whom a large part of it was prepared, interwoven with the work; but it contains a variety of lessons in common, practical life, which will be interesting and useful to parents of other opinions, who are willing to be eclectics.

A large part of it is republished from an English work; and we regret that the word 'prepared' or 'edited' had not been inserted on the title page; for it would have saved many a disappointment, and prevented all danger of associating a name we so highly respect, with that of Blake, whose assumption of the labors of others we have felt compelled to expose.

Angell's Union Series of Common School Classics.

In our number for April we remarked of this series, 'The plan we think good; the selections, so far as we have been able to examine them are interesting and well graduated; but we could not venture to give an opinion of the whole series so extensive and composed of so various materials — without an examination which our duties render impracticable. We observe that several instructors who have introduced them have found them very useful.' In justice to schools, we feel bound to state, that a number of respectable teachers assembled in New York, who profess to have examined them, declare in the public papers that they abound with 'inconsistencies and oversights' in regard to 'orthography, pronunciation, and syllabication,' and that they are 'unworthy of the patronage of teachers.'

AMERICAN

ANNALS OF EDUCATION

AND INSTRUCTION.

JULY, 1834.

AMERICAN MISSION SEMINARY IN CEYLON.

Third Triennial Report of the American Mission Seminary, at Jaffna, Ceylon. With an Appendix and a List of Benefactors. Nellone, Church Mission Press, 1833.

THE heart of an American cannot but throb with pleasure, (for we trust it is not always *pride*), when he encounters in every port which he visits, in every paper which he reads, the traces of that native enterprise which called forth even the eloquence of Burke. It is with kindred and more exalted pleasure, that the American philanthropist sees his countrymen exploring the regions of intellectual and moral darkness, and endeavoring to open the way for the rays of truth to enter. It is a cheering and a striking spectacle, to see this nation, 'yet in the gristle of youth,' carrying back the light of knowledge to its original sources; and, through its missions, sending the rays of temporal and eternal truth to classic Greece, and to the ancient capitol of the Eastern Empire, and to venerable India. We do not speak thus to excite that spirit of 'self-glorification,' to which as a nation we are already too prone; but to arouse the heart of every American to gratitude, that Providence employs his country in so noble a work to direct his patriotic feeling to our enterprises of peace and benevolence, and to urge him to the effort to contribute to this — its only substantial and immortal glory.

All may not agree in approving the *motive* which prompts to such efforts as that we are about to describe, or the *ultimate* object in view; but none can help rejoicing, to see the thousands of children, who were destined to the darkness of ignorance, and the bondage of superstition, brought under a course of instruction in the elements of useful knowledge, and taught the existence and character of the only true God, by the delegates of American benevolence. Especially will every friend of light hail the efforts made to spread the light of science among those nations, where a system of cruel and debasing superstition is founded upon false theories, in regard to nature itself.

The American Missionary Seminary at Ceylon was established for this purpose. The wretched indifference of the natives to education rendered it almost impossible to secure the regular attendance of their children at day schools; and it became necessary to encourage those who were willing to receive knowledge, by engaging to support all who should be placed under the entire direction of the missionaries. In this way, a system of boarding schools was originated. It was found that $12 a year was sufficient to feed and clothe a native child. The benevolence of our countrymen soon furnished the means of receiving a large number; and in 1823 one hundred and twenty boys and thirty girls were sustained in the boarding schools connected with the mission in Ceylon.

The want of native teachers, and the rapid progress and promising talent of many of the pupils, then led their teachers to propose the establishment of a central institution of a higher order, whose third triennial report is now before us.

A leading object of the institution is, to give native youth of promise a thorough knowledge of the English language; not only to give them access to the science and literature of Europe, but to prepare translators, who shall be able to transfer the literary treasures of the West to the languages of the East. To this work, none but natives, thus trained, can ever be fully competent; and without it, the east cannot be fully enlightened.

Another object of primary importance is the cultivation of Tamul literature. In this way only can the poetical and sacred books, which are the national depositories of religion as well as of knowledge, be thoroughly understood by the teachers of European science and Christian truth. Thus, also, writers will be prepared who can produce original and useful works in this language, to gratify the taste for reading which the education of the people will naturally excite.

The Sanscrit, as the depository of the Hindoo mythology and literature, and the Hebrew and Greek as the languages of our sacred books, are taught to a few; and the Latin to such as may need it. It is obvious, however, that if an oriental pupil needs to study any works, purely *as classics*, he should be directed to the poets of Persia and Arabia rather than those of Greece and Rome.

But none of these branches is more important to secure the intellectual and moral illumination of the East, than instruction in the sciences of Europe. The whole system of Hindoo superstition, and folly, and cruelty — so unworthy the name of religion — is based upon false views of Cosmogony, and Astronomy, and Chronology, and Geography, and Chemistry; and so interwoven are these crude and ridiculous theories with the doctrines and rites of Boodhism and Brahminism, that they must stand or fall together. The true theory of eclipses must at once put an end to all the rites and ceremonies which are practised, when they occur; and the proud ignorance which considers the East the centre of the world and the depository of all knowledge, vanishes before the light of Geography.

Such are the grounds which render an institution of this character at once a legitimate object of interest to the Christian missionary and to the lover of science; and on these grounds, it has been liberally sustained by benevolent and enlightened men, in our own country and in the government of India.

It was opened at Batticotta, in Ceylon, in 1823, with 48 pupils. A preparatory school was commenced two years after, at Tillipally, another of the missionary stations, in which pupils were received at an early age, and were thus enabled to acquire the idioms and the pronunciation of the English language with a degree of accuracy which would be impracticable at a later period. This school has lately been transferred to Batticotta, and united with the Seminary, as an Introductory Class.

In 1830, the number of students was sixtythree, divided into three nearly equal classes. Thirty, from the preparatory school, were admitted in the same year, after passing a satisfactory examination. In 1832, sixtythree others were received from various schools, on the funds of the mission. Twenty applications were made in the year preceding the date of the report, for the admission of lads who had the necessary qualifications, but could not be received on the funds; and so great was the confidence inspired in the institution among the prejudiced natives, that several of these were boarded by their friends near the Seminary, and sent to enjoy its privileges. The whole number of pupils, at the date of the report, was one hundred and forty, of whom twentyfive were pursuing the study of theology. In addition to these, ten, who have finished the prescribed course of study, are retained as teachers. The whole number who have been in the Seminary is about two hundred, of whom fifty have finished the course of instruction, and are employed as assistant missionaries and teachers, as tutors in private English families, or as interpreters of government.

The funds of the institution have been derived almost entirely from the American Board of Missions, who have expended on this establishment £2,558 sterling, within the last three years. Since its origin, it has also received liberal donations of more than $3,000, from gentlemen who have witnessed its influence, chiefly members of the government, in Bengal, Ceylon, and Southern India; and the present government of Ceylon has subscribed £60 annually for the support of several pupils. A ruined church, originally built by the Dutch has been granted by the government, and repaired for the use of the mission and Seminary.

This Seminary is so unlike our own institutions in external appearance, that our readers will need some account of it, which we are enabled to give from the description of the Rev. Miron Winslow, of Ceylon, recently the instructor in theology. Instead of a formal row of masses of brick or stone, we must imagine a garden or grove of cocoanut palm trees — furnishing at once both shade and food — surrounded on three sides by a range of low buildings, of the simplest construction, divided into rooms. The central portion of the range is occupied by the rooms appropriated to recitations and lectures. On the left are the rooms for the pupils, one devoted to each class of twenty or thirty, in which they study under the direction of monitors and assistant teachers. These are furnished with the ordinary supply of desks and benches for their use, when they do not prefer the Hindoo posture on the tiled floor; and at night, each pupil unrolls his narrow straw mat, and if the heat does not drive him into the verandah or the open air, stretches himself upon it for repose. On the right, are the kitchen and the eating room, in which the pupils assemble three times a day, and sit upon the floor to receive their simple fare of rice. When the meal is finished, each goes to one of the wells in the garden, to quench his thirst, and wash his *hands* and his *brass plate*, the only articles of table furniture for which he finds occasion; and the important, and, with our habits, laborious business of eating, is finished! Necessity and habit prevent all craving for variety—all desire for what we often term the 'comforts of life;' and in this climate, the expenses of *four* or *five* students may be paid with the sum which is necessary to sustain *one* American youth.

In front of the quadrangular garden we have described, is the new building erected for the library, apparatus, and public rooms of the institution; which has been named *Ottley Hall*, as a tribute of gratitude to the Chief Justice, Sir Richard Ottley, one of the most liberal friends of the Seminary. It is built of hewn stone, (the coral, which is the principal rock of the island,) two stories high in the centre, and surrounded with the verandahs, or porticos, so necessary in a hot climate. Its length, including the verandahs, is one hundred and nineteen feet, and its breadth sixtysix. It contains a small library, and a valuable philosophical apparatus. A tower is to be erected at one end, terminating in an observatory; and a gentleman well qualified for the task was sent out the last year, who will attend to instruction and observations in physical science. We trust the institution will thus aid in promoting the progress of science, as well as in spreading its light.

In addition to the library of the Seminary, a second has been collected by the students, and a third by a society for moral improvement; both small, of course, but indicating the taste of the students for English works. Each student is also furnished with a little library of *class books*, which he retains when he leaves the institution that he may be enabled to review and retain what he has acquired.*

Four public examinations have been held in English, before the commissioners and other members of the British government, and two exhibitions in the Tamul language, before the Brahmins and other natives, which appear to have excited great interest. The officers of government, on some of these occasions, have not only given assurances of official countenance, but have furnished decisive evidence of personal interest and approbation, by valuable donations in books, apparatus, and money.

At the English examinations in 1827, and 1830, the pupils were examined in English Grammar, Arithmetic, Geography, Astronomy, Algebra, Geometry, Trigonometry, and Mensuration; in Mechanics, Pneumatics, and the Evidences of Christianity. The mechanical powers, the properties of the atmosphere, and the principles of the pump, diving-bell, barometer, hygrometer, and other instruments, were explained satisfactorily by the pupils. The projection of Maps, the calculation of Eclipses, and the superiority of the European to the Hindoo system of Arithmetic were illustrated. All the pupils were examined in Scripture History and Chronology. In the examination of 1832, the examination in science was more extensive.

But the most interesting public exercises were the exhibitions in Tamul. They were designed to show that the knowledge of

* We cannot express the mortification we feel, in comparing this plan with that so generally adopted by the students of American colleges, of *selling* their class books, as soon as they have ceased to study them! Is knowledge of no use except 'to pass an examination?' or have they attained the *ne plus ultra* in each study?

European teachers and schools extended to the languages and books and science of India, and to give practical demonstration of the superiority of European science and knowledge, by dissertations and exercises in which they were compared. From an article in the Columbo Journal, republished in the Report before us, it appears that a very respectable assembly crowded the chapel of the Seminary at one of these exhibitions. The pupils were first briefly examined in native systems of arithmetic, grammar, and morals. A prize translation, in Tamul, of a part of Lord Brougham's Essay, prefixed to the Library of Useful Knowledge, was then read. The second class was examined in Trigonometry, and gave popular illustrations of its application ; and a comparative examination of the Hindoo and European systems of Astronomy was made. Several dissertations prepared by the students, were next read, of which we find the following account in the Columbo Journal:

'1. *On the Shape of the Earth.* The object of this was to prove that the statements in the Purana, of the flatness of the earth, cannot be true. This was done by the application of the principles of trigonometry, before explained, to the statements concerning the height and situation of the polar star, in connection with its observed elevation above the horizon at this place. In the Purana, the polar star is supposed to be situated directly over the summit of Mount Meru, or the centre of the earth, at the height of 1,500,000 yojana ; or more than 27,000,000 of miles. Taking the height thus given as one of the sides of a right-angled triangle, and having the opposite angle, which is known here by observation to be nearly ten degrees, by the rules of Trigonometry, we may get the base or distance from us at which the star should be vertical. But this would make Mount Meru, so distant that we instead of being in the first or Jambu Island, as is said in the Purana, must be as far off as the sixth island ! and to cause the star to rise one degree, as it will by our going only to Negapatam, we must, on the supposition that the earth is flat, travel not sixtynine miles only, but more than fourteen millions of miles ! Of course Englishmen, to whom the polar star in London is nearly fifty-two degrees high, never could come from that country here ; and those here could never go there, as it would take for the journey some thousands of years. The conclusion was, that from data taken from the Purana itself, it is clearly demonstrated that the *Earth* CANNOT BE FLAT.

'2. *The principles of the foregoing dissertation applied*, to show the falsity of what is said about Mount *Meru*, and the seven islands that surround it.

'3. *Three proofs that the Earth is round;* to which was added an explanation of the method in which its diameter and circumference are measured, and the importance of knowing the earth's semi-diameter, as a base line, in several important calculations.

'4. *An application of the principles of Trigonometry to Navigation.* Showing the method of navigating a ship, when out of sight of land, by the log, and by observation, with the help of tables formed on the principles of the earth's convexity.

'5. *Method of ascertaining by the rules of Trigonometry the distance of the Sun and planets.* The semi-diameter of the earth and parallaxes of the heavenly bodies being known.

'6. *The real magnitude of the heavenly bodies ascertained,* by a knowledge of their distances and *apparent* magnitudes.

'7. *The motions and phases of the moon, and the cause of eclipses,* illustrated in a familiar manner, and compared, (as were the principles established in other essays), with the absurd doctrines of the Purana.

'*Two dissertations in Tamul,* on themes given out by his majesty's commissioners of inquiry for prize essays in English. 1st, On the advantages, to the natives of this country, of studying the English language. 2d, On the benefits of veracity, both to individuals and society; or the evils of lying and deception. The manner in which deception is practiced by jugglers and others, was shown by a skilful sleight of hand, with cups and balls, by one of the students; who after having 'quite astonished the natives,' and led them to think he had supernatural assistance, explained the manner in which it was done, and in which they are often deceived.

The examination was closed by an address from one of the native instructors, formerly a student in this seminary, giving a short history of the establishment, the number of students educated in it, their present employments and prospects, and the benefits, to the country at large, of this institution.'

The institution now contains one hundred and fifty pupils; and a recent decision of the Board will authorise the officers to receive three hundred hereafter on the foundation. It is under the direction of the Rev. Daniel Poor, as principal, Gabriel Tissera a native, and an accomplished English scholar, as tutors; nine native assistants; the Rev. J. R. Eckard, a teacher of natural science; and two gentlemen attached to the mission, as instructors in medicine and theology.

Such is the little colony of science which American enterprise and benevolence have established on the shores of Ceylon, as a source of illumination to the eight or ten millions of Hindoos, who use the Tamul language, and whose influence may extend to the remote regions of India, carrying with it the knowledge of Christian truth. Who that values science, or that loves Christianity, will not bid it 'God speed!'

[From the Ladies' Magazine.*]

FEMALE EDUCATION.

EXTRACT FROM A LETTER TO THE EDITOR.

'Mrs Hale,—I noticed with peculiar pleasure, in your October Number, an appeal to the philanthropic of the other sex, for equal facilities in the acquisition of knowledge. There is no subject on which I feel so deep an interest as that of *female education,* in all

* We shall endeavor to give in this number some of the examples of articles on education, found in other periodicals, which were excluded from our last.

its bearings; and when I see a writer express herself with such a noble fearlessness in so good a cause, she has the best sympathies of my heart. I would say to her, go forward in earnest effort to enlighten your sex, and the gratitude of many shall cheer you on your way.

Much has been said of the superior privileges of woman in this enlightened age, with regard to education. But not until recently, has it been even *hinted at* that these privileges have been overrated. She has, it is true, in some instances the advantage of knowing what would make her useful and happy, and of seeing the desired good *almost* within her reach, but her energies are wasted in unavailing efforts. Why must woman be denied to drink of the deep fountain of knowledge, and to experience the rich delight it infuses into the mind? What a charm would it throw around her otherwise dull and monotonous cares; what a blessed light would it give to irradiate her path and beguile her sorrows! Trifling as are my own acquisitions, I feel now, while rocking my babe in his cradle, and attending to the wants of two other little prattlers, an unspeakable gratitude that I can now and then sweeten my toils by the pleasures of reading and reflection, of imagination and composition; and I think I can form some *faint* idea of the mine of wealth and enjoyment *she* must possess, whose powers of mind have been *extensively* cultivated. With the blessing of God, *those treasures shall yet be mine;* though years of toil and self-denial be the *sacrifice.*

However varied may be the duties of a woman, if the means of instruction are within her reach, and knowledge be her object, no obstacle can intimidate her. She, who has the faculty to derive happiness from her most painful occupations, will find that the fountain of knowledge, when once tasted, is too sweet to be neglected or forgotten; that it opens to her a source of enjoyment always new and delightful, to which she will gladly repair for relaxation from depressing cares.

I would plead the cause of female education, were it a means only of promoting the *happiness* of my sex. I see many of them enduring their privations and sufferings as wife and mother silently and patiently, and even *submissively*, with scarcely a gleam of unmixed enjoyment to gladden their existence. Their beauty, which once won for them the gaze of admiration, has perhaps deserted them, the vivacity of youth has fled, and their ignorance is a subject of ridicule or mortification to those whose respect and love are dearer *than all beside.*

A husband may regard his wife with kindness, may appreciate her amiable qualities, and especially her readiness to oblige *him;* but if she be ignorant, he may at the same time consider her as rather of an inferior order of beings, and he will *treat* her *as such.* Now there is something in the breast of woman that tells her she is his equal; and if she have any sensibility, without his respect she cannot be happy. No wonder, when there is nothing to excite her interest or encourage her efforts, she should sometimes repine and murmur at her lot. No wonder that her mind, though naturally *strong*, should, by sickness and the dull monotony of her life, become weak and inactive, and thus the idea that 'woman is the weaker vessel,' become a proverb.

A mother's life is one of unceasing care, of laborious effort; and if her burthens can be lightened in any way, and her happiness promoted, it should be done. Education is the very thing she needs. Education, moral and mental, will sweeten her joys and enliven her solitude; will throw a gracefulness around her every employment, and render her not only persevering and useful, but happy and beloved.

An ignorant woman may flatter herself with her privileges, but she is in fact only an upper servant in her family, and pays dearly for the *elevation* of her station by more abundant cares and labors. Her influence is scarcely felt at home or abroad. But let the same female by education be transformed into the intelligent wife and mother, not only will she gladden her home and the hearts of all who know her, but she may elevate the taste and polish the manners of an illiterate husband, and give a character of respectability to her children, which it is not in the power of a father to bestow. Who that has looked much upon the world, has not observed that the respectability of a family depends chiefly on the mother; and that even when her children are worthy, how slowly they force their way in the world, if she be undeserving of regard?

But we need not fear that our claim on appeals for mental culture will be disregarded. The public mind will soon be awake to this subject. Neither do I believe that female influence will be less than it is at present, when she shall have realized the advantages of education. I think too highly of the taste of the other sex to fear such a result. We will give the most charitable excuse for their long inattention to our wants in this respect, by supposing they have concluded us so gifted by nature as to require little aid to render us accomplished. If experience has not already convinced them of their error, my feeble efforts may do something towards producing this effect.

S. F. W.

[From the Mothers' Magazine.]

PHYSICAL EDUCATION OF LITTLE CHILDREN.

'We are gratified to find the Mothers' Magazine takes up subjects connected with Physical education. We extract part of an article on this subject ,with some of the Editor's remarks, which well deserve attention.'

'Before subjoining these extracts we would state that, a few years since, while on an infant school committee, we had opportunity to make our observations upon the different treatment of children, by their mothers, in the article of food.

'It was revolting to the feelings of humanity, as well as of common sense, at the time of their dinner to see their infant board loaded with confectionaries of all kinds, cakes and fruits, and candies of every variety, and in frightful abundance. The committee made several attempts to substitute, in their place, a bowl of simple bread and milk, but in vain. Mothers actually seemed to vie with each other, in furnishing their little darlings, dressed like butterflies, with the greatest variety of dainties. Had Dr Brigham and others, in their severe animadversions upon the early precocity of children, by means of infant school instruction, examined further into the causes of the evils reprobated, and levelled some of their heavy artillery against the practice of *gorging* children and infants with such unsuitable regimen, we believe they would have found that the evils referred to, originated partially at least in improper diet, and overheated rooms, instead of being solely the effect of infant school instruction.'

EXTRACT FROM A MOTHER'S JOURNAL.

"Knowing the intimate connection between the body and soul, and being sensible that the animal feelings have a direct influence upon the heart, we felt the necessity of directing our efforts toward her physical, as well as moral and intellectual education. From her earliest infancy, therefore, we paid particular attention to her diet and regimen. Her food has consisted chiefly of milk, and bread and milk. For the first eighteen months, she scarcely tasted flesh; and since that time, she has had it very seldom. All kinds of rich food have generally been denied her, and her only drink has been cold water or milk. Either of these satisfies her, and if offered tea or coffee she will not drink it; thus showing that the appetite for stimulating drinks is not natural, but acquired.

"We have had an opportunity of testing the influence which this course will have upon the disposition of a child. Although we have already abundant evidence of the existence of native depravity in the heart, yet, we believe, from the experiment we have made, that, by avoiding exciting causes, the development of latent depravity may, in a great measure, be prevented. From the most careful observation, we are satisfied, that her temper is seldom if ever ruffled, except when under the influence of uncomfortable bodily feelings; and we are persuaded also, that these uncomfortable feelings in children more frequently arise from the improper quality or excessive quantity of their food, than from any other cause. With these views we have endeavored, so far as practicable, to confine her to regular and stated meals; and not to indulge her in the propensity which most children manifest, to be constantly eating; nor to permit her to eat all kinds of food indiscriminately, and we think we have reaped a rich reward in the general sweetness and cheerfulness of her temper and disposition. We have noticed, also, that when, through inattention, she has been permitted to eat improper food, or to eat it excessively, it has had a perceptible influence upon her temper, rendering her peevish and fretful. And when, from any cause, she feels uncomfortable, we find her temper more obstinate, and more easily irritated. Indeed, most of the correction which we have been under the necessity of administering, has been while she was under the influence of such feelings; from which we draw the conclusion that, when a child is sick or in any way uncomfortable in body, the utmost care should be taken to avoid all causes of irritation. We have also to record the happiest influence of the course we have pursued, in relation to diet, &c, upon her general health. She has never had any sickness, except from teething and colds; these have been less severe than is common with full fed children. Her appearance is far from indicating any want of nourishment. She is the very picture of health; and although of a full habit, she is sprightly and active.

"This course has also afforded us an early opportunity of moral discipline. At a very early period, she was brought to the table in her mother's arms; but, as she was not indulged with any food from the table, she never expected it; and after she began to be fed, not being allowed to take anything except what was placed before her, she was satisfied with her portion. But we have paid dearly, when, on any particular occasions, we have given her articles of food not proper for a child, and which she is not in the habit of receiving. — The next time we denied them to her, we could not make her understand why she might not as well have them at one time as another. When first brought to the table, she would lay hold of the dishes, and everything within her reach; but at the age of six or seven months, we undertook to correct her by frowns and marks of disapprobation. In this we succeeded beyond our anticipations. In a short time she was so completely broken of the habit, that the most enticing articles of furniture might be placed within her reach, and she would gaze upon them with exclamations of admiration, and yet not presume to touch them.

"About this time we administered our first correction. We had never been in the habit of giving her things for which she cried. On this occasion, she was permitted to take a time-piece in her hand for amusement; but another child being present, and wishing for it, it was taken from her and given to him. She appeared angry at this, and set up a loud cry, with convulsive struggles in her father's arms, manifesting great obstinacy of temper. No efforts were made to pacify her; she was frowned upon, and presently laid in the cradle, where she was suffered to lie apparently neglected. After giving vent to her temper in furious cries, for some time, she at length ceased crying and appeared subdued. For a long time after this she would permit things tobe taken from her without complaining; and since that time, she has very seldom cried when either her father or mother has taken things from her, or denied her things which she wished to have; and her mother has made it her practice frequently to deny her things which she might innocently have, when she was in a particularly happy mood, for the sake of teaching her practical lessons of submission and self-denial. This has been attended with the happiest effects, in teaching her to subdue her feelings, and submit her own will to that of her parents. Before she was quite a year old, we began to correct her for crying. This has been a severe but wholesome discipline. It has taught her a command over her feelings which we trust may be of great service to her in subsequent life."'

[For the Annals of Education.]

ON THE CULTIVATION OF IMAGINATION AND TASTE, AS AIDS TO EXPRESSION.

THE character of modern expression is greatly impaired by a cause distinct from those mentioned in my former communications on this subject, yet not less injuriously operative. I mean the prevailing deficiency of that influence which ought to be instilled into the young mind, from intercourse with the ideal and the spiritual. Let it not be said that I am here wandering from the sphere of practical effect, the great attribute of all felicitous or appropriate expression.

The character of every human soul is uttered in the habitual language of the individual man. Whatever, therefore, tinges the current of the spirit within, or tends to give it a particular direction, in early life, decides whether its waters shall be pure and transparent or turbid and dark; for genuine language is but the flowing of the soul. The mind which has habitually run in the pure channels of spiritual truth and spiritual life, imparts, of necessity, the virtues imbibed from its source, and aggregated in its current. The English language is, from the practical genius of the English people, and the defective and material philosophy, deficient in the free scope and ennobling elevation which characterized the diction of antiquity, and which several of the continental tongues seem to have successfully retained, — whether by their nearer affinity to the Latin, or their closer adherence to their own original Teutonic stock. The forms, too, of English, and, not less, of American life, are peculiarly unfavorable to excursive and expressive power. Human character is, among us, presented, for the most part, in the low attitude of the search after external comfort and convenience; thought is turned chiefly into the channel of acquisition; mental effort is judged by a standard merely practical; the reality *without*, swallows up the reality *within*. We affect to despise all theory. We are willing to forego the sublimest speculation for a single fact in any department of knowledge. We discourage everything metaphysical. We watch every working of the imagination with a suspicious eye. We exalt intellection to the mental throne, and slight and disparage every other part of our nature. Contemplation, and reflection, and spiritual investigation we consign to the regions of obsolete cosmology. Plodding and experimenting are our universal prescription for the health of the intellect.

This exclusive regard to one class of human relations, and its correspondent faculties, deprives us of power of expression, in its higher and its more general forms. It is conceding little to admit, that clearness and precision in the statement of facts, or directness and simplicity in modes of argument, are exhibited in greater perfection, under the influence of modern education, than under the auspices of the ancient philosophy. But, grounding their assertions on this circumstance, the advocates of modern perfection have not unfrequently arrogated for our own times the attainment of a truer eloquence than prevailed in the period of classical antiquity. This view of the case is partial and defective. Power of expression, if justly estimated, must be measured by the ability to give utterance to all forms of thought, and to every aspect of human experience — to the feelings not less than to the understanding. If any preference is to be adjudged to a single department of expression, it must necessarily be in favor of that which enables man to communicate his moral impressions; since these are the most decisive of human action. The enunciation of the truths of pure intellection may be of the utmost importance to the impartation or the acquisition of knowledge. But this is the advancement of a limited class, only, of our innumerable relations, and of a class less influential than others upon human character.

The exclusive pursuit of intellectual objects, as it cuts off the intercourse of the mind with the social sympathies, and with the creations of imagination, entails a dry, narrow, and mechanical mode of expression, reduces language to a mere skeleton of thought, and character to a cold and negative excellence. If there is any unity in the nature and constitution of man, it should be preserved in education, and uttered in the modes of language. Life itself is the palpable expression of this unity; and mental expression should ever be a transcript of it, since thus alone it becomes a fair representation of man.

The mind is not so constituted as to be capable of contemplating even abstract truth, without associated emotion and suggested imagery; and the true representation of thought is that which observes this law of our nature, and communicates conception in its unity and entireness. Genuine expression is that, which issues from the principle of mental life, pervading and inspiring all the powers of the spiritual nature, not that which proceeds from an unnatural analysis and dissection of our constitution, reducing its functions to detached operations, and its faculties to fragmentary and lifeless parts.

Were intellect the influential and ascendant power in the soul, the modifying of language in exclusive adaptation to it, might be expedient. But the office of the understanding is rather to interpret external impressions to the inner arbitrator, conscience, and thus to influence the will, or to enable man to discern and discriminate his internal sensations, so as to provide for the primary wants and aspirations of his nature. The end accomplished by mere intelligence, is therefore secondary and transient. Expression addressed exclusively to this part of the mental constitution can produce, at best, but limited and imperfect results; since the design of mental communication must necessarily be to influence action by the solicitation of motive; and it is to the attainment of this species of power, that the processes of education should be directed, as the end of all culture in the department of language.

To render thought expansive and vivifying, it must partake largely of ideal character. It must operate as a quickening touch. It must descend from a region above the usual level of intellection.

It must come upon the mind with something of creative force, awakening, enkindling, and impelling the various powers which are summed up in that comprehensive word, *mind*. All human beings cannot, it is true, rise, by any discipline, to the highest degrees of expressive power. But the office of education is, by every salutary influence, to aid man's progress towards comparative perfection, in this, as in all other departments of human endeavor. Liberal provision for the development of communicative power, should ever form a part of the educator's arrangements for the early stage of life. The ideal power embodied in fiction, in poetry, and in the romantic associations of the past, in their wide variety of form and effect, should all be made to pass before the young spirit, and disclose to it their inexhaustible treasures of imaginative and creative wealth.

The sources, too, of spiritual life should be early disclosed to the dawning mind. The purifying and inspiring power of religious feeling should be early experienced, in all its ennobling and expansive associations ; and its power perpetually cherished, as the most genial of all the influences which infinite Benignity sheds upon the nature of man. From this region of human experience issue, not only all those truths which lift the mind above the present sphere of existence, but those, also, which amplify and complete and ennoble our present life, and which impart the unity of harmonious design to its manifold interests and events. Breathing an atmosphere tempered and illuminated from above, the associations of the young retain that brilliancy, that freshness and that healthful soundness, which are the life-springs of natural, vivid, and forcible expression. — How defective and how inefficient are our methods for accomplishing this highest end of all education, it would be, perhaps, inappropriate here to discuss.

The preceding remarks on expression, as a branch of instruction, refer principally, it will be observed, to the period of early education. But the subject requires that we trace it higher in the order of tuition, to its connection with the more advanced stages of culture, and observe some of the disadvantages under which this branch labors at our collegiate institutions. One prominent defect here presents itself, in the very inadequate attention paid to the collateral influence of the fine arts, as an aid to the formation of appropriate habits of expression. At our places of learning we seldom observe an entire neglect in regard to those facilities which come in aid of the physical sciences. Libraries, cabinets, and apparatus, of one kind or other, are generally furnished. But there is not one of our numerous colleges, which is yet provided with even the rudiments necessary for a decent gallery. A few models in architecture may be found here and there. But no proper attention has yet been given to secure to the minds of youth that indispensable aid to the formation of correct taste, arising from a suitable collection of casts and copies, or even of superior prints.

The works of accomplished artists being copies and concentrations of natural excellence, — ideal compressions of the infinite, and actual embodyings of the beautiful, their influence on the expanding mind must necessarily be powerful, and vivid. The spirit of the young, springs forward to meet them, and responds instantaneously to their language. No ascendency, perhaps, is so complete as that which is exercised by felicitous delineation, over the heart and the imagination of the young. No discipline is so effectual as that eloquent and impressive instruction which emanates from the silent creations of perfect and irrisistible art. Years of formal essays and lecturing on the theory of expressive beauty, are nothing in comparison to the opportunity of daily contemplating a single production of excellence. Taste, the great arbiter of character and of expression, receives its truest and most effectual impressions from direct contemplation — not from reflective reasoning. The study of the models and delineations of the gallery is to fancy, taste, or imagination, and expression, what the apparatus and the exercises of the gymnasium are to the bodily frame, in its detail of bone, muscle, and nerve ; — correcting, invigorating, and inspiring the whole, and imparting universal grace, force, and pliancy.

The creative efforts of the painter, the sculptor, the architect, the musician, the poet, and the orator, all shed light on every other form of expressive skill ; and the human being who grows up under the influence of their presence, has his nature imbedded in a rich and cherishing soil. The aliment hence imbibed, transfuses itself through the whole nature of the individual, and renovates and sustains all his powers. Expression becomes to him an easy and a natural function : the stream of language flows from a full heart and an affluent imagination. How different from this result is that of our prevalent artificial culture ! The common course of school and college exercises in rhetoric, has ever been a matter of form and routine. A multitude of exercises, both in composition and declamation, must be daily passed in summary review, and a yearly effort patched up between the pupil and the teacher, for the purpose of exhibition ; and here the matter ends. Antecedent and collateral influences receive no attention. The vast power of circumstances, in eliciting expression, is never adverted to. Formal compulsion is substituted for the genuine promptings of feeling, and imagination is either suffered to run riot on the surface of style, through neglect and false taste, or the instructor nips it at once, with the chilling reception of utter scepticism.

A professorship of English literature, competently endowed and competently filled, which would insure to our young collegians a faithful history of our language, and an adequate analysis of our classical writers, leaving the effect to work itself out in the student's own habits of mind and expression, would be a national benefit of incalculable value.

SIMPLICITY OF LANGUAGE IN TEACHING.

We spoke, in a former number, of 'The Inciter,' as an interesting paper published at Lancaster, Pennsylvania, in which the subject of education is prominent. In one of its numbers we find an illustration of the sentiment we expressed under the head of. Notices in our last number of June, that authors would do well to test their writings for children by actual experiment. The editor observes that he had prepared an article with great care, which he considered quite simple, and called upon his boys to read it. He found it difficult, however, to interest them in it, or to make them enter into his ideas, and read it with the proper tones. He gave up the point, and then presented them a dialogue written by one of the pupils. They not only understood it, but entered into it with deep interest, and read it with propriety and spirit. We annex the dialogue as a specimen of a style which children can understand :

SCHOLARS FROM DIFFERENT SCHOOLS.

L. Oh, how glad I am there is no school for three weeks !

H. And I am very sorry. I am already lonesome and tired.

L. You must love school better than play.

H. I do ; I am hardly ever contented without I am learning something.

L. And I am not contented when I am learning.

H. Why not? Do you not wish to grow wiser, and know more than you know now?

L. I would, if I could learn it all at once.

H. That is impossible. You must take pains, and try to understand what you learn.

L. I can't understand ; it is too hard.

H. What book do you read in ?

L. The English Reader.

H. I know the reason, now, why you do not like to go to school.

L. What is the reason ?

H. Because the English Reader is hard for you to understand, and you get discouraged.

L. I do; and if I could have something I understand, I think I should like to read better.

H. It is all important for you to understand what you read, and then you will not get discouraged.

L. I think I will read in an easier book, and try how it will go then.

H. Why, I would advise you to do so; then I dare say you will take delight in reading.

L. But after all, I think I can read well enough.

H. You may be mistaken in that; reading is the main object.

L. I can write too, but I soon get tired of that.

H. Do you write copies?

L. Yes.

H. Then it is no wonder you get tired; would it not be well for you to compose something?

L. I do not know what to write about.

H. Anything that comes into your mind. Could you not write that a cow has four legs, and two horns, and is very useful on account of her milk, &c, as well as to write a copy over a dozen times?

L. I think I could give a description of a cow, and it might improve my writing as well as the other.

H. Not only so, it would learn you to think about what you write, and you would soon learn to compose any other thing.

L. It may be that you are right, and I will go right home and see if I cannot give a description of a cow, and improve my time better than I have several ways. R.

We are reminded by this anecdote of a remark of Father Girard, the benevolent founder of the system of mutual instruction in Friburg, Switzerland. In examining the school he observed to us, that when he met with difficulty in explaining some word or subject to a child, he had often called in a boy more advanced, to aid him, and had usually found him succeed entirely, even when all his own efforts had failed. It is no less necessary than it is difficult, to avoid speaking in an 'unknown tongue,' when we attempt to teach a child; and there are comparatively few authors of children's books who have attained this art.

[From The Inciter.]

'SCHOOLING', NOT EDUCATION.

THE following extract from 'The Inciter,' is in harmony with our views of 'Kitchen and Street Education,' expressed in a number of our last volume.

'Is that education best which teaches children the common branches of education during six or seven hours each day, and then leaves them to all the bad habits which, suffered to run wild, they will acquire? Here in the city, for instance, is that education the best, by which children spend five or six hours out of the twenty-four in the streets, learning rudeness, impertinent manners, vulgar language and vicious habits? Will any advantages in school compensate for these advantages out of it? But let us remember it is not the question whether this half training (too often much less than half) is good enough for the common people. It is the question whether it is the best that can be devised.

'For our own part, we understand education to mean everything which influences, directly or indirectly, the child's character. To see his companions smoke cigars is a part of his education; to hear oaths is a part of his education; to see and laugh at drunken men in the street, is a part of his education. And if any one thinks that an education like this, (which is daily obtained in the streets of our city) will be counteracted by half a dozen hours' daily schooling, we are not of his opinion. We had almost as soon have a child of ours raised among the Indians, as have him frequent a common-day school one half the day, and wander about our streets the other half.'

EDUCATION IN SOUTH AMERICA.

Foreign Correspondence of the American Lyceum.

Translated from Extracts of Letters received by the Corresponding Secretary on Lyceums, from Joaquin Mosquera, Vice President of New Grenada.

Carthagena, Feb. 20, 1833.

'My dear and esteemed friend, — I arrived at this port on the 10th inst., after a passage of twentythree days from New York; and although my country is poor and weak compared with the nations I have lately visited, I could not but salute it with enthusiasm. I was detained by the quarantine in the bay, and spent the night looking at the castles and shores, which recalled the recollections of so many calamities, heroic sacrifices, and glories of my countrymen, and so many acts of Spanish barbarity and cruelty. Between the sea and the land, and affected by the tranquillity of the sky, all these recollections, with thoughts of my family, the old world I have left, and the future, which occupied most of my thoughts, gave me some of the most impressive reflections I ever experienced.

'Everything is proceeding according to my wishes, particularly in regard to public instruction, as you will perceive by the newspapers I send. They mention that two inhabitants of my province, the Cauca, have commenced the translation of Virgil's works in Castilian verse, which is the first literary enterprise of equal magnitude ever undertaken in South America. From this and the published remarks of a citizen of Popayan, on the observance of the Lord's day, our enemies may learn that we are not barbarians.'

'BOGOTA, MAY 21, 1833.

'You will learn from the papers, that I have been elected Vice President; and that in spite of my twice refusing to accept, the Congress have insisted and required me to accept, contrary to my wish, for my disposition inclines me to retirement, and I shall be prevented from devoting myself exclusively to my cherished object, the instruction of the young and the people of Popayan.'

'POPAYAN, OCT. 23.

'I have the pleasure of forwarding to you a copy of the Constitution of the Popayan Society of Primary Elementary Education, which I have founded in this city. My fellow citizens have engaged in the undertaking with enthusiasm, and contributed for it according to their ability. I have given, in books, slates, paper, &c, above $1,000. We are building a school-house for two hundred boys, twentyfour yards in length, which is almost finished; and I am forming a normal school of a master, two general monitors and several class monitors, with thirty children, to furnish the school as soon as the building is completed. I began a subscription for a girls' school of the same size; and when these are in full operation, I propose to found an institution for secondary instruction, to prepare youths for the university. I shall do all that lies in my power, to place Popayan in advance of the cities of New Grenada in education. We are printing a few small books for the use of the schools.

'I have hardly attended to any of my own private concerns since my return here, having been occupied in my exertions for public and intellectual improvement.'

'POPAYAN, OCT. 29.

'In my last I informed you of my exertions in favor of primary education. I am going on, with perseverance, and have succeeded in infusing enthusiasm even among the common people, who have invited me to visit the country, that they may show their gratitude for my exertions in promoting schools. We are about to appoint a committee of ladies, to be employed under the direction of the Popayan Society for Elementary Primary Education, in founding and improving female schools.'

POPAYAN, Nov. 19.

'I am still occupied as when I last wrote, and wish I could communicate all the difficulties and labors I have had to encounter, and such gratifying results as promise great benefit and comfort, and reward me for my trials. The Society is proceeding successfully, and the Ladies' Committee have begun to act with enthusiasm. As soon as the members of the latter shall have obtained sufficient experience to act alone, they will probably be formed into an independent society, to direct female education.

'I hope for great results, to morals and intelligence, from their example. From Chili to Mexico, the Popayan Society, particularly this part of it, is a new model; and I hope in Providence, that it will be effectual, and be generally imitated.

'By the beginning of next month I shall return to Bogota, where I shall undertake to form another similar society of primary elementary education. I have sent on to General Santander some reading cards and other objects, that preparations may be made without loss of time.

'I have opened a friendly enthusiastic correspondence with the influential citizens of Pasto, with the hope of animating them with the same spirit of popular education, which is necessary in this part of the world; and it has succeeded to a miracle. They have worked, even to the women, and that gratis, in erecting a college, which they have already completed. An Augustine friar and a priest, both formerly royalists and fanatics, have become the most active and fervent in this work, and fulfil all my wishes. I have just sent them a present in books and other objects necessary in education, which they have received with great gratification. I hope to do much more, and to deserve well of my country before I die, by a persevering devotion to her with all my powers. But, I have often remarked, I am a founder of new institutions, and find everything to do and overcome. We South Americans are sons of parents who have become bankrupts, and have our social and intellectual fortune to make, as well as to erase the marks of errors, prejudices, and false policy, in which we were educated. How much might the philanthropists of the United States aid us in the task; and how much would they deserve of humanity! May those who have assisted us hitherto, accept the benedictions of myself and my friends!'

From one of the newspapers alluded to above, we derive the following particulars concerning the Popayan Society:

'The committee of ladies having been elected by the society, on the 10th of November, a public meeting was held in the city of Popayan, in the hall of the university. The President made a patriotic address, in which he made known the objects of the meeting, the benefits to be expected from the coöperation of the ladies in the enterprise of restoring and improving the schools, and enforcing the importance of the undertaking by various considerations.

'The ladies then proceeded to elect Lenora Maria Josefa Hartado, their president, and Nocolasa Cozy Villar, vice president. The installation of the committee was then pronounced, and after the choice of two secretaries, and resolving to hold weekly meetings at the president's house, the meeting adjourned.

'On the 13th, the committee met for business; and made arrangements to open a subscription to complete the school-house for girls, and to request the Executive Com. of the Society to add six ladies to their number, whom they nominated.

'The council, on their part, had already, by the middle of November, made progress in printing catechisms and reading cards, and completed that of a collection of hymns, composed by one of their members, a poet of much feeling, to be sung daily by the children at the opening and conclusion of their exercises. Furniture was making, adapted to the mutual and simultaneous systems of instruction; and the normal school was in operation, under rules drawn up by the society, on the basis of certain schools in the United States;'—(meaning, doubtless, the public schools of the city of New York, with whose system they are known to be furnished.)

REPORT ON THE NEW JERSEY LYCEUM.

PRESENTED TO THE AMERICAN LYCEUM.

The New Jersey Lyceum has been but recently organized. For a long time, the friends of education and of intellectual improvement in New Jersey have felt that something was imperatively demanded towards the melioration of their common school system, and the general furtherance of useful knowledge. A convention was accordingly called, which met at Princeton, on the third and fourth days of April, ultimo, for the purpose of devising plans for future action, upon this subject. Though the weather had been unfavorable for several days, yet more than fifty gentlemen attended, representing sixteen different societies or conventions, in seven different counties of the state.

After the Convention had been duly organized, and had heard an interesting essay by Mr Wines, on the state of Primary Education in Prussia, the following questions were discussed: 1. What is the state of Common School instruction in your vicinity? 2. What attention does it receive from the community generally? 3. How may it be improved? These questions were propounded to the members of the convention individually, and were severally answered by them. The delegates, not being prepared to communicate accurate statistical details in answer to the first query, could only state generally their own impressions on the subject. It appeared, however, from the statements made, that there is a lamentable degree of indifference in the public mind on the subject of common school education, and that the system of instruction prevalent throughout the state, is greatly in need of *reform*, in a variety of particulars. In answer to the third inquiry, various suggestions were thrown out by different gentlemen; and among others, the propriety and practicability of founding a seminary for the education of teachers, and of appointing an agent or agents to travel though the state, to communicate information on the subject of elementary instruction, and endeavor to rouse the public mind, and excite it to a more just appreciation of the high value and importance of a more efficient education of the common people.

After the discussion of the foregoing questions, it was resolved unanimously to proceed to the organization of a State Lyceum, which was done accordingly, and a copy of their constitution, and a list of their officers, are herewith submitted.

The following resolutions having been discussed and variously modified, were finally adopted with great unanimity.

Resolved, That we deem a careful and searching inquiry into the state of our Common Schools, with a view to ascertain their defects and apply the proper remedy, an object particularly calling for the attention of all classes of our citizens.

Resolved, That we regard the teachers of our Common Schools as a body on whom the future character and the continuance of our free institutions very much depend; and that suitable efforts ought to be made to increase their usefulness, by promoting a higher order of qualifications, and by holding out pecuniary inducements sufficient to persuade men of talents to engage and continue in the highly honorable and responsible business of imparting instruction to the young.

Resolved, That it be recommended to the Executive Committee of the Lyceum, to appoint in each county a corresponding committee, whose duty it shall be to collect and to transmit to the committee, all the information practicable in regard to the condition of common schools, and in relation to all other matters which usually fall under the notice of Lyceums.

Resolved, That it be earnestly recommended to the inhabitants of this state, to form Lyceums in villages, towns and counties, auxiliary to the State Lyceum.

Resolved, That the Executive Committee be requested to prepare plans for the constitution and management of Lyceums ; and that copies thereof be circulated throughout the state.

Resolved, That it be recommended to the Executive Committee to draft a series of questions respecting the state of common schools, and common school education, to be addressed to lyceums, school committees, and societies or individuals, interested in the subject ; and from the answers to said questions, to digest and prepare a report to be presented to the Lyceum.

Resolved, That the Executive Committee of the Lyceum be requested to engage, if practicable, agents to visit the various parts of the state, and by delivering lectures, collecting information, encouraging the formation of lyceums, and otherwise, to promote the objects of this institution.

The first annual meeting is to be held at Princeton, on the third Wednesday of June next.

The Executive Committee have instructed the Corresponding Secretary to write to several distinguished gentlemen in different parts of the State, requesting them to prepare essays on suitable subjects, to be read on that occasion. And they have requested that answers may be furnished from every township to the following questions :

1. How many schools are there in your township, and its vicinity ? 2. Are these sufficient ? 3. Do all the children in your district or neighborhood, attend school ? 4. What is the average number of pupils in the schools ? 5. Are the sexes taught together ? 6. What proportion of the children in your neighborhood go to no school ? 7. What part of the year are the schools taught ? 8. Are the affairs of your schools conducted by trustees ? 9. Are they subject to any stated inspection or visitation ? 10. What branches are taught ? 11. What is generally the qualification of the teachers ? 12. By whom are teachers appointed ? 13. Are they subjected to any examination ? 14. Are the schools subject to frequent change of instructors ? 15. Are they left for any length of time without a teacher ? 16. Is it found difficult to provide the requisite number of suitable teachers ? 17. What compensation do the teachers receive ? 18. How much money is raised in your township for common schools ? 19. How much is received from the state ? 20. Upon what principle is this distributed ? 21. To what purposes, other than the compensation of the teacher, is it applied ? 22. Has any school more than a single teacher ? 23. Is our present system of common schools found to operate favorably ? 24. What amend-

ments in the legal provisions, seem to be pointed out by experience? 25. Is the present system acceptable to the people at large? 26. Are any of the adult population unable to read? and if so, what proportion of them?

The following are the officers of the New Jersey Lyceum:

President, William R. Weeks, D.D., of Newark; Vice Presidents, Dr Isaac H. Hampton, of Cumberland, Prof. T. Strong, of New Brunswick, Samuel Gummere of Burlington; Corresponding Secretary, Prof. J. W. Alexander, Princeton; Recording Secretary, E. C. Wines, Princeton; Treasurer, J. Van Deventer; Executive Committee, Rev. J. V. Brown, Prof. A. B. Dodd, J. Halsey, J. Loring, W. C. Morris.

[For the Annals of Education.]

RECEPTION AND TREATMENT OF NEW PUPILS.

HINTS TO YOUNG TEACHERS. NO. IV.

It often if not generally happens, that a child derives its strongest impressions, either in favor or against study and education, from the first school he attends, and often more especially, from the first weeks, and even days of his course. This fact the young teacher should never overlook. But here I would warn him, not to suppose that in order to make the first impressions pleasant and useful ones, unbounded indulgence is necessary. By no means; more injury is doubtless done by this idea, than by any other; and indeed, young teachers are in danger of more than one error upon this point; few are successful in finding the 'golden medium'— a medium more important here, than in most of the concerns of life; since, oftentimes the whole success of his school course depends upon it. He is apt to carry, either his indulgence or his strictness too far. If he be too full of tenderness and attention and indulgence at first, the child expects it always, and acts as if he were unjustly treated, if he be not constantly petted and caressed; if on the other hand, he is first greeted with solemn severity, due to him only when he has transgressed or is transgressing the rules of the school, — of which he, as yet, can be supposed to know nothing — he will fear, and if a child of strong passions, be ready to hate his instructor, and imbibe a disgust for the school, which it may take years to overcome. I would endeavor to point out some means, by which both these fatal errors may be avoided. Much, indeed, necessarily depends on the species of preparation the child has had at home, and on the discretion of the parents' general management; but still the result must, after all, depend on the teacher.

I once had a boy of three years old, offered to me, whose violence of apparent passion, on finding out that his destination was a school, would have frightened me into believing him a confirmed little tyrant, had I not seen distinctive marks of an uncommonly fine character, which convinced me, that this violence was but temporary, — a summer shower, rather than a wintry tempest. I had nearly given up this opinion, however. For several successive mornings when he was brought to school, he kept up a strain of incessant tears and violent expostulation against remaining, making use of all his little strength to obtain his release; and my fears were, that his parents would indulge him by taking him home and giving up the experiment as they had done, I found, in several previous instances. But I was agreeably disappointed; his parents were people of good sense. I found that they were aware, as well as myself, of the very bad tendency and effects of giving way to his self-will, and withdrawing him from school, because he insisted on their doing so, and had yielded to him before, only in consequence of delicacy toward the instructor, who, they felt, must be unwilling to encounter such turbulence. I found, the third or fourth day, that in consequence of this feeling in respect to me, the boy was not sent. I saw the parents were satisfied, that their motive was solely consideration toward myself, and warmly expressed my opinion and desire, that on the child's account he might not thus again have his own way; professed my undoubting assurance, that he would be, eventually, happy and good; and my perfect willingness to manage him, if they would entrust him to my care. I received thanks which went to my heart, and what was better, an entire yielding of the child to my judgment; and by means of firm yet gentle decision, he was simply made to be convinced, that he was to stay with me a certain number of hours, if good, to be happy like all he saw around him, and if not, to be deprived of the occupations they had, and which their smiling diligence testified to be pleasant ones. My hopes were not deceived. His good sense, of which all children have more than is suspected, decided him which part to choose. That one storm over — during a period of *several successive years*, I had but a single instance, and that a trivial one of passion, self-will, or, even of temper; he possessed, far the finest mind I ever had to manage, and one of the most attractive dispositions. A few weeks after he had become one of my pupils, I met a teacher in the neighborhood, who said to me, 'I understand you have taken little ——; he came to me for a day or two, but I would not consent to manage such a temper. He had taken a disgust to schools and to teachers, and I politely informed his parents that I could not retain him. *I* would have gained such a scholar at almost any sacrifice.

Such instances as the above, are not rare, but they afford only one view of the case. There are many timid little spirits, who are alarmed at the sight of a school full of children, or at the strange face of the instructor of these. Some will sit perfectly quiet, not daring to move or look up, and making no answer when addressed; while others will weep incessantly; and, without the least self-control — (and the words is *not* too strong to use, even respecting children of three or four years old) will continue to do so in despite of caresses or soothings, or even gentle efforts to engage and interest the attention. With the first of these classes, gentle kindness, steady effort, and persevering attention will infallibly succeed, at least I never knew it fail; but there are different opinions respecting the treatment of the second. People generally believe that these are sensitive and delicate spirits, accustomed to gentleness only at home, and incapable of bearing any thing like firmness; that if they are not moved by the means abovementioned, it is better to 'let them alone, till they get accustomed to the appearance of things;' others think they should be accompanied by some friend, who will stay with them, and sooth them, and gradually draw their attention from their grief. The sensitiveness, delicacy, &c, ascribed to children of this class, rather belong to the other, whose shrinking timidity will always yield to love and kind continued, efforts; but depend upon it, *unless there is bodily indisposition*, the crying, whining complainant, is only indulging a regular habit of self-will. He is afraid perhaps, at first, and troubled, and ends by troubling all around him and making himself miserable. This system of 'letting children alone,' to recover themselves, will do admirably well in cases like that of the violent child, where there is good sense enough to direct them to the wise choice at last, and after kindness, firmness, and perhaps a little severity is tried in vain, it will do. But with those of whom we are now speaking, it seldom answers any effect, save to confirm the habit; for they will, very probably, cry and lament during the whole of school time. As to the other resort, that of friends remaining to pacify them, it is equally ill-judged in them to do so, and in the teacher to permit it. Decision and firmness are the antidotes in such troublesome cases. Let the child plainly see that though you are ready to love, caress, and indulge him sufficiently, if he will govern himself and be good, you are not to be disobeyed, or the school put into confusion, and its laws broken. I have had children of this sort often, who, after resisting every effort of a mild and gentle nature, would stop crying forcibly, when I looked firmly in their faces, and *bid them do it.* I have heard persons say, that children could not thus early command their tempers, much less their feelings. I am, and from experience, of a different opinion. But as soon as this temporary severity has effected its object, let the teacher take advantage of the moment, smile on the child, and show him how happy others are with their lessons, &c, yet tell him gently you will not request him to read or even to look at a book, then, only he *must not cry*. Make this the point, and require no other for that time. You will find that a perseverance in this method, will effect what no other, perhaps, could do. Indeed, in some schools I have seen a child cry itself to sleep, or weary itself sadly by this perpetual indulgence, day after day, because the kind-hearted but mistaken teachers considered it cruel to use authority or severity, or because he would not believe that the child could conquer himself *if he would*. Both these classes of timid children, if amiable and intelligent, will probably, after a time, take pleasing impressions of the school, if it be properly conducted, and on that score, give the teacher little trouble.

There are other children who enter a school, with, it would seem, a determination to have their own way, and who, not afraid, like the last mentioned, and not inherently wise, and only, as it were, experimenting, like the boy I alluded to first, show themselves to be, in reality, petty tyrants. They incline to obey only when it suits them, and are violent in the extreme, and will go all lengths to have their own way, when it does not. Such children, are rarely seen, and when I see them, I cannot help supposing bad management and weak indulgence at home; but with such I can only say, let your watchfulness be unfailing; be careful to demand nothing that is not just, and then show them plainly from the first, that you will never give up to them; — that your laws are not, in any one case, to be violated with impunity. Strive less to gain their love than their fear, (if they have hearts, their love will come by and by) and make them distinctly feel all the inconvenience to themselves, of their turbulence and self-will. But with all this, if possible, be gentle still, not violent. Always fear yourself, for if there be any temptation for the teacher to forget himself, it is from spirits like these. Keep love towards the child always in your heart, since he is but a child, and always realize that you are to act for his good, and not solely for the maintenance of your own power, however important that necessarily must be. Take every opportunity, when there is *any* yielding, even if it be mere matter of necessity, to show this unruly child, that others stand on a different and happier ground with you — that it is his own choice that places him on this. Let him see how happy he may be, by *willing* submission; and while you are gaining on him, step after step, by power and authority, you can easily see how much he can bear of the far better ministry of entreaties, reasoning and affection. But it is a mistaken idea that these can always come first. Such children as I have last described, generally show the worst at the onset; and it is not, therefore, possible that you can *gain* by gentle means what I admit can be *maintained*, *only* by gentleness.

I shall have occasion, by and by, to speak of punishments and arbitrary discipline.

There are still other children, who having been to schools previously, have become accustomed to certain methods of education, and a certain manner of treatment, to certain particular habits, and customs. These it is sometimes difficult to change, because a *first* impression, as we have observed, is almost always the most powerful and lasting; and if a child has learned to consider right, what you consider wrong, the only way is to convince him, by your actions and their effects on him, that you have his best interests at heart in all your regulations concerning him. He will soon judge for himself; and if he be intelligent and amiable, he will gradually learn to prefer your ways, if they really are best. But examine well the difference, and be sure that your own laws and ministrations are really most salutary, before you compel an observance of them; and do not fail to acknowledge that others are better, and to adopt them, if they really are so.

For here I beg leave to remark, that a teacher may gain more on the respect and affection of his pupils by generous and sincere confessions of error or mistake, than by almost any other means. Let his true disinterestedness and real desire for their good once be firmly established in their minds, and his power over them is almost unbounded. There is a certain instinctive faith in the minds of children, when love is fixed in them, on a pure and holy basis, which is truly beautiful and touching. They will be ready to believe without demonstration, that all he does is right, that all he tells them is true, and that all his opinions are correct ones, and that if he is displeased with them, they must be in the wrong. Indeed, they invest him with a sort of infallibility, which becomes to him a kind of guard; which wraps around him a panoply, erects before him a shield, with which he has power and ability to do 'all his work', and may go forth, 'conquering and to conquer', if that indeed can be called conquered which yields with little or no resistance.

There is only one more remark I would make, while on the subject of reception and treatment of new pupils, it is in reference to the painful possibility that there may be some one among the flock who proves indeed a 'black sheep,' that is, one who has some decided and confirmed fault, such as wilful and deliberate lying, or a disposition to take what does not belong to him. Such a child may enter a school with good apparent dispositions, and ready obedience and respect for the wishes of the teacher; but if such a fault is discovered, it should not be a moment tolerated like trifling errors, because he is a new scholar, and unaccustomed to the rules of the school. If the vice prove to be a confirmed one, a fearless appeal to the parents should immediately be made, for their prompt co-operation and assistance in rooting out the evil, since it will require a perfect unity of feeling on all sides. But if they choose to consider it only a childish indiscretion or comparatively unimportant error, the teacher should not hesitate in resigning the charge of such a child at once, unless he be of so pliant a nature, as to yield easily to admonitions and efforts in his behalf; unless it is certain that he will receive more good, than he can do evil to his companions by communicating to them his bad habits. This is a serious subject, and requires more serious thought than a paper like this can supply; but there is no question in my mind, that decided faults of *this kind, if tolerated at home*, cannot be thoroughly corrected at school. At least, in the effort, to do it, more mischief than can well be ascertained may, perhaps, be accomplished. The teacher should give the child up, as he would give up one who had the yellow-fever, or small-pox, — in justice to those whose moral constitutions he has pledged himself to purify and to improve the utmost of his power.

BOSTON ACADEMY OF MUSIC.

Second Annual Report of the Boston Academy of Music; read at the Anniversary Meeting, May 28, 1834. Boston: Perkins, Marvin, & Co.

Only four years have elapsed since the introduction of Vocal Music, as a branch of general education in our country, was proposed, and the rational inductive system of instruction announced to the public. Our pressing engagements at that time, only allowed the oral translation of Pestalozzi's works, to the gentleman who made the first experiments on the system. Our views were regarded by many as visionary; the system was classed among the new inventions for 'royal roads to knowledge;' and indifference or incredulity were the kindest reception then given by most persons to this important subject.

It is with peculiar pleasure, therefore, that we have received the *Second Annual Report* of an institution whose object is, not to amuse or instruct its own members, but to diffuse the knowledge of music, and elevate the standard of taste among *the schools* and *the people* of our country. It is with still greater satisfaction that we find the views, and opinions, and results of experience, announced by the able reporters, who have on this occasion been the organs of the Academy, so fully coincident with our own former statements, and which, in consequence of our absence, we then saw, for the first time, in the pamphlet.

The report commences with a series of important remarks and illustrations of this subject generally; and, on all accounts, it would give us pleasure to republish it entire. We cannot, however, do justice to the subject or to many of our readers whom the report will never reach, without extracting that portion which relates to the methods of instructing in music, and the difficulties which have hitherto prevented its general introduction as a branch of education.

'The course which has been pursued in teaching music and acquiring a knowledge of it, has heretofore been little adapted to carry the cultivation of it to any good degree of perfection, or to give it the rank which it deserves among the other branches of an education.

'Teaching has been commenced too late. Instead of beginning in early childhood, as is the case in regard to most other branches of knowledge, it has been deferred generally till late in youth or to adult years. It has been generally supposed that children could not learn or be taught successfully, and that labor or expense for this purpose would be nearly thrown away. But why is it more impracticable or more difficult to teach even very young children to use their vocal organs in making the sounds required in singing, than those required in conversation? or to teach them the forms, names, and power of the notes in music, than the forms, names, combinations and power of the letters of the alphabet? or to teach them the principles and rules of music, than those of correct reading, or of arithmetic and grammar? Undoubtedly the difficulty in the former case is far less than in the latter, and the susceptibility of feeling an interest in the subject, greater and more universal.

Besides, fondness for music and capacity for performing it require the cultivation of certain bodily organs; and this cultivation, if it is to be carried to a high degree, must be begun early in life, while these organs are most flexible, and before they have acquired rigidity by age. The ear is an organ that is as susceptible of improvement from cultivation and use as any other member of the body. The earlier this is commenced, the more steadily and judiciously it is pursued, the more delicate will its susceptibility become, the keener its power of discernment, and the higher its capacity for receiving pleasure. Similar is the fact in regard to the improvement of the voice. If the cultivation of it is begun early, and wisely continued, almost any voice, if there is no serious physical defect in the vocal organs, may be made good, and most voices may be improved to a high degree of perfection. But the longer either the ear or the voice is neglected, the more difficult does the cultivation and improvement of them become, and the less perfection can be attained to. This is abundantly illustrated in acquiring and speaking new languages, especially by the ear. Children acquire them easily, and pronounce them with purity and correctness; while those who attempt to acquire and speak a new language in adult years, generally find much greater difficulties, and almost without exception, pronounce it imperfectly.

'Hence it is that so many provincialisms and nationalisms in pronunciation, are daily heard in the streets. With few exceptions, and where great and long continued exertion is made, persons do not acquire a good voice for singing or public speaking, who do not commence the cultivation of it early.

'The young ear is more susceptible of pleasure from music, than that which has remained uncultivated till adult years; and of course that fondness for it, which is requisite to secure a continued and successful attention to the subject, is not often contracted after the period of youth is past.

'Too little time has been devoted to the cultivation of music. Daily study, for a long series of years, is deemed requisite for acquiring the common branches of education, and is patiently devoted to the purpose. No one expects to become a proficient without it. But not even an hour or two a week, during the common period of education, is supposed to be necessary for attaining to a competent knowledge of music. It is nearly excluded from, or rather has not been introduced into, the ordinary course of school instruction, and is left to a few nooks and corners of time, amounting to perhaps twenty or thirty evenings, with a repetition of the same round the next year, when the new made musician takes his place in the village choir, with his education completed. To suppose that individuals can become good singers with such a training, or that choirs composed of such members can make good music, is unreasonable. Unless more time shall be devoted to acquiring a knowledge of the subject, we must endure more bad music.

'There has been an entire destitution of suitable elementary books; and scarcely a beginning has been made towards supplying the deficiency. Some small collections of tunes for Sabbath schools, together with the Juvenile Lyre, are the only attempts which are known to have been made in this department, in this country. A good assortment of elementary books, adapted to young minds, containing the rudiments of instruction and practice in music, is greatly needed, and must be provided before this branch of education can be introduced as advantageously and generally as it deserves. With the books now generally in use, the pupil, after learning a few definitions, necessarily involving terms and principles of science with which he is wholly unacquainted, and of which probably the teacher understands little more than himself, is put directly upon the performance of common psalm tunes, often complicated and difficult, and of course uninteresting, if not painful, from the miserable manner in which they are performed. Such a method is as unphilosophical as the exploded one of giving the learner of the Latin language his first lesson in a grammar written in that tongue. Elementary books, adapted to children of the most infantile capacities are, in these days of improvements in education, furnished on almost all other branches of knowledge. They are needed, and why should they not be furnished, on music?

'Nearly connected with the want of suitable elementary books, is the defective and unphilosophical method of teaching music. There is nothing like simplicity in the first lessons; nothing like analysis and the orderly development of principles as the pupil advances; nothing, in short, of the inductive method, which is now introduced into almost every other branch of instruction: but so far as the science or art is concerned, the learner must grapple with the whole subject at once, with a mind utterly unprepared. Nor can it be otherwise, till suitable elementary books shall be provided, or teachers become competent to devise a method of teaching for themselves, and by means of oral instruction, to supply the deficiency of written treatises. Such teachers in sufficient numbers cannot be looked for, till music shall be cultivated far more generally, and to a greater measure of perfection, than it now is—not until the very neglect now referred to, shall be overcome.

'The consequences of these defects respecting the time and the manner of teaching, have been on those who set out to learn something of music, bad ears, bad voices, little correctness or ease of performance, a knowledge limited to a few psalm tunes, no readiness in reading or performing music generally, little taste or judgment in regard to style or adaptation, little pleasure from the practice, and in a few years a weariness which occasions a cessation of all attention to the subject. The consequences in regard to the community generally, have been a corrupted or defective taste, a very low standard of excellence, and a prevailing indifference whether music was cultivated or not.

'As may readily be supposed, therefore, music has received the attention of very few persons, and by those, under very unfavorable circumstances. Those few who have cultivated music successfully and to any considerable extent, have generally maintained such a character, and connected themselves with such professions and pursuits in life, that, instead of commending the subject to the favorable regard of the sober and intelligent part of the community, they have, by occasioning the opinion that a fondness for music and much attention to the cultivation of it were inconsistent with virtue and a due attention to the great business of life, exerted a powerful influence to bring it into disrepute. A fondness for it has, therefore, often been repressed, rather than cherished and rightly directed. That this apprehension of evil from a well directed attention to music is without foundation is rendered pretty evident from the statements given in the former report of the Academy, relating to effects produced in some countries of Europe, where it is made a common branch of education, and cultivated extensively by all classes of society; and from some documents to be inserted in another part of this report.

'A large portion of the community have been thought to be utterly incapable, not only of becoming practical musicians, but even of acquiring any correct knowledge of the principles of music, or of exercising any taste in regard to it, or of becoming susceptible of any impression from listening to its performance by others. This belief has prevented much the larger portion of the community from giving any attention to the subject, at least, from making any proficiency in it. But this belief is probably without foundation. It can hardly be supposed that the ear, which can distinguish with unfailing certainty the inflections which denote an interrogation or a command, or the tones used in irony or supplication, should be unable to distinguish the various sounds of the scale, surely marked no less distinctly, and more protracted. Nor can it be supposed that those organs of voice that can make easily, plainly, and with perfect accuracy, all the inflections and tones required in conversation, are incapable of making the sounds required in a simple melody. The supposed or real difficulty, if it be real, in the way of being able to sing, has its origin, almost without a doubt, in the want of early discipline, and of earnest and persevering effort. That some persons discern differences between sounds, and are able to imitate sounds, more readily than others, who perhaps have had the same training, is not denied. A similar difference is seen among different persons, in the various degrees of facility with which they catch the sounds and become able to pronounce the words of a new language. And it is confidently believed that it is no more impossible, nor even more difficult, to distinguish, or to utter, the sounds required in music, than those required in conversation or public speaking; and that all who labor under no serious defect in the auricular or vocal organs, by giving a persevering and well directed attention to the subject, are capable of making a good degree of proficiency in the knowledge and performance of simple music.

'It is not, however, the expectation or aim of the Academy to make all persons practical musicians; but it does seem desirable that skill and taste in music should be held in just estimation by the public; that all should understand something of its principles and use, and should possess a correct taste and standard, of judging in respect to it; that the facilities for cultivating music should be so diffused as to enable all who are placed in favorable circumstances to acquire a practical knowledge of it; that attention should be given to it much earlier, and the study of it carried to a much greater extent, than it has hitherto been; and that the mass of the community should be rendered susceptible of deep impression from it, and become capable of participating in the enjoyment and benefit which it is adapted to afford. This the Academy is aiming to accomplish.'

The report then proceeds to give the following account of the operations of the Academy for the past year, under several heads:

'*Juvenile and Adult Classes.* One of the first objects of attention with the Academy was the making the study and practice of vocal music a part of the early education of children. Previous to its establishment, some interesting experiments of this nature had been made gratuitously by one of the present professors of the Academy, with very encouraging success. These experiments — if they need now be called experiments — have been continued, and have occupied a considerable portion of the time of the professors. Classes and schools of this description have been formed and taught during portions of the past year, in this city and in Salem, Lynn, and Cambridge, embracing nearly 1,200 pupils, of various ages, from five or six years and upwards. In teaching these, the most simple and philosophical method has been adopted. Very little use has been made of books in the more elementary parts of instruction. The method has been strictly analytical and progressive, and most of the lessons have been given orally or on the black-board. The proficiency of the pupils has been exhibited at the concerts given during the year by these classes, under the direction of the professors, in a far more satisfactory manner than it could be by any description.

Adult classes have been taught in this city, in Salem, and in Harvard University, embracing together about 500 pupils; making the whole number of pupils in classes, formed especially for musical instruction, about 1,700. The number has varied considerably during the year; but that given above may be considered as about the average attendance.

'While the desire to become acquainted with music seems to have in no degree diminished among the adult portions of the community, there is obviously an increasing disposition to obtain the benefits of jevenile instruction in almost every class of society. The rich, as well as the poor; the fashionable and refined, as well as those in the humbler walks of life, are beginning to regard vocal music as an accomplishment, at once attainable, pleasing, and useful; and are becoming desirous that the children iu their families should participate in the advantages and pleasures of it. The constant employment which has been furnished to the professors of the Academy, and the liberal patronage extended to other teachers of music in the city, fully establish this fact.

'*Common Schools.* The professors have been employed during the past year to give instruction in music to the pupils of nine schools, including several of the largest and best conducted private schools in the city, together with one in Cambridgeport and one in Charlestown; embracing together about 530 pupils.

'The whole number of pupils taught by the Academy, is about 2,200.

extensively in the city, for admission to which a reasonable charge for tuition should be made, would be preferred by parents, and would afford opportunity for introducing a more systematical and thorough course of musical education; while at the same time it would relieve the Academy from one cause of expenditure, and enable it to use its funds in other ways for the promotion of its objects. During the past year it has expended in the instruction of free classes, $660, besides $165, the avails of a juvenile concert, which was granted by request to the Infant School Society of this city.

The Academy has ever regarded the introduction of vocal music, as an ordinary branch of study, into common schools — not only those under private patronage, but public schools generally, — as an important object to be aimed at in its labors. Little effort has as yet been made to accomplish this, and no experiment has been tried. The low estimate which is now set on a knowledge of music by the community, and the prevailing impression that attention to this study would seriously interfere with, or divert the attention of children and youth from other and more important branches of an education, will probably, for some time to come, present a barrier in the way of accomplishing all that the Academy desires in this department. It is hoped, however, that some satisfactory experiments may soon be made, which may diminish the indifference or prejudice which now exist on this subject; and that vocal music will, at no distant day, be generally included among the branches of a common school education. This change in public sentiment will not probably, however, be wrought by any elaborate statement of the advantages to be derived from instructing children in music. Instead, therefore, of formally discussing the subject, it is deemed expedient, in addition to the statements given in the last Annual Report of the Academy, of the results of introducing musical exercises into common schools in some European countries, simply to subjoin here the testimony of some of the most respectable teachers of private schools in this city, and vicinity, relative to the effects, as observed by them, of teaching music in their schools by professors of the Academy, during the past year.'

From a number of testimonials, we extract two, as expressing the sentiments of all whom we have known, who have adopted vocal music as a branch of school instruction:

'*From* William B. Fowle, *teacher of the Monitorial School, Temple Avenue, Boston.*

'In reply to inquiries as to the result of the experiment I have made upon the practicability and utility of teaching vocal music to large numbers of children, I would remark, that the experiment has succeeded beyond my expectation. More than a hundred of my pupils, between the ages of four and eighteen, have been under the care of Mr Mason more than a year. I intended the exercise rather as a pastime than a serious study; but, with only two short lessons a week, the children have acquired no inconsiderable knowledge of the elements of music. Before any experiments were made in this country, I had proofs enough of the *practicability* of making simple melody a part of popular education, and I consider this question as demonstrated beyond doubt in my school. Of its *utility*, as *we* use it, I have as little doubt. It is never allowed to interfere with or supersede the common branches of study, and I often use it to call attention, restore order, or promote the innocent recreation of the pupils. I consider music one of the arts of peace which all may cultivate sufficiently to feel its influence upon their manners and dispositions, and in introducing it into our schools we are sowing seeds, which if they do not keep out the tares entirely, will essentially modify them.

'William B. Fowle.

'*Monitorial School, Temple Avenue, May* 1, 1834.'

'*From* E. A. Andrews, *teacher of the Mount Vernon Female School, Masonic Temple, Boston.*

'The following, so far as I have observed, have been the principal effects of the introduction of music into the Mount Vernon school, as a general school exercise.

'It has furnished an agreeable variety in our employments. It is an exercise so different in its nature from all the ordinary employments in the school, that it is generally anticipated as a desirable relaxation from our usual avocations.

'The study of the principles of musical science has appeared to afford as salutary a discipline of the mind, as the other studies usually pursued in school for this purpose, and I have not observed any one successful in becoming acquainted with these principles, without a corresponding success in other branches.

'It has afforded an agreeable amusement during our recesses.

'It has enabled a large part of the school to join with pleasure in the singing of a hymn at the devotional exercises at the opening and close of the school.

'By singing frequently such words as contain useful sentiments, they occur to the mind in those moments when it is not occupied with regular trains of thought, and, in this way, useful associations occupy the place of such as are useless or pernicious.

'By commencing very early in life, most of the difficulties which are experienced at a later period in acquiring the art, are avoided. The propensity to imitation is then strongest, and that timidity, which at a subsequent period prevents the pupil from making a full attempt to imitate musical sounds, is by children scarcely felt. Among the younger members of the Mount Vernon school I have not observed a single instance of failure in learning to sing, while many continually occur among the older members who cannot overcome their timidity so far as to attempt fearlessly to imitate the sounds which they hear.

'From what I have noticed in the Mount Vernon school, and in other classes under the direction of the professors of the Academy, I am satisfied that the general introduction of music into schools will be attended with complete success, if competent instructors are employed for this purpose.

'E. A. Andrews.

'*Boston, May* 8, 1834.'

PRACTICAL LESSONS

ON THE EXISTENCE OF GOD.

VISIBLE ILLUSTRATION.

Dr Beattie adopted the following method, to impress upon the mind of his son, the existence and providence of a God.

'He had reached his fifth or sixth year, knew the alphabet, and could read a little, but had received no particular information with respect to the Author of his being. In the corner of a little garden, without informing any person of the circumstance, I wrote in the mould, with my finger, the initials of his name, and sowing garden cresses in the furrow, covered up the seed, and smoothed the ground. Ten days after, he came running to me with astonishment on his countenance, and told me his name was growing in the garden. I laughed at the report, and seemed inclined to disregard it; but he insisted on my going to see what had happened. Yes, said I, carelessly, on coming to the spot, I see it is so, but what is there in this worth notice? Is it not mere chance?—and as I went away, he followed me and taking hold of my coat, said, with some degree of earnestness, 'it could not be mere chance, for somebody must have contrived matters so as to produce it.'

So you think, said I, that what appears so regular, as the letters of your name, could not be chance? 'Yes,' said he, with firmness, 'I think so.' Look at yourself, I replied, consider your hands and fingers, your legs, and feet, and other limbs; are they not regular in their appearance, and useful to you? He said they were. Came you then hither by chance? said I. 'No,' he answered; 'that cannot be; something must have made me.' And who is that something? I asked. He said, 'I don't know.' I had now gained the point that I aimed at, and saw that his reason taught him, (though he could not express it,) that what begins to be must have a cause. I therefore told him the name of the Great Being who made him and all the world; concerning whose adorable nature I gave him such information as I thought he could, in some manner, comprehend. The instruction affected him greatly, and he never forgot it, nor the circumstance that introduced it.'

ARGUMENT.

We have alluded to the difficulty of adapting our language and style to the capacity and modes of thought of very young children. Some indeed affect to despise a puerile style. It may be carried too far, or applied to those who are capable of understanding something less simple, but we often find these objectors speaking in an 'unknown tongue,' so far as their readers are concerned. We have met with nothing which so well satisfies us, as a model for the style of first instructions to a child, as Todd's 'Lectures to Children,' a work composed of sermons addressed to them, of which he gives the following account:

'I have usually delivered one of my 'little sermons' once in three months, supposing this to be no more, certainly, than the share of the lambs. The following lectures are a selection from such as I have thus delivered to the children under my care. My language and illustrations may seem familiar and common-place; but I have tried to talk in such a manner, that, on pausing several times, and asking my little, bright audience, what point had just been stated and illustrated, the child who could only lisp, should usually be able to throw his voice in with the rest in answering.'

An extract on the existence of God will be appropriate to our work, and serve as a useful model to the parent and infant school teacher:

'You see this meeting-house. You see it is full of things which were planned out, and everything in it, planned for some use. Now look. This pulpit with its stairs and window, and seat — for what are they designed? Why, the window is to let the light in, the seat for the preacher to sit down, and the stairs so that he can get into it; and this place where I stand, that he may stand up so high as to be seen by all in the house. Those seats or pews were made for you to sit in, during the sermon, and all done off and numbered, so that each family might have their own pew, and know it. Those windows were made to let the light in; those posts to hold up the gallery so that it might not fall on those who sit under it. Those doors are made to shut the noise and the cold out, and those stoves to warm the house in winter, and the long pipes to carry off the smoke. That front gallery is for the singers to set in and sing God's praises. Look now, and see if you can find anything to play with. No. There is nothing. Of course, this house was not made to play in. See if you can see anything to sleep on — any couch, or bed? No, none. Of course, this house was not made to sleep in. It is all planned to be a place in which to worship God.

'Suppose now I should tell you this house was never built by any body! It all grew up by chance, just as it is! The brick for the walls on the outside, and the roof on the top, grew just so, making this great square room, with its pews, and pulpit, and windows, and stoves, and everything just as it is! It all grew so by chance! Could you believe this? No, you could not believe it. Why, you would say, this house must be built by some body. True. True. But tell me, did you ever see the man who made these bricks, and spread these walls? No. Did you see the carpenter who built these pews, and pulpit, and doors, and windows? No. Did you ever see the glass-maker who melted the sand and made this glass? No. Did you ever see the silk-weaver who wove this pulpit-curtain? No. Or the man who hammered out the iron and made those pipes? No, no. You never did, and yet you know that all these lived, because you see what they have done. And this is good proof.

'And it is in just such ways that we know there is a God; for he made the clay, which had only been altered by the fire, and it is brick. He made the wood, which has only been altered in its shape, and it becomes pews and seats. He made the iron, which had only to have its shape altered by melting, and it is these stoves. The sand which he made, had only to be melted, and it becomes glass. He made the little worm which spun the silk of which this cushion was made. And he made the light to shine through these windows, and your eyes to see it after it comes in; and your ears to hear voices and sounds. He made that mind of yours, so that it can understand what I say, and your memory so that you can lay it up and keep it, and talk it over after you go home.'

THE TEACHER'S ALMANAC FOR JULY.

THE SCHOOL-ROOM.

The heat is increasing. Remember still, that he is a cruel task-master, who demands as much from the languid and enfeebled as from the vigorous. Watch over your pupils, lest their violence in play, or their too constant exposure in the heat of the day while they are confined in the cooler hours, should impair still more their energy or their health. Give the boys advice, if you can, about bathing — especially to avoid it when exhausted — or after meals. You will find an essay on it in one of our former volumes. Lead out your pupils, when public opinion or circumstances will allow it, to learn and to enjoy in the open air, in a shady spot; and give them sufficient intervals of relaxation. Watch over them in reference to the green fruits which will begin to tempt them, and which may perhaps cost the life of some who are dear to you. Assist them to *govern themselves* by anecdotes, and familiar and frequent explanations of the danger which your physician will teach you how to give. This will do far more good than to say merely — 'You *must* not; it will hurt you.'

THE WORLD.

Do not let the curiosity of your pupils sleep. Take every opportunity to call it forth, and endeavor to establish the habit of recording, in a little journal, the progress of the seasons and the face of nature. The change in plants from flower to fruit, and the formation of seeds, are new and interesting subjects of remark. The nests of the birds will frequently become objects of attention, and lessons should be given which shall excite deep interest in their parental cares, and effectually prevent the cruel robbery in which children so often indulge. If possible, teach them that sweet song of Mrs Hale's, set to music in the Juvenile Lyre, beginning —

If ever I see, On bush or tree
Young birds in a pretty nest,
I must not in my play — Steal the birds away
To grieve their mother's breast.

The predicted seventeen years locust has made its appearance in many parts of our country, and will probably appear elsewhere. Its structure, history, and mode of singing will be interesting to your pupils; but they should be warned to use it tenderly; for its sting has been fatal to children in several instances this season. The world of insects is full of wonders; and your pupils are perfectly capable of observing and describing their appearance and habits. Mudie's Guide in the observation of nature, published by the Harpers, as a volume of the Family Library, well deserves your perusal, as illustrating the ease, and pointing out the mode, of studying science in the book of nature itself.

THE HEAVENS.

The aspect of the heavens is not materially changed from the last month, so far as the planets are concerned. The Scorpion is the sign of the Zodiac now on the meridian in the evening; and it would be very desirable, by the aid of a globe, or Burritt's maps, to make your pupils familiar with each of these signs, that they may be able to trace the paths of the planets. Hercules, also, and Serpentarius, may now be conveniently observed. Let your pupils remark the decreasing length of the days, and the position of the Sun at rising and setting, and his approach to the zenith at noon.

MISCELLANY.

Andover Seminary for Teachers.

We have been favored with the following account of the course of studies in the Teacher's Seminary at Andover.

In the Teacher's department are *three classes.* The course of study can be accomplished in three years. But as the middle and senior classes are expected to be absent to enable them to teach during the winter, the course requires three and a half years. The regular time for admission is at the commencement of the summer term. Candidates for admission to the Junior class must be prepared to pass a satisfactory examination on the sounds of English letters, rules of Spelling, Reading, Geography, first principles of Etymology, and Syntax, Intellectual Arithmetic, History of the United States, Ground rules of Written Arithmetic, and Fractions. The year is divided into *three terms,* and the following studies are pursued at each.

Junior Class. 1st Term. — English Grammar. Intellectual Arithmetic, *reviewed.* History of U. States, *reviewed.*
" 2d Term.—Written Arithmetic. Geography—ancient and modern. History of England.
" 3d Term. — Written Arithmetic, *finished.* Linear Drawing. Construction of Maps. Use of Globes. Book-keeping.
Middle Class. 1st Term. — Algebra. Euclid. Rhetoric.
" 2d Term. — Algebra, *finished.* Trigonometry. Chemistry.
" 3d Term. — Chemistry, *finished.* Surveying. Spherical Geometry. Conic Sections.
Senior Class. 1st Term. — Natural Philosophy. Logic. Civil Engineering.
" 2d Term. — Natural Theology. Evidences of Christianity. Moral Philosophy. Astronomy.
" 3d Term. — Political Economy. Intellectual Philosophy. Art of Teaching.

All the members of the junior class attend to the *Political Class-Book* on Saturdays, and to Declamation and Composition on Wednesdays, through the year. The middle and senior classes write compositions on subjects connected with the Art of Teaching.

Lectures are given, accompanied with illustrations and experiments, on the most important studies; particularly, Natural Philosophy, Chemistry, and School-keeping. Each one who finishes the course, will have attended more than fifty lectures on the latter subject.

Efforts are making to aid indigent students, which, it is believed, will effectually open the benefits of the institution to *every worthy applicant.*

Nautical Schools.

In recent numbers, we have published two articles on the importance of nautical schools. We rejoice to see that a memorial from citizens of Boston to Congress has been presented, and supported by Mr Webster, which proposes that a portion of the duties collected in each port be applied to aid in the establishment of schools for mariners. Unsettled from their very mode of life, these useful men are emphatically the children of the Union, and as such, deserve public aid.

Public Schools in New York.

We have been favored with the twentyninth annual report of the Trustees of the Public School Society in New York. To their care is committed the whole subject of common education in the city of New York; and by their faithfulness, and the indefatigable labors of their superintendent, Mr Seton, who spends his whole time in visiting the schools and destitute families, they have attained a high degree of excellence and usefulness. The state superintendent of schools observes: 'The methods of instruction are highly judicious, and the schools are in every respect of a high order.'

From this report it appears that there are 11,444 pupils in the public schools under the care of this society, of whom about 2,500 belong to the primary departments and primary schools, under the care of 49 teachers, 28 assistant teachers and 75 monitors. The amount expended by the Society during the last year was $91,656, of which $50,000 was paid for instruction and current expenses, and the remainder for buildings, books apparatus, and payments, on former expenditures. The society have acted in the true spirit of economy in raising the salaries of the teachers of the boys' schools to $1000 a year, and of those of the girl's school to $400; for nothing is more dangerous to the energy and success of a teacher, than to be pressed by necessity to engage in some other employment, as has sometimes been the case. The society consists of 600 members, paying $10 as a life subscription. The Board of Trustees consists of 50 members elected, and 27 added by them from members of the society. The Board is divided into sections of four to eight members, each of which is entrusted with the charge of one of the school buildings, and is bound to visit and examine schools weekly by sub-committees. In addition to these weekly examinations, the schools are inspected annually by the Board of Trustees in the spring, and by the Executive Committee in the autumn, and were pronounced at the recent visit, to have been in a state highly satisfactory.

Cumberland College.

This institution, as it appears from a recent report, contains 75 students under the care of a president and two professors, whose annual salaries, with that of the treasurer, amount to $1983. It has a farm of 339 acres under cultivation. Its annual income at $80 for the board and tuition of each student, is $6000; leaving a balance of $4017, which is considered sufficient to meet all the expenses of the refectory and farm, and place the institution in a state of security.

Manual Labor College in Missouri.

Marion College, founded and since endowed by the legislature of Missouri, is soon to go into operation with a system of manual labor, on a peculiar plan. About 1000 acres of land are attached to it, twenty acres of which are to be assigned to each pupil, together with the horses and tools necessary for cultivating corn, grass, and grain, as a means of supporting himself. To facilitate his labors, the vacations are given at seed time and harvest; and it is expected that he will easily pay the $70 required for his board and tuition. Workshops are to be provided for those who prefer mechanical employments.

Lyceums in South Carolina.

During a recent visit of Mr Holbrook to Charleston, S. C. the attention of the Literary and Philosophical Society of that city was called to the subject of lyceums, and a committee was appointed to prepare and circulate an address to the people of that state, on the origin, constitution, operations, and advantages of lyceums. We earnestly wish that they may be successful in introducing some plan of social improvement among our southern brethren; and while the scattered state of the population presents an obstacle to efforts of this kind, we cannot but hope that the social and hospitable spirit for which they are so distinguished will be sufficient to overcome it.

Lutheran Seminary at South Carolina.

The first examination of the Lutheran Theological Seminary at Lexington, S. C., under the care of the Rev. Dr Hazelius, is stated to have been very interesting and satisfactory. The number of theological students is 14; and the classical department has 45 pupils.

Schools in Constantinople.

We have mentioned the establishment of Lancasterian schools in Constantinople, under the direction of American missionaries. From recent accounts in the Missionary Herald, it appears that a fourth school has been established within the walls of the *Seraglio* itself; and so great is the confidence reposed in the benevolent agents in this plan, that the missionaries were allowed to enter its innermost enclosure, usually shut to every stranger. They even found a little school-room, fitted up by one of the officers, for the instruction of his sister and daughter! a novelty unexampled in Turkey.

Improvement in Africa.

Africa presents a recent example of invention similar to that of the Cherokees. 'The Vey people,' says a missionary of the American Board, in the Missionary Herald, 'residing on Grand Cape Mount, have recently *invented a system of writing* entirely new, and altogether different from any other we have yet seen; in which, although it is not more than two years since it was invented, they write letters and books. Some of their characters resemble the Arabic, some resemble the Hebrew letters, others Greek; but all of them, except those resembling the Arabic, are merely fanciful. The alphabet is *syllabic*.' In the last point it resembles that devised by Guess, whose origin was described by Mr Boudinot, in the 2d volume of this work.

The missionaries find that the people along the whole coast, are desirous of *schools*. Wherever the plan of the missionaries was known, urgent applications were made for schools, and a written promise was often requested. In one instance, they would not close a council until this was given; and after travelling 200 miles, the Americans received a message reminding them of this promise! And yet, thousands of parents in our own country, and of our own color, are willing that their children should grow up in ignorance!

The progress and state of several schools in Liberia is also stated to be very encouraging.

Vocal Music in Ceylon.

Since our first article was printed, we have seen a letter from the Rev. W. Hutchins, American missionary at Ceylon, who paid particular attention to the Pestalozzian system of music, under the direction of Mr Mason, before his departure. He found that the principal of the mission seminary at Batticotta fully accorded with him in his views of the importance of vocal music as a means of moral influence, and commenced instructing a class of thirty in Rhythm. On proceeding to Melody, he found two thirds able to sound the eight notes correctly at once. Those pupils were selected who understood English; and so delighted were they with their newly discovered faculty, that some of them arose at night, and walked out, to enjoy the pleasure of singing. We rejoice at this introduction of a new instrument in the great work of enlightening and Christianizing India, and we would remind the missionaries, that the progress of the reformation was not a little promoted by the efforts of itinerant singers of sacred songs composed for the purpose, who thus proclaimed the truths of religion, invested with the charms of poetry and music, to multitudes who would not have listened to a preacher.

Discovery of a New Continent.

It is stated in a newspaper of Hobart's Town, Van Dieman's Land, that a new southern continent has been discovered in latitude 66° 30′, extending from longitude 47° 31′ east to 69° 29′ west.

NOTICES OF BOOKS.

Poetry for Children, by the author of 'How to be Happy.'

'Poetry holds children, from their play,
And old men from the chimney corner.'—*Sir Philip Sidney.*

Hartford: Robinson & Pratt. 1834. 18mo. pp. 102.

The School Song Book, adapted to the School-room. Written for American Children and Youth by Mrs Sarah J. Hale, editor of the Ladies' Magazine, &c. Boston: Allen & Ticknor. 1834. 18mo. pp. 72.

There is no gift to the public for which we feel so much disposed to offer our personal thanks, as poetry for children, and especially from such pure and elevating pens as those of Mrs Sigourney, and the editor of the Ladies' Magazine. We can never forget how much more the *ballads* of a nation can effect than its *laws:* and when such efforts are combined with those now so extensively made, for the introduction of juvenile vocal music, we fondly anticipate the dawnings of a little millennium in our schools. We never feel so much impatience with our narrow limits, as when we are obliged to repress the desire we have to communicate to our readers, by extracts, some portion of the pleasure we feel, in looking at works like these. But the names of the authors are a better passport to public favor than our recommendation; and we will only beg that our readers, who are parents, will not deny the pleasure of reading them to their children, if they do not desire it for themselves.

The Genius and Design of the Domestic Constitution, with its Untransferable Obligations and Peculiar Advantages. By Christopher Anderson. From the Edinburgh edition. Boston: Perkins, Marvin, & Co., and Wm. Pierce. New York, Leavitt, Lord, & Co. Philadelphia, Henry Perkins. 1834. 12mo. pp. 420.

The work before us is not one of a popular, illustrative character, fitted to attract an indolent mind, or fill up an idle hour. It is a work developing principles, and demanding attention, and requiring of all who read it, serious thought and energetic effort. It is written by one of the 'evangelical' school of Great Britain, with constant reference to the sanctions of its religious opinions. It presents in detail the great principles as to the nature and importance of *education*, as distinguished from *instruction*, and of the constitution of the family which have been presented in this journal, but enforced by peculiar religious views, which could not be presented appropriately in a journal, designed, like this, for a country of *common schools*. But there are many among our readers who hold similar opinions. On these we would urge the study of this work, in the hope that principles which we too often see *utterly neglected*, to the dishonor of religion, in families professedly devoted to God, may be so mingled with their views of religious truth and religious duty, that they shall cease to be matters of theory or speculation, and be regarded as no less important than the devotions of the family, or the contributions of benevolence.

Manual of the Boston Academy of Music, for Instruction in the Elements of Vocal Music, on the system of Pestalozzi. By Lowell Mason, Professor in the Academy. Boston: Carter, Hendee & Co. 1834. 18mo. pp. 236.

We are gratified to announce at length a guide for teachers, in the Pestalozzian system of musical instruction. It has been long in preparation, and in its passage through the press, in order to allow a thorough examination of the best German works on this subject, to give ample time for testing its principles and methods, and to give it that practical character which will make it a satisfactory manual. It proposes no royal road to music; its author deprecates the idea of pretending to learn or to teach vocal music 'in a few months,' or without labor. His object is to present a simple and natural mode of conducting that *course of exercises* which is indispensable to the training of any of our organs, and of producing ease and accuracy in the command of the voice. That he has succeeded in this, the inspection and thorough trial of this work, and above all a visit to his schools or choirs, will, we believe, satisfy every candid inquirer. It is one excellence of the book before us, that in accordance with the German models, it gives those directions in regard to little particulars for want of which a teacher often fails entirely in the application of a new method. With the views we have expressed of the importance of vocal music, and with such a guide to parents, we would adopt the language of Mr Mason—'And now, teacher of our country's youth, put your hands with courage to the work, until our schools, and firesides, and play grounds echo with harmony.'

The Musical Cyclopedia, or the Principles of Music considered as a Science and an Art, embracing a Complete Musical Dictionary, and the Outlines of a Musical Grammar, and of the Theory of Sounds, and Laws of Harmony, with Directions for the Practice of Vocal and Instrumental Music, and a Description of Musical Instruments. By William S. Porter. Boston: J. Loring. 1834. 18mo. pp. 430.

The title is an ample description of this work. Of its character, we have decisive testimony in the language of Mr Lowell Mason, by whose request and with whose advice it has been prepared. He observes that Mr Porter has manifested in its preparation, 'science, taste, and judgment;' that it is the result of 'great labor and research;' and that it 'contains a mass of information no where to be found in the same compass, and which could not otherwise be obtained, but at great expense.'

A Guide to the Study of Moral Evidence, or of that species of Reasoning which relates to Matters of Fact and Practice. By James Edward Gambier, Esq. With Illustrative Notes, being an Application of the Principles of the Science to the Divine Origin of the Christian Religion. By Joseph A. Warne, A. M. Pastor of the Baptist church, Brookline, Mass. To which is prefixed an Introductory Essay on Moral Reasoning. By William Hague, A. M. Pastor of the first Baptist church in Boston, Mass. Boston: J. Loring. 1834. 18mo. pp. 246.

The importance of correct views of moral reasoning in practical life is too little appreciated. It is very happily exhibited in the introductory essay before us, and we rejoice to see so valuable a work as that of Gambier, presented in a manner likely to attract general notice. The application to the evidences of Christianity in the notes, is peculiarly appropriate to this day, when so many are disposed to go back to the dark ages of scepticism, with the specious pretence of new light. We should rejoice to see this little book employed as a class book in our high schools; and we are confident, that for the practical and the highest purposes of life, it would do more to invigorate the reasoning powers, than that superfluity of material and mathematical science, which is admitted to be of no practical value, and with which pupils are often overloaded, merely with a view of 'strengthening the mind.'

Sketches of the Prophets and Prophecy, for the Young. Hartford: D. F. Robinson & Co. 1834. 18mo. pp. 180.

The Holy Land and its Inhabitants. By S. G. Bulfinch. Cambridge: T. Munroe & Co. 1834. 18mo. pp. 298.

While urging the use of the Bible as a class book, we have perhaps been deficient in not pointing our readers to books which would assist in illustrating and making it interesting. The Bible dictionaries of Alexander and Malcom have been for several years of essential use to bible teachers. That of Robinson, recently published, is peculiarly valuable for illustrations of another kind. The octavo edition of Calmet, by Robinson, we do not hesitate to say, ought to be on the desk of every teacher in whose school the bible is *read* or *taught*. A number of small but valuable works have been published on biblical antiquities, and biblical geography, by Nevins, Clark, Ingraham, the Sunday School Unions, &c, which will be found on the catalogues of our Sunday Schools. We are gratified to add to this list the first book mentioned, the result of research, on a subject too generally neglected, on account of its supposed difficulties. It is deeply interesting for the old as well as the young, from the condensed view it gives of the character and productions of the prophets; and the overwhelming proof which it affords, indirectly, of the divine origin of the scripture, from the striking fulfilment of its prophecies, will make it, to many minds, a more efficient work on the evidences of Christianity than formal treatises. The second is the third volume of Ware's Sunday Library, comprising a condensed account of the geography, history and antiquities of Palestine. The descriptions are clear and graphic; its style uncommonly simple and beautiful; and the whole peculiarly fitted to interest and inform the young student in the bible.

AMERICAN

ANNALS OF EDUCATION

AND INSTRUCTION.

AUGUST, 1834.

LIFE OF EMERSON.

Life of the Rev. Joseph Emerson, Pastor of the Congregational Church in Beverly, Mass., and subsequently Principal of a Female Seminary. By Rev. Ralph Emerson, Prof. of Eccle. History in the Theological Seminary, Andover, Mass. Boston: Crocker & Brewster. New York: Leavitt, Lord & Co. 1834. 12mo. pp. 434.

The biography before us is not marked with striking events; nor was Mr Emerson so connected with public concerns, as to render it a portion of history, as history is usually written. But if untiring and successful efforts to elevate the standard and improve the state of female education, if the preparation of hundreds of females for the important task of training the young, entitle an individual to the name of a benefactor of his country, it cannot be denied to him.

Neither our limits nor the objects of this work, would permit us to attempt a general delineation of his character, if we were sufficiently familiar with it to justify the attempt. For this, we must refer our readers to the record before us, which approaches more nearly to the standard of scriptural biography in its faithfulness, than any recent work within our recollection. We can only give a brief sketch of his life, and of his plans and efforts as an educator.

The Rev. Joseph Emerson was born at Holles, New Hampshire, in October, 1777, but four days before the surrender of Burgoyne, and in the midst of that struggle for our national independence, which, to his latest years, seems to have roused his feelings to the highest pitch of enthusiasm. At the age of six months, he was attacked with a severe disease, under which he suffered for a year, and which appears to have laid the foundation for that state of suffering in which he passed the greater part of his life. Whether it was the result of unavoidable causes, or of some defect in physical education, we are not informed.

Of the defects of his early instruction, he complains in terms which are too generally applicable to the schools of the present day.

'My parents taught me very little, and my teachers scarcely more. I did indeed attend school several months in the year; but it was attendance rather than attention. I did scarcely anything. Almost my whole business was to sit idly upon my seat through nearly the whole of the six long tedious hours of the school. Fifteen or twenty minutes might have been taken up in reading and spelling alone, four times a day. In all this, there was scarcely any benefit. It conduced rather to dulness than energy.

Even in his years of boyhood, he observes that 'little progress was made compared with what might have been.' His remark that the greatest advantage he derived at school, and the best religious instruction he received, was in '*reading the New Testament*,' is a cheering encouragement to those who require it.

He was early distinguished for frankness and simplicity of character, but was naturally impetuous and irritable. At three or four years of age, his temper burst out in an act of violence towards one of his sisters. An elder sister merely held him still, and remonstrated with him on his conduct. At length, his arms suddenly dropped by his sides, and he submitted; and the fact that she never afterwards witnessed a similar ebullition of passion, strikingly illustrates the importance of employing efficient means of government, at an early period.

At the age of seventeen, he entered Harvard College; and in the same class with such men as Story and Channing, he sustained, throughout his collegiate course, a high character for moral excellence and intellectual attainments. On leaving college, at the age of twentyone, he took charge of an academy at Framingham, Massachusetts, for a year, and then devoted himself entirely to the study of theology, with Dr Emmons, of Franklin. In 1801, at the age of twentyfour, he received the appointment of tutor at Harvard College; and at about the same time commenced preaching. As a tutor, he appears to have been characterized by ardor in the study and illustration of the branches he taught, and a familiarity of manner, not altogether consistent with the code of tutorial dignity; and on both accounts, he gained the affection of his pupils to an uncommon degree.

From Cambridge he went to Beverly, to assume the pastoral care of a new congregation; and passed thirteen years in this station with great usefulness. His interest in education appeared here, in various plans for the improvement of the young under his care. Among other measures, he established one of the earliest classes for the study of the bible, and gave a number of lectures on Sacred Geography and History, with the aid of the black board; a method which, though now familiar, was scarcely known in the schools of our country, thirty years ago.

In 1816, his health became so feeble, that after preaching for sometime in a sitting posture, he found it necessary to relinquish his ministerial labors, and spend a year in a southern climate. During this period, however, he did not lose any opportunity of employing his talents for instruction in giving lectures and teaching private classes. Finding himself still unfit for the labors of his profession, he now resolved to devote himself to an object long cherished, the establishment of a seminary for the education of female teachers, with a view of forming and elevating the system of female education.

We have heard it flippantly asserted in a public assembly, that no man was fit to teach, after the age of forty. It is a remarkable evidence to the contrary, that Mr Emerson did not commence his useful career as a teacher at Byfield, until 1818, at the age of *fortyone.* Arrangements which promised him the opportunity of being useful as a minister, to a feeble congregation in connection with his school, so far as his strength allowed, led him to remove three years after to Saugus, near Lynn. But he found the burden of this double responsibility too great for his health; and in 1824, the solicitation of a number of gentlemen at Wethersfield, in Connecticut, induced him to remove his school to that place, where he closed his life, at the age of fiftysix.

He was one of those who were concerned in forming the American Institute of Instruction, of which he was appointed on the first board of counsellors. He attended the meetings whenever circumstances permitted, and his death was noticed with a tribute of respect by that body.

It was with no small surprise that we found the whole period of Mr Emerson's labors as a teacher, in which he had accomplished so much for his pupils and the cause of education, was limited to *fifteen years.* Through this whole period, he was a great sufferer, and with that class of diseases which usually impair and occasionally almost paralyze the vigor of intellectual effort. He was often obliged to intermit his labors for months; and during the later years of his life, could spend but a small portion of his own time with his pupils. Yet he was enabled to improve the minds and characters of the thousand females who passed under his instructions, to an extent which has gained him an unusual share of their veneration and affection. He has developed and formed many minds which might have slumbered in obscurity; for he sought to bring forward the deserving poor. He has gladdened many a family by the effect produced by his instruction upon their daughters; and exerted a still wider and happier influence, by the preparation of a large number of female teachers.

Although his mind was naturally one of considerable, and, in some respects we learn, extraordinary power, yet taking into account his state of health, we can scarcely regard this success as the result of peculiar intellectual vigor. Much is to be ascribed to the intense ardor with which he prosecuted every object before him; but this often led to an over-estimate of the subject or scheme which immediately occupied his mind, and sometimes to sudden changes of plans and views, (in part, doubtless the result of disease) which were unfavorable to his success. Under these disadvantages we believe he has pointed out the great source of his usefulness, when he says, that the difference of men is very much to be ascribed to their different modes of application and different degrees of perseverance; and it will be interesting to every one engaged in education, to learn something of the principles and plans which guided his efforts, and enabled him to accomplish so much.

As one fundamental principle he contended earnestly for the importance of *knowledge*, as one of the *ends* of education, and not merely, as it is sometimes represented by ultra reformers, as the *means* of developing our faculties; for after all, the only use of these faculties is the discovery and application of truth, and they are exercised only to prepare them for this office.

He was not less decided, however, in conducting the acquisition of knowledge in such a manner as to call every faculty into exercise, and rouse it to the greatest degree of vigor. He thus strove to combine two objects, which no rational educator will ever separate. He possessed uncommon skill in exciting those around him to *think* — a habit which he deemed it especially important to cultivate in the education of females. One of the most essential parts of his lessons was to propose subjects of inquiry, to give out questions to be answered, and topics to be examined and reflected on, and to lead the mind, by an inductive course, to the knowledge he wished to be acquired.

His views of the relative importance of the various branches of female education, differed materially from those which have been fashionable. Some of the accomplishments generally considered indispensable, he regarded as useless, or worse than useless; and embroidery, fancy work, dancing, and fashionable music, he would not tolerate. Drawing he valued very highly ; but he does not appear to have considered it attainable, consistently with the economy of time and expense which his plan required, except so far as the tracing of historical scenes and portraits, by the aid of transparent paper, as a means of aiding the memory and the imagination. Vocal Music, of an elevated and devotional character, he considered as a very important acquisition, and prepared a book of poetical extracts in order to aid in its execution.

He appreciated very highly, a thorough course of instruction in the elements of education. Reading, as comprising the art of uttering the thoughts of others in the most striking and expressive manner, Pronunciation, Spelling, Defining and its extension in the critical interpretation of authors, and Chirography, required, in his view, the most laborious and thorough efforts on the part of the teacher ; and he seemed to consider all neglect of these, for the sake of pressing on to get a smattering of science, as ridiculous vanity. *Geometry* he justly regarded as *an elementary study* ; and maintained that a child could more easily understand the forms and names of simple geometrical figures, than those of the complicated emblems which form the letters of our alphabet.

Among the branches of natural science, he was most deeply interested in Astronomy, not merely from its intrinsic value, but from the use which could be made of it in enlarging the mind, and cultivating the imagination and the taste. As this remark would imply, he did not lose sight of the variety of faculties on the human soul, nor did he permit his instructions to terminate in the improvement of the reason and the memory. He sought to cultivate the imagination and the taste, not merely by the manner in which he presented the wonders of creation, but by the study of poetry and works of taste. In this connection it is a fact well worthy of the attention of those who grow cold-hearted while engaged in study, that Mr Emerson was remarkable for preserving the ardor of his feelings and the warmth of his affections under the pressure of infirmities, and cares, and labors, more chilling than those which are usually connected with age, and that he ascribes it to his constant attention to *poetry as a study*, and the efforts he made to inspire others with a taste for its beauties. We are well acquainted with another instance in which this course was equally useful, in maintaining the full flow of the affections, and the ardor of interest in the passing scenes of life, to an advanced age.

Mr Emerson was much interested in mathematical studies, and valued their influence highly. But he thought that they generally occupied too much of the time devoted to education. He believed, that to exercise the mind in scientific and especially in moral reasoning, would more certainly give that species of vigor of mind which we need for the great purposes of life, than the mere investigation of number and quantity. He perceived also the danger pointed out by Fellenberg, of giving the young false views of the nature of evidence, of teaching them to demand *demonstration*, where *testimony* and *consciousness* are the appropriate grounds of belief, and thus producing a tendency to materialism, and a contempt for all that belongs to our moral or affective faculties, too often found in devoted mathematicians.

He agreed with Locke and Rush, in thinking that the study of the Greek and Latin occupied far too much of the ordinary course of instruction among our youth; and that they were forced upon many individuals whose talents and circumstances would render other pursuits far more useful. He was especially desirous, that authors, whose standard of religion and morals is so debased as that of the pagan classics, should not be the first and incessant companions of youthful study. For ourselves, we owe it to truth to say, that the first licentious ideas which polluted our imagination were derived from the classics which we were required to *study*, and taught to regard with veneration; and that their influence was among the most difficult we found to overcome. Indeed *we can find no apology* for that course of education which allows any but an *editio expurgata* to be placed in the hands of youth. Mr Emerson believed, however, that even to females 'some acquaintance (with these languages) is really desirable,' with a view of understanding better the force of those words of our language which are derived from them. He therefore recommended a short course of Latin, at least, devoted chiefly to the study of the forms and the acquisition of a vocabulary, with some simple and unexceptionable text-book.

History, and especially Sacred History, had, in his view, the highest claims to a prominent place in a course of education. Regarding it as an exhibition of the character of man, and the ways of God, he adopted the maxim, 'Let a person commence with it as soon as he can speak, and pursue it as long as he lives.'

He gave a similar prominence to other sciences which relate immediately to man, and regarded practical instruction in Intellectual Philosophy, Logic and Rhetoric, as highly important. The principles of Education he considered as indispensable in a course of study for females. Could this become *a universal study* among the females of our country, what a change might we not hope for in the character of the succeeding generation!

In reference to the methods of instruction, we have already stated the high value which he placed upon a mode of examination, which calls forth the ideas of the pupil, as well as of the author he studies. He believed, in this view, that questions attached to text books, which are drawn up with the proper degree of skill and care, were much more likely to be useful than those which would occur to most teachers, in the midst of their miscellaneous labors.

It was a favorite object with him to systematise the various branches he taught, and to arrange them, as far as possible, in a *visible* order. As we have before intimated, his ardor and ingenuity often led him to attach too much importance and devote too much time to the minutiæ of a single subject, and to adopt plans which, however useful to his own mind, were only burdensome to others. The same fertility of invention and ardor of feeling led to sudden changes of views and plans. Still his pupils were much indebted to this habit of forming plans, as a means of leading them to feel its importance, and to devise such as were adapted to their own minds.

In our view, the results of Mr Emerson's labors, short, interrupted, and often desultory as they were, in consequence of his infirmities, are to be ascribed rather to the moral than the intellectual influence which he exerted.

He taught his pupils to pursue their studies with *high and noble aims*. While he valued knowledge as an end of education, while he burned with ardor in pursuing and imparting it, to his latest days, it was only as a subordinate end. To his own mind, and to those of his pupils, it was continually presented as a means of moral elevation and usefulness. The constant tendency of his instructions was, to employ truth of every kind in improving the heart. Nature was displayed in all its glories, to elevate the soul to 'Nature's God.' History was traced in its minute circumstances, to make his pupils acquainted with the characteristics of men, and with the moral government of God.

He regarded the ultimate objects and influence of education as belonging to another sphere of existence, whose happiness or misery depend on the moral, and not merely or chiefly on the intellectual character. He gave all his instructions, under the deep impression that their influence, for good or for evil, would be *eternal*. On this principle, no recitation was allowed to pass without its religious application.

On the other hand, he considered *practical utility* an object never to be lost sight of — not indeed in that narrow sense of the terms which embraces only the immediate productions of profit or comfort, but in that wide and true import of utility, which embraces the body and the mind — the benefit of the individual and of all within his reach.

Motives and views so elevated, combined with a temperament naturally warm, and receiving permanent life from his faith in future realities, produced an enthusiastic ardor in his instructions which gave them peculiar interest, and probably constituted the great secret of his influence as a teacher.

It is well known that he strenuously maintained the utility of exciting emulation as a motive to study; and he believed it one means of insuring his success. He was the only one among its advocates, whom repeated solicitations and demands have drawn forth in a defence which our readers have seen in the second volume of this work. His own mind was doubtless much influenced by the love of approbation, a propensity of great value within proper limits, but which rarely endures excitement, and still more rarely needs it. He found the desire of superiority a powerful means of rousing him to study, and preserving him from temptation, amidst the dangers of a college life. But in later years, higher motives certainly stimulated his efforts. His soul evidently burned with the desire to do good. In the course of much familiar intercourse with him, we have often seen the whole ardor of his mind poured forth in desires and efforts for usefulness; but we never saw or heard of an exhibition of the spirit of *rivalry*. Indeed, his own definition of the emulation he approved — *the desire of superiority for the sake of doing good* — removed him from the ranks of those who advocate this desire as the *motive* or *end* — for the end he proposed was usefulness. Indeed, some who heard him discuss this subject at the last meeting of the American Institute which he attended, considered him as abandoning all defence of *personal rivalry*.

We have been confirmed in this view of the case, from the fact that we have never found reason to believe this feeling was strongly excited among his pupils. The testimony of those with whom we have conversed, may be summed up in the remark of one of his pupils, quoted in the volume before us, concerning his school — '*Here I was taught that knowledge was desirable principally as a means of usefulness to others; and that literary selfishness was as sinful as any other selfishness.*'

But his own advice to a brother seems to us to point to other motives, as higher and nobler.

'I used to study night and day, that I might gain the character of a good scholar, that I might finally be a learned man — not that I might do good in the world. My brother, learn wisdom from my folly. When you leave college may your education be worth ten times as much as mine was. Do not study in order to shine as a great man, but in order to do good.'

We cannot but ask, who would feel himself authorized to indulge personal rivalry, if this motto were enacted into a law of our schools, 'DO NOT STUDY TO BE A GREAT MAN, BUT IN ORDER TO DO GOOD!' Who that should act upon it, could feel the need of a motive so inferior, or allow it to influence him without self-reproach? Such practical opponents of emulation accomplish more than labored arguments. May they be multiplied an hundred fold!

A natural result of the views we have described, was the preeminent place he assigned to the Bible, in his course of private studies and public instructions. He regarded it as 'the book of books,' for schools and colleges — as the highest and purest source of knowledge, the best means of discipline for the intellectual as well as the moral powers, and as the best instrument of government. If sound philosophy would not lead the guardians of our youth to assign a higher rank among classics to a book which one of the first scholars the world has ever seen, pronounced to be superior to all that was ever written in all human languages, one would expect at least, that in Christian institutions, the record of our faith, the basis of our morals, would receive more attention; and that a larger space would be assigned to the standard of moral and religious truth, among those works which are employed to invigorate the mind and elevate the taste.

In reviewing all that we have read and known of Mr Emerson, we have been led to the conclusion that his success as a teacher must be ascribed to the great objects of education which he kept in view, and the ardor and earnestness with which he employed every means in his power for their attainment, to the elevated motives which he addressed to his pupils and to his employment of the best of classics, the most perfect of guides, in the mental and moral improvement of his pupils. We hesitate not to express our conviction, that those who will follow his example in these important points, if they astonish less by the brilliancy of examinations and exhibitions, will win a tribute of gratitude, a crown of glory, in the character of their pupils, which shall last when all the trophies of those who profess merely to make perfect scholars, or accomplished ladies, will have vanished away.

EFFECTS OF EMULATION.

From the Addresses of Joseph A. Hill, Esq., and Prof. Anderson, before the Institute of North Carolina.

WE have been gratified to receive frequent evidence of the activity of the Institute of North Carolina. The addresses of Mr Hill and Mr Anderson are the most recent, and both highly interesting. Mr Hill devotes his address to the importance of a thorough education, and in the progress of his remarks expresses the following views of the effects of exciting Emulation as a motive to study.

'The teacher who seeks to awaken this spirit in his pupil, runs the risk of rousing passions, in close alliance with it, and of the very worst character — such as envy, hatred, and the spirit of detraction. A spirit of rivalry, in a long course of competition, is apt to be aggravated into a feeling of hostility, and the opponent comes, at length, to be regarded as an enemy. He, whose example we are bid to emulate, who is often exhibited in injurious contrast to ourselves, whose merit is made the reproach of our unworthiness, whose success frustrates our hopes, and disappoints our ambition — he, in a word, who impresses us with the painful sense of inferiority, will, unless we are watchful of our motives, and keep a guard upon our passions, become an object of envy, and a subject of detraction. Hurt vanity, and mortified self-love, will prompt the disingenuous wish to lessen the merit we have in vain essayed to equal. These effects of a vicious system of education, frequently betray themselves even in youth, the period of candid sentiment and generous feeling; and the young bosom which should be taught to throb only with virtuous emotion, becomes the theatre of contending passions. In after-life, when as the objects of competition are of greater value, the eagerness of desire is increased, and the pang of disappointment more keenly felt, they assume an aspect of darker malignity, and a form more disgustingly hateful. They sometimes mingle in the strife for noble objects, and characters of otherwise exalted worth, are degraded by the littleness of envy and the meanness of jealousy.

'There is another error, which, though not so general as to be fairly considered inherent in our systems of school discipline, is yet sufficiently common to deserve notice and reprehension. It consists in a misrepresentation of the objects and purposes of education; and may be defined to be the suggestion to the learner of a false motive to exertion. The eminences of fame, the heights of power, the applause of contemporaries, and the plaudits of posterity, whatever can flatter vanity or awaken ambition, is presented to the notice of the pupil, and proposed to him as the certain reward of industry and assiduity. There cannot be a more pernicious error. Its effects upon the character of the individual and upon society, are indeed deplorable. The youth, so soon as he becomes capable of observation and reflection, detects the fallacy of the hopes with which his mind has been filled; he discovers that the rewards which have been proposed as certain, are impossible; that the objects at which he has been taught to aim, must remain forever beyond his reach. Hope dies within him, and his exertions relax. Upon the failure of one motive, a more correct but less stimulating one may fail to reanimate his courage. If the delusion be sustained until he has completed his collegiate course, so soon as he enters upon the great stage of life, it is sure to be dispelled. He then discovers that fame must, from the nature of things, be the lot of a very few, and that his must be the fate of the predecessors of Agamemnon —

"Vixere fortes ante Agamemnona,
Multi; sed omnes illacrymabiles
Urgentur ignotique longa
Nocte."

He yields to the feeling of despondency, which succeeds the excitation of hope, and refusing to attempt even that which he has the ability to accomplish, finds in retirement, obscurity indeed, but not contentment: Or, worse still, losing the motive of a lofty ambition, abandoning the pursuit of those higher objects which are seldom sought, because they can never be won but by honorable means, and too long accustomed to the high excitement of stimulating motives, to acknowledge the influence of more moderate hopes, he becomes an unprincipled demagogue, a restless intriguer for petty power and ephemeral distinction, the parasite of power, the flatterer of the people, the pander to prejudice, the advocate of error, acknowledging no principle but expediency, no feeling but selfishness! A political cameleon, changing his complexion with the changing hue of the times. Behold him a Law-giver, illustrating by the vacillations of his unprincipled policy, the description which the poet gives us of one of the worst characters of antiquity,

"Vendidit hic auro, patriam, dominum que
Imposuit, fixit leges pretio, atque refixit." — *Virg. B.* 6. 621.

serving no other purpose than to indicate the caprices of power or the eccentricities of popular whim. If you would not, that these sad effects disclose themselves in the man, deal fairly by the boy. Suggest to him no false motive, let there be no misrepresentation of the purposes, no exaggeration of the advantages of education; let him be told all the good that knowledge rightly used will accomplish for him; that by enlarging his mind and extending his views, it will increase his capacities for happiness, and multiply to him the sources of innocent enjoyment; that education, though it be auxiliary to the acquisition of power and fame, is not proposed as a certain means of becoming powerful and distinguished, but that habits of industry, correct principles, and upright conduct, will certainly be rewarded in after life, by usefulness, respectability, and happiness.'

Prof. Anderson, an officer of the University of North Carolina, was appointed by the Institute to deliver a lecture expressly on the subject of 'Exciting Emulation in Schools, by the use of rewards and punishments.' After alluding to the remarks of Mr Hill, with which he does not agree entirely, as applied to the *male sex* — he reverts to its effect on females, as being after all the most important, because their influence over their sons is such that 'no subsequent neglect or culture can destroy it;' because — 'if we wish to have *Gracchi*, we must first look for *Cornelias*.' He then proceeds to exhibit the effects of exciting emulation which he has observed in female schools.

'For what, then, let us now inquire, is the gentle being destined, whose untainted and flexible mind is to be subjected to the ordeal of elementary discipline? What is the station she is to occupy in after life? What are the peculiar obligations she will be expected to discharge? What the trials and hindrances with which her path will be beset? The answer is obvious. Her station is that of an aid, a counsellor — a subordinate — her peculiar obligations all spring out of her relation to man as her guide and governor — her trials and hindrances for the most part may be traced to that natural corruption of the heart, which she partakes with the rest of her species, and which ever prompts her to deny and resist the great end of her being. In that exquisite picture of female loveliness, for which, as an almost perfect model, the sex owes eternal gratitude to the poet Milton, Eve is made to address her husband in these beautiful words, expressive at once of the relation between them, and her own cheerful acquiescence in the subordinate lot to which she was created:

> "My Author and Disposer, what thou bid'st
> Unargued I obey — so God ordains—
> God is thy law, thou mine; to know no more,
> Is woman's happiest knowledge and her praise."

And what is the discipline by which we seek to prepare this gentle being for the love-inspiring offices of her station? What system of culture do we apply to those affections which are to soothe, by submission and forbearance, the stern austerity of the companion of her pilgrimage? How do we train woman for that relation to man, in which, like the ivy that embraces and embellishes the oak, she at once receives support and imparts beauty? Why, the answer is ready. We prepare her for her gentle offices of love, by bringing her into fierce conflict with the companions of her education — by teaching her to "hate that excellence she cannot reach." We cultivate her submissive and forbearing spirit, by teaching her to exult in the pain and disappointment of those whom the natural impulses of childhood would otherwise prompt her to love. We mould her for that relation to man in which she derives support and imparts pleasure, by stimulating her easily excited passions in the contests for superiority over her fellows — by making it one condition of her exaltation, that her companion should be degraded — of her pleasure, that her rival should be mortified — for the same end is attained, whether the successful competitor excels by the vigorous and well regulated efforts of her own mind, or in consequence of the feebleness or indolence of her antagonist; and as the passions exposed to the influence of such motives belong to a mortal, and are tainted with the universal degradation of our nature, we need not hope they will escape those agitating impulses which

"vex the mind
With endless storm; whence deeply rankling grows
The partial thought, a listless unconcern,
Cold and averting from our neighbor's good;
Then dark disgust and hatred" —

Let us, in imagination, trace the progress of one of these beings, on whose proper culture the happiness of man so largely depends, through the successive positions in which she is prepared for, and fulfils, the destinies of her sex — let us watch the effects of associations and habits on her susceptible mind, in the counteraction of the gentle dictates of her nature, and in the formation of masculine principles of action; and then, when education has thus unfeminized her, let us attend her to the theatre of her peculiar responsibilities. We see her placed in close collision with the companions of her childhood — we hear her called upon to press forward for the foremost place in the contest in which all are engaged — we see the workings of excited passion in the kindled eye, the flushed cheek, the eager step — we discover, with concern, her selfish and exclusive devotion to her own advancement; for, whatever the generous impulses of the girl may prompt her to feel for others, the unnatural, but easily acquired, feelings of the candidate for distinction teach her to suppress. A competitor in the race falls — does the sympathizing girl hasten to the aid of her unfortunate rival, and, thoughtless for a while of herself, lend all her generous cares to the restoration of her friend? Oh, no! this is no part of the system. She is taught to exult that one obstacle to her success has been removed, and that, if she extends assistance, she may convert a disgraced into a triumphant rival — she denies the gentle promptings of her sex, and passing on, urges her strength against some new and envied rival.

'When the gentle girl, with all the affectionate impulses of her nature, and the yielding graces of her sex, has been thus converted, by the operation of the stern system we are contemplating, into the jealous and aspiring woman, we will attend her upon her further progress into life, and see with what feelings she assumes, and with what fidelity she is prepared to fill, her appointed station in the world. She is not fitted for submission, by a discipline which has taught her to regard a station of inferiority as one of disgrace. That distinguishing virtue of the woman — I mean gentleness — which like the fragrance of the flower, alone gives any value to beauty, is greatly impaired, if not destroyed; for the opposite feeling of fierce contentious emulation has usurped its place and withered its affectionate impulses. She is not even fitted for the forbearance and concession demanded of her in every relation of life; for she has been taught resolutely to seek, and boldly to maintain, pre-eminence over all around her. If the excellence of another affects her susceptible mind with admiration, that virtuous feeling is polluted by an admixture of the most selfish regrets; and the disgrace and failure of another do not always fill with tears those eyes which have so often kindled with exultation at the ill success of her fellows. I will not be understood, I hope, Mr President, as meaning *every* woman exposed to the influence of this improper system becomes the unamiable being I have described ; or that even where its evil effects are discovered in the vitiated impulses of the female mind, there does not remain much to redeem the ravages which a vicious culture has made. The rose does not lose its fragrance, though its delicate leaves be torn and polluted by the storm ; yet who does not regret that a flower so sweet should have had its beauty so marred.

As a substitute for a system which is thus unsuited to the female character and station, Prof. Anderson proposes the establishment of fixed points of excellence, easily settled, to which all may attain, and in which all may at once enjoy the first place without the feeling of personal triumph or degradation. He states from his own observation, that this system is entirely efficacious, in leading to the utmost exertion and the highest attainments which pupils are capable, and thus producing on a whole school, that effect which emulation only produces in the favored few, while it banishes 'animosities, envyings and jealousies,' and cherishes 'the benevolent and social affections of those who are trained under it.' What blessing would be greater in a school of the other sex ?

[For the Annals of Education.]

SURE AND INTRINSIC REWARDS OF STUDY.

COMMON SCHOOLS AND COMMON EDUCATION.

NO. V.

IT is useless to attempt any extensive improvement of common schools and common education on the promise of extravagant rewards. My friend Thomas had the right of the matter in my last number. The rewards of mental and moral industry must be attainable by all, or our urgency is a farce : and the public is justly neglectful of a course, which, if pursued, would yield them only their labor for their pains. All our urgency will prove in vain, unless we can fix the minds of the people upon *sure and intrinsic rewards.*

True, there are instances of young persons who began life with only common advantages, and occupied in daily labor for their maintenance, who, in consequence of getting hold of the principles of self-improvement, and taking constant pains, have gained not only knowledge and skill, but have risen to conspicuous rank, and attained the highest fortune and fame. You will find such examples in 'the Biography of self-taught Men,' and in two or three numbers of the Library of Entertaining Knowledge, entitled 'The

Pursuit of Knowledge under Difficulties.' Thus Franklin improved himself, while he learned and practised the trade of a printer, and was so prosperous as well as diligent that he attained great wealth, the highest fame as a philosopher, and the highest places in the civil affairs of his country. Sherman was a shoemaker — studious and self-improving; and being prosperous as well as diligent, he became an accomplished lawyer, judge and politician. Lee, too, now living, was a few years ago a working carpenter, with as little spare time and as little opportunity as any laborer; but he so improved himself, and so prospered, that he is now the far-famed and well-endowed Professor of Oriental Languages in the English University of Cambridge. Parkes, having been unsuccessful in business until he was forty years of age, turned his attention to the manufacture of muriatic acid, for which his previous studies had prepared him; and by his business, and his books on the Science of Chemistry, acquired rapidly great wealth and reputation.

Such examples, however, are few, and do but show what high rewards *may possibly* be attained by just principles and constant pains. Is it not, then, mere mockery to make this *bare possibility* the grand motive by which we are to urge on the improvement of common schools and common education? Can we persuade the parents, can we persuade the children, by the futile possibility? None but the vain-hearted, whose improvement will be a useless pedantry, will listen to us. While we think we are stimulating them with the highest conceivable motive, they will remain in torpid indifference, moved only to the useful knowledge — 'to read, write and cypher!' leaving us to mourn over our inability to move them by a dream. And would it be other than a dream, if we could set the whole district, or the whole town, or the whole people, upon the track of Franklin, or Sherman, or Lee, or Parkes? They might dream of high places, but would one in a hundred thousand obtain them; or, failing to gain them, would they long persevere in search of such improbable rewards? The printer, alas! would soon find himself toiling at the *case* or the *press*, instead of becoming the far-famed philosopher and ambassador to foreign courts. The shoemaker would find himself tied to his last, and the carpenter would be left toiling on the roof, and not on the bench of the judge or in the chair of the Professor. Nay, the very examples referred to would never have persevered to their full and final success, except in view of sure and certain rewards.

But have we nothing but dreams wherewith to stimulate the community, and the whole community? Are we left to the idlest fancies as the motives for the improvement of the people? Has not the improvement of the mind an intrinsic and real value, for the common places of society? Does it not promise rewards which any man may be sure of attaining, in the full proportion of his power and pains? I have no objection to saying to my reader, 'If you will be as diligent, you *may be* as great a man as Franklin;' yet in all honesty, without any intention to discourage him, I must say, *it is of all things the most unlikely.* It is much more probable that you will, with all your industry, remain in some common station, perchance where you are unnoticed and unknown, fifty miles from home. What then? Have I struck a death-blow to your improvement? By no means; for I can still promise you, singly and severally, and to a full million of you too, if you will, *magnificent* rewards. Listen, then; *You will at every stage of progress be wiser than you were* — better fitted for every duty of life — to make the best use of every advantage, and to turn every disadvantage to the greatest profit — to be useful and happy in your day and generation. I will not mock you by the offer of rewards which not one in ten thousand can gain; but I will encourage you by the assurance of those which not one in ten thousand need to miss. The true use of such remarkable examples as have been made conspicuous by their extraordinary success, is to imitate their earnestness and their pains in view of sure and intrinsic blessings. It is a farce to offer to the reader the fame or the fortunes of Benjamin Franklin; but I can say, imitate his earnestness and diligence and you *will be wiser than you were.* This is virgin gold. Are you not willing to dig for it?

If the promise of extraordinary rewards is a deception palmed upon the male community, such is the condition of the *female* portion that we cannot even encourage them to *dream* themselves into a partnership with these high aspirings. High stations, posts of honor and profit in great numbers, are open to men, and any man who will qualify himself *may possibly* rise to them; *may possibly*, qualified or not. But women! —— do what they will — their families — their homes — are their highest posts of honor and profit. Grow wiser and wiser as they may, their wisdom may be known to scarce a thousand people in the wide world. A studious father *may* rise in proportion to his growing attainments; and his son become renowned beyond all the experience and hopes of the family which gave him birth. But a studious mother, after she has doubled and again doubled her acquisitions, and again doubled them, must hold her private station unnoticed and unknown. But without reward? Nay — As she learns, she feels that 'a mother can never know enough' — nor hold her mind too well trained, too alert, in that high office to which nature has appointed her — in that little kingdom of which God has made her queen. And the sister, too, like a minister of state, aiding in the high employment of preparing minds for life and for immortality, in laying the foundation for families for many generations — the sister, as she grows to womanhood, occupied in these high employments, feels, as she improves herself, that she can never know enough for her station, as a ministering spirit in the family that gave her birth, or to which she may be called, as the queen of a future kingdom of her own. Is there a better reward of self-improvement than is gained by a studious mother, who becomes more and more qualified for the education of her children? Is there a goodlier sight than such a mother, qualified to interest as well as instruct her children — surrounded by sons and daughters, growing with her in wisdom and knowledge, and daily rising up to call her blessed?

A regard to the intrinsic and sure rewards of knowledge, is fitted not only to stimulate the people, but it affords the best assurance that the people, in their efforts at improvement, will not 'make fools of themselves,' against the *pedantry* of a 'little learning; against the vainheartedness, and out of place displays of smatterers in knowledge. No doubt the ancient and modern poet had some occasion for their reproach: —

'Ne sutor ultra crepidam.'

'A little learning is a dangerous thing;
Drink deep or taste not the Pierian spring.'

True enough, they are ill employed who are studious to no good purpose — who study only to feed their vanity, or to prate and act out of time and out of place — who study only to be and to appear to be 'great men.' Such learners were indeed better unlearned. Such shoemakers had better limit their science to their lasts. But, whoever will learn for use, will find enough to learn in his own proper sphere; and, rightly learning what is useful there, will become qualified for every advance which Providence may see fit to give him in his path of life.

I cannot forbear to add, how admirably the great principle of popular improvement — a regard to intrinsic value — is cherished by our holy religion. The folly of mankind in all ages has been manifest in their regard to the gloss and the glare, rather than the substance — to the improbable, rather than the certain. No wonder that the mass have been torpid — save here and there one, roused only to vainheartedness and pedantry. No wonder that when knowledge has been commended to the multitude only by its unattainable or most improbable rewards, that the mass have sought it not. Christianity addresses men on a better principle, and invites them to knowledge as useful and agreeable for all conditions and stations in life; cherishes contentment with any lot, however obscure, and demands the best use of our faculties for the right performance of the duties and full enjoyment of the blessings, as well of the lowest as of the highest stations in life. Ambition of high places may stimulate here and there an individual, before whom the path of wealth or fame seems to open as they proceed; but it can never urge on the mass in the improvement of the mind. Christianity, reason, common sense, on the other hand, exalt the rewards which are sure and certain, and call the whole people to earn and enjoy them.

It is impossible to close this number on 'common schools and common education,' without casting a glance at *Colleges* and *professional education*. Alas! are not our learned Professors sadly unlearned, for the lack of the very principle urged in this article? Are not the learned professions, as a mass, in a state of degradation from the absence of this principle? And by it, might they not be exalted to an influence and usefulness far surpassing all that is at present known? The thousands of ministers, lawyers, physicians — can each of them occupy high stations or have extensive fame? What then! Shall they merely jog on, satisfied with the most moderate without growing attainments? Such is, indeed how commonly, the case — the man of forty or fifty scarce exceeding, nay, scarce equalling, his former self at twentyfive or thirty. Christianity, reason, common sense, might they have scope, would introduce a new era in professional life, and in the whole state of society, which the learned professions could, on just principles, be prepared so much the more to adorn and bless. Every professional station is occupied with duties to which the highest knowledge and most improved faculties can never be equal — which call for the utmost diligence for earnest and growing improvements. The most obscure physician would, on just principles, be as studious and self-improving as Boerhave or Rush; the most obscure lawyer would emulate the diligence of Webster or Brougham; and the most obscure pastor be as devoted a student as Dwight or Chalmers. The principles of this number — the principles demanded alike by common sense and Christianity — would add more to professional endowment, than is now ordinarily given by 'professional education.' Still, as they enter upon life, the mass of professional men would find themselves mingled in the multitude, unknown to fame, and without promise of high places or great honors; nevertheless, in spheres which give scope for the highest mental improvement — for the greatest knowledge and the highest faculties; and at every step prepared for any and for every higher place, to which Providence may call them. What physicians, lawyers, clergymen, would society be furnished with, if the rewards, attainable by all, were commended and welcomed? With what lights would the whole firmament of society be lighted up? I confess, as I look upon the history of man for many thousand years, I see no ground to expect this desideratum of professional life, or of common life, except from the influence of Christianity, at once unfolding and applying the principle of improvement, except by its giving power to the intrinsic rewards.

The glance which we have given at higher education may be the more easily pardoned, when the reader is reminded, that we have actually turned our eye upon a 'third estate,' who, of course, are to be called into the service of 'common schools and common education.' I will not now refer to the direct aids which, over the whole land, professional men can render to the cause of popular improvement: I refer only to the influence they would certainly have, in proportion to their diligence in self-improvement, for the purposes of their private and public duties. What examples should we everywhere have, and what means of improvement would be everywhere afforded! This exclamation may be made especially in view of the Ministry, whose intimate connection would make their example universally known, and whose lips, both in public and private, would drop as the rain and distil as the dew, in imitation of that rich and various book which is the guide of their instructions. How different would such teachers be, from those unimproving men who occupy life in repeating the mere common places of their profession, in every place, to every man and every year alike — and in the unthinking routine of mere professional engagements. And how much less of words and more of wisdom should we have in our legislative assemblies, and in the laws and institutions to which they give rise, if every man, who is professionally devoted, and in conscience and in law consecrated, as the guardian of public morals and private rights, were continually pressing forward to higher attainments and wider views in his boundless field, and seeking to advance the science of human government itself? *Who* would then 'despair of the Republic?'

[For the Annals of Education.]

LIBRARY FOR THE POOR.

A VERY intelligent and benevolent gentleman in a remote part of England being in a certain place one evening, inquired if there was any public library in the town. He learned that there were two, one of such extent that the entrance money was five pounds, and the annual payment fourteen shillings. The other was called 'the Tradesman's Library;' the entrance to which was *one* pound, and the yearly payment *four* shillings. The first was wholly out of the reach of the poor; and the other would, by no means, reach all. 'It will not supply the young,' he replied; 'you must try another, to excite the desire of knowledge among the young and poor.'

With the aid of the minister of the parish, his lady, and a few other influential individuals, a subscription of twenty pounds was soon got up, and the donors held a meeting. It was at first proposed to allow people to read the books gratuitously; but it was at length wisely decided to cherish the natural desire of independence in the poorest and youngest, by requiring the payment of a penny monthly. It was also decided that the volumes should be small, that they might be the oftener returned. About one hundred volumes were procured.

The second week after the commencement there were above one hundred applicants, of whom about thirty were poor laborers, or solitary females, and a larger number were under fourteen years of age. Many of them had not read two hours in succession for many years before. At the beginning of the second year, they were allowed, at their own request, to pay for six months at once, instead of a penny monthly.

Among many similar proofs of the beneficial results of this library was the following, related by a member.

'Had I paid you a shilling a week, instead of a monthly penny, myself and family would have been gainers. During the winter months, I, and those like me, got home and took dinner between four and five o'clock. Then an ill-ordered house and a noisy family, induced us to go out. If the weather was favorable, we stood to talk and spend an hour at the Cross; if otherwise, we went into a smithy for shelter, and often to the public house, and though I am not given to drink, yet we had to spend a little when there; and even a little frequently occurring is felt by a poor man. When I took home my first book from the library, I was asked to read aloud, but objected because of the noisy children. After some time the younger were put to sleep, and I began to read. Next morning, and every evening after, my house was clear and in order, the fire-side trimmed, my meal waiting, the children in bed, or allowed to sit up on condition of listening as quietly as their attentive mother. The book we obtained from the library was Goldsmith's Animated Nature, and it has been highly interesting to us. And, Sir, apart from all we have learned by reading, to find week after week my own house the most comfortable, and my own family the happiest I ever saw, shows me that a poor man with a book in his hand may be as happy as the richest and most noble.'

ON THE POLICY OF ELEVATING THE STANDARD OF FEMALE EDUCATION.

ADDRESSED TO THE AMERICAN LYCEUM, MAY, 1834.

THE importance of Education seems now to be universally admitted. It has become the favorite subject, of some of the wisest and most gifted minds. It has incorporated itself with the spirit of our vigorous and advancing nation. It is happily defined by one of the most elegant of our living writers, — as the '*mind of the present age, acting upon the mind of the next.*' It will be readily perceived how far this machine surpasses the boasted lever of Archimedes, — since it undertakes not simply the movement of a mass of matter, the lifting of a dead planet from its place, that it might fall, perchance, into the sun and be annihilated, — but the elevation of that part of man whose power is boundless, — and whose progress is eternal, — the raising of a race, 'made but a little lower than the angels,' to a more entire assimilation with superior natures.

In the benefits of an improved system of Education; the female sex are now permitted liberally to participate. The doors of the temple of knowledge, so long barred against them, have been thrown open. They are invited to advance beyond its threshold. The Moslem interdict that guarded its hidden recesses is removed. The darkness of a long reign of barbarism, and the illusions of an age of chivalry, alike vanish, — and the circle of the sciences, like the shades of Eden, gladly welcome a new guest.

While gratitude to the liberality of this great and free nation is eminently due from the feebler sex, they have still a boon to request. They ask it as those already deeply indebted, yet conscious of ability to make a more ample gift profitable to the *giver* as well as to the *receiver*. It seems desirable that their education should combine more of thoroughness and solidity, that it should be expanded over a wider space of time, and that the depth of its foundation should bear better proportion to the height and elegance of its superstructure. Their training ought not to be for display and admiration, — to sparkle amid the froth and foam of life, and to become enervated by that indolence and luxury, which are subversive of the health and even the existence of a republic. They should be qualified to act as teachers of knowledge, and of goodness. However high their station, this office is no derogation from its dignity, — and its duties should commence whenever they find themselves in contact with those who need instruction. The adoption of the motto, that *to teach is their province*, will inspire diligence in the acquisition of a knowledge, and perseverance in the beautiful mechanism of pure example.

It is requisite that they who have, in reality, the *moulding of the whole mass of mind, in its first formation*, should be profoundly acquainted with the structure and capacities of that mind; that they who nurture the young citizens of a prosperous republic, should be able to demonstrate to them, from the broad annals of History, the blessings which they inherit, and the wisdom of preserving them, the value of just laws, and the duty of obeying them. It is indispensable that they on whose bosom the infant heart is laid, like a germ in the quickening breast of spring, should be vigilant to watch its first unfoldings, and to direct its earliest tendrils where to twine. It is unspeakably important, that they who are commissioned to light the lamp of the soul, should know how to feed it with pure oil; that they to whose hand is entrusted the welfare of a being never to die, should be able to perform the work, and earn the wages of heaven.

Assuming the position that *females are by nature designated as teachers*, and that the mind in its most plastic state is their pupil, it becomes a serious inquiry, *what they will be likely to teach*. They will, of course, impart what they best understand, and what they most value. They will impress their own peculiar lineaments upon the next generation. If vanity and folly are their predominant features, posterity must bear the likeness. If utility and wisdom are the objects of their choice, society will reap the benefit. This influence is most palpably operative in a government like our own. Here the intelligence and virtue of every individual possesses a heightened relative value. The secret springs of its harmony may be touched by those whose birth-place was in obscurity. Its safety is interwoven with the welfare of all its subjects.

If the character of those, to whom the charge of schools is committed, has been deemed not unworthy the attention of lawgivers, is not *her* education of consequence, who begins her labor before any other instructor, who pre-occupies the unwritten page of being, who produces impressions which nothing on earth can efface, and stamps on the cradle what will exist beyond the grave, and be legible in eternity?

The ancient republics overlooked the worth of that half of the human race, which bore the mark of physical infirmity. Greece, so exquisitely susceptible to the principle of beauty, so skilled in wielding all the elements of grace, failed to appreciate the latent excellence of woman. If, in the brief season of youth and bloom, she was fain to admire her as the acanthus-leaf of her own Corinthian capital, she did not discover, that like that very column, she might have added stability to the temple of freedom. She would not believe, that her virtues might have aided in consolidating the fabric which philosophy embellished and luxury overthrew.

Rome, notwithstanding her primeval rudeness, and the ferocity of her wolf-nurs'd greatness, seems more correctly, than polished Greece, to have estimated the 'weaker vessel.' Here and there, upon the storm driven billows of her history, the form of woman is distinctly visible, and the mother of the Gracchi still stands forth in strong relief, amid that imagery, over which time has no power. Yet where the brute force of the warrior was counted godlike, the feebler sex were prized, only in their approximation to the energy of a sterner nature, as clay was held in combination with iron, in the feet of that mysterious image which troubled the visions of the Assyrian king.

To some of the republics of South America, the first dawn of liberty gave a light which Greece and Rome, so long her favored votaries, never beheld. Even in the birth of their political existence, they discovered that the sex whose *strength is in the heart,* might exert an agency in modifying national character. New Grenada set an example which the world had not before seen. Ere the convulsive struggles of revolution had subsided, she unbound the cloistered foot of woman, and urged her to ascend the heights of knowledge. She established a college for females, and gave its superintendence to a lady of talent and erudition. We look with solicitude toward the result of this experiment. We hope that our sisters of the 'cloud-crowned Andes,' may be enabled to secure and to diffuse the blessings of education, and that from their abodes of domestic privacy, a hallowed influence may go forth, which shall aid in reducing a chaos of conflicting elements to order, and symmetry, and permanent repose.

In our own country, man, invested by his Maker with the 'right to reign,' has nobly conceded to her, who was for ages a vassal, equality of intercourse, participation in knowledge, guardianship over his dearest possessions, and his fondest hopes. He is content to 'bear the burden and heat of the day,' that she may dwell in plenty, and at ease. Yet from the very felicity of her lot, dangers arise. She is tempted to rest in superficial attainments, to yield to that indolence which spreads like rust over the intellect, and to merge the sense of her own responsibilites in the slumber of a luxurious life. These tendencies should be neutralized by an education of utility, rather than of ornament. Sloth and luxury, the subverters of republics, should be banished from her vocabulary. It is expedient that she be surrounded in youth with every motive to persevering industry, and severe application; and that in maturity she be induced to consider herself an ally in the cares of life, especially in the holy labor of rearing the immortal mind. While her partner stands on the high places of the earth, toiling for his stormy portion of that power or glory from which it is her privilege to be sheltered, let her feel that to her, in the recesses of the domestic sphere, is entrusted the culture of that knowledge and virtue, which are the strength of a nation. Happily secluded from lofty legislation and bold enterprise, with which her native construction has no affinity, she is still accountable to the government by which she is protected, for the character of those who shall hereafter obtain its honors, and control its functions.

Her place is in the quiet shade, to watch the little fountain, ere it has breathed a murmur. But the fountain will break forth into a stream, and the swelling rivulet rush toward the sea; and she, who was first at the fountain head and lingered longest near the infant streamlet, might best guide it to right channels; or, if its waters flow complaining and turbid, could truest tell what had troubled their source.

Let the age which has so freely imparted to woman the treasures of knowledge, add yet to its bounty, by inciting her to gather them with an unremitting and tireless hand, and by expecting of her the highest excellence of which her nature is capable. Demand it as a debt. — Summon her to abandon inglorious ease. — Arouse her to practise and to enforce those virtues, which sustain the simplicity, and promote the permanence of a great republic. Make her answerable for the character of the next generation. Give her this solemn charge in the presence of 'men and of angels,' — gird her for its fulfilment with the whole armor of education and piety, and see if she be not faithful to her offspring, to her country, and to her God!

L. H. S.

EDUCATION IN MEXICO.

ADDRESSED TO THE AMERICAN LYCEUM BY JUAN RODRIGUEZ.

MEXICO, MARCH 20TH, 1833.

IN comparing the situation of Mexico with what it was at the time the independence of the country was first proclaimed, its bitterest enemy will confess it has made great advances in knowledge. It owes its progress solely to *liberty,* for from a fatality inseparable from political vacillations, government pays little attention to so interesting a subject. To the scandal of philosophers, the administration which has just been deposed, at the same time that in the capital it abolished the free elementary schools, opened one, in which young men prepared themselves for appearing on the theatre. The diplomatic agents of the Republic who were in Europe, in 1830, were commissioned to engage comedians but were never instructed to purchase elementary books which were so necessary to give a new direction to the studies of youth.

An intelligent traveller will be much surprised in visiting the colleges of Mexico, in the 19th century. The Latin grammar is taught in the same way it was eighty years ago; and though indeed, they teach them to construe Cicero and Virgil, they do not analyze them; and the beauties of these justly celebrated authors are undiscovered.

The authors commonly used by the colleges of the Republic for teaching Philosophy, are Alsieni, Jaquier, Guevara, Para, and Roseli, writers, whose day is passed. The same course, however, is pursued for those young men who intend to study theology, those who are preparing for the bar, and those who are to practice medicine. The physics which are found in these books, are, in fact, metaphysics; truths, which are no longer doubted, are in them contradicted; and in studying them, the young men lose the time which might be spent usefully to themselves and the public.

In Ethics months are lost, examining the indifference of human actions, and questions on the system of probabilities of theological casuists; while they neglect the principles of universal morality which ought to be so carefully inculcated on young men in their earliest youth.

The Theology which is learned by those who consecrate themselves to the science, is, what has been forged by ecclesiastics, and disfigured by all the vices with which the learned men of polished nations have painted it. Three or four years are thus employed, and not one in the study of the Holy Scriptures.

Civil Jurisprudence is taught from the Institutes of Justinian, without method and without criticism. The masters expound doctrines which are exploded in the present age, in place of those which are adopted among civilized nations.

The study of the canons is monstrous; it is pursued without consecrating a single day to Ecclesiastical History, and it appears that they do not even aspire to a knowledge of the laws of the church; but only to support the rights of the Pope, and the episcopal jurisdiction. There is but one establishment in which there is the necessary apparatus for the study of Chemistry, Mineralogy, and the other sciences. Botany is taught in a garden attached to the federal palace; and Medicine in the university. The arrangement of this, is worse than of any of the other houses for study. It is, however, the only one in which medical lectures have been given. The professors have had the prudence not to subject themselves to the ancient statutes, and they disseminate among their scholars the more modern doctrines of medical science.

Notwithstanding what I have said in so concise a manner, with regard to the obstacles that science meets with, in these establishments intended for its promotion, the Mexicans have overcome these difficulties, and have made great progress in learning. There is scarcely any student that does not understand French; and English is growing in the estimation of those who are following a literary career. We have learned naturalists, and excellent maps of the state of Mexico have just been finished by a son of the Republic, D. Ramon de Moral. We have lawyers well-instructed in the learned works of Heineccius, and other standard authors. Among our physicians, there are men of skill, whose reputation is the result of their great application. Many persons, who from their age might be expected to be devoted to recreation and amusement, form associations for the promotion of belles-lettres, legislation, Political Economy, Geography, and other branches of equal utility.

During the administration of Yturrigaray, a gazette and a daily paper, were the only periodicals, in all that is called New Spain. Now, in almost all the capitals of the twenty states of the confederation, there are periodicals and printing-presses, multiplying daily. The freedom of the press has brought before *the people*, questions of great political and social importance; and if in Mexico, as in other countries, many things have been published unworthy the public eye, yet many dissertations on important subjects distinguished by their learning and their elegance of style and diction, have also appeared, notwithstanding that in none of the colleges the language of the immortal Saavedra is studied.

There are few schools for young children, and still fewer that are gratuitous. The most noted are those of *la Filantropia*, and that of the college of St Gregorio; in one there is 330, and in the other 520 pupils. In the former, the Lancasterian plan is pursued, and the old system in the other; in both everything necessary for the children is furnished. The first receives 3000 pesos from the public treasury; the other is supported by funds given by D. Juan Chavassia. In many of the schools, children are taught branches, which, twenty years ago, even among civilized nations were not thought of — French, Geography, Writing, Drawing, and Music. Their physical education is not neglected, the gymnastic exercises are used; and ease of manner is thought essential to fit them for society. The girls are taught all that is suitable for their sex, for the necessary business of life, and to make them appear agreeable among those of the most polished education.

There are not so many children in the free schools as might be admitted; for the poverty which induces the Americans to educate them, makes the Spaniard put them to work as soon as they are able to do anything. If the stocks become secure, public wealth will increase, and new funds will be invested for popular education; for the leaders of the democratic party are well convinced of the necessity of disseminating the first principles of learning. The present President of the Republic has sent commissioners to all the colleges of the capital to ascertain their situation, and to devise means for their increase and improvement. Such plans are worthy the attention of those who know how much liberty depends on the diffusion of knowledge.

The Mexicans, notwithstanding the great obstacles they have had to contend with, have progressed respectably though slowly, in the sciences. In a few years legislators, and governors will protect the cause of education; the establishments dedicated to it will be reformed, all obstacles will be removed, and our youth, naturally inclined to investigation, will be crowned with the laurel of Minerva, and will be the ornament of their country.

JUAN RODRIGUEZ.

[For the Annals of Education.]

INDIVIDUAL DEVELOPMENT.

THE obvious tendency of the common methods of instruction is, not to call into exercise the various faculties of body and mind, which our Creator has given to each individual for the acquisition of knowledge and wisdom. All that is done is to communicate to the learners verbal descriptions of what others have perceived, and the reflections suggested by their perceptions. By the common methods of teaching, our children are not led to *observe*, but merely to learn what observations others have made. They are not taught to think, but to receive passively what others have thought. They are not required to weigh evidence, reason and decide for themselves, but to accept the reasonings and decisions of other minds. What I mean to say is, that, in the common processes of education, our youth are not led to see with their own eyes, and hear with their own ears, and understand with their own understandings, but to receive without question the reports of other men's observations and reflections. Mind, consequently, is but the repetition of mind. All the knowledge, that is possessed by mankind, was actually acquired by a very few of the race, and from them has been received and repeated by the many. The field of truth has been entered, and labored in, by only an individual here and there. Others have lived upon the fruits of these solitary investigations. And yet every individual is probably so placed that he might, if he would, survey some portion of the field of truth under peculiar advantages. If all were habituated, as all should be, to use their own senses, and reflect upon their own perceptions, how rapidly would the bounds of science extend on every side! Where now there is one, there would be thousands of accurate observers of the works of creation, the ways of Providence and the manners of men. Thousands who now look about them 'with brute unconscious gaze,' would then be making observations with an intelligent eye, and ascertaining important facts, which might lead them or others to invaluable discoveries, in physical, metaphysical and moral science.

To this result, I repeat, the common modes of instruction do not tend. Our youth are not incited to seek knowledge for themselves, but merely to adopt the knowledge of others, and this often with implicit faith, which is enfeebling to the mind. Language, the language either of books, or of oral instruction, is the means by which alone ideas are suggested to them. Their ideas therefore are necessarily very vague, if not otherwise inaccurate; for language is an essentially imperfect medium for the communication of truth. It is obviously impossible to impart, by the best description that was ever given, the same complete idea which is given to the mind when the thing described is submitted to the observation of the senses. No words, however well adapted and well arranged, are strictly speaking, *the truth;* they can be no more than the representation, which some one may give of his idea of the truth. So that in the common methods of education, our children are not nurtured by those aliments, which our Heavenly Father has provided in rich abundance everywhere; but by such admixtures of intellectual food as human ingenuity has prepared. Thus are their minds confined in their range, and stinted in their growth. And they go through life under the sad mistake that books are the chief, if not the only sources of knowledge, and all the while, the volumes of nature, of providence, and of man, lie open, unread before them. 'Eyes have they, but they see not — ears have they, but they hear not, neither do they understand.'

In consequence, little, very little of the field of truth has yet been explored. Narrow paths are seen here and there; but on either side dense forests stand, which the eye of man has never penetrated. I would not speak disparagingly of the efforts of those who have guided our race to the discovery of what is known among men. They have done much, and deserve our gratitude and admiration. But their achievements lead us to reflect what a multitude of minds have ever been, and still are, dormant or inert. If a few individuals have done so much, what might not soon be accomplished, if all were actively engaged in the pursuit of truth? I am aware that in time past, it was the bad policy or the pride of the few learned, to discourage the pursuit of knowledge by the many. They wrapped up what they knew more than others, in a garb of mystery; and clothed the results of their observations and reflections in unintelligible phrases, which none but the initiated could understand. The day of that aristocracy of learning is past. In New England, at least, it is recognised as the right and the duty of all to seek knowledge, to the utmost extent of their power and opportunities. Nevertheless, even we persist in the general use of methods of instruction, which have come down to us from those ages when the true method of seeking knowledge had not been pointed out; and when the many were permitted to learn, only so much as the few thought proper to teach them.

I cordially grant, that our books are prepared with a more generous aim, aye, with the express intention of assisting the many in the acquisition of truth. There is, however, a fundamental mistake yet to be corrected. It is that too much dependence is placed upon books, although the original fountains of truth are sending out their streams on every side. Let me not be thought unfriendly to books. If I had the power, I should not dare to restrain the multiplication of any but such as are immoral. Those, which contain the records of discoveries, that have been made in any department of science, are of course invaluable. And those which give us discussions or treatises on any points in doubt among the learned, may be of great use in quickening the spirit of inquiry, and directing its aim. But books ought not to be resorted to as the primary sources of knowledge; and our youth should never be suffered to trust implicitly to them. They should be made to depend upon their own powers — first, to make accurate observations upon men and things, and patiently to reflect upon what they have observed. They will then be prepared to derive benefit from the recorded results of inquiries upon the same subjects, made by others, in different or more enlarged fields of observation. If all were thus educated, (as all might be who are educated at all) to be active searchers after truth, instead of passive recipients of what others have found, how fast and how far might human acquisitions be extended!

It may not be supposed, that with the help of the most careful direction of his faculties, every boy would become a Newton. But there is no doubt that each one would become an adept in some branch of science; and all would then be active agents in subduing the yet unexplored fields, where treasures of knowledge are yet to be found. Whenever I behold a group of children, I know that I am looking upon those, who possess powers of observation and reflection, that are capable of efforts, which, alas! but few may ever make — efforts not less astonishing than those which have filled the passive world with admiration. There may be, as is now generally agreed, original differences in the intellectual capacities of the children of men. Still all of them, who are not idiots, possess capacities, which few exert to the extent, which the possession of such capacities renders obligatory.

It ought to be the great purpose of education to do for every individual, what has been left in almost every instance, for accident to do, that is, to direct his faculties to those objects, in creation, providence or the relations and circumstances of man, which will give to each faculty and every affection their appropriate exercise. That education alone can be considered perfect in its kind, which aims and tends to develope the individual being; not merely to train the multitude of learners to think alike, and speak alike, and move alike; which leads the individual to exercise fully the organs of his own body — the powers of his own mind the affections of his own heart — that is, to unfold himself — to become what God has made him capable of being — to avail himself of his own opportunities for observation — to survey the physical and moral world from his own positions, rightly to appreciate the relations, which he individually sustains; and fulfil well the duties which devolve upon *himself*. Now it is obvious that the process, which shall tend to this result, must be instituted with reference to our whole nature, and to the present circumstances of our being.

DERBY.

[For the Annals of Education.]

DISTINCT ARTICULATION.

A DISTINCT articulation and a correct knowledge of orthography are two qualifications, which are too seldom found in any degree of perfection, glaring as the defect may appear. Many persons, even in reading, not to speak of their familiar conversation, mumble and confuse the sound of their words, and drop letters and even syllables frequently; and what is worse, they are often persons of a rank in society, or at least who have received such an education, as would lead us to expect better things of them. I have even heard an address to the Supreme Being completely deprived of its effect for want of a distinct articulation, which, added to the low tone in which much of it was delivered, rendered it in a great measure inaudible.

Now it is rarely the case that *natural* impediments exist in the organs of speech; and all other obstructions are capable of being overcome. Nay, even these may in some degree be ameliorated, by effort and exertion. The truth is, this acquisition is not much thought of, and its importance is not sufficiently weighed. A person can generally be understood by his acquaintances, at least, if his articulation be not perfect, or his pronunciation correct.

Indeed, if we look into the letters, or account books, of such persons, we shall find other marks of their ignorance of their mother tongue, and imagine that their writing is copied from their pronunciation. How difficult it is to find among the common, even the higher classes of a people, those whose writing is free from bad orthography! This would seem to us as inexcusable, as any on the list of common faults. It argues an inattention to the spelling-book, that famed and abundantly useful, though too often hated volume, that is highly unbecoming and derogatory to the reminiscences of scholarship. But to speak seriously; cannot a people so notorious as a *reading* people, whose libraries are well stored, cannot they, reading as much as they do, remember from the time they lay down a book till they take up their pen, how the words of their own language should be spelt? We never found any difficulty in doing this.

But we wish to apply some remedy to these evils. Not the eloquence of Demosthenes could have saved Greece, unless a spirit of action had been roused in Athens, to march against Philip, to conquer or die. The child should be taught to speak distinctly, rather than encouraged to speak rapidly and fluently. Fluency will come of practice. Thus must the evil be nipped in the bud. What the parent will not or cannot do, must be done at school. Pronunciation must be taught as a school exercise, or this evil will not be cured. No wonder, when in a school boy's dialect, the interrogation, 'Sir, may I leave my seat?' as we have practically witnessed is, '*Semme leemy seat?*' (for thus was it by many spoken in the school we had the honor to attend in our boyhood,) — no wonder, we say, that, such being the case, bad articulation should be so common among those of whom boys are said to be the miniature. Much is learned by example. The master should be possessed of a good articulation, and he should thus teach by his example, what it becomes his duty to inculcate by precept.

We would also suggest the formation in academies and schools of societies for mutual improvement, in these acquirements. We think boys might thus be made to do much in some such way to improve themselves in orthography and pronunciation.

We have heard of Lyceums, and 'all sorts of plans for improvement' in *science*, *philosophy*, &c ; but the plan of teaching people how to write and speak their own tongue, which, it is a lamentable fact, a large portion are unable to do, would be, we believe, a novel project, though not less useful than new. Why not defer teaching people Astronomy, Philosophy, Geology and Botany, till they have thoroughly learned the rudiments of their own language?

We might here speak of *bad grammar*, which is not the least disagreeable or the least general of faults in regard to language. Every one, almost, is taught grammar at school, and so every one is taught spelling and reading. But who speaks better grammar for having *studied it*, as the phrase is? Now must these things be so? Is there no way in which people can be taught what, above all things, they ought to know, a thorough knowledge of their own language? We believe there is. We assuredly believe it. We are confident that the people can be 'brought *right*' on this subject. And we feel assured that this neglect is, in a great measure, owing to the indifference and neglect, or the ignorance and disqualification, of those who are appointed to instruct the youth of our country.

Suitable men, then, must in the first place be placed in charge of our youth; and when that is done, and when the people at large feel, in all its strength, the importance of education in its elementary parts, then may we expect the state of things will be such as it ought to be, and not till then.

[From the Academician.]

EXAMINATIONS AND EXHIBITIONS.

In a recent number of the Academician and Southern Journal of Education, published at Milledgeville, Geo., we find an extract from a report by W. Baird, read before the Teachers' Society of Georgia, on the subject of Examinations and Exhibitions. The following are the views in regard to Examinations.

'Examinations should be thorough upon every branch of study, before a select number of literary gentlemen; and be conducted principally by the teachers themselves. The object of an examination being to exhibit the fidelity of the teacher — the standing of the pupils, and the true character of the school — every branch of study should be taken up — every important principle should be brought under review, and the pupil made to exhibit what he *does not know*, as well as what he does know. To effect this, he should be taken off the book as well as on it — out of the ordinary track as well as in it. He should be thrown upon his own resources — be required to take up each principle and wield it himself — to originate examples illustrative of every principle, and give the 'why and wherefore' of everything he advances. All this should be done before a select number of literary gentlemen, fully competent to decide upon the character of every performance, whose special business it should be to attend through the whole course of the examination; with unbiassed minds to mark fidelity where apparent, and collusion, when attempted, to award the palm to merit, and mark the defection of the negligent. An examination of this kind cannot fail to be a test of scholarship, and to answer the ends of its institution.

'A large assembly on such occasions, is perhaps not desirable. For though the attendance of parents and guardians affords encouragement both to teachers and pupils, a very large promiscuous audience tends to create in the minds of teacher and scholar, an unnatural excitement, affords too great a temptation to make an ostentatious display, and frequently interferes greatly with the progress of the exercises.

'Examinations, we have said, should be conducted principally by the teachers themselves. Few persons who are not engaged in imparting instruction, or in some other way unusually conversant with literary and scientific subjects, are sufficiently versed in the higher branches of study, in their minutiæ and depths profound, to go through them with the order, accuracy, and rigid scrutiny above recommended. But if ever so competent, most persons feel a great delicacy in publicly examining the pupils of another. Modest youth also dread to be examined by any but their teachers; and their perturbation of feeling often prevents their exhibiting their real attainments. Hence examinations left to be conducted by parents, guardians, or occasional visitors, can seldom be relied on as accurate tests of real scholarship. The mode of examining is frequently injudicious, generally superficial, and always irregular. An occasional question is put by one and another; the pupil becomes confused, loses confidence, answers at random, forgets, and for the time, is sensible of nothing but the glow of confusion burning on his cheek, and the chagrin consequent upon failure. The great burden of examining should therefore always rest upon the teacher. After he has gone through with a regular course, occasional questions might with propriety be put by others; but no other should be known as the regular examiner. How long a time should be spent in an examination, must depend upon the number of classes to be examined, and the number of studies to which they have attended. But if it required a week, or two weeks, we would say, let the examination be thorough. Time spent in examinations of a proper kind, is never lost. On the other hand, it generally benefits the cause of education tenfold more than the same time spent in teaching would do, were examinations entirely dispensed with. How often they should be held, must also depend on circumstances; but we are of the opinion that general and public examinations should be held at least twice a year. Quarterly examinations of a more private nature, when convenient, would also be desirable. The importance of such examinations must be obvious to every reflecting mind. Every school should rise or fall, according to its own merit. But without examinations, parents must judge principally of the character of schools by the progress of their own children. Insulated examples are seldom a correct criterion. Hence, even if parents were always fully competent to estimate the progress of their children, false impressions would probably be numerous. It is from the progress of a school "*en masse*," we are to judge of its merits; and examinations are the only proper test of that progress.'

These remarks certainly deserve the serious reflection of those who object to these public displays of their pupils, and should lead them to ascertain by inquiry and experiment, whether the evils may not be remedied by changing the mode of conducting them. The reporter then goes on to present in their favor the argument that they serve to excite the ambition of the pupils. As this is beyond debate, and is with us and many of our readers one of the most serious objections to examinations, we pass it over, and present the remarks on exhibitions.

'Exhibitions, like examinations, have their defects; and as they are frequently conducted, we consider them of a doubtful, if not entirely objectionable character, especially where they are upon an extensive scale, and of a theatrical kind. They have recently been much reprobated, and entirely excluded from some of our most respectable institutions. This is however going to an extreme. By judicious management, their objectionable features might be removed, and many benefits derived from them. Public speaking should be attended to by the male members of every school. We think therefore that exhibitions, consisting in the performance of a few, well selected dialogues, with the alternate reading of essays, and the delivering of short, pithy, and appropriate orations, select and original, are calculated to be eminently useful. But those only of the simplest kind we think commendable. Oratory is an all important acquisition, and should be cultivated at an early age; and the performance of simple plays, and spirited dialogues, the adaptation of voice, gesture, countenance, &c, to the spirit of the pieces and the character assumed, is well calculated to inspire confidence, improve enunciation, and give freedom and ease of action. But here the greatest difficulty is to be apprehended. In this adaptation, lies the great art of the successful performer. And if the pieces selected be of a complicated and intricate nature, few boys can be found in common schools and academies, capable of performing them in a proper manner. Failure here ruins all. Hence it is at great hazard that such are attempted; and a great sacrifice must always be made, either of time in previous preparation, on the part of the performer; or a failure must ensue, and a consequent torture, and sacrifice of the feelings of the audience, at seeing superior pieces unmercifully mangled. The ludicrous and riotous scenes attending the performance of such pieces are also much to be deprecated. Pieces selected for such occasions should therefore be of the simplest kind, entirely within the comprehension of the student — free from everything ludicrous, and should have a decidedly moral tendency. They should be accurately committed to memory, and be frequently acted over previous to the exhibition, with great care, and always under the immediate inspection of the teacher, or some other suitable person. Otherwise, incorrect ideas of speaking will be formed, and unnatural tones of voice, and modes of gesture acquired, greatly to the injury of the performer, and which perhaps no future exertion can remedy. Arranged and conducted as above recommended, we do not conceive that exhibitions can do any harm; and we believe that so far as improvement in public speaking is concerned, they may do much good.'

EVILS OF EXHIBITIONS OF PUBLIC SPEAKING.

[The following article from the Journal of the Institute at Flushing will give the results of experience, in regard to the evils of exhibitions, in a school of high standing.]

'We have but little partiality for the public exhibitions of oratory, which are so common in schools like our own. They have their advantages, inasmuch as they interest the pupils engaged in them, and are always abundantly gratifying to parents. Perhaps nothing is better calculated to secure popularity for a school than successful performances of this kind; for when is parental vanity more agreeably entertained than when in the acting of the boy it presages the eloquence of the man? They may serve, too, to cherish a taste for elocution; they supply an innocent subject of excitement, and in several points of view may have their uses. Accordingly, we have sometimes indulged in them ourselves; but we believe that in general they are much overrated. They are attended with serious evils, and are not productive of the principal good effects at which they aim.

'One objection to these exhibitions, is the waste of time which they occasion. Unless they are likely to do credit to the school, of course they will not be attempted. But for this purpose, they require much previous preparation. There must be many rehearsals. Each of the young performers must, by frequent repetition, be made perfect in his piece. Sentence by sentence he is taught to "speak the speech as it has been pronounced to him." All this consumes time, besides that it is apt to withdraw the attention of both instructor and pupil from other, and at least equally important matters. The exhibition being a rare occasion, everything else must yield to it. Nor would the time thus expended be lost were it devoted to instruction in *elocution*, to developing the principles of impressive speaking; but employed as it is in merely drilling a number of boys to their allotted parts in a show, it is time in a great measure thrown away. For what, after all, have the speakers acquired of the science of elocution. A B and C can recite their speeches perhaps to admiration, but in that their attainments end.

'Another objection to these exhibitions is, that they often confer distinction upon the unworthy members of a school. The only requisite for success on such occasions is a talent for declamation, and this, it unfortunately happens, is often a solitary talent. Who knows not, that the most famous spouter may be the poorest scholar, or the most mischievous idler in the community? Nevertheless at the exhibition he is the foremost man. He is the hero of the day. His are the plaudits of the assembly, while his studious and deserving companions are unrewarded and unknown. We do not undervalue a talent for declaiming; but it is manifestly unfair that on the only day in the year in which a school presents itself for public approbation, the palm should be awarded not to genuine merit, but to flourishing gesture, or "vox et præterea nihil."

'In a Christian school it will always be considered a further evil in exhibitions, that they tend so much to the encouragement of vanity and a love of applause. To show off well, to be admired, is the object constantly in view. And when we recollect that to attain this object, mimicry, buffoonery and whatever will excite a laugh are often resorted to, we must admit that the gratification is dearly bought.

'These evils, it may be said, do not always exist in the same degree, and like many other evils should be borne for the sake of the greater good from which they are inseparable. True, but in the present instance the greater good itself is uncertain. We very much doubt whether exhibitions tend to that improvement in true eloquence, which is their professed end. The instruction which precedes them may make good actors, but not genuine orators. *Eloquence is impassioned sincerity.* In its very essence it is opposed to everything artificial. It is pure nature, and indebted, perhaps less than any other excellence, to the tricks of art. Almost the only thing that can be taught with a view to effective speaking is distinctness of enunciation. Here drilling is of service, and good habits may be formed that will last through life; but gesture, emphasis, inflection, &c, must be left very much to individual feeling and manner of expression. Instruction in these points must be given with judgment. General principles only should be inculcated, otherwise the young speaker will do little more than copy his model. As Quintilian, on being asked what was the first, second and third thing in oratory, answered, *Delivery*, so we would say that the first, second and third thing in delivery is *natural manner*. Now in the most successful school exhibitions that we have witnessed, the performances of the boys, so far from displaying any natural manner, have generally been close imitations of the tone, gestures and emphasis of their instructors. They played their part very well; they were excellent automata; but to a discerning eye, gave no proof of their ever attaining to genuine eloquence. Our readers may have observed, as we have ourselves, that boys who have stood at the head of their schools in declamation, are seldom heard of in after life, as eminent men in the pulpit, in the senate, or at the bar. The contrary is occasionally the fact; but we suspect it is the exception rather than the rule.

'These had long been our views, when we met with the following in Whately's Rhetoric. As the authority of the present Archbishop of Dublin will be conclusive on the subject, we give the passage at length.

'One important practical maxim resulting from the views here taken, is the decided condemnation of all *recitation of speeches* by school-boys; a practice so much approved and recommended by many, with a view to preparing youths for public speaking in after life. It is to be condemned, however, (supposing the foregoing principle correct,) not as useless merely, but absolutely pernicious, with a view to that object. * * * If there is, as is evident, much difficulty to be surmounted, even by one who is delivering, on a serious occasion, his own composition, before he can completely succeed in abstracting his mind from all thoughts of his own voice — of the judgment of the audience on his performance, &c, and in fixing on the matter, occasion, and place — on every circumstance which *ought* to give the character to his elocution — how much must this difficulty be enhanced, when neither the sentiments he is to utter, nor the character he is to assume, are his own, or even supposed to be so, or anywise connected with him; — when neither the place, the occasion, nor the audience, which are *actually present*, have anything to do with the substance of what is said. It is therefore almost inevitable, that he will studiously form to himself an artificial manner;* which, especially if he succeed in it, will probably cling to him through life, even when he is delivering his own compositions on real occasions. The very best that can be expected, is, that he should become an accomplished *actor* — possessing the *plastic* power of putting himself, in imagination, so completely into the situation of him whom he personates, and of adopting, for the moment, so perfectly, all the sentiments and views of that character, as to express himself exactly as such a person would have done, in the supposed situation. Few are likely to attain such perfection; but he who shall have succeeded in accomplishing this, will have taken a most circuitous route to his proposed object, if that object be, not to qualify himself for the stage, but to be able impressively to deliver in public, on real and important occasions, his own sentiments. He will have been carefully learning *to assume*, what, when the real occasion occurs, need not be assumed, but only *expressed*. Nothing surely can be more preposterous, than laboring to acquire the art of *pretending* to be what he is *not*, and to feel, what he does not, in order that he may be enabled, on a real emergency, to *pretend* to be and to feel just what the occasion itself requires and suggests: in short, to *personate himself*.'

Aye, to personate himself. This is the art. Study to acquire this; or rather you have it already. Study to unlearn and undo what prevents the exercise of it. Your own manner is always best. Personate yourself.

*'Some have used the expression of 'a *conscious* manner,' to denote that which results (either in conversation — in the ordinary actions of life — or in public speaking) from the anxious attention which some persons feel to the opinion the company may form of them; — a *consciousness* of being watched and scrutinized in every word and gesture, together with an extreme anxiety for approbation, and dread of censure.'

LISTENING TO AN UNKNOWN TONGUE.

Only he that has listened for an hour or two, to an address or exercise in an unknown language, when everything around him was quiet, can appreciate the insupportable weariness of the task. And yet our children are, to a great extent, subjected to it, at every period of public worship. The almost universal consent of the community requires that children should attend on public religious instruction; and yet, by a consent almost as universal, that instruction is given in terms which are generally as unintelligible to them as Arabic. We must confess that our heart often sickens to see intelligent beings, shut up, as 'The Father's Book' describes it, between high walls, on a high seat, incapable of seeing, and unable to understand what they hear; and nothing but the security from evil influences, and the privilege thus gained for the parent, would justify in our view so irksome an imprisonment, on the day of sacred rest — the festival of Christian lands. We have looked around with astonishment, to think that the same collection of people who would rise in indignation, if the attempt were made to force upon them the Latin Liturgy, and who pour upon it ridicule and reproach without measure, never think of providing intelligible prayers and discourses for their children. On no subject have we been more anxious to raise a voice of remonstrance; but we have stopped in despair, when we have thought again, how few were to be found who could speak the language of children, or who would condescend to its weakness. Happily, our Infant and Sunday Schools have compelled some, and induced others, to attempt it; and the attention even of entire congregations has been called to the subject. An effort was made to establish a public service for children in Philadelphia, but we are not acquainted with the final results. We are happy to hear, however, of a few clergymen disposed to devote themselves to this arduous part of their profession; and of some who are ready to sustain them. We cordially wish success to the plan. We cannot better exhibit our views than in the following lively satire from the 'Western Luminary.'

'How destitute of all common sense do some men appear in their addresses to children, to colored people, and ill informed congregations! Not long since a ——— Preacher addressed a country Sabbath School in the following strain, which might as well have been spoken in High Dutch, or outlandish Guinea. With it I send the translation:'

A Juvenile Lecture.

My respected juvenile auditors:

The Deity is an invisible essence. He not only occupies the vast spaces of this mundane sphere, but fills the ethereal blue extended beyond the heavenly concave. Immensity is his antichamber; and by the omnipotent energies of his mighty arm, he conducts the movements of the heavenly orbs. And yet your inmost reins are unveiled in his sight, and he comprehends every mental emotion. Nothing is so complicated that he cannot unravel it. Nothing so minute he cannot comprehend. Nothing so obscure, that he cannot ferret it out. Nothing so insignificant, as to be beneath his ken. Nothing so hidden as to be beyond the reach of his scrutinizing glance. Infinite justice too is an attribute of Divinity;—it is therefore a logical and natural sequence, that every expression of the tongue, every overt action, and every inscrutable emotion of the thinking principle, must sooner or later pass his review. Those which are obnoxious to his immaculate requirements, will have a condemnation awarded them, which shall fully meet the requisitions and threatened penalties of an infinitely holy law; while those who habitually conducted themselves with an eye to his glorification, will be adjudged mete for the welcome plaudit, 'Come ye sanctified, enter upon the full fruition of the Deity's presence, where you shall associate with seraphic legions, be inmates in glory with redeemed myriads, shall join the music of the spheres, and with angel voices shall attune your golden harps to notes of sweeter symphony.

Translation.

An Address to Children.

My Dear Children:

God is everywhere, yet you cannot see him. And although he fills heaven and earth, and holds up the sun and stars, yet he takes notice of you. He knows all that you do, or think, or say, in the dark, as well as in the light. And since he is a just God, who punishes every one who does bad, and loves, and rewards all who do good, he will at the day of judgment, inquire into all you did or thought or said in the world. If it was bad, you will be driven away from him, as the Saviour says, "into everlasting punishment." But if what you now do is good; if what you do is done because the Bible and God tells you to do it, and you love to do as the Bible says, God will call you his children, will say to you, 'come my children, go to heaven with me, to live where I am, with holy angels, and with christians,' and there you may sing and praise and be happy for millions of years.

'The contrast between roundabout bombast, and plain pointed language, will be obvious. Many public addresses as much need a 'translation,' as the 'lecture.' Without that translation, they are in effect of no more service than mere Hottentot gibberish. Let preachers, exhorters, Sabbath school teachers, take a hint from Q.'

THE TEACHER'S ALMANAC FOR AUGUST.

THE SCHOOL-ROOM.

The season of withering heat has come. Many of our schools enjoy a vacation at this season; and for the sake of their panting, fainting teachers, we could wish this privilege were extended to all. But this again would impose a burden almost as heavy, upon each of many parents, in providing them safe employments and amusements at this critical season. Let this thought cheer teachers who are ready to sink under the oppressive heat. Let them show the spirit of sympathy and indulgence towards their pupils, and let them use every effort to preserve the air of the school-room pure, and its temperature comfortable. Neglect of cleanliness is at all times a transgression of the laws of nature — a positive sin; but at this season it may be visited with a fatal penalty. Let the school-room, and all around it, be kept scrupulously clean. Watch every source of corruption to the air in the accumulation of dirt, fermenting vegetables, stagnant water, &c, which an August sun will easily convert into floating poison. Whenever and wherever it occurs, direct immediate cleansing; or, if this is impracticable, apply lime or chloride of lime without delay. Still watch and caution your pupils against fruit; but do not forget an equally important caution, against too much exposure to the sun, a subject which children do not understand; and the improper use of cold water. Repeated instances, even this season, have proved, that the mere exposure to a hot sun may produce what is termed a 'sun stroke,' sometimes terminating in speedy death, sometimes in fever, brain fever, and even insanity. Sudden changes from a very cool place to the hot sun, violent exercise in the sun, especially bareheaded, and above all, the drinking of cold water, when the heat or fatigue have exhausted the body, increase the danger. Your pupils may escape without these cautions; but if one life should be lost for want of them, could you ever forgive yourself? Is it not worth constant care to avoid this hazard.

THE WORLD.

The heat which withers our strength is cheering to the farmer, and necessary to our own existence. A kind Providence sends it to prepare the products of the earth for our use; and every ray that scorches us, is ripening the grain on which we are to feed during the winter. Remind your children of this, when they are impatient with the heat. The general coolness of this season has left our fruits imperfectly ripe; and nothing but intense heat can give them wholesome sweetness, and thus secure one of our highest enjoyments. Insects are multiplying; and even in our climate, patience is sometimes exhausted by their attacks upon ourselves and our domestic animals. Tell your children that they are the *scavengers* provided by a kind Providence to devour the decaying animal and vegetable matter which the heat would soon render a source of pestilence. The tropical air would soon become noisome without them; and it has been remarked, that a season in which insects are scarce is always unwholesome.*

Let your pupils observe the progress of the caterpillar and other insects which injure the trees and fruits; and teach them how to prevent their ravages. Try the various plans you see proposed, or encourage them to try them. It will lead to observation, if not to success. Among other remedies, we have seen it stated, that if a hole be bored in a tree, filled with sulphur and tightly corked, those insects which so often ruin our shade as well as our fruits, may be destroyed. Point out also the birds that are employed in killing noxious insects; and show the folly as well as cruelty of killing them for amusement. If you can root out cruelty from the heart of one of your pupils, it will be more useful than to give him 'all knowledge.'

* Another striking reason is given by some for the prevalence of insects during the hot season. It is said that the heat produces a feverish state in men and animals, and as the physician often cures or prevents fever by irritating the skin with washes or blisters, or drawing blood with leeches, insects are sent to irritate the skin of animals, and thus draw off the internal heat. It is also said that their attacks compel animals to that motion which is necessary to life, but which the languor of the season would otherwise lead them to neglect entirely.

THE HEAVENS.

The season of splendid skies, especially at sunset, has arrived; and never, even in Italy, have we witnessed more splendor than in the evening clouds of the last month. Encourage your pupils to gaze at them and describe them; and try to fill their minds with admiration of the beauties of nature, and especially of the heavens. It will soften and elevate them more than all rebukes for roughness and rudeness. Venus still opens the exhibition of the starry heavens as the evening star. Do your children know that beautiful little song from the German, in the Juvenile Lyre;

'See the light is fading
In the western sky,' &c.

If you have not made the experiment, you have little idea how much these songs will cheer and assist your instructions and discipline.

Do not neglect the study of the constellations. Never go out with your pupils on a starlight evening without calling upon them to point out those they already know, and trying to show them *one new one.* Are they yet familiar with the Great and Little Bear, the Pole Star, and Cassiopeia's Chair, which are almost always visible? The beautiful Lyra is on the meridian and almost on the zenith at nine o'clock in the middle of the month. In the neighborhood of this constellation, and among the stars of the two Bears, you may now trace Draco, or the Northern Serpent. In the zodiac, Sagittarius will be on the meridian. Be advised again to consult Burritt's work; it will assist you to teach and to interest your pupils. Remind them of the immense distance of these suns of other worlds, and repeat to them some of the beautiful poetry which has been written concerning them; such as that addressed by Mr Ware to the constellation of Ursa Major, of which we can give but an extract:

'I wonder as I gaze. That stream of light,
Undimmed, unquenched, — just as I see it now, —
Has issued from those dazzling points, through years
That go back far into eternity.
Exhaustless flood! forever spent, renewed
Forever! Yea, and those refulgent drops,
Which now descend upon my lifted eye,
Left their far fountain twice three years ago.
While those winged particles, whose speed outstrips
The flight of thought, were on their way, the earth
Compassed its tedious circuit round and round,
And, in the extremes of annual change, beheld
Six autumns fade, six springs renew their bloom.
So far from earth those mighty orbs revolve!
So vast the void through which their beams descend!

'Yea, glorious lamps of God! He may have quenched
Your ancient flames, and bid eternal night
Rest on your spheres; and yet no tidings reach
This distant planet. Messengers still come
Laden with your far fire, and we may seem
To see your lights still burning; while their blaze
But hides the black wreck of extinguished realms,
Where anarchy and darkness long have reigned.'

MISCELLANY.

American Institute of Instruction.

The next annual meeting of the American Institute of Instruction will take place on Thursday, August 21st, and continue until the Commencement at Harvard University, the week following. No programme of the exercises has yet been prepared, and we cannot, therefore, give the details. We anticipate, however, a very interesting meeting. An introductory discourse is expected from Gen. Mercer, of Virginia, whose high character and deep interest in the cause of education are well known. Lectures are expected from Judge Story, Mr Sparks, Mr Abbott, Mr Mason, Dr Keaggy, of Philadelphia, Dr Jones of Washington, and other gentlemen familiar with the theory and practice of different branches of education. Several subjects of interest are also selected for discussion, to occupy the intervals of lectures. We hope, however, that every member of the Institute will come prepared to communicate some facts or principles in education from his own observation and experience. One great object of the Institute, the interchange of opinions, has hitherto been imperfectly accomplished. The body of members have expected too much from the acting officers of the Institute who reside upon the spot, and whose leisure is fully occupied in mere business arrangements. Let each member spend half the time devoted by them to this object in preparing to contribute his portion of information, and none will go away complaining of the want of interest and usefulness in our meetings.

Lectures on the Pestalozzian System of Music.

We are gratified to state, that a course of Lectures will be given during the present month, by the Professors of the Boston Academy of Music, on the Pestalozzian system of instruction. It is designed to furnish persons already acquainted with music, who wish to teach singing to juvenile classes or in common schools, with a knowledge of the simple and admirable method of instruction devised by Pfeiffer and Nageli. It will, therefore, require but a short course of lectures. They will commence on the 19th August. Two lectures will be given a day, at such periods as may be convenient to those who attend the lectures of the Institute, and the whole will be completed in ten or fifteen days. Those who desire to obtain a knowledge of this method cannot hope for a more favorable opportunity.

New-York University.

The University of the city of New-York held its first commencement the last month, at which nine young men delivered orations and received their first degree.

Literary Premiums.

A deposit has been made with the Life Insurance and Trust Company of New York to be distributed in premiums for lectures adapted to children, each to occupy half an hour in reading,— on the following topics:

'1. On the application of Science to the useful arts: — for the best course of lectures, on which a premium of two hundred dollars will be paid.

'2. On the the principles of Legislation — the premium will be one hundred dollars.

'3. On the intellectual, moral, and religious instruction of the youth of this State, by means of Common Schools — the duty of affording such instruction — and the improvements of which the system may be susceptible — a premium of two hundred and fifty dollars.

'4. On Agriculture and Horticulture: — a premium of one hundred dollars.

'5. On Political Economy: — a premium of one hundred dollars.

'6. On Astronomy, Chemistry, Mechanics, Electricity, and Magnetism: — a premium of two hundred dollars.'

These lectures are to be published in a duodecimo volume of about 350 pages, in long primer, and to be distributed gratuitously, to be read in the Common Schools of the State of New-York. The first period assigned for giving the premium having expired, and few essays having been received, the period is now extended to June, 1835. Essays are to be addressed to Messrs John C. Spencer, Canandaigua, B. F. Butler, Albany, or Philo C. Fuller, Genessee.

Progress of Schools in France.

We are just informed of some of the results of the law for the establishment of public schools in France during the year 1833. The minister of public instruction despatched circular letters to 39,000 teachers, pointing out to them the nature and importance of their profession. Answers were received from 13,850 of this number, which furnished pleasing evidence of their ability and zeal. Of the normal schools, or seminaries for teachers, long since ordered to be established, there were only three in 1828, and thirteen in 1830, and thirtyseven in 1832. Now, there are sixtytwo, containing 1944 pupils preparing to be teachers, of whom all but 273 are supported by the public purse or by village treasuries. Of 37,187 communes or villages, 20,961 have voluntarily taxed themselves for the establishment of primary schools; 16,126 still neglecting it. Only 760 unions of feeble communes, for the support of a school have taken place. Of all the communes 10,000 only have school-houses, and these expended during the year 1833, in purchasing buildings and repairs, 3,000,000 of francs, or about 600,000 dollars. In the course of 1834, 1,850,277 francs, (about 370,000 dollars) already voted by the municipal councils, will be appropriated to the same objects. The whole sum necessary to furnish every commune with a school-house is estimated at 72,679,908 francs, or about 1,400,000 dollars, which would be paid, however, in fourteen years by a grant of 100,000 dollars annually.

The number of boys' schools increased in one year from 31,420 to 33,695, and the number of pupils from 1,200,713 to 1,654,828.

Church Schools.

The Methodists of Illinois propose to organize their conference into a 'Common School Education Society,' and to establish schools under the direction of teachers of their own denomination. If the anti-religious party of our country succeed in banishing the bible and all religious instruction from our common schools, they will compel other denominations to take the same course. We hear complaints from every quarter, that our common schools are, to a sad extent, schools of vice. To multiply them, without providing some security against the corruption resulting from accumulation, would be to increase the evil; and efforts for their *increase* ought ever to be attended with efforts for their *improvement*.

Investigation of Schools in Connecticut.

We have more than once spoken of the low state of public schools, even in Connecticut, where a fund, now amounting to $1,939,738 and yielding an interest of more than $100,000, secures gratuitous instruction to every child. We are gratified to see that the legislature have appointed a committee, consisting of the Secretary of State, the Comptroller of Public Accounts, and Rev. Wilbur Fisk, D.D., to inquire whether any, and if any, what, alterations in the laws relating to common schools, are necessary to raise their character and increase their usefulness. Such a committee ought to be appointed in every state in the Union, and authorised to examine its schools, if we are to hope for any improvement in the state of public instruction.

Movement in Pennsylvania.

We have stated in a former number the interest which appeared to be excited in Pennsylvania, in the establishment of a system of public schools. We rejoice to see a corresponding voluntary movement on the part of individuals in the wealthy county of Bucks. A few gentlemen at Newtown invited a county meeting, which was well attended, and of which Antony Morris, Esq., a zealous advocate of the manual labor system, attended. A committee appointed at the previous meeting presented a report, developing the wants of the state, maintaining that the only sure method of improvement was in *creating public sentiment*, recommending 'social organisations' as the best means, and advising the formation of a society for the county of Bucks. The report was approved, and a constitution adopted. Resolutions were then passed expressing the opinions of the meeting on the importance of education to the social, political, and religious prosperity of our country, deploring the apathy with which it has been regarded, and 'protesting' against its continuance; and concluding with a resolution, 'that they err exceedingly who suppose that the cheapest education is always the best, and '*that every American citizen has a direct personal interest, in making the business of teaching a profession both of respectability and emolument.*'

The board of managers were then directed to correspond with their fellow citizens on the subject of calling a state convention of teachers and the friends of education at Harrisburg to deliberate on the best means of promoting its progress.

We cannot but regard the course proposed here as the only effectual one for the advancement of the cause. Were the friends of education but half as active as our political partizans, we might, in a few years, call forth a set of voluntary associations, devoted to the cause of education, in every state and every county in the United States; and we believe nothing is wanting but a centre of action, to produce this result at once in the northern states. Will not our readers undertake, each in his own sphere, to promote such an organization, and favor us with an account of the result whether pleasant or painful? It will be accomplishing much to know our own condition.

Education of Africans.

Two young African princes have been sent to this country to be educated by the Maryland Colonization Society. They are stated to be manly, intelligent looking boys of 14 and 16 years, and have excited much interest at meetings of the Society where they have appeared. This circumstance is pleasing not only on account of the hope of good resulting from it; but as an evidence of the confidence of the chiefs on the western coast, in a nation that has so deeply injured Africa.

A school has been recently established at Grand Cape Mount, under the direction of Baptist Missionaries.

Religious Instruction of Slaves.

A report has been made to the Presbyterian Synod of South Carolina and Georgia on the subject of the religious instruction of the colored population, which advocates in strong terms, not merely its safety but its importance. They urge that there will be a better understanding of the relation of masters and servants, which will lead to more kindness on the one hand, and more faithfulness on the other; that it will cultivate principles and feelings which will soften the character of the slave, will banish his superstition, and promote the love of peace and industry; that it will promote the morality and religion of the white population, by diminishing and removing those vices which infect all who witness them, while it will furnish the slave with that light and hope, which it is the highest duty of Christians to furnish them. It is with peculiar pleasure that we see such a report, drawn up by men familiar with slaves in the states where their numbers are greatest, and meeting with boldness and triumphant argument the objections which are brought. May their plea be heard!

Schools among the Choctaws.

Twelve schools are soon to go into operation among the Choctaws, in addition to those previously provided. The teachers and their families are expected to instruct the natives in farming, spinning and weaving, as well as in the ordinary branches of elementary instruction, and are to receive $500 a year. School houses are to be erected at the expense of the government.

Lexington Manual Labor School.

We observe from a recent account of this institution, designed for both sexes, that it combines horticultural with mechanical labors, and that Drawing, Music, the Spanish, French, and Hebrew, are among the branches taught. The examination is stated to have been very satisfactory.

The Bible in Schools.

We find the Bible announced as one of the text-books of the Lexington Manual Labor School. In the female department of Bradford academy, under the care of Miss Hazeltine, it has been studied and illustrated by charts for fifteen years. Among the papers of some of its pupils, have been found extended notes of the instructions received in this way, which proved both their value and the interest they excited. As we have already stated, it was the 'book of books' in the seminary of Mr Emerson; and exerted an influence on the character of its pupils, more valuable than that of the whole circle of sciences.

Number of Teachers required in the United States.

In an article prepared with great care for the Annals of Education, August, 1833, we estimated that the whole number of white children in the United States, south of New York, from 5 to 15, stated in the census of 1830 at 1,840,000, could not then amount to less than 2,000,000. Pennsylvania has but 1 in 3 of its children at school; Kentucky but 1 in 9, according to the best estimates. If we considered the ratio of Pennsylvania as extending over the southern and western States, there are not less than 1,400,000 children destitute of common instruction. To supply these, estimating thirty pupils to a school, (which would probably be too large an allowance in the thinly settled portions of the country) would require 40,000 teachers for fixed schools; or if the plan of circuit schools should be adopted, and we suppose four as the average supplied by a single teacher, 10,000 would still be requisite to instruct those who are destitute of all instruction. To fill the places of those now employed, who are incompetent to their office, and who obtain employment only because no persons of suitable qualifications can be found, would greatly enlarge the number. But in order to keep up the present inadequate supply of instruction, if we leave out of view all over 15 or under 5 years of age, the annual increase of the class of our population between 5 and 15, amounting to 75,000 a year, would require an annual increase of 2500 teachers for the new comers. In order to fill the vacancies which death and change of occupation are continually producing, the estimate must still be enlarged — even if we allow every incompetent teacher to keep his station — even if we neglect the multitude of emigrants, who bring in whole families among us, in absolute ignorance.

The work to be done is indeed great — almost sufficient to discourage all effort. But if we are not prepared to abandon our country to ruin, its magnitude is only an additional reason which commands us to BEGIN, and to trust to Providence for success, in a work which he will approve.

NOTICES OF BOOKS.

The Father's Book, or Suggestions for the Government and Instruction of Young Children, on principles appropriate to a Christian country. By Theodore Dwight, Jr. Springfield: G. & C. Merriam, 1834. 12mo. pp. 200.

The book before us possesses one quality of peculiar value in a work on education. It gives us, in a simple, unpretending series of maxims and examples, the results of a judicious father's experience and observation, and careful study of the habits and feelings of childhood, in his own family, and among successive classes in schools, which his love of infancy led him to instruct. On this ground, we think it claims the attention of every young parent, and we believe it will secure his confidence and interest his feelings. The introductory remarks on the general principles of education are sound and important. The succeeding chapters treat of Health, Moral, Religious and Intellectual Instruction, Playthings, Amusements, Exercise, Discipline, Domestic and Social Influences, Habits and Manners, and Schools. On each of these topics we find many hints, many instructive details, which are rarely met with in works of this kind, accompanied by examples and illustrations, which prove that they are not the invention of a mere theorist. We can cordially recommend it as one of the 'First Books' of the parent's library, and would gladly extract some of its interesting anecdotes, if our limits would allow it. The author considers education, throughout, as involving all the faculties of man and the whole period of his existence. The chapters on religious instruction are based upon the 'evangelical' views of the author.

Remarks on the Classical Education of Boys. By a Teacher. Boston: Hilliard, Gray & Co. 1834. 18mo. pp. 120.

In the small volume under this simple and unassuming title, we have found more good sense, and more practical views on this subject, than in many of great size, and of still greater pretensions. The author advocates with much force, the method of Ascham and Locke in the study of the languages, and urges the employment of every species of oral and visible illustration, in reference to manners, customs, scenery and history. Above all, he urges that the study should be thorough, not of the form and accents of the language merely, but of the spirit of the authors which are studied. The views expressed in regard to other branches of study are generally sound and interesting; and we think that teachers, who have not '*stereotyped*' their opinions and plans, will find this book well worth perusal.

The Young Ladies' Assistant in Drawing and Painting. By Maria Turner, author of Rudiments of Drawing and Shadowing Flowers. Cincinnati: Corey & Fairbanks. 1834. 12mo. pp. 72.

We cordially sympathize with the author in her feelings concerning those 'awful hieroglyphics' so often preserved in 'the best room,' as specimens of progress in the fine arts, which are *interpreted* to mean, pictures of Moses in the Bulrushes, 'Memory weeping over Beauty,' &c, &c; and we fully agree with her in believing, that drawing and painting are highly valuable as branches of education, and that they may be employed, when sufficiently cultivated, in recapitulating and fixing the knowledge of objects and events acquired at schools. We are not qualified to judge whether the directions and recipes of this work are correct, but in regard to its character, we may give the opinion of a correspondent. — 'It appears to have been intended as a manual on all or nearly all the arts connected with drawing and painting, and contains some useful directions, or at least such as might be useful in more complete treatises, devoted to each of its multifarious departments. The book is not sufficiently elementary for the novice, and is too much so for the proficient in the arts. As a text-book, it is evidently deficient; but as a collection of hints, to be accompanied by oral instruction, or to be resorted to by those who are already acquainted with the rudiments, it may prove useful.' From the title-page we presume it is designed to follow some other work.

The House I Live in. Part I. The Frame. For the use of Families and Schools. By William A. Alcott. Boston: Lilly, Wait, Colman and Holden, 1834. 18mo. pp.

We know not how the want of elementary instruction for children on the Human Frame, could be better supplied than by the little book before us. It presents a subject, in itself usually considered dry, in an allegorical manner, which renders it intelligible as well as interesting; and will give to children more distinct ideas of the bony structure of our frame, than their parents have usually possessed. We have already given specimens from it; and the readers of the Juvenile Rambler have seen others. We have heard it spoken of in very high terms by medical men, and the author has lost no opportunity of giving the practical and moral results of his instructions. We know of no work which resembles it; and we cannot but regard it as an indispensable volume in the child's library. We hope the author will go on with his plan, and soon furnish our children with a complete introduction to a study, which it is surprising to find so long neglected — the study of themselves.

AMERICAN

ANNALS OF EDUCATION

AND INSTRUCTION.

SEPTEMBER, 1834.

SKETCH OF EDUCATION IN THE REPUBLIC OF MEXICO.

Communicated to the American Lyceum at its Fourth Annual Meeting, by LORENZO DE ZAVALA, *Mexican Minister to France.*

IN our last number we inserted a brief account of the state of education in Mexico, which presents painful as well as encouraging views of that rich and noble country. We now publish another article, containing additional details on the same subject, addressed to the American Lyceum, by a Mexican gentleman, whose intelligence and character leave us no room to doubt the existence of evils, which we would gladly believe to be over-rated. It enables us to account for the unhappy state of that republic, and of others in the southern part of the Continent, whose struggles and disorders seem rather like the restlessness of a fever, or the contests of rivalry, than like patriotic efforts for rational liberty. Is there no mode in which the philanthropy of our own country can aid, in removing this cloud of darkness from one of the finest portions of our continent, and preventing the evils which it produces and threatens, not only to its inhabitants, but to all surrounding countries? Might not a foreign school enterprise have the same effect on our efforts at home, that foreign religious missions have produced in increasing the zeal and activity for home missions? Is there no one who would delight to visit the imprisoned minds of Mexico? Are there none who would deem this an enterprise worth sustaining? We cannot but hope, that the perusal of this painfully interesting account may excite some interest on the subject.

SKETCH OF EDUCATION IN MEXICO.

DURING the period of one year and eight months, which has elapsed since I became associated with this society, it has not been in my power to fulfil the obligation which I imposed upon myself, to give an account of the state in which we find the instruction of youth in the Mexican Republic. This has been owing to engagements of a different nature, which have occupied my attention, and prevented me from attending to this important object; and although I am still not less employed, I shall devote a few hours to the task of communicating to you some information, that you may lay before the Lyceum a general view of education in my country.

You cannot be ignorant that one of the fundamental principles of the Spanish colonial system was, not only to keep the people in the most entire ignorance, but to pervert their education, even from the first elements. Hence it happened, not only that the greater part of the colonial towns were destitute of schools, but that such as existed were established under a method of instruction which tended to convert the youth into subjects, trained to passive obedience, as well to the ecclesiastical as to the temporal or political power. The consequence was, that those men among us who were called learned, and sages, were those who had best learned the doctrines of the Catholic theologians, and the elements of Aristotle's dialectics, with the commentaries of ignorant critics. It was impossible, in the midst of so great obscurity, to perceive the true principles of enlightened philosophy, to understand social duties, or to improve popular education. The guardians of independence did not know all that was necessary to a people destitute of education, and therefore could not foresee all the consequences of so great a deficiency. Here your society will perceive the cause of the numerous errors, committed in our political and moral calculations.

In proportion as we have become convinced of the impossibility of sustaining any species of free institutions without universal education, we have devoted ourselves with great ardor, to the extension of primary schools. The Lancasterian system was first known in Mexico in 1822, when a school was established, called "The School of the Sun," under the auspices of a society. In the whole extent of that vast territory, there was but a single institution of that character. As the federal form of government had not been adopted, and those which are now states, were then provinces, very little progress was made until 1824, when the states became independent. Since that period, the progress may be regarded as rapid, considering the unhappy circumstances of the country.

In the first place, there was a great want of instructors. The society will scarcely suppose that teachers are not to be found in Mexico, capable of instructing in the first rudiments of knowledge, at least in an imperfect manner. The members of the American

Lyceum can hardly conceive it: yet unfortunately it is a fact. In my own state, Yucatan, the Lancasterian system is not yet known; for there is not a person there who can teach it. The rudiments of arithmetic were hardly known in the three schools which existed in 1822 in Medrida, a city of 36,000 inhabitants. At the same time, the whole state of that name, with more than 600,000 inhabitants, contained at the utmost, a dozen schools! But what schools! It is melancholy to say it: but, in order that your society may be able to know, by comparison, what we were and what we are, I will give a rapid description of the state in which the country formerly was.

The principle by which all movements were excited, was terrorism. The youth saw, not only in the teachers of the primary schools, but even in the colleges, tyrants, who inspired unspeakable terror in the tender minds of the young. I recollect when I saw in my primary school-master, a fierce enemy, and trembled whenever I met him in the street. I also recollect, that the Rector of my college, a professor of theology, attempted to chastise me one day, and would have succeeded if some of his friends had not interfered. I ought to inform you, that the theological class was the highest in my college.

The only books used in the primary schools is that called the "Christian Cato," (it will doubtless be asked by what art Cato could be made a christian, so long anterior to our Saviour,) and the Catechism of Father Ripalda. Both are the most servile and degrading authors to be conceived of, fitted to make men slaves, and at the same time false, revengeful, and flatterers. In those schools, however, which I have spoken of, although so bad, the pupils were taught to read and write. In the villages and smaller towns, the boys and girls were taught only to repeat certain prayers.

What I have said of the state of Yucatan, you are to understand as applying to the other states of the Mexican confederation; for education was in the same condition everywhere, with few exceptions. Among these exceptions was the state of Mexico; for it contained an university and four colleges: but I should prefer the happy ignorance of other parts of the country, to the useless and fallacious learning which was there to be found. In consequence of the influence of such institutions, independence, and more recently, reforms, have constantly encountered the greatest obstacles in Mexico, Puebla, and some other points, where the greatest amount of the false and empty science of the Spanish Theologians and Sophists had been accumulated. Add to this, the precautions taken in former times by the Inquisition, to prevent the importation of all kinds of books calculated to enlighten the understanding, and you may form some idea of our moral condition at that epoch.

Since the establishment of the Federal system, the governments of the states have not ceased to make exertions to establish primary schools, and to improve public education in all respects. From the school established in 1822, many instructors went abroad to different points of the Union; and the Lancasterian system has been propagated with the same rapidity as the benefits of inoculation. The states which have chiefly distinguished themselves are Mexico, Zacetecas, Jalisco and Tamaulipas. In the first, I have the satisfaction of having established more than five hundred schools, with fifty-eight thousand scholars of both sexes, who have been instructed in reading, writing and the first elements of arithmetic. Some of those schools may be compared with the best in this admirable country; and from them, youths will proceed, within three years, prepared to study other branches of education corresponding with their condition and inclinations.

In the city of Mexico, primary education has advanced in an extraordinary manner. Among many others, there are three schools for females, in which are taught Reading, Writing, Drawing, Music, Arithmetic, Geography and History, as well as the useful arts and duties appropriate to the fair sex. It is very gratifying to me to state to your honorable society, that these seminaries of virtuous females will hereafter yield fruits of great value to the Mexican nation. Besides the schools conducted by natives of the country, there are several under the care of French teachers, in which I have had the pleasure of seeing and hearing the pupils speak three languages—the Spanish, French, and English. If to all this is added, the change made in the literary establishments of the capital by the Vice-President, Don Valentino G. Farias, under the authority of the Congress, important improvements may be anticipated in the education of the Mexicans.

The present Vice-President of the Republic has arranged the course of studies as follows.

1. The Preparatory class, in which are taught Latin, Greek, English and French, the elements of Arithmetic, Algebra and Geometry, as well as the principles of Religion.

The 2d. class embraces Ideology and Humanities: Logic, the Morality of nature, Political Economy, Literature, general and particular, and Profane History.

The 3d. embraces the Physical and mathematical sciences; the German language, Mathematics, Natural Philosophy theoretical and experimental, Cosmography, Natural History, Chemistry and Geology.

4th. Medical science, including its various branches.

5th. Jurisprudence: Roman, Canonical, Political, National and Natural law, and the Law of Nations.

6th. Ecclesiastical sciences, embracing duties towards God, the councils, the holy fathers, Practical Theology and Sacred History.

I have thought it proper to give these particulars of the course of general education in my country, because it must produce a great change of ideas within a few years. The spirit breathed by the newspapers of that republic, the spirit of liberty, frankness and tolerance, begins to presage the happy future which awaits us, if we remain as now under a liberal administration.

In Tampico de Tamaulipas, one of the places with which this city carries on much commerce, a school has been established, embracing all branches, from the first elements to Latin and philosophy. And here it is due to Don Tomas Rossell that I should mention him as the chief patron of that institution, which was founded by the municipal authorities.

The second obstacle which we must encounter in Mexico, in attempting to generalize education, is among the indigent class of inhabitants, whose moral capacity is even inferior to that of the savages of the forests; not because they are naturally more deficient in talent, but in consequence of the state of degradation and debasement in which they have long been kept. Among two hundred Indians, scarcely one can be found who knows how to read, in the vicinity of the large towns. Among those who dwell in the villages and remote places, it would be very difficult to find a single person able to read and write. Ninety in an hundred of them are ignorant of the Spanish language. What an insurmountable obstacle is this to their instruction!

We find then three fourths of our population in such a state of ignorance, that we can hardly hope, in two generations, to change the moral aspect of that class of Mexican society. This consideration ought to weigh much in the calculations to be made concerning the stability of democratic institutions in the southern parts of America; because, the will of the majority being the basis of power, it is difficult, if not impossible, to obtain a result which shall be the certain effect of a free and intelligent vote, from a people in such a condition.

The third obstacle to the propagation of instruction among us, is the scattered state of the population. This difficulty is not felt in the United States, of the North, where one or two persons may be found in every place ready to undertake the task of teacher, without interfering with their other occupations. Besides, the desire to learn is so general, and I may say, so inherent in the people of this Republic, that it supplies all deficiencies, and smooths every impediment. In Mexico, on the contrary, our remote villages and small towns, are inhabited by people, who, generally speaking, have no desire to advance in knowledge, nor to learn to read or write. It is also to be recollected, that they subsist by daily labor, are unacquainted with the comforts of life, and still more with the moral enjoy-

33*

ments of civilization; and their ignorance is so great, that they have no conception of the possibility of living better.

Religious education there is none, among this class of the inhabitants, in the meaning of the term in which religious education ought to be understood. On Sundays and festivals, they go to church to hear mass, which lasts twenty minutes or half an hour. It is well known, that although the Catholic mass is a solemn and impressive service, it has no connection with public instruction. After the mass, the parish priest or vicar stammers out a few words on the gospel for the day; but generally speaking, neither does the minister understand the meaning of the text in the Evangelist, nor are the people capable of understanding it.

The Holy Scriptures, being the basis of religious education, and the reading of them being prohibited to the Spanish people, your society may infer what is the state of Christian instruction in the Mexican Republic. Hence results the gross superstition which is generally diffused; the despotic influence of the clergy over the greater part of the inhabitants, and intolerance, which is even sanctioned by the constitutions of the Union and the States. The study of the Bible has been, and is now, confined to a small number of persons; and ten out of a thousand do not know even the signification of the word. They therefore speak of Jesus Christ without knowing his doctrines, and without reading his gospel; and through the explanations of school-masters, they learn a few formularies, and hear the sermons of persons generally little instructed in the Scriptures. The result is, that there is, in fact, very little religion; for it cannot exist without some knowledge of what is believed and professed.

The present influential directors of opinion in Mexico, persuaded that the introduction of other creeds among the Catholics would excite the desire for instruction and study, have maintained, even on this ground, the philosophical doctrine of liberty of worship. The exclusive prevalence of one form of worship by giving, so to speak, a monopoly of the conscience to the Catholic ecclesiastics, renders them despotic, and confident in their power, which is thus erected on the ignorance of the people.

The greatest obstacle to the extension of education among the native population, is the variety of languages. In Yucatan, the Mayan tongue is spoken; in Tabasco, the Mexican, the Zoque and the Chontalpa; in many of the states is found the Otomi; and finally, the Tarazco has more than eighteen different languages, which cannot be traced to any common origin. By what means shall instruction be propagated in such circumstances? Many ecclesiastics are ordained on the ground that they know one of these tongues; and without any other knowledge, are authorized to assume the important office of administering baptism, confession and communion, with other ceremonies of religion. Such, gentlemen, is the deplorable condition of education among the greater part of the natives of the Mexican Republic.

On a future occasion, I shall have the honor to address to your honorable society my observations on our plan for improving the moral condition of my fellow-citizens, hoping for their noble and enlightened co-operation.

I am, Sir, your friend and servant,

LORENZO DE ZAVALA.

REVIEW OF COMBE'S LECTURES ON POPULAR EDUCATION.

Lectures on Popular Education, delivered to the Edinburgh Association for procuring instruction in useful and entertaining Science, in April and November, 1833, *and published by request of the Directors of the Association.* By GEORGE COMBE. First American edition, with additions by the Author. Boston. Marsh, Capen & Lyon. 1834. 12mo. pp. 130.

THE work before us contains much that is sound and interesting and practical on a subject which is *professedly* among the most interesting in our country, but which, as a matter of *practice*, requiring *thought*, and *effort* and *sacrifice*, is treated with shameful apathy, by the mass of parents and citizens.

The first lecture is occupied with an inquiry into the nature of education, and the imperfect character of what is now called by that name. The second discusses the importance of learning more of objects and their relations, gives an account of the German method of education, and urges the importance of the scientific instruction for the laboring classes. Mr. Combe insists that education ought to be so conducted, as to improve *the whole nature of man;* that in our general course, the ancient languages occupy a place far too prominent, that knowledge itself has been too much neglected, from the exclusive attention devoted to those branches which are only the means of knowledge, and that the moral sentiments should be cultivated, no less than the intellectual powers.

One point of the first importance to the improvement of our race is here urged with great force. It is, that the discoveries and inventions of modern times, and the vast amount of labor-saving machinery, are designed by providenee, not to increase the wealth of the few higher classes, or the luxuries of the lower, but to accomplish the object designated in its name,—*to save bodily labor*, to leave the mass of men more at liberty to improve their minds, and cultivate their social affections. He maintains that the laborer, with the ordinary hours of toil, is generally unfit for the active exercise of his intellectual and moral powers, and that the progress of society is intended to secure him this privilege. He asks,

"Can we believe that God has bestowed on us the gift of an almost creative power, solely to increase the wretchedness of the many, and minister to the luxury of the few? Impossible. The ultimate effect of mechanical inventions on human society appears not yet to be divined. I hail them as the grand instruments of civilization, by giving leisure to the great mass of the people to cultivate and enjoy their moral, intellectual and religious powers."

In examining this subject, Mr. Combe observes, that "the industrious classes, or great mass of the people," are rather "organized machines than moral and intellectual beings."

"The chief duty performed by their higher faculties is not to afford predominant sources of enjoyment, but to communicate so much intelligence and honesty as to enable them to execute their labors skilfully and with fidelity. I speak, of course, of the great body of the laboring population; there are many individual exceptions, who possess higher attainments, and I mean no disrespect even to this most deserving portion of society; on the contrary, I represent their condition in what appears to me to be a true light, only with a view to excite them to amend it."

In inquiring whether it is not practicable to elevate them from this semi-rational state, he observes,

"To attain this end, it would not be necessary that they should *cease to labor*; on the contrary, the necessity of labor to the enjoyment of life is imprinted in strong characters on the structure of man. The osseous, muscular and nervous systems of the body all require exercise as a condition of health; while the digestive and sanguiferous apparatus rapidly fall into disorder, if due exertion is neglected."

"Exercise," he adds, "is labor;" and on the well established principles of physiology, confirmed by the experience of our manual labor institutions, that exercise is most beneficial to health, which involves some useful end, without too much thought or responsibility. He admits the importance of agriculture, manufactures, and commerce, but he maintains that they are not the ends of human existence; that the labor necessary to the rational pursuit of these occupations would be salutary and useful; and that it is rendered a source of degradation by its excess.

"My proposition is, that after ten or twelve hours of muscular exertion a day, continued for six days in the week, the laborer is not in a fit condition for that active exercise of his moral and intellectual faculties which alone constitutes him a rational being. The exercise of these powers depends on the condition of the brain and the nervous system; and these are exhausted and deadened by too much muscular exertion. The fox-hunter and ploughman, fall asleep, when they sit within doors, and attempt to read or think. The truth of this proposition is demonstrable on physiological principles, and is supported by general experience; nevertheless, the teachers of mankind have too often neglected it. The first change, therefore, must be to limit the hours of labor, and to dedicate a portion of time daily, to the exercise of the mental faculties."

He argues that this limitation is a necessary result of the improvements in the arts and sciences, when these shall be diffused over the earth. The amount produced by human labor, as at present conducted, will far exceed human wants, and men will be compelled to labor less, because they will receive no reward for excessive effort. And this, he maintains, is the design of our Creator.

"It is clear that muscular power, intellect, and mechanical skill, have been conferred on him (man) with the design that he should build houses, plough fields, and fabricate commodities. But assuredly we have no warrant from reason or revelation for believing that any portion of the people are bound to dedicate their whole lives and energies, aided by all mechanical discoveries, to these ends, as their proper business, to the neglect of the study of the works and will of the Creator? Has man been permitted to discover the steam-engine, and apply it in propelling ships on the ocean, and carriages on railways, in spinning, weaving, and forging iron,—and has he been gifted with intellect to discover the astonishing powers of physical agents, such as are revealed by chemistry and mechanics,—only that he may be enabled to build more houses, weave more cloth, and forge more iron, without any direct regard to his moral and intellectual improvement? If an individual, unaided by animal or mechanical power, had wished to travel from Manchester to Liverpool, a distance of thirty miles, he would have required to devote ten or twelve hours of time, and considerable muscular energy, to the task. When roads and carriages were constructed, and horses trained, he could, by their assistance, have accomplished the same journey in four hours, with little fatigue; and, now, when railways and steam-engines have been successfully completed, he may travel that distance without any bodily fatigue whatever, in an hour and a half: And I ask, for what purpose has providence bestowed the nine hours, which are thus set free as spare time to the individual? I humbly answer, for the purpose of cultivating his rational nature."

The same argument is equally applicable to branches of manufacture.

"Before steam-engines were applied to weaving and spinning, a human being would have required to labor, say for a month, in order to produce the woolen, linen, and cotton cloth, necessary to cover his own person for a year; in other words, the twelfth part of the time of each individual would have been required to be spent in making raiment for himself, or, in case of a division of labor, a twelfth part of the population would have been required to be constantly engaged in this employment. By the application of steam, the same ends may be gained in a day. I repeat the enquiry, For what purpose has Providence bestowed the twenty-nine days out of the month, set free by the invention of the steam-engine and machinery? These propositions are not stated as statistically correct, but as mere illustrations of a proposition, that every discovery in natural science, and invention in mechanics, has a direct tendency to increase the leisure of man, and to enable him to provide for his physical wants, with less laborious exertion. The question recurs, whether, in thus favoring the human race, the object of Providence be, to enable only a portion of them to enjoy the highest luxuries, while the mass shall continue laboring animals; or, whether it be, not to enable *all* to cultivate and enjoy their rational nature?"

He disapproves, however, entirely, the course of those who diminish their hours of labor, and demand the usual wages. He proposes that the hours of labor be diminished an hour at first, and that the laborer give up the price of the hour. The increased demand for laborers will gradually raise the price in a prosperous country, and then there would be room for additional retrenchment.

The third lecture is on the education of females. Mr. Combe urges the importance of making this education conform to the ultimate destiny of woman. Next to the attention required to secure health for herself, he deems it of the first importance to obtain that knowledge which will enable her to secure it to the frail beings committed to her care.

"For many years, the lives of children depend almost exclusively on the care of the mother. Young women, therefore, ought to be taught, not only to regulate their own habits so that they may preserve their health and vigor, but also how to treat children, both as physical and mental beings. This information would be attended with great advantages, whether they subsequently discharged maternal duties or not. The very study of the structure, functions, and proper treatment of human beings, with the view of exercising kindly affection towards them, would be delightful in itself; and the young students, if they did not become mothers, would at least be sisters, aunts, or friends, and could never want opportunities for the practice of their knowledge. Information of this description is not neglected by women with impunity. It appears by the London bills of mortality, that between a fourth and fifth of all the children baptised die within the first two years. There is no example among the more perfect of the lower animals, of such a vast mortality of their young, when external violence is withheld; so that woman, with reason, and morality, and religion as her gifts, makes a poor figure in her maternal character, contrasted with the inferior creatures, acting under the guidance of pure instinct. Much of this mortality arises from imperfect health in the parents themselves, so that the children are born with only a feeble embryo of life; but much is also owing to injudicious treatment after birth.

As one among examples of the results of this ignorance, he mentions the following in the early part of the work.

"Every day affords examples of the truth of this remark. Two young ladies, when in infancy, lost both parents, but sufficient property was left to give them what is called a good education. They were reared in a fashionable boarding school, and in due time the elder was respectably married. When her first child was born, she was extremely perplexed.—Never having lived where there were infants in the family, she had no opportunity of learning *by experience* how to rear such tender plants, and never having been taught any thing of the structure, or functions, or wants, of the human being, she possessed no principles by which she could direct the treatment of her child. In her anxiety to do it justice, she asked the advice of every female visiter, and was speedily bewildered amidst the incongruous recommendations which she received. Unable to decide for herself, she adopted now one plan and then another, till in a few weeks the unhappy infant died. This is an extreme case, but an intelligent female friend, who communicated it to me, had no doubt that the child perished through lack of knowledge."

That the evils resulting from the ignorance of mothers are great and extensive, is known to every intelligent physician. That such evils should be allowed to exist without any attempt to provide a remedy, that a vast amount of time and money should be spent in making females of the higher classes familiar with every other branch of knowledge, and that branch alone be neglected which is necessary to prevent them from shortening the life, or destroying the health of the objects of their care,—is an astonishing instance of negligence and prejudice in our plans of education on this point. Mr. Combe expresses his opinion in the most decided terms.

"One important branch of female instruction, therefore, ought to be the treatment of children as physical beings. Lectures should be instituted to communicate this information, and the basis of it ought to be anatomy and physiology. The minutiæ of these sciences need not be treated of, but all the leading organs, and their uses should be explained. It is a great error to suppose, that this study is necessarily shocking and indelicate. It is so only in the eyes of ignorance and prejudice. Lascivious descriptions of the *abuses* of the bodily functions are extremely injurious to the youthful mind, and the enemies of knowledge have represented this to be the instruction which I recommend. Nothing can be more unlike it. The Creator has constituted every organ of the body, and we contemplate his workmanship in studying its structures and uses. To call this indelicacy, is to libel Eternal Wisdom. The Creator has taught the inferior creatures to rear their young successfully by instinct, but he has not conferred this guide on the human mother. One of two conclusions, therefore, appears to follow. He has intended either that she should use her faculties of observation and reflection, in acquiring all the knowledge requisite for the proper treatment of her offspring, or that she should recklessly allow a large proportion of them to perish. One or other of these conclusions is really inevitable, because, as He has denied her instinct, and as she cannot obtain knowledge to supply its place, without application of her intellect to the study of the laws of nature, which instinct prompts the lower creatures to obey without knowing them, the Creator must have intended either that she *should* study these laws, or give up her offspring in vast numbers to destruction. The latter result actually happens to the enormous extent just mentioned, and if it be the necessary consequence of the Creator's gift of reason, in place of instinct, to women, I submit to condemnation; but if it be the natural effect of their not having employed that reason in a proper direction, I say that He has commanded them to study His works."

Such is an outline of the principal topics discussed in this interesting work. The last two lectures especially, deserve the careful attention of every friend of improvement, and we hope they will be extensively read and carefully weighed, by those to whom they are especially addressed.

EXCESSIVE STUDY IN CHILDREN.

One of our correspondents has made some remarks in reference to the dangers of excessive study in children. We take this method of replying to them, because we have heard them from other quarters.

It is an error to ascribe to *Phrenology*, the views which are now so common, in regard to this danger. They had an earlier origin, and rest on a broader foundation. They are the results of medical observation and physiological research, confirmed by the maxims of experience. Who has not heard the familiar sayings on the short life of forward children? Has our correspondent never seen the medical testimony concerning cases in which disease of the brain existed, which could be ascribed to no other cause? If not, we beg leave to refer him to the lecture of Dr. Reynolds before the Institute, in 1833, and to the little book of Dr. Brigham.

But it will perhaps be more satisfactory to state the grounds on which these conclusions rest. We presume our correspondent is familiar with the fact, that adults, in cases of fever or ill health, or after any accident which affects the head, are often forbidden to read, or think closely; and sometimes even conversation is prohibited. This is done, because the brain is too much excited, and *every effort* of *mind* increases this excitement. The evil is not the less, when there is a disposition to mental effort. On the contrary, the very excitement often increases the disposition and the capacity for reading and thought, while it renders both peculiarly dangerous. The same prohibition is often given to persons who are free from disease, but laboring under that susceptibility of excitement, that comparative weakness of the system, which attends convalescence from sickness.

Now the infantile brain and nervous system always have much of that extraordinary excitability and weakness which belong to the feeble convalescent from a long disease. The very texture of the brain is soft, and the danger of distending its vessels with blood, of producing inflammation or dropsy is far greater than in adults.

This condition renders the brain peculiarly liable to excitement in childhood; and then, it is obvious, that the danger of mental effort is greater than in adult age. The danger is for the same reason, often greatest, where the disposition to reading and study is strongest. It is, therefore, in direct contradiction to the principles of physiology, and the practice of the best physicians, to assume that we may always safely permit a child to study as much, and go on as rapidly, as it is disposed to do *voluntarily*. We are assured on the highest authority, that the brain of a child is often in a state of unnatural excitement from its birth, or from early infancy, and that this is frequently the cause of what is usually called precocity or forwardness. If it be said that the rule is at least safe, in regard to children in health, we answer, that we have more than once known a brain fever come on by steps so insidious, that no one perceived danger, until it was too late to avert it. The unusual energy of body and mind which it often produces, may even lead some to infer extraordinary power of exertion. We have known one most valuable life lost from an error of this kind. We have known a pupil who was a victim to the disease, when its first approaches were so little obvious to common eyes, that all complaints were treated by the parents as merely fanciful, and when it had advanced so far that study became painful, it was ascribed to indolence! What teacher could forgive himself, if ignorance or prejudice should thus lead to the sacrifice of a single pupil, and that one, probably, peculiarly fitted for usefulness!

It is possible that the evil, as a practical one, has been exaggerated; and it would be a perversion of the cautions given, to indulge the mass of pupils in indolence. But we have no doubt of its existence; and we are equally confident that it has shortened many a valuable life, and entailed permanent suffering upon many a feeble constitution, where no *immediate* evil seemed to result. We know more than one instance of this kind.

The fundamental error lies here;—We have formed a plan of education adapted to our own views, calculated to relieve parents as soon as possible from the care of their children, and to gratify their anxiety or vanity, by bringing forward their children as rapidly as possible, and then we conclude, that every thing which interferes with this plan is *wrong!* If children do not accomplish all that *we expect*, it is ascribed to indolence or obstinacy; and that disposition to activity which the Creator has implanted, in order to exercise and invigorate every limb, and which struggles against our artificial plans of confinement to a school bench, is branded as "mischief" or "idleness," is converted by our arbitrary rules into disobedience, and then, a salutary instinct of nature is punished as a crime! We were struck with the remark of a teacher of fourscore, who had acted to some extent on these principles,—"*We often punish children for the faults of their bodies!*"

And let no teacher deceive himself by thinking that he does not urge his pupils on, and that therefore there is no danger. The air and manner of a teacher, the atmosphere and spirit of a school, will often drive on an active, and especially an ambitious mind, more urgently than all the machinery of pedagogical spurs and whips, applied to pupils of a different character. The desire to gain the teacher's smile of approbation, or to give him pleasure, will often urge a susceptible pupil to desperate efforts; and this, where there are neither prizes nor ranks to excite emulation.

We do not attempt to give rules or directions. They must be adapted to individual cases, and they should be founded on knowledge and observation. We only warn against the danger of bringing our plans in collision with those of the Creator, of demanding premature efforts, and "of punishing children for the faults of their bodies."

HEINROTH ON THE EDUCATION OF INFANCY.

(Translated from the German.)

We have often put the question to parents, at what period of infancy moral discipline should begin, and we have heard various ages assigned, from six months to a year. But in watching the management of early infancy, in observing one child incessantly fed and dandled, and yet incessantly fretful, in seeing another burst into distressing outcries, if its wants were not gratified at the instant, in remarking how another would submit, with comparative quiet, to be laid down when it desired to move, and suppress its cries when its gratification was delayed,—above all, in seeing how the infant of poverty, or of savage life, submits to be left unnoticed and unattended, while its mother toils the livelong day for a subsistence, and can only snatch a few moments of repose to feed and fondle her nursling, we could not but ask, whether the *first want* and the *first gratification* do not in fact commence the course of moral discipline. Is not the question often, if not always, settled in early infancy, whether the appetites and passions shall be established with uncontrollable despotism before the dawn of reason, or whether they shall be kept in their appropriate and subordinate place, until reason assumes the throne? On points like this, we are anxious to present the results of wider experience and deeper research than our own; and we have been gratified to find in a work of Heinroth, Professor of Medicine in the University of Leipzig, opinions expressed which entirely accord with those which observation and reflection have led us to form. We present our readers with a translation of the passage, and earnestly recommend it to the attention of mothers especially, as containing the results derived from extensive experience, by a man whose medical knowledge, and whose reputation as a writer on education, give his opinion high authority.

'When a child enters the world, its education is commenced by its physical treatment,—by the manner in which its bodily wants are provided for. As it is the offspring of love, so it should be cherished in the arms of love, from the first moments of its life. We take it for granted that it is blessed with a healthful, virtuous, and affectionate mother. She is the angel who is to watch over that frail existence, and guard it from accident; she should suffer nothing in the elements of nature, nor surrounding circumstances, neither cold air, dazzling light, excessive heat, or oppressive clothing, to excite the child to pain. Even its first nourishment should not be given till the want begins, lest injurious excitement be the consequence; and it should not be given more freely, or more frequently than this want absolutely requires.

'The *first day* of the infant's life must be greeted with *order* and *temperance;* and both must preside over its whole future management. As one sense after another developes itself, each should be supplied with agreeable objects; for cheerful circumstances produce cheerful dispositions. No obstacle should be allowed to the free play of all the limbs and muscles—nothing which will hinder the development of life and strength—and no undue pains must be taken to excite even these; let them advance quietly and naturally.

'The look and voice of the mother's love should be the first food of the infant soul. Life itself is joy; let joy cherish the germs of life. The sight and the touch soon find appropriate objects; but even now must the spirit of education watch over the child. It must not grasp all in its reach; it must not touch the flame, or the knife, or in short, any thing injurious to it. As soon as it learns to hear, it learns to listen to its mother's voice, that is, to obey. The ear gradually becomes the spiritual leading-string of the growing man. The child cannot see and touch, without *desiring*, and does not desire, without exercising *the will*. His first will is *self-will*, and it soon takes root and strengthens, if the will of the mother does not promptly meet, and gently, but firmly check it.

'Here then, education must begin,—with the first want, and its supply. It begins, therefore, immediately, with the physical treatment of the child, for its first wants are only physical. Every mode of treating an infant is wrong which does not satisfy its wants in the right way, and peculiarly wrong is every unseasonable or excessive supply. The first wants of infancy are food, warmth, air, motion and sleep. A greater number of children suffer from an excess of these comforts, than from too scanty a portion of them. It is true, bad nourishment, confined air, want of cleanliness and of free exercise, and unquiet sleep arising from these causes, destroy many children who are left to the care of hireling nurses. But on the other hand, a greater number suffer from the peculiar care of an over-anxious mother, from superfluous nourishment, and excessive wrapping, from guarding against all those influences of air, deemed pernicious, from artificial motion, and from the sleep thus artificially produced and maintained. In this way, many of the most favored nurslings leave the world when they have scarcely entered it. It is not however with the dead, but with the living that we have to do. Few mothers will allow themselves to be charged with too little care or indulgence; and even experienced nurses avoid it from prejudice and disposition. Let us then examine the errors in physical treatment, arising from excess, and particularly from excess in food.

'It is a most pernicious custom to stop every cry of a child with food, whether it is done from the idea that it needs so frequent nourishment, or to make it quiet. Inquire why the infant cries, and remove the cause, if it can be discovered. It will be more rarely the want of food, in proportion as it has been accustomed to regularity. If the child is irregularly fed, it acquires bad habits, it departs from *order*, ("Heaven's first law,") whose first principles should be implanted in man while instinct still governs him. But the infant who is thus accustomed to excess, soon becomes *inordinate* in its demands, and TEMPERANCE and ORDER, the great pillars of life, are both overthrown. It will become greedy when it is unseasonably fed, even with simple food, and the evil becomes still greater when it is pampered with delicacies. An artificial necessity is produced for continual gratification of the palate, so that it will often not be pacified without having something pleasant to the taste constantly in its mouth; and upon this, the whole enjoyment of its young life depends. The sense of taste checks the progress of every noble sense; the child concentrates its whole thoughts on the enjoyment of this single appetite. In this way, it is prepared to become, not only an epicurean, but a sensualist; and the obvious evils of overloading the stomach and producing disease are not the only evils arising from this treatment. The *moral character* is also injured before it is fairly developed. The child thus miseducated, becomes obstinate and self-willed. If its demands are not satisfied, (and its cries are demands,) it will soon learn to fret itself, almost, into childish insanity. See now the seeds of moral corruption implanted in the physical soil, whose roots strike deeper in proportion as they are sown earlier!

'Whence is it that we so frequently see this pernicious physical treatment, and its natural fruits? Why do we see so many over-fed, gormandizing, ill-humored, selfish and self-willed children? The combined power of three great causes are at work:—*maternal love, vanity*, and *ignorance*. We may venture to say, every mother in her senses loves her child more than she loves herself. How can she then refuse to give him any thing! Food is the most obvious comfort, the greatest pleasure he enjoys, and she gives it freely. She wishes her child to *thrive*, to become strong, vigorous and fleshy. And now *vanity* comes in play. Every mother is vain of her child, and would fain have it the finest, and for this purpose also it is excessively fed. Yet this does not happen without the third cause,—*ignorance*. Ignorance does not perceive that the thriving of the child depends upon the quantity which it digests, rather than upon the quantity it swallows, and overlooks the great medium, which it does not understand, the organs of nourishment, whose office it is to prepare *nourishment* for the body, from the food which enters the stomach. Only so much food as the child really digests does it any good; what remains undigested is a source of evil.

'As these bad habits began with blind and injudicious affection, so they end with the same. How *can* one who loves a child so much, give it pain! When the necessary consequences of this treatment appear, and the child becomes ill-humored, selfish and self-willed, and beginning, very early, to worry its mother; this blind and weak love, incapable of resistance, pleads, "*The poor child cannot understand yet.* The understanding is not developed the first year. Let it grow older, and then I will educate it." In the mean-time, before the understanding is developed, the child is *miseducated* and *spoiled.* The first use it makes of the understanding, is in tormenting the mother; and it soon becomes a little tyrant. There are too many mothers of this sort, who are slaves to their children. They reap only what they have sown.'

EFFECTS OF MATERNAL INDULGENCE.

We have expressed more than once the pleasure we felt on finding the subject of education occupy so much more attention of late in other periodicals, &c., and have given several extracts. We add another striking article from the Albany Journal and Telegraph.

'Messrs. Editors,—Of the solemn character of the duties devolving upon mothers, all writers agree to express the same sentiment. Where these duties are neglected, where a mother's fondness controls all without judgment and intelligence, the most unhappy consequences follow. I do not know where these have been drawn out in a more vivid and awful picture than in the late work, entitled Guy Rivers. It does not fall within your line to have to do with such works, yet I trust you will allow me to furnish an extract which does fall in with the practical object of your paper. Guy is a highwayman—a murderer—a cold blooded murderer—an outlaw—of most violent, headlong passions, which pause at nothing where their gratification is concerned, and yet he is a man of great shrewdness and of superior natural intellect. At the point where the extract is made, this man's course is approaching its catastrophe. In his den he sees its approach, and his mind is occupied with bitter reflection. With his Lieutenant this is his conversation; and when I think of what I have known of maternal weakness, I shudder to think how near to the life the picture may be.

'"I do you wrong, Dillon—but on this subject I will have no one speak. I cannot be the man you would have me; I have been schooled otherwise. My mother has taught me a different lesson,—her teachings have doomed me, and these enjoyments are now all beyond my hopes."

'"Your mother!" was the response of Dillon, in unaffected astonishment.

'"Ay, man—my mother. Is there any thing wonderful in that? She taught me this lesson with her milk—she sung it in lullabies over my cradle—she gave it me in the plaything of my boyhood—

her schoolings have made me the morbid, the fierce criminal, from whose association all the gentler virtues must always desire to fly. If, in the doom, which may finish my life of doom, I have any person to accuse of all, that person is—my mother!"

'"Is this possible? Is it true? It is strange, very strange."

'"It is not strange—we see it every day—in almost every family. She did not *tell* me to lie—or to swindle, or to stab. No! Oh no! she would have told me that all these things were bad—but she *taught* me to perform them all. She roused my *passions* and not my *principles* into activity. She provoked the one and suppressed the other. Did my father reprove my improprieties, she petted me and denounced him. She crossed his better purposes and defeated all his designs, until at last, she made my passions too strong for my government, not less than hers; and left me, knowing the true, yet the victim of the false. What is more,—while my intellect, in its calmer hours, taught me that virtue was the only source of true felicity, my ungovernable passions set the otherwise sovereign reason at defiance, and trampled it under foot. Yes—in that last hour of eternal retribution, if called upon to denounce or to accuse, I can point but to one as the author of all—the weakly, fond, misjudging, misguiding woman, who gave me birth. Within the last hour, I have been thinking over all these things. I have been thinking how I had been cursed in childhood, by one who surely loved me beyond all other things beside. I can remember how sedulously she encouraged and prompted my infant passions, uncontrolled by her reason, and since utterly unrestrainable by my own. How she stimulated me to artifices, and set me the example herself, by frequently deceiving my father and teaching me to disobey and deceive him. She told me not to lie, and she lied all day to him, on my account, and to screen me from his anger. She taught me the catechism to say on Sunday, while during the week, she schooled me in almost every possible form of ingenuity to violate all its precepts.

'"She bribed me to do my duty, and hence my duty could only be done under the stimulating promise of a reward. She taught me that God was superior to all, and that he required obedience to certain laws, yet as she hourly violated those laws herself in my behalf, I was taught to regard myself as far superior to him. Had she not done all this, I had not been here and thus: I had been what I now dare not think on. It is all her work. The greatest enemy my life has ever known has been my own mother."

'"This is a horrible thought, captain, yet I cannot but think it true."

'"It is true. I have analyzed my own history, and the causes of my character and fortunes now, and I charge it all upon her. From one influence I have traced another, until I have the sweeping amount of twenty years of crime and sorrow and a life of hate, and probably a death of ignominy, all owing to the first ten years of my infant education, when the only teacher that I knew was the woman that gave me birth."'

This is a fictitious tale indeed, but it is sadly true to nature. We have seen the victim of indulgence trained by the mere neglect of restraint to a violence of passion which reviled and abused the mother that bore him. We have known the abandoned son turn with doubled fist and furious gestures to his mother, and tell her, —"*You* have trained me to all this." We have known those who escaped this dreadful fate, mourn through life, the mental suffering, or the bodily debility, which the mistaken indulgence of a mother's love had entailed upon them. And if the *man* could always look back with the skill of Heinroth to his early childhood, even when no gross neglect of discipline was to be discovered, would he not accuse her early and excessive indulgence of his dawning appetites and craving desires as the source of that violence of passion—that obstinacy, which cost him so much painful discipline in youth, and perhaps still poison the peace of his manhood? Is there no argument, no appeal which can reach the heart of those mothers, who are sacrificing the future peace and character and hopes of their children, to the mere pleasure of gratifying them for the moment?

HABITS OF ORDER IN SCHOOLS.

HINTS TO YOUNG TEACHERS. No. 6.

"ORDER is heaven's first law,"—and in no place, perhaps, is the importance of this truth more decidedly felt, than in a school-room. Nothing can be done without order,—or rather, without it, all that may be accomplished, is not only done ill, but will be more than likely, in a continuance of the same system, to be counteracted. The teacher should emphatically, "have a place for everything, and everything in its place,"—in his own mind, as well as in all the arrangements of his little domain. Regularity and consistency are parts of this order, and he should have every thing governed by uniform rules, though it may not be well always to make these rules apparent; for if his own mind be in perfect subjection to order, it will be a difficult matter for even the most wild and unruly spirits to disarrange the school. But every living being feels and sees the beauty of order, when he finds himself in it, and surrounded by it; and it will become one of the teacher's most efficient helps, if properly brought into play.

In the first place, then, have stated hours of admission, which are *never to be infringed*, without an excuse in writing, from the parent's own hand. The propriety of this regulation, in a school for little children, is often doubted, but it must be by those who have no conception how much depends upon it. Besides, if it be understood to be a regulation, not in any case to be dispensed with, (and this must be enforced by action as well as words,) parents will very soon, for their own sakes, fall into it. They will think it better to rise a little earlier, or be a little more punctual at their breakfast or dinner hour, than to have their child sent home again, or be forced to the trouble of preparing an excuse. But after all, the most efficient method of insuring the performance of this regulation, and indeed of every other, is by a teacher's influence on the mind of the child himself. If his school-room be as dear to him, as it ought and easily may become,—if the face of his Instructor be the face of a friend, and the employments of the school hours those of enjoyment, there will be no difficulty in making it an important point to *him* to be there always in season; and the inclinations of the youngest child generally receive attention at home, when those inclinations are praise-worthy and good ones. The difficulty will be still less, when he grows older, and his little arrangements become of his own choosing. All these minute affairs are considered truly such, when habit has rendered them things of course; but even in trifles, why should not a good as well as a bad habit be formed, and why should it not be formed early? It will be for the lasting benefit of the child as well as the teacher;—and, whatever trouble it may cause parents to regulate so nicely the habits of their children when young, it will be more than repaid afterwards; for their duty will in this respect be done, the seed will be sown; and that parent who knows what it is to see his child, when arrived at years of comparative discretion, constantly tardy in going to school, to say nothing of tardiness in rising, tardiness in obeying, and a habit of procrastinating all the little duties of his life, would think himself richly repaid, could a little additional trouble ensure better habits. As with this, so with other things, apparently trivial. Do not indulge your pupils in carelessly throwing down of their garments, when they enter and leave school, in the careless use, or rather *mis*use or abuse of books, slates, pens and pencils, &c. Do not allow the desks to be disarranged. Many people seem to think, that the same good habits, &c., are not required for infantile minds, which become all important when these minds are more advanced. I cannot be of that opinion, since it is contrary to all the experience of nature to deprive the flourishing sapling of anything necessary to the full grown tree; and a judicious education, will only help out nature by directing and ordering the requisite and *proportionate* quantity of that nourishment, which nature herself ordains and supplies as well for the child, as for the youth. Orderly, healthy habits of mind, come eminently under this head. The teacher should always provide against the necessity of disorder, by having regular places for each child to hang its own things—to arrange its own property. But its attention should not be confined to its own only; it should be taught to feel an interest, if not a care in the property of others, and that harmony of feeling, which it is so delightful to witness, and which is so apt to be wanting in a promiscuous school, at least so far as the kinder and better emotions are concerned. The old worn distich of Pope, on " vice,"—peculiarly applies to habits which ultimately lead to it,—habits of disorder; for the eye and the mind, which has been accustomed to consider neatness as important, and to practice all its maxims, will nevertheless soon become accustomed to the contrary, however " disgusting " and " hateful " at first, particularly if it find, that all the individual care which may be taken, is lost, and hardly needed among a community of contrary habits. There is nothing more easy to fix than habits of order, or the reverse, if precept be constantly attended by example. And when I urge the teacher to insist on these things, I would not be understood to advise the use of arbitrary authority. By no means. I believe there are few children who need to be governed by it,—and comparatively few cases when it need be used. Above all, it is unnecessary as a general principle in regard to things of which we are now speaking. A school may be almost wholly, and almost always, governed by love. I consider it a far more powerful stimulus " in the long run," than fear can be, certainly a more continuous and abiding one, and in every thing relative to daily habits of mind and character, it is, in general, all sufficient. A teacher's grieved look, disapproving tone, or strikingly changed manner, will have ample effect, if he and his pupils are on the proper footing with each other; and even when this conduct has no immediate effect, a continuance of it is usually seen to make its way to the heart of the erring one. The teacher should stand uniformly in the light of a tender and affectionate parent, surrounded by friends and children; the errors of one should be felt by the whole community; and the particular improvement or good behavior of one, should be marked with delight and social pleasure by all. And this is no vain theory; it may become fact, and every teacher can do much toward making it so. As an instance,—suppose the teacher enters his school, and sees the floor of his entry covered with loose garments, against his wishes and his commands. Instead of the customary smile and " good morning "—he remarks the disorder to the scholars. It is probable that each will be eager to affirm, that it was no fault of his—but that *somebody else* must have thrown them down. Suppose without taking notice of this, the teacher should remark emphatically, " It is no matter who did the mischief—since any of you can so easily remedy it. I trust, hereafter, whoever sees *any* article of dress on the floor, he will remember *my wishes* and put it into its place—whether it be his own or belonging to any of his little companions. The one who so remembers me, when I am absent, surely loves me best." If with some remarks of this kind, the teacher *himself*, before the eyes of all, hangs up the disputed articles, it is probable he will see a universal smile of affection on the faces of all, mingled with a little shame on some,—and afterwards, I do not believe the fault will soon again be committed. Most of the children, if not all, will be desirous of pleasing their Teacher, when it can be done so easily. What is at first done from this motive, soon becomes a habit,—and the teacher may thus slide over the difficulty with very little trouble. But should it not be so, should he be disappointed in the good feelings of his little flock, and some be found among them so indifferent to his gentle reproofs, or his affectionate request, I should *enforce* the rule, though on so trivial a subject, quite as much as if it were a more important one. I cannot now speak of arbitrary rewards and punishments, and on the extent to which it appears to me they should be carried, but need only observe that I approve this regimen of love and gentle motives, only so far as these can effect the end proposed.

I have before remarked, that the teacher should never be interrupted while attending to one lesson, by the questions of those otherwise employed,—or, at least, if any accident make it necessary, the lesson going on should be suspended, till they are answered. However young the child, and however trivial his lesson, the *proportionate* vigilance and attention, is to be preserved. It is not trivial to him—and he deserves as much of the teacher's attention, as any of those more advanced in their studies. And the custom in some schools, of putting off the little ones, to be taken care of by the other pupils, or an ignorant assistant, is very unjust, to say no more. It is to avoid this necessity, arising from a want of time, that I have recommended a small number of pupils. I do not here refer to the monitorial system, as a system, or of the regular habit of permitting the elder pupils in small private schools, to assist their teacher; but I allude to the practice of occasionally doing so, carelessly, or from a pressure of business. I am aware that a teacher may acquire a habit of attending to more than one thing at one time, for this I fully learned from experience; but these double employments must be within his own mind, and regulated there. He must not attempt to come in close contact with more than one mind at a time, since, however his own may be enabled to carry on its operations, those of the pupils, with whom he is communicating, may be injured by his doing so. It is certainly far easier to play at two or more games of chess at once, than to carry on two or more separate and subtle philosophical arguments at the same time; and children sometimes make cunning antagonists, if not at philosophy. While, therefore, unimportant questions, asked for the sake of asking, should always be discouraged, sensible ones should be invariably answered with attention; but the children should all acquire the habit of so arranging their own time, studies and thoughts, as to gain all the requisite attention of the teacher, without infringing upon the rights and the comforts of their neighbors; for thus only can order be preserved, and the instructor, with his pupils, be enabled to pursue their duties, unmolested by continual interruptions.

AN UNSUCCESSFUL EXPERIMENT.

THE practical knowledge of mankind has never been advanced without experiments, and seldom has any art or process been rendered in any degree perfect, without many unsuccessful experiments. We believe this is true of education also; and we regard accounts of such experiments, whether successful or unsuccessful, as highly important documents in the Annals of Education. Indeed, we are persuaded, that the account of those which are unsuccessful is often most useful, by preventing the waste of time and effort by others. It is with this view that we insert the following article from the Journal of the Flushing Institute, a periodical to which our readers are already indebted.

' "What harm is there in reading novels?" asks one of our young friends—for novel reading has for the most part been subject to a standing veto in the Institute,—" at home I read as many as I choose." "Have not clergymen," asks another, "delivered eulogiums on Walter Scott? surely then, in a christian and literary institution, we ought to be encouraged to read him." "Yes," adds a third, "and that will do more to improve our taste than all the Greek and Latin. Besides, it is so pleasant a way of gaining information; I am sure I have learned more of English history from Henry Neill's Romances, than if I had read Hume twenty times over." "And then," say a half- a dozen, "we shall be so quiet and orderly in the evening, if you will only supply such entertaining books." These, and similar arguments from our young sophisters, we had listened to and answered an hundred times, and sometimes, with a good nature that was construed into permission of the desired indulgence, when we learned that they had set on foot a Library of "useful and entertaining knowledge." This we thought a very clever project, and were glad to encourage it; for where is the father of eighty children who would not rejoice at every addition of innocent amusement in his family? The Library was opened, and not a little were we surprised to find what a choice collection of tales, novels, annuals, &c. were arranged on its shelves; some thirty or forty volumes of the lightest kind of reading. This would never do. But what was to be done? Shall all these choice volumes be proscribed? That will be robbing the Library of its very attraction. Shall we issue an "index expurgatorius?"—that will be regarded an act of bigotry, as vile as any that ever came from the Vatican. Here was a problem in our politics; for our little world, as well as the great world without, is to be governed by measures of expediency. Our government is necessarily a monarchy, and we have to take care that our loyal subjects do not sometimes suspect it of despotism. Accordingly we determined to try the effect of licensing novels within certain bounds. For a dozen or twenty of inferior volumes, we gave in exchange a complete set of Miss Edgeworth, and sanctioned the Library on condition that its fictitious works should be those only of Scott, Cooper, Washington Irving, and the authoress just named, with such others as should from time to time be authorized. This we thought better than a sweeping proscription. We adopted the opinion of the anti-temperance men,—that moderation in an indulgence not positively wrong, is better than total abstinence. Our young friends of course were pleased with the arrangement. They thought it exceedingly liberal, and for awhile we were quite satisfied with it ourselves. The problem, we hoped, was solved. Only those availed themselves of the license who seemed to have been accustomed to it at home; and the captivating pages afforded a quiet pastime that did not encroach on the hours appropriated to study. Thus it was at first; but by degrees the younger members of the fraternity we found were acquiring a taste for "elegant literature." The history, the moral tale, and the instructive story, were laid aside for "the Pilot," or "the Tales of my Landlord;" and as we walked around the study, on approaching a desk the novel would be adroitly slipped aside that had taken the place of *Sallust* or *Legendre*. Now it was one of the articles in the charter of the Library, that its entertainment should be restricted to the hours of leisure; but after a little while, novels were to be seen open on some desks at all hours. In the meanwhile we constantly preached moderation, prescribed in individual cases how much of a boy's reading might be of the kind in question, and took various measures to ensure the success of our experiment. But it failed; and we came to the conclusion, that moderation in novel reading, however desirable, is not one of the lessons to be learned at school; at any rate, that it is a difficult lesson, which we may be well excused from adding to the tasks of a Christian Institute. We were obliged to make new regulations for the Library, (which, in justice to those who formed it, we must not omit to say, contains also many useful books,) and to tell our youthful literati, that for further acquaintance with fictitious literature they must wait until the vacation. Parents, in their families, may regulate this matter according to their views of propriety, and can control the degree of indulgence; but we are persuaded, that in a seminary of learning, the only safe course to be pursued is the prohibition of such reading altogether. This we wish the friends of our Institution to understand is the course adopted here; and, as they may wonder that we ever deviated from it, and, moreover, may hear distorted accounts of the deviation, we have thought it best to make an honest report of our experiment.'

STUDY OF THE CLASSICS IN GERMANY.

Although the name of the German Gymnasium has been transferred to this country, its spirit has not yet crossed the ocean; or if it has come, it has not gained admission to our institutions, and the details of its methods of instruction are scarcely known among us. We are much indebted to an unknown friend, who enables us to lay before our readers some extracts from an account of a visit to a gymnasium at Halle, by a gentleman now abroad, published in the Baptist Repository of New York.

It is well known that Halle is the seat of the celebrated Orphan-house of Francke, a monument of the faith and prayers and labors of one poor individual. Beginning with a few deserted children, whom benevolence did not dare to reject, and faith undertook to provide for, he laid the foundation of an institution in which 2000 pupils are now constantly receiving instruction. Besides this school, and its university, Halle contains two Gymnasia, the Royal Pedagogium, and the Principal Latin School. The writer gives the following account of the general character of the Gymnasia.

'As the German universities correspond in some degree with our professional schools, so their *gymnasia* correspond in very many respects to our colleges. In general the study of languages is prosecuted farther, and that of mathematics and philosophy less, in their *gymnasia*, than in our colleges. The course of instruction in the gymnasia embraces six years. Neither the universities nor the gymnasia have any anniversary or academical year. Both have a summer and winter *semester* or term, and students may enter in the spring, or in the autumn, as suits their convenience. This arrangement naturally divides the classes of the gymnasia into twelve. The highest class is called the first. With their divisions and subdivisions they stand thus:

Prima	Superior, Inferior,	Secunda	Superior, Inferior,	Tertia	Superior, Inferior,
Quarta	Superior, Inferior,	Quinta	Superior, Inferior,	Sexta	Superior, Inferior.'

The following statement of the course of study in the Principal Latin School will give a more distinct idea of the extent and nature of the education given in a German gymnasium.

'COURSE OF STUDY IN THE PRINCIPAL LATIN SCHOOL IN HALLE.

I. THE CHRISTIAN RELIGION. Catechism, Biblical History of the Old and New Testament, the Doctrines and Duties of Christianity, Introduction to the Old and New Testament, the most important systems of Pagan religion, Christian Ethics, and the Doctrines of the Lutheran Church.

II. THE LATIN LANGUAGE. Ten hours weekly to the lower classes, and six to the middle and higher. All the classes write Latin exercises, and the higher classes speak Latin.

6ta. inf. " sup. 5ta. inf.	Latin Reader.
5ta. sup. 4ta. inf.	Cornelius Nepos.
4ta. sup.	Cicero's Lelius, and Justin.
3tia. inf.	Cicero's Cato Major, and Cæsar.
3tia. sup. 2da. inf.	Cicero's Select Orations, Cæsar and Sallust.
2da. sup. 1ma. inf.	Cicero de Officiis, Quinctilian lib. 10, and Livy.

1ma. sup. Cicero's Tusc. Ques. or De Nat. Deor. and Livy. Latin poets in the middle and higher classes, connected with exercises in Latin prosody.

4ta. inf.	Phædrus.
4ta. sup. 3tia. inf.	Ovid's Metamorphoses.
3tia. sup. 2da. inf.	Virgil's Æneid.
2da. sup. 1ma. inf. " sup.	Horace's Odes, and Terence's Comedies.

III. THE GREEK LANGUAGE. To eight classes six hours in a week.

4ta. inf.	Buttmann's Grammar used in all the classes.
4ta. sup.	Greek Reader.
3tia. inf. " sup.	Xenophon's Anabasis, and Homer's Od.
2da. inf. " sup.	Xenophon's Memorabilia, and Homer's Il.
1ma. inf.	Plato, Lucian, Plutarch, Euripides, Sophocles.
1ma. sup.	Plato, Demosthenes, Soph. and Eurip. alternately.

All but the lowest class write Greek exercises.

IV. THE HEBREW LANGUAGE. 3tia. inf. Gesenius' Grammar and Chrestomathy.

3tia. sup. 2da. inf.	Parts of Genesis or of Joshua.
2da. sup. 1ma. inf. " sup.	Psalms.

V. MODERN LANGUAGES. German Literature, French and English.

VI. MATHEMATICS. In eight Classes. Arithmetic, Plane and Solid Geometry, Algebra, Trigonometry, and Mathematical Geography.

VII. GEOGRAPHY AND HISTORY. 6ta. inf. Survey of general Geography.
6ta. sup. Geography of countries not lying in Europe.
5ta. inf. Geography of Europe.
5ta. sup. Geography of Germany.

4ta. inf. History and Geography of Brandenburg.
4ta. sup. Ancient Geography.
3tia. inf. Ancient History, excluding that of Greece and Rome.
3tia. sup. Roman History.
2da. inf. Grecian History.
2da. sup. Ancient History.
1ma. inf. History of the Middle Ages.
1ma. sup. Modern History.

On all these subjects there are different lectures, and the students take notes.

Vocal and Instrumental Music is also taught.

In this gymnasium there are 300 students, and 24 teachers, of which 17 are licensed, and the remainder are candidates. The Rector has a salary of 1300 Rix Dollars, (a Rix Dollar is about 75 cts.) the ordinary teachers from 400 to 600, and the assistant teachers, or candidates for the office, a mere trifle.

The uniform method of reading the classics is to go through the first half of a work very slowly and critically, and through the last rapidly.'

The writer also gives us an account of a number of exercises which he attended in the Royal Pedagogium, most of which combined the interest of a lecture, with the accuracy of a recitation. One on Roman Antiquities was devoted to the character of the Roman dictators; another was on the Middle ages; a third, on the formation of the Greek tenses, in which the greatest promptitude and accuracy were required, and every demand enforced with severity. Several were devoted to classical authors; one to several Hebrew Psalms; and another to a disputation on Horace's Odes, in Latin, the language universally employed in the recitations of the German gymnasia. We regret that we cannot give his notes at large; but those who are engaged in classical schools would not excuse us for passing over some of the details of recitations in the classics. In visiting the room of a professor, now rector of the gymnasium at Nuremberg, he found the class engaged with Sophocles, and afterwards, with Horace.

'The exercise, as is usual with the higher classes, was in Latin. As the teacher is one of the distinguished later disciples of the great Hermann, we might expect that much of the old Greek and Roman spirit would revive at his touch. Both he and his pupils were enthusiastic in their occupation. The utmost nicety was required in translation. The remarks that were made were full of learning, and were greedily noted down. The explanations of the teacher were preceded by such questions as the following: What is the course of thought in this strophe? What other reading for such a word? Which do you prefer? What are your reasons? Which has the best manuscript authority? Does this authority rest on the number, or on the character of the manuscripts? Which reading agrees best with the usage and spirit of the author? How do you analyse and explain such a phrase? (Your Latin is not good.) How do you express the same idea in Greek prose? Another construction is also admissible; what is it? The whole exercise afforded admirable specimens of classical criticism.

'I attended a recitation, or lecture, (in fact it was both,) of the same on Horace's Satires, 1. 9. I will simply give some of the questions that were proposed, with the answers, when not too long. "What is the subject of this satire?" "A vain and garrulous young man." "In what quarter of the city was the 'via sacra'?" "Why was it called 'sacra'?" "What is the Greek for 'totus in illis'?" ὁλος γινεσθαι. "How else may it be expressed in Latin?" "Omnis in illis." "Is 'rerum' governed by 'quod,' or by 'dulcissime'?" "By the latter." "What is the force of 'occupo' here; How would you express it in Greek?" φθανω ποιων. "To what is the word 'misere' in this case equivalent in sense?" "To vehementissime." "What does 'puer' mean here?" A footman. "What in Greek?" ακολουθος. "What is the Greek phrase corresponding to 'in aurem dicere'?" Εις ους λεγειν. "What is the meaning of 'cerebri,' or of 'homo cerebrosus'?" "An ardent man." "What is the force of 'nil agis'?" "It is equivalent to frustra." "What is the expression used in Greek for 'demittere auriculas'?" Τα ωτα επι των ὠμων εχειν. What does it mean? "Ægre ferre." For what does 'urna divina' here stand? Divination. What is the Greek word? Μαντεια. How does 'hosticus' differ from 'hostilis'? "As *civic* does from *civil*. The former means *pertaining to, externally*; the latter, *having the spirit or nature of*; the one is circumstantial, the other essential." The exercises, which I witnessed, of the same teacher, in Sophocles, and in Homer's Odyssey, were in many respects different, but of the same general tendency.'

He next visited the room of the Rector, whom he found occupied with Eutropius.

'As soon as the teacher entered the lecture room, each member of the class of small boys presented him their little books, which they had made of common paper, where they had written down every new word, with its signification, which had occurred in the lesson, and having committed them to memory were now examined. This is one of the most striking and admirable peculiarities of the German mode of teaching languages. The German students are not always turning to their lexicons to look out words which they may already have had more than a dozen times. As *one* part of acquiring a new language is a work of memory, the early and daily exercise of this faculty is rigidly exacted. Even in the early stages of education, the dictionary begins to be used only in rare cases, and then mostly for critical purposes. An immense deal of time is thus saved, and the foreign air of a Greek or Latin book soon vanishes. This method cannot be too highly recommended; it makes every thing else easy and attractive. The class proceeded to translate, and coming to the phrase "vir ingens," translated it "a great man." "No," said the teacher. "A distinguished man." "No; let another translate it." "An excellent man." "Bewahre," (God forbid) said he, "the next." "An able man." "That is better, but still too weak." "A powerful man." "Right. What emperor of modern times would you call ingens?" "Napoleon." "What is the Latin for the phrase 'with great diligence'?" "Ingente diligentia." "What else?" "Eximia diligentia." "Another still." "Incredibile diligentia." "What have you to say about Constantine?" "He was a distinguished emperor." "What else?" "He was the first Christian emperor." "Any thing further?" "He removed the seat of empire from Rome to Constantinople." A large map of the East was before them, and ample illustrations were given of the political geography of that period. "Why is the subjunctive mood here used?" "Because ———." "Your rule is correct, but inapplicable here. What kind of sentence is this?" ——— "Well, then, what rule?" ——— What is the original meaning of 'affectans'?" "To place one's self upon something." "What case does it govern?" "The accusative." "How do you translate 'affectans viam'?" ——— "'Affectans spem'?"———"'Affectans imperium'?" "What is the meaning of 'bellum inferre'?" ——— "How would you translate this sentence into Latin: Napoleon the emperor of France declared war against Alexander, emperor of Russia?" —— "Can we also say 'denuntiare bellum'?" "Yes, but it is not so good an expression." "'Quamvis esset.' Why is not the indicative 'erat' here used?" "It might have been so; but Cicero always uses the subjunctive with this conjunction." "'Necessitudo et affinitas.' Why is the latter word added?" "To limit or specify the meaning of the former." "What is the meaning of 'necessitudo'?" "A close and inseparable connection, an intimate or *near relation*; but it has a generic meaning, including many kinds of relations." "What means relation by blood?" "Cognatio." "Relation by marriage?" "Affinitas." "How do you translate this into Latin: To have intercourse with any one?" "Commercium habere cum aliquo." "In what instances do the Romans employ adjectives where we employ adverbs?" "When these words refer to time or place." "How would they express: He came suddenly?" "Repentinus venit." "He rose early?" &c. &c. At the close, the teacher called upon one of the class to tell what he had learned during that recitation. Perhaps it was a principle in grammar, or the meaning of a particular phrase, or a nice distinction of words and of constructions. If the student betrayed an imperfect comprehension of the instruction that had been imparted, another was directed to give a full and clear view of the subject. If there was still an important omission, the teacher gave a second explanation. He then passed to another, asking what he had learned, and another, and then another, and so half through the class, when the bell rung, and the boys, though only about twelve years old, seemed to be in no hurry about their dinner.'

The following account of a class employed in Greek exercises, must close our extracts.

'The students came together, after having translated into Greek a passage from some German historian, which had been given out, and the teacher returned to them their written exercises more or less marked with red. He then took his place in the desk with the German book containing the passage before him, and the black board behind. The first sentence began with a particle. "How," said he, "do the Greeks express the force of this particle?" "By a participial form of the verb." "What tense?" "Aorist." "Some of the class have written it as you now see it on the black board. Is that correct? Who will tell me what the error is? The tense is not correctly formed; or, in this verb, that tense is never used. Most of the class have written such a word with such an accent; is this correct; What kind of word is this? What is the rule for the accentuation of such words? How would this phrase be expressed in Latin? How in Greek? What Greek particle corresponds to such a German particle? In a dependent member of a sentence, what would it be? When is the circumflex accent to be used?" After going through the whole passage in this way, although each student had written it previously, the book was delivered to one of the class, to read and translate the first sentence again. Another was called upon to give a rapid repetition of the translation. Then a second sentence was read, and a third called upon to translate it. If he hesitated upon a word, that word was passed to another, and then the former proceeded. This was also repeated, and thus the whole lesson was doubly reviewed upon the spot. I examined the written exercises, and found them neatly and beautifully written, and every word marked with accents.'

After reading this account, and comparing it, in imagination, with such notes as a traveller would take in most of the classical schools of the United States, we need not wonder to hear foreigners say, that we do not *study* the ancient languages. Is it wise, is it rational that so great an amount of funds and so much time and labor should be wasted, in giving superficial notions of the languages, to large numbers who rarely think of them after their course of study is finished, which might be more profitably employed in training a smaller number of thorough scholars, who would retain their acquisitions, and could employ them for the benefit of our country and the world?

EMERSON'S MAXIMS OF EDUCATION.

Those who felt any interest in the sketch of Mr. Emerson in our last number, will be gratified to see an exhibition of his principles of education, in the following maxims extracted from the prospectus of his seminary at Wethersfield. If they are not novel, they contain much practical wisdom, and deserve the attentive study of the young teacher. Let one who is commencing the task, adopt the course which Franklin pursued, in reference to the faults which he had to correct, and the good qualities he wished to acquire. After deciding for himself what maxims are sound, let him commence the practice of one, and when established in this, proceed to another, and finish the series, and we venture to promise him an ample reward for his efforts.

'1. Let it be your grand object, to prepare your pupils for the greatest usefulness and enjoyment.

2. Let their spiritual welfare be regarded, as incomparably their most important interest.

3. Teach for the glory of God.

4. Teach for eternity.

5. Cautiously guard against giving instructions, that will be likely to prove injurious.

6. Never teach useless branches, for the sake of forming useless teachers.

7. Never teach a useless branch, merely because it is fashionable; nor to gratify your patrons or pupils.

8. Teach nothing, but what appears conducive to the usefulness of your pupils, if improved according to its natural tendency and influence.

9. Let every branch receive attention, in proportion to its probable utility.

10. As far as possible, make your pupils perceive and feel the importance of every branch they pursue.

11. Proceed systematically; and, as far as possible, teach those

things first, which are first in the order of nature, and which may be understood, without an acquaintance with other things, to be subsequently acquired.

12. As far as possible, teach those things first, which are easiest in themselves.

This and the preceding maxim must, to a considerable extent, modify each other.

13. In giving instruction, proceed very gradually, and by the shortest steps, from the more easy to the more difficult.

14. As far as may be, see, that your pupils understand each step, before proceeding to the next.

15. Never teach them directly, what they can conveniently learn without such assistance.

It is much better for them to surmount a difficulty by their own ingenuity and efforts, than by the aid of others. It may be much more useful for them to devise a method of obtaining an answer, than actually to perform the operation, that obtains it. When a principle or fact is thus discovered by reflection, or investigation, it is likely to be much more clearly understood in its nature and connection, than when it is learned directly, by means of verbal or printed instructions. This is the way to promote their fondness for study, to foster original genius, and to invigorate and elevate their intellectual powers. It is a most unpropitious symptom for a pupil to be continually asking, "How shall I do this? How shall I do this?" without attempting to discover the method of solution. It is also a cruel kindness, that is incessantly telling and aiding the pupil in doing that, which, without such assistance, she might easily accomplish. If your pupils cannot, or will not, proceed without such abundant aid, it may be expedient to place them in a lower class. To prevent or cure such a mental lethargy, Colburn's Arithmetics are most admirably adapted.

16. Never do for your pupils what they can do for themselves, except so far as may be necessary, to set them an example.

The time that a teacher spends in reading, spelling and reciting for his pupils, in mending their pens, in ruling their paper, &c. is perhaps generally worse than lost. It deprives them, in some measure, at least, of the privilege of learning.

17. As far as possible, prevent your pupils from retarding the progress of one another by affording unnecessary aid in making pens, ruling paper, &c.

18. Never indulge your pupils in saying *Can't*, or expressing inability to perform any exercise required.

They know not what they *can* effect, till they make the attempt; and if one attempt has proved fruitless, another may succeed; and if nine have been unfortunate, the tenth may prosper.

19. Freely indulge and encourage your pupils in asking questions; and as far as possible, lead them to the answers, by questioning them.

This is the method of Pestalozzi; and is perhaps the most distinguishing characteristic of that venerable man, whose well-earned popularity is continually rising. But he did not invent this method; or, if he did, he was not the first inventor. It was practised by Socrates more than 2000 years ago. And it has the sanction of a greater than Socrates. In this way, the Saviour instructed his disciples from day to day. It is agreeable to the direction contained in the sixth of Deuteronomy, "And these words which I command thee this day, shall be in thine heart; and thou shalt teach them diligently to thy children, and shalt *talk* of them, when thou sittest in the house, and when thou walkest by the way; and when thou liest down, and when thou risest up."

20. Teach your pupils to teach themselves.

The benefit of this will be much every way. It will conduce to acquaintance with their own faculties, and render their progress more pleasant and more rapid. It will prepare them to teach others; and it will lay the only foundation for their advancement in science and literature after the close of their pupilage.

Several of the preceding maxims have a bearing upon the subject of self-teaching. Special efforts may also be made for the same purpose.

21. Teach your pupils to teach one another.

This is the grand feature in the system of Lancaster and Bell—a system, by which the most astonishing effects are produced in various parts of the world. In this way, one teacher can conduct the instruction of hundreds at the same time; and, it is said, can carry them forward with great correctness and despatch.

It is yet a question how far the Lancastrian method can be adopted in connection with others. It is particularly a question of great moment, how far this method can be made to coalesce with the Pestalozzian, or rather the Socratic, or more properly, the scriptural method of instruction. That these two methods can be, in some measure, united, is certain; but it is doubtful whether the union can be very extensive.

22. Teach, as much as possible, by example; and let your example in every thing, be such, as may be safely imitated.

Much, though by no means too much, has been said and urged upon the unspeakable importance of ministerial and parental example. Scarcely less important is the example of teachers. This is so obvious, that it may not seem needful to extend the illustration.

23. Endeavor to render your instructions interesting.

If a teacher cannot do this, it is of little consequence what other qualifications he may possess. Whatever be his learning, genius, piety, zeal, patience, faithfulness, &c. &c. if he cannot interest his pupils, he is unfit for his business. The grand question, then, is, How shall instructions be rendered interesting? In the whole art of education, there is perhaps nothing else, at once so difficult and so important. Upon this subject, I would most gladly listen to the instructions of any one. It has become my duty, however, to attempt instructing myself and others. O, that I had more ability to do it.

24. As far as possible, instruct by exhibiting the real objects, or the most perfect natural signs of the objects, to which your instructions relate.

25. Endeavor to discover and correct the bad habits of your pupils.

26. As far as possible, excite your pupils to vigorous and laudable efforts, by inculcating upon them their obligations to God, to

themselves, to their parents, to their associates, to their country, to their ancestors, to the world, to future generations.

27. In exciting in your pupils a sense of honor, shame and emulation, endeavor to guard their minds against that criminal ambition, to which these feelings, or the causes of these feelings, are in danger of leading.

That there may be a virtuous emulation and a laudable regard for character, is certain from scripture. Ec. 7: 1. Prov. 22: 1. Heb. 11 : 2, 39. Phil. 4: 8. Rom. 11 : 14. 2 Cor. 9: 2. 1. Cor. 14: 18. It is equally certain, that those good men have misjudged, who urge us to root up these principles of human nature, as tares sown by the hand of the enemy. These principles seem to be neither good nor bad in themselves, any more than appetite for food, a regard for property, an affection for friends, or the love of happiness in any form. It is certain, however, that there is a love of fame and distinction, which is most hateful to God, and injurious to man. Let us learn to distinguish them, that we may cherish the innocent and the good, and cast the bad away.

28. By no means suffer your faithfulness to be overcome by a fear of wounding the feelings of your pupils.

It may indeed be painful to them, and scarcely less so to you, to mention faults, which they never mistrusted. But remember, it is but the pang of a moment. To neglect this duty might diminish their usefulness and happiness through life. At the same time, the greatest caution and tenderness should be used, that the wound inflicted may be as light as possible. The tender-hearted surgeon, though he may judge it necessary to amputate a limb, will endeavor to avoid giving his patient the least unnecessary pain.

29. Fervently supplicate the divine blessing upon your pupils, and upon your efforts for their improvement, from day to day.'

MEMORIAL OF AN INFANT ON ENGLISH ORTHOGRAPHY.

A LITTLE American stranger in Asia Minor, the child of a missionary, has recently written a letter, by her amanuensis, to a maternal friend in Boston, whom she calls "mother," in which she appeals to us on a subject of great difficulty, and calls upon us to advocate her cause. Now although the right of complaint from one who has yet but a few teeth, in relation to grievances which she has never actually suffered, might well be questioned, yet as we are honestly assured that she writes by the hand of "her next of kin," we are perhaps bound to admit the legal claims of the document, and at least, to receive this petition for relief from future toil, and present it to those who must decide on the point in question. We do it the more readily, as it may soften the hearts, and restrain the impatience, of those who are occupied in teaching the young to find their way through the labyrinth of ambiguous and often unmeaning characters of which our written language is composed, and who, in the course of their duty, call upon them to pronounce letters of which many are obstinately silent, and to divine the power of others, which change as often as any Proteus.

The letter from which we have taken the following extract is dated at Galata, one of the suburbs of Constantinople. In reply, we can only exhort our young friend to arm herself with patience, to encounter the toils by which her predecessors have been trained to perseverance and endurance; for while we lament the loss of time which she must suffer, *we* can offer no hope of relief. There is no tribunal before which this appeal can be prosecuted and decided "in course of law;" we know of no power which could accomplish, if it would venture to attempt, a revolution so radical as the reform of English orthography; and if any individual should dare thus to commit high treason against the majesty of the alphabet, and should succeed in making any impression on its despotic power, a thousand pens would leap from their inkstands, and if they did not overwhelm him with an ocean of obloquy and ridicule, would cover him with stains, as difficult to efface as the spots of the leopard, and, we fear, even cast him out of the pale of literature.

'GALATA, (CONSTANTINOPLE,) MARCH 14, 1834.

'As to *talking*, I have done nothing at it as yet. True, I sometimes, half in jest, and half in earnest, say *Lizah*, which my sister, Eliza, interprets to mean her dear self, while I only smile at her credulity. I do not despair of being able in time to speak the English language well; but the account, which my sisters and others give of its orthography, is very discouraging. I do not see how I am ever going to learn it. They say we can spell a word 20, 40, and even 60 different ways, and spell it right every time, according to the sound of the letters, and still not spell it right once, according to the Dictionary. Do tell me if there be any truth in this. They say, too, that the very best writers in America and England, not excepting even the learned presidents of our Colleges, have to keep a Dictionary constantly at their elbow, and that they never think of writing any thing important without referring to it again and again. Now the Arabs have no occasion for this; nor have the Turks; nor have the Greeks; nor have the Italians. A little Arab, as soon as he has learned the power of the Arabic letters, will, in general, spell correctly every word in his language. The same is true in Italian; the same to a good degree in modern Greek; and altogether the same in Armeno-Turkish. Let an Armenian hear a Turkish word pronounced, and whether he ever heard it before or not, he knows the exact letters he is to make use of in spelling it; and it is impossible for him to spell it wrong, unless he does it on purpose.

'But how different from this is the English, if one tenth part of what they say about it be true! After a little child can spell *ba*, *da*, *fa*, &c., ask him to spell *ha*, and is it possible, that he would ever think of saying, *aitch-a, ha?* I am certain for one, that such a thing would never enter my own little cranium. I should as soon think of spelling it, *wreath-a, ha*; or *hearth-a, ha*; or *sheep-a, ha*; or *hwittch-a, ha*, as of spelling it *aitch-a, ha*. But how would children be likely to spell it? I answer that, judging from what I have seen of my older brothers and sisters, they would very naturally say, *ha-a-ha*, and would not think of saying any thing else. Every child would spell it so. That letter then ought to be called *ha* and not *aitch*. What an uncouth, unintelligible, unmeaning, preposterous name have our fathers given it! Pray where did they ever find such a word! And after they had found it, how in the name of common sense, came they ever to think of applying it to any letter of the alphabet! If it must be retained in the language, let it be applied to designate something in philosophy, or divinity, or no matter what; but let no child, if he appears to have common sense, ever be taught hereafter to say, *aitch a ha*; for *aitch a* does not spell ha, and never did spell it. I assert it confidently, and every child of common sense knows it, that *aitch-a* no more spells *ha*, than it spells *hwilktch*.

'Again; suppose that a thousand of the most intelligent men, collected from different nations, should commence learning the English language together; and suppose, that, when they had learnt the power of the letters, they should be told to spell *wife*. Do you think that if they should try a whole year, any one of them would be likely to say *Double-you-i-ef-e, wife?*—They might perchance contrive to make *Double wife* out of these four letters; but how could they make out simple *wife?*—But almost all of them would say at once *y-f-wife*. That is the most natural way of spelling the word, and unquestionably that is the way it ought to be spelt. How easy it is to say *y-f-wife*. Infant as I am, I can almost spell it myself. Now let the orthography of every word in the English language be regulated in the same way, and we little children can then learn to spell with all ease.

'Pray can you tell me, who made the orthography of the English language; or what in fact it was made for? Was it designed at first to be occult, and to be employed only in affairs of secresy, none but the privileged few, who had been initiated into its mysteries, being at all capable of deciphering it?

'You will perhaps hardly believe it, but I assure you, that it would be adding several years to the intellectual existence of every one of us little ones, if our orthography were as simple, as is that of some other nations. And, among all the reforms of the present day, is this the only thing not to be touched! Shall almost the whole country rise up as one man, in order to prevent some thousands of their neighbors from shortening their lives by intemperance? and is it nothing that some millions of children are reduced to slavery, and compelled to lose several years of their life, by a most arbitrary and despotic orthography? Is there no Howard, or Wilberforce, or Noah Webster, to compassionate our case? Can the able Editor of the 'American Annals of Education and Instruction,' do nothing for us? In looking over some back numbers of his excellent paper, I find that he took up the subject about a year before I was born; for which he has my sincere thanks. And oh! had it been followed up and acted upon in a proper manner, I should have enjoyed the benefit of it, and my existence would have been worth something more to me, than I fear it will be now. And the same is true of some millions of my contemporaries, to say nothing of the unborn generations.

'Foreigners, too, could then learn our language, be introduced at once to a world of good books, and feel the benign influence of our moral, literary, and political institutions. But now, ask a man here to learn Italian, Greek, Arabic, or almost any other language, and he can learn it. But ask him to learn English, and he says, and he says truly, 'I cannot learn your language, I can acquire two or three other languages easier, than I can acquire the English.' And this is not imagination; it is fact. But is it right? Are we not impeding the moral renovation of the world, by surrounding all our libraries, and institutions, our poetry, philosophy and divinity, by an impassable wall of orthography? Let it be broken down at once. It must come to that eventually. Something must be done, and something will be done. I entertain not the least doubt of it. Christian philosophers and philanthropists cannot always sleep over the subject. No; I confidently anticipate the time, when they shall awake to its importance; when they shall rise up as one man, to the mighty task of reforming our orthography; when they shall engage in it with as much conscience, and zeal, and determination, as we see manifested about some of the great subjects, now before the Christian public; and when the indifference of all preceding generations shall ever afterwards be spoken of as a wonder.

'Pardon me, dear mother, for having dwelt so long on this subject. I have a deep and personal interest in it; and in expressing my thoughts to you in this simple way, I feel that I have discharged a duty that I owed to that blessed country which you call yours, and to which I also claim a near relation; and whose language, after all, notwithstanding its horrible orthography, is to me the sweetest and the best in the world. It is the language which conveys to my ear the most soothing tones I ever hear; and it is one in which, more than in any other, the praise of my Redeemer is sung, and my Creator worshipped, in Spirit and in truth. May it never cease to be thus used!'

COLLEGE LIFE.

REBELLIONS in colleges have recently excited much conversation and anxiety. We have more than once expressed our conviction, that there is a radical defect in the plan of our colleges. We have said, and we are still persuaded, that much of the difficulty of governing our colleges, 'arises from *the attempt to educate men and boys in the same establishment.*' It seems to us demonstrable, that 'the same regulations, the same inspection, the same system of discipline cannot be applied to both. We must still repeat what we formerly said of the remedy.

'There seems to be no mode of obviating the evil, but to establish some line of separation. Let our colleges gradually raise their requisitions, until they receive only young men, and let them be treated accordingly. Let them provide gymnasia and higher schools, where younger pupils shall be under constant care and inspection at all hours, and not thrown, into the midst of the temptations and facilities for evil which our colleges present, while neither reason nor experience are sufficiently matured to protect them.*

The following graphic picture of the interior of college life, from Abbott's 'Corner Stone,' will amuse our readers, while it will illustrate the dangers to which we refer.

'I must say a word or two now in regard to the ordinary routine of daily life at college. Very early in the morning, the observer may see lights at a few of the windows of the buildings inhabited by the students. They mark the rooms occupied by the more industrious or more resolute, who rise and devote an hour or two to their books by lamp light on the winter mornings. About day, the bell awakens the multitude of sleepers in all the rooms, and in a short time they are to be seen issuing from the various doors, with sleepy looks, and with books under their arms, and some adjusting their hurried dress. The first who come down, go slowly, others with quicker and quicker step, as the tolling of the bell proceeds; and the last few stragglers run with all speed, to secure their places before the bell ceases to toll. When the last stroke is sounded, it usually finds one or two too late, who stop suddenly, and return slowly to their rooms.

'The President or one of the Professors, reads a portion of Scripture by the mingled light of the pulpit lamps, and the beams which come in from the reddening eastern sky. He then offers the morning prayer. The hundreds of young men before him exhibit the appearance of respectful attention, except that four or five, appointed for the purpose, in different parts of the chapel, are looking carefully around to observe and note upon their bills the absentees. A few also, not fearing God or regarding their duty, conceal under their cloaks, or behind a pillar or a partition between the pews, the book which contains their morning lesson:— and attempt to make up, as well as the faint but increasing light will enable them, for the time wasted in idleness or dissipation on the evening before. When prayers are over the several classes repair immediately to the rooms assigned respectively to them, and recite the first lesson of the day.

* Vol. 4, p. 160.

'During the short period which elapses between the recitation and the breakfast bell, college is a busy scene. Fires are kindling in every room. Groups are standing in every corner, or hovering around the newly made fires: — parties are running up and down the stairs two steps at a time, with the ardor and activity of youth: — and now and then, a fresh crowd is seen issuing from the door of some one of the buildings, where a class has finished its recitation, and comes forth to disperse to their rooms; — followed by their instructor, who walks away to his house in the village. The breakfast bell brings out the whole throng again, and gathers them around the long tables in the Common's Hall, or else scatters them among the private families in the neighborhood.

'An hour after breakfast, the bell rings to mark the commencement of study-hours: — when the students are required by college laws to repair to their respective rooms, which answer the three-fold purpose of parlor, bed-room, and study, to prepare for their recitation at eleven o'clock. They, however, who choose, to evade this law, can do it without much danger of detection. The great majority comply, but some go into their neighbor's rooms to receive assistance in their studies, some lay by the dull text-book and read a tale, or play a game: and others, farther gone in the road of idleness and dissipation, steal secretly away from college, and ramble in the woods, or skate upon the ice, or find some rendezvous of dissipation in the village, evading their tasks like truant boys. They, of course, are marked as absent; but pretended sickness will answer for an excuse, they think, once or twice, and they go on, blind to the certainty of the disgrace and ruin which must soon come.

'The afternoon is spent like the forenoon, and the last recitation of the winter's day, is just before the sun goes down. An hour is allotted to it, and then follow evening prayers, at the close of which the students issue from the chapel, and walk in long procession to supper.

'It is in the evening, however, that the most striking peculiarities of college life, exhibit themselves. Sometimes literary societies assemble, organised and managed by the students, where they hold debates, or entertain each other with declamations, essays, and dialogues. Sometimes a religious meeting is held, attended by a portion of the professors of religion and conducted by an officer; at other times the students remain in their rooms, some quietly seated by their fire, one on each side, reading, writing, or preparing the lessons for the following morning:—others assemble for mirth and dissipation, or prowl around the entries and halls, to perpetrate petty mischief, breaking the windows of some hapless Freshman, — or burning nauseous drugs at the keyhole of his door, — or rolling logs down stairs, and running instantly into a neighboring room so as to escape detection; — or watching at an upper window to pour water unobserved upon some fellow student passing in or out below; — or plugging up the keyhole of the chapel door, to prevent access to it for morning prayers; — or gaining access to the bell by false keys, and cutting the rope or filling it with water to freeze during the night: —or some other of the thousand modes of doing mischief to which the idle and flexible Sophomore is instigated by some calculating, and malicious mischief-maker in a higher class. After becoming tired of this, they gather together in the room of some dissolute companion, and there prepare themselves a supper, with food they have plundered from a neighboring poultry yard, and utensils obtained in some similar mode. Ardent spirits sometimes makes them noisy; — and a college officer, at half past nine, breaks in upon them, and exposure and punishment are the consequences; — disgrace, suspension, and expulsion for themselves, and bleeding hearts for parents and sisters at home. At other times, with controlled and restrain-ed indulgence, they sit till midnight, sowing the bitter seeds of vice; undermining health, destroying all moral sensibility, and making almost sure the ruin of their souls.

'In the mean time, the officers of the institution, with a fidelity and an anxious interest, which is seldom equalled by any solicitude except that which is felt by parents for their children, struggle to resist the tide. They watch, they observe, they have constant records kept, and in fact, they go as far as it is possible to go, in obtaining information about the character and history of each individual, without adopting a system of espionage, which the nature of the institution, and the age of a majority of the pupils, renders neither practicable nor proper. They warn every individual who seems to be in danger, with greater and greater distinctness, according to the progress he seems to be making, and as soon as evidence will justify it, they remove every one whose stay seems dangerous to the rest; but still the evil will increase, in spite of all the ordinary human means, which can be brought against it.'

THE TEACHER'S ALMANAC FOR SEPTEMBER.

SEPTEMBER has stolen upon us, like every preceding month, probably before we were prepared for it. Does the rapidity with which winter and spring, and summer, have just glided by, excite no new impression of the brevity of our days of labor, of the necessity of executing speedily the plans of correction and improvement, which have been so long lying to mature, or waiting for the convenient season? The year has nearly reached its last quarter. It has brought us, as it passed, the flowers and promises of spring, and the warmth and fruit of summer, and nothing remains but to gather the rich harvests of autumn which it has provided. Have you been equally faithful in fulfilling the promises of the spring? How many of your plans of improvement for yourself and your pupils have been commenced? How many have been completed; how many will be, before the year closes? It is better to reflect upon them before the period of unavailing regrets, so generally chosen, on the last day of the old year, or the first of the new. Perhaps a remedy may still be within your reach.

THE SCHOOL-ROOM.

The period of intense heat and its languor and danger is past, and the body and mind begin to recover their activity. Your pupils may begin, if the month has its usual character, to quicken their pace, and regain what they have lost. Let their exercise be more vigorous, so as to enable them better to resist the change of temperature; and do not allow them, when they come in, to be exposed to cool currents of air. The thermometer is not now a sure guide; for, after the system has been enfeebled, and the pores opened by heat, a change of a few degrees will make one feel cold, and produce the effects of cold, and thus prepare us for autumnal fevers. In North Carolina, a scientific man informs us that fires are wanted if the thermometer is below 70°, in consequence of the previous heat; and we have sometimes found the same feeling in all around us, after a few weeks of heat, at the north. Consult, therefore, your own feelings and those of your pupils, as well as the thermometer, especially as you sit still so much of the day. Warn your pupils to be cautious in the cool, damp evenings. Perhaps you are preparing for 'the fall examination.' Let it be, if possible, a course of recitations, in review, for several days, and not a rapid series of questions, for an hour, when the most brazen faced will appear best, and the diffident pupil lose all character for diligence or scholarship, and a large part of the school be agitated with self-conceit, or jealousy, or mortification. Read our last number, before you determine on an *exhibition*.

THE WORLD.

Nature begins to show marks of decline. The splendor of summer has faded away. The relics only of some portion of the crops are to be seen; and the wild plants are sowing their seed for the next year. A large part of the vegetable world is decaying, and in many places producing unwholesome miasma. Let your pupils observe the progress of these changes, and note them, and preserve the record for another year. Let them watch, too, the death and disappearance of insects, and the movements of the birds. We wish some teacher would send us a collection of these notes for insertion in the Annals of Education.

THE HEAVENS.

In the middle of this month, the beautiful diamond of stars which forms the head of the Dolphin, and the splendid cross, which is called the Swan, will be on the meridian at nine o'clock. Do not fail to point them out to your pupils. Capricorn is the sign of the Zodiac now on the meridian. The absence of splendid stars will render close attention to the globe or maps necessary to become acquainted with it; but it will be very useful to teach your pupils each of these constellations as it becomes conspicuous, that they may always know where to find the planets. All their orbits lie within the Zodiac.

We have been gratified to receive a letter from a teacher who has adopted this mode of informing and amusing his pupils, which we hope may encourage others. He first provided a small map of the Great Bear for each of his pupils,* with the stars numbered and named in the margin, and thus describes the course he pursued.

'I now gave one of these maps to each of my pupils and told them the history of the constellation; then directed them how to hold it, while I pointed to the spot in the heavens where they would find the constellation. After this, I read over the names several times so that they might acquire the correct manner of pronouncing them. The next evening, I met some of the younger pupils, and asked them to point to the constellation of the Great Bear. They raised their fingers, and traced it out with the utmost facility, without the least assistance. I then desired them to tell me the names of the individual stars, as I pointed to them. They named them as rapidly as if they had been conversant with them all their lives.

'I did not give them another map until six or seven days after; during which time, I wished them every night to study the constellation attentively, so that the position of the stars, as well as their names might become indelibly impressed on their memory.

'The next I gave them, was a similar one of the Little Bear. I now directed them to find the Polar Star by means of the pointers, and to notice how these constellations *apparently* revolved about the North Pole. I likewise informed them how far the Polar Star is from the North Pole — what it is used for — why the northern regions of the earth are called Arctic, and whatever else I could think of in relation to these asterisms.

* We believe it would have been more useful to require them to draw one for themselves, from a model.

The third map embraced the Dragon and the Little Bear. Since this, I have given them none but those in our zenith. To conclude, my pupils were never more interested with any study, and many are already quite familiar with the names of a large number of stars, and with what is known of the distances, number, and magnitudes of those suns of other worlds.'

MISCELLANY.

Scientific and Literary Anniversary.

We understand that the Executive Committee of the American Lyceum have extended the plan and operations of that society, in obedience to the instructions given them at the late fourth annual meeting in this city. Measures have been taken to form departments for the Natural, and Moral Sciences, Literature, and the Fine and Useful Arts, in addition to that for Education; and a number of gentlemen, distinguished for their devotion to many different branches, have been requested to furnish memoirs or essays on their favorite subjects of investigation, to be read at the fifth annual meeting, in May next, and to be published. Several gratifying answers have already been received; and communications on some interesting topics have been promised.

Such a plan, if successful, cannot fail to be useful.

The results of the labors of many capable minds will be annually secured for the benefit of the public; while the correspondence and the personal intercourse of our literary and scientific countrymen, at the anniversaries, will tend to promote new and wider exertions in the different branches of useful knowledge. This part of the plan of the Lyceum is likely to prove one of the most efficient, and it will be one of the most interesting to our citizens; particularly, if, as is meditated, popular lectures be delivered by members, during the evenings of the annual meetings. — *N. Y. Daily Advertiser.*

Association of Teachers in Kentucky.

The Executive Committee of this Association announced its next meeting on the last Wednesday in August, at which time an address was to be delivered by Pres. Bascom, of Augusta College, and a number of subjects were proposed for discussion; among them are the following: — Whether English Grammar, as taught at present, is as useful as other branches of instruction which are neglected; — Whether 'the art of speaking and writing the English language correctly' is not more frequently acquired by extensive reading of good authors; — Whether a variety of branches should be taught in the same day; — Whether children are not confined too long in school; — Whether a particular series of elementary works ought to be adopted in our schools; — Whether associations ought not to provide means for examining teachers, and to refuse all, who are unqualified, admission to membership.

Teachers' Meeting in Ohio.

A meeting is to be held by the Ohio College of Professional Teachers at Cincinnati, on the 6th of October, on a plan similar to that of the American Institute.

Dr Beecher's Remarks on the West.

We have been favored by a gentleman who heard Dr Beecher's remarks before the Institute in reference to the state of education at the West, with the following imperfect notes on a few points: —

'Men of gigantic intellect are to be found in every country. Nor is it difficult to raise up such men. But to elevate the whole mass, to take society, as it were by the four corners, and lift it up, is a work of more difficulty. In New-England, it has been done. The institutions of these states, planted by our fathers, have thus elevated to a standing, comparatively high, the whole community. The question now is, shall the same thing be done for the West? Shall that immense empire grow up, and become like these Eastern States, or shall it run wild?

'It is said the West will take care of itself, as the East has done. But this is not likely to be done. Is that great territory 8,000 miles in diameter, with a population thrown together from all parts of the world, likely to form itself into little school districts, as flourishing, as those of the East! Impossible.

'Simple as seems to us in Massachusetts, the business of setting up common schools all over the country, it is only simple, as almost everything else is simple, because *we know how it is done.* It is not simple to the people of the West; it is a work of great difficulty. It is believed that the work is to be done, to a very great extent, by the various religious denominations of these states. This, in fact, is the way it has been done in New England. Indeed, take away these churches and other moral bulwarks, and your schools would very soon go down.

'I have attended several Conventions in the West, on the subject of Education; and there seems to be a universal impression that one important means of improvement there is the education and preparation of teachers, in seminaries for the purpose. Teachers will never come from the East, in sufficient numbers to supply our wants; they must be raised up and qualified for the work on the spot.

'Hitherto, teachers have acted as isolated beings. There has been no union — no concentration of effort. There has been no learning from what had been done previously; for every one's experience in this business has perished with him. Much is to be expected of teachers' associations. Raising the wages of teachers is another great object to be accomplished. Good teachers in the western states, say in Kentucky, are probably as well paid as they are in this country; but they ought to be paid still better.

'Dr B. spoke briefly of the motives, to extend to the West the benefits of common school education. The first was their destitute condition. For proof of this he referred, first to Pennsylvania. The western states could not be supposed to be in a more favorable condition. Kentucky, might, perhaps, be considered a fair specimen; and for the state of education there, he referred to the documents procured at the taking of the census, by the legislature, and by Rev. B. O. Peers.

'In reply to one question, Dr B, referred to the popular objection to foreign missions. He first stated that 'charity begins at home,' and appealed to facts on that subject as subsequently developed. in proof of its fallacy. In like manner he observed, the more we emigrate to the West the better we shall go on at home. Whatever raises the West raises also the East, and the contrary. Dr B. would be glad 'to turn New England over and empty all her teachers into the Mississippi Valley.' The East would soon fill up again, and be more full than before. It seems the determination of Divine Providence to populate the great basin of the Mississippi in this way. Here, on this hard, sterile end of the land, they were first planted, to be hardened to labor, that they might then go forth to the work of elevating that mighty empire of mind and heart, and raise the intellect, and form the character of the tens of millions, that ere long will inhabit it.'

Progress of Education in Vermont.

Extract of a Letter from a Teacher in Vermont to the Editor.

'That the Annals will be known, and as extensively circulated in this as in any other State of equal size and population, I firmly believe; for I cannot be insensible to the indications in favor of the cause which they are designed to advance, particularly in the section of the country in which I am located. But a few years since, it was regarded of little consequence who the teacher of a school might be, provided the quality, of 'cheapness,' was considerably developed. Now it is not an uncommon thing to hear a committee say when inquiring for a teacher, that they care not so much about the *price*, provided they can obtain a good one. In short, people are beginning to find out that there is a difference in teachers, and they are by no means backward in manifesting it. Another favorable indication is the filling up of our higher schools, and the establishment of new ones. I think it will not exceed the truth to say, that double the number will have attended our higher schools in 1834 that attended the same in 1833. Indeed, scholars seem to be pouring in from all quarters to these schools; and not a small number, with a view of becoming teachers — permanent teachers.'

Alleghany College.

The College at Meadville is now placed under the direction of the Pittsburg Methodist Conference. It has a library of nine thousand volumes, a good college building and apparatus. Eightyeight students have joined it under the new arrangements.

New Collegiate Institution.

The Manual Labor Academy of Maury county, Kentucky, which was opened in 1830 with seven pupils, has been formed into a College, under the name of Jackson College. The trustees own 310 acres and three substantial brick buildings, with accommodations for 72 students; and are now erecting other buildings. 160 applications for admission have been made during the present year. Two hours' labor a day are required of each student, and $75 in addition to this will pay for his board and tuition. Donations are now solicited for the purchase of a library, apparatus, the erection of a new college building, and the endowment of a professorship. It is a point now conceded, that the west can be supplied with the means of instruction only by educating young men upon the spot.

Liberality to Colleges.

It is gratifying to see so much of public spirit in providing more ample endowments for our colleges. It is known, that a subscription of $100,000 was filled up, two years since, to found additional professorships in Yale College, and that Amherst College received a large addition to its funds. We perceive that one half of the $100,000, proposed to re-establish Dickinson College, under the direction of the Methodists, has been subscribed. Randolph Macon College, under the care of the Methodists, we perceive is enabled to enlarge its buildings and apparatus; and an effort is about to be made to raise $10,000 for their institution in Augusta, Kentucky. The University of Vermont has recently received $25,000 in private subscriptions. Hamilton College in New York has received donations to the amount of $50,000. The Wesleyan University of Middletown, has a grant of $14,000 from the State of Connecticut; and Harvard University, after soliciting in vain from the Legislature of Massachusetts the means for erecting a building, in which its noble library could be safely preserved, has received from the widow of the late Governor Gore a legacy of $50,000, which it is proposed to use for this purpose. Can no individual — no state — be found to endow, with equal liberality, a seminary for teachers of our common schools, to form men who shall be qualified to labor at the foundation of our institutions?

American School Society.

Great Britain has long had her British and Foreign School Society, and National School Society, and France has organised similar institutions. But while we have established several associations whose object it is to collect the experience of teachers, and to promote improvements in the science and the art of education, no general society has been established to investigate and supply those urgent wants of schools and teachers, which we have so often presented to our readers, and to carry home these improvements to our youth. We rejoice to state that an association, long demanded, has at length been formed with this object, under the title of the 'American School Society.' The following gentlemen have been elected its officers, most of whom have accepted their appointments:

President, Francis Wayland. *Vice Presidents*, William Reed, Daniel Sharp, Rufus Choate, Richard Fletcher, Heman Humphrey, Thomas H. Gallaudet. *Directors*, Heman Lincoln, Edward Reynolds, David Greene, Ethan A. Andrews, Samuel R. Hall, Daniel Crosby, Daniel Noyes, Rufus Anderson, Jacob Abbot, B. B. Edwards, Louis Dwight, William C. Woodbridge. *Recording Secretary*, William A. Alcott. *Treasurer*, Samuel H. Walley, jr. As a corresponding secretary has not yet been chosen, a corresponding committee has been appointed, consisting of W. C. Woodbridge, B. B. Edwards, and Louis Dwight, who solicit communications on this subject from the friends of education.

Schools among the North American Indians.

From the report of the Committee on Indian Affairs, presented to Congress in May last, we learn that there are among them 4857 scholars at sixty different stations. The following table will show the number of teachers and pupils under the direction of several different sects, and the amount appropriated to the support of each, from the civilization fund of the United States.

Under the direction of	Teachers.	Pupils.	Amount paid.
United Brethren,	3	20	
American Board of Commissioners for Foreign Missions,	98	1339	$1,690
Methodist Society,	1	47	550
Baptist General Convention,	17	280	2,000
Methodist Episcopal Church,	7	85	
Protestant Episcopal Church,	7	160	
Roman Catholic Church,	4	120	1,300
Total,	137	2,011	5,540
To the Choctaw Academy,			310
" Godfrey, a Pottawattamie Indian,			200
" Choctaws,			300
" Mohegan Indians,			400
Total,			$6,750

The following is a statement of sums provided by treaties with Indian tribes, for the purposes of education, exhibiting the names of the tribes, the amount for each, and the period for which the payment is to be continued.

Names of the tribes.	Amount.	How long payable
Miamies,	$2,000	Pleasure of Congress
Pottawattamies,	3,000	do. do.
Do. of Indiana,	2,000	do. do.
Winnebagoes,	3,000	till 1859
Menomonies,	,500	1842
Chippewas,	1,000	Pleasure of Congress
New York Indians and others,	1,500	do. do.
Sacs, Foxes and Ioways,	3,000	till 1840
Shawnees and Delawares,	,500	1835
Kickapoos,	,500	1835
Choctaws,	12,500	1840
Creeks east,	3,000	1851
Cherokees west,	2,000	1839
Florida Indians,	1,000	1843
	$35,500.	

Progress of Indian Pupils.

The Cherokee children in the school at Brainard, are more forward than the children of New England, who have had no greater advantages of schools. Those who have attended two years could read, write and spell well — are familiar with the elements of geography, arithmetic and grammar, and show great skill and taste in writing composition, for children of their age. Many of the adults, some fifty or sixty years old, have learned to read their language without any teacher but themselves. Children who have an English father and Cherokee mother, can usually speak both languages at three years old. Boudinot and Ridge, who married northern women, have each four or five uncommonly fine children. One, four years old, reads well in the Testament; two other little girls know much about geography, and something of numbers. Ridge's eldest son, who is six or seven, is a fine scholar and a great reader. Major Ridge is known both as a warrior and a statesman; in addition to this he proved himself an orator in a lecture on the history of nations, which he gave through his son as interpreter. The son followed him in an animated address on the present state of the Cherokees. — *Nashville Banner, (abr.)*

Universalist College.

The buildings at Norwich, Vermont, formerly occupied by Captain Partridge, have been procured for a Universalist College, to be placed under the direction of Captain Partridge.

Education and Crime.

From the Warden's Report of the Eastern penitentiary of Pennsylvania, we learn the following facts. The whole number of criminals received since its opening, is two hundred and nineteen, of this number fortytwo could neither read nor write, fiftynine could read but not write, and one hundred and eighteen could both read and write. Of this last class, one had been educated at a University, ten had received a good education, and only two others could only read and write tolerably well, leaving one hundred and five who could read or write very indifferently. Many of them could not read a sentence without spelling every word. They were equally ignorant of trades and occupations. Of the two hundred and nineteen, sixtyeight had been apprenticed to masters, only thirty of whom had served through their apprenticeship, thirtyeight had left their masters for trivial reasons; most had ran away from them; eight were slaves until twentyone or twentyeight years of age, and one hundred and twentyone, more than half the number, were never apprenticed. The late lottery system and the use of ardent spirits were probably the two great causes of crime. From the best information that could be collected it appeared that three quarters of the criminals were addicted to either habitual, or occasional intoxication, and that two thirds of the crimes were *acknowledged* to have been committed while in this state.

American Institute of Instruction.

The American Institute of Instruction commenced its fourth annual meeting on Thursday Aug. 21. By a vote of the Institute, Clergymen and Editors in Boston and vicinity, were invited to attend the Lectures.

At 11½ o'clock, an able and eloquent Introductory Address was delivered by Hon. C. Cushing, of Newburyport, on "*The true uses of Instruction.*"

At 3½ P. M. Rev. Mr. Burton, of Hingham, gave a lecture on "*The best mode of fixing the attention of the young.*"

At 5 o'clock, Dr. Beecher of Cincinnati, Ohio, gave a lecture on "*The condition and wants of the West.*" Of this we have given extracts.

The Institute commenced its morning session on Friday at half past 8. About an hour was occupied in hearing statements from Dr. Beecher in relation to the West, in answer to questions proposed, at the time, by the members of the Institute.

At half past 9, Dr. W. Grigg, of this city, delivered a lecture on Physical Education. In the course of the lecture, several pieces of apparatus, constructed by the lecturer, were exhibited, and their uses explained.

At 11½ o'clock, Rev. Stephen Farley, of Amesbury, delivered a lecture on the importance of Common Schools. Dr. Keagy, of Philadelphia, who was announced in the papers as lecturer for this hour, informed the committee after the commencement of the session, that sickness would prevent his fulfilling his engagements. The same apology was received from several other lecturers.

At 3 P. M. L. Mason, Esq. gave a lecture on Music as a branch of school instruction, and the Pestalozzian method of teaching it. The principles of the lecture were illustrated by a juvenile choir of about twenty of Mr. M's. pupils.

At 5½ M. M. Carll, of Philadelphia, commenced a lecture on "Maternal Instruction and the management of Infant Schools."

The Institute came to order on Saturday, at 7½, A. M.

At 9½, Rev. J. Abbott, gave a lecture on "The duties of Parents in respect to the schools where their children are instructed." By a vote of the Institute, 10,000 copies of this lecture were ordered to be published.

After which Rev. M. M. Carll, of Philadelphia, concluded his lecture on "Maternal Instruction and the management of Infant Schools."

At 12 o'clock Dr. J. V. C. Smith, of this city lectured on "the Mechanism and Philosophy of the organ of sense." (The Ear.)

At 3 o'clock, P. M. Dr. Smith continued his lecture.

At 4 o'clock, Thomas Sherwin, Esq. of this city, delivered a lecture on "Teaching the elements of Mathematics."

At ¼ before 10 o'clock on Monday, a lecture was delivered on "Natural History as a study for the young," by Dr. A. A. Gould, of Boston.

At ¼ before 11, Rev. H. Winslow, of this city, delivered a lecture on the "Danger of unsafe and useless Innovations and the Indications of any tendency to this evil in our country."

At 3 o'clock, P. M. Dr. C. T. Jackson, of this city, delivered a lecture on Chemistry and its uses.

On Tuesday, the 26th, at 9½ A. M. a lecture was delivered by Hon. Joseph Story, of Cambridge, on "The Science of Government as a branch of popular Education."

Immediately after which, Dr. C. Follen, of Cambridge, gave a lecture on "The Study of History, and the best mode of pursuing it."

At 4½ o'clock, P. M. Dr. Barber, of Cambridge, delivered a lecture on "Phrenology as connected with education;" after which a discussion took place on this subject.

We had put aside our ordinary occupations in some measure, in the hope of enjoying the present session of the Institute; but illness has prevented our attending for a single hour. We learn that the audience was respectable, and generally much interested in the lectures. The discussions on several subjects, which were usually held in the evening at Chauncey Hall, are said to have been very interesting also, although both sides of the question do not appear to have been always fully represented. We are gratified to learn, that the lectures will probably appear in a cheap form, so as to be accessible to a greater number of teachers. We regret, however, to hear that any of them presented the sectarian views of the writers. Although some of these were in accordance with our own, we shall not cease to remonstrate against their introduction on neutral ground.

Bristol College.

This institution which was founded by the Episcopal Education Society, and has been endowed with an ample farm for manual labor, and furnished with instructors beyond its present wants, appears to be in a very prosperous state. Numerous applications for admission are rejected for want of room to receive them, a new college building is about to be erected, and twelve hundred dollars were subscribed by members of the board of trustees. A professor of the Greek and Hebrew languages, has been appointed and measures have been taken to procure a chemical apparatus abroad.

NOTICES OF BOOKS.

The Youth's Letter-Writer, or the Epistolary Art made plain and Easy to Beginners through the Example of Henry Moreton. By Mrs John Farrar, author of 'Congo in Search of his Master.' 'The Children's Robinson Crusoe,' &c. New-York: R. Bartlett & P. Raymer. 1834.

We were not a little surprised, to find so respectable a name attached to a title so generally descriptive of a ridiculous collection of absurd forms of letters, as '*The Letter Writer.*' The mystery was solved, however, on examining the book. It is a pleasing story, in the true style of a child's book, exhibiting the difficulties and progress of a young letter-writer, and fitted to impart to young minds the spirit of letter-writing, in connection with the forms which convenience or custom requires. It might be read profitably by many adults; and we are sure Mrs Farrar will have the cordial thanks of every child who reads it for removing the mountains of difficulties which press upon his little brain, in *this dreaded task* of correspondence.

A new Grammar of the English Language. Second Edition. Corrected, enlarged and prepared for use in Academies and Schools. Boston: Russell, Odiorne & Metcalf. 1834. 12mo, pp. 124.

We learn from the preface, that the author, in examining the language, in place of preceding grammars, has been led to compile a work differing from them in the following particulars: — '*First*, (and least important,) it arranges certain words, some usually called articles, others pronouns, in the class of adjectives. *Second*, it denies that the auxiliaries could, might, should, and would usually refer to past time; in other words, that they are signs of a past tense. *Third*, it denies that the potential mode has more than two tenses. *Fourth*, it rejects the subjunctive mode. *Fifth*, it substitutes for it, or rather recognises, a conditional Mode. *Sixth*, it applies new names to several of the tenses. *Seventh*, Rejecting the passive as a *class* of verbs it exhibits the English verb conjugated in three different ways. *Eighth*, the syntax is simplified, considerably shortened, and compiled without reference to the grammar or construction of any other language.'

The preface states one fact which deserves to be remembered by every teacher. 'Our most elegant writers learned the grammar of their language not so much from Lowth or Murray as from studying the purest specimens of English composition, from attending carefully to the meaning of and force of words, and from consulting and regarding more that indefinable sense of propriety, which constitutes good taste, than the precepts of their instructors.'

Grammatical Pioneer, or Rational Instructor. Analytical Grammer; containing the Principles of the English Language, arranged in Progressive Order and Illustrated by Appropriate Examples. By W. Snyder. Winchester: E. W. Robinson. 1834. 12mo, pp. 164.

This work, published in Virginia, as we presume from the frank which enveloped it, aims at improvement also. From the author's 'Proem,' we find that he has made the two first changes of the preceding work. He also rejects the enumeration of persons by first, second, and third, and refers to the *speaker*, *subject*, and *person addressed*. He rejects the possessive case, because *man's* or *Mary's* is not a noun consistently with any definition of that part of speech, but an adjective. He rejects the Latin term *neuter*, in regard to gender, and says such nouns have *no gender*. Nouns of common gender he terms *epicene*. Adjectives are called *adjuncts*. Adverbs, *modifiers*. Pronouns, *substitutes*. Conjunctions, *Conjoiners*, and *Disjoiners*. Interjections, *Exclamations*. The imperfect tense, he maintains, should be called perfect, as implying the same complete action with the *veni*, *vidi*, of the Latin Perfect; and the ordinary perfect, he ranks as imperfect or indefinite.

To the *conservative party* in education both these works will be odious; to the *radicals*, both will be interesting. Those who are *yet*, *only teachers* in grammar, will find profitable topics for the exercise of their minds. Those who have been thorough *students*, would smile if we were to attempt a discussion in the compass of a notice, of points which have called forth volumes of argument and invective.

AMERICAN

ANNALS OF EDUCATION

AND INSTRUCTION.

OCTOBER, 1834.

ON THE MEANS OF CIVILIZING THE INDIANS.

ESSAY ON THE BEST MEANS FOR EXTENDING KNOWLEDGE AND CIVILIZATION AMONG THE WESTERN INDIANS.

Addressed to the American Lyceum, by HENRY R. SCHOOLCRAFT, Author of Travels to the Sources of the Mississippi, &c.

WHATEVER traits of the Indian character may be singled out and held up for admiration, the inquiry still returns upon us: How can those points which best betoken the possession of intellectual capacity, be most advantageously improved?

Knowledge, to be useful to the Indian tribes, must possess a decidedly practical character. All the sources of their moral depression, and all the means of their moral elevation, are such as are peculiar to the earliest stages of human society. Their wants, both intellectual and physical, are of the primary character; and may be sufficiently comprehended in the round of practical truths, which form the basis of civilization. Most of these truths are of the most simple and obvious kind. Lying level with every capacity, and constituting the objects of daily action, they are only in danger of being lost sight of, by straining after some great and sudden efforts to remodel the internal constitution of their society. History gives us very little reason to suppose that such changes will happen, by any other, but the patient and faithful application of the common means. To read and to write, to build and to plant, household economy, dress and address, are among the elements of civil knowledge. And this knowledge may be compared to a series, which begins in the profoundest state of ignorance and barbarism, and terminates in the most polished state of moral refinement.

To depart one step from the former, is to take one step towards the latter. To abandon the temporary lodge, to throw aside the blanket, to discontinue the use of paints, are as certain indications of incipient civilization, as it unquestionably is, at a more advanced stage, to substitute alphabetical, for hieroglyphic signs, or machine, for hand labour. The example of consistent individuals, will become the means of influencing communities. If we can convince them of the superiority of agriculture, over mere gardening; of grazing over hunting—of pacific, over warlike achievements—of written, over oral laws—of temperance, over intemperance—of industry, over inanity, we have gained so many points in their reformation. It will then become easier to convince them, that it is dishonorable to be lazy, and infamous to be dishonest.

Other truths lie in the direct train of these improvements, and are inseparable from them, such as relate to the varied economy of life, the reciprocal duties of society, and the principles of government. To assent to these truths, and to adopt them in practice, cannot, it is conceived, be occurrences very widely separated, in point of time. But in order to the mind's giving this assent, in the true sense, there must be such a previous understanding, appreciation, and application of these important truths, as is totally irreconcileable with the moral condition of Indians living in an idolatrous and irreligious state.

Hence, there is a still higher and nobler duty,—the duty of preparing the Indian mind for giving this assent. And it is one, which, paradoxical as it may seem, is conceived to be alike essential to the commencement, as to the completion of their moral elevation. It is not only deemed a point of primary importance, to teach them their true relation to civilized communities, and the principles which lead such communities to rise and fall in the scale of wealth and power; but a little reflection must make it manifest, that they should, at the same time, be taught the solemn and important relation, in which the volume of inspiration places them, with respect to the Author of their existence.

By imparting this light at the commencement of their career of civilization, they will be enabled to take a view of the whole ground of their responsibilities, and to see whether it is worth their while to commence a moral race, the rewards of victorious competitorship in which, are fully held up, and displayed to their view. If this paramount obligation can be impressed on their minds, while they exist in the state of hunters and warriors, they will be placed in a position, in which they can the more readily judge, whether a continuance in these pursuits, wholly or in part, or the adoption of civilized modes of industry, wholly or in part, will best subserve the fulfilment of the whole circle of their obligations. And, if there be no error in this conclusion, they will thus be led to esteem industry, and the acquisition of property and education, as means essential to the attainment of an end; and not, as they are otherwise apt to become, the end itself.

Christianity every where inculcates order, obedience, wisdom and virtue. Its order, educed from chaos, leads the mind through an infinite and connected series of beautiful creations, of both animate and inanimate classes, 'from nature up to nature's God.' And its maxims of obedience, wisdom, and virtue, are the most perfect and sublime to which the human intellect can refer. Considered merely as a code of morals, and were there no futurity to test their immutability, they would produce the greatest amount of happiness to families, and to communities. They are so interwoven in their practical application with the duties and relations of life, and evince so intimate a knowledge of human nature, that they are found to be adapted to all periods of human life. They form a system which applies to man in his infancy and in his age;—in his weakness and in his strength;—in his joy and in his sorrow;—in his life and in his death. And it is the admiration of this system, that it is equally applicable to every condition of society. The governor and the subject, the master and the servant, the parent and the child, the rich and the poor, the wise and the ignorant, are placed on an equality of faith. Science and learning, splendor and penury lose their distinctions before the two-edged sword of its requisitions. It considers all as subject to its laws. It deems all capable of obeying them. It prescribes no standard of art, or book knowledge. It looks to no necessary amount of human attainment, in the occupations or rank of life. Felix, trembling before the moral majesty of Paul, or Tinda, quailing under the denunciations of Brainerd, are equally just demonstrations of its applicability and power. To love, and to hate, are the ends of its requirement. And these are exercises of the affections, at the command of every rational being, savage or civilized. All its promises; all its denunciations; all the inducements it holds out to obedience; all its solemn threatenings of disobedience, are equally addressed to the 'Jew and the Gentile, the bond and the free.' Were it not so,—if truth could disprove one of its precepts; if justice could point out any portion of the human family, who were exempt from its laws; or if any candid interpretation of language could be made, tending to show, that in the final retribution, one tittle of the just man's reward should be given to the unjust, then the exhibition of this single truth, so established to be a truth, would be, in effect, to knock the keystone from the temple of God, and tumble the whole superstructure in splendid fragments.

If these positions be correct, and I am not aware that they are not strictly so, then it is an object of the highest moment with all, who purpose to better the condition of the Indians, to begin their labors by the introduction of Christianity. This should be the corner stone. We are not willing to stop here. It should also cement the materials of the whole edifice. And it should constitute the capitals and ornaments of its final finish. Without it, there may indeed be corporeal civilization. Several of the States of Antiquity are pronounced to have been eminently civilized before the Christian era. But we are inclined to think it was the civilization of the head, rather than the heart. Body and mind were brought to unite their aid in this effort. Sculpture, painting, and architecture, were carried to their highest pitch. All the arts, which require great physical skill, were successfully cultivated. History and poetry were unexcelled. But they owed no part of their excellence to the virtues of society. Viewed in the era of its highest refinement, it was corrupt to the core. Profligacy, revenge, and refined error, in morals and philosophy, were its striking characteristics. There was an utter destitution of moral loveliness. And we cannot select an era, which will bear the scrutinizing glare of biblical truth. Their very highest efforts were made in times of the greatest turmoil and excitement; affording proof that, while the mind was disciplined for its most extraordinary achievements, the affections of the heart, like an uncaged lion, were left to rage in all their native fury. We merely allude to this species of civilization, for the purpose of pointing out its enormities; and to illustrate the position, that mere civilization of manners, and changes of philosophical opinions, will not, as necessary consequences, produce Christianity; while we may confidently appeal to history to show, that the introduction of the gospel among the rudest nations, has, without producing luxury, been attended by an almost immediate resort to the arts of civilization.

We are aware that we are trenching on disputed ground, and that many have entertained a different theory. By these, Christianity has been deemed the peculiar growth of a more advanced period of human attainment. It has been regarded, so to say, as the *fruit*, rather than the *seed* of civilization. We believe this opinion to be confined to the doctrines of a sectarian philosophy. We do not know that the church of Christ has, at any period of its history, or under any of its phases, had any doubts respecting the perfect applicability of the gospel to uncivilized nations. Paul had none. The Moravians had none, when they entered the missionary fields of India and Greenland. Elliot had none. Brainerd and Martyn had none. And whatever doubts there may have rested on the minds of candid inquirers after truth, on this point, the history and progress of missions, in our own day, and in our own land, has furnished a most triumphant answer on the subject.

So far as my own observation has gone, on the American frontiers, I feel impelled by the force of facts, to affirm that, as a general axiom, Christianity must be regarded as the precursor of civilization That it is a *cause*, and not an *effect*; and that if the action of these appear to be often reciprocal, such reciprocity is, to human view, the result of a belief, and a condition of the affections, which may nevertheless be exercised by individuals the most rude and nomadic in their habits.

(To be concluded.)

GREGG'S ADDRESS BEFORE THE NEW HAMPSHIRE LYCEUM.

Address delivered before the New-Hampshire State Lyceum, in the Representatives' Hall, at their Second Annual Meeting, June 5, 1834. By Jarvis Gregg. Published by request of the Society.

'"Knowledge is Power;" but knowledge is neither wisdom nor virtue. Knowledge is the mere function of the understanding; the material indeed, out of which Reason and Conscience build the fair structures of wisdom and virtue; but the material too, out of which the passions often rear the monuments of folly and vice. Intelligence is to be estimated by its use; applied to wise and virtuous ends, it is the greatest of blessings; to pernicious ends, the severest of curses.'

This is the opening sentence of an address, whose eloquence is no less attractive, than its arguments are convincing. In a preceding essay, we have seen the views of a gentleman, whose scientific attainments and reputation secure him from the charge of enthusiasm, and whose extensive observation gives peculiar authority to his opinions; and we find him expressing the most decided conviction that religion must be the precursor of civilization, even among the savages of the West. In the address before us, the author insists that this is the only conservative influence by which our own state of civilization can be maintained. He remarks, that as light and liberty are almost uniformly seen associated; the inference is very natural, that the last is the consequence of the first; but in this he believes there is a fundamental error. He pays the merited tribute of respect to the efforts of Lord Brougham, and his philanthropic associates, in the promotion of general knowledge; but he considers it demonstrable from the light of reason, and from the history of our race, that they have expected, from the mere diffusion of knowledge, effects which it can never produce.

His first appeal is to the condition of the enlightened, cultivated states of Greece.

'The populace of Athens constituted one grand adult school. Orators, poets, and philosophers were their teachers. The facts of their history, the achievements of their heroes, the glories of their ancestors, were all treasured up in their memories in the enduring forms of eloquence and poetry. The poems of Homer and Euripides and Pindar were inscribed on the living tablets of the Grecian mind, if they were not mouldering in material forms on the shelves of the bookstore, or gathering dust in the unfrequented library. A Grecian ignorant! If he did not know the diameter of Jupiter, or the height of a mountain in the moon, he knew what was far more important for him to know, as a citizen, and a man, the principles of duty as they were then imperfectly developed. His mind was stored with the maxims of philosophy and the sentiments of virtue; his memory was the storehouse of whatever had been wisely said, or felicitously expressed, of the "thoughts that breathed" from the most exalted patriotism, and the "words that burned" upon the lips of the sublimest and sweetest bards.'

And yet Greece is no more.

'Science, art, genius, taste, intelligence, could not save her. In the days of her comparative ignorance and barbarism, she was free. Cultivated, refined, intelligent, Greece was enslaved.'

Rome does not present so striking an example; still, he observes,

'The populace of the Augustan age must have been far more intelligent than that of any previous age. And yet from this point we begin to trace the decline and fall of Rome. If intelligence did not hasten her catastrophe, it did not save her.'

But Modern France affords an overwhelming evidence, that intellectual light may blaze in meridian splendor, without casting one ray of hope upon the darkness of moral pollution.

'They sought to spread the leaven through the whole mass of mind; to draw off from the grand reservoir, innumerable rills, which might water and fertilize the whole face of society. Their conception was magnificent; their visions glorious. Human perfectibility, the supremacy of human reason, the uninterrupted and unlimited progress of human society, were the day-dreams of French philosophy. Their means were wisely selected. A multitude of powerful minds devoted their labors to the preparation of books, treatises, essays and tracts for the people. All France became one great school of philosophy. The stagnant ocean of mind was moved. Its agitation was deep, magnificent and grand.'

And what was the result of this mighty effort of the most powerful intellects, the most skilful managers of the human mind?

'For a while, the philosophers rode proudly and gloriously, like Tritons, amid the waves they had excited. But they had forgotten to provide the only trident of sufficient power to control and allay the storm. Science may excite, and arm, with irresistible might, the powers of the human intellect; but science alone cannot restrain and direct them. So found the misguided philosophers of France, when it was too late. When the disciples of the Encyclopædists, cut loose from all the restraints of conscience and moral obligation, arose in the might of a philosophy, which promised to disenthral the human mind of all political and moral prejudice, and overwhelmed law, order, and civilization with the violence of a torrent, the dreaming speculators on human perfectibility, found that the spirits they had raised would not down at their bidding. The very weapons they had forged in the laboratories of philosophic seclusion, were turned against themselves. They had put the two-edged sword of knowledge into the hands of maniacs, or rather demoniacs, from whose minds were obliterated every sentiment of virtue, every idea of moral accountability. It was not ignorance that deluged France in an ocean of blood, and stained it with crimes at which humanity shudders. It was not an uninstructed, an unreading populace, that perpetrated horrors, which might make the sun in heaven hide his head, and turn the moon to blood. It was the intelligent, philosophical disciples of the Encyclopædists. It was *unbaptized science*.'

Even England has given sad evidence, that the increasing and extending light of knowledge is not the desired panacea for the prevention of crime.

'The fruit of the tree of knowledge, unmixed with that of the tree of life, has been found in England too, to be *unto death*. The process of demoralization and disorganization has kept pace with the diffusion of knowledge. Within the last twenty years, during which these philanthropic efforts have been made, crime in England has more than tripled.

'The parliamentary return, March 29, 1833, shows an increase of criminal committals, which is altogether unprecedented. In 1812 there were 6576—which number, by regular increments during twenty successive years, amounted in 1832 to 20,829. In Scotland and Ireland, the deterioration in morals has been yet more appalling;—crime in the former country having increased during the same period fourfold, and in the latter country sixfold. "If things continue at this rate, (says a writer in a recent review,) we shall have crime going on not as the *square*, but as the cube; in twenty years, the criminals will be 60,000 annually in England; in forty years 180,000; in sixty years 540,000; in eighty years, 1,620,000; in a century, 4,860,000, or nearly a third part of the whole existing population."'

When these facts were recently stated in the English Parliament, it was replied by Lord Brougham, that the inference drawn was by no means just;—that 'the demoralizing effect of the laws—especially of the perpetual oath-taking, and the poor-laws,' and 'the abuse of the poor-laws' were 'counteragents,' which all the efforts yet made for the diffusion of knowledge could not be expected to overcome;—that to these causes, and to the rapid growth of population, was to be ascribed the increase of crime; and that no remedy, however powerful, could be expected at once to neutralize evils so extensive and so inveterate. 'It is,' he remarked, 'like pouring a drop of water into a large quantity of arsenic or prussic acid, thinking thereby to diminish and destroy their noxious and deleterious qualities;' and he urges, that no argument can hence be derived against the acknowledged influence of education, of which even antiquity asserts

'Emollit mores; nec sinit esse feros.'

There is much truth in this reply; and still more in the allusion of the noble reformer to that contracted view of education which limits it to 'reading, writing and accounts.' Let it not be forgotten however, that education, even in the lowest ordinary sense of the term, involves much of *discipline* in connection with instruction; and that the mere communication of the same amount of knowledge through the medium of books, can never produce the same effect on the character. We must also ask again, why the 'great adult school' of Athens, was not purified and preserved by the lessons of its philosophers and historians and poets, and beg the reader to examine still farther, the argument of the address before us.

Mr. Gregg appeals to reason as well as to history. If, he argues, we have two distinct portions of our nature, if there be affections, as well as faculties, both must be cultivated in order to form the complete man.

'There is no tendency in purely intellectual cultivation to moral development. The head and the heart are distinct and independent faculties of the man; each has its appropriate aliment; each demands its own peculiar culture. The neglect to furnish this food and training to the moral powers, leaves one whole department of the human soul uncultivated and waste, to be overspread with a rank growth of noxious and poisonous weeds.'

And what says our experience in regard to individuals within our own sphere of observation?

'Enter our penitentiaries and jails; who are their inmates? The ignorant, the uninformed, the stupid? Alas! how often is the reluctant tribute of admiration extorted from the visiter, as he gazes on the intelligent countenances, keen eyes, and imposing presence of these caged tigers! How often does the suspicion arise in the breast of the admirer of genius, whether virtue be indeed favorable to the development of the highest energies of intellect; whether its proud aspirings, its lofty flights, its bold excursions, be not repressed by the timid prudence of virtue! Who has not gazed with an admiration, amounting almost to idolatry, on a Byron perched in proud scorn on the highest pinnacle of the mount of song—on a Napoleon, by the single might of his genius wielding the energies of half a continent;—though he knew that the former had scattered mildew from his wings, and flung perdition all around him, and the latter sacrificed on the altar of his ambition more than a million of his race?'

These are not indeed new facts or reflections; but when we think of them, how can we but ask, with the author,

'Why then should it ever have been thought, that mere intelligence in the mass of the people would be an infallible guaranty of security and happiness? What is there in diffusion that should change the nature of knowledge? In the case of individuals, whose moral culture has been neglected, knowledge has quickened the propensity, and enlarged the capacity for evil; has let loose the tiger from his cage, and sharpened his appetite for blood. Why then should the experiment, in masses, be expected to contradict all our experience in individual cases? Why should this partial education be expected to do for a nation, what it has never done for individuals? If intelligent, enlightened individuals have been found dangerous to society, why should it be thought that an intelligent community must of necessity be free and happy?'

Is then the flowing stream of knowledge to be checked? This is not our author's view.

'Let the people be instructed. Let the streams of knowledge be sent abroad in copious irrigations over the face of society. But let not these streams water only the wild native growth of the fields, or the poisonous plants, which accident or malice has sown. Let the seeds of moral culture be scattered abroad with a liberal hand, and let their plants be trained by the labors and cares of the diligent cultivator.'—'Let the people then be *instructed;* but let them be also *educated.* Let their intellects be stored with the principles of science, but let their hearts, too, be imbued with the sentiments of virtue. Let the powers of their understandings be developed; but let the faculties of the spirit also be called into exercise.'

In seeking for the means by which this great work is to be accomplished, the writer has no hesitation in presenting that mighty power which gave to Scotland and New England the highest state of education and of morals which the civilized world could present.

'But how, it may be asked, shall this be done? What is the appropriate food of the Spirit? What is the best means of that training which the moral powers demand? To these questions, unhesitatingly, and boldly I answer,—The Gospel of Jesus Christ.'

It is indeed in Christianity alone that the politician will find the long sought check, which shall maintain each portion of the state in its requisite balance, not by the threats of power, or the contests of violence, but by the gentle influence of the law of love, which Christianity inculcates, and the sanctions of a future state which the Bible proclaims. It is here, and here only, that the patriot finds a remedy for the evils which infest his country,—a protection against the dangers which threaten it. Nothing else can check the progress of that spirit of lawless violence, which is stalking through our land, and threatening the safety of our firesides, and the peace of our midnight slumbers.

HOW TO RENDER INSTRUCTION INTERESTING.

Among the maxims of education, which we copied from Mr. Emerson in our last number, one of the most important to success is that which enjoins upon the teacher—'*Endeavor to render your instructions interesting.*' In referring to his life, we had occasion to observe that he made this a special object of attention in his own instructions, and that he was unusually successful. The principles which he adopted, while engaged as a tutor at Harvard University, present some important means of securing the point.

'In order to render the pupil's progress the most pleasing and rapid, it is not enough that the instructor understands the exercises he assigns. He must consult other books; he must think; he must dive into the subject; he must compare; he must be able to illustrate and elucidate, and tell the *why* and *wherefore.*'

The efforts to which the familiar extracts of a letter refer, were not in vain. One of his contemporaries at Harvard observes, that he was 'remarkably clear and satisfactory in his views and illustrations'—'a very popular as well as useful instructor;' and the general testimony of the pupils of his seminary, will satisfy us, that he had attained, to a good degree, the power which he recommends. We have already quoted his remark,—'If a teacher cannot do this—it is of little consequence what other qualifications he possesses;' and the same remarks are not less true of the parent and the religious teacher. Notwithstanding therefore, his modest disclaimer of ability to point out satisfactorily the mode of rendering instruction interesting, we know not to whom we can look so rationally, as to one who was himself successful—and we feel bound to present our readers with the following views, extracted from his prospectus.

'To form an interesting instructor, there must be a foundation in native genius,—an original aptitude of mind. This talent is, no doubt, in some measure, common to all, though dealt out in different portions, to different individuals. As actually possessed by teachers, however, it is probably much more the result of circumstances, of culture, and of effort, than is generally imagined. How then is this talent to be cultivated and improved?

'It may be scarcely needful to remark, that for this end, you should gain a thorough and familiar acquaintance with the branch you teach. It is indeed true, that with the book in your hand, without any knowledge of the subject, you may ascertain, how far your pupil repeats the words of her lesson. But this can hardly be called teaching. At least, it is not your teaching. If any instruction is communicated, it is the book that teaches, and not you. An interesting teacher does much more. He questions his pupils. He hears and answers their questions. He interrogates them again and again. He ascertains, how far they understand the subject. He explains what is obscure. He makes observations, and leads his pupils to make reflections, not contained in the book. In these ways, he enlightens their minds; enlarges their views; gratifies their taste for knowledge; stimulates and delights their curiosity. To do this, he must be well acquainted with the subject.

'The respect, which pupils must feel for such a teacher, will also conduce to increase the interest of his instructions. Their respect and interest may be raised still higher, if he can point out the faults and inaccuracies of the book, state the remarks and opinions of others, and discuss and settle questions, that may appear at once difficult and important.

'To gain the interest of your pupils, you must be ardently engaged in your work. This may be, in some measure, implied in the above remarks. But it deserves a more particular consideration. Our minds are formed to be strongly affected by sympathy. Our feelings are highly contagious. If we exercise and manifest strong feeling, it will be, in some measure, propagated to those around us, though they know not the cause. Much more, when the cause is known; especially if it relates to themselves. Scarcely less contagious are dullness and stupidity. Dull teachers, therefore, must expect to have dull pupils. If, then, you would interest your pupils, you must be ardent yourselves. But how will you kindle and fan such a fire within your own breasts? One method for this, is faithfully to study every lesson, previously to attending recitation. It may have been from neglecting this, more than from any other cause, that those who have long been employed in teaching, are sometimes found to be cold and lifeless in their instructions. Though you may have a good general acquaintance with the branch; though you may have heard the same recitation twenty times before, you should still devote particular attention to the exercise, before meeting your pupils, not only to refresh your mind with thoughts before familiar, but to gain new and more extended views upon the subject. This will excite an interest, which merely reviewing former ideas and reflections, can by no means inspire.

'To excite your interest to the utmost, teaching should be your chief business; at least, it should not be secondary to any other. It should engage your heart and your meditations, by night and by day. It has been remarked, that persons of superior talents and acquisitions, sometimes succeed wretchedly in teaching. One reason of this has probably been, that the current of their vigorous energies has been chiefly directed to other objects,—objects, which they have considered more worthy of elevated genius, than the humble office of a pedagogue.

'If you would keep your own interest continually glowing, let your method of instruction be occasionally varied; mark well the peculiar advantages and disadvantages of each; and exert yourself to the utmost to improve the art of teaching. Reading, writing, and conversing upon the various branches of your employment, will conduce to the same result. Probably nothing has yet been written upon the subject, more worthy of your diligent and frequent perusal, than Watts's treatise on the Improvement of the Mind. Associations of teachers, formed for conversation and correspondence, for mutual improvement in their art, must happily tend to the same effect.

'But scarcely any thing will have a greater influence to render instructions interesting and pleasant, than the mutual attachment of teacher and pupils. To kindle your affection for them, it would seem sufficient to consider the divine requirement to extend your love to all, even to enemies. But in addition to this, you have other excitements, most affecting and powerful. Consider your high obligations to them in particular. They are committed to your special care. Your God, your country, and your patrons are saying to you, "Take these children, and educate them for us." And as you proceed, the very exercise of feeding them with knowledge and understanding, cannot fail to invigorate your attachment. This attachment you must manifest, not so much in profession, as in conduct. "Let it glow in your looks and sparkle in your eyes, and flow forth in all you do and say. By your unaffected smiles, by your condescension, by your affability," by your parental tenderness, "by your assiduity, to assist them to the utmost, make them feel, that you are deeply attached to their welfare—that their improvement is more precious to you than gold." Government you must indeed have. Without this, your instruction will be all in vain. You must constantly maintain your authority. "You must be absolute in your little empires. Your word must be law; but let it always be the law of kindness." As far as possible, govern your pupils, as though you governed them not. While they continually *feel*, let them as rarely as possible *perceive* the hand, that restrains and regulates them. Instead of driving them with the scourge of stern authority, endeavor to draw them with the cords of parental love. Should you be compelled to rebuke, let it be with solemn tenderness—let it be felt, as a faithful wound of a friend—let it be felt, as coming from the wounded, bleeding heart of tenderness. Rarely, if ever, administer a sharp rebuke. Thus you may probably succeed, in some measure, to gain the attachment of your pupils. And you will bear in mind, that this most precious and important boon is to be won, preserved, and increased, by a continued use of the same means.

'Thus, if you have a good general acquaintance with the branches you teach; if you ardently and vigorously pursue your employment; if you make special efforts to be as well prepared as possible, for every recitation; if you strive to improve in your profession, by reading, writing, conversation and reflection; if you cherish an ardent attachment to your pupils, and succeed in gaining and preserving theirs; if you do not attempt too many or too arduous services; if you are favored with a good share of health, and the common smiles of Heaven; you can hardly fail to render your instructions, in a good degree, interesting to your pupils. And thus you will find the task of teaching as delightful to yourselves, as it is profitable to them.'

A YOUNG TEACHER'S HISTORY.

[The following sketch of a teacher's history will illustrate some of the defects in our schools, and we hope, may give salutary warning to those who design to become teachers, as well as to those who employ them.]

When a man enters upon any new scene of action, even if he is well prepared for his duties, he is not so ready in performing them, as he will be when time has given him experience; and it certainly then cannot be expected that one wholly unqualified for his station should pass through his daily avocations without difficulty. Such is the fact with too many individuals who attempt to teach our common schools; and such it was with me when I first entered a New-England school-house as a teacher.

With no direct preparation for the duties devolving upon me, I acted in many respects a very injudicious part. With a mind neither disciplined by study, nor matured by experience, I attempted to lead others into paths wholly untrodden by myself. It is true, that I had made a beginning in study; but all that study would have been as necessary to any mechanical employment. It was a *mere beginning;* for I had pursued an academical course for only one year; previous to which, my pursuits in life had led me far even from the streams of knowledge. I began to '*keep school*,' without an acquaintance with the common branches of education, and what was still worse, I knew *little* of other men, and *much less* of myself. Hence, as might be expected, *self-government* was something to which I was an entire stranger. The teacher's duty was thought to consist in preventing disorder, and 'hearing the boys say their lessons.' Daily experience, however, soon taught me, that it was no easy task to teach others those things of which I was ignorant.

About the time of beginning my course, 'Hall's Lectures on School-keeping' made their appearance; and, fortunately for me, my teacher in the academy recommended the book to my attention. It was of essential service to me; but inexperience and ignorance caused that valuable manual to be of much less value than it would have been in more favorable circumstances. This book, for the most part, was used as a text book by several other teachers and myself, at stated weekly meetings, which we held for conversation on various topics connected with our schools. In these meetings, we gave the results of our own experience, and entered into a full detail of *every* thing that we did. In addition to this, we visited each other's schools, and there saw their everyday operations. Perhaps the course we pursued might have been more beneficial; still it was not unproductive of good. Through the influence of these meetings, of 'Hall's Lectures,' and a few numbers of the Journal of Education, which a friend lent me, I *began* to feel my own deficiencies, and thoughts wholly unknown before, would often pass through my mind. Mr. Hall's ideas, common sense taught me, were correct; but as I was unable to make them my own, they were comparatively of little avail.

In the course of the winter, owing to my extreme ignorance of what belongs to a teacher's duties, I took many injudicious steps. Corporal punishment of the severest kind was the penalty for disobedience to my directions. I endeavored, as I thought, to follow the suggestions of Mr. Hall on the subject of punishment, but I now see, that I greatly erred in the *spirit* of the thing. Though I do not feel authorised to assert that corporal punishment ought wholly to be excluded from common schools, I can say with assurance, that the course I pursued was productive of no good, but of a vast amount of evil. I think it may be further said, that with the exception of *one* boy, with whose parents I boarded, the members of the school had little or no regard for me as a friend or a teacher; and I fear, even to this day, the parents and children of that district cherish towards me feelings of bitter hostility. Although I had to contend with difficulties, I am not inclined to excuse myself in the smallest degree, for no person should ever take upon himself the responsible duties of a teacher, unless he is *well qualified.*

My second attempt at teaching was rather more fortunate than the first; yet it had its difficulties. I trust I was a little better prepared for my employment, but I fear that the preparation was not such as to enable me to do any thing as it ought to be done. I had, in the course of the previous summer, an opportunity of hearing a part of the lectures of the American Institute of Instruction at its first session; but such was the rude state of my mind, that the instructions there given, produced with me but little good. It is true, I began to *think*, but was unable to reduce any thing to practice. As a help in doing my duties, I obtained the 'Education Reporter,' which was indeed a very valuable paper. I read it with much satisfaction, and became more and more impressed with the fact that our schools, to say the least, are badly managed. This paper had the effect of leading me to *think* still more; though I put few of its valuable suggestions in practice. My views of education were still very limited.

I tried, as I thought, while in connection with this school, to treat those under my care as reasonable beings; but I am now inclined to think that reason did not guide me in every thing. Corporal punishment was often inflicted, and in the presence of the whole school, though never at the time the offence was committed. I believe a want of self-government on my part, tended much to increase the faults for which it was inflicted. With a few exceptions, I passed through the time allotted to the school, without bringing upon myself the displeasure of parents and children, and so much better was this second attempt at teaching than the first, that I was invited to take the school the following winter.

Previous to my third trial in school-keeping, the 'Education Reporter' was united with the 'Annals of Education.' This change brought 'the Annals,' which I had not before read, into my hands. The day that first led me to a perusal of this valuable work, was to me a new era in my views of education. Whatever correct views I may now have on this subject in all its bearings, I consider myself mainly indebted for them to the 'Annals of Education.' I first read the work with pleasure, then with profit. The 'Sketches of Hofwyl,' and the Editor's reply to the inquiry 'What is Education?'

were probably more beneficial to me than all other reading on the great subject of man's improvement. I ought not, in this connection, to neglect to say a word respecting the Juvenile Rambler,* and the benefit which resulted to me from its perusal. Though it was a work designed expressly for the young, no number of it came to me without giving much instruction, as well as pleasant reading. I am confident that no teacher of our common schools, situated as I was, could read this little paper without much benefit.

This third attempt at teaching was more satisfactory to myself and others, than either of the former. There was less of corporal punishment, than before, and when inflicted, it was never in the presence of the school. The time was spent more agreeably, and I trust more profitably, both to myself and pupils. I endeavored to act on the principles of Salzmann, whenever difficulties occurred, to '*seek the cause in myself;*' and I think I may say with truth, that the single remark of that teacher has effected more for me in the management of the young than any other one thing.

When that school closed, I entered another of higher order as an assistant. In this I remained a year, at the close of which Providence led me to a new scene of action. I commenced a select school of *five* boys, in the spring of 1833, and continued with it till the present time. The number, at times, has been increased to *thirty-five.* Whether the time spent with this school has been beneficial to my pupils or not, perhaps others can determine better than myself, though it has passed away very pleasantly, both to them and myself. In the course of the last few months, days have often passed without causing an *unpleasant thought*, so far as the school is concerned. For the last two years, I have made use of corporal punishment but once. In that instance, I think a different course would have been better for the individual. My school, it is true, has not been a common district school, and hence it may be said that the experiment is not a fair one. Be this as it may, I am now persuaded that it would be far more beneficial if there were much less of this kind of punishment, than is now inflicted in many schools, and families. If the young cannot be led to do their duty without coercive measures, this may be the *last* resort, but it seems to me this should never be tried until all other means have failed. I meet my pupils as rational, immortal beings, destined with me to live through an existence of countless ages, of which this life is a mere introduction. They come to me as a friend,—one who can sympathise with them in all their difficulties, and who will lend them his aid whenever it is in his power. Hours, days, and weeks glide away, and I hardly know that they pass,—I only realize that they are gone. Perhaps it may be said, that time passed agreeably is no test of a teacher's usefulness.

* A paper for children, established under the direction of the Editor of the 'Annals,' but now united with Parley's Magazine.

I grant it, but I believe the pupil's moral feelings will be little benefited, unless his time in school is pleasantly employed.

Such is the outline of the last few years of my life. I have been guilty of many imprudent measures, but I hope in some degree to atone for them, by future diligence in the performance of duty. Difficulties arose with *men*, from an ignorance of their nature, and with *children*, from an ignorance of *myself*. At first, time was spent unprofitably and unhappily, because I knew not how to spend it. Experience has taught me many severe lessons, which I should desire no young person to learn so painfully; and if this account produces no other good, I hope it may deter the young from entering upon the duties of teaching without a previous preparation.

A YOUNG TEACHER.

STATE OF SCIENCE AND LITERATURE IN RUSSIA

In a former number, we gave an account of the state of Education in Russia, with which we were favored by our correspondent at St. Petersburg. We have received from the same source the following particulars in regard to the condition of Science and Literature in that great empire.

SCIENTIFIC UNDERTAKINGS OF THE GOVERNMENT.

The determination of Triangles, for measuring the degrees of Northern latitude, commenced in 1830, was continued by Mr. Struve, the astronomical professor of Dorpat, assisted by Captain Oberg and Lieutenant Melin, officers of the Imperial Staff. They determined all the points for a chain of 70 triangles, between the Island of Hoghland, in the Gulf of Finland, and the city of Tornea. This chain begins at the northern side of Hoghland, passes through the town of Lovisa, along the lake great Peyan, then to the Westward by Uleaborg, and from thence, by the islands of the Gulf of Bothnia. It embraces six degrees of latitude, stretching more than 600 versts. At sixty of the most Southern points, beginning at Hoghland, signals are placed, and all preparations arranged, so that next year, it may be possible to begin the exact measurement of degrees, by means of the exact determination of the angles between the signals.

Researches on the Cholera, were made by the medical faculties of the Universities of Moscow, Casan and Karkoff, the results were communicated to the ministers of the Interior, in the works of thirteen Professors of the Universities of Moscow, Karkoff and Casan.

The Minister, deeming it advisable that the teachers of the Gymnasia should collect information respecting the natural productions of the places of their abode, and forward the result of their researches to the Academy of Arts and Sciences, caused instruction for this object to be prepared.

Stroelf, the Archeograph, continued his travels and researches in various governments, in order to collect, for the public arch ves, documents relative to the history of Russia.

Professor Arseniesf was appointed to collect, from all sources, official information, in order to give a full course of lectures, on the statistics of the Russian empire, for the instruction of the Heir apparent.

PRIVATE LEARNED AND LITERARY SOCIETIES.

In St. Petersburg, the Society of Mineralogy published four works during the year 1831. Owing to arrangements made by this society, the academician Hess, gave a public course of lectures on Chemistry, with its application to Mineralogy and Technology.

The Society of Apothecaries, consisting of 112 members, in 1831, was engaged in publishing a complete Pharmacologia. This society has a school for training assistants, in which there are 14 pupils.

In Moscow are the following Societies,—The Society of Amateurs of Russian Literature, with 71 members; the Medico Physical Society, with 121 members; the Society of History and Russian Antiquities; and Society of Natural History, with 231 members. This last Society published, in 1831, the 2d and 3d volumes of the Imperial Society of Naturalists.

In Casan, is the Society of Amateurs of Russian Literature. In Karkoff, the Society of Science—17 actual members. In Wilna, the Imperial Medical Society. In Riga, the Free Society of Literature and Practice. They publish the result of their labors in the State Gazette.

In Mittau, are the Society of Amateurs of Literature and Arts, with 98 native, and 112 foreign members; the Society called "Masée et Athénes," with 40 members, employed in collecting books and manuscripts; and a Society for Latin literature.

In Arensburg is a Society for Esthenian literature.

PERIODICAL PUBLICATIONS.

In 1831, under the censorship of the Ministry of Public Instruction, 16 Newspapers and 24 Journals were published in the empire. Of these, 1 was a daily publication, 2 every other day, 9 twice a week, 1 every 5 days, 10 weekly, 6 twice a month, 3 monthly, 2 every two months, and 6 quarterly. Six of these publications were on Politics and Literature; 20 exclusively literary; 4 on Trade, Manufactures and Mineralogy; 2 on Agriculture; 1 on Statistics; 4 on the Art of War; and 3 on Natural Science and Medicine.

Besides these, are the Invalid or Military Newspaper, in Russian and German; the "Journal de St. Petersburg," in French; the

Petersburg and Moscow newspapers, in Russian and German; the Senate newspapers, and sundry Provincial gazettes.

BOOKS.

The annexed Table soews the result of the literary and scientific labors of 1831. By a comparison, it appears that in this year, there was an increase of 101 original works, and 10 translations.

BOOKS IN THE CHIEF LIBRARIES UNDER THE MINISTER OF PUBLIC INSTRUCTION.

		1830.	1831.
In the Public Library,	vols.	272,191	273,776
In the Academy of Arts,	"	100,000	101,116
In the Russian Academy,	"	2,379	2,435
In Wilna University,	"	50,417	51,837
In Dorpat do.	"	51,437	52,449
In Moscow do.	"	20,474	22,777
In Casan do.	"	22,993	23,930
In St. Petersburg do.	"	6,315	7,535
In Romantsoff's Museum,	"	28,910	28,921

BOOKS PUBLISHED IN 1831.

	Original.	Translations.		Original.	Translations.
For learning languages,	58	1	Politics, - - -	3	5
On History, Philology and Criticism, - -	10		Political Economy, - -	2	2
On Poetry, - -	104	15	Commerce, - -	10	
Prose and literary works,	105	50	Mathematics, - - -	13	5
Philological, - -	14	1	Physics, Chemistry, and Natural History, -	21	6
Philosophy, - - -	13	5	Agriculture and Technology, - - - - -	11	2
Religion, - - -	40	2	Science, - - - -	4	
Geography and Statistics,	18	2	Medicine, - - -	45	10
Universal and Russian History, - - -	38	12	Sundries, - - - -	72	6
Legislation, - - -	11				
				592	124

Of which were in Russian, - - - - -	479
In Russian with other languages, - - - - -	10
In German, - - - - - - - - - -	97
In Polish, - - - - - - - - - - -	40
In French, - - - - - - - - - -	33
In Italian, Esthenian and Finnish, - - - - -	25
In Latin, - - - - - - - - - -	23
In Ancient Greek, - - - - - - - - -	2
In Modern do. - - - - - - - - -	4
In Hebrew, - - - - - - - - - -	8

BENEFACTIONS.

In 1827, the Emperor approved of the offer made by the chamberlain Demidoff, to give 20,000 roubles, annually, to be distributed by the Imperial Academy of Arts and Sciences, as rewards. Afterwards Mr. Demidoff made a further grant of 5000 Ro. annually, to defray the expense of printing such works as the Academy thus approved, provided the authors have not the ability to do it at their own expense. He further declared, that by a legal deed, he would bind his heirs to continue these annual payments 25 years after his decease.

Of the benefactions granted in aid of the Schools, the most remarkable for the situation in life of the donors, though not for the amount bestowed, are 1st, The Carrier Revin, 5500 Ro. for the District School of Morshansk. 2d, The Don Cossack, Dunderkoff, 1000 Ro. to the District School of Aksaysk, and 1000 Ro. to the Gymnasium of Novo Cherkask.

REWARDS.

Of the various rewards granted by the learned Societies, on examining the works submitted to them, it may not be improper to notice the grant of a medal, awarded by the Imperial Academy, to the peasant Alipanoff, for the poetical productions which he published.

CULTIVATION OF THE SENSES.

MUCH as we value ourselves upon our intellectual faculties and moral affections, we may not with impunity forget that these are now resident in a tabernacle of flesh,—a body,—the functions of which should always be the subjects of our care, and which claim the earliest and most assiduous attention of those, to whose charge we are committed in infancy. Physical education has ever been, and still is, wofully neglected or misdirected in all its parts. Much of the mental imbecility and moral degradation, as well as bodily derangement and suffering of the human family, may be traced to this neglect. One astounding fact alone may suffice as proof that the neglect or mismanagement of the bodies of children is general, and lamentably great. It is, that more than one half of them die before they have attained the age of 7 years. How unavoidable the inference, then, that a great part of the debility, disease and consequent suffering of that portion of our race, which survives the treatment of childhood, may be deduced from the same cause. That many mental and moral evils also flow from this source may not be at first so evident. But I think a little consideration will show it to be even so.

Our senses, it is allowed, are the means by which we get most, if not all, of the elements of our ideas. Is it not then reasonable to infer that the correctness of our ideas must depend upon the accuracy, with which our senses perceive external things? Surely if our perceptions be wrong, the reflections to which they give rise cannot be right; and the complex ideas which may be formed in the mind, and the emotions awakened in the heart, will of course partake of the inaccuracy. Let me give a familiar illustration of my meaning.

Two boys go out to play, when the thermometer indicates that water will freeze. One of them has been habituated to exercise and exposure to the air. His skin is consequently in a healthful state. The other has been kept from the air, confined most of his time to a warm apartment. The action of his system is consequently feeble. Now is it not reasonable to suppose, that the organs of touch, which are diffused over the body in or near the skin, will in these two boys be very differently affected? And will not the perceptions of their minds be necessarily alike dissimilar? Surely. Their reflections and emotions therefore cannot be the same. One will pronounce the air to be at the right temperature for a game at ball. His body and his mind will be elastic and joyous. He will bound like the roe, and make the welkin ring with his merry shout; and return to the bosom of his family with a gladdened heart, ready to impart and to receive pleasure. The other boy will be too keenly affected by the contact with the air; and think it is too cold to play out doors. He will thrust his hands into his pockets, and curl himself up like one decrepit with age. His teeth will chatter, and his whole frame tremble. Of course very different reflections will be awakened in his mind. He will hurry back to the fireside, thinking winter a dismal season; and will be apt to fret himself and all about him, because of the confinement, from which he has not the resolution to break out.

This may not be so good an illustration as might be found. It is the first that occurs to my mind, and will answer my purpose. For it shows the moral as well as intellectual differences, which may result from the sense of touch, if it be in a different state of health, in two individuals similarly placed. The cheerfulness of one boy and the fretfulness of the other are the opposite moral effects produced by the same temperature, owing to the opposite sensations caused in the mind by the contact of the air.

The other senses are also affected greatly, though not probably so much as the touch is, by the general health and vigor of the body. The number, variety and correctness of their communications to the mind, depend more upon the particular discipline they have each received. Let us consider this matter more particularly.

A perfect infant is undoubtedly born with all the senses, which are at any time possessed by a man. But all of them are to be developed. Necessity awakens, exercises, and therefore unfolds them, to a certain extent. For as all our senses are necessary to our comfortable existence in this world, they will soon be affected more or less by the objects, with which we are perpetually surrounded. Whether we take any pains with them or not, the touch, the taste, smell, sight and hearing of a child will be exercised. But who can doubt that the exercise of these senses may be so directed and regulated by a judicious guardian, as to ensure a much more complete development of them, than they can otherwise attain? And who does not know that they are each of them susceptible of a far higher measure of improvement, than they commonly receive? How exquisite, for example, does the touch of the blind become, whose loss of sight compels them to seek a substitute in this other sense! or the touch of those who have been long employed in some of the more delicate mechanic arts? How far stretching is the sight of men, who are occupied often in watching for very distant objects; and how keen the sight of those who are continually engaged in the examination of minute ones! The worthless native of the forest, and the half savage hunter of our western wilds, 'tis said, can follow the game or their foe through the pathless wilderness, guided merely by the little twigs that were broken, or the leaves turned aside by the fugitive, who to other eyes than theirs has left no trace behind. So too, how delicate are the perceptions of the ear, which has often dwelt upon the harmony of sounds! or how discriminating does the hearing become in our common factories! There, where we are so deafened by the whirl and buzz, that we cannot hear ourselves speak, those who are accustomed to the din, learn so to distinguish between the noise of the machinery and the human voice, that they can converse together with ease in their natural tones.

Thus we see, that necessity and the influence of adventitious circumstances disclose a power in the senses of some men, which we should not suppose it possible for them to have acquired. Now, although we may not thence infer, that the senses of persons in general, could be made to attain such perfection, without the urgency of similar circumstances, yet who can doubt that the senses of all persons might be improved, by proper exercise, to a much higher degree than they usually are? When therefore we contrast what might be done with what is done for the improvement of these avenues of thought, knowledge, and sentiment, how can we avoid the conclusion that the very general neglect of them must have injurious effects upon the intellectual perceptions of men, and thence upon their moral sentiments, feelings, and principles? How such effects may be produced, will need some further illustration. I will attempt to give it, in respect to the senses of sight and hearing.

First, of sight. Those persons, who have been long accustomed, either by the necessity of their situation, the example of those about them, or the judicious care of the guardians of their childhood, to observe attentively the relations of parts, the symmetry of forms, or the contrasts or blendings of color, have eyes that are perpetually soliciting their minds to notice some beautiful or grand perception. Wherever they turn, they espy some new and therefore curious arrangement of the elements of shape, some striking combination of light and shade, or some delicious peculiarity of coloring. The multiplicity and variety of their perceptions must of course increase in proportion the number of their thoughts; or give to their thoughts greater compass or definiteness, or new associations. Such persons are likely to be poets or painters, or sculptors or architects; or at any rate they will duly appreciate and enjoy the productions of others, who have devoted themselves to the practice of these arts. And do we not find persons of this description, with some most melancholy exceptions, to be most readily awakened to descry and adore the power, the skill, and the beneficence of the great Architect who reared the stupendous fabric of the universe, who devised the infinite variety of forms which diversify creation, and whose pencil has so profusely decked his every work with myriads of mingling hues, resulting all from a few parent colors?

But to an unpractised eye the beauties and wonders of creation are lost. The surface of the earth is a blank, or at best but a confused and misty page. Such an eye passes over this scene of things, and makes no communications to the mind, that will awaken thought, much less enkindle the spirit of devout adoration, and fill the soul with love of Him, 'whose universal love smiles every where.' There is a very pertinent and pleasing illustration of my meaning, adapted to young readers, in the story of 'Eyes and no Eyes,' given in the 'Evenings at Home,' and I believe also in the 'Parent's Assistant.'

The effects, which may follow from the due cultivation of the sense of hearing are not less apparent, and certainly not less important. How extravagant to one whose ear is uncultivated may seem the extacy of the amateur in Music! He whose ear has been accustomed to dwell on the melody and harmony of sounds, perceives in them a meaning and a power of expression, which the neglected ear can in no wise comprehend.

'Music! Oh how faint, how weak
Language fades before thy spell!
Why should feeling ever *speak*,
When thou canst *breathe* her soul so well!'

This explanation must be wholly intelligible to one, whose ear has been so much neglected, that he perceives not the significancy of sounds, that are not articulated. How little too can such a one enter into the spirit of the inspired Psalmist, when he tells of the valleys and the hills singing for joy in the wisdom and goodness of their Creator! Music was cultivated so universally among the Hebrews, that we find the Sacred Scriptures abound with allusions to that extatic art. Indeed the most highly wrought descriptions of the heavenly felicity appeal to the charms of music, that they may give us the plainest intimations we can now receive of that seraphic bliss, which yet no eye hath seen, no ear hath heard, nor heart of man hath conceived. But what pleasing thoughts, I fain would know, can be suggested to the mind of him whose ear is deaf to harmony, when he reads of the heavenly choir singing praises to the

Most High,—of the host of the redeemed with golden harps, and voices, all in sweet accord chanting their Hallelujahs,—of the 'Angels, who with songs and choral symphonies, day without night, circle his throne rejoicing.' I may be much mistaken, but while I have been reading the writings of the Hebrew Prophets, who communed so intently with nature and with nature's God, it has seemed to me impossible that any one could enter fully into all the tenderness, the beauty, the sublimity of their language, or receive into his heart all its peculiarity of meaning, unless his eye has been used to trace the skill of that hand, which formed and fashioned every thing that is, and to descry the delicacy of that pencil which has painted all the flowers of the field; nor unless his ear has learnt to perceive the melody and harmony of sounds.

In like manner, I think, might be shown the losses which the soul sustains, and other evil effects which flow from the very general neglect of the other senses. But there is not room nor time for further detail at present. Nor is it needed.

Let it ever be borne in mind by parents, who are appointed of God to the guardianship of the young, and by those who undertake to assist them in the work of education, that their object should be not the communication of the mere knowledge of facts stated, and things described by others; but the development of the faculties of the mind and the affections of the heart, and the unfolding of these in harmony with the divine will. These faculties and affections can be thus developed but by their appropriate exercise; and this is to be had only in direct intercourse with the works of Deity, and by holding individual communion with that Spirit, which breathes throughout them, revealing the holy will of Him who made and who sustains creation. Children ought therefore to be directed, in the outset of their career, to use with care their own senses, and notice attentively their own varied perceptions. Thus should they be introduced to the study of nature. I do not mean that they should be put to study any treatises on natural and moral sciences; I would have them begin long before they are able to use a book with facility. They ought to read, first of all, the volume which is writ by God's own finger. They may very early be made familiar with the alphabet of Creation, form and number, and color and tune; and soon after may be led to notice more and more the endless variety of the combinations of the elements of each of these. Then the perfect order which presides throughout this endless variety, and the exact adaptation of every thing to its use, may be made the objects of their delighted contemplation. Their own observations and reflections will naturally awaken an eager curiosity to know what others have seen and thought upon the same subjects. So soon, and not before, will it be time to introduce them to the scientific treatises which men have written. And they will then be prepared to appreciate the use, aye, even feel the necessity of the technical terms, the nomenclatures, which philosophers have devised, in order that they may arrange what they gather, and communicate to each other, and to their disciples, the results of their researches.

Without presuming to give even an outline of a course of education, I mean now only to insist that the careful cultivation of each of the senses ought to precede all other exercises—that we should ever deem it more important to direct a child to his own perceptions, and awaken him to reflection thereon, than to impart to him the verbal knowledge of the reflections of others. For he will always be imbecile, if not gross, who has not learnt to hear with his own ears, and see with his own eyes, and understand with his own heart. It is not the possession of words, though they be the words of the wisest of men, that will make the learner wise. He must have come to perceive the truth in the exercise of his own faculties, ere he can know its worth, or see its beauty, or feel its power. Language is but the artificial instrument, by which men communicate their thoughts to one another—a very imperfect instrument at best—and used so badly that we are perpetually misunderstanding one another. Our senses and powers of reflection are the instruments, by which we may draw knowledge from its own pure fountains; by which, alone, we can learn the character of God, and hold communion with his Spirit. Think not a child has learnt there is a God, because you have told him so, until he can repeat your words. The most incontrovertible argument for the existence of Deity, the most touching descriptions of his character, are lost upon a wooden or a marble man. It is because your pupil has the same faculties, by which others have discovered the being and perfections of that One, who created and upholds all else, that you may hope he will learn the glorious truth. Why then do you not, from the beginning, induce the child to use these faculties? If you would have him know God, you should let him feel after him, and find him. His first essays may not result in the discovery of the truth, as it appears to your mind; but his subsequent inquiries will lead him to correct his mistakes. Repeated and varied observations will enlarge his range of thought, and lead him at last to perceive and grateful own that there is One,

> 'Parent of good, Almighty,
> To us invisible, or dimly seen
> In these his lowest works; which yet declare
> His goodness beyond thought, and power divine!'

Beyond thought? How much beyond expression, then! Why therefore should we feed our children's souls so much on mere expressions,—on words, the faint, imperfect signs of man's poor, dim conceptions—while they are surrounded with things, which God has made, bearing the impress of Himself?

I am sure the common modes of teaching, are sadly wrong, in this particular especially; and therefore have I endeavored to point it out.

DERBY.

THE STUDY OF THE ENGLISH LANGUAGE,

OR SPELLING, READING, DEFINING, GRAMMAR AND COMPOSITION.

Our labors in the instruction of the deaf mute, first led us to see clearly a truth, for which we had long been groping, when we were expected in ordinary schools to 'transfuse' the theories and rules of Murray into the brains of boys, with all the pompous array of names by which the branches of instruction are designated. Spelling, Reading, Defining, Grammar and Composition, Etymology, Syntax and Prosody, mean nothing more than '*the study of the English Language*.' It is a false refinement, in our view, which has thus divided a simple and comparatively easy and interesting study into several dry and difficult branches, each one of which sometimes costs more labor than the whole actually requires, when pursued in a simple method. After attempting to pursue this same artificial course with the deaf mute, and finding it insupportably wearisome, and absolutely stupifying to the intellect, the simple plan of nature was adopted. The pupil was taught to write sentence after sentence, was told the meaning of the words in a simple phrase, the mode of spelling them, and their proper order, and was required to write a new phrase composed of the same words,' and thus like the gentleman who had 'spoken prose all his life without knowing it,' these ignorant deaf mutes were soon familiar with Spelling, Reading, Defining, Grammar and Composition; and attained a degree of accuracy which surprised all who witnessed it, without being aware of the number of their studies.

On visiting the best schools of Switzerland, we found this same plan adopted. A class of little boys were called upon to *speak* a phrase; they were taught *orally* to spell the words which composed it: they *wrote* it, and thus spelled it again: they were then called upon to *read* it; and to repeat it, and to spell the words again; and then to speak and write a *new phrase*, and to explain the words. On this plan while these simple children only supposed they were '*learning German*,' or rather learning to express their thoughts, they were acquiring five distinct 'studies' besides Chirography! And they acquired them in *fact*, and not in name. We received a letter from a boy of nine years of age, taught in this manner, which surpassed in all its characteristics those of our schoolmates at fourteen years of age, and some of those of our fellow students at college. The same mode of instruction applied to the ignorant adults of our country, would remove half the difficulties of this important, but laborious, and on the ordinary plan, almost impracticable task.

We ought to add, that in this mode of instruction, where the examples of a particular inflection or combination of words became sufficiently numerous, the pupils were taught to remark the general form or principle which pervaded them, and thus imbibe, imperceptibly, all of the theory of language which the young or ignorant can comprehend.

We leave our readers to decide which plan is the most rational and simple. We will only assure them, that so far as our observation has extended, this produces greater accuracy in far less time than the ordinary course. We beg them to recollect the key to all just views on this subject — that language was established before grammarians or lexicographers existed — that its rules and principles are to be found in the practice of the best writers, and that the study of these is the best mode of learning them practically. Our best writers are formed by the study of our best authors.

ON THE PROPER DEGREE OF STUDY IN CHILDHOOD.

HINTS TO YOUNG TEACHERS. NO. VI.

A GREAT deal has, of late years, been said in relation to the quantity and kind of study, which should be permitted to young children. There was a time, and not very long since, when the rage for early development, and the admiration for precocious talent, was extreme; children were pressed a great deal too much, — brought forward too far, and not allowed sufficient time for exercise and recreation. The dangers arising, possibly, (or as some are convinced, *probably*) from this mistaken system, are so dreadful, that it is not surprising that some should feel a blind horror of everything which bears the name of application, and prefer that their children should acquire absolutely nothing, during the earlier period of their lives, — lest they should labor too hard, and essentially injure their health of body or brain. Were there no alternative, I should say that these last were correct and judicious in their opinion on the subject, — and as it is, I should almost fear to advance any argument on the other side of the question, did I not feel entirely convinced that this, among other approved and rational theories, may be carried too far, — and sometimes perverted by *ignorance* or *indolence* (*a* p. 466)

When pupils have reached the period of youth, which is sometimes at ten or twelve years of age, (for it is strictly those under that age that I denominate children, and of whom I generally speak) — when they begin to discover the immense field of acquisition before them, the advantages of which, hard labor will alone procure for them — besides the conviction that the very labor, when successful, carries with it its own reward, — when ambition, and emulation, (which

I consider as two distinct passions) with other incentives, begin to exert their full power, then there is the greatest liability to injurious application. But I am inclined to think that this is *rarely*, at least, the case with the very young (even taking into view, the greater delicacy of all their organs,) — from the exceeding volatility of their minds, — the never ceasing action of external objects upon them; their proneness to fly from everything which would confine their attention for any length of time, and the small comparative power which external motives exercise over them.

Watch the very best and most industrious child while learning a lesson which he perhaps has really a great desire to acquire; how easily is his attention diverted, how volatile are his thoughts, how readily, because how unconsciously, are the head and the eye turned, if anything foreign from the book he is conning, attract his attention. I do not mean to say that children do not often make great efforts, I have reason to *know* that they *do*, — or that they may not be exceedingly stimulated by affection, by fear, and even by ambition; but I think instances are rarely found when any of these inducements lead them far enough in advance of their strength to do them any real injury, — at least, if the teacher constantly watch, as he should do, the effects of every employment on the opening mind, and delicate frame of his pupil. (*b* p. 467.)

It appears to me then, that the degree of study and application of each child should depend wholly upon his peculiar character, constitution, and tendencies: all are not of one organization, and we should be careful not to fall into the too common error of treating them as if they were. I should advise every teacher to examine carefully the various capacities of the children committed to his care, and to govern himself and them accordingly.

It is acknowledged by all, that some constitutions can bear uniformly a much greater quantity of food than others, and so it is with their mental nourishment.

While in health, therefore, nature will best direct the degree of exercise proper for each of their physical and mental organs (*c* p 467.) as long as they are purely natural, — as long as they are children; and while too much care cannot be taken to keep back those who are feeble and can bear but little, but who are at the same time anxious to learn, we should not extend that restraint to others, whose strong and active capacity, *both bodily and mental*, crave and require a great deal of exercise. See, in both cases, that the food be wholesome in itself, and appropriate to their age and state. There are many plays which children engage in, as a recreation, far more laborious both to body and mind, than some of the exercises to which an intelligent instructor will lead the attention of his pupil; and who would be apt to fancy that a child could injure his mental system by too much play. (*d* p. 467.)

While therefore the teacher should aim to blend amusement so happily with instruction, as to render the latter truly a pleasure, he should be careful not to fall into the great mistake of supposing that instruc-

tion can always be rendered an *amusement*. There is such a thing as hard study, study which is a labor, but which cannot be dispensed with, in the path of knowledge; yet it brings its own reward even to quite young children, and they have sense enough to find it out. (p. 167.) They will not at the present, or in future time, thank the teacher who should remove from before them, step by step, every difficulty which it may require strength and zeal to overcome; because there must come a time when this labor will begin, and it comes hardest, because distasteful to that mind which has been carefully kept from perceiving and preparing for it. Nothing good can be acquired in this world without effort, and great effort; but it does not follow that this effort, this labor, is irksome or painful. On the contrary, I maintain that it may always be rendered a pleasure of itself.

In the case of quite young children, teachers have been too apt to do for them all or nothing. To prove the sum, to solve the question, to find the result for the scholar, or, on the contrary, to leave him alone and unassisted to perform all these wonders for himself, and by this means to become perhaps discouraged and weary; instead of firmly insisting on his doing his duty, but at the same time gently and kindly putting him in the right way to it by assisting him to look around, or *within himself*, to discover the means; and these remarks may refer to the youngest pupils. *There is no period when the mind [illegible] only and spontaneously by a [illegible] dependent on itself*, it always has it in a certain proportion and quantity, and it matters little whether the work to be done be spelling a hard word, or solving a question in algebra, the principle is the same; and if a little child acquires the habit of thinking that he may, parrot-like, repeat from the teacher the letters of his infant lesson, he will expect, and with reason, that his mind shall remain equally passive when it arrives at the difficult studies of mature years. I will readily admit, that it is far easier for the instructor himself to carry his pupil along in this soft and easy manner; but by doing so, he encourages indolence in himself, and discourages every good and useful energy of the child. Better let him read one page a day, manfully mastering it himself, word by word, than twenty, with the teacher to prompt, and spell, and pronounce for him. Still, he should never be left to his own unassisted efforts. The teacher should give him his whole attention, and testify the kindest interest, ever ready to throw in a little timely aid that he be not discouraged before he has finished. Let him recollect too that nothing can be more discouraging to an intelligent well disposed child, while doing his best to satisfy his conscience and his instructor, than to perceive that instructor's attention taken off, even by the necessary and equally important employments of others. I can myself remember numerous instances of disappointments and discouragements from this cause, when a child at school. The custom of helping him *too much*, has precisely the same effect upon his mind, since it inspires him with a belief that a teacher has not patience with his little mistakes, and is in a hurry for him to get through his lesson. He consequently makes a thousand more than he would otherwise have done; and ends with feeling dissatisfied, both with himself and his instructor. A teacher should always preserve such perfect order in his school, and induce such universal kind feeling between his pupils, that each will give way on occasion to the other, so that the regular business shall never be interrupted, unless by some unforeseen or accidental occurrence. In such a case he should stop the reading or the lesson, till his attention can be given again entire; for this will clearly show the child to whom he is at the moment attending, that he is devoted to him and to his improvement, and that neither his attention nor his negligence can escape his notice. I have observed children, while reading or reciting, take a direct advantage of their teacher's momentarily distracted attention, to run on in their lesson with utter carelessness, making innumerable unobserved mistakes,—and when the teacher attends again, unless required to repeat, go on as if they had been reciting correctly. Let me observe, that this never would be done, unless an instructor were in the habit of such culpable negligence, for though every one, even with the best order, may be subject to occasional, unexpected interruptions; yet children will respect the known laws of their teacher, if he has been in the habit of enforcing them.

I have had previous occasion to remark, that as far as I have been able to judge of *Infant Schools* I should decidedly not prefer them for any but infants in fact. I have had more than one instance of their highly injurious tendency when acting on the mind, after a very early period of childhood. They are indeed truly Christian institutions, and many a parent may bless them for having kept his child from utter ignorance or vice; but it seems to me that they should, like public schools, be left to that large class of persons in every community, who *cannot* give their children the superior advantages of a *small* private school, or of that tuition, perhaps still better, which the conscientious and judicious parent can administer amid the pure and holy influences of the domestic circle. I say *perhaps*, because I am aware that it is still a question, whether the advantages of particular attention and care at home, are not over balanced by the want of that association inseparable from a school life.

As it will probably be inferred, from my preceding remarks, I am of opinion that children have as often too little, as too much to do in common schools: that they are happier, as well as better, when all their energies are in healthy action, and that they are generally capable of greater exertion without danger of over exercise, than is generally required or expected of them; if, as I before observed, (and it cannot be insisted upon too strenuously) that action be of an appropriate and judicious kind, and if watchful care of their bodily health be constantly taken; if that action too be spontaneous, free, the result of their own wills, after those wills have been biassed to high and good desires. Be this then the part of the teacher, train up your pupils to regard the *quality* rather than the quantity of what they acquire — to incite their own wishes to what is good; to industrious exercise, to active duty, to progressive steps in wisdom and virtue, and you will give them an impulse which will go with them, through this life, to another and a better.*

REMARKS OF THE EDITOR.

(*a.* p. 462.) We fully agree with our correspondent that this principle in education, like every other, is liable to abuse, and that there is danger of banishing hard study from our schools; but we feel it necessary to make some remarks on a few points in which our own experience and views do not coincide with his.

It is only among the few, and the highly cultivated, among those who have witnessed or experienced the effects of excessive application, or those anxious and indulgent parents who dread every breeze, or humor every caprice, that we have met with this 'horror.' The tendency of our countrymen, is, more than that of any other nation we have seen, 'to drive on,' in this, as in every other object. The most rapid methods of instruction are the most popular. Parents are ready to complain if their children do not 'learn fast,' and expect to receive *so much knowledge* for every dollar of tuition.

We have known a mother ignorantly accuse a child of idleness, who was disqualified for study by a fatal disease of the brain which study had produced. We have known an intelligent parent reproach the teacher of an infant school, because a feeble child, of four years old, did not learn to spell and read as fast as he anticipated. We have heard more than one teacher mourn, that parents would not allow him to adapt the employment of their children to their condition, but demanded more than he was satisfied they could safely perform. Some of the most judicious and thorough teachers we have known, have complained, that they could not give the thorough instruction they desired, because parents insisted on hurrying their children on.

We regret to believe that the 'rage for early development' — 'the admiration for precocious talent, is still unsubdued; and that we must speak of it in the *present* and *future* tense, as well as the past. Nor can it cease, until our national character, our universal anxiety to press forward into life is checked — nay, until parental vanity shall be brought more under the influence of religious principle, and of sound views in reference to the structure and offices of the human frame. That the apprehensions of precocity alluded to are not new, our correspondent may be satisfied by turning to old works on education. We happen to have at this moment before us, a work by Caroline Rudolphi, one of the most distinguished German writers on education, in which she advises that a child should read no books until six years of age, but only hear them read. This opinion is common in Germany; and where do we find more profound scholars?

* This number was intended to appear previous to the last one, which will account for the reference made in that to some of the remarks in the present paper.

(*b* p. 463.) We would merely observe here, that ambition in study, in ourselves, was never more strongly excited than at five years of age, — that we never witnessed it more powerful in its influence than in a school-mate of the same *age*, — that no visible evil was produced upon either of us for several years — that our companion was an early victim of epileptic fits, and died a premature death; — and that the habits thus produced, and the seeds of debility and disease thus implanted, have rendered a large part of our life a course of bodily and mental suffering.

(*c* p. 463.) If by 'nature' our correspondent means the *disposition, or inclination* of children, we suspect that it would not direct their confinement for six hours in a day to a school-room, until the first seven years of life were past. If he means their *constitution* or *formation*, Physiologists, who have studied it most, assure us, that it is perpetually overtasked by the present plans of early education; and they appeal, not only to individual cases, but to the feebleness of the present generation, compared with the vigor of our forefathers, who spent a large portion of their early years in activity, in the open air, as an experimental proof of the justness of their views.

(*d* p. 463.) We would beg leave to remind our correspondent, that to adults, the absorbing novel, and the absorbing study are, at the moment, very often, a delightful amusement — and that they still produce the worst consequences. It is only to adapt the novel or the study to the capacity of childhood, and you may produce the same absorption, the same amusement, or 'play' in the child, and the same evil. It is nothing extraordinary for a child to neglect his meals, and *active* games for the *intellectual* '*play*' he finds in an engaging book.

(*e* p. 464.) If our correspondent employs the word 'study,' as it is commonly used, for *intense and continued application to books*, we would remark that the most judicious parents, and educators, and writers within our knowledge, think that 'study' ought not to be required before six years of age — that there is enough, and more than enough to be learned by observation, and moral instruction, and reading, until that period. Physicians, (not phrenologists,) inform us, that until that age, the brain does not acquire its consistency, and that it is totally unfit for 'study.'

The remainder of the article, if applied to a later age, contains in our opinion, just and important views on a subject now too much overlooked; not so much as we believe from the abuse of truth, as from that mental indolence, which scarcely allows a modern adult to read anything, more substantial than a newspaper or magazine. Other remarks on the general subject will be found in an article on Excessive Study in our last number, and in the following sketch of Caldwell's discourse.

CALDWELL ON PHYSICAL EDUCATION.

Thoughts on Physical Education, being a Discourse delivered to a Convention of Teachers in Lexington, Ken., on the 6th and 7th of Nov., 1833. By CHARLES CALDWELL, M. D. Boston: Marsh, Capen & Lyon. 1834. 12mo. pp. 133.

THEY who have felt the difficulty of bringing an important subject within the compass of an hour will not be surprised that on a subject so extensive and important as physical education, Dr Caldwell was led to expand a lecture into a volume. The discourse before us was delivered before the first General Association of Teachers in Kentucky, and the most important of which we have heard in the Western States.

Dr Caldwell commences with lamenting the abuses of the press in our country, and the corruption and falsehood which they are producing. He regards *education* as our only means of safety, and *physical education* as an essential part of it — as the basis upon which a sound education must rest. In regard to the care of infants, he urges the necessity of pure air, scrupulous cleanliness, and a proper temperature. He allows no improper food under pretence of strengthening the stomach; and he believes that even ripe summer fruit, without cooking, produces, on the average, more evil than good.

In regard to cleanliness, he observes, that this minor virtue is sadly neglected even by adults, in our country; and that if they would *wash the whole body* much more frequently, they would be purer, more comfortable, and more healthy than they are. He repeats the remark of Dr Rush, that 'crying, within proper bounds, is good exercise for the lungs and other vocal organs of children' — that 'to cry and be fat,' is often as true as 'laugh and be fat.' He warns against premature efforts to teach them to walk; he urges the necessity of early restraining the passions; and enjoins that 'children should never be allowed to obtain what has once been denied them by breaking into a passion about it.'

In accordance with the warning already given, not to injure the limbs by premature use in walking, Dr C. urges, with more anxiety, that we should not endanger the safety of an organ, far more delicate, by premature or too severe demands upon the brain. He assures us, that the anxiety of parents may do irremediable mischief to this organ, that until the seventh year, all its energies are necessary for its own healthy development, and that of the other portions of the body. He remarks that it is *not the mind*, but *the brain* that toils and is oppressed by the studies of the school; and that if parents were fully aware of the danger, they would no more overload the infant's brain with the studies of a school, than they would his limbs, by compelling him to carry burdens. On these grounds Dr C. disapproves of infant schools, on any plan but that which seeks to occupy and amuse, without requiring confinement and effort of mind. He goes so far as to say;

'It would be infinitely wiser and better, to employ suitable persons to superintend the exercises and amusements of children, under seven years of age, in the fields, orchards and meadows, and point out to them the richer beauties of nature, than to have them immured in crowded school-rooms, in a state of inaction, poring over torn books and primers, conning words of whose meaning they are ignorant, and breathing foul air.'

In passing to the maxims of physical education which relate to the school-room, Dr C. insists particularly, that children should not be allowed to sit in currents of air, or with damp feet or clothes; for that exposure which is perfectly safe, while in motion, will injure the most vigorous constitution, when at rest.

In his observations upon diet, he endeavors to guard us against the besetting sin of our country, in strong terms.

'Eating too much, and of unwholesome articles, is a national evil in the United States; and were I to add, a national disgrace, the charge would scarcely be too severe. I confidently believe, that the thirteen or fourteen millions of people, inhabiting this country, eat more trash *for amusement*, and *fashion's sake*, and to *pass away the idle time*, than half the inhabitants of Europe united. Unquestionably they consume a greater amount of such articles, in the proportion of *five to one*, than an equal number of the people of any other country I have ever visited. Shame, if not prudence, should drive them from a practice, which might well be called disgusting.'

To this cause he ascribes the frequent dulness of children in their afternoon tasks; but while he cautions parents against allowing excess in their children, it seems to us, he ought to have warned teachers, that it is not safe to occupy the mind *vigorously*, while the stomach is employed in digestion, even if the meal has been moderate.

In treating of the education of the lungs, he urges the importance of healthy, dry, and elevated situations for school houses; and of careful ventilation, as not less necessary to the formation of healthy blood, and to the vigor of body and mind, than proper food. Singing and declamation he deems highly important as exercises for the lungs, muscular exercise is equally important to secure the proper circulation of the blood; and 'without this,' he remarks, 'even the brain itself cannot receive its full supply of well-formed blood.' In literary men, therefore, he observes,

'The vigor of the brain is diminished by a twofold cause, "exhaustion from its excessive labors, and a defective supply of sound arterial blood, which is its *vital food*." Though in a given time, then, a literary man may accomplish a greater amount of work, by inordinate and unremitting cerebral toil, he cannot do it so well. In a particular manner, the product of his mind will have less brilliancy and power. It will be like the fruit of advanced age, contrasted with that of the meridian of life — like the Odysey of Homer, compared to the Iliad, or Milton's Paradise Regained, to his Paradise Lost.'

We have not time to examine Dr C's. speculations concerning the connection of matter and mind; but we were struck with the thought, that the Creator has given the body to be *the instrument* and not *the clog* (as it is too often termed) of the mind, and that it is ungrateful to ascribe to Providence that interruption of our mental labors, which is generally owing to our abuse of the wonderful organs which are appointed to be its servants.

In addition to the connection of the mind with the brain as its organ, Dr C. maintains, as a phrenologist, that the various faculties perform operations through distinct portions of the brain. By considerations of this kind he urges with more force, and explains with more appearance of reason, some maxims which have become established among those who have thought deeply upon education.

One of these, which we have formerly exhibited in our views of the system of Fellenberg, is, that pupils should pursue several studies at the same time, in order that no single faculty should be excessively fatigued by continued application. In connection with this, are two other important points. The attempt to burden moderate faculties wtih a task to which they are not adequate, either by urging on a youth to studies for which he has no talent, or by attempting to make him a literary man, whom nature obviously designed for an active or mechanical employment, not only disappoints the end which was aimed at, but endangers the health of the body, and the soundness of the mind. It is not less dangerous to excite one who possesses some peculiar talent in the highest degree, to devote himself exclusively to its cultivation; for Dr C. assures us, that inflammation of the brain, and madness itself, are often produced in this manner. On the other hand, it must not be forgotten that a temperate exercise of the brain is as important to the vigor of the body as of the mind. Experience does not need the aid of phrenology to assure of what that science distinctly teaches and explains, that *the neglect of mental occupation* will often produce stupidity or imbecility, and that those who abandon all attempts at improvement in later life, only hasten the decay of age.

To maintain the body in its vigor, it is of still greater importance to maintain the proper balance of the feelings. The proverbial longevity of mathematicians and philosophers, compared with that of poets, we have formerly noticed in illustrating the influence of strong emotions.

'Passion,' observes Dr C.' 'when fierce and unrestrained, resembles intemperance in the use of strong drink. It inflames or otherwise deranges the brain, hastens the approach of old age, and curtails life, on the same principles. In delicate and irritable systems, it often excites convulsions, and sometimes palsy, apoplexy and madness.'

On the other hand he observes;

'The influence of strong and well cultivated morals and intellectual organs on the general health of the system, is soothing and salutary, and feeds and strengthens it, instead of ruffling and wearing it out. Compared to the influence of the organs of passion, it is as mild and wholesome nourishment, contrasted with alcohol, or like the genial warmth of the spring and autumn, to the burning heats of summer. Life, and health, and comfort may last long under the former, while all is parched and withered by the latter.'

It is remarkable that of the fiftysix signers of the Declaration of Independence, all of them men of well-cultivated and well-balanced minds, fifty four attained an average age of sixtysix years and nine months. The two others died from accident. It is a confirmation of the same general views, that the periods of revolution and excitement, and the countries most agitated by conflicts of opinion and feeling. produce the greatest number of insane persons. While England has but one lunatic in 820 inhabitants, the state of Connecticut has one for every 262 of its inhabitants ; and our country generally has a far greater proportion than any other in the world — a result no doubt of the intense excitement of feeling — the constant pressure *onward*, which marks every period, every pursuit, and every station in life. Dr C. ascribes much of it to the intense eagerness for wealth, which he considers peculiar to us.

In connection with the effect of excessive intellectual effort or excitement, in producing insanity, Dr C. observes, that that sad disease of literary men — *dyspepsia* — is to be ascribed, to a great extent, to the same train of causes. Like insanity, this complaint is more prevalent in our country than in any other known. In Europe it is confined chiefly to the higher classes; but in the United States it invades every portion of society. Like insanity, he observes, it 'commences as often in the brain as in the stomach, possibly oftener.' The American savage, and the English laborer, who eat an immense quantity of food, and even the Esquimaux, who eats ten or twelve pounds of solid animal food in a day, and swallows with it a gallon of train oil, rarely, or never, suffer from indigestion : while, on the other hand, the literary men, public officers, and speculators of civilized nations, give melancholy proofs of the ravages of dyspepsia ; although they often use the most select and judicious diet. When the stomach alone is tasked, it is obvious that it will sustain an extraordinary burden. It is only when it is robbed of its nervous energy by the abuse of the brain, that it produces the intense sufferings of which the literary man complains. And even if the anxious dyspeptic undertake to balance excessive effort of mind by attempting at the same time that bodily toil which he supposes gives the laborer his iron organs, he will usually only succeed in wearing out body and mind together. '*Be temperate in all things, — be anxious for nothing*,' are maxims no less important to health than to piety. The anxieties of the exchange or the counting-house, or even of the voyage or journey of business, are often more ruinous to health, than the intellectual labors of a quiet student.

As an additional evidence of the truth of this position, Dr C. refers to the well known fact that many a dyspeptic, after trying in vain the effects of the whole *Materia Medica*, with the most rigid diet, and regular habits, is relieved at once by throwing off his occupations and cares for a few weeks, although he encounters every species of irregularity with regard to sleep, diet, and weather. Were we gifted with the talent of the author of 'the Miseries of Human Life,' we could utter many a dolorous groan in response to the remarks of Dr C.; but we will only say, that he who returns from such a journey, ascribing its results merely to exercise, to company, or above all to indulgence, and attempts to maintain health, by pursuing the same courses in connection with his usual cares or studies, will only plunge himself deeper in sorrow.

The remainder of this discourse, is chiefly occupied with the subject of dress, in which the great principle is, that nothing should be so tight as to restrict the motion of *any* organ, or the free circulation of blood. Dr C. remonstrates in the most feeling manner against the use of corsets; he shows that they destroy that symmetry of form which is admired in the models of antiquity, that they injure, by compression, the most important vital organs, and that thus they often produce the most dangerous diseases, the sad heir-loom of succeeding generations. '*The descendants*' he observes, '*of tight-corsetting mothers, can never become the luminaries and leaders of the world.*' It can only be expected that they will 'inherit a *corset-broken* constitution.' If all other arguments fail, cannot *female vanity*, or *womanly affection* be enlisted in checking this suicidal practice?

We have thus given a brief analysis of a discourse which we hesitate not to pronounce the most comprehensive and valuable treatise on this branch of education, that has appeared in our country. We shall rejoice if our remarks induce our readers to study it, and to reduce to practice some of its important principles, principles which may be tested without adopting the theories with which they are connected in the mind of the writer, and which the nature and limits of our work do not allow us to examine.

ABBOTT ON THE DUTIES OF PARENTS.

The Duties of Parents in regard to Schools where their Children are instructed. A Lecture delivered before the American Institute of Instruction, at their fifth Annual Meeting. By Jacob Abbott. Published by order of the Institute. Boston: Carter, Hendee & Co., 1834.

This lecture relates to a topic more important to the welfare of our schools, and the progress of education, than any other which can be named. If those who *provide the teacher, and direct the school,* fail in their duties, the best 'school system' may become a curse, and even if they provide the best teacher, and secure the best methods, and the best books, their children may still be ruined if parents do not do their duty continually to the pupils and the school. Mr A. presents to parents the following as their principal duties in reference, to schools, and illustrates them in his own clear and simple manner.

I. The first duty which you have to discharge in respect to the school, is to feel yourselves, and do what you can to awaken in others, an interest in it before it is commenced.

II. Make proper efforts, and be willing to incur the necessary expense, to secure the best teacher whom you can obtain.

III. You can co-operate very powerfully with the teacher whom you shall employ, by taking an interest in his plans and labors, after he shall enter upon his work.

IV. Submit cheerfully to the necessary arrangements of the school which are required for the general good.

V. Do not judge the teacher on the testimony of your children, (alone).

VI. When the teacher has done wrong, do not condemn him too severely.

VII. Set your children such an example, too, as you wish them to imitate.

We believe most friends of education would admit on reading this simple, practical view of a subject so important, whose neglect leads to so much difficulty and sorrow, that it merited the high compliment paid it by the Institute, in directing ten thousand copies to be printed, at a low price, in the hope that it would be circulated extensively — a compliment which no elegant writer, or accomplished scholar need envy, for it is paid to its plain, common sense character — its adaptation to do good to the mass of the community.

Mr Abbott concludes his lecture with some remarks on the necessity and mode of government at home, in which he observes that ' almost every case of gross failure in education on the part of virtuous parents,' which he has known, may be traced to the neglect of one of two principles. 1. ' Keep your children from bad company. 2. Make them obey you.'

We are not fond of reducing a complicated course of duty to maxims so simple as to produce mechanism or indolence; and we regret that Mr Abbott was prevented by the desire for brevity, and the haste of publication, required by the Institute, from bringing out more distinctly the idea evidently intended, that they are but two of the most essential, among many important maxims. Still, this very lecture requires a variety of duties which are rarely alluded to. It is also true, that we rarely find a child corrupt, who ' is made to obey,' and ' kept from bad company :' and yet it is certain, that some parents who follow these directions to the letter, are only the tyrants of their children, and prepare them to run wild, as soon as this fetter system is destroyed.

We can find, however, no adequate foundation for the fears entertained of its effects, or the violent attacks made upon it by some. The ground of both is found, in *two sentences only*. ' Make them obey you. If parents ask how shall we make our children obey, we answer, in the easiest and pleasantest manner you can, but at all events, MAKE THEM OBEY.' A comment is previously given, ' they must be governed at home — or they are ruined.' It is said in opposition to this, that Jehovah does not *make* men obey. We ask whether he did not punish the Jews, when they disobeyed, and until they obeyed ; and does common sense understand anything else by ' MAKE them obey ?' To be held down by force, is not to obey an order to be still. In the law which Jehovah himself gave, it is written, that he that obeys not his father or mother, shall die. Is there any higher sanction to obedience?

'But this simplification of duties will give indulgence to lazy parents.' We confess, we rarely find such disposed to take this trouble; but if they are induced to do it by this lecture, we think even the reviewer may rejoice. And if the multitude of those who '*will* be rich,' and find no time to train their children, could thus be led to find time to '*make them obey*,' many teachers in the land would bless the day in which it was delivered. In propounding one simple subject of attention, Mr. A. has required a long course of labor, and 'training,' which we should think the reviewer's eye would at once have perceived to be inevitable. He only claims that compulsion is '*usually inapplicable*,' but admits its necessity *sometimes*. He wishes that mild means may be employed, or, in other words, 'make them obey in the pleasantest manner you can.' But if this does not succeed he must admit, and we think does admit, with Mr Abbott, 'at all events MAKE THEM OBEY.'

The complaint, after all, amounts to this, and we think it one to which Mr Abbott's rapid course of authorship often exposes him, that principles which are important, have not been brought out with sufficient distinctness to guard against misapprehension and abuse. We could wish that influence like his, might never be exerted in an unguarded manner.

[For the Annals of Education.]

THE ORIGIN AND VALUE OF 'THE PICTURE SYSTEM.'

IN the May No. of the 'Annals of Education,' there is a communication signed X, on what is there called the 'Picture System;' that is, the use of engravings in education. This writer affirms that there is a numerous and increasing class of persons, interested in education, who are possessed with a *mania* for pictures, and insist that the parlor and the school-room shall be covered with them, and that the pages of all juvenile books and papers shall be illustrated with cuts. There are some, he says, who go so far as to reject ordinary engravings, and are satisfied only with good ones! To such an extent indeed has the evil already gone, that not only are our youth imagined to be in danger of ruin, but our adults are said to be affected with mental and moral disease; and as an awful evidence of the extent of its ravages, it is stated, that there is, throughout the land, a cry for short chapters, short articles in the newspapers, short prayers, and short sermons! Such is the fearful state of things, according to X; and a large share of these evils, it appears, is attributed to the 'Picture System.'

Now for myself, I freely declare, that, if there is such a cry in the land, and if it is to be attributed to the 'Picture System,' important as I believe that system to be to the great cause of education, it has produced one benefit that I had not credited to the proper source. I believe that short articles in the newspapers, short prayers, and short sermons, are in general, better than long ones. The best example of a prayer that has ever been furnished is short, and if we recollect right, it was the Pharisees, and not the disciples, who used long ones. The best specimen too of a sermon (it may be found in the forepart of St Matthew's Gospel,) is also short, and if the 'Picture System' has brought people to prefer short prayers, and short sermons, it has so far tended to cultivate good taste, sanctioned by those beautiful models which Christ has afforded. If then the author of 'Peter Parley's tales' has been, as affirmed by the writer in question, a leading promoter of the 'Picture System,' and its consequences, common sense, taking the accusation of X. from his own mouth, will award him a degree of praise, which I suspect he would not himself be disposed to claim.

But although I can see little justness, or consistency in the communication of X. so far as it blames the 'Picture System,' I am free to admit that all good things are liable to abuse; and those which are the most obviously valuable, are perhaps most likely to be abused, either by being carried to an extravagant length, or turned to pernicious uses. It may be that there are foolish people who are for making education a mere matter of play; who are unwilling to task the eyes and intellects of children with study, and would rather teach them by pictures and other facilities. It may be, too, that there are books of which the pictures constitute the only merit. But it is to these seeming evils, that X. attributes the pervading taste for short sermons, and short prayers, a taste which every person of sense will commend. Thus the bad tree, is, by this logic, made to produce good fruit;' thus we gather grapes of thorns, and figs of thistles. Let us rather be consistent, and admitting the facts, allow that some real evil may flow from them. But let us not permit a comparatively few instances to swell into the greater number; nor dwell upon the backward current of the eddy, till we forget the quiet, but deep onward movement of the stream. Let us not take abuses of any system, exceptions rather proving the rule, for a test of its utility; and let us not allow the kaleidoscope of a heated fancy to multiply the few who are disposed to carry the 'Picture System' to extremes, into a dangerous legion.

Let us consider, that, if there are extremes on one side, there are also extremes on the other. If there are persons who would make education all play, there are those who would make it all work. There are some 'ripe scholars' who are opposed to all facilities in education, and I believe to this very hour, it is the practice of many eminent teachers in England, to require boys to begin the study of latin, by giving them a grammar written in latin. This absurd system, in a greater or less degree, is still fostered by the University of Oxford, and I doubt not, there are many educated in the spirit of the olden time, who maintain that this is all right, and the new views all wrong.

The truth in this case as in others seems to lie between the extremes. The training of the mind should like that of the body, consist not wholly of either play or toil, but of the mingling of both. If a child is never required to study a dry and difficult lesson; if he is never made to apply himself with patience and energy to the mastering of some extensive subject, his mind, like an arm tied up in a sling, will become weak and indisposed to exertion. But if, on the other hand, he is compelled to bend steadily over a repulsive task, and inch by inch to creep through pages which reward him with no clear ideas, no gratification suited to his taste and years, he is condemned to suffer a species of tyranny at which a Russian peasant would revolt. We once heard of a beggar who was willing to work, and being offered a dollar a day to pound with the head of an axe upon a log, after trying it for an hour, quitted it in disgust, choosing rather to run the risk of starvation, than labor without witnessing any result from his exertions. And children, thus tasked and driven, though they may seem to plod on, and master page after page, are still working with an averted mind; they disrelish the book; their faculties instead of being enlarged and developed, are dulled and stunted. A few, stimulated by ambition, or aided by ready powers of acquisition may advance; but the greater number will learn to shuffle at their recitations, and either get into the habit of learning mere words without ideas, or get accustomed to being content with dim and partial knowledge; and, finally, if the master uses the rod, they will probably learn to cheat. Thus, if on the one hand, there is mischief in the system of all play, on the other hand, there is still greater evil in the system of all work.

The picture system seems to be regarded by some persons as a modern invention. The golden age of instruction, according to X. was thirty years ago. But did not Dilworth and the New England Primer have pictures? And was not Emerson's Primer, a few years later, embellished with some 75 wood cuts? Yes, and shocking things they were. I was among the number educated in those golden days, and well remember the notions which I acquired from the grotesque representation of Nebudchadnezzar, creeping like a beast on all fours, and sundry other illustrations of scripture. Yet these books had a vast circulation, and constituted a large part of the juvenile literature of the golden age. They were full of pictures, as full as the books of the present day; the great difference is, that the kinds of books are now more numerous; the engravings too are improved, and are to a greater extent used as illustrations in aid of the text. Many of them are spirited and just representations of things, and are calculated to impart knowledge, and communicate correct and vivid ideas. The juvenile books, too, are more devoted to matter of fact, than formerly; and the engravings are therefore less designed to excite the imagination, than to store the memory.

Great as has been the improvement in the arts of instruction within a few years, we must not suppose that the power of pictures was unknown to earlier ages. At first, all language was imitative or descriptive; if oral, it mimicked sounds, if written, it drew pictures. Mankind at once saw the power of these representations, and as the readiest and most effectual mode of communicating their ideas, copied, as well as they could, the objects of their knowledge. This was a natural language, and though it was superseded by the invention of letters, and artificial language, still the effect of paintings and drawings has never in any age been overlooked. As the arts have advanced, pictures have been multiplied; and as no one till recently seems to have doubted their utility, their introduction into books has kept pace with the progress of the arts. The recent invention of lithography has resulted in an immense improvement in the art of sketching, and this, in connection with the great progress made in the art of wood-engraving, rendering it a cheap and beautiful style of illustration, has led to the present state of the picture system, of which some persons complain.

To many, it may appear incredible that the utility of pictures in instruction is seriously controverted; but such is the fact. It is so obvious to most minds, that a good picture of a lion, a tiger, or giraffe, will give more clear and vivid ideas than volumes of written description, that it seems absurd to condemn their use in books, particularly in books for youth. Still, such condemnation, with greater or less reserve, has been uttered by persons, who consider their opinions worthy of respectful consideration, and it shall be met with a more full reply when your limits will permit. Y.

THE TEACHER'S ALMANAC FOR OCTOBER.

THE SCHOOL ROOM.

The languid heats of summer, and the unhealthy period of autumn, are now past; and the temperature and the air are calculated to revive the vigor of body and mind. In those schools whose vacations are already past, the labors of the winter may now be commenced with energy and success. But in order to secure these to the full extent, ample time must be given to active sports, and provision must be made, by rendering the school-room tight and comfortable, and preparing fuel for days which render fire necessary, to prevent that chill of body, and chattering of teeth, which impair cheerfulness, or take away the power of mental activity. To require study from pupils in this condition is tyranny; and nothing is more absurd than to regulate the period of fires by the almanac, instead of attending to the temperature of the air, or the state of the body. Many an autumnal fever, and many a winter's cough, may be traced to ridiculous precision, or mistaken economy on this subject.

Nor is such a course always without moral influence. Dr Combe remarks with great justice and sarcasm, 'What advances in morals and religion can be expected under the charge of one, who says, "*Do unto others as you would be done by*," and then leaves his dependants (pupils) to suffer pain, chilblains, and disease, for want of fire to warm the room in which they sit; he, himself coming into it with features flushed by the heat of the blazing fire which, for weeks, has been provided for comfort in his own apartment?'

In a large number of our schools, this is a period of recess. Let their teachers employ this favorable season in gaining vigor of body for their winter's labors, and in laying up a store of instruction and amusement for their pupils, by careful observation of the scenes and events which pass under their notice; and when this point is effected, let them be diligent in preparing to teach well, all that they attempt to teach.

THE EARTH.

It is the month of the fall of the leaf; the foliage which was the ornament and shelter of the trees in the heat of summer, is now about to drop as a useless incumbrance, to allow the more free access of the sun to their trunks and branches. In this, as in every change of nature, the kindness of the Creator has not forgotten to provide pleasures for the eye; and the very pall-bearers of the year, are adorned with the gayest and most beautiful livery. It is a simple and easy branch of the observation of nature, with children, to collect the leaves of plants and trees, and dry them in folds, or books of wrapping paper; and it would be no small addition to the interest of such a collection, if you could induce your pupils to gather those of each tree as they are fading, with each successive change, till they reach that skeleton state, which is often produced by the decay of winter.

THE HEAVENS.

Aquarius is the sign of the Zôdiac on the meridian at nine o'clock in the evening, during this month. Four stars forming the letter Y, are the only ones which can be distinctly pointed out, without examination of the map. Immediately beneath them is the Southern Fish. The most beautiful star in it is *Fomalhaut*, which is much used by navigators to find their longitude at sea. East of the Swan and the Dolphin, four remarkable stars, in the figure of a square, will now become conspicuous, which form part of the constellation of Pegasus, or the flying horse. The two eastern stars mark the equinoctial colure which is the first meridian of the heavens.

Venus is performing her last duty as the evening star, during this month, and will appear most brilliant at its close. Herschel will be on the meridian in the course of the evenings of October.

Let your pupils still keep up the habit of observing the progress of the sun by the shadows at its rising, noon, and setting. Above all, let them not forget Him who appoints the passing seasons in regular succession, and let them read if they do not learn, the beautiful hymn of Thompson, whose first lines ought to be written on our hearts;

> 'These, as they change, Almighty Father! these,
> Are but the varied God. The rolling year
> Is full of thee! —— '

MISCELLANY.

Addresses on Education.

It is gratifying to see the increasing number of addresses and reports on the subject of education, in the various parts of our country. We have been recently favored with the addresses of the Rev. Stephen Olin, president of Randolph Macon college; the lecture of Dr Drake before the literary convention of Kentucky, on the 'Importance of Literary and Social concert in the valley of the Mississippi;' Mr Grimke's address 'on the value and power of the Sunday School System;' Mr Key's oration at Bristol college on 'The power of literature in its connection with religion;' Mr Clarke's poem on 'The past and the present,' delivered at the same institution; the Inaugural address of Pres. Babcocks'; a Sketch of the Oneida Institute; a spirited report of the Buck's County Society, for the advancement of general education, and several interesting accounts of private institutions. All of them contain much which we wish we could present to our readers, but the extent of our general subject, and the narrow limits to which we are confined, and the necessity of providing something for the various classes of our readers, compels us to pass them by for the present, with only this notice. They well deserve the attention of those who have the opportunity of perusing them.

Teachers' Course at Hofwyl.

Recent letters from Switzerland informed us that the course of instruction for teachers was in successful progress, and that instruction was given in Religion, Language, Chirography, Linear Drawing, Arithmetic, Geometry, the elements of Philosophy, Chemistry, and Natural History, Geography, the History of Switzerland, Agriculture, and Music. Teachers were received and taught gratuitously, and assistance was afforded to the families of those who were indigent. More than a hundred teachers were in attendance. We regret to find that the institution established by the state is continued under the direction of a person not experienced in teaching, and whose instructions have met with great disapprobation from most of those who heard them. It appears that the number of teachers who frequent it is small. From public documents we find that Fellenberg was appointed president of the republic of Berne, but has now retired from the office, in order to devote himself exclusively to Hofwyl and the cause of education. We are not surprised that views so extensive and elevated as his, should not meet with sympathy and encouragement in a canton, where the pride of the aristocracy, and the prejudices of an uncultivated people, are equally unfriendly to enlarged views of improvement. Such has ever been the fate of reformers.

Marietta Collegiate Institute and Western Teachers' Seminary.

This institution, which was briefly described in our last years' volume, is now under the care of four Professors; and if we may judge from the 'First Annual Report,' with which we have recently been favored, is flourishing. It is in three distinct departments; a Preparatory, a Teachers', and a Collegiate Department. The whole number of scholars who have been entered, in all the Departments, during the past year, is 110; of whom 93 were members at the close of the second term. A farm of sixty or seventy acres is attached to the establishment, for the agricultural labor of the students, and two work shops for those who prefer mechanical labor. One of these 100 feet long is adapted to the coopering business, and will accommodate 30 students. The other shop is for such mechanical labor as the student prefers. It is three stories high, and will accommodate a considerable number. Those who labor in the cooper's shop have their timber and tools found them, and receive half the avails of their merchandise. Those who labor in the other shop, furnish their own tools and timber, and have the entire avails of their labor. These shops are under the direction of suitable persons, who aid, as far as is necessary, those who work in them. During the past year, 44 students have engaged, more or less in manual labor, and the average amount of their earnings for the time they have been employed, is a fraction over six cents an hour. The result of the experience of this Institution, thus far, is, that three hours labor a day, will not impede the literary progress of the student.

Baltimore Union Lyceum.

We have collected from the Baltimore, Charlestown, and other papers, the following account of this interesting Institution.

It is divided into twelve branches or ward Lyceums, and these into departments, such as ladies', mothers', teachers', apprentices,' and seamens' lyceums. These last are again subdivided into classes.

One of the most useful departments, it is thought, will be the ladies' lyceums, in their operations for the improvement of girls who are now, to a lamentable extent, acquiring bad habits in the schools which they attend. One of the first steps contemplated is to ascertain what number of children there are in the city who do not attend school, the causes of their neglect, the best methods of bringing them within the pale of their instruction, what instruction they most need, &c.

The plan of instruction about to be commenced by the ladies, is to establish weekly schools, in which needle-work will be particularly attended to by all the girls, together with reading, writing, and such other studies as their age or other circumstances may render proper. A few schools for adult females, where they are taught reading, writing, and arithmetic, are already in operation; and more it is expected, will be commenced, after the present season.

The Curators of the Baltimore Union Lyceum, are about making arrangements, on the one hand, for securing the efforts of the schools, in collecting specimens of Natural History: and, on the other, for exchanging them and other specimens, with similar societies. The Board are about to assign the subject of Natural History to three or four of their number, whose special duty it will be to collect and exchange specimens, or rather to put the schools in the way to do it. All the labor, both of collecting and exchanging, can be done by lads, aided, in some of the specimens, by the misses in the schools. In the room of the society there are, at present, several thousand geological specimens, collected principally by the boys in some of the schools.

It is gratifying to see Episcopalians, Methodists, Presbyterians, Baptists, Quakers, Lutherans, and Catholics, all engaged in efforts to promote the same object.

Worcester Manual Labor School.

This institution appears to be flourishing. The examination at the close of the first term is represented to have been highly satisfactory. Mr Bailey, late a member of Brown University is the teacher. The second term is about to commence under favorable auspices.

Education in Missouri.

Within a few months past, there have been several interesting movements among the people in several counties in Missouri, in favor of Education and common schools. Several associations have been organised, and among the rest, at a meeting of citizens, at Loutre Island Academy, on the *fourth of July*, one by the name of the *Loutre Island Education Society*.

The object of this Society, as we perceive from their constitution, is 'to take into consideration the best method of teaching, and to seek out and circulate information upon this subject.' They are to meet quarterly. At the meeting abovementioned, among several important resolutions passed, were several which contemplate the appointment of delegates from the society to visit various literary institutions; meetings of citizens in different parts of Warren county, on the subject of education; and the adoption of measures by the several counties in the state for the formation of a state society.

Movements in Illinois.

It is stated in the Pioneer and Western Baptist that most of the candidates for the legislature, during the late contest in Illinois, have come out decidedly and unequivocally in favor of a system of common schools. From this circumstance the editor of the Pioneer concludes that something efficient will be done at the next session. We hope that time will show his expectations to be well founded.

We observe also in another number of the same spirited paper, a communication from Mr Holbrook, on the subject of lyceums and lyceum seminaries, and recommending an education convention to be held throughout the Union, on the first Wednesday of November next. In pursuance of the general train of remark of Mr Holbrook, the editor suggests the importance of a State Education Convention at Vandalia, the first Friday of December next; which is also the time for the annual meeting of the Illinois Institute of Education.

Peterboro' Manual Labor School.

This is an institution for young men of color, established at Peterborough, Madison County, N. Y. by Gerrit Smith, Esq. It originated in the belief that it is the duty of the whites to elevate the condition and character of the colored people, and is intended to afford advantages for obtaining either a good common or a classical education. The teacher is Mr C. Grant, formerly Principal of Whitesborough Academy.

Mr Smith provides, at his own expense, instructors, books, stationary, rooms, bedding, fuel, lights, and boarding; as a partial compensation for which the student is expected to labor four hours, daily, in some agricultural or mechanical employment. Labor is estimated at about twelve and a half cents a day, upon the average, for each student. The student furnishes his own clothing.

The living of the pupils is very plain. Neither tea nor coffee is allowed them, and they have meat but once a day. They sleep on mattresses of straw. They do their own cooking and washing, under the superintendence of a respectable colored woman, who was formerly, for many years, in the family of Gov. Trumbull, of Conn. This labor, however makes a part of the four hours per day. Every scholar, on entering this school, is required to subscribe a promise of abstinence from all intoxicating drinks, including cider and strong beer; and also from tobacco in every form. There is a reading table in the school-room, supplied with many periodical publications. Accommodations are furnished, thus far, for only eighteen students; none of whom are received under fourteen years of age.

Telescopes.

Mr Amasa Holcomb, of Southwick, Mass. has been engaged, several years, in the construction of Telescopes. He is a self-taught man, and has at length brought his instruments to a high degree of perfection. Mr. H. does probably what no other man has ever done, casts and grinds his mirrors and lenses, makes the tubes, and founds and fits all the mountings and finishings.

We learn from the journal of the Franklin Institute of Philadelphia, that one of these telescopes, of six feet focal distance, has been examined by a committee of the Institute. It is constructed on the plan of Herschel's great telescope, which requires the observer to stand with his back to the object, and look directly into the speculum. It was compared with two fine English telescopes, and was found much superior. The waved appearance of the edges around the craters of the volcanoes in the moon were distinctly visible, and yet land objects could be clearly seen at the short distance of a quarter of a mile. The committee state that Mr Holcomb can furnish for $100, with plain mounting, or for 150 to 200 with more expensive mounting, telescopes, whose performance equals that of Gregorians and Achromatics hitherto imported into the country at an expense of five hundred dollars.

The Academican and Southern Journal of Education.

We are sorry to record the orbituary of another periodical on education. 'The Academician,' which has been struggling for an existence nearly a year, is about to be discontinued, for want of patronage. The editor has felt himself gradually compelled to adapt his paper to that popular taste, which will not admit of the sober discussion of important topics to any considerable extent, but must needs be gratified by a large proportion of light reading, as the modern palate must be tickled by dainties in the place of wholesome and solid food. We had fain hoped that the good sense and intelligence of the people of Georgia would have sustained a journal of only eight semimonthly pages, to be devoted exclusively to education and instruction; and above all, that they would not suffer it to perish in its very infancy. But thus it is. Periodicals on trifling or comparatively unimportant subjects receive the cheerful and liberal patronage of thousands, and perhaps tens of thousands; especially if they will enlist in the service of sect or party, while those which aim at giving solid and useful instruction on the highest interests of man are suffered to languish and die. Parents and teachers! guardians of the republic! ought these things so to be?

Female Education in Greece.

The annual meeting of the Troy and other co-operating Societies for the advancement of Female Education in Greece, was held in this city on the 20th inst. After an anthem, suitable for the occasion, was sung by the choir, and prayers by the Rev. Mr Paddock, a Report of the past transactions of the Societies, from Mrs Emma Willard, Corresponding Secretary of the Troy Society, was also read by him. A Poem from the pen of Mrs Sigourney, written for the meeting, was read by Mr T. H. Vail. We regret that ill health prevented Miss Beecher from preparing her anticipated address. The concluding prayer was made by the Rev. Mr Newton. A liberal collection was taken up, in aid of the object of the Society.

Norwich Courier.

Improvement in Africa.

Africa presents a recent example of invention similar to that of the Cherokees. 'The Vey people,' says a missionary of the American Board, in the Missionary Herald, 'residing on Grand Cape Mount, have recently *invented a system of writing* entirely new, and altogether different from any other we have yet seen; in which, although it is not more than two years since it was invented, they write letters and books. Some of their characters resemble the Arabic, some resemble the Hebrew letters, others Greek; but all of them, except those resembling the Arabic, are merely fanciful. The alphabet is *syllabic*.' In the last point it resembles that devised by Guess, whose origin was described by Mr Boudinot, in the 2d volume of this work.

The missionaries find that the people along the whole coast, are desirous of *schools*. Wherever the plan of the missionaries was known, urgent applications were made for schools, and a written promise was often requested. In one instance, they would not close a council until this was given; and after travelling 200 miles, the Americans received a message reminding them of this promise! And yet, thousands of parents in our own country, and of our own color, are willing that their children should grow up in ignorance!

The progress and state of several schools in Liberia is very encouraging.

Teachers in Hindoostan.

A native Hindoo paper states, that two students have recently been selected from the Hindoo College, and sent to Moorshedabad as teachers of the English Language, in the Nizamut College, and that the natives at Santipore are desirous of engaging a well qualified teacher, either christian or native, to reestablish a deserted English school among them.

College of the Propaganda in Rome.

The zeal and diligence of the Roman College of missions, in providing instruction and books in every language of the world, deserves the imitation of Protestants. At a recent public recitation, speeches were made in thirtytwo languages. The Chaldee, Samaritan, Syria, Arabic, Coptic, Ethiopic, Greek, Armenian, Georgian, German, Highland Scotch, Irish, Persian, Curdic, English, French, &c, were recited or spoken by students, generally natives of the countries in which they are vernacular or best understood.

Hottentot Schools.

In connection with the charge of the missionaries in South Africa, there are eight schools, containing five hundred Hottentot children. It is stated by the superintendent that 'they are not by any means deficient in capacity,' but 'shrewd, lively, intelligent and good-tempered,' and most of the schools are taught by *Hottentot* teachers, under the direction of the superintendent! If the 'brutish Hottentot' as he was once termed, is found, on cultivation, capable of being a useful school-master, is it not time to subject our prejudices against the African race to the test of thorough impartial experiment?

NOTICES OF BOOKS.

The Intellectual and Practical Singing-Book; embracing the Elements of Vocal Music, and a Selection of Pleasing and Popular Tunes, designed for the use of Beginners, particularly the Children connected with the Sunday Schools of the Protestant Episcopal Church: also, for Teachers and Sunday Schools in general. By Charles Dingley. New-York. N. B. Holmes. 1834. pp. 80.

This little work adopts, to some extent, the Pestalozzian plan; and far surpasses in simplicity any of the *ordinary* elementary books for children. We think, however, it partakes too much of the character of the old system, especially in the rapid progress required, and in the introduction and explanation of technical terms. We hope that this very circumstance may be a means of introducing a more rational method of instruction into schools where a system completely inductive would not be received.

The Family Minstrel. A semi-monthly Newspaper. By Charles Dingley. New-York.

This new periodical is designed to excite and gratify the taste for Music of a social and religious kind, and to advocate its introduction as a branch of study in all our seminaries, from the primary school to the university and its important religious influence. Each number is to contain from two to four pieces of music, adapted to the school and the family, which is intended to be of a medium character, between the light and frivolous, and the solemn and devotional. We are much gratified with the sentiments of the editor expressed in the first number, and cordially wish success to the enterprise. The terms are $3; or $2 in advance.

The Third Class Reader. Designed for the Use of the Younger Classes in the Schools of the United States. By B. D. Emerson, late Principal of the Adams Grammar School, Boston. Boston: Russell, Odiorne & Metcalf. 1834. 18mo, pp. 160.

In a former number we have expressed the pleasure we found in examining the 'First' and 'Second Class Reader,' by the same author. The present work is designed for the younger class of pupils, and affords the same evidence of experience and taste, in the selection and arrangement. There is much that is instructive combined with many amusing lessons, and the selections are unusually simple in their style. The moral tendency is excellent, but we could wish to see more lessons of an elevating religious tendency, like those found in the previous works, in one that is adapted to the most susceptible years of childhood.

The Mother's Friend; or Familiar Directions for Forming the Mental and Moral Habits of Young Children. New-York: Leavitt, Lord, & Co. Boston: Crocker & Brewster. 1834. 18mo, pp. 240.

This volume is a republication of an English work, selected and edited by Mr Abbott, as one of a series. Its chief object is 'to show how good principles in the heart are to be carried out to amiable and praiseworthy manners and habits.' It is simple and unpretending in its character, and without those numerous illustrations which excite so much interest in the original works of Mr Abbott; but it is full of valuable principles and maxims, which appear to have been derived from close observation in the nursery itself. 'Early associations,' 'Justice and Generosity,' 'Manners, and Order,' 'Early Lessons, and Amusements,' 'Rewards and Punishments,' 'The Nursery Maid,' are among the titles of its chapters, and will furnish some idea of its contents. We find the *spirit* of the editor throughout the work, but we do not find any of his own peculiar religious views, except in the concluding chapter on 'Religious Instruction.'

AMERICAN

ANNALS OF EDUCATION

AND INSTRUCTION.

NOVEMBER, 1834.

REVIEW OF COMBE'S PHYSIOLOGY.

The Principles of Physiology applied to the preservation of Health, and the improvement of Physical and Mental Education. By Andrew Combe, M. D., Fellow of the Royal College of Physicians of Edinburgh. New York: Harper & Brothers. 1834. 18mo. pp. 291.

It is more than four years since we began in this work, to press the subject of Physical Education upon the community; to urge them to consider the mutual connection and dependence of mind and body; and the consequences which have resulted, and which still result from overlooking this connection in practice. We have been sustained in our views, by many of the most able periodicals of the day, and have been encouraged by the appearance of several interesting books on the same general subject. "The Constitution of Man, as related to external objects," by George Combe, Esq., of Edinburgh; "The Influence of Mental Cultivation on Health," by Dr. Brigham, of Hartford; "The Principles of Physiology applied to the preservation of Health," by Dr. Combe, of Edinburgh; and a recent work by Dr. Caldwell, of Kentucky, are among this number. In addition to this, three school books, "The Anatomical Class Book," by Dr. Smith; "The Outlines of Physiology," by Dr. Hayward; and "The House I live in," an allegorical description of the human frame, by Dr. Alcott, have appeared in Boston; and a fourth work of this same general character is expected from Dr. Drake, of Cincinnati. We might also mention, in this connection, the many valuable lectures and addresses on this subject, especially at Conventions of Teachers in various parts of the United States, which have been delivered, and the many manual labor schools which have been established.

We had promised ourselves the pleasure of reviewing another of the same general tendency, the recent interesting work of Dr. Alexander Combe, one of the most valuable of a popular kind, we have yet seen upon physiology; but ill health has compelled us to relinquish the hope. We are happy, therefore, to have received an article, which we can present as cordially as if it were our own, and in which we preserve the editorial style which we have ceased to admit in the articles of others, since our early associates have been compelled, one after another, to leave us.

"The phrase 'physical education,' in the title page of any book," said a friend not long since, "is alone sufficient to secure it a favorable reception." But he was mistaken. The philosopher Locke, who said one hundred and fifty years ago, that a 'sound mind in a sound body is a short but full description of a happy state in this world," might have advanced the same opinion, and with his own estimate of the value of a sound body, nothing would have been more natural. Yet the observation and experience of every friend of physical education, both before and since the days of Locke, must, it seems to us, lead to a far different conclusion. For ourselves, we feel assured that the subject has not obtained a permanent hold on the public mind. There is yet a propensity almost every where to exalt the intellect, and leave the body to shift for itself; and not a few of those who press the subject with the utmost earnestness, and are resolved never to cease from doing so, till they cease from their earthly labors, are still regarded as enthusiastic or visionary.

It is this view, among many others, that induces us to welcome the appearance of such a work as that to which we have referred, by Dr. Combe. The interesting, we might say captivating, manner, in which the subjects of that work are treated, and the wide circulation which the manner of its publication almost inevitably secures, have led us to hope that it will do more towards awakening the public mind, than any other work which has yet appeared; the abler one, by Dr. Caldwell, not excepted. We hope so, because it will be read by more individuals than any previous work; and its style is more of a popular cast than any kindred work which has been published, either before or since. Dr. Combe is evidently no visionary; and his work will do much, we trust, to relieve others who have used language no stronger than his, from that imputation.

"Society groans," says he, "under the load of suffering inflicted by causes susceptible of removal, but left in operation in consequence of our unacquaintance with our own structure, and of the relations of the different parts of the system to each other, and to external objects. Every medical man must have felt and lamented the ignorance so generally prevalent in regard to the simplest functions of the animal system, and the consequent absence of judicious co-operation of friends in the care and cure of the sick. From unacquaintance with the commonest facts in physiology, or incapability of appreciating their importance, men of much good sense in every other respect, not only subject themselves unwittingly to the active causes of disease, but give their sanction to laws and practices destructive equally to life and morality, which, if they saw them in their true light, they would shrink from countenancing in the slightest degree."

He then goes on to adduce examples in support of his position. The heated and impure atmosphere of factories, cabins of vessels, hospitals, jails, and those jails of mind, — school rooms, — with the unreasonable tasking of the body which exists in factories, the almost universal mortality among infants, with those daily abuses of the lungs and other vital organs of the body which every medical man sees and deplores, are among the evils to which he would direct the public attention.

Dr. Combe adverts, with peculiar earnestness, to those anomalies in practical life, in the case of individuals little accustomed, while in health, to observe or reflect on the influence of external circumstances and modes of life in disturbing the action of the various animal functions, but at the same time easily and deeply impressed by all *extraordinary* occurrences affecting them.

"One cause of such anomalous conduct," he observes, "is the dangerous and prevalent fallacy of supposing that because glaring mischief does not *instantly* follow every breach of an organic law, no harm has been done." "What is more common," he adds, "than to hear a dyspeptic invalid, who seeks to gratify his palate, say that vegetables, (crude ones) for example, or pastry, or heavy puddings, do not disagree with him, as he ate them on such a day, and experienced no inconvenience from them? And the same in regard to late hours, heated rooms, insufficient clothing, and all other sources of bad health." * * * * "As the breach of the law is limited in extent, and becomes serious by the frequency of its repetition, rather than by a single act, so is the punishment gradual in its infliction, and slow in manifesting its accumulated effects; and this very gradation, and the distance of time at which the full effect is produced, are the reasons why man, in his ignorance, so often fails to trace the connection between his conduct in life, and his broken health. But the connection subsists, although he does not regard it; and the accumulated consequences come upon him when he least expects them."

Again the Doctor adverts to the indispensable importance of pure air, and the injurious consequences which often slowly, but always certainly follow from every exposure to the bad air of heated rooms, or crowded parties, theatres, churches, or school rooms.

How much it were to be wished that every teacher and nurse in the land would read—and not only read, but appreciate the importance of Dr. C.'s remarks on this subject. Especially important is it to those teachers who have the charge of large numbers of very young pupils in the confined rooms of our cities, towns, and villages. In these situations, teachers are generally satisfied, if no immediate inconvenience is perceived; and yet on the principles of Dr. Combe, if the air be impure in any degree, suffering must sooner or later follow, even though no individual on earth should ever be able to trace the evil consequences to their legitimate source.

It is, indeed, indispensable to ventilate school rooms when the air becomes *perceptibly* injurious, as teachers are accustomed to do. So far they do well. But to make their own feelings the test of security, is wrong, for two reasons. 1st. The bad air, especially the carbonic acid, made by breathing, will be found in greatest abundance nearest the floor. So that while the teacher himself may range above it, in a better atmosphere, the pupils may be inhaling, at every breath, the seeds of disease and premature dissolution. 2d. Neither the feelings of teacher or pupil, at the time, are any certain test of the security of either.

Here is the difficulty; — a difficulty which mere preaching to instructors, will, we fear, never remove. The teacher must be induced to study his own constitution, and its laws, and relations. Until this is effected, but little is done. Teachers are told of their danger and the danger of their pupils; they assent, but do not feel. They must study the organic laws, as Dr. C. calls them, for themselves; and draw their own conclusions. We hope much from Dr. C.'s book, because we are confident many parents and teachers will read it, and that it will be the means of leading them to a farther and deeper investigation of the same subjects.

But not only will the work be likely to interest parents and teachers, and lead them to a judicious method of managing those who are committed to their charge; — there is good reason to hope it will do much for every individual who peruses it, in aiding him to take care of himself. Much is said, in these days, of the importance of self-education, and of the work never being finished; but there are none of the three great departments of education, in which more can be, and should be done by the adult, than in physical self-education.

Let us consider, for a moment, the subject of cutaneous exhalation. The surface of a middling sized body is usually estimated at about fifteen superficial feet. In a state of health, every part of this, excepting, of course, those small portions covered with nails, is pierced with little holes, and is constantly emitting vapor, in a quantity that would astonish many who have not attended to the subject. It is, moreover, a fact well established, that the internal surface of the lungs, which is about as extensive as the surface of the body, exhales, also, a moisture like the skin; and that when this exhalation is checked on the surface of the body, an increased task is imposed on the lungs. Dr. Combe says:—

"We find the skin endowed with the important charge of removing from the system, about twenty ounces * of waste matter every twenty-four hours; and when we consider that the quantity not only is great, but is sent forth in so divided a state as to be invisible to the eye, and that the whole of it is given out by the very minute ramifications of the blood vessels of the skin, we perceive at once why these are so extremely numerous that a pin's point cannot touch any spot without piercing them; and we see an ample reason why checked perspiration should prove so detrimental to health,—because, for every twenty-four hours during which such a state continues, we must either have twenty ounces of useless and hurtful matter accumulating in the body, or have some of the other organs of excretion grievously overtasked; which obviously cannot happen without disturbing their regularity and well being. People know the fact, and wonder it should be so, that cold applied to the skin, or continued exposure in a cold day, often produces a bowel complaint, a severe cold in the chest, or inflammation of some internal organ; but were they taught, as they ought to be, the structure and uses of their own bodies, they would rather wonder that it did not always produce one of these effects."

In the third chapter of the work before us, is a very full and interesting account of bathing, in all its varied forms, cold, tepid, warm and vapor. The author insists on bathing, in some form or other, as *indispensable to all, at all seasons*; and in all, or nearly all climates. His directions are so minute, as well as clear, that none, we should think, need mistake, in regard to their application to his own case. Those who are unable to sustain, or are obviously not benefitted by the cold bath, should use the warm or tepid. The latter is considered as the best for general use, especially in the cold season, and in cold climates. Sometimes, where the cold bath in the common form cannot be borne, or *enjoyed*, the shower bath produces the happiest effects; and for those who are not robust, daily sponging of the body with cold water and vinegar, or salt water, is an excellent substitute for cold bathing. Friction of the skin is also highly commended. We should be glad to transcribe the whole chapter, but as our limits do not permit, we must content ourselves with here and there a striking extract. The following is not only striking, but important; and rather amusing:—

* This is the lowest estimate. Generally it is much greater; and in a state which we call *sweating*, greater still.

"If one tenth of the persevering attention and labor bestowed to so much purpose in rubbing down and currying the skins of horses, were bestowed by the human race in keeping themselves in good condition, and a little attention were paid to diet and clothing,—colds, nervous diseases, and stomach complaints would cease to form so large an item in the catalogue of human miseries. Man studies the nature of other animals, and adapts his conduct to their constitution; himself alone he continues ignorant of, and neglects. He considers himself not subject to the laws of organization which regulate the functions of the inferior animals; but this conclusion is the result of ignorance and pride."

We have had before our eyes, during the present season, a full exemplification of the truth of the foregoing remarks. Every day, while the hot season lasted, have the horses of a gentleman in this vicinity been taken to a brook, in full view of our own window, and thoroughly washed and cleansed, while we are well assured that neither the groom nor the master has washed his own body in water once a month. And there are thousands who never do it once in their whole lives.

While all the various forms of bathing may be used in such a manner, in the case of different individuals, as to prove salutary, Dr. C. does not deny that any of them may, by ignorance or inattention, produce the opposite effects. He therefore devotes much of this chapter to the task of showing when and under what circumstances, one or another kind is indicated. Most of his rules are in entire accordance with the views which have formerly been expressed in this work, under the heads, Cold Bathing, Swimming, &c.; though much more varied and extended, and more fully illustrated by cases and anecdotes.

The uses and abuses of dress; its results, in particular to the skin; the effects of the various forms of exercise,—walking, riding, sailing, &c.—on the skin, and of course on a free perspiration, also occupy a conspicuous place in the work. The use of flannel next the skin, in cold climates, and some of the more common mistakes which prevail in regard to dressing thinly with a view to harden ourselves against the evil effects of changes of temperature, are most clearly and ably shown. We have one extract to make on wet feet. The remarks are of universal application, though the author evidently had in view the inmates of school rooms, factories, &c.

"It is well known that a person in ordinary health may walk about or work in the open air, with wet feet, for hours together, without injury, provided he put on dry stockings and shoes immediately on coming home. It is, therefore, not the mere state of wetness that causes the evil, but the check to perspiration, and the unequal distribution of blood to which the accompanying coldness gives rise. Wet and damp are more unwholesome when applied to the feet than when they affect other parts, chiefly because they receive a large supply of blood to carry on a high degree of perspiration, and because their distance from the heart or centre of circu-

lation diminishes the force with which this is carried on, and thus leaves them more susceptible of injury from external causes."

Several chapters of this interesting work treat of muscular action, and of the laws relating to it. The appropriate time, place, and kind of exercise, and the adaptation of the latter to the peculiarities of constitution, and the varying employments of individuals, are pointed out in the most admirable manner. One chapter of more than forty pages, is devoted to the consideration of the lungs and the various functions which they perform, or in which they are concerned; on pure air, and the importance of ventilation; and on diseases of the lungs, and the precautions which are required of those who are peculiarly exposed to them. One of the closing chapters treats of the brain and nervous system; the connection between the mind and the brain; and the conditions on which alone the health of both can be preserved. This last portion of the work is especially important to the sedentary and studious.

But our readers must not judge of the merits of Dr. Combe's book from this imperfect sketch, and a few insulated extracts. The whole work should be read, again and again. It will richly repay the labor; and if what we have here said should be the means, in any degree, of bringing it into more extensive notice, and lead to a more thorough study of the laws of physiology, it is all we expect, and all we could desire. Dr. C. seems to regard the present universal ignorance of the human frame, as in some degree pardonable, because it is not voluntary; but when we consider the flood of light which has recently been poured on the subject, especially by the work in question, is it not obvious that no parent or teacher can longer justly plead involuntary ignorance?

ON THE MEANS OF CIVILIZING THE INDIANS.

ESSAY ON THE BEST MEANS FOR EXTENDING KNOWLEDGE AND CIVILIZATION AMONG THE WESTERN INDIANS.

Addressed to the American Lyceum, by Henry R. Schoolcraft, Author of Travels to the Sources of the Mississippi, &c.

[CONCLUDED.]

The true inquiry respecting these tribes, is not, whether the duty of instructing them be an imperious one, but how this duty can be most speedily, usefully and efficiently performed. And the question, which we take to be the pressing one, in the present condition of Christian operations, is, *whether there be any thing, in the condition and dispersion of the Indians, which requires a peculiar adaptation of the means of instruction, or whether the ordinary modes should be exclusively pursued.*

On this point we may be allowed to speak rather from the results of personal observation, than from preconceived theory. The time has gone by, with us, when we regarded the conversion of an adult Indian, as an anomaly in religion. The course of missionary exertions, on the frontiers, has brought numerous examples of such conversions before us. It has afforded the opportunity of observing, that the plain and striking doctrines of the Scriptures may be declared to them, in a language which they understand, with as promising prospects of their being understood and assented to, and adopted as the governing axioms of life, as to other classes of individuals, not farther advanced in the scale of intellectual improvement. Coming, as these doctrines do, to their minds with the charm of novelty, (a principle as deeply implanted in the Indian as the white man,) they are the more readily led to consider them. The principal impediment, aside from external bias, arises from the acquisition of the languages — an object demanding the earliest attention, in all attempts at instruction.

It has been found that the most simple and direct mode of conveying instruction, moral and religious, has been attended with the best success. The mode of lecturing on the Scriptures to the Indians, should be of the plainest character, and as little as possible left to inference. What is not plainly told, will generally not be inferred at all. Books should be as simple, as elementary books can be made. Orthography should be simple and uniform. No rules are likely to facilitate early instruction, but those of the most obvious necessity. Much of the dicta, laid down in our elder school books, are rather suited to puzzle, than inform the beginner. Children are not capable of metaphysical analysis, and least of all, Indian children. Indeed, if the spirit of teaching be present, and there be perseverance, and discrimination in the order in which facts are presented to the youthful mind, it is of little moment, how much of the external circumstances and customary forms, be dispensed with. Personal exertion and ingenuity on the part of the instructor, must often compensate for disadvantages of time and place. A circle of Indian children, gathered under a grove, might be as certainly taught the alphabet and digits, as if they were covered with a costly canopy. Buildings become necessary only to avoid the common changes of the atmosphere, and to ensure the observance of order. But such buildings require nothing beyond the simplest arrangement of a school house. It has been found that children and parents are better kept from the sources of jealousy and suspicion, if the scholars come from their parents' lodges in the morning, and return to them in the evening.

In the system of instruction, the monitorial plan, as it is most economical of time, and makes a more direct appeal to the spirit of emulation, (which the natives, in an eminent degree, possess,) is preferable. There are also some features in the plan of Infant schools, highly calculated to interest Indian children. It is found that their attention is quickly attracted to forms representing astronomical and other bodies. And the apparatus may be dismissed, at the precise point, where the idea is retained in the memory. But every school, whatever aid it may derive from monitors, should be placed under the strict and constant care and personal supervision of a white teacher.

Large expenditures in the shape of buildings and fixtures, diminish the means applicable to Christian instruction, and are precisely those features, which either excite jealousy on the part of the Indians, or animadversion on the part of the whites. And it is on this account, that boarding schools should be confined, as closely as possible, to the sites of academical instruction. To teach a scholar is one thing; to board, clothe, and lodge him, another. There is no comparison, in point of expense, between the first and second objects. There is no necessary connection between them. And we believe, that in schools, located in the territories of the tribes, the furnishing of both, in the form of free boarding schools, has been a positive injury, instead of a benefit to both parents and children. No system is so exclusively right, as that which begins right. It is a position which forms the very basis of civilization, that each member of society must support himself by his own industry. And it seems important to teach this truth early to the Indians. If they ever exist, as a happy and independent community, it must be through faithful individual exertions on their own part. And were the question between the adoption of manual labor and free schools, we should think there could be no hesitancy, in point of policy, as to the preference of the former.

Schools, to be greatly beneficial to the tribes, must be local. A school situated without the boundaries of the tribe, is also measurably without the boundary of a moral influence upon it. Experience has fully demonstrated the futility of attempts to change the moral condition of tribes, by educating a select number of their youth, at remote points, while no simultaneous efforts were made with the body of the tribe itself. The learning of colleges has thus, in a measure, been thrown away upon individuals, who, on returning to their tribes, have found them, in no way prepared for appreciating their acquirements. Did they labor to convince their erratic countrymen of the advantages of learning over ignorance, of farming over hunting, of letters over rude signs —

> " ——— all
> Doubt, few aid, and fewer understand."

Neither could they themselves maintain the state of artificial elevation, in which adventitious circumstances had placed them. Their first efforts have been received with coldness and indifference. And they have, at last, themselves yielded to despondency. Like partial efforts in other departments of human knowledge —

> " Teach one, in fifty, and the one shall stare,
> To see how blind, the nine and forty are;
> But teach a band, and there are none behind
> To mark how want of knowledge sinks the kind."

The whole failure, in these cases, has resulted from the want of local schools, and other sources of instruction. And whatever degree of objection arises to them, from this cause, wholly ceases the moment the cause is removed. And this may be regarded as the plain reason, why some of the tribes who have enjoyed the double advantage of academical and primary local instruction, have made more rapid advances in civilization.

Of the same era with the policy of educating, at remote points, the few, while the many remained in gross ignorance at home, is the opinion that the native languages should be neglected. The theory on this subject is, that it is easier to teach the Indians the English language, than to learn theirs. Connected with it, we have heard of projects for their melioration, in which it was maintained, " that the Indians must sink the distinction of languages." As if it were an easy thing to induce a whole nation to lay aside its mother tongue.

A stronger reason for the disuse of the native languages, arises from their crude and imperfect state, and their consequent maladaptation to the purposes of moral instruction. An Indian who has been all his life in the habit of supplying the deficiencies of speech by gesticulation and circumlocution, may not be aware how far he comes short of the purposes of exactness and precision in the conveyance of thought. But when such a language comes to be written and cultivated, there will be found numerous deficiencies and redundancies. The pertinacious distinction of matter into animate and inanimate classes, while it destroys the distinction of gender, has imparted to the vocabulary a cumbrous load of inflections, which greatly extend its limits, while there is but little gained in obvious utility. This extension in space is still further increased by the most besetting evil of the languages — their *tautological forms*, by which not a particle of new meaning is conveyed. These defects will have been observed by those who have given any attention to Scripture translations, *which, from the days of Zeisberger to those of Peter Jones, are rather numerous.* The most obvious external trait of these, is, that the Scriptures require nearly double the space in the translations, which they occupy in either the Hebrew, Greek, or English languages.

These defects weigh much against the substantial claims of the languages to cultivation. They do not, however, interpose a bar to it. On the contrary, it is a field in which the genius of missionary enterprize is invited to enter, and may be expected to triumph. All that relates to the conversion and improvement of the adult population, must be done in the native languages. And it is a question of practical importance, to what extent they may be employed in primary schools, and at what point they may be laid aside. On this subject, an experiment, on a large scale, is in progress, and we may confidently look to the active laborers in the missionary field for information.

In advancing the subject of moral and religious instruction among the Indians, it is not improbable to my mind, that the peculiar branch of modern benevolence which is comprehended by the subject of Tracts, may open a means of extensive usefulness. An appropriate series of school and missionary Tracts, in the native languages, might prove valuable helps to teachers now in the field, both in their preparation and distribution. And one or two missionary papers on the frontiers, (say one in the north-west, and one in the south-west,) would quadruple the powers of every active laborer.

In the preparation of such Tracts, it is obvious that a brief and simple system of alphabetical notation is required. And to be generally useful, it should provide for the whole circle of the languages. How far this object may be attained, without such a departure from the primary sounds of the English alphabet, and without, at the same time, admitting any of its inexactitude and partiality of application, is, perhaps, a question of importance. For, it must be recollected, that the literature of the Indians, when they come to require it, is one which they will find recorded in the English language. And it will therefore be an advantage that the sounds of its alphabet be not such as shall grate on the Indian ear, in repulsive and foreign tones.

Many subjects are connected with the education and conversion of the Indians. The organization of the element of a civil government among the tribes who have emigrated to the west banks of the Mississippi, is one of the number which claims missionary aid. But there is none, of more practical importance, than the subject of temperance. Without temperance, nothing can be accomplished. There can be no christianity—no well-attended schools — no well-cultivated farms — no comfortable buildings — no comely dress — no personal cleanliness — no adequate means of subsistence — no general health, or sound prosperity. Without temperance, the bible and the school book may be carried to the Indians, but they will be carried as sealed books.

[For the Annals of Education.]

INFLUENCE OF MOTHERS.

A GREAT and important change in the public sentiment is silently advancing; and if the breaking up of old opinions, and the establishment of new, on several important points, cannot be effected without a temporary agitation of the elements, still I would say, let the change come.

I allude to the mode of operation and kind of influence which ought to be exerted in the formation of human character. Let me not be misunderstood. I meddle not with the past, to complain of it. I speak only of the present and future.

The notion very generally prevails, that the greatest concentration of talent, natural and acquired, is, and ought to be, demanded of the presidents and professors of colleges, of those who sit on benches, for thousands a year, and plead at the bar for sums still larger, and of those who deal with fevers and consumption, and fractures; and that as you *descend* (as it is called) from these higher to the more common walks of life, talent, both native and acquired, — wisdom and excellence, become less necessary.

We were going to say, that our own belief is, that this order ought to be inverted. But we do not mean so. No devoted minister, no learned counsellor, no wise physician is a whit too wise or too good, at present. Let them stand where they are, as we have already hinted. But let parents and teachers be educated to fill a sphere of action, as much more elevated than that of president of a college, judge of a supreme court, or professor of medicine, as these are now deemed more elevated than the profession of parent or teacher.

"Any body can teach or take care of very young children," said the public sentiment but a little while ago; "any body" can plead a law case where the amount of property at stake is small; "any body" can prescribe for a cold, or other slight affection, especially in infants.

But is it so? Does not the voice of human experience inculcate views somewhat different? Does it not say, Bring your youngest infants under the influence of the wisest and best of mankind?

1. *Moral Influence.* Is it not here, at the earliest possible age, that a gospel ministry can be most efficacious? Is it not in preparing the ground, sowing the seed, nurturing the young plant, and directing the tender twig? In proportion as the human being is more advanced, does not the character of its teachers become of less and less comparative consequence?

2. *Intellectual Influence.* The younger the child, the wiser and better—whether male or female—should be its instructor. To put the mind upon the right track at the outset, is pre-eminently important. As it comes to act for itself, and consequently gets beyond our reach, its teachers, though they cannot be too wise, absolutely, may, with more safety, be ignorant.

3. *Civil Influence.* Those judges and counsellors who sit in parlors and kitchens, and plead at the bar of the tenderest infancy, need the greatest amount of true legal knowledge, as well as the greatest share of integrity.

4. *Medical Influence.* Any body, comparatively, may take the charge of a patient in a straight forward fever, or in rheumatism, or consumption; or in the case of a fractured limb—diseases which, if overcome at all, must be overcome by the force of nature, unsolicited, but only not interfered with. But the wisest and most judicious medical advice and aid which you can possibly obtain should be procured when your child has catarrh, or sore mouth, or bowel complaint, or eruptive disease; or any little affection which it is supposed "any body," especially any *mother* can manage almost as well as the physician.

I am aware that the great truth which is developed in these desultory remarks is still, to some extent, unpopular. There are mothers who have all confidence in their skill in managing the tender infant, and yet they would shrink from the charge of a case of typhus fever. But if all the diseases of adults were left wholly to nature and female nurses, the latter would not lose, for want of skill, half so many patients as female nurses of infants now do. On this subject I speak with confidence, for I know where I stand when I make the statement.

Mothers bring about more physical and moral destruction, (unintentionally, of course, but not the less certainly,) than all other causes put together. It is useless to attempt to evade the force of this conclusion; we have attempted evasion too long. The truth must be spoken. They are most powerful for good or for evil, who have most influence. But is not the *amount*, if we may so express it, of maternal influence, greater than the amount of all other human influence? It cannot be questioned. Then if evil results, in human conduct, is the general rule, and good the exception, is not our position confirmed?

But why is this so? Simply because mothers, though they may admit the force of our position in the abstract, after all, do not feel it; and because men, their nominal lords, will not give them an opportunity to feel.

We speak of the folly of European females who consign their infants to the care of nurses and hired servants; and yet our own ears were shocked the other day, to hear of a widowed mother, in this country, who has a perfect hatred, and always had, for her own children. Yet if every mother hated her children, we cannot believe the results would be much worse than they now are. But to what purpose is it that a child is fed from its own parent, if this is all? I grant this is very well, so far as it goes; but it does not go far. It has something to do with the physical frame of the infant; but other causes undo much which is here done, as we shall see presently. To what purpose is it that a child bears its mother's name, and receives its food, and perhaps its medicine at her hands, if it never sees her smiling countenance, or enjoys her company in the best hours of her life,—if her sweetest smiles and most vigorous efforts are to receive and entertain transient adult company, and her child is her associate only when she can find none more fashionable?

Can she mould a child's character, who, for the sake of work or company, turns it off, for three fourths of its waking hours, to "any body," no matter who? How much better is this than to trust its nursing to a hireling? Does she expect to form the character of her offspring, or does her husband expect it at her hands, who plies the wheel, or the needle, or the wash bench, nearly her whole time, and not only consigns her infant to foreign influence, but what is worse, gives it cordials, and elixirs, and other stupifying draughts as a substitute? She forms character, alas! but it is of a depraved sort, whether physical or moral. She forms character,—but it is to *un*form again, or the child's body, mind, and heart are ruined. She forms character indeed; but it is of a kind which can hardly hope for happiness, either here or hereafter.

A.

DOMESTIC SEMINARY FOR YOUNG LADIES.

No name could convey more fully the conception of such an institution, as we believe the education of the female sex requires. We have recently been favored with a catalogue of the Seminary at Clinton, which bears this title, under the direction of the Rev. H. H. Kellogg. It presents so much that is true and interesting on this subject, and the Principal appears to have advanced so far towards the completion of a plan which shall enlarge the intellect of our female youth, without interrupting the formation of a domestic character, which shall teach them how to combine elevation and improvement of the mind with the most humble labors of the hands, that we are persuaded it will interest our readers to learn from himself its "objects, and principles, and results."

Mr. Kellogg enters into no argument to show the necessity of educating in the best manner, the mothers who are to form the mind and character, and ought to command the respect, of the rising generation. But he urges that the sex have a claim to education not less strong, and even more extensive, because we need them as teachers of the young.

"If the youth of our widely extended country shall ever be instructed, it will be chiefly done by them. They are better qualified by nature than the other sex. They better know how to secure the attention, confidence, and hearts of the young. They can better exercise that patience which is necessary to success.

"But if men could do the work as well, they could not be obtained. So various and promising are the fields of usefulness, enterprise and ambition which lie before them, few will engage in the work of instructing children and youth for a compensation such as the community are prepared to allow."

Mr. K. then argues that in order to furnish this preparation, we must have institutions more extensive and better patronized than those we now have, not to make learned females, but to afford them a thorough education, on terms as reasonable as are afforded to the other sex.

"There are colleges and academies founded by public munificence, and sustained by permanent funds and legislative appropriations, for the education of young men,—but where are there similar institutions for young ladies? And are they not needed? Are females so much more wealthy—are their means and opportunities for self-support so much more abundant that they can educate themselves, while the widow's mite, the abundance of the rich, and the resources of the state, must all be put in requisition to educate young men? We have been accustomed to regard the former as the dependant class. We have felt that man was the lord, and to him the eye of woman, conscious of her weakness and her dependence, was to be directed. But here we have a practical inversion of these views, or a denial of the importance of female education. Are the public aware that their education is, and must necessarily be, upon the present system, more expensive than that of males? Those institutions which are, in part, sustained by public funds, are, with very few exceptions, not calculated to give young ladies that training which they need, either as it respects their minds, their manners, or their hearts."

In regard to the institutions which exist, the same circumstances obstruct their progress which have proved fatal to almost every institution which attempts to advance a step beyond the actual state of public opinion — the necessity of ample endowment—a circumstance, we may add, which would have been fatal to the noble institution of Fellenberg, had he not devoted his large fortune to its support. On this point, Mr. Kellogg observes :—

"Those institutions which are designed exclusively for females, are, with scarcely an exception, the fruit of private enterprise. Founded and sustained upon individual responsibility, with no other dependence for the support of the principal and teachers, for remuneration for the capital invested, or for the payment of rents, in short for meeting all the expenses of such an institution, than the income derived from pupils. The expenses must be far greater than in similar institutions, for young men. For them, buildings are erected, apparatus and library provided, public money received from the state, and in most instances a permanent fund, the interest of which is appropriated towards the support of teachers."

The list of studies in the Domestic Seminary furnishes ample means of intellectual improvement; and Vocal Music, Linear Drawing and Calisthenics are among the exercises. Religious instruction is based upon the study of the bible, and the review of public discourses. But the chief peculiarity of this institution is in its domestic arrangements.

"The pupils engage a portion of each day in domestic avocations. This portion is greater or less according to a variety of circumstances, as the age, health, and wishes of the pupils, and the wishes of their friends.

"The work consists of the various business of the family, together with sewing and spinning. It is divided into six departments; 1st. Care of the house. 2d. Of the clothes. 3d. Of the dishes. 4th. Cooking. 5th. Nursing. 6th. Sewing. The young ladies are distributed from time to time in these departments. All who spend any considerable time in the institution, have an opportunity of engaging in each department of labor.

"At the head of each department is placed a young lady competent to the entire charge of it; her duties consisting of the supervision of the work, and the instructing and directing those placed under her charge. She is responsible to the mistress of the family for everything connected with the department.

"These monitors keep an account of the number of hours spent in work by each young lady under their charge, and together, form a board to determine the relative value of each pupil's time and work. This is credited to the pupils respectively, and deducted from their bills."

As one result of these arrangements, we have learned from Mr. Kellogg's conversation, as well as from the prospectus, that they have tended to produce more contentment, and domestic enjoyment, than is common at our boarding schools — and to banish that spirit of complaint and jealousy which is too common.

"We wish our house to be the home of every young lady who enters it. The tendency of this feature is to do away those feelings of distance and separate interests which prevail to so great an extent in boarding establishments, and to promote a spirit of united devotion to the general good. The pupils being engaged in every part of the establishment, in preparing the meals, in keeping the house neat and in order, cannot but take an interest (unless under the influence of supreme selfishness and disaffection) in the welfare of the family, similar to that which they take in the prosperity of the families to which they more properly belong."

That such a system, well executed, secures and maintains a practical acquaintance with housewifery, will be one of its highest recommendations to those "lords of creation" who value merely their own comfort, and especially, to those mothers who do not wish to entail their own mortifying "*accomplished ignorance*" upon their daughters, and their daughters' husbands. To this, Mr. Kellogg adds:—

"Another very interesting result is, labor is made to appear respectable. When literary pursuits are disconnected with domestic duties, there is great danger that females will not only lose their relish for those duties, but that they will associate in their minds respectability with literature, and degradation with labor. Indeed, this effect has been lamentably apparent in the case of many educated ladies. There has been an erroneous public sentiment in respect to female industry; but it is even now undergoing a change, as is manifest in the fact that families of the first respectability have sought situations in this institution for their daughters."

But Mr. Kellogg states that the saving of expense to the pupils, on this plan, is an important advantage.

"It ought not to be supposed that this can be, in most cases, very great; for most young ladies are not in a situation to earn very much when they enter such institutions. Their age and their slight acquaintance with business forbid any large expectations from this source.

"But there are those who from their capacity for business are able to earn that which is not only very acceptable, but without which their connection with the institution would cease, or be very much abridged. And it is worthy of notice that those persons who most need this pecuniary aid are those who are most thoroughly acquainted with business, and consequently qualified to derive the greatest degree of benefit from this source. The amount earned during the hours assigned to work, and which do not interfere with their progress in study, varies with varying circumstances from ten to thirty dollars per year."

Of that part of the plan which proposes to associate several young ladies in a hired room, to provide their own food, we cannot speak with approbation. Nothing but the most pinching necessity ought to be allowed to place them in a position so unlike that which belongs to a domestic seminary. But as the economical result of the labor required, Mr. K. assures us, that while he is obliged to require $110 a year for board and tuition, those who labor, often procure an education for $50 or $75 — a saving far less than is claimed for manual labor schools of the other sex, but still as great as could be expected from the comparatively low price of female labor.

We shall rejoice if, in this way, the many noble females in the middle classes of life, can be furnished with the means of making themselves worthy to be *the teachers and mothers of American citizens.* But this, in our view, is but the dust in the balance, compared with other effects of the combination of manual labor with study on the body, and the mind, and the character. Our country will have reason to bless those who shall succeed in persuading parents who have no need of this economy, to educate their daughters, as well as their sons, in this way, and thus prevent that excessive exercise of the mind which is called for by interrupting all the peculiar duties and studies of woman, in order to attend exclusively to books, for this course too often destroys the vigor of the body, and endangers even the ultimate derangement of the brain itself, and the awful fate to which the talented female is so frequently the victim. Happy will he be, who can teach the domestic mother to avoid that mortifying neglect of all improvement — that dwindling of the mind — which so often follows her entrance on the duties of a family, who can show the talented and wealthy, that domestic duties may be regularly and well performed, without the sacrifice of dignity or intellect.

But we hope much more will be done for the education of female teachers, than can be done by an unassisted individual. There are numbers of females among the poorer classes, who have the best natural qualifications for the office of teachers, but who could not procure an education on the most moderate terms afforded by such an institution as that at Clinton. They are compelled to resort to the manufactory, or to domestic service, as the means of support, and thus are lost to the more important service for which providence has fitted them. Some institutions are already founded, and some societies already in existence, for the preparation of young men as teachers. We hope ere long, to see associations of females engaged in supporting and preparing those of their own sex for this office; for we have heard the conviction of its necessity and its practicability expressed in the strongest terms. Nor do we despair of seeing female labors employed in furnishing means for the accomplishment of this design. We have mentioned, in a former volume, an ancient institution in Guatemala, in which pupils were provided with buildings and means of instruction, and were enabled to provide for their own support by the culture of a garden and the management of bees; and the culture of silk has been proved in our country, to be highly profitable as well as perfectly simple.

But without resorting to any new branch of industry, we would ask what more is necessary to accomplish the object proposed, than that some proprietor, resembling Fellenberg in wealth and liberality, (and surely there are many such in our country,) should have his attention turned to this subject, and should be induced to invest his capital in a manufactory connected with an institution of this nature, where he could secure the requisite amount of work by an alternation of laborers, provide them with the means of immediate support, and allow them, during their hours of leisure, to avail themselves of the means of instruction? Recent calculations in a city of England, led to the belief that the efforts of one female in a benevolent object, were equivalent to those of thirteen males! We would therefore ask again, whether it would not be practicable for an association of females to organize an institution in one of our manufacturing villages already existing, to make arrangements for the selection and alternate labors of the females connected with it, and thus improve the character of that increasing class of the community, and secure the benedictions of thousands of neglected children?

REPORT OF THE ONTARIO COUNTY ASSOCIATION OF TEACHERS.

[The following Address to the Teachers and Patrons of Common Schools in Ontario County, New York, has been long on our files; but it has lost none of its practical value. It certainly deserves a place among the "Annals" of Education, and we earnestly bespeak the attention of School Committees, Parents and Teachers to the subjects which it so ably presents.]

The undersigned, a committee appointed by the Association of Teachers of this County, to present to you some suggestions for the improvement of our system of common school education, feel that they address you on a subject of high importance. As citizens of this great state, we justly boast of the liberal provision which has been made for the education of every child. We view our system of common school instruction, not only as necessary to promote the intelligence of our citizens, but essential to the preservation of that civil liberty, which has cost the blood of our fathers, and which they have bequeathed to us as a legacy more valuable than life.

Our district schools furnish the only means of education to the great body of our citizens. Not more than one in fifty of our children attend any other school. To improve our common schools, then, is to increase the facilities of education to the great mass of our people.

That our district schools have not been made to yield that amount of good to the community, which the system is capable, under different management, of giving, we need not say. We shall briefly lay before you the results of the deliberations of our Association.

1. Some obstacles which greatly prevent the usefulness of our schools. — These are, small school houses, poorly constructed; with inadequate arrangements for warming them; with desks and seats not suited to children. Most of our school houses are not furnished with maps, globes, or apparatus of any kind. Parents are often unwilling to furnish suitable books for their children, not thinking that a good book may save weeks or months of time to a pupil. "*Time is money.*" Parents almost universally neglect to visit schools. Inspectors rarely visit them. In our villages, many of our most respected citizens pay no attention to our district schools, as though general education was not a public blessing and common good. In many school districts, contentions, arising from various causes, have nearly destroyed the usefulness of schools.

2. What the supporters of schools should furnish. — In addition to spacious school houses, well built and made warm, each school should be furnished with a map of the County, of the State, and of the United States; a small globe, a numeral frame, geometrical and alphabetical cards, geometrical blocks, and a black-board. Each pupil, however small, should have a slate and pencil. In many schools, improved books should be introduced. We venture to say that $15 expended in maps and apparatus for a school, would increase the value of the services of a competent teacher, at least one third, during the term of one winter. Parents should encourage the teacher, and aid him by their support, in cases when called to the discipline of turbulent und ungoverned youth. We confidently affirm, that no man, in whatever vocation he may labor, suffers greater exhaustion of body and mind than the teacher — spending his days in a small crowded room, breathing an impure and unwholesome atmosphere, laboring with ceaseless activity to accomplish his daily routine of duties, dealing often with perverse spirits who have been taught to honor neither father nor mother, and much less teacher; leaving the scene of his labors at night, every muscle relaxed and his spirits exhausted, with the reflection that to-morrow the same routine is to be repeated. Were it not that the dawning of intelligence in the youthful mind, the developement of the intellectual man, and the kindling up of love for study in some of his pupils, and their affectionate interest in all he says and does, cast a charm over him, and make him forget his toils und his exhaustion, many a teacher would relinquish forever an employment, in which success is crowned with so little profit or praise, and failure is accompanied with so few circumstances of alleviation. Let parents, then, aid, encourage and sustain teachers in

their laborious efforts to advance the good of those whom they commit to their charge.

3. We would respectfully suggest a few considerations to Teachers.

1. Labor assiduously to improve yourselves in the business of teaching. Study how to teach. Watch the operations of the mind; observe the effect of different modes of teaching the same branch. Devise new arts to interest children in study. We commend to your notice and careful study, Hall's Lectures on School-Keeping, a work which every teacher should read. We commend to your patronage the Annals of Education, a monthly publication of great value. We also respectfully and earnestly urge teachers to form associations for their special benefit. If a few teachers, situated in the neighborhood of each other, would meet weekly or semimonthly, and discuss those subjects which daily concern them; if the teachers of towns would form such associations, great good would result. In those towns in which Lyceums are organized, Teachers' Associations might be organized in connection with them; and a portion of each evening, on which the Lyceum meets, the teachers might spend by themselves, and devote it especially to their improvement in the business of teaching. We should add no more on this subject, did we not know, that many teachers in those towns in which Lyceums have been organized and ably sustained, have not aided and encouraged them. We do hope the time will quickly arrive, when no teacher will find patronage or employment in this county, who will not attend and aid in sustaining these voluntary associations for improvement. We do hope that school districts will hesitate to employ such men as teachers, who will not interest themselves in efforts for improving the intelligence of the community around them. We seriously propose the question to parents, whether they can place their children, with any fair prospect of intellectual improvement, under the charge of those who manifest no disposition to advance the intellectual improvement of the society with which they associate.

2. We consider one of the greatest defects in the present mode of managing schools to be, the almost entire want of employment for small scholars. The story which has circulated in our newspapers, of the little boy, who, on being asked what he did at school, replied, *he said his A B and C, and sat on a bench,* is too true a description of a portion of many of our district schools. Schools become places of extreme weariness to children; and a disrelish for everything connected with them, is created from the actual want of something to do. We would recommend that every child should have a slate and pencil; that geometrical diagrams and cards of

letters be placed before them, and they be permitted to imitate them, and show their teachers from time to time the results of their attempts. Children will thus learn to write, and will be greatly delighted with the employment.

As soon as children can read, we would recommend to teachers to put them to mental arithmetic, beginning with Emerson's North American Arithmetic, and then taking Colburn's First Lessons. This course will furnish employment for them, make them happy, and fit them for the study of larger systems of arithmetic.

3. We would recommend to teachers the practice of asking their pupils questions, to excite them to the examination of subjects, and to form early habits of close observation. We will explain our meaning by an example.

Mr. B. one morning, as he called his school to order, asked his pupils the following questions.

T. Can any one of you tell me if there is any thing in the room which you cannot see?

The children looked at each other and at their teacher. A lad who was once in an infant school, answered; There is; it is the *air.*

T. How do you know that?

A little girl replies; When I move a fan, I *feel* the air.

T. What is the use of the air?

C. We cannot breathe without air.

T. Would fire burn without air?

C. We think not.

T. Can you think of any other use of air?

No answer.

T. What is wind?

C. Air in motion.

T. What does the wind do to ships?

C. It blows against their sails and moves them.

T. Did you ever read or hear of wind mills?

C. Yes, sir.

Mr. B. then told his pupils to find their lessons, and study; and if they were diligent, he would ask them more questions at noon. The scholars studied far better than usual. Noon soon came. He then asked the children the use of an ox; beginning with the smallest boy in school. He replied, to draw wood; a second, to draw hay; a third, to plough the ground; a fourth said, his flesh was good for food, his fat for candles, his horns for combs and knife handles; a fifth, his hide for leather, his hair to put into mortar, his feet to make glue, &c. The children went home pleased, told their parents the history of the half day, and many a smiling parent replied to his little one; You have a good teacher.

We would recommend to teachers, to prepare sets of questions on various subjects, for the instruction and amusement of their pupils. To aid them in this, we would refer them to a small book, called "The little Philosopher," and also to the "Pestalozzian Primer."

4. We would recommend to teachers, the introduction of Signs into their schools, to avoid the many questions asked. The raising of the hand may be understood to mean a request to leave one's seat; raising the hand with all the fingers shut but one, a request to speak; with two fingers up, to go out, &c. These simple signs will be found to save much trouble, and will be quickly learned by children, who will adopt the use of them, with great pleasure.

5. In many school districts, Libraries have been organized, in the following manner. The scholars, under the direction of their teacher, form an association, each agreeing to take one or more shares, at 25 or 50 cents. The money is paid in — books are purchased suitable for children and youth — each one draws a book on his share. The effect is, to create in children a love for reading and gaining information. A parent, perhaps, cannot give his children a few shillings which will benefit them more than in this way.

6. Let the teacher labor to make the school pleasant to the scholars. Let them be told what they are capable of becoming. Tell them of the powers of the mind; how they will expand by culture; how subjects which are now difficult, they will, by improving their time, soon comprehend with ease. Tell them that a little learned every day, will amount to much in a few years. The boy who will read ten pages a day, will in ten years, read seventy volumes of five hundred pages each; that it is by diligent and persevering attention, that anything useful or great is accomplished. Tell them that there are no bounds set to the human mind; that it will expand and expand — that it is *immortal*. Relate to your pupils the lives of great men, who have risen from low stations; and tell them that they, by the same diligence and perseverance, may acquire equal knowledge and equal respect. The teacher should impress upon his pupil, that the acquisition of knowledge will promote his happiness and usefulness; and that, next to the improvement of the feelings of the heart, the pursuit of knowledge is the noblest employment of man.

7. To render a school truly pleasant, and study interesting, the teacher should instruct *understandingly*. In the first steps of the education of a child, the teacher should take unwearied pains to make him understand every word he learns. The first book used should allude only to objects familiar to the child. To explain our meaning, we refer teachers to Worcester's Primer. Every lesson in this little book is about things familiar to a child of four years of age. In selecting books to follow this, let the same object be kept

in view; that they are composed of stories suited to children of this age. The teacher should pay very particular attention to the meaning of words, not requiring exactly such a definition as a dictionary furnishes, but rather that the child refer the word to the *thing* intended by it. The teacher, in pursuing this course, must, at first, require the definitions of such words only as are the names of objects familiar to the child. From the names of objects, he may proceed to those qualities of them which the senses of sight, feeling, and hearing, reveal to the child. In this manner, every lesson will become more and more interesting to the little learner.

8. We strongly urge teachers to improve the moral feelings of their pupils; to teach them to be kind and affectionate to each other, to respect the aged, to honor their parents, and to reverence the name of GOD. Teach them to love truth, and to despise deception. Let these topics be frequently conversed upon, in a familiar manner, before your pupils, and illustrated and enforced by interesting anecdotes, suited to excite the attention of children and youth.

In conclusion, and as one of the results of the meetings of the Ontario Association of Teachers, and of the information laid before them, we would say to parents and teachers, that increased and united efforts on the part of both, are necessary to bring our common schools to that state of usefulness which the friends of improvement desire; that the active co-operation of the patrons of our schools with the laborious exertions of teachers, is indispensable to the success of our system of primary education. We cannot estimate how much parents would aid in the business of education, by early encouraging in their children the practice of reading, and improving their leisure hours in a profitable manner. Every father, in the winter evenings, should have his domestic school. Here the first love of learning should be kindled up; the mind should be early supplied with its appropriate nourishment. The rising generation, thus trained up to intelligence and usefulness, under the united efforts of parents and teachers, will be eminently qualified to take the place of their fathers, and to succeed to the responsible trusts which must soon pass to their hands.

[For the Annals of Education.]

ON THE USE OF PICTURES IN SCHOOL BOOKS.

IN a former number of the "Annals," I offered a few remarks, introductory to the discussion of the question now agitated, as to the utility of pictures in books of education. The subject is interesting, and the arguments, if drawn out at full length, would occupy a space beyond what can fairly be assigned to it. I must therefore be content with hinting at them, leaving the reader to follow out the trains of thought that are thus suggested.

In the first place, it is proper to observe that I do not vindicate the idle use of pictures in books for embellishment, though I believe that tasteful and spirited designs, with a view to give a book an attractive and pleasing aspect, may be lawfully carried to a considerable extent. The real points at issue are, 1. Are pictures useful in juvenile books? 2. What is the proper limit to their use?

1. Are pictures useful in juvenile books? The great objects of intellectual education or instruction are, 1. to communicate knowledge; 2. to enlarge and strengthen the mind; 3. to establish good mental habits. If the picture system tends to secure any or all of these objects, it is so far useful; if not, it is useless.

The natural impulse of a child is to exercise his senses; he wishes to touch — to taste — to hear, and above all, to see. The eye is the most active and grasping of all the faculties. It brings more ideas than all the others — and how active is it in children? Bring a child to the school room — to the book. How does his eye wander from the alphabet; it steals to the faces of the other children; it gazes through the open door or window; it pursues the fly along the wall, or the spider to the corner of the room. All these things give him ideas, and his Maker has so constituted him, that everything around is a natural book, and he is earnest to read it. But the artificial book of letters and words — all this to him is an unintelligible mummery, in which he takes no interest, and from the study of which, he feels an impulse in every limb to escape.

How then shall you induce him to learn? Shall you entice or drive him? If you drive him, will you not sour his disposition, and create an aversion to books, by rendering them, at the threshold, sources of fear and punishment? But how shall you entice him? There are two means. In the first place, children are very imitative, and one child will try to do what another does. Place him therefore by another child, nearly of his own age, who has learned to read, and he will soon be inoculated with a desire to do the same. In this humor, give him a book with simple pictures. These he will understand. Connect with them letters and words; these he will readily learn, and in a short space, the meaning of words, the significancy of a book, will dawn upon the infant intellect. The printed paper will cease to be mummery, and the first reluctance will give place to an earnest love of reading. All this is too obvious to need illustration, and thus far, both as tending to communicate knowledge, enlarge the mind, and give good mental habits in the important era of a beginning, pictures are decidedly serviceable to education.

Suppose the child has learned to read; how many subjects of study are now before him? In the first place, geography is presented. This consists almost wholly of ideas of visible objects — rivers, hills, valleys, mountains, lakes, oceans, cities, edifices, animals, races of men, customs, &c. What would be the most effectual method of getting correct and vivid ideas of these things? Doubtless, to travel and see them. But this course cannot be pursued. What then is the next best? Certainly to present maps, plans, and pictures of these visible objects. These will not only shorten the study by an abridgement of time and labor, communicating at a glance what it would require pages to describe, but they give clear and distinct ideas of what mere words cannot portray. Thus, in the second stage of education in the most important of all juvenile studies — Geography — pictures are an invaluable auxiliary. They communicate knowledge, they give ideas, and thus awaken and expand the intellect; they give distinct and strong impressions, and these tend to establish the habit of understanding and retaining what is studied.

We might proceed to apply similar observations to the farther progress of the pupil, particularly in the study of Natural History. How few animals can he actually see, and yet how perfectly may he know the forms, the aspect, the attitudes, the motions of them all, by the help of pictures? And in the study of History, too, how great may be the aid of pictures! You may describe a crusader or a knight errant by well chosen words, but a simple wood cut will give a better idea of his appearance; you may tell of Cromwell dissolving the parliament; you may dilate upon his rigid form and features; you may detail his dress, and paint his air and his aspect — a wood-cut will accomplish more with the young student than all your eloquence.

In the study of the Bible too, how important is the use of pictures! Suppose you wish to convey an idea of the dress of a high priest — will not an engraving do it better than verbal description? And cannot a multitude of the objects mentioned in scripture, animals, trees, plants, edifices, as well as many points relative to the manners and customs of the Jews, all of which it is necessary to understand, in order to comprehend the sacred volume, be better represented by cuts than words?

There can be no question then, that, as an auxiliary, pictures are of the greatest importance in education; as before remarked, they often do effectually what words can do but imperfectly; they give vivid and lasting ideas of things, of which written language can only impart obscure and feeble impressions. They serve therefore not only to communicate knowledge, but to communicate it in such a manner as to invigorate the faculties, and lead the mind into the important habit of understanding things thoroughly, and recollecting them with ease and clearness.

We believe every person who has paid close attention to children will concur in these views. Pictures are indeed a far more natural language — a vehicle of instruction much more adapted to the nature of children, than the artificial language of letters; and so far as they can be used, they are effective instruments of education. The best method of communicating knowledge is to place before the child the objects of knowledge. If you would give the most accurate idea of a lion, bring the lion himself. If you cannot do this, give a picture of him. Why is travelling esteemed a great advantage? And why are the descriptions of an eye-witness listened to with such interest? The reason is that the eye has a scope beyond all the other senses; it flies on wings of light, and busy as the bee, brings home images from every visible thing, and stores them away in the cells of memory. These are the most vivid of all ideas, and he who is speaking of things he has seen, speaks with a clearness and animation which fascinate the listener. And shall we in education be denied the use of an art, which, if it cannot bring into the study the objects which a traveller sees, may at least, place before the eye lively delineations of them? If there is an art which is the best substitute for the best method of acquiring exact knowledge, and if it is peculiarly suited to the taste and faculties of childhood, shall not childhood profit by it?

Knowledge has a gravitating power like that of matter — a little, provided it is clear and distinct, constantly attracts more; and a single idea implanted by seeing a wood-cut, has often led the mind from one step to another, till it has mastered a whole science. This principle in the human mind is of infinite importance in education. We believe it is too much overlooked. Give a child a little knowledge of Natural History, and as his intellect advances, like a wheel that is set in motion upon a declivity, it will speed onward with an accelerating velocity, till it compasses the whole subject. This is the natural tendency of the mind — but a false system of education may check, or turn it aside. Let a book become hateful by being associated with the rod and a scowling brow; or let its pages speak in such a style, that the reader only gets faint and obscure ideas, and instead of aiding, you hinder the progress of the mind; instead of accelerating the wheel, you sink it in the sand; instead of cultivating the plant, you trample upon it, you crush it. If these things are so, how important is the use of pictures, properly applied, in giving the first impulsive knowledge, and in assisting the young mind to gain clear ideas, where verbal language fails!

It would be easy to produce examples, and multiply arguments to strengthen the ground here taken, but it would seem hardly necessary to say more on a subject so clear. A few observations upon the proper limit to the use of pictures in education, and we have done.

In England, this system is carried much farther than in this country. The Society for the Diffusion of Useful Knowledge are expending sums of money in their various publications, for maps, plates and cuts, which surpass anything ever attempted in this country. Not only are the juvenile books illustrated by engravings of great spirit and beauty, but all other publications, as voyages and travels, books of history, zoology, and other branches of natural science abound with lithographs, steel-plates and wood-cuts. There is now in a course of publication, in London, an extensive Encyclopædia of Geography, in which there are to be nearly 2000 fine engravings. And will any one say this is going too far? How can this be so? So long as these engravings impart knowledge in a better manner than words, who can with reason condemn them? Let it not be said that pictures tend to cultivate indifference to reading, and aversion to study. They cannot have such an effect, either on the young, or on the adult. Thousands have had their curiosity excited, and thus been stimulated to read, and read with interest and effect, by seeing a picture; but no one can testify from his own experience, that his interest in any subject was allayed or weakened by a good picture of it.

The only restrictions, then, which the present state of things would lead us to impose upon the use of pictures are these. Poor, or indifferent, or inaccurate engravings should be discouraged; correct and spirited engravings, illustrative of all subjects, whether in books of instruction or amusement, which convey ideas with more accuracy and effect than words can do, are deserving of encouragement, so far as they do not interfere with the necessary cheapness of this class of publications; it being however understood that a preference is always to be given to those which communicate knowledge over those which illustrate fancy scenes. The low price at which juvenile books are afforded is a sufficient proof that the picture system has not yet touched upon the above-mentioned ground of restriction, and we believe there is still room for carrying it beyond its present limits with a salutary influence. Let us teach all we can by every art and facility — there is still enough to learn — there are still difficulties enough to overcome — still ample fields in which the diligent and faithful teacher may exercise the patience, and task the faculties of his pupils. If the rising generation become impatient of study, and weary of mental toil, it must arise from some other source than the picture system, or from an abuse of that system. It would be as wise to complain of railroads and cotton gins, and other inventions to abridge labor, and accuse them of a tendency to encourage indolence and weakness, while it is well known that they are excitements to enterprise and exertion, as to complain of the use of pictures in education, while they are as surely calculated to stimulate the intellect, and give it strength and courage, as well in its first steps, as its onward progress. A fair wind may prove destructive to a ship ill managed, but let us not impute such misfortune to the fair wind.

The writer, under the signature of X, to whom we have referred in a preceding number, considers the author of Peter Parley's tales as particularly obnoxious to the charge of having carried the picture system to excess. As we take a different view of the subject, we should deem that a merit, which X condemns. But as to the matter of fact, this writer is in the wrong. The author of Peter Parley's Tales has never carried the Picture System so far as the Editor of the Annals himself, in connection with Mrs. Willard, in their work entitled the Rudiments of Geography. In that, pictures are avowedly a prominent part of the means of instruction, and constitute a larger, and more essential portion of the book than of any other we are acquainted with. This work preceded the editorial labors of the author referred to, and more than any other single publication, has contributed to promote the picture system in this country. We say this to the credit of the authors, and rejoice that the good sense of the public has led them thus signally to approve the picture system, by selecting as the object of their particular favor, one of the most highly-pictured school-books in the United States. Y.

ON THE PHYSICAL TREATMENT OF CHILDREN, AND ITS EFFECTS ON THEIR CHARACTER.

From the Journal of Heinroth, Professor of Medicine at Leipsic.

In the first number of this work, published in August, 1830, we inserted an essay on the subject of Infant Education, and made the following remarks :—

"The manner of directing the child in the common actions and concerns of life, will have an influence even more direct, upon his future character. We may pamper his appetite until we make him value the pleasures of the senses more than all others. We may measure his need of food, rather by some arbitrary rule, than by his constitution and appetite, and thus lead him to *habitual excess upon principle*, which we have known to produce and perpetuate disease in later life. There can be no doubt that many have been plunged into the gulf of intemperance by the habit so prevalent, of giving cordials even to the infant in the arms of its mother, to palliate a momentary inconvenience, or with the false idea of their giving him strength; or what we cannot but deem still worse, by administering an opiate merely to relieve the mother from the care of the infant, and thus, not only endangering his constitution, but producing the habit of using these insinuating poisons."

To this, we added :—

"As soon as the day can be divided into periods, in reference to rest and occupation, and the supply of his wants, the character of his future life may be seriously affected by the regularity or irregularity with which the little affairs of his life are conducted. It is scarcely credible that the child of a family where order is neglected, and everything that concerns him is conducted with irregularity and confusion, should ever acquire those habits of system and order so necessary to success and usefulness in life."

In a former number, we inserted an article translated from the German of Heinroth, an eminent Physician at Leipsic, confirming the same views, especially in reference to the food of children. The Professor next goes on to speak of the other great wants of childhood; — warmth, air, and sleep.

In regard to warmth, he observes that it is highly important that the infant should be guarded from currents of air, and cold, which often produce, in a few moments, the seeds of dangerous disease. But on the other hand, excessive warmth, either of the room, or of clothing, will render it feeble, and more susceptible of cold even to a painful and dangerous degree.

But an evil of still greater magnitude often arises from keeping an infant too warm. The first and most necessary means of ascertaining and increasing its own strength, is *the inborn propensity to motion*. This serves to wake up the interior being. On this propensity depends the subsequent disposition to action — in short, the love of occupation — the habit of industry. For it cannot be too often repeated, that the true life of man consists in action. Then the foundation of moral nature is laid in the earliest physical wants — and to check this early propensity, will obstruct the subsequent developement.

Now the disposition to keep an infant warm, often leads the mother to interfere with this propensity. Wrapped, and rolled, and packed in a variety of garments and coverings, the poor child can scarcely turn its head, much less move its limbs; and in some countries, it passes the first months of its fresh and joyous existence in the state of a mummy, without being able to carry off, by its limbs, the strong stream of life and strength which flows in upon it. Its uneasiness or suffering is strongly manifested by its cries and fretfulness, which no excessive nourishment, or artificial nursing and rocking into forced slumbers can relieve.

It is to little purpose to have the child, thus packed up, carried out in the arms of the nurse, or in a little wagon; and however well covered it may be, its limbs will be chilled sooner in cold air, in proportion as they are kept motionless. The motion which it needs, is *the use of its limbs;* and for this purpose, it should be laid, several times a day, upon a bed, and allowed to move its hands and feet with perfect freedom. Its smiles, and joyous cries will soon show how agreeable it is; and where no attention is paid to this, evil consequences almost certainly follow.

Another indispensable want of the infant, is air. It is, indeed, a part of its nourishment, for it is necessary to prepare the blood to communicate nourishment to the body. The child needs pure air, which it can never have, if it is perpetually shut up in the nursery; and without pure air, it will soon lose its color, and appetite, and sleep. One who is kept in impure air, becomes heavy, cheerless, fretful, and self-willed, and injury is done to the moral character in this way, also, by the neglect of its physical wants, while an important means of developing that character is taken away. The confined air of chambers, especially if it is rendered impure by the want of cleanliness as well as constant breathing, has none of that life-giving quality which tinges the cheeks of the peasant, and whose absence bleaches the complexion of the citizen. This air is the more injurious in proportion as it is less frequently renewed, from thoughtlessness, or the fear of chills. Even from antiquity, it has been a common opinion, and with much reason, that the want of fresh air tends to produce dulness, and stupidity of feeling.

Heinroth next treats of the subject in a manner so unusual, that we present his views entire, and earnestly recommend them to the attention of every mother.

"Sleep is, in fact, a part of the necessary nourishment of the child. In sleep, its vegetation, or growth, proceeds most rapidly. In its waking hours, its strength is taxed in other ways, especially by the continual activity of the senses, and the never-ceasing motion of its limbs, when this is allowed. The vigor of life, during the waking hours, is rather spent in the exercise of its infantile powers, than in the enlargement and completion of its organs and limbs. In this view, no amount of nourishment, no other excitement, can supply the place of sleep. It is, indeed, the opposite of excitement — it is, so to speak, the principle, the spirit of *rest,* the ground on which all *activity* depends.

"The child needs more *sleep* in proportion as its powers of body and mind are less developed, for in *sleep*, the organs of sense and motion strengthen themselves by rest for greater activity, while the business of nourishment goes on with undisturbed efficiency. The supply, (but not the oversupply,) of the simplest and most nutritious food, the enjoyment of fresh air, and free bodily exercise, will ensure a sound and refreshing sleep, because the supply of these wants produces a natural weariness. If this is not brought about naturally, or is prevented by artificial excitement, there will be either no sound sleep, or the child will suffer unnatural and painful wakefulness. The guardians in the nursery are often in the deepest ignorance of the causes of disturbed sleep, because they do not call their understanding into exercise on such occurrences, an effort which does not require medical knowledge, but only observation and daily experience. Hence they ascribe it to accident, a convenient resort for those who wish to save themselves the trouble of seeing and thinking.

"The sources of the uneasiness will be more obvious in proportion to the neglect of the mother. Excessive warmth, want of fresh air, want of motion of the limbs, neglect of cleanliness, (which sometimes produces a permanent eruption,) or above all, excessive or improper food, are sufficient to account for restlessness. When the mother or nurse frequently gives way to passion, even the nourishment of her own bosom is poisonous to the infant; and the same consequences will follow when she neglects her own diet or health. Either of these causes is sufficient to produce the colic, and other diseases with which children suffer, and even the convulsions, to which those that are ill-managed are subject. In short, all the food which ferments, instead of digesting in the child's stomach, gives rise to those accidents, which should be called by their true name, the effects of negligence.

"When any of these causes produce unnatural wakefulness, the mother or nurse is urged on by the blind impulse that the child needs *sleep*, as well as by the laborious attention which is necessary to an infant thus unnaturally excited, and by sympathy with its sufferings to try every method to produce it. She will tell you that '*the want of sleep* is the source of his troubles,' and that 'if the little sufferer could only sleep, all would be well,' forgetting the very evils she has, herself, entailed upon it. She tries then to lull him with singing, or rocking in the arms, or in the cradle,—a motion which drives the blood into the head, and by its pressure on the brain, produces stupifying slumbers.

"If this fails, other means are resorted to. The child is allowed to drink as much as it can and will; and it often drinks from the heat and thirst of fever until it sleeps from weariness, or from the pressure upon the stomach and brain produced by the quantity of food. Or, finally, if nothing else will answer, they resort to anodyne powders or drops. Now, the child will sleep from stupor; and having attained these objects, its mistaken guardian breathes freely.

"In this way, the child is poisoned with artificial sleep, as he was before with excess of food. But the nature of our sleep has great effect on the manner of awaking, and on the vigor of the soul. If we awake from healthy sleep, we are refreshed, and go cheerfully to our day's labor. But if our slumbers are weary, dead, or interrupted, we are gloomy, languid, unfit for thought, and discontented with ourselves, and the whole world. These last are the results of artificial sleep on a child, and a course of such treatment, and such consequences, has the most pernicious influence on the character as well as the health of the child; for it forms these unpleasant feelings into a habit. How can the soul be rendered cheerful, when so much interrupted and embittered by the defects of the body, when life is thus rendered painful from its outset?

"We thus see new evidence, that errors in physical treatment of children, lie at the root of false education; for when a plant finds no healthy nourishment in the soil from which it grows, how can it produce a vigorous stem, and healthful branches, or cover itself with leaves and blossoms? The fruits of life exist in the seed, and are already prepared in the very commencement of its germination."

AMERICAN INSTITUTE OF INSTRUCTION.

In a former number we gave a sketch of Dr. Beecher's remarks before the Institute, and of Mr. Abbott's Lecture, which was published during the session. As the hope of a speedy publication of the Lectures is disappointed, we avail ourselves of the following sketch of them, furnished by one of our correspondents who attended, and who is, himself, much indebted, on some points, to a correspondent of the Hingham Gazette.

Hon. Caleb Cushing, of Newburyport, in his introductory Address, labored with much ability, to show the absurdity of the sentiment, that the poor are happy in proportion to their ignorance. His views afford a striking contrast to those which were lately presented in the British Parliament, where a member endeavored to show, — and a member, too, who owes his elevation to early elementary instruction — that all the efforts for educating the common people better than they were twenty or thirty years ago, were misplaced.

In speaking of the best, and at the same time the most efficient motives that can be employed to induce the young to make proper application to study, Rev. Warren Burton, of Hingham, dwelt at considerable length, on emulation. He adverted to the injustice to which its use, in our schools and colleges, gives rise; of the injury which it often occasions to the health; of its great danger to the spiritual nature of man, by substituting anxiety, discouragement, despondency, disappointment, despair, envy, detraction and malignity, for better feelings and passions; and of its tendency to divert the student from what should be the great end of study, the acquisition of knowledge, the discipline of the mind, and the improvement of the heart. He did not doubt that emulation, in past times, in consequence of the absence of better motives, had been of considerable use. But now that the philosophy of the youthful nature has become better understood, and better motives can be brought to bear on the conduct, with efficiency, he thought that this primitive, coarse, *heathen* stimulant should, as a general rule, be let alone.

Mr Burton would substitute for this doubtful principle, another, which, for want of a better name, he would call Self-Emulation. Let the child compare himself with himself; let him strive to *excel* himself; to do more than he has ever done before. Let the teacher acquaint himself, when a pupil enters the school, as far as may be, with his natural capacities, and with the acquisitions he has already made; and let a record of the same be made in a book kept for the purpose. Let this be the starting point from which his future progress is to be measured; and in all his progress, let him be constantly referred to this, instead of being compared with those around him. Mr B. did not deny, that there were individuals, still to be found, on whom emulation, of the coarsest kind, would have a good effect; but he insisted they were only as exceptions to the general rule.

But he also appealed to other, and higher motives to effort than even self-emulation — to the benevolent affections, and to conscience. He spoke, too, of the motives by which they should be actuated, who assume the responsibilities, and take upon themselves the holy vocation of educators and teachers.

Dr Grigg, of Boston, dwelt with much ability and force on the mutual dependence of body and mind; and on the injury which must necessarily follow, if either of the two are neglected. He dwelt with an unusual, but just severity, on the fatal tendency of those fashions which lead otherwise sensible females to sacrifice health to obtain the enviable accomplishments of a pale countenance and slender waist. He exhibited, on the one hand, a model of the chest as developed in a healthy person, and, on the other hand, the model of a female chest, contracted and disfigured, and the spine distorted by a fatal and alarming fashion. We know not how a single mother, who heard this lecture, can go and dress her female children as formerly. Our only regret was, that the chest which was well formed, happened to be that of a large healthy male, rather than a female; for there is no necessity of overrating or exaggerating the deformity in question. If the true state of the case, made known by fair comparisons, cannot awaken the public mind, we should almost despair of doing it at all.

Mr Lowell Mason earnestly recommended that music be made an indispensable branch of education in common schools; that it be taught by the masters generally, whether they can themselves sing or not, though they would teach much better, of course, in the former case than in the latter. He showed, by the clearest reasoning, and by the examples of a juvenile choir present, that there was no difficulty in acquiring the principles of the Pestalozzian plan of teaching music; and that little children are capable of learning music, and ought to be instructed in the art, as soon as they are old enough to read. The only thing objectionable in this gentleman's lecture, as far as we could judge, was the omission of all reference to female instruction. It was *male* instructers who could do all this. Not a word was said of what could be done by females; nor a word of encouragement given, in this respect, to a class embracing almost all the teachers of young children, at least in summer, in New England.

Of Mr Abbott's excellent lecture, the late review renders any farther account unnecessary.

In the lecture on Maternal Instruction and the management of Infant Schools, by Rev. Mr M. Carll, of Philadelphia, the subject of female education, and female instructers was brought fully into view, and every omission of Mr Mason fully supplied. If there were some faults in the lecture, we are not sure but it will appear as well, when published, as any one of the whole series. Mr C. dwelt, at great length, on the qualifications of a mother to discharge her duties as the intelligent guardian and teacher of those pupils whom Providence commits to her keeping. He insisted that woman must not only understand Physics, but Metaphysics. She must know how to treat both body and mind, and to train them up in such unison, that subsequent years may develope both, in their highest symmetry and beauty. He spoke of the painful contrast which is now witnessed in the ghastly countenance and distorted shape, so common, but so portentous. Mr Carll opposed the doctrine, that the infant mind may be compared to white paper, and introduced some of his peculiar views in theology. He proposed, among other things, that the Institute should take the subject of Female Education into consideration, and offer Premiums for the best dissertation on female schools, and the manner in which they might be improved,—a measure which we hope will be early attended to.

Mr Sherwin, of Boston, gave a simple, but full exposition of a successful mode of teaching mathematics, as pursued by himself. It was plain and practical. There was no soaring into the visionary fields of speculation, no hypothetical deductions, no straining after pompous epithets or startling propositions. He made a practical illustration of his method, by introducing a class, and instructing them before the audience. Those who heard a plain, practical discourse of the deceased Colburn, at one of the first sessions of the Institute, and which secured such warm approbation even in a foreign country, could hardly avoid being reminded of it by the lecture of which we are now speaking.

The two lectures on the eye and the ear, by Dr J. V. C. Smith, of Boston, were exceedingly interesting. The lecturer presented apparatus on a large scale, for showing the whole structure of these delicate and wonderful organs; and we should be surprised to learn that there remains a doubt in the mind of any one who attended the lecture, of the importance of introducing the study of Anatomy and Physiology into all our schools.

Professor Follen, of Cambridge, delivered an extemporaneous discourse on the study of History and the best mode of pursuing it. His lecture was all that might have been anticipated from a deep read scholar, profound thinker, and clear reasoner.

Dr Gould, of Boston, insisted on the study of Natural History, by children, for the sake of their health. He particularly recommended, for this purpose, two branches of this great subject, Entomology and Botany. These, he said, ought to be commenced in the garden, and pursued together. In our pursuit of the insect, we are led to the discovery of the plant on which it prefers to feed; and thus, knowing the plant by sight, it is convenient and important that we should be able to assign to it its proper name, and become acquainted with its nature and distinctive qualities. The study of Mineralogy was also strongly recommended. The reasoning of Dr G. on the importance of these studies, was striking, if not conclusive.

Dr C. T. Jackson treated of the rise and progress of Chemistry; and of its uses. We thought the lecture more profound than useful, especially to a company of teachers; though enough was said, it seems to us, to show the importance of making the study of this useful science a part of common education.

The lecture by Rev. S. Farley, of Amesbury, insisted on a more enlightened, faithful, and candid supervision of Common Schools, as one of the more important means of raising their character, and increasing their usefulness; and that the school agent ought to feel a deep interest in his employment.

Rev Mr Winslow, of Boston, lectured on Unsafe and Useless Innovations, and the indications of any tendency to this evil in our country. We are not prepared to doubt, with him, the utility of Manual Labor Schools. There is the most satisfactory evidence to be obtained, that students may labor three or four hours a day, and yet make as much progress, and at the same time take as deep an interest in their studies as those who do not labor. We also consider the opinion of Mr W., that great muscular power is incompatible with high mental development, as wholly unsupported by facts. We think the lecturer's views on government were far more just. He was no advocate for severity in schools or families; but he believed that the rod, or something equivalent thereto must, sometimes, be resorted to,—and that the coaxing, wheedling system of governing, now very common, is as unreasonable as it is ineffectual.

It was maintained by Judge Story, in an able and eloquent lecture, that the science of government, to some extent, ought to be made a branch of popular education. The subject was urged with a spirit bordering on enthusiasm, and with the ability of one deeply versed in the science which he recommended.

Dr Barber, on Phrenology, was learned; perhaps too much so for a popular audience.

The discussion which followed on this subject was among the most interesting which occurred during this session of the Institute, and was ably sustained both by the friends and opponents of Phrenology. The discussion on the utility and inutility of pictures in school books elicited some interest; though it does not appear to have been thoroughly discussed. The same remarks apply to several topics of discussion. Among these, were "The expediency of endeavoring to induce children to regard their studies as an amusement, rather than a labor;" and "The use and abuse of recommendations in reference to subjects connected with education." On "The safety of dispensing wholly with corporal punishments," much more of both talent and interest were elicited, though the subject was by no means exhausted.

THE PICTURE SYSTEM.

Mr Editor,—Your correspondent Y. has given us much interesting and valuable information in his series of remarks on what was recently said in your journal, on the use and abuse of the Picture System. He has, however, fallen into a few mistakes in regard to the writer's object, as well as his sentiments. Will you permit me — in a manner as brief as the nature of the case will permit — to try to set him right? Is it not a pity that he should waste the fire of his artillery?

He appears to take it for granted that I would gladly maintain the following opinions. 1. That the use of pictures in school books is a modern invention. 2. That they ought not to be used as means of instruction. 3. That education should be made "all work." 4. That the golden age of instruction was about thirty years ago. 5. That long prayers and sermons are the most valuable.

Now I must confess my surprise, Mr Editor, that any one should make such inferences. I am quite sure not one in a hundred of your readers ever would have done so. It was certainly no part of my purpose to advance or defend either of those sentiments. The views of the community differ widely on all those points; and my object was to arrange the various opinions which prevail in regard to pictures, in two classes; and to show that while the "excess," if I may so call it, of a good thing, has been productive of some evil; yet the source of a large share of the evils which have been charged upon even the *abuse* of the "picture system" lies deeper, and can easily be traced to the change in the domestic and social manners and habits of our country which has been going on for half a century.

Will not your correspondent Y. read the article a second time? Will he not discriminate, fairly, between that which the writer advances as his own opinion, and what he quotes as the opinions of others? Will he make a distinction between what others are said to think, and what the writer himself thinks? And when he has done this, and also made a fair discrimination between what the writer regarded as the use and what the abuse of a good thing, will he not show wherein I have, as he intimates, been guilty of a want of consistency?

If the "Annals" were the place for subjects of this kind, I would ask Y., since he has favored us gratuitously with a part of his creed, and has advanced certain doctrines respecting prayers and sermons, what proof there is that "the best example of a prayer which has ever been furnished, is short," and that the best model of a sermon "is also short." But this point must, of course, be left for discussion elsewhere.

I do not, therefore, see the least occasion for retracting one tittle of what I have said, to which Y. has adverted. I will avail myself, however, of this occasion, to explain some remarks which I find have been misunderstood, concerning that popular writer, Peter Parley, who has done much — perhaps more than any other individual — to introduce pictures into general use; and which may seem to border upon severity. Now I certainly never, for one moment, supposed that writer would *willingly* "mislead," either by his pictures or his statements. But can it be supposed that the influence of such numerous works should be unexceptionable? When many of those authors whose influence upon the world has been most valuable and permanent, have been ten — fifteen — twenty years in preparing a volume of moderate size; and have written and rewritten fifteen or twenty times, what can he expect, who, on the contrary, prepares fifteen or twenty volumes, almost, in a single year? Whether he prepare the whole himself, or employ others to assist him, must there not be room for much error in the result?

Now I do not allude, Mr Editor, to errors which have not originated with, nor been confined to Parley. I do not refer to such instances as that at page 51, 54 and 56 of his Book of Curiosities, (and many others of the same general character,) where the dog, the prong-horned antelope, and the duck-billed platypus of New Holland, are represented in the engravings as nearly of the same size, except that the legs of the latter are shorter than those of the others; where, after being told that the length of the latter is only thirteen inches, the pupil is left to form his own opinion of the size of the others; while he is as liable, perhaps, to compare the antelope with the platypus, for size, as with the dog. I do not refer to this, I say, because Parley is not alone; and because all the blame that can attach to him, in this matter, is on account of his not having reformed a practice so grossly erroneous.

But let us look, for example, at his First, Second, and Third Books of History. The First Book contains sixty-two engravings; and they are generally correct and beautiful. The second contains, also, numerous engravings, some of which are good; others, besides being coarse, are wretched. The engravings of the Third Book are almost all bad. Perhaps the defects, in this case, are chiefly owing to neglect in stereotyping. Be this as it may, they are unpardonable. Let the reader examine the awkward Grecian and Roman figures on pages 21, 44, 48, 56, 69, 83 and 98. The pictures of Brutus and Cato are a burlesque upon humanity. Nor are the representations of Moses, and Jepthah, and David, and Goliath, and many others, much better.

This is not all. In the stories about Ancient and Modern Greece, historical facts are so confounded with fable, that it is extremely difficult, if not actually impossible, for an adult, who has read no other Ancient History, to discriminate between truth and fable; or to know what the author intended. But if adults are thus exposed to the danger of forming wrong conclusions, are not children much more so? Will not many who read about the Trojan wooden horse, for example, and see the picture, believe it to be historical truth? True, we are told that the story is given by "the poets;" and subsequently, that it is most probable that the place was betrayed by some of the Trojans. But before the reader is apprized of the writer's own opinion, thus tardily given, he has seen the picture, and a strong impression has been made, which the statement on the following page, *if ever read*, will hardly eradicate.

But we have a more striking example. The expedition, under Jason, to Asia Minor, is spoken of, in such a manner, that an ordinary reader would think the writer himself regarded it as a historical fact, and of course meant to have his readers believe it. But Hercules, one of the company, is expressly said, at page 47, to be a man, in strength, "not inferior to Samson." And again, at page 59, the story of Hercules, with his club, killing the lion, is so associated with the stories of Samson and the lion, and Putnam and the wolf, that any unbiassed reader must, I should think, be led to suppose that the writer regarded them all, as of equal authority, and equally wonderful. Can he seriously intend to place Samson, who pulled down, almost instantaneously, a large building, with three thousand people on its roof, on a level with Hercules? If this was the intention, will it not have the tendency to confound, and even to mislead? X.

OBJECTIONS TO THE ANNALS, CONSIDERED.

"I SHOULD like the Annals of Education, better," said a friend to me one day, "if it contained more for teachers." "But, my dear Sir," said I, "it is *all* for teachers. The great object of the work, is their benefit and elevation." "That may be," he replied; "but I want plainer and more direct instructions. I want to have the Editor give us his opinions in full, what are the best methods of governing, — the best motives to action, — the best rewards, punishments, &c. I want him to say what are the best methods, and the best books for teaching spelling, reading, writing, arithmetic, grammar, geography, &c.; and also what are the best kinds of recreation."

"But, my good friend," I replied, "I am a teacher, as well as yourself; and, like you, I take the Annals of Education. I have read every number of the work, from the beginning; and, if I live, I shall be likely to read every future number. I have found it to contain precisely the kind of information you speak of. Not in the precise order, at all times, which you have presented, it is true. But what have its two thousand and five hundred pages contained but facts, or the details of facts, from every one of which, a teacher may derive principles to help him forward, and strengthen him in his work?"

"Sometimes, it is true, the bearing of a fact on my own case, has been more, and at others, less obvious. Sometimes I have been forced to learn what I could do, from hearing what others could *not* do. In other instances, I have been obliged to learn what I *could not* do, by ascertaining from the experiments of others what they, in different circumstances, *could* do. When I have heard what Legislatures and Associations were attempting, every step of their progress has shown me more and more how much they could do, — the power and influence of public sentiment, — and consequently what remains for individuals, like myself, to accomplish. When I have heard what methods of instruction in a given branch were adopted, successfully, I have considered how far they were adapted to my own condition; or, if only partially applicable to my case, — to what extent. If methods of recreation or discipline have been reported, I have considered, or endeavored to consider, how far the character of the subjects for whom they were intended or used, corresponded to the character of the pupils of my own charge, and wherein it differed. Thus I have been acquiring strength, as I trust, from day to day, to prosecute, successfully, my employment, although the editor has never presented a single plan of his own, or of any other individual which I have adopted fully, since the commencement of his work. Every improvement I have made, seems, on the contrary, to be a thing of my own originating. I say it *seems* so; — but then I know that I never should have originated it without the assistance of the Annals.

"I might, it is true, have taken a very different course. For example, when he described the Infant School of Geneva, I might have adopted the methods of Mr Monod, with my infantile classes, without considering the difference of circumstances which existed. Of course, I might, too, have been successful, as well as Mr M.;

but *I might, also, have failed.* So when we have been told of a method of teaching spelling or arithmetic in a certain school, which was attended with very great success, I might, without considering the age, capacity, progress, number of pupils, or any of the circumstances of the school referred to, have gone and adopted them at once, with results entirely different from those which attended that experiment.

"But I do not believe, my dear Sir, that this last is the best way of elevating the standard of our profession, or of accelerating our own, or our pupils' progress. I do not believe it will make us thinking, understanding teachers. It might make us successful in parrot work; but never in forming mind and heart. As well may we expect the bleeding and warm water of Dr Sangrado, or Swaim's Panacea, to cure every patient of every disease, as that any given plan of teaching can be alike applicable to all teachers and schools. Besides, if a plan were ever so applicable to my own condition and circumstances, there is a difficulty of adopting it at once. It is better that we should come into a plan by little and little. You remember how awkward David felt, newly clad in Saul's armour."

My friend seemed to feel the force of this sort of reasoning, in some measure; and yet he was unconvinced. He said it seemed to him a pity that *some methods* of teaching every branch, whatever may be the age, capacity, or circumstances of pupils, or the wishes of parents, and some methods of discipline and modes of recreation alike applicable to all places and circumstances, could not be adopted. The whole work of instruction and education, including also the instruments, the books, &c., seemed to him a complete chaos; and he only wished there were some creating, or at least *re*forming hand to place them in an appropriate order, and educe beauty and harmony from deformity and confusion. He had long hoped — and could not but still hope that the Editor of the Annals of Education would be the agent of accomplishing this mighty work. He believed it was only for him to say, "Let there be light," and light would beam forth.

Now, for my own part, I entertain no such expectations of sudden reformation in the work of education. I anticipate great improvements; but not in a miraculous manner. They must, after all, be the work of the individuals themselves who are engaged in the business of teaching. We have too many leaders — too many theorists — already. What we want, is more thinking, feeling educators — more parents and teachers whose hearts and hands are practically engaged in making experiments; or at least in adopting those which have been successfully made. To such persons, a work on education must be an important aid. To all classes, it may, indeed, be useful; but to such, it must be indispensable. And to all who are engaged in the work of improvement in the right spirit, *principles* will be more valuable in proportion as they are shown in connection with practice; exactly in the way which the Annals of Education has pursued, ever since its commencement. I do not mean here to say, that in every instance the editor has pursued his plan in the most perfect manner; but only that the *general course and plan* which he has adopted, has been the best — not for machines, or teachers or parents who wish to be machines merely, but — for moral agents; men who wish to form intellectual and moral character.

On looking over the volumes of the Annals, I have been struck with the vast amount of information for teachers which the work contains. Those, even, who wish to imitate with the utmost degree of servility, need not be at a loss for something to follow. If I thought it would not aid in the work of making more educating machines than we now have, I would endeavor to sum up, or draw out, in a future article, or series of articles, the results to which a careful examination of the work in question would lead. It might be done under three heads. 1. Things which *every teacher* can do or adopt. 2. Things which *many* teachers can do. 3. Things which *no* teacher can do. Under each of these heads, we should find a very large list of things, facts, or principles; and though there should be nothing new, on the whole, yet such a bird's-eye view of the ground which the Annals has taken, and the work which it has consequently accomplished, would, in my own view, be satisfactory to many teachers, and to some, highly instructive.

A Teacher.

THE TEACHER'S ALMANAC FOR NOVEMBER.

Every one has heard of the consternation into which the community were thrown, in days of yore, by a famous Almanac maker, whose servant, as the story goes, being employed to write down the prognostications of the weather, wrote, in the column for July, "Snow about these days." We should be sorry to make as serious a mistake in our Teacher's Almanac, for November. And yet, were we to state that the million of parents, and the twenty thousand teachers in New England and New York were now on the alert in making preparations for winter schools, we are not sure that we should be much nearer the truth.

During this cold month, many thousand male teachers will take the places which, two or three months ago, were vacated by as many females. "New lords, new laws," is an old saying; and how often is the young teacher forward to promulgate his new code of enactments, and careful to see that not a few of them are diametrically opposed to those of his predecessor. However, he alone will act the wise part, who takes care to repeal no wholesome laws, and to enact no new ones, till urgent circumstances seem to call for them.

A recess of two months, with the younger pupils, and of eight with the older, will have given them time to forget much which they once knew, and to acquire many idle or mischievous habits, in the streets, if not at home. These habits, it will require a fund of wisdom and patience, and much time, to correct. But let no precious moments be spent in reforming and undoing, without necessity.

No teacher should enter upon the duties of his station, without a plan, both as regards methods of discipline, and modes of instruction. None should enter a school house without remembering, that though the bodies of the pupils are the habitations of immortal spirits, they are, nevertheless, related to, or affected by, external objects. The temperature and purity of the air, the quantity and quality of food and drink, the nature and amount of clothing, and a thousand other circumstances, independent of peculiarities of constitution, — all affect the mind and spirit. The teacher should take his pupils as they are, study their constitution of body, mind, and spirit, and endeavor to make the most of them. He should do his utmost, for the time he is with them, to make them comfortable, cheerful, virtuous and happy; and should leave undone nothing which will promote their virtue and happiness in time to come.

THE ANIMALS, AND VEGETABLES.

In the progress of this month, the hybernation, or winter's sleep of many an animal will commence. The birds, except a few of the more hardy, have already winged their way to more genial climes; and the few downy tribes that remain, are making preparation for their departure. The insects have suspended their "busy hum," and the reptiles have gone to their dark quarters. The fishes, many of them, have retired to the deeper and warmer ocean. The furred animals which remain, and continue active, generally put on a whiter and thicker coat, and thus are better defended against the severity of the cold. Vegetation, too, is suspended. The leaves of the trees have fallen, the sap has descended, the flower is withered, and the grass is faded. Will not every teacher remind his pupils of the changes which are going on, and refer him to their Divine Author?

THE EARTH.

Frost begins to bind in chains the silver streams, and spread its mantle over the faded earth; ever and anon the fleecy flakes descend — the winds howl around, and all puts on the appearance of approaching and desolating winter.

THE HEAVENS.

On the 10th of November, at 10 o'clock, the beautiful constellation of Andromeda will be immediately overhead, containing a nebula or little cloud of very small stars, which is sometimes called the hair of Andromeda. Between this and the north star is the chair of Cassiopea in the shape of an inverted 4. The sign of the Zodiac on the meridian is Pisces, which must be studied on the map.

On Sunday, Nov. 30th, there will be a total eclipse of the Sun in the United States, at Charleston, Savannah, Milledgeville, Little Rock, and places in the same range; the Sun will be entirely covered. The whole duration of the eclipse will be 4 1-2 hours, beginning at Washington 1-4 before 1; at 1-2 past 1 in Augusta, Me.; and at 1-2 past 11 in New Orleans.

MISCELLANY.

Rutland County School Convention.

A Convention of Teachers, Parents, and others interested in Education, was held at Castleton, Rutland County, Vermont, on the 23d of Sept. last. The Chairman of the Convention, Mr. Thomas H. Palmer, of Pittsford, addressed the Convention — the teachers especially — on the best modes of teaching Arithmetic to very young children.

The Convention also passed several resolutions, one of which recommended Libraries of School Books as valuable and economical appendages to District Schools. Another resolution was, that it is not only the duty of parents to furnish schools with proper school books and apparatus, and with competent teachers, but that it is a matter of economy. It was also resolved, that the common practice of changing teachers every season, is a great injury to our primary schools. Several resolutions were passed on the importance and necessity of raising the standard of attainments on the part of Teachers of District and other Primary schools, and urging upon parents and professional men, and teachers themselves, the importance of uniting their efforts for this purpose. They also resolved to appoint two persons to meet with teachers and parents in the several towns in the county, about the time of commencing the winter schools, and address them on the subject. The expense, they observe, ought to be defrayed by those for whose benefit the lectures or addresses were given. The Chairman of the meeting, and Mr L. F. Clark, a teacher in Castleton, were designated as the Lecturers.

One resolution, rather novel in its nature, was adopted by the Convention; which was to make trial, in Rutland County, of the *Central School System*. By Central Schools, is meant schools for the larger pupils of two or more adjoining districts, to be kept by a man, during the winter. Some of the reasons urged in favor of this measure were, that by taking some of the larger pupils out of the district schools, the latter might be continued, under the care of female teachers, throughout the year; and the division would be alike advantageous to both. Those who have experienced the evils which at present exist, and which gave rise to this new measure, will be anxious to know its results, when submitted to the test of experiment.

Virginia Institute of Education.

The second Anniversary of this Society was held at Prince Edward Court House, Sept. 25, and was well attended. It will be remembered, that the object of this Association is to collect and diffuse information on the subject of education. A Report was read, showing the alarming destitution of Virginia, in regard to regular instruction. It was accompanied, however, with a few cheering facts, in regard to the state of female education, and the increase of permanent and native teachers. The report was followed by a lecture, by J. M. Garnett, Esq., of Essex, "On the Advantages of Associations for the Promotion of Education." We understand that the interest in this lecture was so great, that measures are taken to secure its speedy publication.

School Law in Pennsylvania.

We have mentioned the School Law in Pennsylvania, and congratulated this noble State on its prospects of improvement. We regret to receive the following information in a letter from a gentleman in that State.

"This law, which is to be accepted or not by the people, was submitted to them a fortnight ago, and I very much fear it will be rejected by a large minority, if not by a majority, and place it in a situation so embarrassing to its friends, as to lead to its repeal. The opposition comes chiefly from the German counties, where the most excessive aversion to taxation is coupled with the darkest ignorance. In the West and North West, the law has met with favor, and been generally adopted. Should it fail, ultimately, Pennsylvania will remain, for many years, in her present destitute situation, in regard to a general system of Education."

Instruction of the Colored People in Bermuda.

During the past year, considerable effort has been made in behalf of the colored population of Bermuda. Mrs Holt, a highly respectable and benevolent lady, in a letter to a friend in the United States, has ably set forth the advantages which would result to the whole American community, from a permanent establishment at Bermuda, for the education of colored missionaries and teachers of the African race. Mr Crofts, a Wesleyan missionary there, has also advocated, with much ability, the same plan, in a letter to Mr Cookman, of N. J. Mrs Holt is now training four or five persons for teachers. She thinks there is no time to be lost, and closes her remarks by saying, that "the West Indies need teachers instantly;" that after a small expense to purchase land and house to begin with, the students might easily pay their way at the Seminary, by manual labor; and that the only expense, annually required, would be to pay the salary of the Principal. Mrs H. also speaks of the very great anxiety manifested, both by parents and children, in Bermuda, for books, and refers to the success which has attended her efforts to establish a small library.

This benevolent lady has also a school for the young in one of these islands, which she calls the "Wilberforce School." The following is an extract from her letter.

"I teach the small colored boys from 6 to 8 in the morning; — from 9 to 3, I attend to my own private school; — from 4 to 6 P. M. teach colored women and girls, at which time from 40 to 60 attend; — and from 7 to 9 in the evening, teach large boys and men.

"Last night, I formed a class of boys in Arithmetic, twenty-three in number. Never were any people more completely ready for instruction; and although we have been teaching only a fortnight, already we see great improvement. We teach all to read, spell, write, and cipher."

We are exceedingly mortified to be compelled to say, that the first school for the colored population of our own free states, established a short time since in Canterbury, Connecticut, and which has met with constant opposition from the public sentiment, has, at last, been violently assailed, and the proprietors have thought it expedient to discontinue it, and sent the pupils — twenty in number — to their homes; while in Bermuda, where more than half the population are colored, and where the most enlarged and liberal efforts have been made, and are still making for their education, the public peace and prosperity has never been greater, nor the state of society happier.

Education in Greece.

The efficacy of the operations of the missionaries in the schools established at Athens, the confidence of the government, and its favor towards them are confirmed by recent letters from that city. Greece looks to these schools as models, and also as the means of furnishing the country with competent teachers. A recent letter from Mr Hill, who has the charge of the female and infant school department, to the editor of the New York Daily Advertiser, under date of July last, states as follows:—

"It is just three years since we commenced, actively, the work which we hoped would shed intellectual, moral, and religious light on this people, and it has been made to prosper. We have just been highly encouraged by testimony of the confidence of the king and government, in a "Royal Ordinance," communicated to us, and accompanied by a letter of the Minister of Instruction. Twelve girls are to be placed at the Institution, under our charge, to be educated for teachers, at the expense of the government. This measure will, we hope, stimulate the friends of the work we are engaged in, to greater exertions for its support and extension. There are no bounds to the good that may be done here, if the means are provided."

We also learn from the "Report of Mrs Emma Willard, Corresponding Secretary of the Troy Society for the advancement of Female Education in Greece," with a copy of which, we have recently been favored, that the Troy Society, during the year and a half of its existence, have forwarded to Greece $1600, besides expending nearly as much in printing and circulating information in regard to their object.

Benevolence and Enterprize.

Mr James P. Allaire, of New York, who is so extensively engaged in the manufacture of Steam Engines as to have about 2000 persons dependent on him for support, has a school connected with his works at Howell, N. J., which accommodates nearly 100 scholars, and is supported at his own expense.—*N. Y. Daily Adv.*

NOTICES OF BOOKS.

The Third Book of History; containing Ancient History in connection with Ancient Geography. Designed as a Sequel to the First and Second Books of History. By the Author of Peter Parley's Tales. Boston: Carter, Hendee & Co. 1834. pp. 189.

This work will unquestionably derive a degree of popularity from that of its predecessors, which it resembles in character. So far as we have examined it, we are pleased with its style and spirit. Its typography appears to be remarkably correct; but we are sorry to find the type, like that of the Second Book of History, and indeed a large proportion of all our books for the young, much too small. The eyes ought not to be tried more than they are with that of the First Book, which is a size larger. This Third Book, like the First and Second Books, is furnished with maps at the end, and is illustrated with numerous engravings; but we suspect that both our correspondents, X and Y, would find fault with the stereotype impressions of the latter.

The Intelligent Reader; designed as a Sequel to the Child's Guide. Springfield: G. & C. Merriam. 1834. 18mo. pp. 252.

This volume is compiled by the same judicious hand that prepared the Child's Guide; and on the same principles. Great care was taken that the moral tendency of the selections should be excellent, and every lesson is preceded by a short vocabulary of its more difficult words, with definitions. There is, also, a series of questions for examination, at the end of each article. The mechanical execution of the Intelligent Reader is creditable to its enterprising publishers; and the type is generally of tolerable size. The work contains ten or twelve engravings, which are obviously better than those of the Child's Guide.

A Fourth Book of Lessons for Reading; with Rules and Instructions. By Samuel Worcester, Author of the Primer, Second Book, Third Book for Reading and Spelling, &c. Stereotype edition. Boston: Carter, Hendee & Co. 1834. 12mo. pp. 408.

This work is intended as the completion of a series of books for teaching children how to read, of which series, the three first are named above, from the title page. It is constructed on the same plan with the Third of that series; each selection, whether of prose or poetry, being preceded by a Rule for reading, and followed by a list of common errors in pronouncing some of the words included in it. The object of these peculiarities of Mr Worcester's Third and Fourth Books, is to make Reading a STUDY in our schools, instead of a mere exercise. The style and sentiments of some of the lessons, even the compiler admits, are not of a very high order, but his apology is, that they were selected with primary reference to teaching children how to read.

We regard the Fourth Book as, on the whole, a useful compilation for the classes for whom it was intended. There is a large fund of valuable information embodied in the Rules and Instructions at the beginning, and in the Errors and Questions at the end of each chapter; as also at the close of the work;—even more than the author, in his modesty, has ventured to claim.

ERRATA.

We regret that errors have crept into some of the articles of our correspondents, from too great reliance on former printers, and in some instances, from our inability to read the proof.

In the article on Expression, in the April No. Vol. 4. p. 153, last line, read "healthful" for "beautiful;" and in the May No. p. 204, last line but one, for "importations," read "impartations." In one of our own articles, in the same No. p. 231, we are made to say magazines of "*philosophy*," instead of "philology." In spite of reiterated corrections, the compositor has persevered in spelling the respected name of Pres. *Duer*, of New York, most strangely; and has also given us the new orthography of "*children*," for the offspring of man, in the title of The Father's Book, p. 387. We regret, more than any errors we have discovered, that "*Derby*" (Oct. No. p. 458) is made to say, "This explanation must be wholly intelligible," in place of "This *exclamation* must be wholly *un*intelligible;" and on page 457, "*worthless* native of the forest," instead of "ruthless native."

We are mortified with these and other errors, which our readers have, doubtless, noticed; and can only atone for them, by the new measures we have taken, to secure more accuracy.

AMERICAN

ANNALS OF EDUCATION

AND INSTRUCTION.

DECEMBER, 1834.

INFANT ASYLUMS.

It would probably have been attended with happy effects upon the cause of early education, if the institutions formed for the care and education of infants had been called *Asylums* instead of *Schools*, as indeed, they originally were. Names influence, very much, the expectations of parents and the public, and the conceptions of teachers in regard to their duty. The name of a Female College, for example, has excited extravagant expectations in some parents, ridiculous vanity in others, and equally unfounded prejudices in others; while those institutions which are called by the unassuming, but correct name of Seminaries, or Academies, though in some instances of equally high claims as to studies and usefulness, receive universal approbation, and excite none but proper feelings. In the same way, the mere name of an Infant School, has seemed to furnish a kind of pledge, that the half formed minds, introduced into them, should be compelled to perform mental labor — should be returned to their parents little prodigies of early improvement. It has not less excited the benevolent vanity of some of their patrons, and we have been pained to see how they would bring forward little victims of mistaken kindness to excite the applause of a large assembly, by showing how excessively their brains had been made to grow and act, beyond any other part of their diminutive frame. For ourselves, we have no more patience with this abuse of benevolent feeling to produce premature advances in one part of the system at the expense of the rest, than we have with the method employed at Strasburg, of shutting up their geese in a coop so small that they cannot move, and feeding them with fat meat, in order to render their livers peculiarly large and delicate for the famous pies of Strasburg. We have expressed, too fully, our views of premature development, to render it necessary that we should again say how much we are opposed to a system of hot-house forcing, under whatever name.

Infant Asylums owe their origin to the benevolence of a German Princess, and were intended to provide better air, food, attendance, and training for the children of the poor, than they could otherwise receive, together with such instruction as their age allowed.

The same spirit appears to have actuated the founders and patrons of the institutions described in the following circular, issued at Paris. Our readers may recollect the description of this Asylum, as given at page 140 of our first volume; and will be gratified, we doubt not, to learn that the expectations of its founders have been more than realized.

"PARIS, FEBRUARY 6TH, 1834.

"Among the charitable institutions of Paris, is one which all persons who are interested for the laboring and poor classes of society will appreciate; it is that called the Asylum Rooms.

"The first years of life, the period so important for moral and physical development, are for the children of the poor and for those of most mechanics, a season of every kind of dangers. Too young to be admitted into the schools, these unfortunate little ones are left to themselves, whilst their parents go to their daily employments. Confined in an unhealthy hovel, they are exposed to a thousand accidents, and are frequently burned, or else they run the streets, where they find other dangers and learn lessons of immorality; soon the vicious propensities are developed, and cannot be eradicated.

"In the Asylum Rooms, children, from the age of two to seven years, are kept during the day. Collected under a common superintendence, they contract habits of obedience and honesty, and the principles of religion and morality are imbibed. Their mothers, during this time, can devote themselves to lucrative occupations, and contribute to the support of the family.

"A committee of ladies, appointed by the general council of the *Hospices*, have opened, since 1825, ten asylums, which contain more than seventeen hundred children of both sexes; but there are still thousands who suffer without our being able to admit them; for more than twenty-four asylums* would be necessary in Paris

*Fourteen had been opened previous to 1825.

to meet the pressing wants of the population. The aid of public charity is indispensable to accomplish this, and the ladies of the committee solicit your assistance on behalf of the existing asylums and those which are yet to be opened; and if you consent to renew your subscription annually, you will ensure the continuance of establishments worthy of your care. Any sum, however small, will be received with gratitude.

THE COUNTESS OF BONDY, *President*,
EMILE MALLET, *Secretary*."

There is, however, a demand for such institutions beyond the mere limits of suffering poverty, and for the same reasons as for other schools. There are, in all the classes of Society, parents, whose circumstances render them unable, or whose character renders them unfit to take the care of their children, even at an early age. Many a life is lost, many a child is ruined, many a bad citizen formed, by the want of proper training. It is far easier to find two faithful, able guardians for twenty or thirty infants, than fifty competent parents; and we believe, therefore, that Infant Asylums, properly conducted, aiming chiefly at the care of the body and the character, and giving instruction only as it can be easily and cheerfully received,—in short, extensive *public nurseries*,—would be a great blessing to the community.

It is in this view, that we insert the following extracts from the "Sixth Annual Report of the Infant School Society of Boston." The schools of this Society are represented as more flourishing than at any former period.

"It is now six years since the first infant school was established in this city. During this period, hundreds of children have been taken from the streets, and instructed in useful knowledge. Hundreds of industrious mothers have been relieved from the care of their young children during the day, and have thus been enabled to gain a comfortable subsistence.

"Though our rules do not oblige the teachers to take children under eighteen months of age, they have, in many cases, taken them when not more than sixteen, and even twelve months old.

"Viewed simply in the light of *neighborhood nurseries*, these schools are valuable institutions—as every mother knows how much attention such children require.

"During these six years, we have reason to think that much good has been done, and more evil prevented. How much, we cannot tell. Our schools have made better *children*, and it remains for future years to show whether they will make better *men* and *women*. But if the earliest impressions are most lasting, there is much to hope. They are expensive institutions, it is true—but we believe *they are worth all they cost*. It is earnestly recommended to those who have any doubts on the subject, to visit the schools, and the parents of the scholars.

"The object of our infant schools is the same with that of the 'Society for the Moral and Religious instruction of the Poor.' The only difference is, that we commence 'the moral and religious instruction of the poor' at an earlier age than they do.

"No Christian parent thinks it safe to let his child roam the streets, and mingle with bad company, till he is old enough to go to the Sabbath school. It is found that the seeds of folly, which are bound up in the heart of a child, may spring to a premature maturity in these hotbeds of vice, and before they are four years old, may bring forth bitter fruits. While the city missionary is laboring to reform the parents, the infant school endeavors to prevent their children from ever needing reform.

"The phrenologist fears we shall learn the children too much, and the primary school teachers and committees complain that we learn them too little. Our great aim has been, to teach them to 'fear God and keep his commandments;' and we sometimes have cheering evidence that our efforts are not in vain.

"Infant schools appeal to the feelings of every *mother*, in the character of *neighborhood nurseries* for neglected children. They appeal to the *Christian*, for they are designed to carry the gospel to the poor. They appeal to the *friend of Sabbath Schools*, for they are kindred institutions—having the same object in view, and using the same means. They appeal to the *friend of the poor*, for they are calculated to bring permanent relief, by removing the *causes* of poverty. They appeal to the *ministers of the gospel*, for they preach to a class of immortal beings, whom the eloquence of the pulpit cannot reach. They appeal to the *city missionary*, for if they succeed, he will soon have no work to do. They appeal to the *political economist*, for they hope to do more than any thing he has yet devised, to prevent pauperism, and supersede almshouses and prisons. They appeal to the *patriot*, for if suffered to have their perfect work, our country, instead of degenerating, will stand yet higher among the nations. Finally, they appeal to *Him*, who, when he was on earth, took little children in his arms and blessed them, and said to his disciples, 'Feed my lambs.'"

The first Annual Report of the "Richmond, (Va.) Infant Free School Society" is a document of much importance and interest; and contains much that is adapted to our present purpose. Though the Society has but recently commenced its labors, they have much to encourage them. A school was opened on the first of July, 1833, with only twelve children; but in June, 1834, the number had increased to seventy-three. Perhaps the following extract will best serve to show the object and character of this school, and what should be a prominent object of those who have the care of every Asylum for Infants.

"The immediate results of an Infant School, are not of a character to be definitely described, or very obviously perceived. The system of instruction, when faithfully applied, may be likened to clipping the sprouts, as they shoot from noxious roots, and depositing seed in a soil which, though in many respects favorable, yet time alone, by the blessing of God, can secure the growth. Many circumstances connected with this school, are peculiarly calculated to prevent obvious results; such as the unfavorable influence to which most of the children are exposed, when out of school, and the short time many of them are connected with it, owing to frequent change of residence. Yet, it is believed, sufficient success has attended the undertaking, to warrant a continuance of similar effort. The general aspect of the children is improved; they are neater in personal appearance, and more orderly and mild in their deportment. In several cases, there is a decided change apparent in the temper and disposition. A little girl, remarkable for giving way to her passions, by knocking her head, pulling her hair, &c., when any command, unpleasant to her, was given, now needs only to hear the command, to secure cheerful obedience. Another child, considered quite unmanageable by his parents, who, in fits of anger, would fiercely throw stones through the windows, and curse his mother to her face, is now kind and amiable in his deportment, and seldom manifests anything like anger."

The following statement, and list of anecdotes, is by no means the least interesting part of the Report. We are aware that great care should be used by the conductors of Infant Asylums, not to array children against their parents, though ever so intemperate. Perhaps they would do well to remember the caution once given to those, the scene of whose ministry was chiefly among adults; "Be ye wise as serpents, and harmless as doves." In the present instance, no evil appears to have arisen, for we are expressly told, that the influence of the school on the parents, is not only very happy, but that the parents themselves feel that their situation at the school is a favor.

"Early in the autumn of 1833, it was discovered, that a great proportion of the children were in the habit of getting morning drams. It was evident that, unless this could be counteracted in some way, the beneficial efforts of moral instruction would be looked for in vain. Measures were taken to enlighten the minds of the children, by simple illustrations, presenting to them the drunkard, and the sure process by which he became so, together with the dreadful consequences of drunkenness, here and hereafter. It was quite surprising to see how quick were their perceptions, how proper their applications, and how correct their reasoning upon this subject.

"A gentleman furnished them with a series of cuts representing the progress of the drunkard from infancy to the gallows, the exhibition of which made a deep impression on their minds. A little girl, after looking at one of the pictures where a child was in the act of asking its mother for a dram, said, 'O, that is just as I used to do before I knew it was so bad to drink drams; but I never mean to drink any more.' It is believed she has kept her resolution. Her mother says she cannot prevail on her to take even cordial. A little boy said, one morning, 'I did not drink a dram, for I thought of the little boy who teased his mother for a dram, and at last came to the gallows.' A little child, on being asked why she would not take drams now, replied, 'for fear it will make me a drunkard, and God says no drunkard shall inherit the kingdom of heaven.' Another would not take her coffee out of a cup in which there had been whiskey, lest it should taint her breath."

The experience of the Richmond Infant Free School Society confirms the increasing sentiment, that the number of infants assigned to the care of a single teacher has often been too large; and that if it be limited to forty, a greater amount of good will probably be secured in the increased attention which the teacher will be able to afford, not only to the health and personal comfort, and moral habits of each individual, but to their intellectual cultivation.

The Asylum for Female Orphans,—infants, among others,—to be located at Fredericksburg, Va., of which mention is made in another part of this number, and the views of its founders, afford increasing evidence that the true end of infant schools is beginning to be better understood in the United States, and that while less effort is making to form intellectual prodigies, much more pains are taken in reference to health and personal comfort, and to improve the body, and develope and cultivate the social and moral feelings.

ORPHAN ASYLUM AT HALLE.

Among charitable institutions of the kind, none is more justly celebrated than Franke's Institution at Halle, in Germany. This institution is also sometimes called the *Orphan Asylum*, or Orphan Hospital. Augustus Hermann Franke, the founder of this and several institutions connected with it, and who was otherwise greatly distinguished in the history of philanthropy, was born at Lubec, in 1663. Having entered the University in his fourteenth year and passed through it with great rapidity and success, he became, at the early age of eighteen, a distinguished lecturer, and was soon after appointed a professor of Oriental Languages and Theology in the new University of Halle. At the same time, he became, also, the pastor of Glaucha, a suburb of the city of Halle, where his institutions were subsequently established.

The ignorance and poverty of the inhabitants of the village of Glaucha, filled the benevolent heart of Franke with the deepest distress; and in 1694, when he was scarcely thirty years of age, he began a plan for their reformation, which succeeded beyond his fondest hopes and most sanguine expectations; and which, when we compare the present results of the undertaking with the smallness of the beginning, can hardly fail to astonish us.

He first instructed a few destitute children in his own house, and gave them alms. After this, he received several orphans into his family. Their number soon increased; and several benevolent individuals of Halle assisted him in his charitable work.

The number of orphans increasing every year, it was found necessary, in 1698, four years after the plan was begun, to erect buildings for their accommodation. But how was the money to be obtained for this purpose? The resources of the philanthropist were very inconsiderable. Franke however commenced, and the buildings went on. Money was sent to him from all quarters, sometimes when he least expected it. Indeed, it frequently happened, that when his means were wholly exhausted, and he was, apparently, unable to proceed a step farther, he received such unexpected supplies, as gave him the most ample proof of the divine protection and favor. It is also worthy of remark, that this unlooked for assistance often came immediately after he had been engaged, as is confidently stated, in the most fervent prayers for the orphans and poor. Among other benefactions, was one from a chemist, who, on his death bed, gave him a recipe for compounding several medicines, which afterwards yielded an income of from $20,000 to $30,000. It was these frequent and liberal donations which enabled him to erect and complete stone buildings, which form two rows eight hundred feet long; and without the least assistance from the government.

The number of orphans in that part of the institution of Franke which is devoted to their accommodation is, at present, about one hundred. The greatest number which it has ever contained at once, is two hundred. Since its foundation, it has been the happy means of educating, gratuitously, no less than four thousand and five hundred orphans, of whom three fourths were boys. Such of the boys as manifest talents, are here prepared for the university.

Connected with the Orphan Asylum, are, 1. The Royal Pedagogium, an institution for the education of young men. Since its establishment, in 1697, it has educated two thousand seven hundred and ninety individuals. They pay for their education, which is of a very high standard. 2. The Latin school, for pupils less wealthy than the former; and for boys of the city of Halle. The number of boarding scholars in this department has sometimes been very large. 3. The German school, for boys and girls whose parents do not wish to give them a learned education. 4. The Canstein Bible Press, instituted in 1712, by one Canstein, a friend of Franke, the object of which was, to furnish the Bible, at a cheap rate, by stereotyping it.* From this press have already been issued two millions of copies of the whole Bible, one million of the New Testament. The profit belongs to the press, and is devoted to rendering every new edition still cheaper than the former. 5. A large library, and collections of natural history and philosophy. Its income is derived from the extensive apothecary's shop

* Canstein died in 1719, leaving to the orphan asylum his library, and a part of his fortune.

of the orphan asylum; from the book establishment, which is one of the largest in all Germany, and publishes all sorts of school books, at very low prices; from the pedagogium; and from charitable contributions.

The benevolent founder of such a combination of charitable institutions, died in June, 1727, after devoting himself to his favorite establishment for thirty-three years.

The following letter, from a correspondent of the Baptist Register, shows the actual condition of the Orphan House at Halle, in March, of the present year; which, though it should repeat some of the statements we have already made, we choose to insert entire.

"Halle, March, 1834.

"The Orphan House, at Halle is, to the stranger, an object of peculiar interest, as exhibiting the fruits of an enlarged Christian benevolence, which has immortalized the name of Franke. Though it rose from the smallest beginnings, it has grown to a large, literary establishment, embracing all the public schools at Halle, except the university. At present, more than two thousand scholars are there receiving daily instruction, though, alas! under the influence of Rationalism. It has two gymnasia, to prepare young men for the universities; one called the Pedagogium, designed for the rich, — the other, called the principal Latin School, designed for the common people; a scientific school to prepare young men for business; and four day schools, two of which are free. The number of orphans, supported by the institution, is fixed at one hundred; of which two thirds are to be males. There is, also, a considerable fund appropriated to the support of those in the Latin School, who distinguish themselves by their scholarship.

"The Bible Institution, founded by Von Canstein, and the press connected with it, are too well known by the Christian public to need description. The public library, to which the students have access, contains nearly thirty thousand volumes. The orphan house bookstore is one of the most respectable and substantial in Germany, and annually sends to the United States, large quantities of German books. The profits of this, as well as of the extensive apothecary shop, go to the support of the institution. But, alas! the spirit of its pious founder is no longer the presiding genius of the place.

"The 'Franken Stiftungen,' (charitable establishment,) as it is called, is situated in the south part of the city. Its principal building fronts a large street and public square, and another of nearly equal size stands directly in the rear, at the distance of eight hundred feet. These are so joined together by two rows of buildings, as to leave a beautiful enclosure of about fifty feet in width. As one enters it from the street, he ascends a large flight of stone steps, and finds himself in a spacious entry, with a stone floor. On the right, are large windows, and a door leading to the bookstore ; on the left, a corresponding department for the fine apothecary shop. Passing directly forward, he comes to a portico, from which, a flight of side steps leads to the upper stories, in which, are the numerous steps of the Latin School. Another flight, directly in front, descends to the beautiful large area within. Passing along this elegant walk, he has, on his left, the row of buildings containing the common schools, and the residences of the teachers, and on his right, the other row of buildings containing the Library, Bible Institute, dining hall, &c. Still continuing his course, he finds the walk gently ascending, and at the end, a broad terrace with stone steps, upon which is erected a large bronze statue of Franke, with an orphan boy, standing on each side. Here he reaches the Royal Pedagogium, which closes up the space."

WHAT EVERY TEACHER CAN DO.

Mr Editor,—In a former communication, I spoke of the importance of a recapitulation, or summing up of some of the prominent doctrines taught in the volumes of your Journal, under three heads. The first, or "Things which every teacher can do," I now beg leave to present to your readers, in as condensed a form as possible.

1. Every one who engages in school keeping, can open his school precisely at the appointed hour. There is no one thing, which, at first view, appears to promise so little, that will ultimately accomplish so much good, as this. I have seen an indifferent teacher inspire his pupils, and many of their parents, with confidence, and effect a thorough reformation in this respect, by commencing his exercises every morning at exactly nine o'clock, the time appointed, and persevering in this practice. I have known him dispense with his usual meal, when the lateness of the hour was likely to prevent his being at the school room in due season.

2. It is in the power of every teacher to have the school room comfortable every morning, in regard to temperature. There is so much of suffering in school, from late, or inefficient, or smoking fires, that this is a point of more importance, than many are accus-

tomed to suppose. The work of heating a school room does not properly belong to a teacher; and it is a most mistaken economy which leads his employers to suffer him to perform it, when those whose time is worth far less than his, could do it just as well. Still, if effectual measures are not taken by others, it is best for the teacher to see the work done, or do it himself. There are *instructors* who have made their morning fires for six months together, and always with great advantage, both to themselves and their pupils. Every teacher can do this, — I mean if he is furnished with a sufficient quantity of good fuel; and if not, he ought to relinquish his employment.

3. All teachers have it in their power to welcome their pupils to the school room when they arrive, and to see that they are provided with seats, books, &c., if they *have* them. It is true that such marks of attention and interest will consume time; but is that time misemployed which is spent in measures calculated to promote the happiness of a school, and impart to it a tone of good feeling which is not likely to be wholly lost during the day?

4. Every teacher has it in his power to consult the health and comfort of his pupils while they remain with him. If the air is bad in the school room, he can ventilate the room by means of doors or windows. If the temperature is too high or too low, he can regulate it. If the pupils are tired of sitting, he can let them stand, or walk out; either single, or by classes. If they are thirsty, he can furnish them with drink, without exposing their health by suffering them to pour down large quantities of water when greatly heated with exercise.

5. Every teacher can make constant and unremitting effort so to gain the affections and confidence of his pupils that he can control them, properly, without violence. He can labor hard to govern by persuasion, rather than force; by kindness, rather than severity; and by love, rather than fear. But when all other measures fail, with certain individuals who have never been accustomed to restraint, without violence, — and such cases may occur in very large schools — every teacher can, as a last resort, use severity. Nor need he fear with some fastidious and over-philanthropic individuals, so much the moral degradation which a little bodily pain may produce in the subject of punishment, as the more intense pain, and deeper degradation which must inevitably result from a habit of insubordination, either to parents or to higher authority.

6. Every instructor can and should see that what he teaches, is taught thoroughly. If a school consists of eighty or an hundred pupils, the time which, in three hours, can be appropriated to an individual, is, of course, very trifling, and unless what is done for

an individual be thoroughly done, he will derive little benefit from attending, except in so far as he learns from hearing others. But even here, *thorough* teaching is equally indispensable; for the more he learns from imitation, the greater the necessity that the example which he imitates, should be excellent.

7. Every one who has the care of the young, can strive to furnish them with constant employment. This is so indispensable, that when we have once considered the matter, we wonder why any teacher should ever have been so unreasonable as to require children to sit like statues an hour, or two hours, at a time; and why the latter should not have rebelled against such tyranny, much oftener than they have.

8. It is, also, within the power of every one to try to make children interested in what they learn. He has not the first qualification of a teacher, who supposes the child to be benefited to the utmost, when he is wholly passive in the work of education, like a vessel which merely receives and contains what is put into it. It is as necessary that the mental palate should be gratified, as the physical.

9. He who takes a school, should remember that he is not only responsible to those who are committed to his charge, and to their parents, but to God. He should, therefore, devote himself wholly to the business; attending to nothing else, except so far as may be necessary, in order to preserve his health. His school is to have a place among his first thoughts in the morning, and his last in the evening, as well as those of every hour between. If a teacher cannot *afford* to teach thus, then let him betake himself, at once, to some other employment. But I have seen an experienced and approved teacher devote himself wholly to the work of managing and instructing a school for six dollars a month, and his board, (about half the usual compensation in the place,) besides expending a part of even this scanty pittance for conveniences for the pupils.

10. Every teacher, whatever may be his religious opinions or creed, and whatever may be the difficulty of inculcating religion, or even morality in his school by precept, can set a pure and spotless example before his pupils. Now, although I think few teachers, at least in New England and New York, are guilty of open immorality, yet I am compelled to believe, that multitudes fail to set such an example on all occasions as they ought. And it is owing to this fact, in no small degree, that many observing men have come to the conclusion, — strange and unwarranted, as it appears, — that our common schools are doing more harm than good. It is not that the pupils do not learn to read, and write, and cipher, —

better, perhaps, than formerly, — but that the moral habits which they acquire, are often extremely unfavorable.

Perhaps they reason thus, "I send my child to school for four months in the summer, and four in the winter, from the age of four to sixteen. During this time, he learns to spell, read, and write, and gets a little knowledge of arithmetic, grammar and geography. But he does not appear to me to acquire more knowledge, in the whole time, than he *might* gain in about one year of constant and faithful instruction. And this is not the worst of it, either. He comes from the school with many bad habits, which I labor morning and evening, and during vacations, with all my might, to eradicate; but always without success. In spite of all I can do, he carries these habits with him from year to year, from childhood to youth, and from youth to maturity; and it is to be feared, he will then be likely to carry them with him through life. Well for him if he do not carry them and their consequences with him, beyond the grave!"

But all the moral evils thus complained of, — and they are certainly numerous, — need not discourage us. Though there is much that common school. teachers *cannot* accomplish, there is, also, much they *can* do. We might as well "despair of the republic," as of common schools. They can be reformed, and probably will be. Such, even, as they now *are*, and such as they can be *made*, they constitute, in no small degree, the hope of the country, the church, and the world.

Let me not be understood, Mr Editor, as attempting to give a complete enumeration of the *things* which, according to the doctrines of the "Annals of Education," *every teacher can do.* I have only selected a few, — such as it seems to me, are the more prominent ones. What has been said, is intended to apply to all teachers; whether of Infant, Primary, Common, Select, or Academic Schools, — whatever the name may be, — and whether they include the child of two years, or the youth of twenty.

In my next communication, I am to present a *compendium* of the "things which *many* teachers can do." They are much more numerous than those which are within the power of *all;* and may demand more space. A TEACHER.

INAUGURAL ADDRESSES.

Inaugural Address delivered by the Rev. Stephen Olin, *President of Randolph Macon College, on the occasion of his introduction into office.*

Inaugural Address of Rev. Rufus Babcock, Jr., *President of Waterville College, July 29, 1834.*

Randolph Macon College is founded and sustained by the Wesleyan Methodists, — and Waterville college, by the Baptists. It is peculiarly interesting to receive from two denominations, who so recently dreaded the influence of human learning, and now, in Mr Olin's language, are "roused from a long reverie," the inaugural addresses of presidents of colleges, which aim at a high standard of liberal education. Both addresses give evidence of talent and sound judgment; and we are desirous to make them better known to our readers.

President Olin commences with a just tribute of gratitude and respect to those who have contributed to advance the arts and the physical sciences, as among the most valuable patrons of intellectual enterprise, by diminishing the labor, and increasing the profits of human toil, and rescuing much of time and talent from the material world.

He next goes on to point out what should constitute a course of liberal studies. After stating, distinctly, the high claims of the mathematics, he argues, with no less zeal, the importance of the ancient languages.

"Throughout the whole progress of modern literature, from its dawn to its present state of maturity and comparative perfection, classical learning has been its safest guide, and its most liberal benefactor. With an unalterable constancy, it has held forth its masterly performances and authoritative examples to human observation, to correct the eccentricities of genius, to restrain the aberrations of taste, and to rebuke the waywardness of imagination, and the extravagancies of fashion. Its graceful specimens of eloquence and poetry, of style and sentiment, embody and exemplify the immutable laws of composition and the mind. They constitute an unexceptionable standard of good writing, above envy or controversy, which acts, at once, as the inspirer and counsellor of genius; the model and test of excellence.

Whilst the classical student secures, in an eminent degree, the most valuable ends of education in the discipline of his intellectual faculties, his labors are amply rewarded by the acquisition of valuable knowledge. It is not true, as often asserted, that the classics impart nothing to the mind but a dry vocabulary of obsolete words and idioms, utterly useless for all the purposes of speech and reason. Language, as well as mind and matter, has its philosophy, not formed to suit its particular cases, but applicable, with few modifications, to the dialects of all ages and nations. The regularity, the copiousness, the elegant refinement, and the profound logic of the Greek and Roman tongues, give facilities for the investigation of these universal laws, unknown to the defective and anomalous languages of modern times; and the youth, who has once thoroughly mastered the difficulties and the mysteries of classical literature, has imbibed those unchangeable principles of speech and of thought, which are alone able to guide him on the great occasions, in active life, when eloquence and reason exert a controlling influence."

He remonstrates against the disposition to swell the list of collegiate studies, already burdensome, to the immature minds found in our public institutions; and considers, that with such minds, mere lectures on a variety of topics, can never take the place of thorough recitation, on a judicious selection of subjects.

In regard to the discipline of public institutions, President Olin has no confidence in anything short of the influence of christianity to maintain it in any degree.

"I venture to affirm, that this generation has not given birth to another absurdity so monstrous, as that which would exclude from our seminaries of learning, the open and vigorous inculcation of the religious faith which is acknowledged by our whole population, and which pervades every one of our free institutions. Our governors and legislators, and all the depositaries of honor and trust, are prohibited from exercising their humblest functions, till they have pledged their fidelity to the country, upon the holy gospels. The most inconsiderable pecuniary interest is regarded too sacred to be entrusted to the most upright judge or juror, or to the most unsuspected witness, till their integrity has been fortified by an appeal to the high sanctions of Christianity.

"Even the exercise of the elective franchise is usually suspended on the same condition. The interesting moralities of the domestic relation; the laws of marriage and divorce; the mutual obligations of parents and children, are all borrowed from the christian scriptures. The fears of the vicious, and the hopes of the upright; the profane ribaldry of the profligate, no less than the humble thanksgiving of the morning and evening sacrifice, do homage to the gospel, as the religion of the American people. Our eloquence and our poetry; our periodical and popular literature in all their varieties; the novel, the tale, the ballad, the play, — all make their appeal to the deep sentiments of religion that pervade the popular bosom. Christianity is our birthright. It is the richest inheritance bequeathed us by our noble fathers. It is mingled in our hearts with all the fountains of sentiment and of faith. And are the guardians of public education alone 'halting between two opinions?' Do they think that, in fact, for practical purposes, the truth of Christianity is still a debatable question? Is it still a question, whether the generations yet to rise up and occupy the wide domains of this great empire, to be the representatives of our name, our freedom, and our glory, before the nations of the earth shall be a Christian or an Infidel people?"

He alludes, with great justice, to that source of insubordination, which we have formerly pointed out in our colleges, the too early age of the students.

"The internal discipline of a college is a subject of great practical importance, as well as of great delicacy and difficulty. The regulations of society which fix the period of minority, are formed upon the constitution of nature, and dictates of experience. The controlling authority of the parent is maintained, till the formation of proper habits, and some maturity of judgment, are presumed to have fitted the child for subjection to the positive institutions of society, and the general restraints of moral obligations. In our places of learning, this period is usually anticipated, and this salutary arrangement disturbed. The youth passes from a government of authority and influence, to a government of laws, before he is prepared to appreciate the value and the reason of the restrictions that are imposed upon him, or to respect their sanctions. Dislike and contempt for regulations deemed frivolous or arbitrary; reckless indifference to consequences, and practised ingenuity in evading the penalty, whilst it violates the spirit of the law, are the two common results of this premature and unnatural substitution of positive enactments, for that discretionary power with which God has invested the parent. The evil is one of portentous magnitude; but it is not easy, perhaps not possible, to prescribe a remedy."

He proposes that less of positive laws should exist, and more of discretionary parental power be vested in the officers; but he also shows clearly, that great dangers attend this; and we do not hesitate to say, that so long as a part of the power is entrusted to a changing body of tutors, advanced but a few years beyond their pupils in experience, we believe it would only increase the evil. It is certainly startling, to hear from a presidential chair,

"Of the whole number of those who enter college, it is believed that less than half remain to complete their education. The majority are arrested in their career of improvement by idle or vicious habits; by extravagance and discontent; and sometimes by unwise laws and mal-administration. This result of the prevailing systems of public instruction is truly appalling."

President Olin looks, with much confidence, to manual labor as the source of great and salutary reform in the morals and manners of our schools of learning, and hopes it will render education more accessible to those in the middle classes, especially at the south, where they have hitherto been unable to enjoy its advantages. He concludes with an earnest appeal to the body of Methodists, to put forth all their energies in the great work of education, to which they are just roused.

President Babcock has chosen a most important topic. "The object of the teacher's office," he remarks, is three fold; to secure mental discipline, to communicate useful knowledge, and to give all our powers a right direction. The last, in his view, is the preeminent duty.

In regard to the topics of instruction, his views of the classics coincide entirely, with those of President Olin.

"The purposes of healthful discipline may, for the most part, be happily secured in those very studies which are of useful tendency. Such, eminently, is the study of the ancient and modern languages. Neither of these would have been decried, as they are, had a more just and philosophical view been taken of their direct and indirect utility. What! shall a man, whose great business through life is identified with the right use of language, be told that it is needless and preposterous for him to study its constituent elements? Or shall he be told that as much advantage may be derived from the perusal of an author in his vernacular tongue, as by the careful study of one equally valuable in his thoughts, but written in a language which requires, at every step, comparison, judgment, precision, taste; and which, by their very exercise, tend to strengthen all these powers? Let it be granted, that some of the reasons which were formerly much relied on, as requiring the study of the ancient languages, are no longer valid; or, in the same degree valid, as at the time when most of the elementary instruction, in some important branches, was accessible only through this channel. Let it be freely conceded, that what is chiefly valuable in them, has been laid open to the mere English scholar by translations, or has been superseded by original treatises of equal or superior value, in our own tongue. Still, you leave untouched reasons of paramount importance, for giving to these studies a share of attention. I cannot, therefore, sympathise with that innovating rage, which would exile the study of ancient, or even of modern languages from our literary institutions. The kind of influence which this study indirectly produces, is greatly needed by all educated men. They also need to improve their precision and copiousness, their taste and correctness in the use of their own language; and no more ready and certain method for securing this object can be devised, than the study of those from which ours is principally derived."

He presents one reason, which is not hackneyed, for the study of mathematics.

"Let it never be forgotten, that the best exercises for the mind, and especially for the judgment, are always found in those subjects which do not bias us for or against them. Such, eminently, are the mathematics, several branches of philosophy, and the natural sciences generally. Vigorous application to these, will happily prepare us for the important, complicated, and otherwise embarrassing emergencies of actual life, in which this discipline is most necessary, and its deficiency utterly irreparable. William Tell could never have gained such surprising skill in markmanship, if his early exercises had been of a character to agitate his heart, like the requirement to shoot the apple on his son's head."

He insists, not less earnestly, on the importance of the study of man, himself,—of his body as well as of his mind, and asks, "why should not the principles of physiology, at least, be taught in every course of liberal study? Will those who neglect it for the sake of adding one more classic to the course, furnish us with an answer?

"But," he remarks, "more will depend on the manner of teaching, than on the subject of instruction." Interest in the teacher, simplicity of manner, practical application of truth, and a course adapted to keep the faculties in constant activity, are the principal directions he gives.

In treating of the requisites for the teacher's office, he places a firm and vigorous constitution at the foundation. A well-disciplined and energetic mind, blameless morals, entire self-control, and above all, true benevolence, he considers indispensable to a teacher. On the last point, he observes:—

"This affection for pupils, in order to produce its legitimate results, must be based on permanent principles, and must have a like permanency or continuity of exercise. Fitful manifestations of affectionate regard, separated by long intervals of coldness, will not, probably, secure any happy results. The affection of the teacher, like that of the parent, should be a happy medium between fondling weakness and repulsive austerity,— pure, quenchless, and ennobling. He who is a stranger to such affection for his pupils, does not deserve to have a pupil; nor will the relation which thus exists be productive of happy consequences. It may be sustained with tolerable decency on both sides; but its termination will be a mutual relief; and no tear of regret or swelling of tender emotions will mark the hour of separation. And can it be possible that a relation thus sustained, can realize the results which ought to flow from it? As well might we expect 'grapes of thorns, or figs of thistles.' How certain it is, on the other hand, that the unaffected interest and affection of the teacher, will beget its own image in the heart of the pupil,—that it will prepare him to receive, with incomparably greater advantage, the lessons of instruction which are imparted to him, and will secure him against many of his most formidable dangers! By planting deeply in his bosom the conviction that his teacher is warmly interested in his happiness and advancement, the exercise of government, in its odious sense, will be rendered unnecessary."

He recommends a free and affectionate mode of intercourse between teachers and pupils, and observes:—

"Let him not fear the loss of personal dignity, in thus mingling with those committed to his trust. Let him not do violence to the tender and generous impulses of his own nature, by shutting himself away from their sympathies, and severing the ties of a tender affection, which should make the interests and happiness of both, mutual and indispensable."

He considers the spirit of Christianity the best security for these moral qualities, and in regard to the jealousy of sectarianism, observes:—

"He that can, and does sincerely delight in the increase of true piety and virtue, in whatever form it appears, or by whatever name it is called, who delights in seeing and promoting the increase of love to God and love to our neighbor; and who, while fully believing, that without the spirit of Christ we are none of his, remembers that Christ severely rebuked the impertinent zeal of his own followers, for hindering those who followed not with them,—such an one, I am sure, need not be dreaded for his sectarianism, nor unconstitutionally excluded from the office of instruction in literature and science, even though he be also a teacher of the religion of Christ."

We cannot close our sketch of these interesting addresses, without begging the attention of those who would put out the lights of science, because they are not kindled in every street, to the following passage:—

"The attempt which has been made to raise a popular clamor against the higher seminaries of learning, for the alleged purpose of giving more aid to common schools, is as wise and consistent, as it would be to sever the head from the human body, in order to favor the limbs. *The one cannot long flourish without the other; and mutual hostility between their friends will be suicidal to the best interests of both.*"

EXERCISE OF MIND IN CLASSICAL STUDIES.

One source of difference of opinion in regard to the utility of classical studies, arises from the different modes of pursuing them. In our country, the ancient languages are studied, to a sad extent, as a mere exercise in the technics of etymology, syntax and prosody; and when thus pursued, there can be no good reason for so great a sacrifice of time and labor, or for that *mechanization* (if we may make a term) of mind which is the natural result. It is true that much of this drilling is indispensable as a part of the exercise; and it is also true that when not carried to excess, it gives the pupil a habit of application, and a command of his faculties, which more agreeable but less laborious pursuits could not bestow.

But those who advocate these studies, have another, and a higher standard of instruction in view. They propose that young men should study, not the *languages* merely, or chiefly, but the author's models of thought and expression, whose superiority to other uninspired writings is admitted by most literary men. It will assist our readers to understand and appreciate these views, if they are familiar with the details of the best modes of instruction. We have already made some extracts from the correspondence of a gentleman abroad, ascribed to a professor of the Newton Theological Seminary. Other extracts will illustrate the manner in which the judgment, and reason, and taste, are called into exercise in studies which, among us, are so often made to stupify every faculty but memory, and check every feeling but disgust. The following is an account of an exercise with a young class in a German Gymnasium, on Cornelius Nepos.

"Dr E——n, with a young class on Cornelius Nepos.—The exercise, which was in German, was distinguished by a remarkably clear exhibition of ultimate grammatical analysis. The *principle* of every rule referred to was searched out and sifted, till it was distinctly seen, and then a multitude of examples were given in German, which were required to be put into Latin. In the course of the reading, the students were frequently directed to tell in what other way the same idea could be expressed in good Latin; to explain the principle of the different constructions; and to specify what constituted the peculiarities of this author's style."

Another, on works which few of our Greek scholars see, exhibits topics of which they rarely hear.

"Dr S——t, author of a good work on the life, character, and writings of Aristotle, heard a class of thirteen advanced students, on the Œdipus Coloneus, of Sophocles, Excepting the translation, which was into German, the Exercise was in Latin. The students spoke this language with great ease and fluency. A full exposition of the passage; an examination of the higher principles of grammar; a nice discrimination between poetry and prose, whether in language or in thought; a discussion of the comparative claims of different readings, occupied the chief attention. In these discussions, the teacher threw out many valuable hints, and abounded with instructive remarks. The classical acquisitions were of a very high order, and he seemed to understand the art of making scholars."

A third is equally removed from the ideas of most teachers and pupils in the United States.

"Dr Sch——t, rector of the Latin School, on Plato's Symposium. In nice, metaphysical distinctions, and in translations, both the teacher and the class employed German; in all the rest, Latin. First, an explanation of the preceding paragraph, not by way of review, but for the sake of connection, was demanded. Then the whole of the twenty-ninth section was read and translated. The teacher insisted on great exactness of expression. He required the student to tell in which of his writings Cicero treated of the same subject; what the views of that philosopher were; what Latin terms he employed to express the same ideas which were contained in the Greek of Plato; and what were the philosophical doctrines of their author. The teacher then gave an admirable exposition of the author's theory of 'ideas,' and particularly his doctrine respecting 'the beautiful.' He then retranslated the whole passage with masterly skill; gave out certain passages to be translated into Latin, for the purpose of comparing the idioms of the two languages; and closed with a short extemporaneous lecture."

We need not say how few American students of Horace, even in our colleges, ever dreamed of such recitations as the following, upon that poet.

"Dr S——t, in a Latin disputation with nine students on Horace's Odes, lib. 4, ode 6. — The disputation appeared to have a twofold object; to exercise the students in speaking Latin, and to train them in the art of criticism. There was a long argument about the design of the poet in this ode. The teacher would give no hints as to the right way of explaining the subject, but would merely show the incongruity and absurdity of the imperfect or incorrect views presented by the students. They, of course, would often go very long upon a point before they would stumble upon it, but in the mean time acquire much information respecting what the ode was *not*. It was like a fencing master exercising the sword with others, in order to impart his skill. The teacher was the most eloquent and accomplished Latin speaker I have yet heard."

"Dr L——n, in Horace's Odes. — The teacher took his place in the desk, with his author and manuscript before him. Of the latter, however, he made very little use. The Latin only was spoken. After the usual course of translation and correction, words and phrases were closely examined with regard to lexicography, grammar and structure. The students were required to strip the ode of its poetical garb, and put it into pure Latin prose. This was a matter of some difficulty; for one is, in such cases, very liable to retain a poetical word, or poetical construction, or to employ a word or phrase not sanctioned by good usage. Recitation and lecture were combined. I found that the students were capable of giving the literature of Horace, specifying the best editions and the most valuable essays that had appeared on different portions of his works. This is a kind of knowledge as common in Germany, as it is rare in America."

THE CONTRAST; OR THE PERVERSION OF CLASSICAL STUDIES.

We cannot better enforce the remarks of the preceding article, than by requesting our readers to peruse that and the former extracts from the account of recitations in the same institution, and then read the following account of the waste of time in the pursuit of the very same studies arising from the absurd methods which are adopted. We find it in an article on "Boy's Education," in the Southern Academician, over the signature of Alpha, prefaced by the following judicious quotation: —

"It is not the waste of intellect, as it lies torpid in the great multitude of our race, that is alone to be regretted. * * * It is, in many cases, the very industry of intellect, busily exerted, but exerted in labors that must be profitless."

The following account is then given of a course of classical study, if we may thus misuse the words, which is but too just a specimen of that which has been generally pursued in our country: —

"At seven years old, I was compelled, by my teacher, to drudge at Latin Grammar, — and many times have wept over the hated task; with a persuasion, that any thing on earth was more tolerable than my situation, in this respect. Again and again I recited this jargon through, and I may safely say, without being one whit the wiser, — and surely much less happy for the labor. At length, 'Mair's Introduction' was put into my hands, and turning bad Latin into *good*, alias worse, constituted my daily toil. My grandfather, who had attended to Latin, and who had a tolerable knowledge of the language, was living near me, and often have I repaired to him with a prayer for assistance. It was his custom, on these occasions, to tell me, word for word, just what I had to repeat to the master; and on my way to school, earnestly and carefully would I struggle to exclude every other thought, and over and over repeat the recitation. Not a thought, not a wish, not a word, would I suffer to draw from my mind the phrases thus gathered, until I had recited my lesson, which I generally did, without much trouble or disgrace. And then, — as if with one fell swoop, — away was driven all the rubbish which had cost so much toil and vexation to collect. After a few years, my father's circumstances changed, and I, with others of our family, was compelled to seek my fortune on the world's wide tide. I have lived long, — and never, in all my life, have I regretted anything more, than the circumstance of having had my early education so badly conducted. Had the same labor, and the same means been employed on more useful branches of knowledge, — and my mind been stored with information calculated to fit me for business, I should have suffered less mortification, and derived abundantly more benefit. As it is, I look back on my early days with regret, and feel, that with all my after labor, I have not been able to compensate for the loss and mental injury I then sustained."

The correspondent of the Academician then adds the following just remarks: —

"This was the sum of a conversation recently held with a gentleman of respectability and talents. And it needs no comment to show, that it is only one of the ten thousand instances of the folly connected with the conduct of a boy's education. And while I would again assert, that I am a friend to classical instruction, yet I would again write, that this course, (and many others which vary only in the minutiæ of matter,) can never enlarge the mind; and retards, rather than promotes, profound scholarship in those destined to letters; while it totally destroys the most desirable points of good attached to the prospects and usefulness of those who are to struggle with a world of duties and toils."

So long as such a course is pursued, what can be anticipated, but an increasing and well founded prejudice against classical studies?

LITERARY INSTITUTIONS OF THE UNITED STATES.

In 1830, the number of students in all the Colleges in the United States, independent of Theological, Medical, and Law students, was estimated by the Editor of the American Quarterly Register of Education, at 3,475. The Theological students were estimated at 663; Medical students, about 2,000; Law students, 88. Total, 6,216. The same invaluable work for Feb., 1834, makes the exact number as follows: Classical students, 4,100; Medical, 1,863; Theological, 709; Law, 88. Total, 6,760. But this enumeration is probably derived from the catalogues for the year 1833.

The increase of these several classes of students, since that time, will be perceived by a comparison with the tables, on the two following pages, which also contain other important information. They are copied — with some additions and variations — from the American Almanac for 1835.

There are a few smaller institutions in which a thorough classical or collegiate course of study is pursued, and which we believe, are chartered; but we have been unable to obtain particular information concerning them, in time for our present number. Such are the Oberlin Collegiate Institute of Ohio, the Universalist College in Vermont, and several others. The number of the Scientific Tracts for Sept. 15, states — we know not on what authority, — that there are, in the whole United States, seventy-eight chartered Universities and Colleges. Perhaps this number includes some which we have here reckoned among the schools of Theology and Medicine.

COLLEGES IN THE UNITED STATES.

The number of students belonging to the Colleges, consists of UNDERGRADUATES only; and it excludes also, medical, theological, and law students. The number of instructors mentioned, does not include the presidents. In the column of denominations to which the Colleges belong, those which are not marked, are generally supposed to be either Congregational or Presbyterian. The greater part of the students in the Catholic Colleges, belong to the preparatory department.

Name.	Place.	Denomination.	Instructors.	Students.	Vols. in College Libr's.	Vols. in Students' Libraries.
Bowdoin,	Brunswick, Maine,		10	140	8,000	6,000
Waterville,	Waterville, do.	Baptist.	8	100	4,000	600
Dartmouth,	Hanover, N. H.		10	150	4,500	8,500
University of Vermont,	Burlington, Vt.		7	50	1,000	1,000
Middlebury,	Middlebury, do.		5	129	2,300	3,100
Harvard University,	Cambridge, Mass.		30	217	40,000	4,500
Williams,	Williamstown, do.		7	133	3,800	2,300
Amherst,	Amherst, do.		9	227	4,300	6,250
Brown University,	Providence, R. I.	Baptist.	8	157	6,000	5,140
Yale,	New Haven, Conn.		20	373	8,500	10,500
Washington,	Hartford, do.	Epis.	8	53	2,000	2,500
Wesleyan University,	Middletown, do.	Meth.	5	60	3,000	
Columbia,	New York, N. Y.	Epis.	11	100	8,000	6,000
Union,	Schenectady, do.		9	225	5,250	8,150
Hamilton,	Clinton, do.		6	97	2,500	3,700
Geneva,	Geneva, do.	Epis.	8	41	821	1,150
University of N. Y.	New York, do.		16	226		
College of New Jersey,	Princeton, N. J.		12	170	7,000	4,000
Rutgers,	Brunswick, do.		8	85	3,750	2,500
Univ. of Pennsylvania,	Philadelphia, Penn.		20	94	2,000	
Dickinson,	Carlisle, do.	Meth.			2,000	
Lafayette,	Easton, do.		3	51		
Jefferson,	Canonsburg, do.		9	175	1,000	2,400
Bristol,	Bristol, do.	Epis.	1	85		
Washington,	Washington, do.		7	47	1,500	
Allegheny,	Meadville, do.	Meth.	3		8,000	
Western University,	Pittsburg, do.		4	50	500	
Pennsylvania,	Gettysburg, do.		–			
Newark,	Newark, Delaware.		3			
University of Maryland,	Baltimore, Md.		7			
St. John's,	Annapolis, do.	Epis.	5	82	2,700	400
St. Mary's,	Baltimore, do.	Catholic.	24	193	10,500	
Mount St. Mary's,	Emmitsburg, do.	Catholic.	25	90	7,000	
Columbian,	Washington, D. C.	Baptist.	9	25	4,000	
Georgetown,	Georgetown, do.	Catholic.	17	134	12,000	
William and Mary,	Williamsburg, Va.		6	15	3,500	600
Hampden Sydney,	Prince Ed. Co., do.		6	75	5,000	3,200
Washington,	Lexington, do.		4	40	1,500	
University of Virginia,	Charlottesville, do.		10	205	8,000	
Randolph Macon,	Boydton, do.	Meth.	4			
Univ. of North Carolina,	Chapel Hill, N. C.		7	90	1,800	3,000
Charleston,	Charleston, S. C.	Epis.	7	30	3,000	
College of S. Carolina,	Columbia, do.		7	50	10,000	
University of Georgia,	Athens, Georgia,		9	97	3,200	3,000
Alabama University,	Tuscaloosa, Ala.		6	101	3,000	
Jefferson,	Washington, Miss.					
Louisiana,	Jackson, Louisiana.		4	15	350	
Greeneville,	Greeneville, Tenn.		1	38	3,500	
University of Nashville,	Nashville, do.		6	70	2,000	1,200
East Tennessee,	Knoxville, do.		2	28	1,100	200
Transylvania,	Lexington, Ky.		11		2,400	1,500
Centre,	Danville, do.		8	65	1,600	
Augusta,	Augusta, do.	Meth.	6	75	2,000	500
Cumberland,	Princeton, do.		3	72	500	
St. Joseph's,	Bardstown, do.	Catholic.	14	130	5,000	
Georgetown,	Georgetown, do.	Baptist.	4	36	1,200	
University of Ohio,	Athens, Ohio.		5	15	1,000	1,000
Miami University,	Oxford, do.		8	126	1,200	2,500
Western Reserve,	Hudson, do.		5	46	1,400	300
Kenyon,	Gambier, do.	Epis.	10	71	2,300	
Franklin,	New Athens, do.		4	40	1,200	
Indiana,	Bloomington, Ind.		4	31	400	200
South Hanover,	South Hanover, do.		6	35		
Illinois,	Jacksonville, Ill.		5	8	1,200	
St. Louis University,	St. Louis, do.	Catholic.	11	154	4,500	
St. Mary's,	Barrens, Missouri.	Catholic.	15	124	6,000	
		Total,	547	5,702	241,600	97,121

THEOLOGICAL SEMINARIES.

Denomination.	Name.	Place.	Professors.	Students.	Libraries.
Cong.	Bangor Theological Sem.	Bangor, Maine.	2	6	2,000
Cong	Theological Seminary,	Andover, Mass.	5	139	11,000
Cong. Unit.	Theological School,	Cambridge, do.	3	36	
Baptist.	Theological Institution,	Newton, do.	3	53	1,800
Cong.	Theological Institute,	East Windsor, Ct.	4		
Cong.	Theol. Dep. Yale College,	New Haven, do.	3	55	
Episcopal.	Theol. Ins. Epis. Church,	New York, N. Y.	6	65	3,880
Presbyt.	Theol. Seminary of Auburn,	Auburn, do.	3	54	4,500
Baptist.	Hamilton Lit. and The. Inst.	Hamilton, do.	4	38	2,250
Lutheran.	Hartwick Seminary,	Hartwick, do.	2	9	1,000
Dutch Ref.	Theol. Sem. Du. Re. Church,	New Brunswick, N. J.	3	24	
Presbyt.	Theol. Sem. Pr. Ch. U. S.	Princeton, do.	3	119	6,500
Evang. Lu.	Seminary Luth. Ch. U. S.	Gettysburg, Pa	2	20	7,000
G. Ref. Ch.	German Reformed,	York, do.	2	21	
Presbyt.	West. Theol. Seminary,	Allegany T. do.	2	29	4,000
Episcopal.	Theological School,	Near Alexandria, D. C.		30	2,000
Episcopal.	Epis. Theol. School, Va.	Fairfax County, Va.	2	39	2,000
Presbyt.	Union Theol. Seminary.	Pr. Ed. County, do.	2	50	4,000
Presbyt.	Southern Theol. Seminary,	Columbia, S. C.	3	21	1,800
Lutheran.	Theological Seminary.	Lexington, do.	2	1	
Baptist.	Furman Theol. Seminary,	High Hills, do.	2		1,000
Presbyt.	South West Theol. Sem.	Maryville, Tenn.	1	22	6,000
Presbyt.	Lane Seminary,	Cincinnati, Ohio.	3	42	
		Total,	**62**	**872**	**60,730**

There are Roman Catholic Theological Seminaries at Baltimore, and near Emmitsburg, Md.; at Charleston, S. C.; near Bardstown, and in Washington Co., Ky.; and in Perry Co., Mo.

MEDICAL SCHOOLS.

Name.	Place.	Professors.	Students.
Maine Medical School,	Brunswick.	5	80
New Hampshire Medical School,	Hanover.	3	100
Vermont Med. School, Univ. Vt.	Burlington.	3	14
V. Academy of Medicine,	Castleton, Vt.	6	62
Mass. Med. School, Harv. Univ.	Boston.	6	82
Berkshire Med. Inst. W'ms Coll.	Pittsfield, Mass.	5	85
Medical School, Yale College,	New Haven, Ct.	5	73
Coll. Phys. and Surgeons, N. Y.	New York.	7	158
Coll. Phys. and Surg. West. Dist.	Fairfield.	5	199
Med. Department, Jef. College,	Philadelphia, Penn.	6	121
Med. Department, Univ. Penn.	do. do.	9	431
Med. Department, Univ. Md.	Baltimore.	6	150
Washington Medical College,	do.	6	
Medical Dep. Columbian College,	Washington, D. C.	6	30
Medical Dep. University, Va.	Charlottesville.	3	40
Medical College, State of S. C.	Charleston.	7	150
Medical College, of S. C.	do.		
South School Pract. Med.	do. S. C.	6	
Medical College of Georgia,	Augusta.	6	
Medical College, Trans. Univ.	Lexington, Ky.	6	211
Louisville Medical College,	Louisville, Ky.	6	
Medical College of Ohio,	Cincinnati.	6	110
Ref. Medical College, Ohio,	Worthington.		
	Total,	**118**	**2,067**

LAW SCHOOLS.

Location.	Professors.	Students.
Cambridge, Mass.	**2**	**40**
New Haven, Ct.	**2**	**39**
Philadelphia, Pa.		
Baltimore, Md.		
Williamsburg, Va.		
Staunton, do.		
Charlottesville, do.		
Lexington, Ky.	**1**	**39**
Cincinnati, Ohio.	**3**	
Total,	**8**	**118**

Grand Total, Instructors, 735. — Students, 8,779. — Volumes in Libraries, 399,450.

[For the Annals of Education.]

BOSTON PUBLIC SCHOOLS.

The Boston Public Schools consist of sixty-seven Primary Schools, ten Grammar and Writing Schools, including one for Africans, one English High School, and a Latin Grammar School. From printed documents in relation to the subject, and from other authentic sources of information, we are enabled to present the following account of them.

In all the primary schools, and in six of the grammar and writing schools, instruction is given to pupils of both sexes. In two of the latter, girls only are admitted; in the remaining two, and in the English high school, and the Latin school, boys only. The Infant schools — of which there are several in Boston, — form no part of the public school system. These are sustained by the contributions of benevolent individuals or associations.

Though the primary schools of Boston are usually spoken of as forming a part of the system of public schools, they are almost entirely under a government of their own. They are of comparatively recent origin, having been instituted in 1818, while the Latin school, and several of the grammar and writing schools have been in operation more than a century.

The government of the schools is vested in twenty-one gentlemen, twelve of whom, — one from each ward in the city, — are chosen annually by the citizens; the other nine consist of the Mayor of the city, and eight Aldermen. These constitute a general school committee; but are divided into sub-committees for the more convenient examination of the schools. They have also a standing committee on School Books, and a standing committee of conference with a like committee from the government of the primary schools. The only control which this general committee have over the latter schools, except that they appoint a Board for their general management, is advisory, through this committee of conference. In other respects, as we have already intimated, they are independent.

The number of children in the primary schools is believed to be at present, about four thousand; and there are not far from the same number in the higher public schools. This includes, it is true, but about half the children in Boston, between the ages of four and sixteen years; but there is a very large number of infants and older pupils in private schools; besides a few of the children of the poor who do not attend any school at all. But the public school system is intended to make provision for all these, provided they could be induced to attend. The poorest inhabitant of Boston may thus have his children gratuitously instructed, — his boys, at the least, — from the age of four to seven, in the primary schools; from seven to nine in the grammar and writing schools; from nine to twelve in the Latin school; and from twelve to seventeen in the English High school. In these different schools, the pupils will go through a course of instruction, supposed, by the patrons of the schools, to be equal to that which is provided at many of our respectable colleges.

We will first mention a few regulations which are common to the primary and higher schools, and afterwards proceed to speak of each separately.

The instructors are appointed at a particular time of the year, and hold their office for one year unless sooner removed by the government. In general, they are continued in the schools for many successive years. Every instructor is required to be punctual in regard to the hours appointed for opening and dismissing his school. The morning exercises of all the schools but the primary, are required to be commenced with reading the Scriptures and Prayer; and the same course is *recommended* to the teachers of the primary school. Every instructor is to keep a daily record of admissions, ages, attendance, absence, tardiness, negligence, and such other particulars as may be useful to the committee at their visitations, in forming a correct idea of the state of the schools.

The instructors are required to pay attention to the cleanliness, comfort, and moral character of their pupils, and on all suitable occasions to inculcate upon them the principles of truth and virtue. No pupil can go from one school to another of a higher grade, without a certificate from the committee, setting forth his qualifications, as well as general standing and character.

The Primary Schools.

Regulations. For the appropriate government and direction of the primary schools, the city is divided into eight districts, each district including from seven to ten schools. They are governed by a committee consisting of one member to each school in a district, who hold their regular meetings, and appoint their chairman, secretary, &c.; but the general care of each school is confided to the particular committee of that school, who performs the duties which are usually assigned to both the district and visiting committees of single schools in the country. The whole committee of each district is so subdivided for this purpose, that each individual shall visit the school of his own charge, at least once a year; but every school is to be visited by one of the body at least once a month. Written reports of these visits are to be made to the secretary of the district.

The standing committte, consisting of one member from each of the eight primary school districts, are required to visit and examine all the schools semi-annually, viz: in the months of April and October. A district is usually assigned to each of their members, in regular rotation.

The teachers of the primary schools are to conform to the directions of their committee, respectively. The teachers are, without exception, females; though we do not know that male teachers are excluded by anything but the expense. They are to govern as much as possible by mildness and persuasion; but they are also to govern effectually and thoroughly.

The teachers are not to permit visitors to remain in their schools, unless introduced by the district committee, nor to allow tracts or any other publications to be distributed in them. The afternoons of Thursdays and Fridays are assigned to tuition in needle-work, to those who come provided with suitable materials; but both the teacher and the pupils are forbidden to employ themselves in needle-work at any other time.

During the summer, the schools are opened at 8, and closed at 11 o'clock in the forenoon; and opened at 2, and closed at 5 in the afternoon. In the winter, the forenoon hours are 9 to 12; and the afternoon hours, 2 (or at the discretion of the committee, 3) to 4 1-2.

The primary schools are designed to include pupils from four to seven years of age. But none are to be admitted of any age whatever, till they have been vaccinated, or otherwise secured against the small pox.

Course of Instruction. The pupils in each of the Boston Primary Schools are arranged in four classes; and the third and fourth classes are in two divisions each, viz:

Fourth Class, 2nd Division. Cards; Alphabet. — 1st Division. Cards continued; Monosyllables and Dissyllables.

Third Class, 2nd Division. Spelling book; words of two or more syllables. — 1st. Division. Spelling book continued; Spelling and Easy Reading Lessons; the Lord's Prayer; Abbreviations and Numbers commenced.

2nd Class. Spelling book continued; Spelling, Reading, and all the other lessons in the same, to the end; the Commandments; Reading book.

1st Class. Spelling book continued; Spelling, Punctuation, Abbreviations, Numbers, Arithmetic; words of similar sound but different in spelling and signification; Reading book continued.; New Testament.

Rule 1. The second division of the fourth class shall first stand up, and after an appropriate address, shall read from the Cards with a distinct and audible tone of voice, the letters of the Alphabet. In like manner, the first division of the same class, shall read in words of one and two syllables; and no one of this class shall be advanced to the third or higher class, who cannot read deliberately and correctly in monosyllables and dissyllables.

Rule 2. The third class must be furnished with the Spelling book adopted by the Board, and the second division of it must be taught to read therefrom in words of three, four, and five syllables. The first division of the same must be continued in their spelling, and advance to the easy reading lessons of the same book, and learn the Lord's Prayer; the learning of Abbreviations and Numbers is to be commenced, and no one is to be promoted to the second class, who cannot spell with ease and propriety words of the above number of syllables, and read well in the easier lessons of the Spelling book.

Rule 3. The second class must proceed in the Spelling book through all the spelling, reading, and other lessons of the same, and be taught to recite well the Ten Commandments; must be provided with the book of Reading Lessons, and make progress therein; and no one of this class can be advanced to the first, who has not learned and recited, as far as practicable, all the lessons in the Spelling book, including the stops and marks, and their uses in reading; the use of the common abbreviations; the letters used for numbers, and their uses; and the catalogue of words of similar sound, but different in spelling and signification. They must be able also to recite the Ten Commandments and the Lord's Prayer, and to read correctly and readily in the book of Reading Lessons.

Rule 4. The first class shall be continued and perfected in the lessons of the Spelling book and book of Reading Lessons; be furnished with the New Testament, and taught to read therein fluently and correctly, and be instructed in the elements of Arithmetic; and no one of the first class shall receive a recommendation of the examining committee, to be admitted into an English Grammar School, — unless he or she can spell correctly, read deliberately and audibly, has learned the several lessons taught in the second class, and is of good behavior.

The number of pupils in the primary schools varies, but in general, averages about fifty or sixty. Some of them are provided with inferior school rooms; but within a year past, several large and commodious rooms, well lighted, and susceptible of free ventilation have been erected, and others are now erecting.

Grammar Schools.

These schools, ten in number, and containing an average of from three hundred and fifty to four hundred pupils each, are located in large and commodious houses in different parts of the city. They are designed to receive children from the primary schools, and give them such an acquaintance with reading, writing, English grammar, geography, and arithmetic, as shall be sufficient for the ordinary purposes of life. They are admitted at the age of seven years.

These schools are separated into two rooms, the upper being occupied for the reading, and the lower for the writing department; these two branches being kept entirely distinct. Each room designed exclusively for boys, is provided with a principal and an assistant teacher, and is large enough to accommodate about three hundred children. The principal teachers are selected with special reference to their qualifications in these branches; but the law requires that the master of the grammar or reading school shall have been "educated at some college or university, and be a citizen of the United States by birth or naturalization." In those schools where none but females attend, there are a master and three female assistants in each department, and in those where both sexes are found, the place of one of the assistants or ushers is supplied by three female assistants.

Regulations. The masters must commit their requirements and prohibitions to writing, and read or cause them to be read aloud in school, at least once a month. Both the masters and the assistant teachers under them, are required to give their pupils constant employment, and to endeavor, by judicious and diversified modes, to render the exercises of the school pleasant and profitable; to use firm, prudent, and vigilant discipline, but to punish as sparingly as is consistent with securing obedience; and to govern, as much as possible, by persuasion and gentle measures. For obstinacy on the part of the pupil, or a determination not to submit to the authority of the teacher, he may be excluded from the school for a time; but the parent or guardian must be immediately informed, and the sub-committee consulted on the subject. Whenever he manifests symptoms of undoubted regret for his error, he may, with the consent of the committee, be reinstated in the privileges of the schools: but for habitual neglect of his duties, any pupil may, with the advice of the committee, be finally expelled. No pupil is admitted to the privileges of one school who has been expelled from another, or while under sentence of suspension.

Though the Lancasterian or Monitorial system is not, at present, pursued in any of the public schools, every teacher may avail himself of the assistance of advanced pupils, whenever it can be faithfully and judiciously applied. The teachers are to exercise a general care and inspection over the pupils, as well out of school as within its walls; and on all occasions to prevent injury being done to the apartments of the buildings, the furniture, &c.

No instructor in the public schools is allowed to keep a private school; or to attend to the instruction of any private pupils before 6 P. M. except on the afternoons of Wednesdays and Saturdays. No subscription for any purpose whatever may be introduced into any public school. No books may be used, or studies pursued, but those authorized by the Board. And no pupils are allowed to retain their connection with any of the public schools, (except by permission of the sub-committee) unless they are furnished with the books and utensils regularly required to be used in the schools respectively.

No pupil is allowed to leave school before the appointed hour, except in case of sickness or pressing emergency, of which the master is to be the judge. There is a recess of from five to ten minutes allowed in each half day, *that the pupils may not be injured by too long confinement.*

In every school, the grammar master and the writing master shall each have the regulation and control of his particular department, so far as regards the classification, the mode of instruction, and the discipline of his pupils, provided the regulations of one department do not interfere with those of the other. But in all cases involving the interests of both departments, where a difference of opinion or question of authority arises, the grammar master is considered the head of the school, and his decision settles the question.

The pupils are required to be present within five minutes after the opening of the school. Those who arrive late, are received, but not without notice of their fault. No new pupils are admitted, except on the first Monday of every month.

These schools are to be visited quarterly. At the semi-annual visitation in August, from two to six silver medals, furnished from a fund, bequeathed for this purpose by Dr. Franklin, are distributed to the most distinguished boys in each of the reading schools, and the same number in each of the writing schools. In 1822, medals were extended to the girls, in equal numbers to each school.

Course of Instruction. The grammar department of these schools is divided into four classes, subject to such subdivisions as the master may judge expedient. The course of studies is the following.

Class IV. Spelling. Reading. Class III. Spelling and Reading, continued. English Grammar. Class II. Spelling, Reading, and Grammar, continued. Geography. Parsing. Class I. Spelling, Reading, Grammar, and Geography, continued. History of the United States. Composition. Declamation.

Natural History, Natural Philosophy, and General History may be introduced at the discretion of the master; — and on Thursdays, the first class, in place of their ordinary class books, read in the Bible.

The pupils of the writing department are also divided into classes according to their progress, for the study of arithmetic and book-keeping.

All the pupils are taught writing and arithmetic daily; and the teachers are required to furnish the pupils with copy slips written, or from good engravings; or to write the copies themselves in the writing books. — The pupils of the first class are taught to make their own pens. It is also deemed desirable that oral instruction should be combined with the use of books, in all the exercises.

Latin Grammar School.

Regulations. The instructors of this school are a master, a sub-master, and so many assistants that there shall be at least one teacher to every thirty-five pupils. At present, there are one hundred and seventy pupils, and three assistants. Every instructor in this school must have been educated at some respectable college.

Candidates for admission to this school must bring from the masters of the schools they last attended, certificates of good moral character; must be able to read common English authors correctly and fluently, and to write a running hand; and they must have some knowledge of either the English or Latin grammar. They must also be at least nine years old. Candidates are examined for admission but once a year. The regular course of instruction continues five years.

The hours for opening and closing the school correspond, very nearly, with those of the grammar schools; but from April to October, the three lowest classes may be dismissed from the school in the forenoon of each day, at 11 o'clock. Tardiness, beyond five minutes, is regarded as a violation of school hours, and excludes the delinquent.

The school is divided into five classes, with such minor divisions as the master and sub-committee of the school may think advisable. The master is required to give his occasional services to each portion of the school, and also once a month to institute a rigid examination of his pupils in the different departments in all the studies to which they have attended since his last examination. The studies required in this school are the following: —

Class V. Latin Grammar. English Grammar. Reading. Class IV. The same studies continued. Reading and writing exercises from Latin. Declamation. Roman Antiquities, and Ancient Mythology. Modern Geography. Intellectual Arithmetic. Writing Translations from Latin into English. Class III. Same exercises continued. Written Arithmetic. Greek Grammar. Greek Authors. Ancient Geography. Class II. Same studies continued. Grecian Antiquities. Algebra. Cicero's Select Orations. Gould's Virgil. Jacob's Greek Reader. Greek Lexicon. Writing Translations from Greek into English. Committing to memory portions of Latin and Greek. English Composition. History. Geography and Trigonometry. Juvenal Expurgata. Gould's Horace Expurgata. Homer's Iliad. Greek Testament, the Four Gospels. Xenophon's Abasis. Writing and Composing Latin Themes and Verses. Constitution of the United States. Paley's Natural Theology.

All the classes in the school receive instruction in writing.

The English High School.

This school was established in 1820, with the design of furnishing the young men of Boston, who are not intended for a collegiate course of study but who have enjoyed the usual advantages of the other public schools of the city, with the means of completing a good English education to fit them for active life, or qualify them for eminence in private and public stations.

Regulations. The same qualifications are required, and the same proportionate number of instructors, as in the Latin school. In addition to these, there is a teacher of the French language. The institution is furnished with a valuable mathematical and philosophical apparatus, for the purposes of experiment and illustration.

No boy is admitted a member of this school under the age of twelve years. Examinations for admission take place only once a year. The school is divided into three classes; and these into as many sub-divisions as may be found expedient. Individuals are advanced according to their scholarship, and no faster. Each class or section is occasionally reviewed; but there is a general review once a quarter. No pupil is allowed to remain in the school more than three years. — Tardiness in arriving at school, beyond five minutes, subjects the pupil to the same inconveniences as at the Latin school.

Course of Instruction. The exercises and studies required during the course of instruction in this school, are the following: —

Class III. Intellectual and Written Arithmetic. Ancient and Modern Geography. Elements of General History. History of the U. States. Constitution of the U. States. Reading. Grammar. Declamation. Composition. Algebra. — Class II. The same studies continued. Book-keeping, by single and double entry. Geometry. Natural Philosophy. Natural Theology. Class I. Same studies continued. Moral Philosophy. Evidences of Christianity. Practical Mathematics; comprehending Navigation, Surveying, Mensuration, Astronomical Calculations, &c.; together with the construction and use of Mathematical Instruments. A course of experimental lectures on the various branches of Natural Philosophy. — All the classes receive instruction in writing.

The following studies are also allowed in the first class if the master thinks proper to introduce them. Philosophy of Natural History; Chemistry; Intellectual Philosophy; Linear Drawing; Logic.

Expenses.

The schools in Boston are sustained at the public expense. In the twenty-first Annual Report of the receipts and expenditures, we find the following account of the sums paid for the support of schools.

Salaries of Instructresses for 63 primary schools, with a part of rent, &c.	$13,430 00
Rents of school rooms hired by the city, and repairs,	2,673 16
Ten dollars per school for fuel, ...	630 00
Rewards for schools, $2 per school, ...	126 00
Total, Primary Schools,	16,859 16

Salaries of instructors in other schools.

Latin School, ...	4,695 28
English High School, ...	4,686 66
Eliot School, *(a grammar and writing school,)* . .	3,378 21
Other Grammar and Writing Schools, ...	21,257 25
Instructor of African School, ...	375 00
Total of other Schools,	34,592 40
Expended for repairs and supplies of all Schools, .	3,880 73
Paid for fuel for all the Schools, ...	1,150 94
Expenses of examinations, medals, &c., ...	274 18
Supply of Ink for all the Schools, ...	90 00
Salary of Secretary of School Committee, ...	100 00
Total,	56,947 41

CENTRE DISTRICT SCHOOLS IN WORCESTER.

Worcester, in Massachusetts, contained, in 1830, about 4,000 inhabitants. Besides schools supported throughout the town generally, as in other parts of Massachusetts, and sustained at the public expense, and besides a Central Grammar school, which is also supported at the expense of the town, the Centre District has been incorporated for the purpose of paying more special attention to the education of its citizens. It now has eight permanent schools, and one temporary one, viz:

1. Two schools for the youngest and lowest grade of scholars, denominated the North and South Infant Schools.

2. Two schools, one grade higher, to which pupils are promoted from the Infant Schools. These are called the North and South Primary Schools. These last and the Infant Schools are for both sexes, indiscriminately.

3. The next two schools, are the Second Female School, and the English School for Boys; to which promotions are made from the Primary Schools.

4. The seventh and highest in rank of the permanent schools of the District, is the Female High School, to which promotions are made from the Second Female School.

Corresponding to this last, is the Boys' Latin Grammar School, supported, as we have already mentioned, at the expense of the town, to which promotions are made from the Boys' English School.

The eighth permanent school for the district, is that for the children of color, in which are taught all the useful branches of a common education, but from which there are no promotions to any school of a higher grade.

All these eight schools are to be kept during the whole year, with such vacations only as may be required for the accommodation of the teachers, or as may be directed by the Board, who have the general direction of them.

In addition to these, a school for apprentices and clerks, and such other boys as attend only a part of the year, is kept three months in the winter.

These schools are under the superintendence and direction of a Board of Overseers whose duty it is "to determine upon the qualifications of instructors, and to contract with them for their services; to determine upon the attainments of scholars to be admitted into the said schools respectively; to prescribe the course of instruction therein, and all necessary rules and regulations for the government thereof; to determine upon all complaints of instructors, of parents or of scholars, which may arise in relation to said schools, or either of them; to visit and examine said schools respectively, at stated periods during the year; to encourage, in every suitable manner, both instructors, and scholars in the performance of their relative duties; and to make a report, in writing, annually, to the district, of the condition of the schools, during the period of their office."

For the purposes of visiting, the Board is formed into nine divisions, one to each school. The schools are to be visited and thoroughly examined once in three months. Minutes of these examinations are to be made in a book kept for the purpose, designating the whole number of scholars and the number present; the exercises of each class, with the number of scholars belonging to it present, the number absent, &c.; and any other particulars necessary to give information of the state of the school. A Report, embracing these particulars, is made to the next subsequent meeting of the Board of Overseers. At each examination, they also report to the Board the names of candidates for promotion to higher schools.

General Regulations. The instructors of the schools, before vacating their office, are to give the Board of Overseers three months notice of their intention, and the Board cannot discontinue the services of a teacher, without giving the same notice. Scholars belonging to the Female High School, the Second Female School, or the Boys' English School, whose absence has been of more than one month's standing, may not be readmitted by the instructors, without a certificate from the visiting committee of the schools to which they respectively belong. The visiting committee are authorized to regulate the time and duration of the vacations in their respective schools.

Needle work is permitted in the primary schools two half days in each week; and in the higher female schools, one half day. Writing is taught in all the schools above the primary, two half days in each week. Instruction on the terrestrial Globe is also given in all the schools above the primary schools. Written or printed questions are prohibited in the same schools; except that Emerson's Questions on Goodrich's History are allowed in the Second Female School.

No scholar is admitted into any of the schools under three years. All transfers and promotions from one school to another, except when the transfer is made to another school of the same grade, shall be by a vote of the Board, to be certified by the secretary.

System of Discipline, &c. The schools are expected to commence with devotional exercises, at precisely nine o'clock in the morning throughout the year; and to recommence at half past one in the afternoon in the winter, and at two in the summer. They are to continue three hours in each half day. The school bell always rings fifteen minutes before opening, and five minutes before closing the schools.

Every teacher is required to take cognizance of the conduct of his pupils, not only while in school, but during recess, and while going to, and returning from school. None are to be admitted into the schools, after commencement, either in the forenoon or afternoon, or after absence half a day or more, without a written or verbal excuse from the parent or guardian. Nor is any one permitted to leave, till school closes, except in case of illness or some necessary cause obvious to the teacher, without similar verbal or written excuse. And in neither of these cases, can the scholar be the bearer of such excuse.

The crimes which are regarded as punishable are, impertinence to teachers, obstinacy, neglect of duty, falsehood, obscene and profane language, quarrelling, and injury done to a school house, or to the property of any teacher or scholar. In case of delinquency, recourse is first to be had to persuasion, reproof, and admonition; but when these fail to produce reformation, reasonable corporal punishment with the rod is to be inflicted. In case of any scholar's leaving school when under censure for misconduct, notice thereof is to be immediately given to the Board by the instructor, and such scholar cannot be readmitted to the school he left, or to any other school in the district, till he shall have made such satisfaction as shall be prescribed by the teacher, or on appeal from him, by the Board. It is, moreover, required or expected, that teachers will keep accurate lists of their scholars in the order of their classes, containing a daily account of their attendance and absence, of their good and bad behaviour, with the manner in which their lessons are recited, as good or bad; — which lists are to be submitted to the visiting committee at each examination.

Each grade of schools has its appropriate set of school books, presented, of course, by the Board, but subject to variation, as circumstances may seem to them to require.

COMMON SCHOOLS AND COMMON EDUCATION.—NO. 6.

Dialogue iv. — Scene, *The Autumnal Fireside.*

Robert. — Well, Thomas, how have your studies fared these four months? Have you succeeded in continuing them all summer?

Thomas. — Why, not exactly, Robert. You know I never expected to do much.

R. Ah, I thought how it would turn out. — Why, Thomas, there 's no time for study in summer. "Work, boys, work," is all the song, now-a-days. Ploughing, and planting, and hoeing, and haying, and harvesting, — these are the summer lessons. There 's no time, at this season, "to trim the midnight lamp," as they say. Now the lesson is, "Work while the day lasts;" — "Make hay while the sun shines." We have to work all day, and sleep all night. So you will have to give it up.

T. Not so fast, Robert. I did not say I had done nothing, nor did I say I had not done about what I expected; though I should be ashamed to call it *much*. True enough, I have had something else to do, at midnight, besides trimming the lamp; as well as a great deal of hard work by day. But then you know nobody works *all* day, from sunrise to sunset; and sunlight is as good, for what I know, as lamplight, if one will only use it.

R. Yes; but midday is the time to rest, — for the oxen to rest, and the horses to rest, and the men to rest.

T. Why, Robert, do you mean to say that oxen, horses, and men are all to rest in the same way? I cannot think that a brute's rest, and a man's rest should be *exactly* alike!

R. Sure enough, I should not quite like to say that; but then you know they say that study is very hard work: that nothing will break the constitution faster than *hard study.*

T. That may be; but then I have not tried *hard study.* I have only studied a little every day, and I must say that I have rested the better for it: a great deal better than if I had rested only like the oxen and horses.

R. Well, Thomas, if I could rest any better for it, I should like to know how to study a little myself; for I have been prodigiously tired sometimes, before noon. I 'll think about that before next summer. But then, after all, you will be obliged to confess, that you have not studied enough to learn anything. If you can rest better, why, very well; but as to knowing any more in October than in June, that is out of the question. Let us see, then; how much time have you had for study?

T. Oh, sometimes more, and sometimes less. Sometimes two hours, sometimes one; always half an hour at least.

R. *Half an hour!* Quite a long time for study. Half an hour a day! So then, I was right, as to knowing any more in October than in June.

T. Not *much* more, Robert, you should say; and then you would be right; I do'nt know much more than I did last June, it is true; but I have learned a little. It is *but* little, sure enough; but after all, it is something. Why, let us see; I have reviewed the whole of my arithmetic, from beginning to end. As I had not forgotten what I learned in the winter, it came easier; and I can now see into it a great deal better than before; and it seems as if it was all at my finger's ends. I do 'nt believe I shall ever forget it.

R. Well, then, I must confess that you *can* learn something in midsummer. But then I should not like to have my head full of figures and nothing else, — to turn my head into a complete multiplication table. I should think your brains would need to rest by this time.

T. Oh, but that is not all I have done in arithmetic; for I kept myself to half an hour exactly by the clock; and then you see I had half an hour, or an hour, for something else. So that if my brains, as you say, got a little tired, they were soon rested again. Then I have read Plutarch's Lives, and part of Rollin's History, into the bargain: yes, and that prettiest of all books for a farmer's boy, Thompson's Seasons. There 's another thing; I could not help thinking of what I had read when I was about my work.

R. Well, Thomas, I believe there is one member of your body, that has rested all summer. I do not believe that your tongue has had anything to do. For my part, I like a little *tongue* work.

T. Why surely, Robert, I am talking fast enough now, to show that my tongue has not been still all summer. Why, I never chatted so much in my life time; and you would have found it out, had there been winter evenings, but the summer evenings have been so short, and the days so busy, that we have not often met. But really, Robert, I have become a greater talker this summer than ever. We have had a good deal to talk about at our house, I assure you; and without complaining of our neighbors, either. Father says that the more we read and think, the less we shall be inclined to find fault with others. Little time as I have had, I have accomplished about as much as I ever did in a winter, in my life. True, that is not much.

R. I expected it would come to that. So now, I suppose you will use your influence in the district to have no more schools. We shall not need them any more, for a boy in summer by himself, can learn as much as he can in the winter, with ever so good a teacher!

T. No, Robert; I did not say that. But if, by means of a teacher, winter after winter, he has learned a little how to study, and got into a regular way, and can make himself *stick to the business*, — why then, he is a poor fellow if he can 't learn something by himself afterwards. I am quite sure, that without what little school learning I have, I could not have done even the little I have been speaking of.

R. Yes, yes; and now for a hint, which you know I am always willing to give when it comes in my way. Without the *key*, you could not have got into the fine house. If you had not known how to read English fluently, you could not have read Plutarch, or Rollin, or Thompson; and without a little previous knowledge in ciphering, you could not have reviewed the whole arithmetic; and if you had not known, that "many a little makes a mickle," you would not have husbanded those half hours so nicely. To use the old proverb, "*He has leisure that uses it.*" There 's a lesson for you, Thomas. So you need not mince the matter any longer; use leisure and you will have leisure; keep learning and you will increase in knowledge. Am I not a good adviser, Thomas?

T. Yes, Robert; I must own you have given me a great many good hints; but you are a real rogue after all. I see by your look, that you have been as busy, and learned as much as I, after all your talk. So out with the truth, at once.

R. Why, Thomas, to be sure I have not quite forgotten our talk in the spring; how I helped you along with a hint now and then; and I have taken some of them to myself. Perhaps I have found something to do that is worth doing, though I do 'nt see my way clear to be as great a man as Franklin. I have brought a little more to pass than I expected, though I have not followed your track exactly.

T. Well, Robert, let us hear what you have been about?

R. Why, first of all, as I am a farmer, and am like to be, I have read all I could find about farming, the New England Farmer, and I have got hold, too, of White's History of Selbourne, that Lucy mentioned last spring, and that has kept me reading and looking, and reading and looking, all summer; so that I know birds, beasts, and fishes, and insects, and plants and trees much better than I did three months ago.

T. Well done, Robert, you have followed your own hints better than I have, after all. Why, you have been a real Solomon; for if I recollect, he spake of trees from "the cedar tree that is in Lebanon, even unto the hyssop that springeth out of the wall;" he spake also of "beasts, and of fowls, and of creeping things, and of fishes." You have *turned scholar out of school* with a witness. So the next thing is, as you told me, to turn *scholar the whole year round.* So it is you, I see, who are going to use your influence to break up the schools. Now, Robert, I beseech you, spare them a little longer, for I have determined to go to school one more winter; though I thought last winter I had done.

R. Never fear, Thomas. I'll join you; for I find I want more *keys.* You know what I mean. Why there are Botany, and Chemistry, and Mineralogy. Why, if I can have a teacher that can help me a little to an insight into these, then I can get along.

T. And I want more *keys.* I scarcely know enough to tell what, — but Algebra and Geometry. I should like a teacher that would give me a start in these matters. Then there is Composition. Father says that three quarters of the people cannot write a common letter in a pleasant and intelligible way. I should like to know how to write a letter. Well, Robert, how shall we make the most of school next winter? Let me have a little more of your advice.

R. Here it is. Wash well, in the first place. Do n't be one of those who only wash the ends of their fingers and noses. They cannot study well. Wash all over, Thomas, then you can study. Work, saw, split wood; — do anything that is necessary; — play, run, and jump. These stupid fellows, they cannot study. And what rule was it that we read in the papers sometime ago? Can you remember it, Thomas?

T. Yes, yes; "One thing at a time."

R. That's it, Thomas. You need not trim the midnight lamp. The best place for a scholar at midnight, I think, is the bed, — the best study, a nice sound sleep.

MUSICAL REVOLUTION IN SWITZERLAND.

[Abridged from the London Evangelical Magazine.]

In the south-west of Switzerland, a *Musical Revolution* is rapidly taking effect. Its object is to give a new direction to popular singing; and its means may be found wherever there are persons willing to take a little pains, and who can find a leader to give them a little instruction, and to guide their voices in singing the charms of their country and the praises of their God. Long was it thought that French Switzerland could not march with the German cantons in vocal music. Long has the lake of Geneva heard little along its shores but coarse, vulgar, and obscene ballads. Lately, the students of Geneva and Lausanne have labored to counteract this evil, by composing, and endeavoring to circulate patriotic songs. The effort has been happily successful, but within a small circle. New methods have been adopted in many schools, to train the children to the execution of hymns, with a fine and simple harmony; and the effect has been so far pleasing. But something was wanted to reach the mass of the people; and that, the kindness of providence has supplied.

About two years ago, M. Kaupert, a Saxon gentleman, proposed to teach gratuitously the whole population of young and willing persons in any village or small town, to sing together. The rumor attracted considerable attention, and drew forth a variety of opinions. But soon his promises were realized, and all scepticism was silenced. At Morges and in the neighboring villages, concerts of the voice alone were heard, producing such a noble and simple harmony as no person in the whole country had before the least idea of. He was induced to extend his benevolent labors. He electrified, as it were, the whole side of the Lake down to Geneva. Everywhere, the *Magician of Song* was followed by crowds. The *moral* effect of this is beyond calculation.

M. Kaupert commonly began in schools and other large rooms. Persons of all ages and of every rank in society flocked to these meetings. It was soon necessary to ask for the use of the churches; and sometimes, large assemblies have been held in the open air. In the former places, hymns are sung; and in the latter, songs, patriotic or descriptive, but all free from any immoral taint.

His plan is, to trace in a simple and clear manner upon a large black board, the notes of each lesson; and he furnishes each one of his pupils with a card or paper, containing what he judges fit for each step of instruction. He usually succeeds in ten lectures, to qualify these vast masses to execute the simple and touching hymn or song in parts and full concert, enrapturing all who witness the scene.

In the introductory lectures, he strongly affects the imagination and the sensibility of his bearers, by his descriptions of the powers and the intention of music, to breathe noble and generous sentiments, to harmonize the minds and hearts of men, to honor our country, to excite admiration of the works of God, and, as the highest point of all, to show forth his praises. — These large assemblages follow his instructions, and catch his manner of execution with an enthusiasm perfectly astonishing. His kind manner and untiring patience have a great share in producing the effects which so surprise us.

The great and learned city of Geneva invited the musical philanthropist to visit and charm its population. Some of the higher classes became alarmed; but in the result, they too were carried down the stream. Pastors, professors, magistrates, ladies of the first rank, persons the most distinguished for learning and science, were seen side by side with children and poor people, listening and learning. When the grand meeting took place, no church could receive the multitude, and they repaired to the Plein Palais, in number, four thousand singers. Here, however, the success did not answer expectation; the wind acted unfavorably upon the vibrations of the air, and perhaps the distance of the extremes made it impossible to keep time. But M. K. was loaded with expressions of admiration and thanks, and a medal was struck in honor of him: a mark of respect, which, in Switzerland, is never conferred but upon what is judged to be in the highest order of merit.

At Lausanne, his instructions were sought with universal avidity. Many who had been accustomed to spend their evenings in dissipation, began to employ them entirely in learning the new style of music. Children and their parents, all the schools, the professors and students of the college, servants and mistresses, workmen and masters, persons who had been the most opposed to each other, in religion and politics, the inhabitants of different villages distinguished by banners, — all were attracted, all seemed to be of one heart and soul. When the previous training was complete, a day was fixed for the grand concert. — More than two thousand singers arranged in the great church, the noblest Gothic building in Switzerland; the flags of villages and societies were tastefully arranged on an ivy-clad tower; the vast multitude who came to hear were disposed within and without: and then was sung a hymn and its air, of Luther's composing, — simple, grave, noble. — But O the effect! — No words can utter it! — The impression will never be forgotten.

The happy fruits of this *Musical Revolution* show themselves almost everywhere. The people in the different places keep up their singing meetings. In the summer evenings they are seen in the church-yard, or on the village-green. In the streets and on the roads, the ear of the passenger is met by the sweet sounds. In these groups we perceive some failures of execution, compared with the fine style when led by M. Kaupert; but attention and practice will remedy them.

THE TEACHER'S ALMANAC FOR DECEMBER.

THE SCHOOL ROOM.

Many teachers smile when we venture to speak of the importance of duly ventilating the school room; and some no doubt shrink back in disgust or horror, lest we should repeat to them the old story of the black hole at Calcutta.

But if there are teachers to be found, — and undoubtedly there are, — who do not believe that breathing renders atmospheric air unfit for respiration at the rate of a gallon a minute, (as we have so often insisted,) we do not ask them at once to relinquish their scepticism; but we do ask them to make an experiment, and then reflect on the consequences of inhaling bad air for a longer period, and by lungs more tender than their own.

Let them confine themselves in a small tight closet, or cask, holding just sixty gallons besides the space occupied by their own persons, and there remain exactly one hour. At first they will breathe with considerable freedom; but after the lapse of sixty minutes, respiration will be more difficult. We do not ask them to continue in it longer than one hour, lest it should do their lungs permanent injury.

Let teachers, then, look well to the purity of their school rooms. If they do not fear for themselves, let them at least fear for others. If they have no mercy on their own lungs, let them have mercy on those of the children committed by God and parents to their charge. Temperature is important; but terrible as is the catalogue of evils which result from its neglect, they are hardly to be named on the same day with poisoned lungs, and deranged vital organs, generally. The one is a mere attack upon the suburbs, or outposts of human existence, the other is destroying the citadel.

THE EARTH.

The world we inhabit is now wrapped in the gloom of winter. The *vegetable* kingdom as well as a part of the more highly elevated *animal* world is apparently sunk in death. How cold, how cheerless! But is this the *end* of so large a portion of the great Creator's works! Will there be no renovation, — *no* cheerful resurrection? Yes; when the winds of a few wintry months have whistled over the temporary tomb of millions of organized beings, the "powerful king of day," returning from the chambers of the south, shall reanimate the slumbering tribes, restore the sleeping dead, and Nature shall once more put on her beautiful robes.

Even so is it with man. Though he sleep not during the winter with the bat and the marmot, and the hedgehog, and the woodchuck, yet his long sleep must sooner or later, come. He must lie down in the grave to awake no more, till the Sun of Righteousness, rising in glorious strength, and awful majesty, shall rouse all who sleep, and animate them with new life. What teacher will fail occasionally to remind his pupils of this brighter and better resurrection?

THE HEAVENS.

Aries is the constellation of the zodiac now immediately north of the Pleiades; and east of Andromeda, is the constellation of Perseus. The Whale may also be studied through this month. Jupiter will be visible during the evenings. Venus will become the morning star at the close of December.

MISCELLANY.

Education Convention at Cincinnati.

The third session of the "Western Literary Institute, and College of Professional Teachers," commenced at Cincinnati, on the 6th of October last, and continued in session four days. The following Lectures were assigned for the session.

1. On the moral character and influence of Teachers; by Rev. J. Van Doren, Lexington, Ky.
2. Against the Classics and Mathematics as part of a scheme of general Education in this country; by Thomas S. Grimke, Esq., Charleston, S. C.
3. The influence of the regular study of the Bible on intellectual and moral improvement; by Rev. W. H. McGuffy, Oxford, Ohio.
4. The best method of teaching the languages; by W. Hopwood, M. A., Cincinnati.
5. The application of principles to practice, in the various departments of physical science; by Rev. E. Slack, Oxford, Ohio.
6. Anatomy and Physiology, as a branch of study in Schools and Academies; by A. Kinmont, A. M. Cincinnati.
7. The proper method of teaching Geography and History in connection; by J. L. Tracy, Esq., Lexington, Ky.
8. Constitutional and Criminal law, as a branch of study in schools and Academies; by B. Storer, Esq., Cinncincinnati.
9. College Discipline; by Prof. M. A. H. Niles, South Hanover, Ind.
10. The nature and moral influence of Music; by W. Nixon, Esq., Professor of Music, Cincinnati.
11. Institutions for Teachers; by Rev. Dr. Beecher, Lane Seminary, Ohio.

Besides the Lectures, several reports were to be made from Committees on topics mentioned in our last volume, at page 591. We have been unable to learn from the public papers, whether the lectures were all delivered; though one was given which had not been announced, by E. D. Mansfield, Esq., on Mathematics. We find, however, that the meeting was well attended, the audience sometimes consisting of 1500 persons; and that the interest was greatly enhanced by a most able discussion, by Mr. Grimke, and Mr. Kinmont, of the question, Whether the Classics ought to be studied as a branch of general Education: the former maintaining the negative, and the latter the affirmative. These efforts of Mr. Grimke were among the last acts of his public life. He died in a day or two after the close of the Convention.

Evening Education Party.

On the evening after the "Western Literary Institute and College of Teachers" adjourned its late session at Cincinnati, Dr. Drake, of that city, threw open his doors to the Teachers present in the city, and to many other gentlemen, and a kind of Education party was convened. Here the conversation turned almost solely on subjects connected with Education. Partly for the sake of ascertaining the opinions of the company on certain topics, and partly for amusement, many votes were taken on the questions which were agitated. The following are a few of the questions, with the results.

What is the nativity of each individual comprising the company? England, 7; New England, 27; New York, 8; New Jersey, 2; Pennsylvania, 9; Virginia, 3; North Carolina, 1; South Carolina, 2; Kentucky, 2; Ohio, 8.—69.

Has a spirit of *emulation* a favorable or unfavorable tendency, employed as a means to promote improvement among young persons?—Affirmative 62; Negative 7.

Is it expedient to employ the *rod* in restraining youth.—Affirm. 44; Neg. 25.

How many pupils can one instruct to the best advantage?—30.

Should the Bible be adopted as a school-book?—Affirmative unanimously. Should it be studied at particular times set apart for the purpose, or indiscriminately with other studies? At particular times.—One dissenting voice.

Should the study of the ancient classics be required as a necessary branch in our colleges and universities?—Affirm. 32; Neg. 26; Neutral 6; several of the company having retired. Should the studies in regular institutions be uniform, and all the students required to pursue the same course?—Affirm. 28; Neg. 30.

Should the study of *mathematics* be required in every regular institution?—Affirm. 36; Neg. 23.

Should anatomy and physiology constitute a part of popular education?—Affirm. 57; Neg. 1.

Should the system of giving diplomas as now practised in colleges be abolished, and certificates substituted?—Affirm. by a decided majority,—not counted.

Should female education be confided exclusively to females?—Affirm. 5; Neg. 18.

Should chemistry and natural philosophy be studied by females?—Affirm. 21; Neg. 3.

Should the government of the teacher extend beyond the bounds of the school-room and school-yard?—Affirm. 27; Neg. 5.

At another meeting on a similar occasion, the question, Has the system of instituting printed questions in elementary school-books, a favorable or unfavorable tendency?—Affirm. 8; Neg. 6; Neutral, 3.

Instruction of the Colored Population.

Evening schools for adults.—We learn that the "Association of Friends," in Philadelphia, formed three years ago, of which a brief account was given at page 284 of our third volume, continues to be the instrument of much good to that class of the population for whom it was designed. It was the means of opening, in the autumn of 1833, two schools, one for men and the other for women. They commenced in October, and continued till the end of February last, and the female school till sometime in April. The male school had an average of thirty-five attendants during the winter, and the female of fifty; making a total of 85.

Renewed efforts have been made during the present autumn, in this sphere of Christian benevolence and right legislation. These efforts have resulted in the establishment of four schools, instead of two; of which one half are for males, and the other half for females.

Instruction for all Classes. — Efforts are making in Kentucky to form a State Association for the Religious and Moral Improvement of the colored population. The kinds of instruction proposed are, 1. Special preaching; 2. Oral instruction from the Bible, in something like Bible classes; 3. In places where the public sentiment will permit it, reading. The leaders in this movement adopt the principle, that slavery cannot be terminated *peaceably* in any other manner than by the religious and moral instruction of the slaves themselves.

Indian Academy, near Georgetown, Ky.

This is under the superintendence of Col. Richard M. Johnson. It embraces one hundred and forty pupils of all ages, from ten different tribes. Among them are Choctaws, Chickasaws, Cherokees, Pawnees, Winnebagoes, Sacs, Foxes, &c. &c. It is an affecting sight to see the youthful remnants of these once powerful tribes, as arranged two and two, they slowly march to and from their meals, with drums beating and colors flying. Where are their proud ancestors, with iron frames and elastic nerves, who called the great valley "their own, their native land?" A few stragglers in the "far west," and these youths, are all that remain.

Col. Johnson is said to receive $250 per annum for the instruction of each pupil. This amounts to an immense sum, which must leave a handsome profit. The lodging rooms are constructed of logs one story high, and differ not, except in their size, from the common dwellings of new settlers in Indiana and Illinois. The school house is also constructed of logs, two stories high. By leaving out one log, and inserting in its place panes of glass, sufficient light is admitted. The school is furnished with philosophical and mathematical apparatus of the plainest kind. Four teachers and a superintendent control the school. The superintendent is the Rev. Mr. *Henderson*, of the regular Baptist Church. He is an intelligent and amiable man, deeply solicitous for the welfare of his interesting charge. The other teachers are respectable. The pupils are taught to sing by a *native* teacher.

This school promises to be of solid utility to the young sons of the forest who enjoy its privileges. It is desirable to see all the present buildings supplanted by large, airy, and convenient edifices like those of other literary institutions. This would have a vivifying influence on the students, and render them still more solicitous to introduce among their countrymen, the arts and elegancies of civilized life. — *Cincinnati Journal.*

American Institutions.

Dickinson College. — We have recently received a pamphlet, containing the Inaugural Address of the Rev. J. P. Durbin, Principal of Dickinson College, Carlisle, Penn.; and another embracing the Statutes of the College, including the course of Studies, &c. The Address is rich in valuable thought, on the general subject of Education, as well as replete with sound views in regard to college instruction and discipline.

Dickinson College, under the direction of the new Principal, is to give the student a more extended course of instruction than formerly; and to unite manual labor with study. A well organized grammar school is also to be connected with the college. There are to be seven professors, including the Principal, four of whom are already appointed.

Willoughby University of Lake Erie.—This is an institution, recently incorporated, and to be located at Chagrin, 15 miles East of Cleaveland, Ohio. It is to consist of three departments. 1. A Medical School, with six professors, who have all been designated, and the first course of lectures was to have commenced on the first Monday of November. 2. A male Collegiate Department. In this, four Professors are appointed. It is to be opened on the first Monday of April next. 3. The female Collegiate Department, to be opened at the same time with the latter, under a competent female Professor. It is intended that the female Department shall not be inferior to any institution of the kind in America.

New College.—The Manual Labor Academy of Maury county, Kentucky, which was opened in 1830 with seven pupils, has been formed into a College, under the name of Jackson College. The trustees own three hundred and ten acres, and three substantial brick buildings, with accommodations for seventy-two students; and are now erecting other buildings. One hundred and sixty applications for admission have been made during the present year. Two hours' labor a day are required of each student, and seventy-five dollars in addition to this, will pay for his board and tuition. Donations are solicited for the purchase of a library, apparatus, the erection of a new college building, and the endowment of a professorship. It is a point now conceded, that the West can be supplied with the means of instruction only by educating young men upon the spot.

Steubenville Female Seminary.—The leading peculiarity of the Female Seminary at Steubenville, Ohio, is its large number of teachers, in proportion to the pupils. For while the latter seldom much exceed a hundred, the number of teachers is no less than twelve, besides three assistant teachers, three assistant pupils, and a matron; making in the whole, *nineteen*. This looks like making provision,—so far as the number of Instructors can go,—for female education. From the remarks appended to a Catalogue which has been sent us, the course of instruction at the Seminary appears to be extended and thorough; and the moral influence very superior.

Dayton Academic and Manual Labor Institution.—This institution, located at Dayton, Ohio, has been in operation one year, and with happy results. A considerable proportion of the students who have labored, have earned from thirty-six to fifty-five dollars; and the experience of this institution, thus far, goes to prove, unequivocally, that labor is beneficial to progress in literary pursuits; and instead of enervating the mind, serves to invigorate and quicken it.

Boston Seminary.—A new literary institution has been proposed, in Boston, to go into operation as soon as sixty scholars can be obtained, the object of which is to give a liberal education to young men who are not destined to the professions, and who do not desire instruction in the ancient languages. The latter, however, will be taught if desired. The whole control of the Seminary is to be vested in four teachers, or professors, viz: a Teacher of History and Moral Philosophy, a Teacher of Mathematics and Natural History, a Teacher of English Literature and Composition, and a Teacher of the Ancient Languages.

Education in Tennessee.

The following facts are interesting, because they serve to show that the subject of education is becoming popular in Tennessee.

At the Annual Commencement of the University of Nashville, Oct. 1st, the following were four out of the five Orations delivered by the senior members of that Institution. "On the Inducements held out to young men of talents," by John P. W. Brown, of Ky.; "On the Union of Moral and Intellectual Culture," by Jos. B. Hadden, of Ky.; "On the Power and Influence of Voluntary Associations," by Le Roy D. Halsey, of Ala.; and "On the Importance of rightly educating children," by Andrew Ewing, of Tenn.

Charleston Free Schools.

We learn from the Carolina Gazette, of Charleston, S. C. that the system of Free Schools in two of the parishes in that city, embraces five schools, containing, in the whole, five hundred and thirty-eight children of both sexes, who are taught Reading, Writing, Arithmetic, and the Elements of Grammar and Geography.

Examination of Teachers.

In the Kortland Observer, for Oct. 31st, we find a notice of the Inspectors of Common Schools for the town of Homer, N. Y., stating the day, hour, &c. when they will meet for the purpose of examining teachers. The notice closes with the following paragraph:—

"The Inspectors take this opportunity to observe to those who expect to be employed in the instruction of our district schools, and to trustees and proprietors of school districts, that an effort will be made by the Inspectors to elevate the standard of common school instruction in our town. They have come to the determination to license only those who, upon a most thorough examination, shall be qualified in every respect contemplated by the laws for the regulation of common schools."

This is precisely the stand which has occasionally been taken within three or four years, in a few towns in New England, and which has often kindled a violent war with public sentiment. It is worthy of remark however, for the encouragement of those who may take the same course hereafter, that the Inspectors have usually come off victorious, in consequence of the change thus produced in public opinion.

Female Orphan Asylum, in Virginia.

We learn from the Southern Religious Telegraph, that the Ladies of Virginia have lately obtained from the Legislature of that State, a charter for a Female Orphan Asylum; and in pursuance of their plan, have erected a large and convenient edifice at Fredericksburg, to be used for that purpose. It is intended for destitute female orphans, without regard to party or sect; and to be, in the largest sense of the term, a *place of education*. They would not only save them from the seductions and the miseries of vice, but would give them the advantages of maternal superintendence, a pure example, judicious instruction, and moral and religious influence. Such an effort is worthy of those who have attempted it; and we cannot doubt that the warm heart and the open hand will be ready to second their laudable exertions.

Chatham Academy.

We have received a Catalogue of the Trustees, Instructors, and Students of Chatham Academy, Savannah, Georgia. It consists of three Female Departments, — primary, junior, and senior; — an English Department of Boys; a Classical and Mathematical Department; a French Department; and a Drawing and Painting Department. There are one or more teachers or professors in each of these several Departments, and a Principal, who has the superintendence of the whole. The institution appears to be flourishing. The number of pupils is three hundred and fourteen; of whom two hundred and three are females. The course of instruction appears, from the Catalogue, to be *systematic and thorough*; but we see nothing in it very peculiar, except a liberal supply of teachers.

The Young Ladies' Lyceum, connected with the Institution, is highly interesting in its character and useful in its results. Its meetings are held on the first and third Saturdays of every month. The exercises are essays, lectures, the exhibition of specimens in nature and the arts, &c. Since February last, the Lyceum has collected a Library of one hundred and sixty-five volumes. The general influence of the Lyceum is represented as thus far highly salutary. It has aided and assisted the regular school exercises; it has rendered not only the school, but their homes and boarding houses more pleasant; it has been the means of collecting a cabinet of specimens of plants, and minerals, and works of art; and by correspondence and exchange of specimens with other Lyceums and Schools, has also been a means both of very great pleasure and profit.

Foreign Donations for Libraries.

The British Government have recently made the liberal donation of 80 folio volumes to each of fifteen of the principal college libraries in the United States, and also to six other important city libraries, including the Atheneum, of Boston. These volumes contain a collection of ancient documents and state papers, recently printed by order of Parliament.

Literary and Historical Society of Quebec.

This Association will, on the last Thursday of April next, award "four first prize silver medals, and four second prize silver medals," to the best Essays which shall be presented, post paid in the usual manner, to the County Secretary before the 20th of February, on some subject to be selected from a list of subjects just published by the Society.

This list embraces, 1. Literature and History; 2. Natural History; 3. Science; 4. Arts. Under the first head, eighteen topics have been selected; under the second, six; the third, four; and the fourth, seventeen. Two of the medals are to be given for the best essays under each of those four heads. The subjects, or topics are all truly Canadian; but the prize productions may be in the English, French, or Latin language, and are open to all persons residing on the Continent, or Islands of North America. The list of topics is too long for this place; but we may mention among those on Literature and History, the civil and political history of Canada, its antiquities, geography and statistics, and language; Indian oratory, the progress of literature, means of inducing the Indians to apply themselves to agriculture, water color paintings of landscape scenery, and oil paintings of historical subjects. In Natural History, a catalogue of indigenous plants; on the fishes of the St. Lawrence; and on the migrations of the salmon. In Science, on the state of heat existing in living trees, and the best account of any unexplored river not less than fifty miles long.

Garden School.

A school in which boys will be taught gardening, agriculture, and rural economy, generally; and girls, sewing, cookery, and domestic economy in all its details, is about to be established at Fordhook, Eng., by Lady Noel Byron. She has engaged a head master of the establishment, who is now gone to Switzerland, to inspect the establishment of Fellenberg, at Hofwyl.

Institutions of Vienna.

A late New York Mirror gives a particular account of some of the institutions of Vienna; among which are the following.

Polytechnic School. — This is designed to give "a practical Education for the trades, commerce, and manufactures." It is divided into three departments. The first is preparatory, and resembles our high schools; but the terms of tuition are only fifty cents a month. It occupies two years. The two other courses last but one year. In the manufacturing course, the principal study is chemistry, as applied to arts and trades generally. The school is under the direction of a Principal, who has associated with him thirty professors.

Private Penitentiary. — To this institution, respectable parents are permitted to send, privately, for reformation, those children whom they are unable to govern at home. "The name of the family and pupil is kept a secret, and the culprits are returned after a proper time, disciplined without disgrace. Pride of character is thus preserved, while the delinquent is corrected."

Education at the Sandwich Islands.

The number of natives of the Sandwich Islands, who were able to read with more or less facility in June, 1803, according to the Boston Recorder, was

Kailua,	1,099	Kaluaaka,	500
Kaawaloa,	2,500	Honolulu,	3,100
Hilo,	3,859	Waialua,	1,600
Waimea,	3,000	Kauai,	2,977
Lahaina,	1,818		
Wailuku,	731	Total,	20,184

The amount of printing, during the year ending June, 1833, was 166,000 copies, and 8,436,000 pages. The copies of books printed from the beginning of the mission have been 776,000; pages 33,501,800. About 368 pages of new matter were added the past year, to the Sandwich Islander's Library, making the whole number of pages, 1,988. About 3,000 geographies and 200 historical catechisms were bound in cloth.

There is still a great deficiency of books adapted to schools. Select schools have been established at most of the stations, which are taught by the missionaries themselves. The first session of the High school at Lahaina, (of which mention was made in a former volume of this work,) commenced July 2d, 1833. In the course of the year, there were 91 scholars in the school. Great embarrassments have been experienced for want of school books.

Class Book of Anatomy and Physiology.

The Executive Committee of the American Lyceum have extended until May, 1835, the time for receiving communications from competitors for the prize of three hundred dollars, which the Society have offered for the best Text Book for the use of Schools, on Human Anatomy and Physiology. The following gentlemen are the committee to award the premium: Dr. J. Kearney Rodgers and Dr. John D. Russ, of New York; Dr. John C. Warren, of Boston; Dr. Samuel Harris, of Philadelphia, and Rev. Thomas H. Gallaudet, of Hartford, Conn.

The Rudiments of Geography and the Picture System.

In the last article of Y, on the use of pictures, a sentence was added which escaped the Editor's notice, in which the writer alludes to the "Rudiments of Geography," and ascribes to Mrs. Willard, in connection with the Editor, the introduction of pictures into that work. It is proper, therefore, to state that the "Rudiments" was in press before Mrs. Willard's plan was known to its author, and that a few slight alterations only were made at her suggestion—that a part of the copy-right was transferred to Mrs. Willard, not on account of any share in its authorship, but because it contained principles and methods which that lady had also adopted, and whose separate publication she was thus induced to relinquish,* and particularly that the introduction of pictures did not form a part of her original plan. For this feature of the work, especially, the author alone is responsible, and indeed is perfectly ready to answer. He agrees both with X and Y in believing the use of pictures, not only allowable, but indispensable to thorough instruction in many branches of knowledge, and highly useful in impressing facts and truths upon the young mind. He has acted on the principle that every engraving is valuable which will give more distinct ideas of the subject illustrated, or fix it more deeply in the mind; but he cannot consent that this opinion should be adduced to sanction the introduction of pictures as a mere trick of trade, to promote the sale of a work, or as an expedient to give circulation to a useless, pointless tale, without regard to their significance or accuracy. He is obliged to defer to a future occasion a full exhibition of his views.—The Editor.

* "The system of modern geography here presented to the public contains that method; yet strange as it may appear, *Mr.* Woodbridge originated and wrote it."—"*Mr.* Woodbridge has also relinquished a part of a copy-right obtained solely by his invention and industry."—*Mrs. Willard's Preface to the Rudiments.*

CORRESPONDENCE.

Statistics of the Blind.

Dr. Russ, the Principal of the Asylum for the Blind, in New York, favored us some time since with the following remarks on the number of these unfortunate individuals for whom public benevolence ought to provide. They have been accidentally laid aside, and deferred, after being sent to the printer; but we hope they may serve to excite and direct public attention on this subject.

"I am very sorry not to have it in my power to comply with your request in relation to the Statistics of the Blind; but I believe we have as yet no data upon which anything but a conjecture can be hazarded in regard to the relative proportion of cases of congenital, or original blindness to those in which it is the result of subsequent disease; or as to the ratio of yearly increase. My friend, Dr. Howe, will probably be able to furnish you with all the information that can at present be obtained, and I take the liberty to refer you to him.* My own opinion, (and I would be understood as expressing merely an opinion) is that congenital blindness bears about the same proportion to the population, as does congenital deafness. The proportion of the blind from all causes, however, is I believe in this State at least one tenth greater.

About one eighth of the whole number are capable of receiving instruction. Admitting this to be a correct estimate, and it is certainly a low one, this State will supply us with from 120 to 130 pupils. Assuming seven years as the ordinary term of pupilage, the natural increase during that period may be computed at 30. At the expiration of seven years, probably not more than one half the pupils will be qualified to support themselves *out* of the Institution. The other half, though they may be, by the economy of an institution, enabled to earn their living as inmates, would not probably do this, when thrown upon the world; so that an institution for the blind must almost necessarily become a permanent Asylum, to at least a portion of its pupils.

Viewing the subject in this light, New York, alone, will probably furnish 90 pupils, 30 of which will continually need instruction. New Jersey will probably supply from 12 to 15 more, so that we can, I think, safely calculate on one hundred pupils from the two States. This, I conceive, will be as many as can be profitably or advantageously instructed or employed in one establishment. Should the number be materially increased, the limited number of trades or occupations in which the blind can be profitably employed would force so many into the same occupation, (as is the case, I understand, to a limited extent at the present time in Edinburgh) that much difficulty would be experienced in effecting sales of these manufactures. I am therefore of opinion, that one institution for every 2,500,000 inhabitants will be no more than is required,— which will give about six to the United States.

* For Dr. Howe's opinion, see Annals of Education, Dec. 1833.

NEW PUBLICATIONS.

A Universal History, in twenty-four books, translated from the German of John Von Muller. In four vols. 12mo. Boston: Cottons and Barnard. 1834.

Good's Book of Nature, abridged from the original work; adapted to the reading of Children and Youth; with Questions for the use of Schools, and Illustrations from original designs. Boston: Allen and Ticknor. 1834. Square 16mo. pp. 224.

The Intellectual and Practical Singing Book; embracing the elements of Vocal Music, and a Selection of Pleasing and Popular Tunes, designed for the use of Beginners, particularly the Children connected with the Sunday Schools of the Protestant Episcopal Church; also, for Teachers and Sunday Schools in general. By Charles Dingley. New York: N. B. Holmes. 1834. pp. 80.

The Third Class Reader. Designed for the Use of the Younger Classes in the Schools of the United States. By B. D. Emerson, Late Principal of the Adams Grammar School, Boston. Boston: Russell, Odiorne and Metcalf. 1834. 18mo. pp. 160.

Remarks on the Classical Education of Boys. By a Teacher. Boston: Hilliard, Gray & Co. 1834. 18mo. pp. 120.

The Mother's Friend; or, Familiar Directions for Forming the Mental and Moral Habits of Young Children. New York: Leavitt, Lord & Co. Boston: Crocker & Brewster. 1834. 18mo. pp. 240.

The Constitutional Class Book; being a brief exposition of the Constitution of the United States, designed for the use of the Higher Classes of Common Schools. By Joseph Story, L. L. D. Boston: Hilliard, Gray & Co. 12mo. pp. 166.

The Father's Book; or, Suggestions for the Government and Instruction of Young Children, on principles appropriate to a Christian country. By Theodore Dwight, Jr. Springfield; G. & C. Merriam. 1834. 12mo. pp. 200.

The Teacher's Gift, for 1834. Boston: Brown & Peirce.

The Class Book of Anatomy; designed for Schools; explanatory of the first principles of Human Mechanism, as the basis of Physical Education. By Jerome V. C. Smith, M. D. Boston: Allen & Ticknor. 1834. 12mo. pp. 280.

The School Song Book; adapted to the School Room. Written for American Children and Youth, by Mrs. Sarah J. Hale, Editor of the Ladies' Magazine, &c. Boston: Allen & Ticknor. 1834. 18mo. pp. 72.

Manual of the Boston Academy of Music, for Instruction in the Elements of Vocal Music, on the system of Pestalozzi. By Lowell Mason, Professor in the Academy. Boston: Carter, Hendee & Co. 1834. 18mo. pp. 236.

Berquin's Childrens' Friend. 4 vols. 18mo. Munroe & Francis.

The Youth's Letter Writer; or, the Epistolary Art made plain and easy to Beginners through the Example of Henry Moreton. By Mrs. John Farrar, author of "Congo in Search of his Master," "The Childrens' Robinson Crusoe," &c. New York: R. Bartlett and P. Rayner. 1834.

A New Grammar of the English Language. Second Edition. Corrected, enlarged, and prepared for use in Academies and Schools. Boston: Russell, Odiorne & Metcalf. 1834. 12mo. pp. 124.

Grammatical Pioneer; or, Rational Instructor. Analytical Grammar; containing the Principles of the English Language, arranged in Progressive Order, and Illustrated by Appropriate Examples. By W. Snyder. Winchester: E. W. Robinson. 1834. 12mo. pp. 164.

Lessons in Greek; a familiar Introduction to the Greek Language as a living Tongue. By Theodore Dwight, Jr. Springfield: G. & C. Merriam. 1833. 12mo. pp. 104.

The Young Man's Guide. Third Edition. Boston: Lilly, Wait, Colman & Holden. 1834. 18mo. pp. 354.

The Young Ladies' Assistant in Drawing and Painting. By Maria Turner, author of Rudiments of Drawing and Shadowing Flowers. Cincinnati: Corey & Fairbanks. 1834. 12mo. pp. 72.

The House I live in. Part 1. The Frame. For the use of Families and Schools. By William A. Alcott. Boston: Lilly, Wait, Colman & Holden. 1834. 18mo. pp. 144.

A Compendium of Natural Philosophy, adapted to the use of the General Reader, and of Schools and Academies. By Denison Olmsted, A. M., Professor of Mathematics and Natural Philosophy in Yale College. New Haven: H. Howe. Boston: Carter, Hendee & Co. 1833.

Mental Culture; or, the Means of Developing the Human Faculties. By J. L. Levison. Boston: Allen & Ticknor. 1834. 12mo. pp. 264.

Outlines of Human Physiology; designed for the use of the higher classes in Common Schools. By George Hayward, M. D. Boston: Marsh, Capen & Lyon. 1834. 12mo. pp. 217.

A Lecture to Young Men. By Sylvester Graham. Providence: Printed by Weeden & Corey. 1834. pp. 80.

The Family at Home; or, Familiar Illustrations of the various Domestic Duties; with an Introductory notice. By G. D. Abbott. Boston: Carter, Hendee & Co. 1834. 12mo. pp. 363.

Poetry for Children. By the author of "How to be Happy." Hartford: Robinson & Pratt. 1834. 18mo. pp. 102.

The Third Book of History; containing Ancient History in connection with Ancient Geography. Designed as a Sequel to the First and Second Books of History. By the author of Peter Parley's Tales. Boston: Carter, Hendee & Co. 1834. pp. 189.

The Intelligent Reader; designed as a Sequel to the Child's Guide. Springfield: G. & C. Merriam. 1834. 18mo. pp. 252.

A Fourth Book of Lessons for Reading; with Rules and Instructions. By Samuel Worcester, author of the Primer, Second Book, Third Book for Reading and Spelling, &c. Stereotype edition. Boston: Carter, Hendee & Co. 1834. 12mo. pp. 408.

The High School Reader; designed for a First Class Book, consisting of extracts in Prose and Poetry. By Rev. J. L. Blake, A. M. Boston: Allen & Ticknor.

Youth's Sketch Book. Lilly, Wait & Co. 1834.

The Genius and Design of the Domestic Constitution, with its Untransferable Obligations and Peculiar Advantages. By Christopher Anderson. From the Edinburgh Edition. Boston: Perkins, Marvin & Co., and Wm. Peirce. New York: Leavitt, Lord & Co. Philadelphia: Henry Perkins. 1834. 12mo. pp. 420.

The Musical Cyclopedia; or, the Principles of Music considered as a Science and an Art, embracing a complete Musical Dictionary, and the Outlines of a Musical Grammar, and of the Theory of Sounds, and Laws of Harmony, with Directions for the Practice of Vocal and Instrumental Music, and a description of Musical Instruments. By William S. Porter. Boston: J. Loring. 1834. 18mo. pp. 430.

Progressive Exercises in English Grammar. Part I. Containing the Principles of Analysis, or English Parsing. By R. G. Parker, A. M., Principal of the Franklin Grammar School, author of Progressive Exercises in Composition;

and Charles Fox, A. M , Principal of the Boylston Grammar School. Boston: Crocker & Brewster. New York: Leavitt, Lord & Co. 1834. 12mo. pp. 96.

Sketches of the Prophets and Prophecy, for the Young. Hartford: D. F. Robinson & Co. 1834. 18mo. pp. 180.

The Holy Land and its Inhabitants. By S. G. Bulfinch. Cambridge: J. Munroe & Co. 1834. 18mo. pp. 298.

The Child's Annual. Boston: Allen & Ticknor. 1834. 18mo.

Neuman's Spanish and English Dictionary. New edition in one vol. 16mo. Philadelphia: Carey, Lea & Blanchard.

The Popular Reader; or, Complete Scholar. Intended as a Reading Book for the Higher Classes in Academies and other Schools in the United States. By the author of the "Franklin Primer," the "Improved Reader," and the "General Class Book." Greenfield, Mass.: A. Phelps. 1834 12mo. pp. 336.

The North American Arithmetic, Part Third; for Advanced Scholars. By Frederick Emerson, Late Principal in the Department of Arithmetic, Boylston School, Boston. Boston: Russell, Odiorne & Metcalf. 1834. 12mo. pp. 288.

An Essay on Moral Culture. Addressed to Parents and Teachers. By M. Carll. Philadelphia: Carey & Lea. 1833. 18mo. pp. 59.

The Every Day Book, for Youth. By Peter Parley. Illustrated by numerous Engravings. Boston: Carter, Hendee & Co. 1834. Square 12mo. pp. 414.

First Lessons in Algebra; being an Easy Introduction to that Science. Designed for the use of Academies and Common Schools. By Ebenezer Bailey, author of the Young Ladies' Class Book. Second improved Edition. Boston: Carter, Hendee & Co. 12mo. pp. 252.

Sunday School Anecdotes. Springfield: G. & C. Merriam. 18mo.

First Foreign Mission; or, Journey of Paul and Barnabas to Asia Minor. By Wm. A. Alcott. Mass. Sab. School Union. 1834. 18mo. pp. 144.

Conversations on Vegetable Physiology, comprehending the Elements of Botany. By J. L. Blake. Philadelphia: Carey & Hart. 12mo.

The Book Keeper's Atlas, &c. By Wm. Edwards, Practical Accountant. New York: Harper & Brothers. 4to.

Geography Made Easy and Interesting. By C. G. Peyton. With 8 Maps and 44 Engravings. Baltimore: Joseph N. Lewis. pp. 94.

American Universal Geography for Schools, &c. By J. L. Blake. Boston: Russell, Odiorne & Co. Small 4to. pp. 144.

Introductory Discourses and Lectures before the American Institute of Instruction at Boston, August, 1833. Boston: Carter, Hendee & Co. 8vo. pp. 317.

Parents' Cabinet of Amusement and Instruction. No. 1. Boston: Lilly, Wait & Co. 1834. 18mo. pp. 282. — No. 2. 18mo. pp. 282.

Introduction to the Grammar of Elocution. Designed for Schools. By Jonathan Barber. Boston: Marsh, Capen & Lyon. 1834. 12mo. pp. 176.

The Child's Reader; intended as an introduction to Porter's Rhetorical Reader. Andover: Gould. 18mo.

Lectures on Popular Education. By George Combe, M. D. Boston: Marsh, Capen & Lyon. 1833. 12mo. pp. 130.

Right and Wrong; or, Familiar Illustrations of the Moral Duties of Children. Boston: Wm. Peirce. pp. 162.

French Fables, with a key for beginners. By F. M. Surault. Cambridge: Munroe & Co. 1834. 12mo. pp. 240.

Prize Essay on Penmanship, new Edition. By B. F. Foster. Boston: Otis Clapp.

Uncle Philip's History of Virginia. New York: Harper & Brothers. 18mo.

The Mother's Friend; or, Familiar Directions for forming the Mental and Moral Habits of Young Children. By Jacob Abbott. New York: Leavitt, Lord & Co. 1834. 18mo. pp. 236.

Lectures to Children. By Rev. J. Todd. Northampton: J. H. Butler. 1834. pp. 218.

The Wesleyan Harp; a collection of Hymns and Tunes suitable for Social Worship. Compiled by Rev. A. D. Merrill and W. C. Brown. 12mo. Boston.

Youth's Treasury. By a Young Lady. Boston: J. Dowe. pp. 72.

Stories from Scripture on an improved plan. 2 vols. 18mo. Boston: Munroe & Francis.

The Principles of Physiology applied to the preservation of health, and to the improvement of Mental and Physical Education. By A. Combe. New York: Harper & Brothers. 1834. 18mo. pp. 291.

Lectures on Phrenology. By Amos Dean. Albany: O. Steele. 1834. 12mo. pp. 252.

Thoughts on Physical Education. By Charles Caldwell, M. D. Boston: Marsh, Capen & Lyon. 1834. 12mo. pp. 133.

The Nurse's Manual, and Young Mother's Guide. Hartford: 1834. Cooke & Co. 12mo.

The Botanical Teacher. By Laura Johnson, under the Superintendence of Prof. Amos Eaton. Albany: O. Steele. 1834. 12mo. pp. 264.

The Alcestis, of Euripides, with notes for the use of Colleges. By T. D. Woolsey, Professor of Greek, in Yale College. Cambridge: James Munroe & Co. 1834.

Key to History. Part III. By Elizabeth P. Peabody. Boston: Marsh, Capen & Lyon. 1834. 12mo. pp. 430.

English History; designed for the use of Schools and Young Persons. By the author of American Popular Lessons. New York: R. Lockwood. 1834. 12mo. pp. 387.

The Child's Daily Food. Prepared by a Father. Springfield: G & C. Merriam. 1834. pp. 189.

The American Almanac and Repository of Useful Knowledge for the year 1835. Boston: Charles Bowen. 12mo. pp. 334.

The District School. By J. Orville Taylor. New York: Harper & Brothers. 1834. 12mo. pp. 336.

A Geography for Children. By H. N. Brinsmade, A. M., Late Instructor in the American Asylum. Third Edition. Boston: Allen & Ticknor. 1834. pp. 122.

Second Foreign Mission; or, Journey of Paul, Silas, Timothy and Luke, into Europe. By Wm. A. Alcott. Mass. Sabbath School Union. 1834. 18mo.

Life of John Knox, the Reformer. American Sunday School Union. pp. 144.

Parley's Book of Stories in the Bible. Boston: Lilly, Wait & Co. 1834. pp. 256.

The Pilgrim's Progress, from this World to that which is to come. By John Bunyan. Abridged for Sabbath Schools. Mass. Sab. Sch. Society. 1834. pp. 179.

INDEX TO VOLUME IV.

NOTICES.

JUL 25 1946		
[illegible]		
[illegible]		
	3.65	
	.80	
	2.20	
	.80	
	.70	
	.30	
	8.20	

CPSIA information can be obtained
at www.ICGtesting.com
Printed in the USA
BVHW061246160819
556068BV00020B/1837/P

9 781406 972252